World Economic and Financial Surveys

WORLD ECONOMIC OUTLOOK
April 2008

Housing and the Business Cycle

International Monetary Fund

Production: IMF Multimedia Services Division
Cover and Design: Luisa Menjivar and Jorge Salazar
Figures: Theodore F. Peters, Jr.
Typesetting: Choon Lee

Cataloging-in-Publication Data

World economic outlook (International Monetary Fund)
    World economic outlook : a survey by the staff of the International Monetary
Fund. — Washington, DC : International Monetary Fund, 1980–
    v. ; 28 cm. — (1981–1984: Occasional paper / International Monetary Fund,
0251-6365). — (1986– : World economic and financial surveys, 0256-6877)

Semiannual.
Has occasional updates, 1984–

    1. Economic history, 1971–1990 — Periodicals. 2. Economic history, 1990– —
Periodicals.   I. International Monetary Fund.   II. Series: Occasional paper
(International Monetary Fund).   III. Series: World economic and financial
surveys.

HC10.W7979   84-640155   338.5'443'09048—dc19
                                                        AACR2 MARC-S
ISBN 978-1-58906-719-6

Subscription price (published twice yearly): $94.
Individual report price: $57 (academic rate: $54).

Please send orders to:
International Monetary Fund, Publication Services
700 19th Street, N.W., Washington, D.C. 20431, U.S.A.
Tel.: (202) 623-7430   Telefax: (202) 623-7201
E-mail: publications@imf.org
www.imf.org

CONTENTS

Tables

Figures

ASSUMPTIONS AND CONVENTIONS

A number of assumptions have been adopted for the projections presented in the *World Economic Outlook*. It has been assumed (1) that real effective exchange rates will remain constant at their average levels during January 30–February 27, 2008, except for the currencies participating in the European exchange rate mechanism II (ERM II), which are assumed to remain constant in nominal terms relative to the euro; (2) that established policies of national authorities will be maintained (for specific assumptions about fiscal and monetary policies in industrial countries, see Box A1); (3) that the average price of oil will be $95.50 a barrel in 2008 and $94.50 a barrel in 2009, and remain unchanged in real terms over the medium term; (4) that the six-month London interbank offered rate (LIBOR) on U.S. dollar deposits will average 3.1 percent in 2008 and 3.4 percent in 2009; (5) that the three-month euro deposits rate will average 4.0 percent in 2008 and 3.6 percent in 2009; and (6) that the six-month Japanese yen deposit rate will yield an average of 1.0 percent in 2008 and of 0.8 percent in 2009. These are, of course, working hypotheses rather than forecasts, and the uncertainties surrounding them add to the margin of error that would in any event be involved in the projections. The estimates and projections are based on statistical information available through end-March 2008.

The following conventions have been used throughout the *World Economic Outlook:*

. . .   to indicate that data are not available or not applicable;

—   to indicate that the figure is zero or negligible;

–   between years or months (for example, 2006–07 or January–June) to indicate the years or months covered, including the beginning and ending years or months;

/   between years or months (for example, 2006/07) to indicate a fiscal or financial year.

"Billion" means a thousand million; "trillion" means a thousand billion.

"Basis points" refer to hundredths of 1 percentage point (for example, 25 basis points are equivalent to ¼ of 1 percentage point).

In figures and tables, shaded areas indicate IMF staff projections.

If no source is listed on tables and figures, data are drawn from the World Economic Outlook database.

When countries are not listed alphabetically, they are ordered on the basis of economic size.

Minor discrepancies between sums of constituent figures and totals shown are due to rounding.

As used in this report, the term "country" does not in all cases refer to a territorial entity that is a state as understood by international law and practice. As used here, the term also covers some territorial entities that are not states but for which statistical data are maintained on a separate and independent basis.

This report on the *World Economic Outlook* is available in full on the IMF's website, www.imf.org. Accompanying it on the website is a larger compilation of data from the WEO database than in the report itself, consisting of files containing the series most frequently requested by readers. These files may be downloaded for use in a variety of software packages.

Inquiries about the content of the *World Economic Outlook* and the WEO database should be sent by mail, electronic mail, or telefax (telephone inquiries cannot be accepted) to:

World Economic Studies Division
Research Department
International Monetary Fund
700 19th Street, N.W.
Washington, D.C. 20431, U.S.A.
E-mail: weo@imf.org   Telefax: (202) 623-6343

PREFACE

The analysis and projections contained in the *World Economic Outlook* are integral elements of the IMF's surveillance of economic developments and policies in its member countries, of developments in international financial markets, and of the global economic system. The survey of prospects and policies is the product of a comprehensive interdepartmental review of world economic developments, which draws primarily on information the IMF staff gathers through its consultations with member countries. These consultations are carried out in particular by the IMF's area departments together with the Policy Development and Review Department, the Monetary and Capital Markets Department, and the Fiscal Affairs Department.

The analysis in this report has been coordinated in the Research Department under the general direction of Simon Johnson, Economic Counsellor and Director of Research. The project has been directed by Charles Collyns, Deputy Director of the Research Department, and Subir Lall, Acting Division Chief, Research Department. Tim Callen helped coordinate the early stages of the project before moving to a new assignment.

The primary contributors to this report are Roberto Cardarelli, Kevin Cheng, Stephan Danninger, Selim Elekdag, Thomas Helbling, Deniz Igan, Florence Jaumotte, Ben Jones, Tim Lane, Valerie Mercer-Blackman, Paul Mills, Gianni De Nicolò, Jonathan Ostry, Rodney Ramcharan, Alessandro Rebucci, Alasdair Scott, Nikola Spatafora, Jon Strand, Natalia Tamirisa, Irina Tytell, Toh Kuan, Gavin Asdorian, To-Nhu Dao, Stephanie Denis, Nese Erbil, Angela Espiritu, Elaine Hensle, Patrick Hettinger, Susana Mursula, and Bennett Sutton. Ercument Tulun provided research assistance. Mahnaz Hemmati, Laurent Meister, and Emory Oakes managed the database and the computer systems. Sylvia Brescia, Jemille Colon, and Sheila Tomilloso Igcasenza were responsible for word processing. Other contributors include Eduardo Borensztein, Marcos Chamon, Hamid Faruqee, Lyudmyla Hvozdyk, M. Ayhan Kose, Kornélia Krajnyák, Michael Kumhof, Douglas Laxton, Jaewoo Lee, Paolo Mauro, Steven Symansky, Stephan Tokarick, and Johannes Wiegand. External consultants include Warwick McKibbin, Tommaso Monacelli, Ian Parry, Luca Sala, Arvind Subramanian, Kang Yong Tan, and Shang-Jin Wei. Linda Griffin Kean of the External Relations Department edited the manuscript and coordinated the production of the publication.

The analysis has benefited from comments and suggestions by staff from other IMF departments, as well as by Executive Directors following their discussion of the report on March 19 and 21, 2008. However, both projections and policy considerations are those of the IMF staff and should not be attributed to Executive Directors or to their national authorities.

FOREWORD

This World Economic Outlook *presents the IMF staff's view of the world economy in spring 2008, with our assessment of current conditions and prospects and with an in-depth analysis of several key elements that will affect conditions and prospects in the months and years ahead. This report has been prepared by a team composed primarily of the staff of the World Economic Studies division, ably led by Charles Collyns and, since January, Subir Lall. I would also like to recognize the particular contribution of Tim Callen, who led this division for three years and who helped shape this issue of the* World Economic Outlook *during its design and development. In addition, I must emphasize, as always, that other IMF staff, both within the Research Department and across the organization, have played critical roles in producing this report, through direct contributions to all the chapters and through a continual process of collegial interaction and productive feedback.*

The world economy has entered new and precarious territory. The U.S. economy continues to be mired in the financial problems that first emerged in subprime mortgage lending but which have now spread much more broadly. Strains that were once thought to be limited to part of the housing market are now having considerable negative effects across the entire economy, with rising defaults, falling collateral, and tighter credit working together to create a powerful and hard-to-defeat financial decelerator.

In addition to serious problems at the intersection of credit and the real economy, the United States remains plagued by profound errors in risk management among its leading financial institutions. Problems that were once thought to be limited to issues surrounding liquidity in short-term money markets—and thought capable of being dealt with as such—have cascaded across much of the financial sector, triggering repeated waves of downgrades,

upward adjustment of losses for both U.S. and European banks, and now an apparently unstoppable move toward some significant degree of global deleveraging.

This cutback in lending and the associated attempt to reduce risks played a major role in a most dramatic pair of events—both of which happened as this *World Economic Outlook* entered its final stages of preparation. First, one of the five largest U.S. investment banks, Bear Stearns, was sold under difficult circumstances—including the presumed imminence of a far-reaching default. Second, and just as headline-grabbing, were the virtually unprecedented steps taken by the Federal Reserve to prevent Bear Stearns's problems from spreading. These steps have had a definite stabilizing effect, at least for now.

In our view, the continuing deep correction in the U.S. housing market and the unresolved financial sector problems have led the U.S. economy to the verge of recession. In fact, we are now anticipating that the United States will indeed slip into recession—meaning that it will experience two or more quarters of negative growth—during the course of 2008, before starting a moderate recovery at some point during 2009.

The effects on the rest of the world are likely to be significant. We have already reduced our expectations for growth in Europe and much of the emerging world. Our revised global growth forecast is 3.7 percent, down from 4.9 percent in 2007, which represents a pronounced slowdown. However, I would stress that achieving growth even at this level will require that most advanced economies experience only mild slowdowns and that many emerging economies be able to keep their rapid pace of growth largely on track.

In addition to problems within the financial sector, there are two main short-run vulnerabilities for the global economy, both of which

House Price Gaps
(Percent)

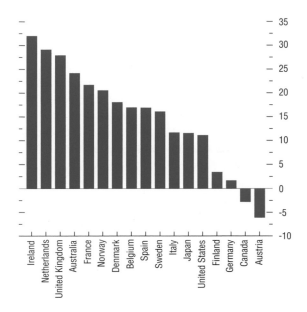

Source: IMF staff calculations, as described in Box 3.1.

Number of Major Commodity Groups in Boom Phase and Global Industrial Production[1]

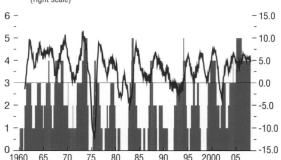

Sources: IMF, Commodity Price System; IMF, *International Financial Statistics;* and IMF staff calculations.
[1]Major commodity groups are defined as oil, metals, food, beverages, and agricultural raw materials.

are covered in considerable detail in this *World Economic Outlook.* The first is that housing prices may adjust downward significantly in many other advanced economies (first figure). Although Chapter 3 shows that the particular dynamics of the housing market in the United States are not matched by those in other countries, it also shows that housing may now play a more marked role in the business cycle more broadly—as the nature of mortgage financing has changed and as valuations have increased almost everywhere over the past 10 years.

The second potential vulnerability is, of course, commodity prices. Chapter 5 examines the role of commodity prices in contributing to the strong performance of many emerging and developing economies in recent years. It is striking how the surging tide of commodity prices over the past five years (second figure) has lifted almost all commodity-based boats around the world. Although there is some reason to believe that the countries exporting commodities are now better able than in the past to withstand a serious downturn, we continue to urge caution: commodity prices have fallen, on average, by 30 percent during significant global slowdowns over the past 30 years.

All eyes now turn to the world's leading emerging economies. They have come of economic age in the past half-decade—diversifying their exports, strengthening their domestic economies, and improving their policy frameworks. It is conceivable that their strong momentum, together with some timely policy adjustments, can sustain both their domestic demand and the global economy.

At this moment, however, these emerging economies find themselves beset not by impending recession, but rather by inflation pressures. In particular, the financial dynamics of dollar depreciation and increasing financial market uncertainty have combined with continuing strong demand growth in the emerging economies and sluggish supply responses by commodity producers in such a way as to keep upward pressure on food and energy prices despite the darkening clouds over the global economy.

Therefore, at the very time when preparations for countercyclical measures would seem to be warranted, leading emerging economies find themselves trying hard to take the edge off inflation.

These immediate issues are compelling, but we must not lose sight of the longer-term challenges, including the global challenge of climate change. The IMF can contribute to the important current debate by analyzing the macroeconomic consequences of climate change, which can be far-reaching and quick-acting. Chapter 4 has a particular focus on the macroeconomic impact of mitigation strategies and argues that well-designed policy frameworks can limit carbon and related emissions without having a major negative effect on growth.

In addition to the compelling medium-term case for containing emissions, we urgently need a more coherent global approach to energy pricing. It is essential that increases in fuel prices be passed on to final consumers, thus allowing the price mechanism to play an appropriate role across the global economy in reducing demand (and limiting inflation pressure) whenever supply conditions or financial events push commodity prices up. Attempts to protect consumers from the true short-, medium-, or long-run costs of using fossil fuels are likely to prove worse than futile.

Simon Johnson
Economic Counsellor and Director, Research Department

EXECUTIVE SUMMARY

Global Economic Environment

The global expansion is losing speed in the face of a major financial crisis (Chapter 1). The slowdown has been greatest in the advanced economies, particularly in the United States, where the housing market correction continues to exacerbate financial stress. Among the other advanced economies, growth in western Europe has also decelerated, although activity in Japan has been more resilient. The emerging and developing economies have so far been less affected by financial market developments and have continued to grow at a rapid pace, led by China and India, although activity is beginning to slow in some countries.

At the same time, headline inflation has increased around the world, boosted by the continuing buoyancy of food and energy prices. In the advanced economies, core inflation has edged upward in recent months despite slowing growth. In the emerging markets, headline inflation has risen more markedly, reflecting both strong demand growth and the greater weight of energy and particularly food in consumption baskets.

Commodity markets have continued to boom despite slowing global activity. Strong demand from emerging economies, which has accounted for much of the increase in commodity consumption in recent years, has been a driving force in the price run-up, while biofuel-related demand has boosted prices of major food crops. At the same time, supply adjustments to higher prices have lagged, notably for oil, and inventory levels in many markets have declined to medium- to long-term lows (see Appendix 1.2). The recent run-up in commodity prices also seems to have been at least partly due to financial factors, as commodities have increasingly emerged as an alternative asset class.

The financial shock that erupted in August 2007, as the U.S. subprime mortgage market was derailed by the reversal of the housing boom, has spread quickly and unpredictably to inflict extensive damage on markets and institutions at the core of the financial system. The fallout has curtailed liquidity in the interbank market, weakened capital adequacy at major banks, and prompted the repricing of risk across a broad range of instruments, as discussed in more detail in the April 2008 *Global Financial Stability Report*. Liquidity remains seriously impaired despite aggressive responses by major central banks, while concern about credit risks has intensified and extended far beyond the subprime mortgage sector. Equity prices have also retreated as signs of economic weakness have intensified, and equity and currency markets have remained volatile.

These financial dislocations and associated deleveraging are affecting both bank and nonbank channels of credit in the advanced economies, and evidence is gathering of a broad credit squeeze—although not yet a full-blown credit crunch. Bank lending standards in the United States and western Europe are tightening, the issuance of structured securities has been curtailed, and spreads on corporate debt have risen sharply. The impact is most severe in the United States and is contributing to a further deepening of the housing market correction. In western Europe, the main spillovers have been through banks most directly exposed to U.S. subprime securities and disruptions in interbank and structured securities markets.

Recent financial market stress has also had an impact on foreign exchange markets. The real effective exchange rate for the U.S. dollar has declined sharply since mid-2007 as foreign investment in U.S. bonds and equities has been dampened by reduced confidence in both the liquidity of and the returns on such assets, as well as by the weakening of U.S. growth prospects and interest rate cuts. The decline in the value of the U.S. dollar has boosted net exports and helped bring the U.S. current account deficit down to less than 5 percent of GDP by the fourth quarter of 2007, over 1½ percent of GDP lower than its peak in 2006. The main counterpart to the decline of the dollar has been appreciation of the euro, the yen, and other floating currencies such as the Canadian dollar and some emerging economy currencies. However, exchange rate movements have been less marked for a number of countries with large current account surpluses—notably China and oil-exporting countries in the Middle East.

Direct spillovers to emerging and developing economies have been less pronounced than in previous periods of global financial market distress, although capital inflows have moderated in recent months and issuance activity has been subdued. A number of countries that had relied heavily on short-term cross-border borrowing have been affected more substantially. Trade spillovers from the slowdown in the advanced economies have been limited so far and are more visible in economies that trade heavily with the United States. As a result, growth among emerging and developed economies has continued to be generally strong and broadly balanced across regions, with many countries still facing rising inflation rates from buoyant food and fuel prices and strong domestic demand.

Underpinning the resilience of the emerging and developing economies are their increasing integration into the global economy and the broad-based nature of the current commodity price boom, which have boosted exports, foreign direct investment, and domestic investment in commodity-exporting countries to a greater degree than during earlier booms. As explored in Chapter 5, commodity exporters have been able to make progress toward diversifying their export bases, including by increasing manufacturing exports, and the share of trade among the emerging and developing economies themselves has increased. Strengthened macroeconomic frameworks and improved institutional environments have been important factors behind these favorable developments. As a result, the

growth performance of emerging and developing economies has become less dependent on the advanced economy business cycle, although spillovers have clearly not been eliminated.

Outlook and Risks

Global growth is projected to slow to 3.7 percent in 2008, ½ percentage point lower than at the time of the January *World Economic Outlook Update* and 1¼ percentage points lower than the growth recorded in 2007. Moreover, growth is projected to remain broadly unchanged in 2009. The divergence in growth performance between the advanced and emerging economies is expected to continue, with growth in the advanced economies generally expected to fall well below potential. The U.S. economy will tip into a mild recession in 2008 as the result of mutually reinforcing cycles in the housing and financial markets, before starting a modest recovery in 2009 as balance sheet problems in financial institutions are slowly resolved (Chapter 2). Activity in western Europe is also projected to slow to well below potential, owing to trade spillovers, financial strains, and negative housing cycles in some countries. By contrast, growth in emerging and developing economies is expected to ease modestly but remain robust in both 2008 and 2009. The slowdown reflects efforts to prevent overheating in some countries as well as trade and financial spillovers and some moderation in commodity prices.

The overall balance of risks to the short-term global growth outlook remains tilted to the downside. The IMF staff now sees a 25 percent chance that global growth will drop to 3 percent or less in 2008 and 2009—equivalent to a global recession. The greatest risk comes from the still-unfolding events in financial markets, particularly the potential for deep losses on structured credits related to the U.S. subprime mortgage market and other sectors to seriously impair financial system balance sheets and cause the current credit squeeze to mutate into a full-blown credit crunch. Interaction between negative financial shocks and domestic demand, particularly through the housing market, remains a concern for the United States and to a lesser degree for western Europe and other advanced economies. There is some upside potential from projections for domestic demand in the emerging economies, but these economies remain vulnerable to trade and financial spillovers. At the same time, risks related to inflationary pressures have risen, reflecting the price surge in tight commodity markets and the upward drift of core inflation.

Policy Issues

Policymakers around the world are facing a diverse and fast-moving set of challenges, and although each country's circumstances differ, in an increasingly multipolar world it will be essential to meet these challenges broadly, taking full account of cross-border interactions. In the advanced economies, the pressing tasks are dealing with financial market dislocations and responding to downside risks to growth—but policy choices should also take into account inflation risks and longer-term concerns. Many emerging and developing economies still face the challenge of ensuring that strong current growth does not drive a buildup in inflation or vulnerabilities, but they should be ready to respond to slowing growth and more difficult financing conditions if the external environment deteriorates sharply.

Advanced Economies

Monetary policymakers in the advanced economies face a delicate balancing act between alleviating the downside risks to growth and guarding against a buildup in inflation. In the United States, rising downside risks to output, amid considerable uncertainty about the extent, duration, and impact of financial turbulence and the deterioration in labor market conditions, justifies the Federal Reserve's recent deep interest rate cuts and a continuing bias toward monetary easing until the economy moves to a firmer footing. In the euro area, although cur-

rent inflation is uncomfortably high, prospects point to its falling back below 2 percent during 2009, in the context of an increasingly negative outlook for activity. Accordingly, the European Central Bank can afford some easing of the policy stance. In Japan, there is merit in keeping interest rates on hold, although there would be some limited scope to reduce interest rates from already-low levels if there were a substantial deterioration in growth prospects.

Beyond these immediate concerns, recent financial developments have fueled the continuing debate about the degree to which central banks should take asset prices into account in setting monetary policy. In this context, Chapter 3 looks at connections between housing cycles and monetary policy. It concludes that recent experience seems to support giving greater weight to house price movements in monetary policy decisions, especially in economies with more developed mortgage markets where "financial accelerator" effects have become more pronounced. This could be achieved within a risk-management framework for monetary policy by "leaning against the wind" when house prices move rapidly or when prices have moved out of normal valuation ranges, although it would not be feasible or desirable for monetary policy to adopt specific house price objectives.

Fiscal policy can play a useful stabilizing role in advanced economies in the event of a downturn in economic activity, although it should not jeopardize efforts aimed at consolidating fiscal positions over the medium term. In the first place, there are automatic stabilizers that should provide timely fiscal support, without jeopardizing progress toward medium-term objectives. In addition, there may be justification for additional discretionary stimulus in some countries, given present concern about the strength of recessionary forces and concern that financial dislocations may have weakened the normal monetary policy transmission mechanism, but any such stimulus must be timely, well targeted, and quickly unwound. In the United States, where automatic stabilizers are relatively small, the recent legislation to provide additional stimulus for an economy under stress seems fully justified, and room may need to be found for some additional public support for housing and financial markets. In the euro area, automatic stabilizers are more extensive and should be allowed to play out fully around a deficit path that is consistent with steady advancement toward medium-term objectives. Countries whose medium-term objectives are well in hand can provide some additional discretionary stimulus if needed. However, in other countries, the ability to allow even automatic stabilizers to operate in full may be limited by high levels of public debt and current adjustment plans that are insufficient for medium-term sustainability. In Japan, net public debt is projected to remain at high levels despite recent consolidation efforts. In the context of an economic downturn, automatic stabilizers could be allowed to operate, but their impact on domestic demand would be small, and there would be little scope for additional discretionary action.

Policymakers need to continue strong efforts to deal with financial market turmoil in order to avoid a full-blown crisis of confidence or a credit crunch. The immediate priorities, explored in more detail in the April 2008 *Global Financial Stability Report*, are to rebuild counterparty confidence, reinforce the capital and financial soundness of institutions, and ease liquidity strains. Additional initiatives to help support the U.S. housing market, including possible use of the public sector balance sheet, could help to reduce uncertainties about the evolution of the financial system, although care would be needed to avoid inducing undue moral hazard. Longer-term reforms include improving mortgage market regulation, promoting the independence of rating agencies, broadening supervision, strengthening the framework of supervisory cooperation, and improving crisis resolution mechanisms.

Emerging and Developing Economies

Emerging and developing economies face the challenges of controlling inflation while being alert to downside risks from the slowdown in the advanced economies and the increased stress in financial markets. In some countries, further monetary policy tightening may be needed to keep inflation under control. With a flexible exchange rate regime, currency appreciation will tend to provide useful support for monetary tightening. Countries whose exchange rates are heavily managed vis-à-vis the U.S. dollar have less room to respond because rising interest rates may encourage heavier capital inflows. China and other countries that have diversified economies would benefit from moving toward more flexible regimes that would provide greater scope for monetary policy. For many Middle Eastern oil exporters, the exchange rate peg to the U.S. dollar constrains monetary policy, and it will be important that the current buildup in fiscal spending be calibrated to account for the cyclical position of these economies and that priority be given to spending aimed at alleviating supply bottlenecks.

Fiscal and financial policies can also play useful roles in preventing overheating and related problems. Expenditure restraint can help moderate domestic demand, lessen the need for monetary tightening, and ease pressures from short-term capital inflows. Vigilant financial supervision—promoting appropriately tight lending standards and strong risk management in domestic financial institutions—can pay dividends both by moderating the demand impulse from rapid credit growth and by reducing the buildup of balance sheet vulnerabilities.

At the same time, policymakers should be ready to respond to a more negative external environment, which could undercut trade performance and stifle capital inflows. In many countries, strengthened policy frameworks and public sector balance sheets will allow for more use than in the past of countercyclical monetary and fiscal policies. In China, the consolidation of the past few years provides ample room to support the economy through fiscal policy, such as by accelerating public investment plans and advancing the pace of reforms to strengthen social safety nets, health care, and education. In many Latin American countries, well-established inflation-targeting frameworks would provide the basis for monetary easing in the event of both a downturn in activity and an alleviation of inflation pressures. Automatic fiscal stabilizers could be allowed to operate, although there would be little room for discretionary fiscal stimulus, given still-high public debt levels. Some emerging and developing economies that have large current account deficits or other vulnerabilities and are reliant on capital inflows may need to respond by tightening policies promptly to maintain confidence.

Multilateral Initiatives and Policies

Broadly based efforts to deal with global challenges have become indispensable. In the event of a severe global downturn, there would be a case for providing temporary fiscal support in a range of countries that have made good progress in recent years in securing sound fiscal positions. Providing fiscal stimulus across a broad group of countries that would benefit from stronger aggregate demand could prove much more effective than isolated efforts, given the inevitable cross-border leakages from added spending in open economies. It is still early to launch such an approach, but it would be prudent for countries to start contingency planning to ensure a timely response in the event that such support becomes necessary.

Reducing risks associated with global current account imbalances remains an important task. It is encouraging that some progress is being made in implementing the strategy endorsed by the International Monetary and Financial Committee and the more detailed policy plans laid out by participants in the IMF-sponsored Multilateral Consultation on Global Imbalances aimed at rebalancing domestic demand across countries, with supportive movements in real exchange rates (see Box 1.3). This road map remains relevant but should be used flexibly to take account of the changing global context. Reducing trade barriers also remains an important priority, but the slow progress toward completing the Doha Round has been disappointing. Rising trade has been a key source of the recent strong performance of the global economy—and the recent progress toward global poverty reduction—and a renewed push in this area remains essential.

Recent commitments to developing a post-Kyoto framework for joint action to address climate change are very welcome. As discussed in Chapter 4, efforts to adapt to and mitigate the buildup of greenhouse gases have important macroeconomic consequences. The chapter finds that these macroeconomic consequences can be contained, provided efforts to limit emissions are based on effective carbon pricing that reflects the damages emissions inflict. Such carbon pricing should be applied across countries to maximize the efficiency of abatement, should be flexible to avoid volatility, and should be equitable so as not to put undue burdens on the countries least able to bear them.

GLOBAL PROSPECTS AND POLICIES

The global expansion is losing speed in the face of a major financial crisis. The slowdown has been greatest in the advanced economies, particularly in the United States, where the housing market correction continues to exacerbate financial stress. The emerging and developing economies have so far been less affected by financial market turbulence and have continued to grow at a rapid pace, led by China and India, although activity is beginning to moderate in some countries. In the baseline, the U.S. economy will tip into a mild recession in 2008 as a result of mutually reinforcing housing and financial market cycles, with only a gradual recovery in 2009, reflecting the time needed to resolve underlying balance sheet strains. Activity in the other advanced economies will be sluggish in both 2008 and 2009 in the face of trade and financial spillovers. Growth in the emerging and developing economies is also projected to slow, although it should remain above long-term trends in all regions. Risks to the global projections are tilted to the downside, especially those related to the possibility of a full-blown credit crunch, while emerging and developing economies will not be insulated from a serious downturn in the advanced economies. Against this background, policymakers in the advanced economies must continue to grapple with the task of restoring stability to housing and financial markets while addressing downside risks to growth, without jeopardizing inflation performance or longer-term policy goals. Many emerging and developing economies still face the challenge of avoiding overheating or any buildup in vulnerabilities, but policymakers should be ready to respond judiciously to a deteriorating external environment.

Overview of Recent Developments and Prospects: Divergence but Not Decoupling

The course of the global economy over the past six months has been shaped by the interaction of two powerful but opposing forces: the burgeoning financial crisis that has shaken the advanced economies and the rising tide of the rapidly globalizing emerging economies. Overall, global GDP measured at purchasing-power-parity weights is estimated to have increased 4.9 percent in 2007—well above trend for the fourth consecutive year (Table 1.1 and Figure 1.1).[1] Following a stronger-than-expected third quarter, activity in the advanced economies decelerated quite sharply toward the end of the year, particularly in the United States, as the debacle in the U.S. subprime mortgage market had knock-on effects across a broad range of financial markets and institutions (Figure 1.2).

By contrast, the emerging and developing economies continued to grow robustly, notwithstanding some slowing in activity toward the end of the year. China and India—which grew 11.4 percent and 9.2 percent, respectively, in 2007—continued to lead the way, but all regions maintained robust rates of growth. The growth momentum is being provided by strong productivity gains as these countries progressively integrate into the global economy, by terms-of-trade increases for commodity producers as oil and other raw material prices continue to soar, and by strengthened policy frameworks.

Headline inflation has increased around the world, boosted by the continuing buoyancy of food and energy prices (Figure 1.3). Rapid increases in commodity prices have mainly reflected continued strong demand growth in the emerging economies, which has accounted

[1]Global and regional aggregates use country weights calculated from the new purchasing-power-parity (PPP) data published by the International Comparison Program (ICP) in December 2007. This has resulted in a downward shift in estimates of global growth in recent years by about ½ percentage point relative to estimates in the October 2007 *World Economic Outlook.* See Appendix 1.1 for more details.

Table 1.1. Overview of the *World Economic Outlook* Projections[1]
(Annual percent change unless otherwise noted)

	2006	2007	Current Projections		Difference from January 2008 WEO Update	
			2008	2009	2008	2009
World output	**5.0**	**4.9**	**3.7**	**3.8**	**−0.5**	**−0.6**
Advanced economies	3.0	2.7	1.3	1.3	−0.6	−0.8
United States	2.9	2.2	0.5	0.6	−1.0	−1.2
Euro area	2.8	2.6	1.4	1.2	−0.2	−0.7
Germany	2.9	2.5	1.4	1.0	−0.1	−0.7
France	2.0	1.9	1.4	1.2	−0.1	−1.0
Italy	1.8	1.5	0.3	0.3	−0.5	−0.7
Spain	3.9	3.8	1.8	1.7	−0.6	−0.8
Japan	2.4	2.1	1.4	1.5	−0.1	−0.2
United Kingdom	2.9	3.1	1.6	1.6	−0.2	−0.8
Canada	2.8	2.7	1.3	1.9	−0.5	−0.5
Other advanced economies	4.5	4.6	3.3	3.4	−0.4	−0.4
Newly industrialized Asian economies	5.6	5.6	4.0	4.4	−0.4	−0.4
Emerging and developing economies	7.8	7.9	6.7	6.6	−0.2	−0.4
Africa	5.9	6.2	6.3	6.4	−0.7	−0.2
Sub-Sahara	6.4	6.8	6.6	6.7	−0.3	−0.2
Central and eastern Europe	6.6	5.8	4.4	4.3	−0.2	−0.8
Commonwealth of Independent States	8.2	8.5	7.0	6.5	—	−0.1
Russia	7.4	8.1	6.8	6.3	0.2	−0.2
Excluding Russia	10.1	9.6	7.4	7.0	−0.6	0.2
Developing Asia	9.6	9.7	8.2	8.4	−0.4	−0.4
China	11.1	11.4	9.3	9.5	−0.7	−0.5
India	9.7	9.2	7.9	8.0	−0.5	−0.2
ASEAN-5	5.7	6.3	5.8	6.0	−0.2	−0.2
Middle East	5.8	5.8	6.1	6.1	0.2	0.1
Western Hemisphere	5.5	5.6	4.4	3.6	0.1	−0.4
Brazil	3.8	5.4	4.8	3.7	0.3	−0.3
Mexico	4.8	3.3	2.0	2.3	−0.6	−0.7
Memorandum						
European Union	3.3	3.1	1.8	1.7	−0.3	−0.7
World growth based on market exchange rates	3.9	3.7	2.6	2.6	−0.4	−0.7
World trade volume (goods and services)	**9.2**	**6.8**	**5.6**	**5.8**	**−0.8**	**−1.1**
Imports						
Advanced economies	7.4	4.2	3.1	3.7	−1.3	−1.2
Emerging and developing economies	14.4	12.8	11.8	10.7	—	−1.1
Exports						
Advanced economies	8.2	5.8	4.5	4.2	−0.4	−0.9
Emerging and developing economies	10.9	8.9	7.1	8.7	−1.3	−1.0
Commodity prices (U.S. dollars)						
Oil[2]	20.5	10.7	34.3	−1.0	13.0	1.3
Nonfuel (average based on world commodity export weights)	23.2	14.0	7.0	−4.9	7.1	1.2
Consumer prices						
Advanced economies	2.4	2.2	2.6	2.0	0.2	−0.1
Emerging and developing economies	5.4	6.4	7.4	5.7	1.0	0.3
London interbank offered rate (percent)[3]						
On U.S. dollar deposits	5.3	5.3	3.1	3.4	−0.9	−1.0
On euro deposits	3.1	4.3	4.0	3.6	−0.2	−0.4
On Japanese yen deposits	0.4	0.9	1.0	0.8	−0.1	−0.2

Note: Real effective exchange rates are assumed to remain constant at the levels prevailing during January 30–February 27, 2008. See the Statistical Appendix for details on groups and methodologies.

[1]Country weights used to construct aggregate growth rates for groups of countries were revised from those reported in the October 2007 *World Economic Outlook* to incorporate updated PPP exchange rates released by the International Comparison Program.

[2]Simple average of prices of U.K. Brent, Dubai, and West Texas Intermediate crude oil. The average price of oil in U.S. dollars a barrel was $70.95 in 2007; the assumed price is $95.50 in 2008 and $94.50 in 2009.

[3]Six-month rate for the United States and Japan; three-month rate for the euro area.

for the bulk of the increase in commodity consumption in recent years, and a sluggish supply response, with financial factors also playing some role (Appendix 1.2). In the advanced economies, core inflation has edged upward in recent months despite slowing growth. In the emerging economies, headline inflation has risen more markedly, reflecting both strong demand growth and the greater weight of energy and particularly food in consumption baskets.

Global growth is projected to drop to 3.7 percent in 2008 and to continue at about the same pace in 2009. Financial market conditions are likely to remain extremely difficult until there is greater clarity about the extent and distribution of losses on structured securities, until core financial institutions are able to rebuild capital and strengthen balance sheets, until the framework for structured finance and related investment vehicles is made more robust, and until the risk of widespread deleveraging and associated asset price declines is more clearly contained. The continuing housing correction in the United States will remain a drag on demand and a source of uncertainty for financial markets. As a result, the U.S. economy is projected to tip into mild recession in 2008, despite the substantial monetary and fiscal support that is now in train. Other advanced economies will also slow in the face of trade and financial spillovers, with housing markets a source of drag in some European countries. Emerging and developing economies are also expected to decelerate, reflecting efforts to prevent overheating in some countries, as well as spillovers from the advanced economies and some moderation in commodity prices, although growth will continue to be above trend in all regions. The risks around this lower baseline remain tilted to the downside, particularly from possible further negative financial developments.

The next sections of this chapter examine two key issues: first, the likely magnitude of the impact of financial turbulence on economic activity, focusing on the advanced economies, and second, the extent to which emerging and developing economies can decouple from a

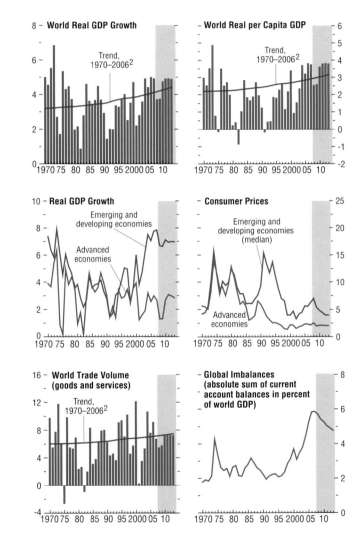

Figure 1.1. Global Indicators[1]
(Annual percent change unless otherwise noted)

While the global economy continued to grow robustly in 2007, for the fourth consecutive year, performance has diverged: activity in the advanced economies slowed, while emerging and developing economies continued to grow rapidly. Looking ahead, growth is expected to decline in 2008 and 2009 in both advanced and emerging and developing economies.

Source: IMF staff estimates.
[1]Shaded areas indicate IMF staff projections. Aggregates are computed on the basis of purchasing-power-parity (PPP) weights unless otherwise noted.
[2]Average growth rates for individual countries, aggregated using PPP weights; the aggregates shift over time in favor of faster-growing countries, giving the line an upward trend.

Figure 1.2. Current and Forward-Looking Indicators

(Percent change from a year ago unless otherwise noted)

Industrial production has moderated in the advanced economies, where there has also been a marked deterioration in business and consumer confidence indicators in recent months. Activity indicators for emerging economies have remained buoyant, while trade has rebounded in early 2008 as a result of commodity price increases.

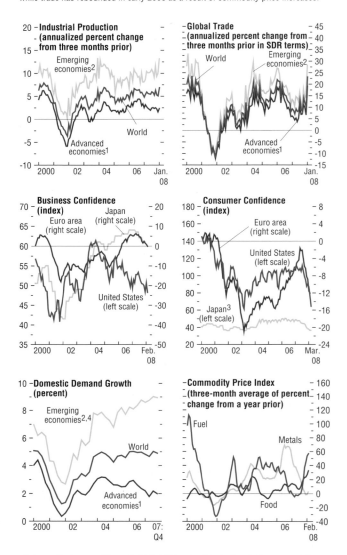

Sources: Business confidence for United States, Institute for Supply Management; for euro area, European Commission; for Japan, Bank of Japan. Consumer confidence for United States, Conference Board; for euro area, European Commission; for Japan, Cabinet Office; for all others, Haver Analytics.

[1] Australia, Canada, Denmark, euro area, Japan, New Zealand, Norway, Sweden, Switzerland, United Kingdom, and United States.

[2] Argentina, Brazil, Bulgaria, Chile, China, Colombia, Czech Republic, Estonia, Hong Kong SAR, Hungary, India, Indonesia, Israel, Korea, Latvia, Lithuania, Malaysia, Mexico, Pakistan, Peru, Philippines, Poland, Romania, Russia, Singapore, Slovak Republic, South Africa, Taiwan Province of China, Thailand, Turkey, Ukraine, and Rep. Bolivariana de Venezuela.

[3] Japan's consumer confidence data are based on a diffusion index, where values greater than 50 indicate improving confidence.

[4] Data for China, India, Pakistan, and Russia are interpolated.

downturn in the United States and western Europe. The chapter then discusses the risks to the outlook and the policy implications.

Financial Market Turbulence: Rocky Ride for the Advanced Economies

The financial market crisis that erupted in August 2007 has developed into the largest financial shock since the Great Depression, inflicting heavy damage on markets and institutions at the core of the financial system. The turmoil was initiated by rapidly rising defaults on subprime mortgages in the context of a major U.S. housing correction (discussed in Chapter 2) and the consequent blowout in spreads on securities backed by such mortgages, including on collateralized debt obligations structured to attract high credit ratings. However, the fallout rapidly spread through an excessively leveraged financial system to curtail liquidity in the interbank market, to weaken capital adequacy and force the emergency resolution of major financial intermediaries, to deeply disrupt structured credit markets, and to prompt a repricing of risk across a broad range of instruments, as described in more detail in the April 2008 *Global Financial Stability Report*.

One of the most dramatic aspects of this crisis has been an unprecedented loss of liquidity, with three-month interbank rates shooting up far in excess of policy targets for overnight rates (Figure 1.4). This occurred as banks sought to conserve their own liquidity in the face of pressures to absorb assets from off-balance-sheet vehicles for which they were no longer able to obtain funding and amid rising uncertainty about the extent and distribution of banks' losses on holdings of subprime-mortgage-related securities and other structured credits. Liquidity shortages spread more broadly as increasingly cautious banks cut back on credit lines and increased haircuts and margin calls on other financial intermediaries.

Major central banks responded aggressively to the loss of liquidity by providing large-scale access to short-term funding through existing facilities, with mixed initial success. With liquidity premiums remaining at high levels, in December the European Central Bank (ECB) further expanded its operations, the Federal Reserve and the Bank of England substantially broadened both the range of collateral accepted and the range of borrowers with access to central bank funds, and major central banks announced a coordinated initiative to ensure adequate liquidity, including the provision of swap lines by the Federal Reserve to allow European central banks to extend dollar liquidity. The Federal Reserve took further actions in March, including opening an effective discount window for prime dealers. A number of central banks have also eased monetary policy stances in reflection of increasing downside risks to the growth outlook over this period. Most dramatically, the Federal Reserve has lowered the federal funds rate by 300 basis points since August 2007, while the Bank of Canada and the Bank of England have also reduced policy rates and the ECB and the Bank of Japan have forgone further interest rate increases. In the United Kingdom, the authorities also provided a full deposit guarantee to help restore depositor confidence after the collapse of a major mortgage provider. Term premiums remain substantially higher than usual more than seven months after the initial outbreak of turbulence.

The persistence of liquidity problems has been due in large part to increasing concerns about credit risks. Credit spreads have continued to widen in recent months, amid increasing gloominess about the outlook as well as mounting concern about the general soundness of structured products and investment vehicles (Figure 1.5). With continuing deterioration of U.S. housing market conditions, particularly in the subprime market segment, prices of mortgage-related securities have continued to fall. Moreover, spreads have risen sharply across other related market segments, including securities backed by credit cards, auto loans, student loans, and commercial mortgages, as a result of concerns about rising default rates, excessive leverage, and questionable securitization tech-

Figure 1.3. Global Inflation
(Twelve-month change of the consumer price index unless otherwise noted)

Headline inflation spiked in late 2007 and early 2008, reflecting the impact of rising energy and, particularly, food prices. Core inflation and inflation expectations have edged upward.

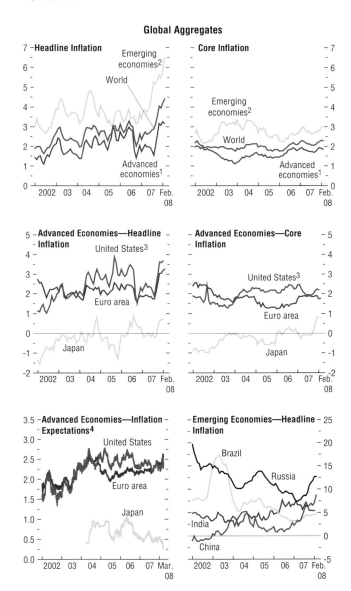

Sources: Haver Analytics; and IMF staff calculations.
[1]Australia, Canada, Denmark, euro area, Japan, New Zealand, Norway, Sweden, United Kingdom, and United States.
[2]Brazil, Bulgaria, Chile, China, Estonia, Hong Kong SAR, Hungary, India, Indonesia, Korea, Malaysia, Mexico, Poland, Singapore, South Africa, Taiwan Province of China, and Thailand.
[3]Personal consumption expenditure deflator.
[4]Ten-year government bond yield minus ten-year inflation-linked government bond yield.

Figure 1.4. Measures of Monetary Policy and Liquidity
(Interest rates in percent unless otherwise noted)

Central banks have responded aggressively to a drying up of liquidity in interbank markets by providing large-scale access to short-term funding. The Federal Reserve responded to increasing downside risks to activity by cutting the federal funds rate rapidly, while the European Central Bank and the Bank of Japan have kept policy rates on hold.

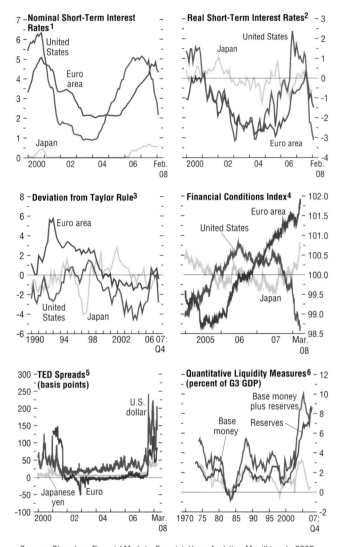

Sources: Bloomberg Financial Markets; Eurostat; Haver Analytics; Merrill Lynch; OECD *Economic Outlook*; and IMF staff calculations.

[1]Three-month treasury bills.

[2]Relative to headline inflation. Measured as deviations from 1990–2007 average.

[3]The Taylor rate depends on (1) the neutral real rate of interest, which in turn is a function of potential output growth, (2) the deviation of consumer price inflation from the inflation target, and (3) the output gap. See Chapter 2 of the September 2004 *World Economic Outlook.*

[4]Weighted average of change in nominal effective exchange rate, overnight LIBOR, three-month LIBOR, 10-year government bond, and corporate high-yield bond rates. Weights estimated by IMF staff.

[5]Three-month LIBOR rate minus three-month government bill rate.

[6]Change over three years for euro area, Japan, and United States (G3), denominated in U.S. dollars.

niques. In this context, there has been intensified concern about counterparty risk as banks have been only partially successful in sustaining capital in the face of mounting losses, with a major U.S. investment bank being sold on an emergency basis with support from the Federal Reserve. Moreover, a number of hedge funds and other highly leveraged institutions have run into serious difficulties as banks increased margin calls on their lines of credit, raising the threat of forced asset sales. At the same time, there are rising questions about the soundness of the credit-default-swap market, particularly given the weakening financial positions of the monoline insurers that provide cover for credit defaults.

Equity prices also have retreated, particularly in early 2008 when signs of economic weakness intensified, and financial sector stocks have been hit particularly hard (Figure 1.6). Measures of volatility in equity and currency markets have remained elevated. By contrast, rates on government bonds have declined sharply, and investment in commodity markets has escalated, as investors seek alternative asset classes.

What will be the overall economic impact of these financial market dislocations? Recent episodes of turbulence in securities markets generally have not had a major impact on activity (see Box 1.2 of the October 2007 *World Economic Outlook*). There is somewhat more evidence to suggest that episodes of banking distress have put a squeeze on credit, but even in these cases it is hard to disentangle the consequences of restraints on credit supply from those of the declining credit demand that accompanies recession (Box 1.1). During previous periods of turbulence, various segments of the financial system have been able, at least partly, to compensate for difficulties experienced in others.

However, experience during these episodes may not provide much guidance for the current unprecedented situation. Of particular concern, the global economy is now facing a widespread deleveraging as mechanisms for credit creation have been damaged in both the banking system and the securities markets—that is, both of the financial system's twin engines are faltering at the same time (Tucker, 2007). Moreover, further broad erosion of financial capital in a climate of uncertainty and caution could cause the present credit squeeze to mutate into a full-blown credit crunch, an event in which the supply of financing is severely constrained across the system.

Looking first at the banking system, the IMF staff estimates reported in the April 2008 *Global Financial Stability Report* suggest that potential losses to banks from exposure to the U.S. subprime mortgage market and from related structured securities, as well as losses on other U.S. credit classes such as consumer and corporate loans, could be on the order of $440–$510 billion out of total potential losses of $945 billion. Such losses would put significant pressure on the capital adequacy of U.S. and European banks, and in fact, losses of this magnitude have already been priced into capital market valuations and rising credit spreads on major financial institutions. Capital adequacy and leverage ratios are also being adversely affected by the reintermediation onto bank balance sheets of off-balance-sheet structures such as conduits and leveraged buyout financing underwritten by major banks.

To be sure, the impact on bank lending need not be calibrated one for one with the deterioration in capital adequacy. U.S. banks in particular have been active in raising capital—about $85 billion relative to declared losses of $190 billion to date—including from sovereign wealth funds, although the cost of raising new capital is increasing rapidly as concerns about bank balance sheets have mounted. Most banks hold sizable capital cushions in excess of regulatory requirements and have some ability to rebuild capital by lowering dividends and costs, although they are likely to be under pressure from markets to restore their capital positions relatively quickly. As described in Box 1.1, lending standards have tightened considerably throughout the advanced economies, which is likely to constrain loan growth.

Figure 1.5. Developments in Mature Credit Markets
(Interest rates in percent unless otherwise noted)

Risk spreads have continued to widen in recent months as financial market uncertainties have continued amid intensifying concerns about the outlook. At the same time, rates on long-term government paper have come down further.

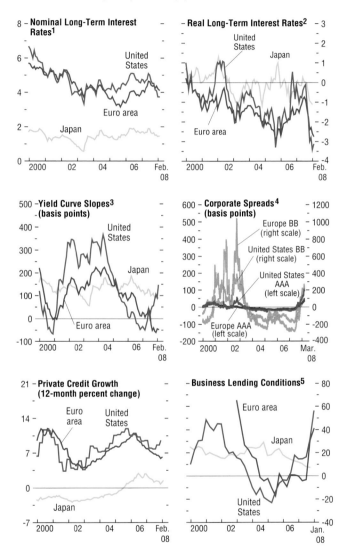

Sources: Bank of Japan; Board of Governors of the Federal Reserve System; Bloomberg Financial Markets; European Central Bank; Merrill Lynch; and IMF staff calculations.
[1]Ten-year government bonds.
[2]Ten-year government bonds relative to headline inflation. Measured as deviations from 1990–2007 average.
[3]Ten-year government bond minus three-month treasury bill rate.
[4]Measured as deviations from 2000–07 average.
[5]Percent of respondents describing lending standards as tightening "considerably" or "somewhat" minus those indicating standards as easing "considerably" or "somewhat" over the previous three months. Survey of changes to credit standards for loans or lines of credit to enterprises for the euro area; average of surveys on changes in credit standards for commercial/industrial and commercial real estate lending for the United States; average of changes in credit standards for small, medium-size, and large firms for Japan.

Figure 1.6. Mature Financial and Housing Market Indicators

Broader financial market indicators reflect the impact of continuing market uncertainties and increasing concern about the economic outlook. Equity markets have turned downward while volatility measures have remained elevated. Residential property prices have moderated in a number of major markets.

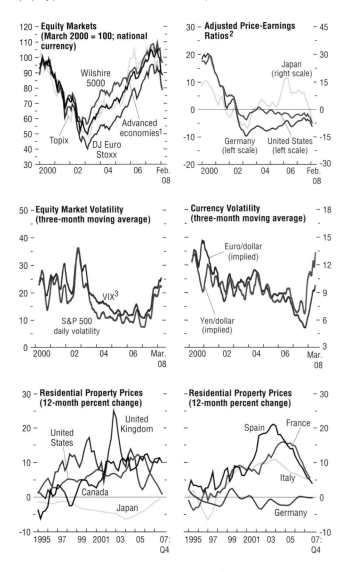

Sources: Bloomberg Financial Markets; CEIC Data Company Limited; Datastream; Haver Analytics; IMF, *International Financial Statistics;* OECD, *Economic Outlook;* and IMF staff calculations.
[1]Morgan Stanley Capital Index for industrial countries.
[2]Adjusted price-earnings ratio is the ratio of stock prices to the moving average of the previous 10 years' earnings, adjusted for nominal trend growth. Adjusted price-earnings ratios are measured as the three-month moving average of deviations from the 1990–2008 (January) average.
[3]VIX is the Chicago Board Options Exchange volatility index. This index is calculated by taking a weighted average of implied volatility for the eight S&P 500 calls and puts.

Although the impact may be at least partly offset in the United States by the sharp lowering of the policy interest rate, this effect has been mitigated because reduced possibilities for securitization of bank credits—including even conforming mortgages—have widened loan spreads considerably.

Turning to securities markets, the most straightforward measure of financial tightening relevant for business conditions is the rise in spreads on corporate securities. As shown in Figure 1.5, such spreads have widened noticeably in recent months. For higher-risk borrowers, the rise has still been somewhat less pronounced to date than during the 2001 recession following the collapse of the dot-com bubble. Spreads facing prime corporate borrowers are close to 2002 highs, although overall yields still remain lower given the decline in government benchmarks. Issuance of complex structured credits is likely to be very limited until underlying weaknesses in the securitization process can be adequately addressed, and former activity levels are unlikely to be recovered even afterward.

The other key factor affecting the macroeconomic impact of tightening financial conditions relates to the financial situations of household and corporate borrowers. The recent slowdown in personal consumption in the United States likely reflects to some degree the diminished ability of households to borrow using home equity as collateral in the face of softening house prices, wider spreads, and tightening lending standards. The pressures on household finances in the United States are likely to be augmented by the correction in equity prices in early 2008 and by deteriorating labor market conditions. Although net assets still remain high, levels of gross indebtedness relative to income are significantly higher than in western Europe. By contrast, U.S. corporates show generally strong balance sheets and robust profitability, which puts them in a position to self-finance investment if needed to avoid high borrowing costs. This safety valve may be less available in parts of Europe (outside Germany

Box 1.1. Is There a Credit Crunch?

Credit conditions in financial markets have tightened and there has been a weakening of the capital positions of many major banks in the wake of recent financial market turbulence. These developments raise the question of whether a "credit crunch"—a severe decline in the supply of credit—is looming in the United States and other advanced economies and, if so, what adverse impact this will have on economic activity. Past periods of financial market stress have not generally had a major impact on broader economic activity, largely because different segments of the financial system have been able, at least partly, to compensate for difficulties in others. However, there have been episodes associated with major bank strains and sharp declines in asset prices when activity has been more seriously affected. In the current context, an overarching concern is that credit creation may have been impaired because of the faltering of the twin engines of the financial system—the banking system and the securities markets.

This box provides a historical perspective on the issue. Because banks remain at the core of financial intermediation, it first examines key features of bank credit cycles in major advanced economies in recent decades, making a clear distinction between bank credit squeezes and credit crunches. This helps assess whether the current financial market turmoil portends risks of a bank credit crunch. Second, the box examines recent developments in capital market financing, notably related to the corporate debt market, with a view toward assessing whether there is a risk of a broader credit crunch.

Bank Credit Cycles and Lending Premiums

Bank credit cycles arise naturally as a result of business cycles. Specifically, bank lending typically rises during an expansion and declines during a contraction. In a downturn, firms' demand for credit normally declines, reflecting a curtailing of investment plans in response to weaker economic prospects and greater spare capacity. Similarly, demand for credit by households moderates if consumption is reduced in response to lower expected real incomes and wealth. The price of bank credit also varies with the business cycle because it incorporates a risk premium. During a growth slowdown, the risk of insolvency increases in both the corporate and household sectors. Banks typically respond by charging higher risk premiums and tightening lending standards, particularly for riskier borrowers.[1] Hence, expansion of bank credit is typically procyclical, whereas risk premiums and lending standards are countercyclical (see Weinberg, 1995).

Simple correlations illustrate these relationships. Specifically, based on data over the last five decades, bank lending growth is positively correlated with real GDP growth, whereas lending premiums—proxied by the difference between an average lending rate and an average of future short-term interest rates—in most cases exhibit a negative correlation (first figure).[2] U.S. lending survey data going back to 1990 show even more clearly these relationships, with current changes in lending standards, demand, and spreads exhibiting patterns in line with the historical experience (first figure, lower panel).

Note: The main authors of this box are Gianni De Nicolò and Selim Elekdag.

[1]Lending standards include all the "nonprice" conditions stipulated in lending arrangements, such as the size and type of collateral requirements and the size, limits, frequency, and duration of drawdowns against credit lines.

[2]Bank credit growth is measured in nominal terms. As discussed in Bernanke and Lown (1991), this measure is most appropriate in proxying the real value of credit extensions in the context of long-term bank-borrower relationships, where the effective maturity of loans is very long.

Box 1.1 *(continued)*

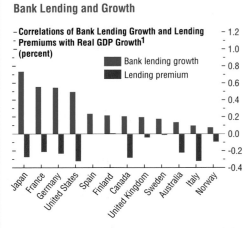

Bank Lending and Growth

Correlations of Bank Lending Growth and Lending Premiums with Real GDP Growth[1]
(percent)

- Bank lending growth
- Lending premium

(Japan, France, Germany, United States, Spain, Finland, Canada, United Kingdom, Sweden, Australia, Italy, Norway)

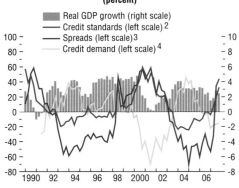

Standards, Spreads, and Demand for U.S. Commercial and Industrial Loans
(percent)

- Real GDP growth (right scale)
- Credit standards (left scale)[2]
- Spreads (left scale)[3]
- Credit demand (left scale)[4]

Sources: Board of Governors of the Federal Reserve System, Senior Loan Officer Survey; and IMF staff calculations.

[1] The sample for the entire period starts in 1957:Q1, except for Italy and Sweden (1970:Q1), Spain (1972:Q1), United Kingdom (1962:Q1), and United States (1952:Q1).

[2] Percent of respondents reporting that credit standards have tightened either "considerably" or "somewhat" minus those reporting standards have eased "considerably" or "somewhat" over the previous three months.

[3] Percent of respondents reporting that loan spreads over cost of funds have tightened either "considerably" or "somewhat" minus those reporting spreads have eased "considerably" or "somewhat" over the previous three months.

[4] Percent of respondents reporting demand for loans as either "substantially" or "moderately" stronger minus those reporting demand as either "substantially" or "moderately" weaker over the previous three months.

Bank Credit Squeezes and Crunches

There can be episodes when the growth of bank credit fluctuates significantly more than is commonly associated with a given phase of the business cycle. This can occur when large swings in asset prices have a significant impact on collateral valuations and the balance sheets of firms and households, inducing borrowers to contract credit demand and banks to rapidly adjust the provision of credit in response to significant changes in borrowers' creditworthiness.[3] In the context of the current financial market turbulence, a particularly relevant issue is the significant increase in (and persistence of) uncertainty concerning asset valuations and borrowers' creditworthiness. Accordingly, a bank *credit squeeze* can be defined as a *slowdown in the growth rate of the bank credit-to-GDP ratio sharper than that experienced during a normal business cycle downturn.*

The amplification of economic downturns triggered by a bank credit squeeze can be particularly severe if banks' access to funds and capital is impaired—either because widespread losses incurred by many banks impair their overall capital position or because large systemic shocks damage depositors' confidence in the banking system. In particular, the inability of banks to either retain or collect deposits and issue debt or equity could constrain the lending capacity of important portions of the banking system, making banks either unwilling or unable to extend credit. In turn, the inability of creditworthy borrowers to tap bank credit in the absence of substitute sources of finance could amplify a growth slowdown and/or lengthen its

[3] The role of collateral valuations, balance-sheet effects, and information asymmetries in amplifying credit cycles is at the heart of the financial accelerator mechanism modeled by Bernanke, Gertler, and Gilchrist (1999) and is the focus of the models of Kiyotaki and Moore (1997), Suarez and Sussman (1997), Cordoba and Ripoll (2004), and Matsuyama (2007).

duration.[4] In the extreme, even a temporary failure by the banking system to channel savings to investment could have longer-lasting, adverse real effects. Thus, a bank *credit crunch* can be defined as a *severe bank credit squeeze driven by a significant decline in the banking system's supply of credit*.[5] Factors that could limit the banking system's supply of credit, and therefore transform a squeeze into a crunch, include banks' inability to raise core funding or retain them due to a run, as well as banks' inability to raise funds through debt or equity issuance on capital markets.

Historically, particularly sharp declines in real GDP growth have been associated with bank credit squeezes, here identified as occurring in all quarters during which the growth rate of the bank credit-to-GDP ratio was in the lowest decile of its distribution over the last few decades (table). In all cases, bank credit squeezes are associated with sharp downturns in real activity, suggesting their potential role in amplifying growth slowdowns. Moreover, large drops in real GDP took place in almost all credit squeeze episodes in which the banking system was in distress, and especially in Finland, Japan, Norway, and Sweden, which all experienced systemic banking crises.

Identifying bank credit crunches is difficult, however, particularly because many factors simultaneously affect supply and demand. However, using a simple diagram of the demand and supply of bank lending indicates whether a decline in bank lending is underpinned by demand or supply factors. If a decline in bank lending is primarily demand driven, there are declining lending rates, whereas lending rates rise if it is driven by supply factors. It is evident that in most cases of a credit squeeze, lending rates have tended to decline, suggesting that adverse shocks to the demand for credit have been the dominant factor underpinning bank credit squeezes (see table).

A word of caution is warranted. A decline in lending rates does not necessarily imply that supply factors play no role in the decline of credit, notably because underlying policy rates may have been lowered in response to weakening growth prospects in the economy. Moreover, evidence based on aggregate data on lending may also mask credit crunches for particular sectors of the economy or for particular borrowers. For example, the credit squeeze in the United States in the early 1990s turned into a credit crunch for bank lending to commercial real estate.[6] Similarly, during the Japanese banking crisis in the early 1990s, capital impairment of banks that incurred large losses on real estate exposures—following the large decline in land prices of the late 1980s—led to a localized credit crunch for firms that were dependent on these banks for financing and were unable to find credit in capital markets.[7]

Where Are We Now?

Signals that a credit squeeze is now under way include tightening bank lending standards and lending spreads, a large increase in

---

[4]Green and Oh (1991) describe a model emphasizing inefficiencies potentially associated with a credit crunch.

[5]This definition is similar to that used by Bernanke and Lown (1991), who define a bank credit crunch as "a significant leftward shift in the supply of bank loans, holding constant both the real interest rate and the quality of potential borrowers" (p. 207).

[6]See Bernanke and Lown (1991) and Owens and Shreft (1995).

[7]See Gan (2007); Peek and Rosengren (2005) also document the absence of a shortage of bank capital leading to a credit crunch in Japan during the 1990s. They also stress that one important factor explaining the persistence of the crisis's real effects was banks' continued financing of borrowers in distress, a kind of credit crunch in reverse.

Box 1.1 *(continued)*

Credit and Real GDP Growth during Bank Credit Squeezes

| | Entire Sample Period[1] | | Periods of Bank Credit Squeezes | | | |
	Annual growth in bank credit-to-GDP ratio	Annual real GDP growth	Annual growth in bank credit-to-GDP ratio	Annual real GDP growth	Average quarterly change in lending rates	Average quarterly change change in policy rates
Australia	9.2	3.8	1.2	1.2	−0.5	−0.4
Canada	6.8	3.9	−4.2	1.7	−0.1	−0.2
Finland	7.7	3.1	−10.6	1.2	−0.2	−0.2
France	7.3	2.5	−2.2	0.7	−0.1	−0.1
Germany	5	2.8	−1.7	0.9	0.2	0.1
Italy[3]	8.2	1.8	−0.6	0.8	−0.1	0.0
Japan	4.3	4.8	−6.4	0.5	0.0	0.0
Norway[3]	8.3	3.5	−3.4	1.6	−0.2	0.3
Spain[3]	11.2	3.2	0.6	0.8	−0.5	−0.2
Sweden[3]	6.7	2.3	−12.1	1.1	−0.4	−0.3
United Kingdom[3]	11.7	2.5	−0.2	0.8	−0.1	−0.2
United States[3]	5.1	3.4	−2.2	0.8	−0.2	−0.2
Average	**7.6**	**3.1**	**−3.5**	**1.0**	**−0.2**	**−0.1**

Source: IMF staff calculations.
[1]The sample for all countries ends in 2007:Q2.
[2]The banking distress and (systemic) banking crises (Finland, Japan, Norway, and Sweden) dates and classifications are based on Caprio and others (2005).
[3]The sample for the entire period starts in 1957:Q1, except for Italy and Sweden (1970:Q1), Spain (1972:Q1), United Kingdom (1962:Q1), and United States (1952:Q1).

risk premiums in capital markets, and sharp contractions in both bank and capital market credit relative to real GDP growth. The mutation of a squeeze into a crunch could be indicated by an increase in risk premiums for all categories of borrowers, including those

typically considered the most creditworthy, reflecting a significant leftward shift in the supply of credit by both financial institutions and investors.

Following the onset of the current financial market turbulence in August 2007, bank

| Periods of Bank Credit Squeezes | | | | | |
| Periods of banking distress and crises | | Periods of bank credit squeezes without distress | | | Credit squeeze quarters with banking distress or banking crisis (indicated in bold)[2] |
Annual growth in bank credit-to-GDP ratio	Annual real GDP growth	Annual growth in bank credit-to-GDP ratio	Annual real GDP growth	Credit squeeze quarters	
1.67	0.75	1.03	1.38	1961:Q4–1962:Q4 1970:Q2–1970:Q4 1991:Q4–1993:Q2	1991:Q4–1992:Q4
−3.18	1.50	−4.22	1.74	1958:Q2–1958:Q4 1983:Q2–1984:Q1 1998:Q4–1999:Q4 2001:Q1–2001:Q2	1983:Q2–1984:Q1
−13.79	0.75	−8.95	1.49	1993:Q4–1997:Q4	**1993:Q4–1994:Q4**
−2.01	0.47	−1.69	0.80	1993:Q4–1995:Q2 1996:Q3–1997:Q4	1993:Q4–1994:Q4
—	—	−1.7	0.9	2003:Q4–2005:Q4 2006:Q3–2007:Q2	
−0.96	1.00	1.15	−0.30	1993:Q4–1996:Q2	1993:Q4–1995:Q4
−2.82	0.22	−6.51	0.44	1999:Q2–2001:Q2 2002:Q3–2004:Q4	**1999:Q2–2004:Q4**
−4.68	1.05	0.04	2.06	1991:Q2–1991:Q4 1993:Q3–1994:Q4	**1991:Q2–1993:Q4**
3.05	0.71	−0.15	0.86	1984:Q3–1985:Q2 1993:Q3–1995:Q4	
−9.65	0.51	−6.36	1.60	1992:Q1–1992:Q2 1993:Q3–1995:Q4	**1992:Q1–1992:Q2** **1993:Q3–1995:Q4**
13.13	0.23	−0.12	0.68	1966:Q4–1967:Q3 1975:Q4–1976:Q1 1991:Q2–1992:Q3 1993:Q2–1994:Q4	1975:Q4–1976:Q1
1.01	0.50	−2.25	1.15	1975:Q4–1976:Q1 1983:Q2–1983:Q3 1990:Q2–1994:Q3	1990:Q2–1991:Q4
−1.7	**0.7**	**−2.5**	**1.1**		

lending standards, based on surveys of loan officers, tightened sharply in the United States and the euro area, and somewhat more modestly in Japan (second figure). In the United States and the euro area, tightening standards are particularly notice-able for lending to the real estate sector (which accounts for more than half of bank lending). Although standards have tight-ened for bank lending to enterprises and households, notably in the United States, it appears that demand for such credit has

Box 1.1 *(continued)*

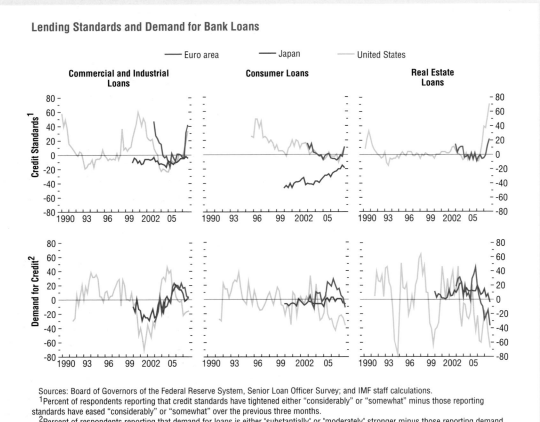

Lending Standards and Demand for Bank Loans

Sources: Board of Governors of the Federal Reserve System, Senior Loan Officer Survey; and IMF staff calculations.
[1]Percent of respondents reporting that credit standards have tightened either "considerably" or "somewhat" minus those reporting standards have eased "considerably" or "somewhat" over the previous three months.
[2]Percent of respondents reporting that demand for loans is either "substantially" or "moderately" stronger minus those reporting demand is either "substantially" or "moderately" weaker over the previous three months.

also declined considerably. How does this evidence match quantitative information on bank lending?

Although slowing, bank credit growth in the United States and the euro area has remained robust thus far, whereas in Japan, the decline in credit growth began at end-2006 and predates the recent global turmoil (third figure). The data are hard to interpret. In the United States, credit growth spiked after August 2007, owing to a surge in commercial and industrial (C&I) loans, which reflected in part the disbursement of leveraged-buyout-related credits that banks had underwritten before the financial market turmoil but were

unable to syndicate or sell afterward. However, since then credit growth has declined, led by a noticeable decline in lending to the real estate sector, although it remains broadly in line with average growth rates observed during the past five years. At the same time, growth in bank security holdings has significantly increased, in part owing to banks' absorption of assets from off-balance-sheet entities back onto their balance sheets.

Is There a Squeeze in Capital Market Financing?

Although the evidence is mixed as to whether a credit squeeze is emerging in bank lending, the dislocations in capital market

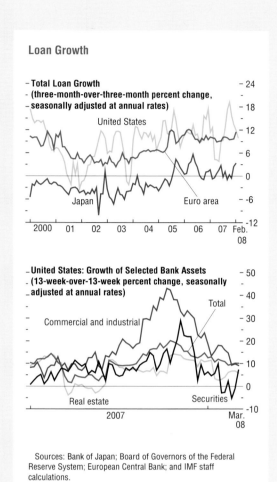

Loan Growth

Sources: Bank of Japan; Board of Governors of the Federal Reserve System; European Central Bank; and IMF staff calculations.

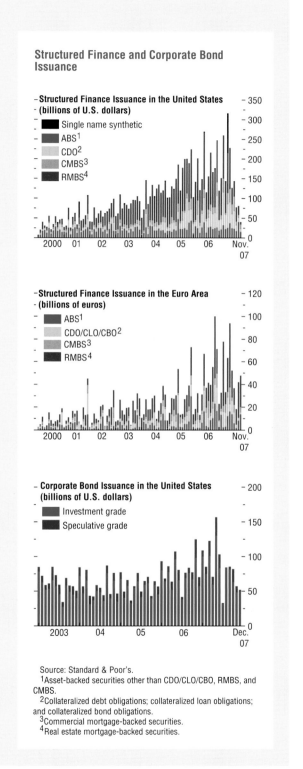

Structured Finance and Corporate Bond Issuance

Source: Standard & Poor's.
[1]Asset-backed securities other than CDO/CLO/CBO, RMBS, and CMBS.
[2]Collateralized debt obligations; collateralized loan obligations; and collateralized bond obligations.
[3]Commercial mortgage-backed securities.
[4]Real estate mortgage-backed securities.

financing could portend a broader credit squeeze. What is the evidence?

The current market turmoil has been accompanied by a more general repricing of risk, reflected in a sharp rise in risk premiums across a range of credit markets (Figure 1.5 in main text). In particular, continuing financial market strains as well as uncertainty about growth prospects have led to a severe contraction in the issuance of structured finance products and to higher spreads and reduced issuance of corporate bonds. The loss of confidence in the securitization model has been particularly severe in

Box 1.1 *(concluded)*

certain sectors. Notably, losses in residential mortgage-backed securities have negatively affected other structured products, with new issuances—particularly those linked to commercial real estate—declining sharply both in the United States and Europe (fourth figure).[8]

At the same time, uncertainty surrounding the growth prospects of the United States and the euro area have adversely affected longer-term capital market financing.

- Risk premiums in corporate bond markets have widened markedly across the entire credit-quality spectrum, suggesting the emergence of a capital market credit squeeze in longer-term debt finance (Figure 1.5 in main text). Although wider spreads on lower-rated bonds can be expected during an economic downturn, spreads on mid-quality and investment-grade bonds have also increased sig-

nificantly. If this trend continues, a credit crunch in longer-term bond financing could be in the making.

- Turning to quantity indicators, U.S. corporate issuance has also declined, amid a complete drying up of speculative-grade bond issuance (see fourth figure). It is important to recognize that demand conditions have changed as well, as a result of the aggregate conditions of nonfinancial firms' and households' balance sheets.

Conclusions

There are now clear signs of a broad credit squeeze affecting a wide range of financing from both banks and securities markets. Evidence to date of a credit crunch is more localized—limited to the U.S. real estate sector and to structured finance products. However, rising uncertainty about growth prospects and asset valuations, further steep declines in asset prices, and—most important—an abrupt reduction in the lending capacity of systemically important segments of the banking system could transform a credit squeeze into a credit crunch, with potentially severe consequences for growth.

[8]Furthermore, during August 2007, and again three months later, spreads on asset-backed commercial paper—particularly paper backed by U.S. nonprime mortgages—widened markedly and with a trend decline in issuances, whereas issuance and spreads of financial and nonfinancial entities were largely unaffected.

in particular) where corporate positions are generally less strong.

Recent financial strains are also affecting foreign exchange markets. The real effective exchange rate of the U.S. dollar has declined sharply since mid-2007 as foreign investment in U.S. securities has been dampened by reduced confidence in liquidity and returns on such assets, as well as by the weakening of U.S. growth prospects and interest rate cuts (Figure 1.7). The progressive decline in the value of the dollar since 2001 has boosted net exports—a key support to the U.S. economy in 2007—and has helped to bring the U.S. current account deficit

down to less than 5 percent of GDP by the fourth quarter of 2007, down more than 1½ percent of GDP from its peak in 2006 (Box 1.2). Nevertheless, the U.S. dollar is still judged to be somewhat on the strong side. Given the limited upward flexibility in the currencies of a number of countries that have large current account surpluses—notably China and oil-exporting countries in the Middle East—the main counterpart of the decline in the U.S. dollar has been appreciation of the euro, the yen, and other floating currencies such as the Canadian dollar and some emerging economy currencies. As a result, the euro is now also judged to be on the strong side, although the yen still remains somewhat undervalued. This experience contrasts strongly with that during 1985–91, a period of rapid external adjustment, when the patterns of exchange rate adjustment and current account imbalances were more closely matched (see Box 1.2).

What then is the bottom line? The pervasive impact of financial market turbulence on both banks and securities markets, coming on top of the continuing housing correction, clearly represents a broad credit squeeze that had already dampened activity in the United States toward the end of 2007 and has prompted an aggressive policy response, although the initial strength of corporate and household balance sheets has provided some protection. The financial conditions index (FCI) shown in Figure 1.4 suggests that the combination of exchange rate depreciation, easing by the Federal Reserve, and declining long-term rates on government securities should be supportive of future activity, notwithstanding rising spreads. However, such a measure does not take account of rapidly tightening bank lending standards and the collapse of complex structured credit markets, which had been supporting credit growth. On balance, adverse financial conditions are likely to have a continuing negative impact on activity in the United States, notwithstanding the Federal Reserve's strong response.

Western Europe is also being affected by the losses incurred by banks with U.S. exposures, spillover effects on interbank and securities markets, and upward pressure on the euro—reflected in a tightening of the FCI. Although the impact on demand has been less evident to date, activity is likely to face considerable drag from tighter bank lending standards and wider spreads for riskier borrowers. By contrast, Japan's financial institutions have been much less directly affected by the financial turbulence, and the economic impact seems likely to be felt through broader spillovers from a global slowdown. However, all the advanced economies are expected to face serious consequences if deepening losses to bank capital and a further

Figure 1.7. External Developments in Selected Advanced Economies

The U.S. dollar has continued to depreciate, helping to bring down the U.S. current account deficit in recent quarters. The yen's value has rebounded since August 2007 as turbulent financial conditions led to some reversal of "carry trade" flows. The euro has remained on an appreciating trend.

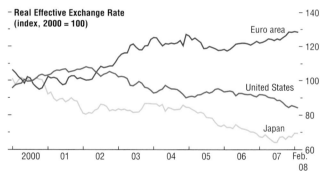

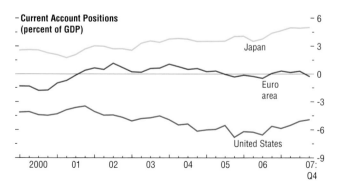

Sources: Haver Analytics; and IMF staff calculations.

Box 1.2. Depreciation of the U.S. Dollar: Causes and Consequences

The U.S. dollar has depreciated by about 25 percent in real effective terms since early 2002, in what has been one of the largest dollar depreciation episodes in the post–Bretton Woods era (first figure). At the same time, the U.S. current account deficit remains above 5 percent of GDP, still leaving considerable uncertainty about the prospects for the resolution of global current account imbalances. Against this backdrop, this box reviews the main factors behind the current episode of dollar adjustment and discusses associated risks and policy challenges.

What Has Contributed to the Dollar's Depreciation?

Similar to the previous major depreciation episode during 1985–91, the current decline in the dollar started against the background of a large U.S. current account deficit and has spanned several years. During both episodes, the pace of depreciation was gradual and orderly, with daily changes below 2–3 percent in nominal effective terms. However, there is a clear contrast between the evolution of U.S. current account balances during the two episodes. During 1985–91, the current account deficit had begun to narrow within two years of the initial depreciation and reached near-balance by 1991. In contrast, during the recent episode starting in 2002, the current account deficit initially continued to widen, reaching an all-time high of almost 7 percent of GDP in late 2005. It began to moderate only in 2006, and remained at 5½ percent of GDP in 2007.

What factors have contributed to the large and widening U.S. current account deficit despite the sustained dollar depreciation since 2002?

• The rise of emerging economies: The dollar's real effective depreciation may exaggerate the improvement in U.S. competitiveness by failing to capture fully the erosion of U.S. competitiveness caused by the rapid shift in trade toward low-cost emerging and developing economies since the 1990s. The

Note: The main authors of this box are Selim Elekdag, Kornélia Krajnyák, and Jaewoo Lee.

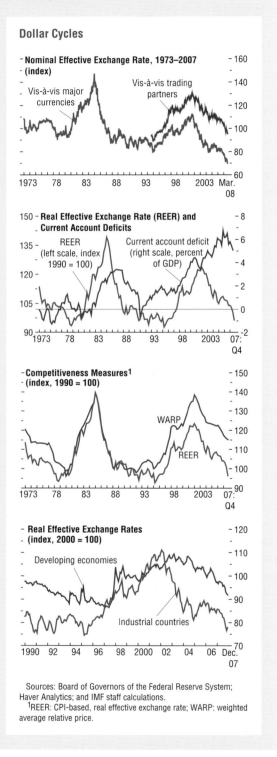

Dollar Cycles

Sources: Board of Governors of the Federal Reserve System; Haver Analytics; and IMF staff calculations.
[1]REER: CPI-based, real effective exchange rate; WARP: weighted average relative price.

weighted average relative price (WARP), which better reflects the growing importance of low-cost trading partners, shows a trend erosion of U.S. competitiveness compared to real exchange rate indices (Thomas, Marquez, and Fahle, 2008).

- The U.S. business cycle: Until 2006, the U.S. economy had a more robust growth performance than other advanced economies—spurred by buoyant consumption reflecting the rising value of housing wealth (see Chapter 3)—and this boosted U.S. imports over this period.

- Oil prices: Driven by strong global growth, including in emerging economies, oil prices have soared to historic highs in recent years, adding to the current account deficits of oil-importing countries, including the United States.

- Financial market factors: Large current account deficits have been financed by steady capital inflows into the United States, mostly through fixed-income instruments, including asset-backed securities. These inflows included large purchases of corporate and agency bonds by private investors attracted by the perceived liquidity and innovativeness of U.S. financial markets, as well as significant official purchases of U.S. Treasury and agency bonds.

Since mid-2007, however, financial and cyclical developments have intensified the dollar's depreciation. Market turbulence has increased uncertainty about the valuation and liquidity of U.S. securitized assets, leading to sharp declines in private demand for corporate and agency bonds (previous areas of strength), depressing net portfolio inflows, and increasing pressure on the dollar (second figure). At the same time, the increasing cyclical weakness of U.S. growth, interest rate cuts, and expectations of further monetary easing have also weighed on the dollar.

Is the Dollar's Adjustment Complete?

With the dollar now close to its historic low in real effective terms, is the adjustment now complete, or perhaps excessive? The analysis of the Consultative Group on Exchange Rate Issues

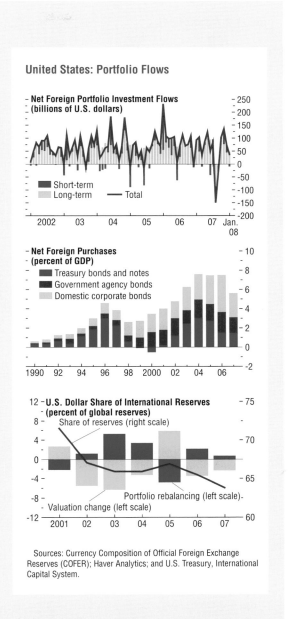

United States: Portfolio Flows

Sources: Currency Composition of Official Foreign Exchange Reserves (COFER); Haver Analytics; and U.S. Treasury, International Capital System.

(CGER) of the IMF suggests that the U.S. dollar has now moved closer to its medium-term equilibrium level but still remains somewhat on the strong side. The CGER analysis is based on three complementary approaches (Lee and others, 2008):

- The macroeconomic balance (MB) approach still finds some misalignment, based on the difference between the projected medium-

Box 1.2 *(continued)*

term current account balance and a "sustainable" level of current account. The sustainable current account of the United States is estimated to be a deficit in the range of 2 to 3 percent of GDP, determined as a function of medium-term fundamentals including demographics and the structural fiscal position. The U.S. current account deficit is projected to come down to about 4 percent of GDP in 2013, but will still exceed the estimated sustainable deficit level. This gap is substantially reduced relative to estimates made a year ago but still suggests that further real depreciation may be needed to bring the current account deficit to a sustainable level.

- The external sustainability (ES) approach indicates a substantial misalignment. For the United States, this approach is based on the difference between the projected medium-term trade balance and the level of trade balance that would stabilize the U.S. net foreign assets (NFA) position at its 2006 level. The NFA-stabilizing trade balance is calculated to be a deficit of about 2 percent of GDP, well below the projected 2013 trade deficit of almost 4 percent of GDP. This gap suggests that sizable real depreciation may be needed to bring down the trade deficit to the NFA-stabilizing level.

- The reduced-form equilibrium real exchange rate regression (ERER) approach finds that the dollar is closer to its medium-term equilibrium value than under the MB or ES approaches. Under this approach, an equilibrium value is estimated directly as a function of medium-term fundamentals including productivity, NFA, and the terms of trade. The real effective depreciation since 2002 reduced the larger overvaluation estimate for the early 2000s, as actual exchange rate depreciation outpaced the more gradual decline in the equilibrium exchange rate that reflected the deterioration in the U.S. NFA and terms of trade.

The CGER analysis thus suggests that the U.S. dollar still remains somewhat on the strong side. However, two mitigating factors could limit

the exchange rate pressure. The first is valuation gains that could moderate the decline in U.S. external indebtedness—measured by the NFA position—implied by current account projections. According to preliminary estimates, the U.S. NFA position at end-2007 was broadly unchanged from its end-2006 level, despite a current account deficit of 5½ percent of GDP, owing to valuation gains on U.S. holdings of foreign equities and the depreciation of the currency. Indeed, favorable valuation gains have supported the U.S. NFA position for many years, offsetting a large part of the cumulative current account deficit.[1] Given historical experience, valuation gains—albeit smaller than in the past few years—may continue to support the U.S. NFA position in the future.

The second mitigating factor is uncertainty regarding the pace and size of the current account adjustment that will follow from the recent depreciation. The narrowing of the deficit since 2006 may well be the beginning of a belated but full-scale adjustment. For example, changing trade and financial practices, including extensive outsourcing and currency hedging, may have delayed adjustment to exchange rate changes relative to lags in earlier trade equations.[2] Thus, the current account deficit could narrow more significantly over time, even with the dollar staying near the current low level. During the adjustment phase, however, the still-large deficit would continue to be a potential source of further downward pressure on the dollar.

What Are the Risks from a Weak Dollar?

The continued perception of downside risk to the dollar has rekindled concerns about the dollar's role as the world's primary reserve currency and has drawn attention to the decline in the dollar's share in official reserve holdings since 2002. In fact, the bulk of this decline is

---

[1]For further details, see Box 3.1 in the April 2007 *World Economic Outlook.*

[2]For related discussions, see Greenspan (2005) and Chapter 3 of the April 2007 *World Economic Outlook.*

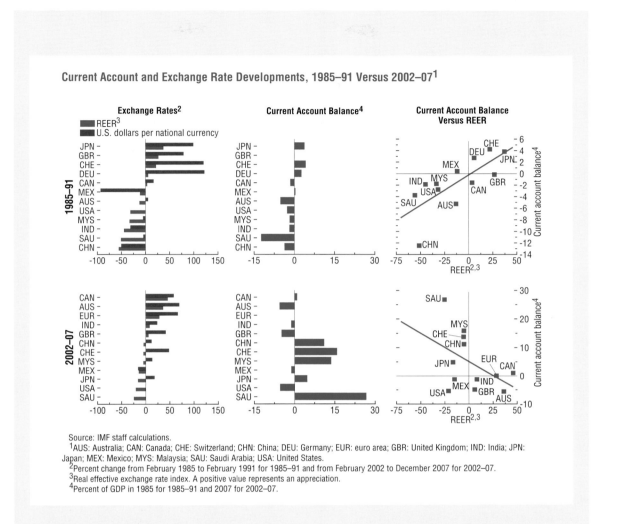

Current Account and Exchange Rate Developments, 1985–91 Versus 2002–07[1]

Source: IMF staff calculations.
[1]AUS: Australia; CAN: Canada; CHE: Switzerland; CHN: China; DEU: Germany; EUR: euro area; GBR: United Kingdom; IND: India; JPN: Japan; MEX: Mexico; MYS: Malaysia; SAU: Saudi Arabia; USA: United States.
[2]Percent change from February 1985 to February 1991 for 1985–91 and from February 2002 to December 2007 for 2002–07.
[3]Real effective exchange rate index. A positive value represents an appreciation.
[4]Percent of GDP in 1985 for 1985–91 and 2007 for 2002–07.

estimated to reflect valuation changes from the dollar depreciation rather than active diversification away from the dollar by official reserve managers (see second figure). Nonetheless, further dollar weakness could diminish the appeal of dollar assets sufficiently to encourage more active portfolio reallocation away from dollar assets, including by U.S. investors.[3] Given the continued large external financing needs of the United States, even a gradual diversification away from dollar assets could trigger a sharp

[3]Currently, U.S. investors display significant home bias, especially with respect to bonds. However, if concerns about securitization and the quality of U.S. assets linger, there could be sizable U.S. outflows.

dollar depreciation, particularly in the context of continued uncertainty and turbulence in financial markets.

Sovereign wealth funds, whose assets have grown to a significant size in many countries, have helped stabilize financial markets and support the dollar by means of capital injections into several financial institutions since summer 2007. Because they are likely to have longer investment horizons than many private funds, sovereign wealth funds could continue to be a stabilizing force in global financial markets. At the same time, managers of these funds could put greater weight on investment returns than do managers of official reserves, and the increase in (reserve) assets under their manage-

Box 1.2 *(concluded)*

ment could facilitate diversification of official assets away from dollar assets and add to the downward pressure on the dollar.

Another concern stems from the fact that, though orderly, the current episode of dollar depreciation has been disconnected from the pattern of global imbalances in several cases. Bilateral and multilateral exchange rate movements since 2002 have borne little semblance to the distribution of current account surpluses, in contrast to the previous dollar depreciation

episode over the late 1980s, when the currencies of the major surplus countries all went through larger appreciations than other currencies (third figure). In the current episode, a number of countries with large current account surpluses have linked their currencies tightly to the dollar, thereby hindering adjustment. A continued mismatch in this regard could result in a reallocation of—rather than a reduction in—global imbalances and could eventually produce new imbalances.

loss of confidence in structured financing were to transform the current credit squeeze into a full-blown credit crunch.

Can Emerging and Developing Economies Decouple?

In strong contrast to earlier periods of global financial disruption, the direct spillovers to emerging and developing economies have been largely contained so far. Issuance activity by these economies has moderated since August 2007, compared with the very high rates experienced during the previous year, but overall foreign exchange flows have been largely sustained, and international reserves have continued to rise (Figures 1.8 and 1.9). Foreign direct investment and portfolio equity flows have generally remained strong, although there have been sharp portfolio outflows during periods of market nervousness. Most emerging markets have significantly outperformed those in advanced economies since last summer, even though spreads on emerging economies' sovereign and corporate debt have widened and equity prices retreated in early 2008.

Within this broad picture, a number of countries that had been heavily reliant on short-term cross-border borrowing—either lending by foreign banks or offshore borrowing by domestic banks—were affected more dramatically by the tightening of liquidity conditions in August

2007, and many faced disruptions in local interbank markets. The immediate dislocations were handled effectively, but capital inflows slowed in some countries—including Kazakhstan and Latvia—constraining domestic credit and slowing GDP growth. To date, none of these economies has faced an external crisis of the sort seen in previous episodes of emerging economy turbulence.

Similarly, on the trade side, spillovers from slowing activity in the advanced economies have been limited to date. There has been some impact on exports by a number of economies that trade heavily with the United States. Moreover, export revenues for metals exporters have flattened as prices have come down from their peaks in mid-2007. Overall trading activity has been well sustained, however, with important support from the strong growth of domestic demand in emerging economies' trading partners.

Against this background, although there were signs of slowing activity in some emerging and developing economies in the latter part of 2007, for the year as a whole growth remained a robust 7.9 percent, even faster than the rapid pace achieved in 2006. Moreover, as in recent years, the strong growth has been maintained across all regions, including Africa and Latin America, as discussed in greater detail in Chapter 2. Indeed, many countries continue to face the challenge of dealing with rising inflation rates, driven by strong domestic demand, rapid credit growth, and the heavy impact of buoyant food and energy prices. Thus, central banks have generally continued to tighten monetary policy in recent months (Chile, China, Colombia, Mexico, South Africa, Peru, Poland, Russia, and Taiwan Province of China have all raised interest rates since the October 2007 *World Economic Outlook*), although some central banks have begun to unwind earlier tightening (the Philippines, Turkey). For some countries, however—notably China and the Middle Eastern oil exporters—monetary tightening has been constrained by the relative inflexibility of their currencies vis-à-vis the weakening U.S. dollar. In China, the renminbi's rate of appreciation against the dollar has increased appreciably since August, but its movement has been more modest in effective terms, and the currency is judged to be still substantially undervalued.

What explains the resilience of the emerging and developing economies? Will they be able to effectively decouple from the substantial slowdown—and possible recession—in the advanced economies in 2008? There are two main sources of support for these economies: strong growth momentum from the productivity gains from their continuing integration into the global economy and stabilization gains from improved macroeconomic policy frameworks. What is important is not just how these factors have evolved in individual countries, but also how they have interacted across countries to change the dynamics of global growth.

Previous issues of the *World Economic Outlook*, as well as a growing literature more broadly, have analyzed in some detail how a combination of market reforms and advances in technology have allowed an unbundling of the production process and a global harnessing of underutilized labor resources, particularly in China, India, and emerging Europe. In turn, this process has promoted the sustained rapid increases in productivity that have underpinned the striking divergence in GDP growth performance between advanced economies and developing economies since 2000.

Figure 1.8. Emerging Economy Financial Conditions

Capital flows to emerging economies have moderated since August 2007, coming down from previous very high rates. Prices on emerging economies' sovereign bonds and equities have softened, but by less than the drop in advanced economies' securities.

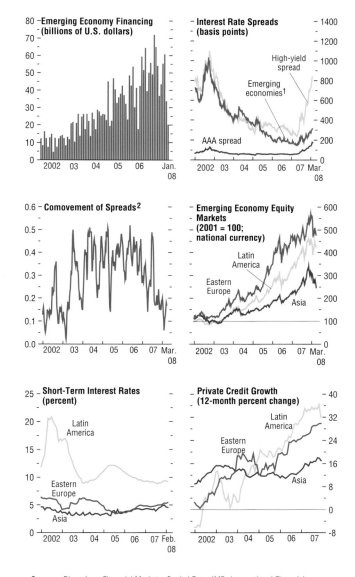

Sources: Bloomberg Financial Markets; Capital Data; IMF, *International Financial Statistics;* and IMF staff calculations.
[1]JPMorgan EMBI Global Index spread.
[2]Average of 30-day rolling cross-correlation of emerging economy debt spreads.

Figure 1.9. External Developments in Emerging and Developing Economies

(Index, 2000 = 100)

Exchange rates in emerging and developing economies have generally continued to appreciate, in the face of strong foreign exchange inflows and despite heavy intervention, which has pushed reserves up to record levels.

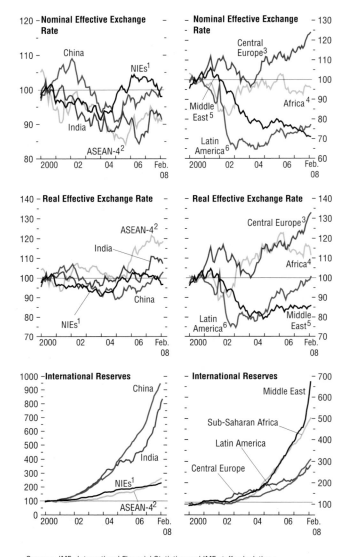

Sources: IMF, *International Financial Statistics;* and IMF staff calculations.

[1]Newly industrialized Asian economies (NIEs) comprise Hong Kong SAR, Korea, Singapore, and Taiwan Province of China.

[2]Indonesia, Malaysia, Philippines, and Thailand.

[3]Czech Republic, Hungary, and Poland.

[4]Botswana, Burkina Faso, Cameroon, Chad, Republic of Congo, Côte d'Ivoire, Djibouti, Equatorial Guinea, Ethiopia, Gabon, Ghana, Guinea, Kenya, Madagascar, Mali, Mauritius, Mozambique, Namibia, Niger, Nigeria, Rwanda, Senegal, South Africa, Sudan, Tanzania, Uganda, and Zambia.

[5]Bahrain, Egypt, I.R. of Iran, Jordan, Kuwait, Lebanon, Libya, Oman, Qatar, Saudi Arabia, Syrian Arab Republic, United Arab Emirates, and Republic of Yemen.

[6]Argentina, Brazil, Chile, Colombia, Mexico, Peru, and Rep. Bolivariana de Venezuela.

As a result, there have been two important shifts in the growth dynamic of the global economy. The first is that growth in global activity over the past five years has been dominated by the emerging and developing economies—China has accounted for about one-quarter of global growth; Brazil, China, India, and Russia for almost one-half; and all the emerging and developing economies together for about two-thirds, compared with about one-half in the 1970s (Figure 1.10). Growth in these economies also is more resource-intensive, given their patterns of production and consumption (see Chapter 5 of the September 2006 *World Economic Outlook*). One consequence of these trends is that the increasing demand for key commodities such as oil, metals, and foodstuffs is now driven by growth in these economies—they account for more than 90 percent of the rise in consumption of oil products and metals and 80 percent of the rise in consumption of grains since 2002 (with biofuels representing most of the remainder). This has contributed to the sustained strong increase in commodity prices observed over the past year, despite moderating growth in the advanced economies, and has been an important factor behind the strong recent performance of commodity-exporting countries in Africa and Latin America, as well as oil exporters in the Middle East.

The second, related shift is the growing importance of emerging and developing economies in the structure of global trade. These economies now account for about one-third of global trade and more than one-half of the total increase in import volumes since 2000. Moreover, the pattern of trade has changed. Almost one-half of exports from emerging and developing economies is now directed toward other such economies, with rising intraregional trade within emerging Asia most notable. And, as explored in more detail in Chapter 5, countries in Africa and Latin America are also achieving some success in diversifying the destinations of their exports and in broadening their export bases, leveraging more successfully than in the past the benefits of the present commodity price boom to increase exports of higher-value-added manufactured products. As a result, the advanced economy business cycle may play a less-dominant role in driving swings in activity for the emerging and developing economies, even as these economies become increasingly open to trade.

Turning to policies, most emerging and developing economies have maintained disciplined macroeconomic policies in recent years, bringing down fiscal deficits and reducing inflation. Public balance sheets have been strengthened, and external vulnerabilities have been substantially reduced as international reserves have risen to historic highs and reliance on external borrowing has been largely contained—for example, see Chapter 2 for a more detailed discussion of Latin America, a region that had been heavily affected by sudden stops in capital flows. Indeed, in the aggregate, these economies have become significant exporters of savings, in strong contrast to the decades before 2000. To be sure, concerns remain, including that government spending has been allowed to rise too quickly on the basis of rapidly rising tax revenues that may be unsustainable when growth slows, that domestic credit booms could weaken financial institutions' balance sheets, and that some countries, particularly in emerging Europe, have built up large current account deficits financed at least in part by short-term and debt-related flows (again, see Chapter 2). But, although pockets of vulnerability certainly remain, the overall framework of macroeconomic policy has been substantially improved in these economies.

The combination of strong internal growth dynamics, a rising share of the global economy, and more-resilient policy frameworks seems to have helped reduce the dependence of emerging and developing economies on the advanced economy business cycle—but spillovers have not been eliminated. This overall assessment is supported by recent work by Akin and Kose (2007), which estimates that growth spillovers from advanced economies to emerging and developing economies have decreased substantially since

Figure 1.10. Growing Global Role of Emerging and Developing Economies

Emerging and developing economies have contributed about two-thirds of growth in output (in purchasing-power-parity terms) and more than one-half of growth in import volumes since the recent upswing in 2002. These economies have also registered large current account surpluses, in contrast to the usual collective deficit prior to 2000.

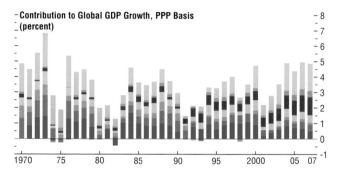

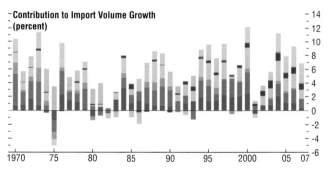

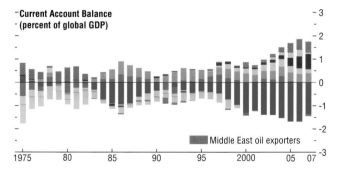

Source: IMF staff calculations.

the mid-1980s, but remain sizable (about 35 percent pass-through for emerging economies and 45 percent pass-through for more commodity-reliant developing economies). Similarly, work on spillovers in the April 2007 *World Economic Outlook* concluded that spillovers remain substantial, particularly for highly open economies, and that spillovers are nonlinear—mild during advanced economy slowdowns but more severe during recessions. One cause of this nonlinearity may lie in the importance of financial channels, including the high synchronization of global equity prices during a correction and the potential for "sudden stops" in financial flows to emerging economies that are seen to be vulnerable at times of financial stress.

The shift to a multipolar world that is much less dependent on the United States as the locomotive for global growth has affected the dynamics of the global economy and carries implications for the analysis of risks to the outlook and policy responses, which are taken up later in this chapter. Three trends are particularly striking:

- The strong dynamism of domestic demand in emerging and developing economies has provided a "trade shock absorber," enabling a robust expansion of U.S. exports over the past year even as U.S. domestic demand has slowed. These same factors, however, have muted the "commodity price shock absorber" that in the past has effectively cushioned the impact of downturns in aggregate demand in the advanced economies. Most strikingly, the rise of oil prices to record highs in early 2008, despite slowing demand in the advanced economies, has simultaneously dampened consumption and raised inflation concerns in the advanced economies, thus constraining the potential for a monetary policy response.
- The shift of the emerging and developing economies as a group to become net savers has contributed to the increasing global availability of savings and has put downward pressure on real interest rates. Arguably, the resulting abundance of liquidity helped to spur the rapid financial innovations and

fund the excesses in global financial markets witnessed in recent years, thereby sowing the seeds for the current financial market turbulence. Recently, the infusion of financial resources from sovereign wealth funds from emerging and developing economies to recapitalize U.S. banks has provided a valuable "financial shock absorber." Looking ahead, an important issue is whether the dislocations in U.S. financial markets could boost the flow of funds into other markets, contributing to the development of asset price bubbles or market excesses elsewhere. For example, little is known about how the large petrodollar surpluses of recent years have been invested. Box 2.2 presents evidence that a substantial portion of these resources has been channeled to emerging economies, particularly emerging Europe. Such flows could rise further, particularly if energy prices stay high, but they could also dwindle if a global downturn were to bring oil prices down.

- The processes of external adjustment and policy coordination have become more multifaceted and complex. An effective response to a deepening downturn in global activity would need to involve the large emerging economies as well as the advanced economies, in recognition of both their increasing share of global aggregate demand and the policy space they have earned through disciplined policy implementation. Similarly, unlike in the 1980s, global current account imbalances are no longer an issue relevant only to the large advanced economies—the Multilateral Consultation on Global Imbalances organized by the IMF last year involved China and Saudi Arabia in addition to the major advanced economies in recognition of this development. Progress is being made to implement policy plans discussed during the Multilateral Consultation, but the coexistence of flexible with more heavily managed and fixed exchange rate regimes among major economies has compromised the effectiveness of exchange rate movements in reducing global imbalances (Box 1.3).

Box 1.3. Multilateral Consultation on Global Imbalances: Progress Report

In the nine months since the report on the Multilateral Consultation on Global Imbalances (MC) was published, the global economy has been buffeted by a series of shocks that were not fully anticipated at the time of the consultations.[1] Most notably, financial turmoil—precipitated by the U.S. subprime mortgage crisis—has gripped money and credit markets in the United States and Europe since summer 2007. Concerns about a credit crunch and a sharper slowdown in the economy have drawn policy attention to monetary easing and fiscal stimulus in the United States. At the same time, with a weaker dollar and moderating growth, the U.S. current account deficit has narrowed and its outlook has markedly improved. Against this backdrop, is the MC policy framework still relevant, or has it been overtaken by recent events?

Although financial market dislocations raise important issues for policymakers, the policy objectives of the MC remain relevant to help mitigate the risks attached to still-high global imbalances. If anything, the dual objectives of the MC—to help facilitate an orderly unwinding of imbalances and to do so in a manner supportive of global growth—have gained increased relevance in light of recent financial market disruptions and a possible slowdown in global growth. The U.S. slowdown, for example, highlights the importance of ensuring strong domestic demand elsewhere to support growth in the global economy. In addition, the abrupt and unexpected nature of recent financial disruptions underscores concerns of a disorderly market adjustment that IMF policy advice has long sought to avoid. Against this background, this box reviews recent progress made in implementing MC policy plans. It also assesses the outlook for adjustment in global imbalances and the

evolving risks in light of recent economic and policy developments. Although the outlook has improved, the continuing risks associated with still-large imbalances—particularly at present—argue for continuing progress on the relevant policy plans to mitigate such risks, but with the flexibility to take due account of the changing global context.

What Progress Has Been Made?

A key achievement of the MC was the set of policy plans set out in some detail by participants, which were congruent with their domestic objectives and the International Monetary and Financial Committee (IMFC) strategy to narrow imbalances.[2] Given the continued relevance and importance of these policy plans, what steps have been taken?

China has made some progress in rebalancing growth toward domestic consumption, including through increased public spending on social programs and financial sector reforms, and has taken incremental steps toward greater currency flexibility.

- Public spending continues to be reoriented toward social programs, which are anticipated to be a major focus of the 2008 budget. This includes the continued rollout of the rural cooperative health system, free-of-charge rural compulsory education, and several enhanced social security programs.
- Financial reforms include easing some restrictions on foreign participation in domestic securities companies, streamlining the process

---

Note: The main author of this box is Hamid Faruqee.

[1]The Staff Report on the Multilateral Consultation on Global Imbalances was publicly released on August 7, 2007, and is available at www.imf.org (see Public Information Notice (PIN) No. 07/97). Background information is summarized in Box 1.3 of the October 2007 *World Economic Outlook*.

[2]As stated in the IMFC Communiqué of September 17, 2006, this strategy comprises "steps to boost national saving in the United States, including fiscal consolidation; further progress on growth-enhancing reforms in Europe; further structural reforms, including fiscal consolidation, in Japan; reforms to boost domestic demand in emerging Asia, together with greater exchange rate flexibility in a number of surplus countries; and increased spending consistent with absorptive capacity and macroeconomic stability in oil-producing countries." Country-specific policy plans consistent with the IMFC strategy were jointly announced by MC participants on April 14, 2007; plans can be found in the appendix to the MC Staff Report.

Box 1.3 *(continued)*

for bond issuances for listed companies, and allowing foreign invested companies (that is, companies that are locally incorporated) to issue bonds and equities in China.[3] Tax reform in the external sector includes lower tariffs on imports of several raw materials and agricultural products, higher export taxes on energy-intensive industries, and a unified corporate tax rate for domestic and foreign-funded enterprises.

- Exchange rate flexibility has increased incrementally. Since the currency band for daily exchange rate fluctuations was widened (from 0.3 percent to 0.5 percent) in mid-2007, the renminbi has shown a greater degree of bilateral appreciation against the dollar, albeit less so in effective terms given the dollar's multilateral depreciation. Since last summer, China's currency has appreciated by about 4 percent against the dollar and about 1 percent in real effective terms.[4]

In Saudi Arabia, the authorities have ramped up spending on needed social and economic infrastructure. Total spending in the 2007 budget increased by 11 percent relative to 2006. Staff projections suggest that the 2008 budget outturn will be more expansionary. Outlays in economic infrastructure include oil-related investment aimed at boosting production and refining capacity and public-private partnership projects, for which medium-term plans have been expanded by 60 percent since 2006. There is a high import content associated with these projects. With domestic inflation pressures rising, it will be important to prioritize spending in areas such as infrastructure to help relieve supply bottlenecks.

Japan has made progress in reforming product markets, and fiscal consolidation has also advanced faster than anticipated.

- Some reforms have been introduced to liberalize product markets. Japan-Post became a joint-stock company in 2007. With respect to trade openness, several economic partnership agreements were also signed.
- Some steps have been taken to level the playing the field for inward foreign direct investment. The government removed a perceived impediment by granting capital gains tax deferrals in "triangular" mergers (through which a foreign company acquires a Japanese target via a local unit).

In the euro area, member states have taken measures to accelerate financial integration and to better align incentives in labor markets. Progress in product market liberalization has been more limited, although implementation of the Services Directive is ongoing.

- There has been notable progress at the EU level in reducing national barriers to a single market in financial services, including passage of the Payment Services Directive, which is needed to create a single European payments area. A new code of conduct has been introduced to help address fragmented clearing and settlement services in Europe.
- EU member states have moved on recommendations to improve flexibility and security in labor markets. Wage-bargaining systems in some countries are gradually moving in the direction of greater wage and working-time flexibility through less-centralized bargaining and more differentiated agreements.[5] However, there has been much less progress (with a few exceptions) on promoting cross-border labor mobility.
- Progress to enhance competition in services is visible, though in a limited number of countries.[6] Some measures have been carried out to open up network industries in the rail, tele-

---

[3]The quotas for the Qualified Domestic Institutional Investor program and for the Qualified Foreign Institutional Investor program were also substantially increased in 2007.

[4]Based on the average January 2008 exchange rate versus the August 22–September 19 period average (October 2007 *World Economic Outlook* reference period).

[5]Related initiatives include limiting minimum wage increases and relaxing the 35-hour-workweek restriction in France and lowering payroll taxes in Germany.

[6]In France, initiatives include a reduction in legal barriers to the establishment of large retail shops, restaurants, and hotels.

com, and energy sectors in several member states. Fewer countries have taken measures in the retail sector.

In the United States, alongside a narrowing current account deficit, the major advance has been the continued decline in the federal budget deficit, ahead of earlier projections. The unified federal budget deficit was reduced to 1.2 percent of GDP in fiscal year (FY) 2007, significantly smaller than originally budgeted. Looking ahead, the deficit is expected to widen temporarily to 3¼–3½ percent of GDP in FY2008 and FY2009, as a result of the cyclical downturn and the $170 billion temporary stimulus package and other spending increases (mainly security related). The administration's budget aims to bring down the deficit and to achieve a small surplus in FY2012, although attaining this will require very tight control in the face of serious budgetary challenges. The IMF staff's medium-term projections foresee the budget gap narrowing modestly toward the administration's goal—which remains an essential objective for addressing longer-term pressures on public finances.

What Are the Outlook and Risks for Global Imbalances?

Overall, MC partners have made welcome progress on several fronts with respect to their policy plans. Reflecting various economic and policy factors, the outlook for global imbalances has also moved in the right direction (see figure). Global imbalances appear to have peaked in 2006–07 and are projected to narrow somewhat faster than earlier projected, although they remain large by historical standards.

Looking specifically at the United States, its current account position and trajectory have improved markedly since the MC. As discussed in more detail in Box 1.2, with moderating growth and a weaker dollar, the U.S. external current account deficit has narrowed faster than expected (to about 5½ percent of GDP in 2007), while the U.S. net foreign asset position has remained remarkably stable. The improvement in the current account's projected trajectory

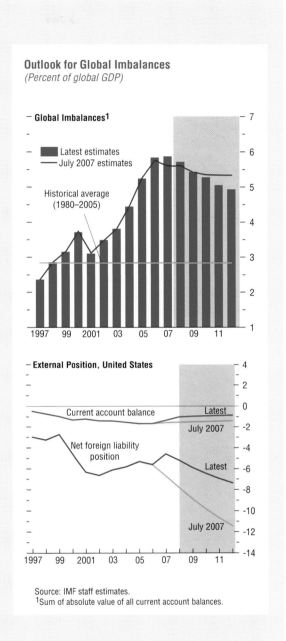

Outlook for Global Imbalances
(Percent of global GDP)

Global Imbalances[1]

Latest estimates
July 2007 estimates

Historical average
(1980–2005)

External Position, United States

Current account balance   Latest
                           July 2007

Net foreign liability position   Latest
                                  July 2007

Source: IMF staff estimates.
[1]Sum of absolute value of all current account balances.

over the medium term partly reflects weaker residential investment and some gradual recovery in personal saving rates amid tighter credit availability and slower growth. The improved trajectory for U.S. net external assets reflects smaller flow deficits, as well as a stronger starting point, given strong valuation gains and return differentials in favor of U.S. foreign investment.

Box 1.3 *(concluded)*

Counterparts to the U.S. external adjustment include China's shift to a modestly lower trajectory for its current account surplus compared with earlier projections, given that domestic consumption is projected to strengthen over the medium term (from 51 percent to 57 percent of GDP). In addition, reflecting exchange rate appreciation and weaker growth in partners, the euro area's current account deficit is projected to widen. And external surpluses in Saudi Arabia are expected to moderate, reflecting higher investment and infrastructure spending that raise the non-oil trade deficit.

However, risks related to imbalances have not dissipated. Indeed, some risks have become more acute in light of economic developments and recent financial disruptions. Key reasons include the following:

- In a period of fragile market confidence, risks of a disorderly market adjustment remain a clear concern. Although dollar depreciation has been orderly thus far, the level of imbalances remains much larger than in past episodes of significant dollar adjustment (see Box 1.2). Moreover, sustained large losses on foreign holdings of U.S. external assets, together with reduced confidence in some securitized assets and structured finance products, suggest that foreign financing could be less forthcoming.
- The recent asymmetric pattern of currency movements against the U.S. dollar—which has depreciated noticeably less against the currencies of some key surplus countries—continues to underscore the need for a broad-based adjustment (see Box 1.2). Disproportionate adjustment, on the other hand, could fuel protectionist sentiments, especially in the context of slowing global growth.[7]
- In the United States, tighter lending standards, declining house prices, and slower growth may support some normalization in household saving from low levels. But prospects for softer U.S. demand would need to be offset by stronger domestic demand elsewhere to avert a deeper global slowdown.
- Despite some slowing in advanced economies, volatile oil prices—which have ascended to new highs—could slow any narrowing of global imbalances. Given strong demand growth from emerging markets and ongoing concerns of supply disruptions, tight market conditions imply continued risks of oil price spikes which could add to the imbalance problem.

This suggests that the MC road map for policies remains relevant and argues for continuing progress on these plans, though with the flexibility to account for the changing global context. From a global perspective, against the background of ongoing financial turmoil and a clouded outlook for the global economy, tangible further progress on these policy plans by all participants would facilitate a smoother shift in the global pattern of demand to ease global risks attached to imbalances and provide needed support to the global economy at a time of heightened market uncertainty.

---

[7]For analysis on the countercyclical nature of trade protection, see Bagwell and Staiger (1997) and the references cited therein. Beyond tariff and nontariff barriers, Leidy (1996) finds that a weaker macroeconomy may also spur antidumping measures and countervailing duties.

Outlook and Risks for the Global Economy

The spreading crisis in financial markets has further dampened the global outlook since the publication of the January 2008 *World Economic Outlook Update*. Under the IMF's current baseline projection, conditions in financial markets will stabilize only gradually during the course of 2008 and 2009, risk spreads will remain substantially wider than the exceptionally low levels that prevailed prior to August 2007, and bank lending standards will continue to tighten. Commodity prices will remain roughly at the high levels of end-2007. Under the baseline, global growth will slow from 4.9 percent in 2007 to 3.7 percent in 2008 and 3.8 percent in 2009.

Among the major advanced economies, the United States is projected to tip into a mild recession in 2008, despite aggressive rate cuts by the Federal Reserve and timely implementation of a fiscal stimulus package. The restraint on demand from the housing cycle, as falling home prices prompt rising foreclosures and further price declines, is being reinforced by an interconnected financial cycle: pressure on capital and credit forces asset sales, which lowers market values and further intensifies the downward swing of the credit cycle. As macroeconomic and financial weakness feed off each other, residential investment will continue to fall; consumption will decline as households retrench in the face of falling home prices, reduced employment, and tighter credit; and business investment will also take a hit. The incipient recovery in 2009 is likely to be slow, held back by continued household and financial balance sheet strains, consistent with the historical experience after major housing busts (Figure 1.11 and Chapter 2 of the April 2003 *World Economic Outlook*). Other advanced economies, particularly in Western Europe, will slow to well below potential, dampened by both trade and financial channels. Growth in emerging and developing economies will also ease but will remain robust during both 2008 and 2009. Headline inflation will remain elevated in the first half of 2008, but will moderate gradually thereafter, reflecting the receding impact of recent increases in commodity prices and the emergence of slack in some economies.

Although these projections now incorporate some of the negative risks identified earlier, the overall balance of global risks remains tilted to the downside. As shown in the global outlook fan chart, the IMF staff now sees a 25 percent chance of growth slowing to 3 percent or less in 2008 and 2009, equivalent to a global recession (Figure 1.12). The greatest uncertainty comes from the still-unfolding events in financial markets, particularly the potential for the deep losses related to the U.S. subprime mortgage sector and other structured credits to further impair financial system capital and cause the

Figure 1.11. Global Outlook
(Real GDP; percent change from a year ago)

The global economy is projected to cool in 2008, before staging a modest recovery in 2009. Among the advanced economies, growth would slow the most in the United States, dipping into recession, but activity in the euro area and Japan would also moderate. Growth in emerging and developing economies would ease but remain at a rapid pace, with continued strength across all regions.

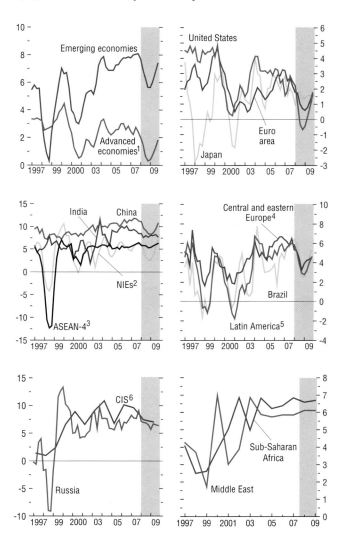

Sources: Haver Analytics; and IMF staff estimates.
[1]Australia, Canada, Denmark, euro area, Japan, New Zealand, Norway, Sweden, Switzerland, United Kingdom, and United States.
[2]Newly industrialized Asian economies (NIEs) comprise Hong Kong SAR, Korea, Singapore, and Taiwan Province of China.
[3]Indonesia, Malaysia, Philippines, and Thailand.
[4]Czech Republic, Estonia, Hungary, Latvia, Lithuania, and Poland.
[5]Argentina, Brazil, Chile, Colombia, Mexico, Peru, and Rep. Bolivariana de Venezuela.
[6]Commonwealth of Independent States.

Figure 1.12. Risks to the Global Outlook

Risks to the global outlook remain on the downside with about a 25 percent risk that global growth will fall to 3 percent or less. The largest adverse risks relate to global financial conditions and domestic demand in the United States. Global imbalances remain a concern.

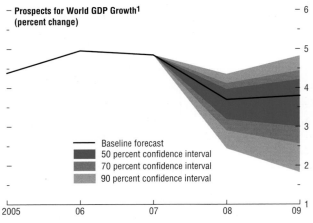

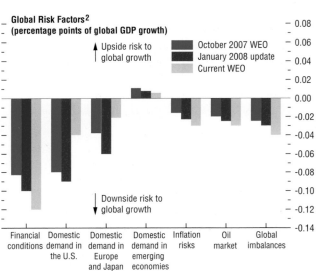

Source: IMF staff estimates.

[1]The fan chart shows the uncertainty around the *World Economic Outlook* (WEO) central forecast with 50, 70, and 90 percent probability intervals. As shown, the 70 percent confidence interval includes the 50 percent interval, and the 90 percent confidence interval includes the 50 and 70 percent intervals. See Box 1.3 in the April 2006 *World Economic Outlook* for details.

[2]The chart shows the contributions of each risk factor to the overall balance of risks to global growth, as reflected by the extent of asymmetry in the probability density for global GDP growth shown in the fan chart. The balance of risks is tilted to the downside if the expected probability of outcomes below the central or modal forecast (the total "downside probability") exceeds 50 percent (Box 1.3 in the April 2006 *World Economic Outlook*). The bars for each forecast vintage sum up to the difference between the expected value of world growth implied by the distribution of outcomes (the probability density) shown in the fan chart and the central forecast for global GDP growth. This difference and the extent of asymmetry in the probability density in the fan chart also depend on the standard deviation of past forecast errors—which, among other factors, varies with the length of the forecasting horizon. To make the risk factors comparable across forecast vintages, their contributions are rescaled to correct for differences in the standard deviations.

current credit squeeze to mutate into a credit crunch. The interaction between negative financial shocks and domestic demand, particularly through the housing market, remains a concern for the United States and to a somewhat lesser degree for western Europe and other advanced economies. There is some upside potential for domestic demand in the emerging economies, although these economies are exposed to negative external risks through both trade and financial channels. At the same time, there are increased risks related to inflationary pressures and high oil prices, despite slower projected growth, reflecting prospects for continued tight conditions in commodity markets and the recent upward drift of core inflation. Finally, risks related to global imbalances remain a concern.

Turning first to financial risks, the increasingly protracted market turmoil poses the key downside risk for the global economy. Estimates of expected losses from the U.S. mortgage market have been revised upward repeatedly since the outbreak of turbulence, and they could escalate further if the U.S. housing sector continues to deteriorate more than currently expected under pressure from a slowing economy and the resetting of variable-rate mortgages. Moreover, financial system losses from other structured credits are also rising and could multiply if other market segments suffer subprime-like damage. As discussed in the April 2008 *Global Financial Stability Report*, rising pressure on the capitalization of monoline credit insurers related to the falling prices of structured securities has disrupted the U.S. municipal bond market and raised concerns about counterparty risks in the credit-default-swap market, where they are substantial net sellers of protection. More generally, the cyclical slowdown is raising default rates, and there are increasing concerns about the possible deterioration of creditworthiness in other markets, including consumer credit, commercial property, and corporate debt. There is also potential for losses on exposure to housing markets outside the United States, including in western Europe and emerging Europe.

A crucial question is whether there is a serious credit crunch on the horizon. The baseline projections already reflect a substantial tightening of lending standards as U.S. and European banks work to rebuild their capital bases. However, total losses could rise substantially above current estimates—particularly if other market segments suffer extreme damage and capital in the core of the financial system is seriously impaired. Moreover, markets for complex structured products could remain heavily disrupted and well-established market sectors could come under further strain from global deleveraging. In such an event, higher-risk corporates and households in the advanced economies would indeed be faced with a sustained credit crunch involving both higher borrowing costs and constraints on market access that could have a seriously detrimental impact on growth.

Relative to the lower growth baseline—with the U.S. economy now projected to grow 1 percent a year more slowly than at the time of the January *World Economic Outlook Update*—the potential for further downside surprises to domestic demand in the United States has moderated. The substantial policy stimulus now in train should provide support for the economy in 2008. However, downside risks remain a concern, especially for 2009, when the projected recovery could be stifled by a confluence of continuing financial strains, a deep housing market correction, and the deteriorating financial position of U.S. consumers. Although U.S. residential construction has been contracting for almost two years, private consumption remained resilient until recently. However, with house prices declining and labor market conditions deteriorating, household finances are becoming more of a concern. Chapter 3 examines past housing cycles and finds that the increasing ability of households to borrow against housing equity as mortgage markets have evolved has increased the sensitivity of consumption to house prices. A sharp drop in house prices—going well beyond the 14–22 percent decline built into the baseline for 2008–09—could have serious repercussions, both through a direct impact on household net

wealth but also through the impact on bank capital of mortgage-related losses from rising default rates as an increasing proportion of householders' equity becomes negative.[2]

Risks for other advanced economies also have been partly incorporated in the baseline since the January 2008 *World Economic Outlook Update* but remain tilted to the downside, particularly for 2009. Western Europe is subject to spillovers from slowing trade with the United States and will also be vulnerable to deteriorating financial market conditions, given the substantial exposure of banks—notably British, French, German, and Swiss banks—to structured products originated in U.S. markets. Domestic risks are now judged to be on the upside relative to the new baseline, because domestic demand could remain more resilient than projected, supported by a moderation in energy and food price increases and a relatively strong labor market. At the same time, however, several countries, including Ireland, the United Kingdom, and Spain, have experienced their own housing booms, and these are starting to turn (see Box 3.1). A sharp deceleration in house price growth in these countries has clouded the outlook for residential construction and has increased financial sector vulnerabilities. Moreover, although European households are less heavily leveraged than their U.S. counterparts, corporate balance sheets and profitability are less strong in Europe than in the United States, increasing the potential impact on business investment of a tightening of credit. In Japan, both external and domestic risks remain tilted to the downside, mainly owing to concerns about external demand, tighter financial conditions, and weakening consumer confidence.

Overall, risks to the emerging economies seem on the downside, with some residual upside risks to domestic demand but larger downside risks from the external side through

---

[2]Different indices have different coverage, implying different rates of change. Specifically, the projections assume a 14 percent decline as measured on the U.S. Office of Federal Housing Enterprise Oversight (OFHEO) index and a 22 percent decline according to the Case-Shiller index of 20 metropolitan areas.

Figure 1.13. Measures of the Output Gap and Capacity Pressures[1]

Various measures of the output gap suggest that gaps largely closed during 2007, in both advanced and emerging economies. However, the projected slowdown in the United States and other advanced economies would lead to rising slack in 2008, helping to counter price pressures. Elsewhere, resource constraints are projected to remain more binding, although moderating commodity prices should take the edge off inflation pressures.

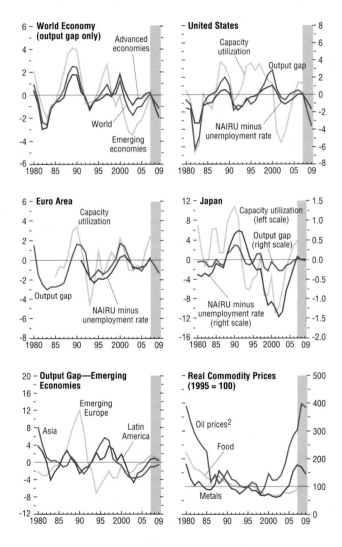

Sources: OECD, *Economic Outlook;* and IMF staff estimates.
[1]Estimates of the nonaccelerating inflation rate of unemployment (NAIRU) come from the OECD. Estimates of the output gap, in percent of potential GDP, are based on IMF staff calculations. Capacity utilization measured as deviations from 1980–2007 averages for the United States (percent of total capacity) and Japan (operation rate index for manufacturing sector), and deviations during 1985–2007 for the euro area (percent of industry capacity).
[2]Simple average of spot prices of U.K. Brent, Dubai Fateh, and West Texas Intermediate crude oil.

trade and financial channels. Increasing concern about asset quality in advanced economies and high external surpluses in some economies, including oil exporters, could spur—rather than depress—capital flows to some emerging and developing economies in the short term as investors search for new opportunities. This could fuel continued rapid growth of credit and domestic demand. More generally, growth in the large emerging economies in Asia and Latin America could slow by less than projected, carried by the robust momentum of domestic demand. However, a protracted weakening of growth in the advanced economies would have negative effects on the growth prospects of emerging and developing economies. Significantly weaker global growth would likely slow their exports and trigger a decline in commodity prices, with knock-on effects on domestic demand and especially investment. Moreover, the financial market crisis could constrain financial flows to emerging economies that are considered particularly vulnerable. In particular, countries in emerging Europe that have benefited from large banking inflows in recent years could face difficulties if western European banks curtail lending to the region in response to rising pressure on their balance sheets.

Growth risks from inflation and the oil market have intensified, notwithstanding the slowing trajectory of the global economy. The concern is that persistent inflation in the advanced economies may reduce the room to maneuver in response to slowing output and that sustained inflation pressures in rapidly growing emerging economies could require policies to be tightened further. Rising commodity prices have been an important source of inflation pressure in both advanced and developing economies. Global oil markets remain very tight. With spare capacity still limited, supply shocks or heightened geopolitical concerns could cause oil prices to rise further from current high levels, unless there is a significant softening in demand in the emerging as well as the advanced economies (see Appendix 1.2). Similarly, food prices may continue to rise in response to strong demand growth in emerging economies and increased biofuel production.

In the advanced economies, slowing growth has somewhat alleviated the pressure on resources, but rising inflation remains a concern. In the United States, unemployment is rising and the output gap is projected to widen further in the year ahead, but headline inflation has jumped in recent months and core inflation has edged above the Federal Reserve's implicit comfort zone (Figure 1.13). In the euro area, the unemployment rate is now at its lowest level since the early 1990s, raising concerns that rising headline inflation could push up wage settlements. Inflation risks are of continuing concern in many emerging and developing economies, where food and oil account for a large share of consumption baskets and where rapid growth has reduced output gaps and brought capacity utilization to high levels.

Finally, large global imbalances remain a worrisome downside risk for the global economy. On the plus side, the projected path for the net foreign assets (NFA) of the United States is now less extreme than it had been (Figure 1.14). The U.S. current account deficit declined to 5½ percent of GDP in 2007, owing largely to the depreciation of the U.S. dollar and a more balanced pattern for global demand growth, and it is projected to come down further, nearing 4 percent of GDP by 2013. In fact, the U.S. NFA position has not deteriorated in recent years despite the large current account deficits—owing to valuation effects related to U.S. dollar depreciation and the underperformance of U.S. equity markets relative to those abroad. Thus, under the latest projections, with a lower starting point and smaller continuing deficits, U.S. net foreign liabilities rise from an estimated 5 percent of global GDP at end-2007 to 7½ percent of global GDP in 2012, compared with the 12 percent of GDP in 2012 projected in the April 2007 *World Economic Outlook*.

Against this, the disproportionate pattern of adjustment in exchange rates since the summer means that certain emerging economy currencies remain overvalued and that new

Figure 1.14. Current Account Balances and Net Foreign Assets
(Percent of global GDP)

Assuming unchanged real effective exchange rates, the U.S. current account deficit is projected to continue to moderate over the medium term, but to remain above 1 percent of global GDP in 2013. As a result, U.S. net foreign liabilities would rise to about 8 percent of global GDP. The main counterpart would be rising net foreign asset positions in emerging Asia and oil-exporting countries.

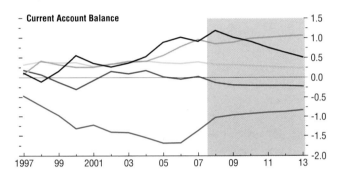

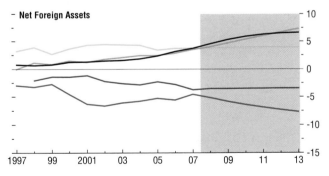

Sources: Lane and Milesi-Ferretti (2006); and IMF staff estimates.
[1]Algeria, Angola, Azerbaijan, Bahrain, Republic of Congo, Ecuador, Equatorial Guinea, Gabon, I.R. of Iran, Kuwait, Libya, Nigeria, Norway, Oman, Qatar, Russia, Saudi Arabia, Syrian Arab Republic, Turkmenistan, United Arab Emirates, Rep. Bolivariana de Venezuela, and Republic of Yemen.
[2]China, Hong Kong SAR, Indonesia, Korea, Malaysia, Philippines, Singapore, Taiwan Province of China, and Thailand.

misalignments may be emerging. At the same time, as discussed in Box 1.2, there is a concern that financial market dislocations have reduced confidence in liquidity and risk-management characteristics of U.S. assets and institutions. Coming on top of prolonged weak returns in U.S. markets relative to those elsewhere, investors and fund managers (including of international reserves and sovereign wealth funds) may increasingly seek to diversify their portfolios. This would make it more difficult to obtain the flows needed to finance the U.S. current account deficits and may even trigger a disorderly adjustment. There are also concerns about increasing protectionist sentiment in the advanced economies, particularly in the context of deteriorating labor market conditions.

To further explore the downside risks to the global economy, the IMF staff has constructed an alternative scenario based on a combination of negative shocks, using a new multicountry general equilibrium model, the Global Integrated Monetary and Fiscal Model. Assessing the impact of multiple shocks is difficult because of significant interactions between sectors within an economy, across economies, and over time. These interactions generate positive and negative feedback, leading to nonlinear reactions. A model-based approach allows a more systematic examination of these interactions and of the potential effects of alternative policy responses, although of course no single model can possibly capture all aspects of a situation.

The downside scenario presented in Figure 1.15 is based on a combination of three related shocks. First, it includes a temporary shock to consumption and investment from a further tightening of credit conditions while the financial system goes through a protracted rehabilitation period during which capital and credibility are repaired after extended financial turmoil. Equity and real estate prices would be reduced relative to baseline (by 30 percent and 20 percent, respectively). The economic impact of this shock is felt most directly in the United States and western Europe, but it also affects parts of the world that have heavily relied on

borrowing. Second, the scenario builds in a permanent downward shift in expectations for long-term productivity growth in the United States, which would tend to raise the U.S. saving rate as households and businesses adjust their expectations for capital gains and lower investment. Third, the scenario incorporates a shift in investor preferences away from U.S. assets, raising their risk premiums and reflecting investors' diminished confidence in the U.S. financial system and their downscaled expectations for U.S. potential growth.

Under this scenario, as shown in Figure 1.15, the U.S. economy would experience a deeper and more extended recession as negative effects from lower asset prices and lower longer-term growth expectations continued to depress aggregate demand, even with a gradual improvement of credit availability and with substantial support from monetary easing and fiscal stabilizers. Slower domestic demand growth, together with exchange rate depreciation, would contribute to an improvement in the U.S. current account. The euro area would undergo an extended period of weakness, as the economy faces the negative financial shock and upward pressure on the exchange rate, although the subsequent rebound would be more robust, because the scenario does not build in the longer-term adverse shift included for the United States. The rest of the world would also experience a slowdown in the aggregate, albeit less intense, reflecting both weaker growth in global trade and the impact of tighter credit conditions.

Although the global model does not explicitly model housing markets or commodity prices and includes only limited country detail, the negative effects appear most intense in countries with particularly large exposure to house price and commodity cycles. Thus, countries in western Europe that have experienced rapid house price appreciation in recent years—such as Spain and the United Kingdom—as well as some emerging economies with booming housing markets—would be vulnerable to sustained housing corrections that would amplify their business cycles. Commodity prices would

Figure 1.15. Two Scenarios for the Global Economy

Based on a multicountry general equilibrium model, a downside scenario has been developed to illustrate the possible impact of a deeper financial shock than incorporated in the *World Economic Outlook* baseline projections. The shock has the greatest impact on the U.S. economy but also has substantial spillovers on the euro area and the rest of the world.

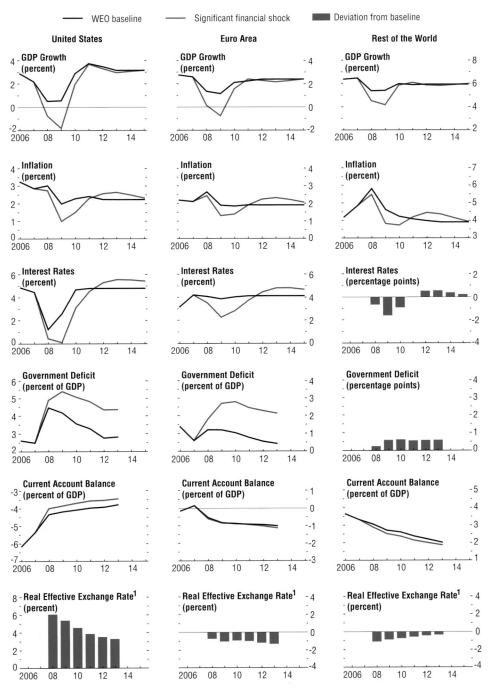

Source: IMF staff estimates.
[1] A positive value represents a depreciation.

also be expected to weaken in the context of a global downturn that slowed growth in the large Asian emerging economies that have accounted for the bulk of the increase in demand for commodities in recent years. Such a shift would have consequences for exporters of food and metals in Africa and Latin America, as well as for oil exporters in the Middle East and elsewhere.

This scenario is intended to be illustrative, but it underlines two key points. First, a downturn would be expected to have global consequences, leading to more moderate rates of growth in emerging and developing economies and exposing some of them to greater external financing strains. Second, a downturn could be followed by a slow rather than rapid recovery, as financial system constraints take time to dissipate and as negative wealth effects continue to dampen activity.

Policy Challenges in a Multipolar World

Policymakers around the world face a fast-moving set of challenges, and although each country's circumstances differ, in an increasingly multipolar world it will be essential to meet these challenges broadly, taking full account of cross-border interactions. In the advanced economies, the pressing tasks are dealing with the financial market crisis and responding to downside risks to growth—but policy choices should also take into account recent high inflation indicators and longer-term concerns. Many emerging and developing economies continue to face the challenge of ensuring that current strong growth does not build up inflation or vulnerabilities. However, a number of countries are already experiencing fallout from the advanced economy slowdown, and an intensified or prolonged global downturn would inevitably strain a widening group of countries, requiring judicious responses from policymakers. Many emerging economies would have more room than in the past to apply countercyclical measures in the event of a severe global downturn, but those that are still highly vulnerable or have

large external financing needs might need to tighten policies.

Advanced Economies

In the advanced economies, monetary policymakers face a delicate balancing act between alleviating the downside risks to growth and guarding against a buildup in inflation.

- In the *United States*, rising downside risks to output, amid considerable uncertainty about the extent, duration, and impact of financial turbulence and the deterioration in labor market conditions, justify the Federal Reserve's rapid interest rate cuts and a continuing bias toward monetary easing until the economy moves to a firmer footing. Although the recent jump in headline inflation caused by higher energy and food prices, and the uptick in core inflation, are of concern, softening labor markets and a rising output gap have alleviated inflation risks.

- In the *euro area*, while current inflation is uncomfortably high, prospects point to its falling back below 2 percent during 2009, in the context of an increasingly negative outlook for activity. Accordingly, the ECB can afford some easing of the policy stance.

- In *Japan*, there is merit in keeping interest rates on hold for now. Monetary policy remains highly accommodating, but there would be some scope, albeit limited, to reduce interest rates from already low levels if there is a substantial deterioration in growth prospects.

Beyond these immediate concerns, recent financial developments have fueled the continuing debate about the degree to which central banks should take asset prices into account in setting the monetary policy stance. The prevailing orthodoxy is that asset price movements would be one factor to consider in assessing price and output prospects, but that targeting asset prices would not be an appropriate policy objective, because central banks have no particular insight into equilibrium price levels and lack the tools to ensure that desired levels are achieved (Mishkin, 2007). Against this, there are concerns that sustained asset price swings can lead to large imbalances in an economy, which are not immediately reflected in short-term price developments, especially when inflation expectations are well anchored. Moreover, perceptions that policymakers will respond vigorously to limit the negative impact of asset price corrections can serve to reduce risk premiums and thus increase the amplitude of the asset price cycle.

These issues are analyzed further in Chapter 3, which looks at the connections between housing cycles and monetary policy. Recent experience seems to support the case for giving significant weight to house price movements in the context of a "risk-management" approach to monetary policymaking, especially in economies with more developed mortgage markets where "financial accelerator" effects have become more pronounced, particularly when house prices move rapidly or move out of normal valuation ranges. Such leaning against the wind would not necessarily prevent large asset price movements—particularly when price dynamics are given some support by changing fundamentals—but it can help to limit the amplitude of such swings (Bordo and Jeanne, 2002). There are two important caveats. First, such an approach must be applied symmetrically: an aggressive easing might be justified in response to increasing concerns about the consequences of a house price correction, but it is also essential to unwind such easing promptly when the downside risks dissipate. Second, monetary policy alone certainly cannot bear the full weight of responding to possible house price bubbles; regulatory policy has a critical role to play in guarding against an inappropriate loosening of lending standards, which may fuel extreme house price movements.

Fiscal policy can play a useful countercyclical role in a downturn in economic activity, although it would be important not to jeopardize efforts aimed at consolidating fiscal positions over the medium term in the face of population aging. In the first place, there are automatic stabilizers during a cyclical downturn—declines in tax revenues and increases in safety net spending—and these should provide timely fiscal support, without compromising progress toward medium-term objectives. In addition, there may be justification for extra discretionary stimulus in some countries, given present concerns about the strength of recessionary forces and perceptions that financial dislocations may have weakened the normal monetary policy transmission mechanism, but any such stimulus must be timely, well targeted, and quickly unwound.[3]

- In the *United States*, automatic stabilizers are quite low, because the overall size of government is relatively small and social safety net spending is limited. Although tax revenues (particularly capital gains) could be affected by a downturn in activity, demand effects might be mitigated because the benefits would accrue mainly to higher-income groups. Given the serious risks coming from sustained financial market dislocations, the recent legislation to provide additional fiscal support for an economy under stress is fully justified, and room may need to be found for some additional public support for housing and financial markets to help stabilize these markets, while care is taken care to avoid inducing undue moral hazard. At the same time, it will be important not to jeopardize achievement of longer-term fiscal consolidation, which is necessary to help reduce global imbalances as well as improve the U.S. fiscal position in the face of an aging population and rising health care costs.
- In the *euro area*, automatic stabilizers are more extensive and should be allowed to play out fully around a fiscal deficit path that is consistent with steady advancement toward medium-term objectives. Countries whose medium-term objectives are well in hand can also provide some additional discretionary stimulus. Indeed, in Germany, where the

---

[3]Box 2.1 assesses the circumstances under which fiscal policy can be most effective, based on empirical and analytical approaches.

public accounts were brought into balance in 2007, tax reforms are already providing some fiscal support for the economy in 2008, and a number of smaller euro area members also have adequate room under the revised Stability and Growth Pact (SGP) to provide stimulus if needed. However, in other countries, including France and Italy, the ability to allow even automatic stabilizers to operate in full may be limited by high levels of public debt and current adjustment plans that are insufficient for medium-term sustainability. Unless these countries face recession, the stabilizers should be allowed to play out only insofar as underlying deficits are being reduced by at least ½ percent of GDP a year, in line with commitments under the revised SGP.

- In *Japan*, net public debt is projected to remain at very high levels despite consolidation efforts. Speeding up such efforts would buy "policy insurance" against shocks and help meet the challenges associated with an aging society. In the context of an economic downturn, automatic stabilizers could be allowed to operate, but their impact on domestic demand would be limited, and there would be little scope for additional discretionary action.

Policymakers in advanced economies also need to continue strong efforts to deal with financial market turmoil in order to avoid a full-blown crisis of confidence or a credit crunch. Priorities include rebuilding counterparty confidence, reinforcing the financial soundness of institutions, and easing liquidity strains, as described in greater detail in the April 2008 *Global Financial Stability Report*. Initiatives to support the housing sector could also play a useful role to reduce the negative interaction between house prices, delinquency rates, and financial losses. Forceful action is essential to avoid the protracted problems that could imply a lingering drag, such as was experienced in Japan in the 1990s after the collapse of its equity and housing bubbles.

- Improve disclosure: A loss of confidence has been at the core of the market turmoil, and financial supervisors must make concerted efforts to ensure timely acknowledgment by regulated financial institutions of their losses from exposures to structured instruments, both directly and through off-balance-sheet entities.
- Reinforce bank capital: Weakly capitalized institutions should continue to rebuild capital cushions and reduce leverage, in order to quickly restore confidence and lending capacity.
- Provide liquidity: Central banks should continue to provide liquidity as needed to ensure the smooth functioning of markets, even as they develop strategies to wind down private sector reliance on central bank actions.
- Support the housing market: Initiatives could be considered to facilitate the refinancing of mortgages in the United States in the face of house price declines, including through the judicious use of government funds, in order to reduce risks that rising foreclosures would put further downward pressure on house prices.

It is too early to draw definitive conclusions about the fundamental reforms that will be needed to safeguard financial stability for the long term, but some preliminary areas for improvement can be identified.

- Improve regulation of the mortgage market: It has become clear that underwriting standards in the U.S. subprime mortgage market were inadequate. Although bank originators have now adopted guidance issued by federal supervisors in 2006 and 2007 to address some areas of concern, there would be considerable merit in improving coordination among federal supervisors to ensure that any future guidance is promulgated more quickly and efficiently. Moreover, there are still gaps in the oversight of nonbank originators that must be addressed. Other countries should review lending standards in their own markets.
- Review the role of rating agencies: Applying a differentiated rating scale to structured credit products, and providing indications of the sensitivity of ratings to underlying assump-

tions, would better inform investors about the risks related to these products. Consideration could also be given to reforms that would prevent conflicts of interest within rating agencies.

- Broaden the risk perimeter: The heavy losses to banks from off-balance-sheet entities during this current episode suggests that the relevant scope of risk consolidation for banks should be widened. Disclosure should be improved so that investors can better assess the risks to sponsoring banks from off-balance-sheet entities, including through contingent credit lines.

- Strengthen supervisory cooperation: The very rapid pace of financial innovation and the increasing complexity of cross-border activities pose a substantial challenge for supervisors seeking to monitor the activities of regulated institutions. This underscores the need to strengthen the framework for cooperation among supervisors, regulators, and central banks, including to share experiences and expertise, both within jurisdictions and across borders, to fill gaps in information flows and facilitate crisis management. It is encouraging that financial regulators in the European Union have recognized the need for progress in this area.

- Improve crisis-resolution mechanisms: The experience with the collapse of a major U.K. bank, the rescue of two German regional banks, and the near-failure of a major U.S. investment bank has raised broader questions about how best to manage financial distress, design financial safety nets, and use public funds. These experiences have illustrated that well-designed deposit insurance systems and mechanisms for swift and effective bank resolution are critical for ensuring that strains in an individual institution do not lead to a broader loss of confidence that could pose a systemic threat. They have also suggested a need to consider carefully how to handle deep stress on large banks whose failure could have systemic consequences. At the same time, bailouts can raise moral hazard, and it is thus

important that infusions of public capital occur only after private sector solutions have been ruled out and that, when state support does prove necessary, shareholders and managers bear appropriate losses.

Emerging and Developing Economies

Emerging and developing economies face the challenge of controlling inflation while being alert to downside risks from the slowdown in the advanced economies and the increased stress on financial markets. In some countries, further tightening of monetary policy stances may be needed to keep inflation under control, recognizing that even though higher headline inflation may be driven initially by rising food and energy prices, it could quickly lead to broader price and wage pressures in a rapidly growing economy. With a flexible exchange rate regime, currency appreciation will tend to provide useful support for monetary tightening, although concerns about competitiveness can limit policymakers' willingness to follow this path. Countries whose exchange rates are heavily managed vis-à-vis the U.S. dollar, however, have less room to respond because raising interest rates may encourage heavier capital inflows, and the real effective exchange rate may depreciate along with the U.S. dollar, exacerbating the problem. China and other countries in this situation that have diversified economies would benefit from moving toward more flexible regimes that would provide greater scope for monetary policy. For many oil exporters in the Middle East, the exchange rate peg to the U.S. dollar constrains monetary policy. It will be important that the current buildup in spending be calibrated to reflect the cyclical position of these economies, and that such spending be aimed toward alleviating supply bottlenecks that have contributed to inflationary pressures.

Fiscal and financial policies can also play useful roles in preventing overheating and related problems. Restraint on government spending can help moderate domestic demand, lessen the need for monetary tightening, and ease pressures from short-term capital inflows attracted by high interest rates.[4] Sustained fiscal consolidation would also provide the basis for further strengthening public sector balance sheets, which is important for reducing the vulnerabilities of countries with high public debt. Similarly, vigilant financial supervision—promoting appropriately tight lending standards and strong risk management in domestic financial institutions—can pay dividends both by moderating the demand impulse from rapid credit growth and by reducing the risk of a buildup in balance-sheet vulnerabilities that could be costly in a downturn. Continued structural reforms aimed at providing the basis for sustained high growth also remain important.

At the same time, policymakers in these countries should be ready to respond to a more negative external environment, which could well emerge in the months ahead and could involve both weaker trade performance and a reduction of capital inflows. In many countries, strengthened policy frameworks and public sector balance sheets will allow for more use than in the past of countercyclical monetary and fiscal policies. The appropriate mix will need to be judged country by country. In China, the consolidation of the past few years provides ample room to support the economy through fiscal policy, such as by accelerating public investment plans and advancing the pace of reforms to strengthen social safety nets, health care, and education. In many Latin American countries, well-established inflation-targeting frameworks provide the basis for monetary easing, and automatic fiscal stabilizers could be allowed to operate, although there would be little room for discretionary fiscal stimulus given still-high public debt levels. However, faced with a severe global downturn and a disruption of external financing flows, some countries that have large current account deficits or other vulnerabilities may need to respond by tightening policies

[4]See Chapter 3 of the October 2007 *World Economic Outlook*.

promptly in order to maintain confidence and avoid the type of external crises experienced in earlier decades.

Multilateral Initiatives

In an increasingly multipolar world, broadly based efforts to deal with global challenges have become indispensable. In the event of a severe global downturn, there would be a case for providing temporary fiscal support in a range of countries that have made good progress in recent years in securing sound fiscal positions. Although fiscal support could be in each country's individual interest, providing stimulus across a broad group of countries could prove much more effective in bolstering confidence and demand, given the inevitable cross-border leakages from added spending in open economies. It is still too early to launch such an approach, but it would be prudent for countries to start contingency planning in the event that such support becomes necessary. IMF staff estimates suggest that countries representing about half the global economy would have fiscal room to provide additional discretionary fiscal stimulus on a temporary basis if needed. These include the United States, Germany, Canada, and China, a number of small advanced economies, emerging economies in East Asia and Latin America, and commodity exporters in the Middle East and Central Asia. Furthermore, most countries (90–95 percent of the global economy) would be able to allow automatic stabilizers to work, at least in part.

Reducing risks associated with global current account imbalances remains an important task. Therefore, it is encouraging that some progress is being made in implementing the strategy endorsed by the International Monetary and Financial Committee and the more detailed policy plans laid out by participants in the IMF-sponsored Multilateral Consultation on Global Imbalances aimed at rebalancing domestic demand across countries with supportive movements in real exchange rates (see Box 1.3). This road map remains relevant, but should be used flexibly to take account of the changing global context. Thus, some reversal of recent progress toward fiscal consolidation in the United States can provide insurance against a worldwide slowdown, but it will be important that the fiscal support be strictly temporary, and not be allowed to jeopardize achievement of medium-term consolidation goals. The continuing depreciation of the U.S. dollar has been helpful in cushioning the impact of adjustments in the domestic economy, but there is concern that the weight of the dollar's adjustment has been largely borne by countries with flexibly managed exchange rates, which has put pressure on other advanced economies that are also slowing. In China, further tightening of monetary policy alongside upward flexibility of the renminbi would contribute to rebalancing the Chinese economy and containing inflation pressures while easing downward pressure on other major currencies in response to the depreciating dollar. For the oil-exporting countries, priority should be given to tackling supply bottlenecks, which have contributed to rising inflation pressures as domestic spending has built up. And in the euro area and Japan, more rapid progress with structural reform of product and labor markets could provide an additional boost to confidence and help sustain growth.

Two other priorities for multilateral action are to reduce trade barriers and combat climate change—both of which promise potentially large returns to collective action. The opportunity provided by the Doha Round to advance multilateral trade liberalization should not be squandered, given the substantial benefits that can be realized, particularly from improving access for agricultural products in advanced economy markets and from increasing trade in services. Rising trade has been a key source of the recent strong performance of the global economy—and the recent progress toward global poverty reduction—and a renewed push in this area remains essential.

Recent commitments to developing a post-Kyoto framework for joint action to address climate change are very welcome. Although the effects of climate change will be evident mainly over the long term and are hard to quantify, there is an imperative to act because the costs will fall largely on poorer countries, because the process is irreversible, and because the costs to the global economy of catastrophic events are potentially very high. Moreover, as discussed in Chapter 4, efforts to adapt to and mitigate the buildup of greenhouse gases have important short-term economic consequences. The fact that expanded biofuel production has raised food prices and inflation pressures is a concrete example of both the immediacy of the risks involved and the need for a multilateral approach. The implementation of a comprehensive framework for carbon pricing and carbon trading would also have a potentially large macroeconomic impact—on global saving and investment patterns and on foreign exchange flows—which will need to be considered carefully to avoid unintended consequences. Chapter 4 finds that these macroeconomic consequences can be mitigated, provided efforts to contain emissions are based on an effective carbon-pricing system that reflects the damages emissions inflict. Such carbon pricing should be applied across countries to maximize the efficiency of abatement, should be flexible to avoid volatility, and should be equitable so as not to put undue burdens on the countries least able to bear them.

Appendix 1.1. Implications of New PPP Estimates for Measuring Global Growth

The main authors of this appendix are Selim Elekdag and Subir Lall.

Following the release of new estimates of purchasing-power-parity (PPP) exchange rates by the International Comparison Program (ICP) in December 2007, global growth estimates in this *World Economic Outlook* have been revised downward by about ½ percentage point over the 2000–07 period (Figure 1.16).[5] It is important

---

[5]For further details on the ICP revisions, see www.worldbank.org/data/icp.

to underscore that changes to the historical estimates reflect mainly the effect of the PPP revisions, but that global growth projections for 2008–09 reflect both the effects from PPP revisions and changes to the overall outlook. This appendix highlights key aspects of the revised PPP estimates and their implications.

The Relevance of PPP Exchange Rates

PPP rates are an alternative way of calculating exchange rates between countries using a comparison of prices for similar goods and services in different countries. The PPP rate is defined as the amount of a particular currency needed to purchase the same basket of goods and services as one unit of the reference currency, usually the U.S. dollar. The PPP rate can—especially in the short run—deviate by a large amount from the market exchange rate between two currencies, given the influence of trade, capital flows, and other factors on market exchange rates. A well-known but less comprehensive measure of the PPP exchange rate between countries is *The Economist*'s Big Mac index, which calculates the exchange rate at which the eponymous hamburger would cost the same across all countries in the index.

PPP exchange rates are important in evaluating aggregate economic activity across the world. Because they adjust for the difference in price levels across countries, they tend to provide a more meaningful estimate of global economic activity than market exchange rates. For example, developing economies typically have relatively low prices for nontraded goods and services, and a unit of local currency thus has greater purchasing power within a developing economy than it does internationally. PPP-based GDP takes this into account, but conversions based on market exchange rates typically underestimate the value of domestic economic activity and the output of a developing economy relative to an advanced economy.

PPP-based GDP estimates also provide a more consistent picture of the relative contributions of advanced economies to aggregate economic

Figure 1.16. Purchasing-Power-Parity (PPP) Exchange Rate Revisions and Global Growth

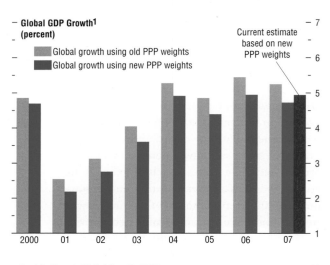

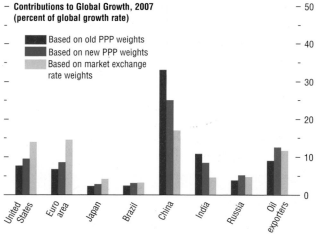

Source: IMF staff calculations.
[1]Based on October 2007 *World Economic Outlook* estimates except where noted.

activity. This is because bilateral exchange rate movements can distort individual economies' contributions to global economic activity. For example, given the depreciation of the dollar over the past few years, comparing GDP using market exchange rates would imply that the contribution of the United States to global economic activity has diminished substantially relative to that of the euro area.

This said, it is important to underscore that PPP exchange rates are not designed to assess potential currency misalignments, but rather to provide a more accurate estimate of economic activity across countries.

Are the New PPP Estimates More Accurate?

The 2003–07 ICP round, coordinated by the World Bank, represents the most extensive and thorough effort ever to measure PPP rates across countries. The PPP revisions were released December 17, 2007, and are preliminary estimates for the 2005 benchmark year. An extensive collection of detailed price data from across more than 100 emerging and developing economies replaces previous benchmark PPP estimates, which date to 1993 or earlier in most cases. Moreover, China participated in the survey program for the first time and India for the first time since 1985. For advanced economies, the Eurostat-OECD PPP program, which updates rates on a more frequent basis, provided the revisions for 46 other economies.

Why Did the PPP Estimates Change?

The first-time participation of China in the ICP resulted in the downward revision of China's PPP-based GDP by about 40 percent. This is because previous estimates were extrapolated from a bilateral comparison of 1986 prices between China and the United States, which failed to adequately reflect the increase in domestic prices over time. In particular, these previous price extrapolations assumed a constant basket of goods and services (with a relatively

Table 1.2. Shares of Global GDP, 2007

Country	At PPP exchange rates[1]	At market exchange rates
United States	21.36	25.51
China	10.83	5.99
Japan	6.61	8.08
India	4.58	2.02
Germany	4.34	6.12
United Kingdom	3.30	5.11
Russia	3.18	2.38
France	3.17	4.72
Brazil	2.81	2.42
Italy	2.76	3.88

Sources: IMF, World Economic Outlook database; and IMF staff calculations.
[1]PPP = purchasing power parity.

limited set of items), which did not account for the changing structure of the Chinese economy. In addition, the extrapolations did not account for the shift away from necessities such as food toward products and services that were not included in the 1986 survey basket. Finally, the new estimates are based on data collected in 11 cities across China, including some rural districts, which facilitates more accurate cross-country comparisons and therefore better PPP estimates. The data for India also include both urban and rural prices for food, clothing and footwear, and education. Incorporating these revisions, China still ranks as the world's second largest economy, with about 11 percent of world output in 2007, and India (which also had a sizable downward GDP adjustment in PPP terms) is the fourth largest, with more than 4 percent of the world total (Table 1.2).

Implications for Global GDP Growth

The revisions to PPP exchange rates imply a substantial reduction in the PPP rates of some key emerging economies and an upward revision in others—including oil exporters. The changes have implications for both aggregate global growth based on PPP exchange rates and the share of global GDP accounted for by individual countries and groups.
- Global growth based on the new PPP exchange rates is now estimated on average

to be some ½ percentage point lower than previous *World Economic Outlook* estimates for 2002–06. The estimated global growth of 4.9 percent in 2007 reflects the 0.5 percentage point reduction purely due to PPP weights (from 5.2 percent global growth forecast in the October 2007 *World Economic Outlook*) and a 0.2 percentage point upward revision based on revisions to the estimates of country growth rates since the last *World Economic Outlook*.

- Although PPP estimates have been revised substantially for a large number of countries, the impact on global growth estimates is driven to a large extent by the implied changes in the relative shares of China, India, and the United States in global output. China's share of global output in 2007 is now estimated at 10.8 percent (down from 15.8 percent), and India's share has declined to 4.6 percent (from 6.4 percent). Reflecting the overall reduction in GDP in PPP terms of other countries, the share of the United States in global GDP has been revised up from 19.3 percent to 21.4 percent.

Notwithstanding these changes, it remains true that emerging economies have been the main recent driver of global growth in PPP terms, led by China, which contributed nearly 27 percent to global growth in 2007 (see Figure 1.16).

Appendix 1.2. Commodity Market Developments and Prospects

The main authors of this appendix are Kevin Cheng, Thomas Helbling, and Valerie Mercer-Blackman, with contributions from To-Nhu Dao and Nese Erbil.

The commodity price boom picked up in 2007 and has shown little sign of abating so far in 2008, notwithstanding financial market turmoil and concerns about slowing growth in the major advanced economies. The IMF commodity price index rose by 44 percent from February 2007 to February 2008. Many prices—including those of crude oil, tin, nickel, soybeans, corn,

and wheat—reached new record highs in current U.S. dollar terms (Figure 1.17, first panel).[6] Nevertheless, in constant terms, prices of many commodities remain well below their highs in the 1970s and early 1980s, with those of crude oil, lead, and nickel being the main exceptions (Figure 1.17, second panel).[7]

Tightening market balances have been a common factor behind the price run-ups for many commodities. Prices have been propelled by positive and rising global net demand (consumption minus production) against the backdrop of already-low inventory levels in some markets. Strong demand from emerging economies, which have accounted for much of the increase in commodity consumption in recent years, remains a main driving force, with seemingly little impact so far from the slowing growth in some advanced economies, except for some softening of base metals prices from their mid-2007 peaks. Biofuel production has added to the demand for some food commodities, especially corn and rapeseed oil, which has affected demand for other foods through cost-push and substitution effects.

Financial trends have also contributed to commodity price increases. The effective depreciation of the U.S. dollar in 2007 pushed up prices

[6]In January 2008, the IMF issued a revised commodity price index, with updated weights based on average export values over the 2002–04 period (previously it was 1995–97) and using 2005 as a base year (compared with 1995 previously). The greatest difference between the old and new index is the change in the weight of energy in the basket, which has risen to 63.1 percent (from 47.8 percent), reflecting higher oil prices and global trade volumes. In terms of composition, rapeseed oil has been added to the index and coconut oil has been removed.

[7]In constant prices, the comparison depends critically on whether the price index used for deflation includes prices of nontraded goods. Because prices of nontraded goods have risen much more than for traded goods, the prices of some commodities—notably oil—are still below their 1970s peaks for 2007 if they are deflated by a broad-based index. In the second panel of Figure 1.17, prices are deflated by a unit value index for industrial countries' exports of manufactures, which is a measure of the so-called commodity terms of trade—that is, the price of commodities relative to prices of manufactures.

by increasing the purchasing power of oil users outside the dollar area (oil and other commodities are priced in U.S. dollars), raising the costs of inputs priced in other currencies and stimulating demand for oil and other commodities as inflation and currency hedges (Box 1.4). Falling policy interest rates in the United States have also played a role, as lower short-term real interest rates tend to push up spot commodity prices—everything else being equal—by reducing inventory holding costs and inducing shifts from money market instruments to commodities and other higher-yielding assets.

More generally, with the prospect of persistently tight fundamentals, commodity financial markets have benefited from favorable investor sentiment. Investors have also increasingly used commodities for portfolio diversification, as commodity returns have typically not been strongly correlated with those of other asset classes, notably equity. Related inflows into commodity investment vehicles have thus risen rapidly in recent years. These inflows have enhanced market liquidity and price discovery in commodity futures markets, including at the long end, but they can also contribute to short-term price volatility and may have led to an overshooting of prices.

Commodity prices are expected to give up some gains later in 2008 and in 2009 with the slowing of global growth. In the baseline projections, the price declines are generally small, reflecting the expected moderate pace of the growth slowdown in major emerging economies. Moreover, tight market balances—because of factors such as increased demand for biofuels and delayed supply responses—should continue to support prices of many commodities well above recent averages, especially for grains and edible oils. Factors such as temporary supply problems and geopolitical concerns, as well as declining short-term interest rates and a depreciating dollar, could again create upside potential for prices, particularly for metals and oil. Nevertheless, if global growth were to slow more than expected—which would involve a large decline

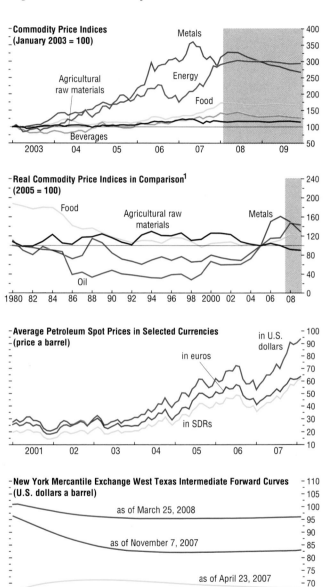

Figure 1.17. Commodity and Petroleum Prices

Sources: Bloomberg Financial Markets; and IMF staff estimates.
[1]Based on a unit value index for industrial countries' exports of manufactures.

Box 1.4. Dollar Depreciation and Commodity Prices

Over the past few years, dollar depreciation has coincided with soaring commodity prices. In March 2008, both crude oil and gold reached fresh highs within a short period after the U.S. dollar set new record lows against some other major currencies. These comovements are no coincidence. Over the past 20 years, commodity prices have generally been negatively correlated with the U.S. dollar—both in nominal and real effective terms—with the notable exception of crude oil during the 1980s (first figure). However, dollar depreciation has been only one factor affecting commodity prices in recent years, and this box attempts to put the role of the dollar fluctuations in perspective. Specifically, it discusses channels through which the dollar exchange rate may affect commodity prices and gauges the impact of U.S. dollar movements on prices of key commodities.

How Does the Dollar Affect Commodity Prices?

There are a number of channels through which a fall in the nominal effective value of the U.S. dollar can raise commodity prices in dollars.

- The purchasing power and cost channel: Most commodities—notably crude oil, precious metals, industrial metals, and grains such as wheat and corn—are priced in U.S. dollars. A dollar depreciation makes commodities less expensive for consumers in nondollar regions, thereby increasing their demand. On the supply side, price pressures arise from declining profits in local currency for producers outside the dollar area.
- The asset channel: Given the purchasing power and cost channel, a falling U.S. dollar reduces the returns on dollar-denominated financial assets in foreign currencies, which can make commodities a more attractive class of alternative assets to foreign investors. Moreover, a dollar depreciation raises risks of inflationary pressure in the United States, prompting investors to move toward real assets—such as commodities—to hedge

Note: The main author of this box is Kevin C. Cheng.

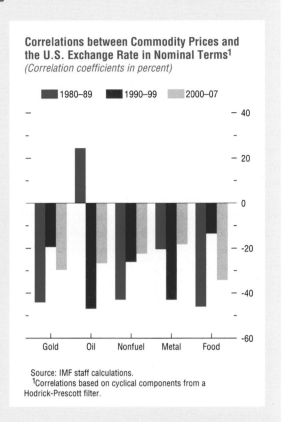

Correlations between Commodity Prices and the U.S. Exchange Rate in Nominal Terms[1]
(Correlation coefficients in percent)

■ 1980–89 ■ 1990–99 ■ 2000–07

Source: IMF staff calculations.
[1]Correlations based on cyclical components from a Hodrick-Prescott filter.

against inflation. For example, commodity markets rallied in the 1970s amid high inflation.

- Other channels: A dollar depreciation could lead to monetary policy easing in other economies, especially in countries with currencies pegged to the dollar. This could result in lower interest rates and increased liquidity, thereby stimulating demand for commodities and other assets.

How Large Is the Dollar's Impact?

To gauge the relationship between the U.S. dollar and commodity prices, a simple reduced-form price equation was estimated for six commodities—gold, crude oil, aluminum, copper, corn, and wheat—together with a nonfuel commodity index. The equation is based on a simple demand-supply framework for commodities along the line of Borensztein and Reinhart

(1994).[1] Specifically, the equation assumes that for each commodity, there is a relationship between the price, the trade-weighted U.S. dollar exchange rate, and three other variables:

- World industrial production: Increases in production require more commodity inputs; this variable should thus be positively correlated with commodity prices.
- Federal funds rate: This variable should be negatively correlated with commodity prices. Frankel (2006) suggests three channels through which a higher interest rate reduces commodity prices: first, it increases the incentive for extraction today rather than tomorrow, thereby increasing supply; second, it elevates costs of holding inventories; and third, it induces shifts in asset demand from commodities to treasury bills.
- Market balance of the particular commodity: This variable captures the impact of inventory holding on commodity prices, with a high level of stocks depressing commodity prices.[2]

The equation was estimated for commodity prices in both current and constant dollars using the IMF's nominal effective exchange rate and real effective exchange rate, respectively.[3]

[1]Given the reduced-form nature of the estimation, the framework can identify only the average responses of commodity prices to exchange rate movements during the sample period; it does not, however, identify a structural relationship that may be time variant or the channels through which the exchange rate affects commodity prices.

[2]For crude oil, Organization for Economic Cooperation and Development (OECD) inventories were used. For corn and wheat, global stocks were used. For gold, aluminum, and copper, global production was used for lack of reliable data on consumption or stock.

[3]The equations were estimated in an error-correction framework. The dynamic ordinary least squares (DOLS) estimator proposed by Stock and Watson (1993) was used to estimate the cointegrating relationships among the variations in levels, with all variables in logarithms except the interest rate. Real commodity prices and real interest rates were deflated by the U.S. consumer price index. Monthly data since the early or mid-1980s

Impact of a 1 Percent Decline in the U.S. Dollar Exchange Rate on Commodity Prices[1]
(In percent)

Months after the Shock	1	4	12	24	60
In Current Dollars (based on U.S. NEER)					
Gold	1.17	1.22	1.30	1.36	1.39
Oil	0.89	0.97	1.13	1.27	1.43
Nonfuel commodity index	0.48	0.47	0.47	0.47	0.46
Aluminum	0.53	0.53	0.53	0.52	0.52
Copper	1.11	1.02	0.80	0.55	0.18
In Constant Dollars (based on U.S. REER)					
Gold	1.12	1.12	1.13	1.14	1.17
Oil	0.48	0.58	0.81	1.08	1.58
Nonfuel commodity index	0.47	0.48	0.51	0.54	0.64
Aluminum	0.55	0.58	0.65	0.74	0.95
Copper	1.23	1.28	1.38	1.52	1.80

Source: IMF staff estimates.
[1]Dynamic multipliers implied by the error-correction equations for individual commodities. NEER: nominal effective exchange rate; REER: real effective exchange rate.

The main results are as follows (see table):

- The nominal U.S. dollar exchange rate has a significant impact in both the long run and the short run on crude oil and gold prices. In the long run, a 1 percent depreciation of the U.S. dollar is associated with increases for gold and oil prices of more than 1 percent. In the short run, the elasticity is close to 1, but higher for gold than for crude oil.
- For other nonfuel commodities, as measured by the IMF's index, the U.S. dollar impact is significant but smaller in magnitude over both the short and long runs. For metals, U.S. dollar movements also have a significant impact. In contrast, the impact on grains is not significant.
- The long-run impact of the real exchange rate is stronger than that of its nominal counterpart across most commodities. Specifically, a 1 percent real depreciation of the dollar

were used because data on many key variables were unavailable before then. The precise year varies from commodity to commodity, depending on data availability.

Box 1.4 *(concluded)*

would result in an increase of greater than 1 percent in the real prices of gold, crude oil, aluminum, and copper in the long run. The real exchange rate also has a significant impact on corn prices, which do not respond strongly to the nominal exchange rate. The stronger impact of real effective exchange rates likely captures that the importance of the purchasing power and cost channel over the long run is better reflected in real variables.

What explains the varying exchange rate impact across commodities? The variation likely reflects that some commodities such as gold and crude oil are more suitable than others as a "store of value." In general, nonrenewable commodities such as crude oil are a better store of value than perishable or renewable commodities.

To gauge the actual impact of the dollar depreciation on commodity prices during 2002–07, an alternative scenario was simulated.[4] Using the estimated equations, the exercise simulated commodity prices under a scenario in which the U.S. exchange rate remained at its peak of early 2002 until end-2007. The study suggests that under such a scenario, by end-2007, nominal gold prices would have been lower by around $250 a troy ounce, crude oil prices would have been lower by around $25 a barrel, and nonfuel commodity prices would have been lower by around 12 percent (second figure).

In summary, U.S. dollar fluctuations have a significant impact on most commodity prices—both in nominal and in real terms. The magnitude, however, varies across commodities and time horizons. The impact is particularly strong on gold and crude oil, followed by industrial metals. For grains, however, U.S. dollar fluctuations do not appear to be an important determinant.

[4]As a caveat, the simulation (as well as the estimated equations) assumes that the U.S. dollar exchange rate and other variables are exogenous to commodity prices.

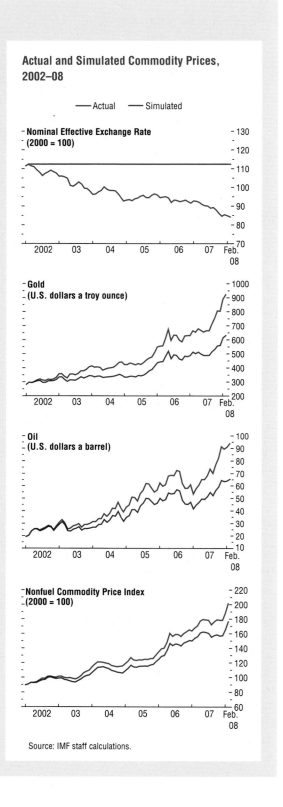

Actual and Simulated Commodity Prices, 2002–08

— Actual   — Simulated

Source: IMF staff calculations.

in growth in emerging markets—commodity prices could fall substantially, as they have in past global downturns.

Tightening Balances Shaping Oil Market Dynamics

After rising rapidly in the first half of 2007, oil prices experienced another strong run-up from late August to early January 2008. Over the year, spot prices for West Texas Intermediate (WTI) rose from $58 a barrel on January 3, 2007, to more than $100 a barrel on January 2, 2008. Although prices eased thereafter around concerns about slowing global growth, prices recovered in February and have stayed above $100 a barrel since end-February on a string of news signaling short-term supply problems and financial factors, as discussed above.

The price surge in the second half of 2007 was sparked by heightened geopolitical concerns about tensions in the Middle East and some weather-related production shutdowns. These events, taken by themselves, are not unusual, but they occurred against the backdrop of a noticeable tightening of oil market balances, and prices became highly sensitive to news that signaled future supply shortages. Nevertheless, the macrofinancial factors discussed in the previous section, such as the depreciation of the U.S. dollar, also played some role (Figure 1.17, third panel).

Global oil demand remained robust and increased by about 1 million barrels a day (mbd) in 2007, about the same as in 2006 (Table 1.3). As in recent years, growth continues to be driven by rapid income growth in emerging economies, supported in part by below-market domestic fuel prices (especially in the Middle East region and in China). Overall, demand from non-OECD countries (particularly India, China, and countries in the Middle East) increased by an estimated 1.3 mbd, whereas OECD demand declined by 0.1 mbd. In regional terms, demand fell in Europe and the former Soviet Union (FSU), but increased everywhere else (Figure 1.18, first panel).

Table 1.3. Global Oil Demand and Production by Region[1]
(Millions of barrels a day)

				Annual Percent Change		
	2006	2007 Est.	2008 Proj.	2006	2007 Est.	2008 Proj.
Demand						
OECD	49.3	49.1	49.3	−0.7	−0.5	0.3
North America	25.3	25.5	25.4	−0.7	0.9	−0.4
Of which:						
United States	20.7	20.8	20.7	−0.5	0.6	−0.5
Europe	15.6	15.3	15.4	0.1	−2.2	0.7
Pacific	8.4	8.3	8.4	−1.9	−1.6	1.9
Non-OECD	35.6	36.7	38.3	4.0	3.2	4.2
Of which:						
China	7.2	7.5	8.0	7.8	4.6	5.6
Other Asia	8.9	9.2	9.5	1.2	3.4	2.8
Former Soviet Union	4.1	4.0	4.1	4.4	−4.3	3.6
Middle East	6.4	6.7	7.1	5.8	4.8	6.1
Africa	2.9	3.1	3.2	−0.4	4.3	3.6
Latin America	5.3	5.5	5.7	3.7	4.7	3.7
World	84.9	85.8	87.5	1.2	1.1	2.0
Production						
OPEC (current composition)[2]	36.3	35.9	. . .	0.7	−1.0	. . .
Of which:						
Saudi Arabia	10.4	10.0	. . .	−1.5	−4.3	. . .
Algeria	2.1	2.2	. . .	1.7	2.5	. . .
Non-OPEC	49.1	49.7	50.6	1.1	1.1	1.8
Of which:						
North America	14.2	14.3	14.2	0.5	0.4	−0.7
North Sea	4.8	4.6	4.2	−7.6	−5.0	−8.7
Russia	9.8	10.1	10.2	2.2	2.4	0.9
Other former Soviet Union	2.4	2.7	3.0	11.1	11.9	12.3
Other non-OPEC	17.9	18.1	19.1	2.3	1.1	5.5
World	85.43	85.62	. . .	0.9	0.2	. . .
Net Demand[3]	−0.53	0.20	. . .	−0.6	0.2	. . .

Sources: International Energy Agency, Oil Market Report, March 2008; and IMF staff estimates.

[1]Covers consumption and production of crude oil, natural gas liquids, and nonconventional oil.

[2]OPEC = Organization of Petroleum Exporting Countries. Includes Angola (which joined OPEC in January 2007) and Ecuador (which rejoined OPEC in November 2007, after suspending its membership from December 1992 to October 2007).

[3]Difference between demand and production. Values reported as percent changes reflect net demand as percent of annual demand during the previous year.

Global oil supply increased only slightly in 2007, reflecting a combination of slightly lower production by Organization of Petroleum Exporting Countries (OPEC) members and shortfalls in non-OPEC production. The latter increased only by 0.6 mbd compared with an average increase of 1.0 mbd during 2001–06, with most of the increase accounted for by rising production in FSU countries. In

Figure 1.18. World Oil Market Balances

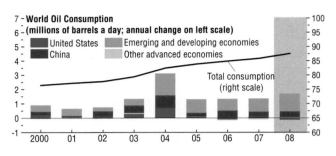

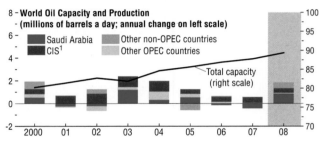

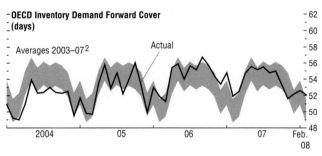

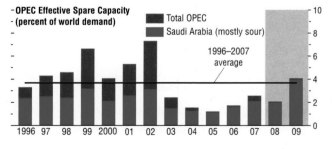

Sources: International Energy Agency; U.S. Energy Information Agency; and IMF staff estimates.
[1]CIS is the Commonwealth of Independent States.
[2]Band is based on averages for each calendar month during 2003–07 and a 40 percent confidence interval based on deviations during this period.

contrast, production in new offshore fields in Brazil and the Gulf of Mexico remained broadly unchanged, while greater-than-expected declines in production in Mexico, Alaska, and the North Sea more than offset modest gains elsewhere in the OECD countries (Figure 1.18, second panel). In general, non-OPEC production growth continues to be held back by frequent production outages and project delays—in some cases prompted by changes in contract terms by host governments.[8] Underlying this trend are major challenges facing all upstream investors, particularly increasingly complex geological and technological challenges as well as soaring costs (including from higher tax rates and royalties). Because some of these factors are expected to persist, supply constraints are likely to remain a dominant factor behind oil price fluctuations during the next few years (Box 1.5).

OPEC production declined by an estimated 0.4 mbd in 2007 compared with 2006. The decline reflected OPEC's decisions to cut production quotas by 1.2 mbd starting in November 2006 and by an additional 0.5 mbd starting in February 2007. Indeed, actual OPEC production would have been even lower in 2007 had it not been for increases in Angola and Iraq, which were not subject to quota limits during 2007.[9] Following OPEC's September 2007 decision to raise output by 0.5 mbd starting in November, estimated actual OPEC production rose by 0.3 mbd between October 2007 and February 2008.

---

[8]A few recent examples include (1) the efforts of Kazakhstan to increase the state oil company's equity in Kashagan, requiring contract renegotiation; (2) the hefty increase in royalties for oil companies in Alberta, Canada; and (3) the forcing out of Shell and BP from the Russian joint-venture projects in Sakhalin and Kovytka, respectively.

[9]Starting in 2008, Angola's output is subject to OPEC quotas, with its initial allocation of 1.9 mbd (below the estimated potential capacity of at least 2.2 mbd). In addition, Ecuador has rejoined OPEC. Although OPEC currently controls about 42 percent of global production, this share is expected to increase over the medium term, as its members own 76 percent of conventional reserves and have large planned additions to capacity.

Box 1.5. Why Hasn't Oil Supply Responded to Higher Prices?

Markets and analysts alike increasingly expect high oil prices to endure.[1] An important factor behind the firming of these expectations has been weaker-than-expected prospects for an expansion in supply. Indeed, the increase in long-dated futures prices over the past three years has coincided with steady downward revisions to projections for non-OPEC supply (figure, top panel). Although initial uncertainty about how long high oil prices would last was plausibly an important reason for oil producers not to rapidly ratchet up their investment, the sluggish supply response has become increasingly puzzling in light of persistently high prices. This box examines recent patterns in oil investment based on company and field data and considers prospects for capacity expansion. It concludes that there are geological, technological, and policy constraints that are unlikely to abate soon.

Soaring Investment Costs Point to Technical Supply Constraints

The sluggish response to higher oil prices is clearly not the result of a lack of investment. During 2004–06, nominal oil investment grew by about 70 percent (figure, bottom panel). However, soaring prices for investment meant that this did not translate into large real investment increases. The higher investment costs were due to a global scarcity both of equipment such as rigs and of services such as skilled engineers and project managers and to higher average exploration and development costs.[2]

Many of the factors contributing to higher costs are cyclical in nature and should moder-

Note: The main author of this box is Valerie Mercer-Blackman, with contributions from Lyudmyla Hvozdyk (Cambridge University).

[1]In their recent long-term reports, the International Energy Agency and the U.S. Department of Energy predicted that prices would remain around current levels (in 2005 dollars) in 2030 under current policies.

[2]According to Goldman Sachs (2007), field exploration and development costs of a sample of the most important projects have soared from $5 a barrel of oil equivalent in 2000 to about $10 in 2007.

Diminished Expectations

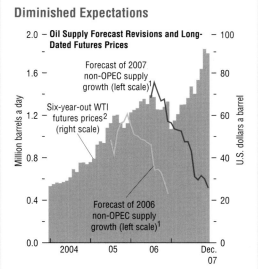

Oil Supply Forecast Revisions and Long-Dated Futures Prices

Forecast of 2007 non-OPEC supply growth (left scale)[1]

Six-year-out WTI futures prices[2] (right scale)

Forecast of 2006 non-OPEC supply growth (left scale)[1]

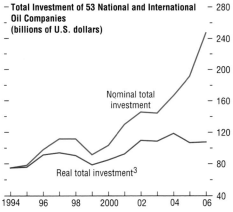

Total Investment of 53 National and International Oil Companies (billions of U.S. dollars)

Nominal total investment

Real total investment[3]

Sources: Bloomberg Financial Markets; Goldman Sachs Group, Inc. (2007); International Energy Agency, *Oil and Gas Journal;* Organization of Petroleum Exporting Countries (OPEC); U.S. Bureau of Statistics; U.S. Energy Information Administration; and IMF staff calculations.

[1]The forecast refers to a simple average from OPEC, the International Energy Agency, and the U.S. Energy Information Administration at the time of forecast. Futures prices are from New York Mercantile Exchange.

[2]WTI is West Texas Intermediate crude.

[3]Nominal capital investment in exploration deflated by the U.S. oil cost producer price index (weighted average of oil and gas wells' drilling services, operational support services, and oil and gas fields' machinery and equipment indices).

ate as input supplies adjust to the increased demand. However, based on evidence presented below, a significant component of these costs is

Box 1.5 *(continued)*

the result of geological constraints—a more permanent rigidity—implying that the responsiveness of supply to high prices is likely to remain low for some time.

Oil Investment Response Lags

To assess prospects for supply, the IMF staff estimated a model of investment to gauge whether the impediments to investment in the oil sector were technical or geological in nature, or whether they were associated with the investment environment. The model postulates that real investment by a company depends on net revenues (profits), expected future prices (proxied by spare capacity or long-dated futures prices), per-unit exploration and production costs, and technical risks, as well as variables characterizing the host-country investment environment, namely political stability (derived from the World Bank governance indicators) and fiscal balance to GDP (intended to capture the possible need of a host country to raise additional revenues through the oil sector).[3] By disaggregating investment at the field and company levels, it is also possible to investigate how quickly supply responds to price signals and whether investment behavior varies by such characteristics as company size, the type of exploration, or majority ownership (private versus public). The conclusions from this analysis are as follows.

- The data suggest that oil companies' investment—in particular that of major international firms—was slower to respond to the price signals in the current boom than in earlier periods. Using a panel of company data for investment between 1993 and 2006, IMF staff estimates show that the lag between spare capacity (a proxy for the price signal) and investment is about three years.[4] However, this lag increased in recent years. For international oil companies, this may reflect

limited given oil sector foreign direct investment restrictions in an increasing number of countries, as well as a reluctance to quickly switch to a risk-taking mode following the consolidation and cost-cutting strategies implemented during the 1990s, when oil prices remained low.[5]

- Comparing investment across companies suggests that the largest companies are also those that take on the greatest technical risks, even after controlling for higher costs. Indeed, regression estimates using company-level data suggest that increased technical risk significantly raises real investment.[6]

- Political variables in the host country were somewhat important in explaining investment. Political stability and the fiscal balance of the host country had positive coefficients in the regressions, as expected, but they were not always statistically significant. It is possible that fears of "resource nationalism" have increased uncertainty about investment in a less-tangible way that is not yet being captured by the data.[7] There could also be

[5]The median share of G7-listed oil and gas companies' cash earnings spent on asset acquisitions and dividend payouts increased from 35 percent in 1990–95 to 57 percent in 2000–04, leaving a lower share to be spent on new investment.

[6]The technical risk variable is an index that takes into account factors such as water depth, environment, geography, climate, technology dependence, stakeholder issues, geological issues (including American Petroleum Institute (API) performance level and reservoir complexity), and, if subject to OPEC quota compliance, infrastructure dependence and project development status. See Goldman Sachs (2007).

[7]Investment data span the 1993–2006 period and are limited. Data for Iraq are not available and are limited for Iran. Moreover, the data do not fully reflect the possible negative effects of recent nationalizations on investment (for the case of República Bolivariana de Venezuela, investment data for PDVSA, the national oil company, are unavailable after 2003). The variable would also fail to capture localized problems within countries. For example, Nigeria's onshore production has been hampered by frequent violent attacks, but investment in offshore production, which is less vulnerable to attacks, has grown steadily. Jojarth (2008) has shown that fields affected by hostilities do

[3]Additional control variables were past investment, reserves, and size.

[4]The oil sector is an industry with long planning horizons and high sunk costs, and so long lags are not unusual.

some self-selection: the strong positive correlation between exploration and production costs and political stability may suggest that oil companies would prefer to gamble on difficult geology than to take the necessary steps to hedge against political uncertainties.

- Increased tax assessments by governments have raised the costs of international joint-venture projects. In 2007, payments to governments (including royalties) represented more than half the cost of a barrel of oil. It was not possible to isolate the specific effect of higher taxes, but after-tax profits were found to have a positive and very significant effect on investment. In other words, to the extent that high tax rates affect companies' bottom lines, they adversely affect investment.

- Comparing investment behavior across companies, there is no evidence that national oil companies were investing less than international oil companies. On the contrary, some emerging, outwardly oriented national oil companies are increasing foreign and domestic investment very rapidly, in some cases with strong political and financial support from their governments. However, traditional national oil companies—which are typically smaller—have been struggling with high costs and aging infrastructure.

- Smaller oil companies are investing more as a share of revenues than larger ones, but they are much less likely to embark on technically risky projects. Soaring costs have been particularly taxing for smaller, independent companies with limited cash flow, which are less diversified than larger ones. In some cases, an important consequence of rising investment costs is that some projects have become unviable.

Turning to results obtained from analyzing field-level investment data, the analysis found

that the amount of time it takes, on average, for investment to translate into output has also increased, as more complex projects have become the norm. The projects attracting most of the marginal investment—such as deep-water offshore drilling in Brazil, the Gulf of Mexico, and West Africa; Canadian oil sands projects; and Siberian projects—take longer to explore and develop than more traditional projects. According to estimates based on field-level investment data of about 150 projects during 2003–07, these projects showed roughly twice the lag before the start of production as conventional projects. The lags likely reflect the complexities of working with emerging technology and are intrinsically related to soaring exploration and development costs. In some cases, projects have been delayed because governments have refused to renew some contracts in their current form in the face of higher-than-expected cost overruns.

In sum, the evidence suggests that although investment eventually does respond to prices, it does so with a greater lag and more slowly than in the past.

Geological Factors Make Supply Rigidities More Persistent

In addition to slow investment responses, there are two other factors that suggest that capacity growth will be more constrained by geology than in the past.

First, although peak production rates in major fields are attained earlier—because extraction methods have become more efficient—"decline rates" are also higher in major fields.[8] The International Energy Agency suggests that almost two-thirds of the additional gross capacity needed over the next eight years will be required just to replace declines in output from existing fields.

---

experience statistically significant higher costs. That said, the IMF staff has found a positive relationship between oil production growth and good governance indicators since 2000 (see Box 1.4 of the September 2006 *World Economic Outlook*).

[8]Decline rates refer to the natural rate of depletion once an oil field reaches its peak and are estimated at between 4 and 8 percent for conventional non-OPEC fields.

Box 1.5 *(concluded)*

Second, oil will increasingly come from unconventional sources, because output has declined from peak levels at conventional fields in many countries, and the size of oil fields is getting smaller on average.[9] This does not mean that the world is about to run out of oil, but it suggests that higher oil prices are needed to induce the additional investment required to balance the market over the medium term.

The rigidities that are currently preventing an adjustment toward greater supply growth suggest that the current cycle will be different from the major oil boom of the late 1970s. The table shows many of the underlying oil market factors associated with both episodes: in the late 1970s oil companies had ample opportunity to expand geographically, more oil fields were conventional, and production was located close to the main consuming centers.

Ultimately, policy and technology will determine the size of the supply and demand responses to high prices this time around. Although both demand and supply will eventually adjust, a policy-induced demand response can be implemented faster and is likely to

[9]See the International Energy Agency (2007), National Petroleum Council (2007), and van der Veer (2008).

Then and Now: Average Values of Oil Market Variables during Two Major Oil Booms
(In percent unless otherwise stated)

	1977–80	2004–06
Supply-related factors		
Oil capacity growth rate	2.5	1.6
Share of production by seven major international oil companies[1]	21	15
Share of production in conventional oil fields to total[2]	93	52
Share of production in the OECD to total global production	61	38
Memorandum item:		
OECD oil intensity (million barrels a day consumed as a ratio of GDP)	1.07	0.57

Sources: Goldman Sachs (2007); International Energy Agency; British Petroleum, Statistical Review of World Energy 2007; and IMF staff estimates.
[1]Data for 1977–80 estimated based on major operations of seven largest companies.
[2]Nonconventional defined as offshore, Siberian, and oil sands.

have a more immediate impact than a supply response, because many of the output constraints are geological and technological. Specifically, policies that lead to higher vehicle fuel-efficiency standards and the elimination of domestic fuel subsidies in some countries have the greatest potential to ease market tightness. It will also be important to remove investment obstacles and foster efficient and stable tax policies for companies.

The increased global net demand (consumption minus production) in 2007 was accommodated by declining inventories. OECD inventories fell through the second half of 2007 to a level below the five-year average (in millions of barrels) and forward cover (in days). During the first two months of 2008, however, inventories started to increase on weakening demand in some OECD economies (Figure 1.18, third panel).[10] With some capacity buildup and

[10]There are no data on non-OECD commercial stocks. China and India have begun to build official oil stock facilities.

declining production, OPEC's spare capacity increased slightly to about 2.7 percent of global demand (Figure 1.18, fourth panel), but remains below recent historical averages and is largely concentrated in Saudi Arabia (consisting mostly of more difficult-to-refine sour crude). However, substantial additions to capacity are projected to raise spare capacity to levels closer to historical averages during 2009.

With the tightening market balance, spot prices rose much faster than futures prices in the second half of 2007, and the oil price futures curve at the front end has been more downward sloping than usual since then. This constellation of above-average backwardation implies that markets expect future spot prices to be below current spot prices, which provides inventory holders with incentives to reduce their stocks below usual levels to accommodate short-term supply disruptions.[11] As inventory levels recovered somewhat in the first six weeks of 2008, the futures curve began to flatten (Figure 1.17, fourth panel). These developments are in contrast with much of 2005–07, when near-term futures were above spot prices—referred to as "front-end contango"—which provided incentives for increased inventory holdings in anticipation of higher prices.

Oil market balances are expected to remain tight on the basis of current demand and supply projections. Most forecasters expect a pickup in demand growth in 2008 by around 1.6 mbd under the assumption of more normal (colder) winter weather, with growth in non-OECD countries broadly unchanged at about 1.3–1.5 mbd. This projected increase in global demand is likely to be only partly met by higher non-OPEC supply. The latter is expected to rise by 0.8–1.0 mbd, but given the recent pattern of over-prediction of non-OPEC supply trends, actual production increases could again fall short of expectations. OPEC has so far resisted pressure to increase production quotas beyond last November's increase, given concerns that prices may fall rapidly with slowing global growth.

As a result, oil prices are projected to remain at around $95 a barrel in 2008–09 (as measured by the IMF's average petroleum spot price, see Box 1.6), broadly consistent with futures market prices. As shown in the fan chart based on options prices, the balance of risks to future spot prices is slightly tilted to the downside, likely reflecting downside risks to global growth (Figure 1.19, first panel). Nevertheless, price spikes remain a concern, as options mar-

[11]Slight backwardation (spot prices above futures prices) has been the norm in oil markets, reflecting the convenience yield required for inventory holdings with stable prices and the incentives needed for producers to extract oil now rather than in the future.

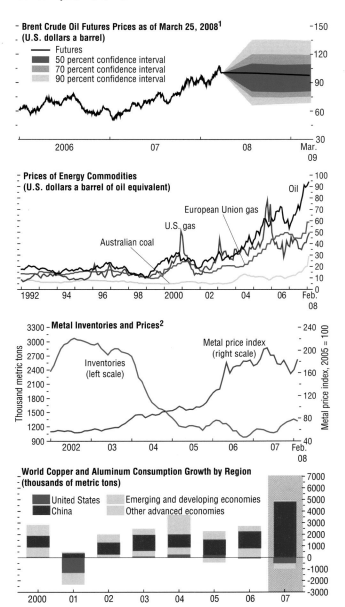

Figure 1.19. Energy and Metal Prices and Metal Consumption Growth

Brent Crude Oil Futures Prices as of March 25, 2008[1] (U.S. dollars a barrel)
- Futures
- 50 percent confidence interval
- 70 percent confidence interval
- 90 percent confidence interval

Prices of Energy Commodities (U.S. dollars a barrel of oil equivalent)
- Oil
- European Union gas
- U.S. gas
- Australian coal

Metal Inventories and Prices[2]
- Inventories (left scale)
- Metal price index (right scale)

World Copper and Aluminum Consumption Growth by Region (thousands of metric tons)
- United States
- China
- Emerging and developing economies
- Other advanced economies

Sources: Bloomberg Financial Markets; World Bureau of Metal Statistics; and IMF staff calculations.
[1]From futures options.
[2]Inventories refer to the sum of global stocks of copper, aluminum, tin, zinc, nickel, and lead monitored by the London Metal Exchange. Price refers to a composite index of those metals.

Box 1.6. Oil Price Benchmarks

There are three main regional crude oil price benchmarks against which crudes in the various regions are priced based on quality differentials. West Texas Intermediate (WTI) is primarily used as a benchmark for much of the Western Hemisphere. North Sea Brent is a marker for crudes from Europe, Africa, and Central Asia, as well as for Middle Eastern crudes heading into Western markets. Dubai Fateh is mainly used as a benchmark for markets in Asia.

All three benchmark prices generally are useful gauges of global oil market conditions, except during times of large localized disturbances. Because the crudes underlying the benchmarks are of different quality, their prices differ. Nevertheless, with arbitrage possibilities across markets, the price differentials are broadly constant on average, and the price benchmarks are typically highly correlated (figure). The main exceptions are times with large localized disturbances, owing to regional specialization in supply chains. For example, in the summer of 2007, WTI traded at a discount to Brent owing to refinery problems in the U.S. Midwest.

The IMF uses an average petroleum spot price (APSP) for projections in the *World Eco-*

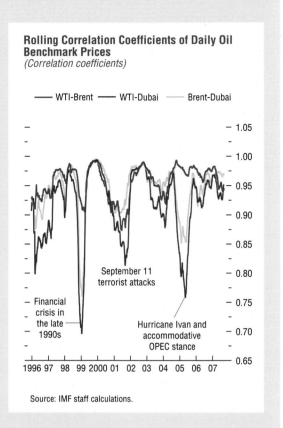

Rolling Correlation Coefficients of Daily Oil Benchmark Prices
(Correlation coefficients)

— WTI-Brent   — WTI-Dubai   — Brent-Dubai

Source: IMF staff calculations.

nomic Outlook. The APSP is a simple average of the three major price benchmarks. Using such an average reduces the risk of misrepresenting the underlying global oil market conditions because of localized disturbances.

Note: The main authors of this box are Kevin Cheng and Valerie Mercer-Blackman.

kets still expect oil prices of $100 a barrel or higher on delivery dates during 2008–09 with a risk-neutral probability of about 40 percent. On the downside, current estimates of long-run average production costs of $50 a barrel in marginal fields effectively constitute a lower bound.

Despite record-high oil prices, U.S. gasoline prices are only slightly above their highs of mid-May 2007, with U.S. retail gasoline prices hovering around $3.30 a gallon, reflecting lower crack spreads as refinery runs returned to normal levels and inventories rose to more comfort-

able levels. However, heating fuel prices in the United States hit a record high in March 2008, as stocks fell to critically low levels.

Coal Prices Soaring with Increased Substitution Away from Oil

The steady increases in crude oil prices since 2004 have changed fuel consumption patterns, which for the past two years have increasingly been characterized by a substitution for oil of other, cheaper energy sources. The substitution is particularly noticeable in electricity production, where fuel oil has increasingly been replaced by coal and, to a lesser extent, natural gas. This is in stark contrast with the consumption rigidities in transportation, where there are no large-scale alternative sources under current technologies (Figure 1.19, second panel).[12]

At a time of rising demand, coal supplies have recently been adversely affected by overextended supply chains,[13] in particular by major bottlenecks in Australian ports and weather problems in South Africa. As a result, coal prices increased by 83 percent over the 12 months ending January 2008. Overall, coal has become the world's fastest-growing hydrocarbon source.

In contrast, natural gas prices remained mostly flat during 2007. In the United States, this reflected ample inventories, notwithstanding greater demand through most of 2007 and two consecutive winters of warmer-than-normal temperatures. Prices are expected to stay near current levels during the next two years, but beyond that horizon, supplies are expected to tighten, as the current inventory overhang is expected to disappear. In Europe, however, energy consumption has shifted from natural gas to coal and nuclear energy, prompted by energy security concerns (Russia is the sole gas supplier for many markets).

Base Metals Prices Soften but Still Benefit from Strong Emerging Economy Growth

After surging in the first half of 2007, metals prices eased in the second half on concerns about slowing global manufacturing and increas-

ing inventories. In early 2008, they recovered some of their losses in light of supply concerns (primarily owing to the effects of power outages on production in China and South Africa) (Figure 1.19, third panel). Tin was the main exception to the general trend, with prices remaining close to recent highs because of continued supply tightness and export restrictions in major Asian producers.

Overall, however, the fall in metals prices from the mid-2007 peak has been relatively narrow, because of continued strong demand from emerging economies, especially China. Prices of many metals—in particular of those used as inputs in steel production (nickel and zinc)—have been strongly correlated with China's industrial production during the past five years, and China accounted for almost 90 percent of global consumption increases in four main base metals during 2005–07 (Figure 1.19, fourth panel).

Metals prices—which tend to be the most sensitive to business cycle fluctuations among commodity prices—are expected to reverse their gains from early 2008 later in the year and to ease further with slowing global growth. That said, as in the oil market, supply problems could limit downward pressures, especially over the medium term, as reflected in the increased spread between five-year-ahead futures and spot prices for copper and aluminum in early 2008. Copper production in particular could remain vulnerable to labor-related disruptions, technical difficulties, and deteriorating ore quality, while other metals—particularly nickel and aluminum—could be affected by escalating costs and the latest bout of industry consolidation.[14] Such merger activity could negatively affect new investment because funds are being diverted from possible greenfield investments to acquisitions, a process generally followed by

---

[12]A recent study by Hughes and others (2007) suggests that the price elasticity of demand for transportation fuels in the United States may be up to 10 times smaller now, compared with the late 1970s. In emerging markets, moreover, transportation fuel demand has become less income elastic with increased vehicle ownership.

[13]Transport bottlenecks for both wet and dry freight have become more prevalent in recent years with rapidly increasing commodity demand, as reflected in sharply higher bulk shipping rates.

[14]Recent notable mergers and acquisitions in metals include Alcoa with Alcan and Arcelor with Mittal. This follows a trend toward greater concentration in mining of the main base metals, with the five largest companies in 2005 producing an estimated 43 percent of metals output combined (compared with 33 percent in 1985).

Figure 1.20. Recent Developments in Major Food Crops

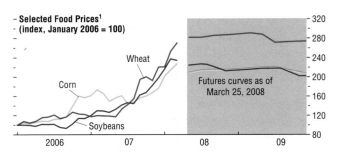

Selected Food Prices[1]
(index, January 2006 = 100)

Wheat

Corn

Soybeans

Futures curves as of March 25, 2008

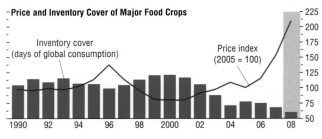

Price and Inventory Cover of Major Food Crops

Inventory cover
(days of global consumption)

Price index
(2005 = 100)

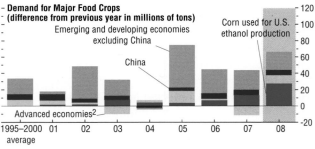

Demand for Major Food Crops
(difference from previous year in millions of tons)

Emerging and developing economies excluding China

Corn used for U.S. ethanol production

China

Advanced economies[2]

1995–2000 average

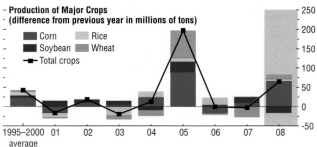

Production of Major Crops
(difference from previous year in millions of tons)

Corn   Rice
Soybean   Wheat
Total crops

1995–2000 average

Sources: Bloomberg Financial Markets; U.S. Department of Agriculture; and IMF staff estimates.
[1]Major food crops are wheat, corn, rice, and soybeans.
[2]Excludes corn used in U.S. ethanol production.

conservative financial strategies as firms attempt to reduce new debt levels.

Prices of Major Crops Propped by Biofuels and Rapid Emerging Economy Growth

Food prices rose by 39 percent from February 2007 to February 2008—led by wheat, soybeans, corn, and edible oils, all of which reached new highs. As in the oil market, price strength reflects tight market balances, with inventories of major food crops at a two-decade low despite generally robust production growth (Figure 1.20, top panels). The tightening reflects a number of factors.

Rising biofuel production in the United States and the European Union has boosted demand for corn, rapeseed oil, and other grains and edible oils. Although biofuels still account for only 1½ percent of the global liquid fuels supply, they accounted for almost half the increase in the consumption of major food crops in 2006–07, mostly because of corn-based ethanol produced in the United States (Figure 1.20, third panel). Biofuel demand has propelled the prices not only for corn, but also for other grains, meat, poultry, and dairy through cost-push and crop and demand substitution effects.[15] Strong per capita income growth in China, India, and other emerging economies has also buoyed food demand, including for meats and related animal feeds, especially grains, soybeans, and edible oils.

On the supply side, drought conditions in a number of countries reduced global wheat production in 2007 (Figure 1.20, fourth panel). Moreover, higher oil prices have also increased production costs for many foods products.

Policies may also have contributed to upward pressure on global prices. In view of political concern about the social implications of rising food prices, some countries have resorted to measures to reduce exports and increase imports of food, thereby contributing to global

---

[15]See Box 1.6 of the October 2007 *World Economic Outlook.*

market tightness. For example, in 2007, China, Russia, Ukraine, Kazakhstan, and Argentina imposed export taxes on grains and lowered tariffs on edible oils, while India banned basmati rice exports and raised export taxes on palm oil.

Food prices are expected to peak in 2008, and they are forecast to ease only gradually thereafter. In the short term, price risks are on the upside, as demand is expected to remain strong. More generally, although food price cycles in the past typically averaged three years, with supply responding quickly to changes in demand conditions, the current cycle is likely to last longer. The reason is that food demand is expected to continue increasing rapidly for some time with rising biofuel production in the United States[16] and the European Union, and with continued strong demand from emerging and developing economies.

Macroeconomic Implications of Rising Commodity Prices

Rising fuel and food prices have boosted headline inflation in many countries in recent months. Food price increases are of particular concern, especially for emerging and developing economies, because the corresponding expenditure shares exceed those of oil-related spending by a substantial margin. Indeed, food price increases accounted for almost 45 percent of global headline inflation in 2007 for major industrial and emerging economies, compared with around 27 percent in 2006, and the impact on emerging economies (almost 70 percent) has been much larger than on advanced economies (around 20 percent) (Figure 1.21, top panel; Table 1.4). The impact on headline inflation

[16]Corn-based ethanol supplies, for example, are expected to be spurred by the mandate in the 2007 U.S. energy bill to quintuple the production of ethanol by 2022. If the mandate under the bill is met on schedule, about half of the entire U.S. corn crop will have to be set aside for ethanol by the middle of the next decade (up from about 31 percent in 2008), even assuming cellulosic ethanol becomes commercially viable in about five years.

Figure 1.21. Macroeconomic Implications of High Commodity Prices

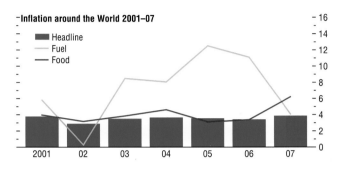

Inflation around the World 2001–07

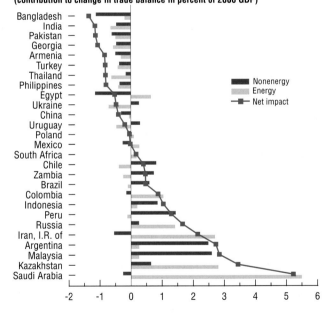

First-Round Impact of Commodity Price Changes on Trade Balance of Selected Countries, 2007
(contribution to change in trade balance in percent of 2006 GDP)

Source: IMF staff calculations.
[1]Assuming full pass-through is allowed.

Table 1.4. Food, Fuel, and Headline Inflation[1]

(In percent)

	2006					2007				
	Headline Inflation	Food		Fuel		Headline Inflation	Food		Fuel	
		Inflation[2]	Contribution[3]	Inflation[2]	Contribution[3]		Inflation[2]	Contribution[3]	Inflation[2]	Contribution[3]
World	3.4	3.4	27.0	11.2	19.9	3.9	6.2	44.3	4.1	8.0
Advanced economies	2.3	2.0	12.4	11.1	28.0	2.2	3.0	19.5	3.8	12.1
Africa	7.2	8.5	46.6	8.7	22.3	7.4	8.7	43.6	6.7	6.5
CIS[4]	9.3	8.5	40.0	17.1	7.6	9.6	9.2	41.1	11.7	7.2
Developing Asia	3.7	4.4	37.7	12.3	19.4	4.9	10.0	67.5	3.1	3.4
Central and eastern Europe	5.2	4.6	22.0	9.7	18.2	5.4	8.2	34.9	6.9	11.8
Middle East	3.4	5.1	57.0	1.9	5.3	10.1	13.6	42.3	10.1	24.4
Western Hemisphere	5.4	4.5	23.1	8.7	9.8	5.4	8.5	40.8	2.3	3.4

Source: Data on food and fuel price inflation are based on 137 countries submitted by country desks and data banks.
[1]Figure may differ from those in the Statistical Appendix tables because of limited country coverage.
[2]Changes in food or fuel-related consumer prices (or closest equivalents).
[3]Contribution to headline inflation in percent.
[4]CIS: Commonwealth of Independent States.

of the recent large oil and food price surges will persist through much of 2008 even without further price increases, and the potential for second-round effects on inflation remains a concern.

Higher commodity prices have benefited many emerging and developing economies, but they have adversely affected external balances of the net commodity importers among them (Figure 1.21, lower panel). IMF staff estimates suggest that the adverse first-round effects of sharply higher oil and food prices in 2007 on external current account balances exceeded 1 percentage point of GDP in a number of developing economies. Because much of the increase in the prices of grains and oil occurred in the second half of 2007, for some low-income economies external balances may deteriorate significantly in 2008, which could contribute to increasing their external vulnerabilities and slowing domestic demand and activity.

The sharply higher commodity prices have also increased cost pressures on producers and reduced household purchasing power in commodity-importing countries. These effects are likely to amplify the downdraft from the credit market crisis on consumers in advanced economies. At the global level, the effect of these subtractions from aggregate demand is unlikely to be fully offset by higher expenditure in commodity-exporting countries in response to the substantial terms of trade gain.

References

Akin, Çigdem, and M. Ayhan Kose, 2007, "Changing Nature of North-South Linkages: Stylized Facts and Explanations," IMF Working Paper 07/280 (Washington: International Monetary Fund).

Bagwell, Kyle, and Robert W. Staiger, 1997, "Collision Over the Business Cycle," *Rand Journal of Economics*, Vol. 28 (Spring), pp. 82–106.

Bernanke, Ben, Mark Gertler, and Simon Gilchrist, 1999, "The Financial Accelerator in a Quantitative Business Cycle Framework," in *Handbook of Macroeconomics*, Vol. 1C, Chapter 2, ed. by John B. Taylor and Michael Woodford (Amsterdam: North-Holland), pp. 1341–93.

Bernanke, Ben S., and Cara S. Lown, 1991, "The Credit Crunch," *Brookings Papers on Economic Activity: 2*, Brookings Institution, pp. 205–47.

Bordo, Michael, and Olivier Jeanne, 2002, "Monetary Policy and Asset Prices: Does 'Benign Neglect' Make Sense?" IMF Working Paper 02/225 (Washington: International Monetary Fund).

Borensztein, Eduardo, and Carmen Reinhart, 1994, "The Macroeconomic Determinants of Commodity Prices," IMF Working Paper 94/9 (Washington: International Monetary Fund).

Caprio, Gerard, Daniela Klingebiel, Luc Laeven, and Guillermo Noguera, 2005, "Banking Crisis Database," Appendix in *Systemic Financial Crises*, ed. by Patrick Honohan and Luc Laeven (Cambridge, United Kingdom: Cambridge University Press).

Cordoba, Juan-Carlos, and Marla Ripoll, 2004, "Credit Cycles Redux," *International Economic Review*, Vol. 45 (November), pp. 1011–46.

Frankel, Jeffrey, 2006, "Commodity Prices, Monetary Policy, and Currency Regimes," paper presented at the NBER Conference on Asset Prices and Monetary Policy, Cape Cod, Massachusetts, May 5–6.

Gan, Jie, 2007, "The Real Effects of Asset Market Bubbles: Loan- and Firm-Level Evidence of a Lending Channel," *Review of Financial Studies*, Vol. 20 (November), pp. 1941–73.

Goldman Sachs, PLC, 2007, "170 Projects to Change the World," a report prepared by the Goldman Sachs Global Equities Group (London, February).

Green, Edward, and Soo Nam Oh, 1991, "Can a 'Credit Crunch' Be Efficient?" Federal Reserve Bank of Minneapolis *Quarterly Review*, Vol. 15 (Fall).

Greenspan, Alan, 2005, "Current Account," speech given at the Advancing Enterprise 2005 Conference, London, February 4. Available via the Internet: www.federalreserve.gov/boarddocs/speeches/2005/20050204/default.htm.

Hughes, Jonathan, Christopher R. Knittel, and Daniel Sperling, 2008, "Evidence of a Shift in the Short-Run Price Elasticity of Gasoline Demand," *Energy Journal*, Vol. 29 (January).

International Energy Agency, 2007, *World Energy Outlook 2007: China and India Insights* (Paris, November).

Jojarth, Christine, 2008, "The End of Easy Oil: Estimating Average Production Costs from Oil Fields Around the World," Working Paper No. 72 (Palo Alto, California: Stanford University Program on Energy and Sustainable Development, November).

Kiyotaki, Nobuhiro, and John Moore, 1997, "Credit Cycles," *Journal of Political Economy*, Vol. 105 (April), pp. 211–48.

Lane, Philip, and Gian Maria Milesi-Ferretti, 2006, "Capital Flows to Central and Eastern Europe," IMF Working Paper 06/188 (Washington: International Monetary Fund).

Lee, Jaewoo, Gian Maria Milesi-Ferretti, Jonathan Ostry, Alessandro Prati, and Luca Antonio Ricci, 2008, *Exchange Rate Assessments: CGER Methodologies*, IMF Occasional Paper No. 261 (Washington: International Monetary Fund).

Leidy, Michael, 1996, "Macroeconomic Conditions and Pressures for Protection Under Antidumping and Countervailing Duty Laws—Empirical Evidence from the United States," IMF Working Paper 96/88 (Washington: International Monetary Fund).

Matsuyama, Kiminori, 2007, "Credit Traps and Credit Cycles," *American Economic Review*, Vol. 97 (March), pp. 503–16.

Mishkin, Frederic, 2007, "Housing and the Monetary Transmission Mechanism," paper presented at the Federal Reserve Bank of Kansas City 31st Economic Policy Symposium, "Housing, Housing Finance and Monetary Policy," Jackson Hole, Wyoming, August 31–September 1.

National Petroleum Council, 2007, "Hard Truths: Facing the Hard Truths About Energy" (Washington, July). Available via the Internet: www.npchardtruthsreport.org.

Owens, Raymond, and Stacey Schreft, 1995, "Identifying Credit Crunches," *Contemporary Economic Policy*, Vol. 13 (April), pp. 63–76.

Peek, Joe, and Eric Rosengren, 2005, "Crisis Resolution and Credit Allocation: The Case of Japan," in *Systemic Financial Crises*, edited by Patrick Honohan and Luc Laeven (Cambridge, United Kingdom: Cambridge University Press).

Stock, James H., and Mark Watson, 1993, "A Simple Estimator of Cointegrating Vectors in Higher Order Integrated Systems," *Econometrica*, Vol. 61 (July), pp. 783–820.

Suarez, Javier, and Oren Sussman, 1997, "Endogenous Cycles in a Stiglitz-Weiss Economy," *Journal of Economic Theory*, Vol. 76 (September), pp. 47–71.

Thomas, Charles P., Jaime Marquez, and Sean Fahle, 2008, "Measuring U.S. International Relative Prices: A WARP View of the World," FRB International Finance Discussion Paper No. 2008–917 (Washington: Board of Governors of the Federal Reserve System).

Tucker, Paul, 2007, "Money and Credit: Banking and the Macroeconomy," speech presented at the Monetary Policy and Markets Conference, London, December 13.

van der Veer, Jeroen, 2008, 'Two Energy Futures" (Royal Dutch Shell plc, January).

Weinberg, John, 1995, "Cycles in Lending Standards?" Federal Reserve Bank of Richmond *Economic Quarterly*, Vol. 81 (Summer), pp. 1–18.

CHAPTER 2

COUNTRY AND REGIONAL PERSPECTIVES

As discussed in Chapter 1, a global slowdown in activity, led by a sharp downturn in the United States and the spreading crisis in financial markets, will create more difficult external conditions for all regions of the world. This chapter examines in more detail how different regions are likely to fare in this environment and the policy challenges that are likely to arise.[1]

United States and Canada: How Long Will the Slowdown Last?

The U.S. economy slowed markedly to grow 2.2 percent in 2007, down from almost 3 percent in 2006 (Table 2.1). The pace of activity weakened sharply in the fourth quarter to only 0.6 percent (at an annualized rate). With the housing correction continuing full blast, the contraction of residential investment sliced a full percentage point off growth in 2007. Consumption and business investment also softened markedly toward the end of the year, as sentiment soured and lending conditions tightened significantly after the outbreak of financial turbulence in August, despite the Federal Reserve's aggressive turn to monetary easing.

Rising oil prices helped dampen consumption, while also boosting 12-month headline inflation to 3.4 percent in February (measured using the personal consumption expenditure deflator). Core inflation has remained at about 2 percent, the top of the Federal Reserve's implicit comfort zone. The one area of strength has been net exports, which have grown in response to the dollar's sustained depreciation and the sluggishness of the U.S. economy relative to those of its trading partners. As a result, the current account deficit declined to less than 5 percent of GDP in the fourth quarter of 2007,

down 1½ percent of GDP from the peak in 2006 (Table 2.2).

The economy is slowing rapidly in early 2008, as falling house prices and tightening credit availability take a toll on consumption even as residential investment continues to drop, with inevitable knock-on effects on business investment. Credit spreads have widened markedly since late February, despite some recent improvement after the Federal Reserve widened access to the discount window to investment banks. The near-collapse of the fifth largest investment bank, Bear Stearns, in early March further heightened concerns about counterparty risk and put additional pressure on bank capital in an environment in which bank lending standards were already being tightened rapidly. At the same time, there are clear signs that housing weakness is now feeding through into labor markets and consumption. Nonfarm payrolls fell in January and February, real consumption has been at a standstill since December, and rapidly weakening consumer and corporate sentiment suggest that downward pressure on domestic spending and incomes will intensify.

The key question is how long the present downturn will last. Previous U.S. recessions have typically been followed by quite vigorous recoveries, as sharp corrections generally help resolve imbalances and monetary and fiscal stimuli kick in. Key determinants of the economy's ability to rebound quickly from the current period of weak performance are the future course of the housing correction and the financial sector crisis, and the ensuing impact on household and business finances.

Looking first to the housing market, the relationship between housing activity and the business cycle has changed markedly in recent years. Until recently, as observed by Leamer (2007), swings in residential investment have been at the core of the cycle—eight of the ten

---

[1] Further analysis of trends and prospects in different regions is provided in the spring 2008 issues of *Regional Economic Outlook*.

65

Table 2.1. Advanced Economies: Real GDP, Consumer Prices, and Unemployment
(Annual percent change and percent of labor force)

	Real GDP				Consumer Prices				Unemployment			
	2006	2007	2008	2009	2006	2007	2008	2009	2006	2007	2008	2009
Advanced economies	**3.0**	**2.7**	**1.3**	**1.3**	**2.4**	**2.2**	**2.6**	**2.0**	**5.7**	**5.4**	**5.6**	**5.9**
United States	2.9	2.2	0.5	0.6	3.2	2.9	3.0	2.0	4.6	4.6	5.4	6.3
Euro area[1]	2.8	2.6	1.4	1.2	2.2	2.1	2.8	1.9	8.2	7.4	7.3	7.4
Germany	2.9	2.5	1.4	1.0	1.8	2.3	2.5	1.6	9.8	8.4	7.9	7.7
France	2.0	1.9	1.4	1.2	1.9	1.6	2.5	1.7	9.2	8.3	7.8	7.9
Italy	1.8	1.5	0.3	0.3	2.2	2.0	2.5	1.9	6.8	6.0	5.9	5.8
Spain	3.9	3.8	1.8	1.7	3.6	2.8	4.0	3.0	8.5	8.3	9.5	10.4
Netherlands	3.0	3.5	2.1	1.6	1.7	1.6	2.4	1.8	3.9	3.2	2.8	2.9
Belgium	2.9	2.7	1.4	1.2	2.3	1.8	3.1	1.9	8.2	7.5	7.6	8.3
Austria	3.3	3.4	1.9	1.7	1.7	2.2	2.8	1.9	4.8	4.4	4.4	4.5
Finland	4.9	4.4	2.4	2.1	1.3	1.6	2.8	1.9	7.7	6.8	6.7	6.7
Greece	4.2	4.0	3.5	3.3	3.3	3.0	3.5	2.7	8.9	8.3	7.5	7.4
Portugal	1.3	1.9	1.3	1.4	3.0	2.4	2.4	2.0	7.7	7.7	7.6	7.4
Ireland	5.7	5.3	1.8	3.0	2.7	3.0	3.2	2.1	4.4	4.6	5.3	5.0
Luxembourg	6.1	5.4	3.1	3.2	2.7	2.3	2.9	2.1	4.5	4.4	4.8	4.9
Slovenia	5.7	6.1	4.1	3.5	2.5	3.6	4.0	2.4	5.9	4.8	4.8	5.0
Cyprus	4.0	4.4	3.4	3.5	2.2	2.2	4.0	2.9	4.6	3.9	3.9	3.9
Malta	3.4	3.8	2.2	2.0	2.6	0.7	3.4	2.5	7.3	6.3	6.5	6.8
Japan	2.4	2.1	1.4	1.5	0.3	—	0.6	1.3	4.1	3.9	3.9	3.9
United Kingdom[1]	2.9	3.1	1.6	1.6	2.3	2.3	2.5	2.1	5.4	5.4	5.5	5.4
Canada	2.8	2.7	1.3	1.9	2.0	2.1	1.6	2.0	6.3	6.0	6.1	6.3
Korea	5.1	5.0	4.2	4.4	2.2	2.5	3.4	2.9	3.5	3.3	3.1	3.0
Australia	2.8	3.9	3.2	3.1	3.5	2.3	3.5	3.3	4.8	4.4	4.3	4.3
Taiwan Province of China	4.9	5.7	3.4	4.1	0.6	1.8	1.5	1.5	3.9	3.9	3.9	3.8
Sweden	4.1	2.6	2.0	1.7	1.5	1.7	2.8	2.1	7.0	6.1	6.6	7.1
Switzerland	3.2	3.1	1.3	0.9	1.0	0.9	2.0	1.4	3.3	2.5	3.2	4.1
Hong Kong SAR	7.0	6.3	4.3	4.8	2.0	2.0	3.6	4.5	4.8	4.1	3.9	3.8
Denmark	3.9	1.8	1.2	0.5	1.9	1.7	2.3	2.0	4.0	2.8	3.1	3.2
Norway	2.5	3.5	3.1	2.3	2.3	0.8	3.1	2.6	3.4	2.5	2.5	3.0
Israel	5.2	5.3	3.0	3.4	2.1	0.5	2.6	2.0	8.4	7.3	6.7	6.7
Singapore	8.2	7.7	4.0	4.5	1.0	2.1	4.7	2.5	2.7	2.1	2.1	2.2
New Zealand[2]	1.5	3.0	2.0	2.1	3.4	2.4	3.4	2.7	3.8	3.6	4.1	4.4
Iceland	4.4	3.8	0.4	0.1	6.8	5.0	5.5	2.7	1.3	1.0	3.2	2.9
Memorandum												
Major advanced economies	2.7	2.2	0.9	0.9	2.4	2.2	2.4	1.8	5.8	5.5	5.7	6.0
Newly industrialized Asian economies	5.6	5.6	4.0	4.4	1.6	2.2	3.0	2.7	3.7	3.4	3.3	3.2

[1]Based on Eurostat's harmonized index of consumer prices.
[2]Consumer prices excluding interest rate components.

postwar recessions were preceded by a housing downturn, and all major housing downturns since 1970 have been followed by recessions (Figure 2.1). However, the liberalization of bank regulations and the shift of housing finance into securities markets has broken the tight link between rising interest rates, the availability of mortgage financing, and residential investment (Bernanke, 2007). At the same time, as discussed in Chapter 3, the increasing development of the mortgage market seems to have strengthened the "financial accelerator" impact of rising

house prices on consumption. The house price boom continued even as monetary policy was tightened from 2002, as financing availability was maintained through securitization techniques that allowed a weakening of loan conditions (rising loan-to-value ratios, use of low "teaser" interest rates, and inadequate documentation) and rising financial sector leverage.

After peaking in the latter part of 2005, the housing market has already undergone a major correction, with house prices dropping 0–10 percent during 2007, depending on the measure

Table 2.2. Advanced Economies: Current Account Positions

(Percent of GDP)

	2006	2007	2008	2009
Advanced economies	**−1.5**	**−1.2**	**−1.1**	**−1.1**
United States	−6.2	−5.3	−4.3	−4.2
Euro area[1]	−0.1	−0.2	−0.7	−0.9
Germany	5.0	5.6	5.2	4.9
France	−1.3	−1.3	−2.4	−2.5
Italy	−2.6	−2.2	−2.4	−2.3
Spain	−8.6	−10.1	−10.5	−10.3
Netherlands	8.3	6.6	5.9	5.6
Belgium	2.7	3.2	2.9	2.8
Austria	2.4	2.7	2.9	2.9
Finland	4.6	4.6	3.8	3.9
Greece	−11.0	−13.9	−13.9	−14.1
Portugal	−9.4	−9.4	−9.5	−9.5
Ireland	−4.2	−4.5	−3.2	−2.9
Luxembourg	10.3	9.5	8.2	7.3
Slovenia	−2.8	−4.8	−4.8	−4.9
Cyprus	−5.9	−7.1	−7.7	−7.1
Malta	−6.7	−6.2	−6.1	−5.8
Japan	3.9	4.9	4.0	3.9
United Kingdom	−3.9	−4.9	−4.8	−4.4
Canada	1.6	0.9	−0.9	−1.2
Korea	0.6	0.6	−1.0	−0.9
Australia	−5.5	−6.2	−6.3	−5.3
Taiwan Province of China	6.7	8.3	7.8	8.1
Sweden	8.5	8.3	6.4	6.7
Switzerland	15.1	17.2	15.4	13.8
Hong Kong SAR	12.1	12.3	9.9	8.3
Denmark	2.7	1.1	0.7	1.3
Norway	17.3	16.3	20.0	20.4
Israel	6.0	3.1	1.8	1.7
Singapore	21.8	24.3	20.6	18.9
New Zealand	−8.6	−8.1	−7.1	−7.1
Iceland	−25.4	−15.6	−8.0	−5.3
Memorandum				
Major advanced economies	−2.3	−1.8	−1.6	−1.5
Euro area[2]	−0.2	0.1	−0.5	−0.8
Newly industrialized Asian economies	5.2	6.0	4.5	4.3

[1]Calculated as the sum of the balances of individual euro area countries.

[2]Corrected for reporting discrepancies in intra-area transactions.

Figure 2.1. United States: Housing Cycles in Perspective

The current housing cycle is already the longest since the 1970s. Moreover, various valuation indicators remain elevated, suggesting that the downswing still has a substantial way to go.

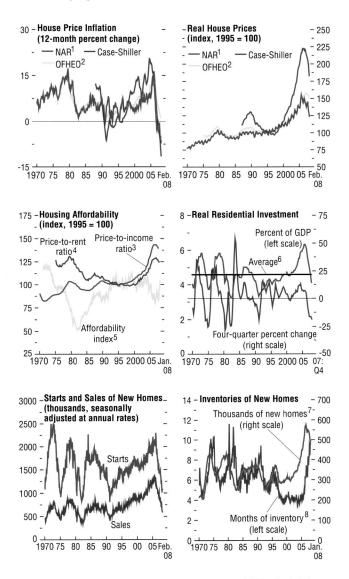

Sources: Davis, Lehnert, and Martin (2007); Haver Analytics; and IMF staff calculations.
[1]National Association of Realtors; three-month moving average of 12-month percent change.
[2]Office of Federal Housing Enterprise Oversight (OFHEO).
[3]Ratio of OFHEO house price index to personal disposable income per capita.
[4]Inverse of the rent-price ratio for the aggregate stock of owner-occupied housing.
[5]Index equal to 100 median family income qualifies for an 80 percent mortgage on a median-priced existing single-family home, reindexed to 1995 = 100.
[6]Percent of GDP average during 1970–2007.
[7]Thousands of new single family homes for sale.
[8]Months of inventory at current sales pace.

used, and house starts dropping over 50 percent from their peak by early 2008. Nevertheless, the market remains far from equilibrium, with inventories of unsold houses still close to record levels and home value indicators still elevated well above historical norms (see Figure 2.1). Moreover, the adjustable-rate sector of the subprime mortgage market has virtually disappeared, and spreads have now widened even on conforming mortgages. Rising negative equity on home ownership and resets of variable-rate mortgages are likely to push defaults and foreclosures up still higher, putting further downward pressure on house prices, which will ratchet up incentives to default. Reflecting these concerns, the baseline scenario for the U.S. economy assumes a 14–22 percent drop in house prices during 2007–08 (depending on the index used)—unprecedented for the United States, although not elsewhere.

Turning to financial markets, the question is how much of a drag will be imposed on activity by the spreading financial market crisis. The concern is that financial and housing markets are in mutually reinforcing cycles of tightening credit conditions, falling asset values, and weakening activity. Risk spreads have widened, notably on high-yield bonds, although the impact has been somewhat cushioned by the decline in risk-free rates and the lower cost of funds. Moreover, capital is being eroded—the baseline scenario envisages that losses to U.S. bank capital from mortgage-related exposures and structured credits will amount to about 2 percentage points of risk-weighted assets. Pressure on capital is being further exacerbated as banks absorb special-purpose vehicles and intended securitization deals back onto their balance sheets. Bank lending conditions have already been tightened, certain types of financing—such as asset-backed commercial paper and credits for leveraged buyouts—have largely dried up, and spreads on other types of asset-backed borrowing—notably credit cards and commercial real estate loans—have widened sharply. All these effects threaten to have a significant restraining effect on activity, pushing up default rates and lowering underlying asset values, with further adverse impact on financial markets.

Partially counteracting these forces, capital in commercial banks had built up to comfortable levels after 2000, and banks have been able to tap new sources to raise additional capital in recent months, helping to keep the ratio of tier 1 capital to risk-weighted assets for the commercial banking system above 10 percent at end-2007. Corporate profitability and balance sheets remain strong, reducing their need for financing. Finally, resources for provision of mortgage financing have been made available to banks by the Federal Home Loan Banks and by an easing of constraints on the main government-sponsored enterprises. Thus, although credit has been squeezed, a full-blown credit crunch has not developed so far (see Box 1.1).

Reflecting these considerations, the baseline projections envisage that the economy will tip into modest recession in 2008, followed by a gradual recovery starting in 2009 that will be somewhat slower than that following the 2001 recession as household and financial balance sheets are repaired. (Chapter 2 of the April 2003 *World Economic Outlook* analyzed how balance sheet problems in the wake of housing busts were responsible for particularly slow recoveries.) On an annual basis, growth will slow to 0.5 percent in 2008, before rising modestly to 0.6 percent in 2009. The trajectory is clearer when measured on a fourth-quarter-to-fourth-quarter basis. On this metric, the economy is projected to decline 0.7 percent during 2008—down from the 0.9 percent increase projected in the January 2008 *World Economic Outlook Update*—before recovering to grow a still-below-par 1.6 percent during 2009. All major components of domestic demand will be sickly during 2008. Residential investment will continue to drop; consumption will decline in the face of adverse wealth effects, tight credit, and deteriorating labor market conditions, despite tax credits in the recently enacted fiscal stimulus package; and business investment will also turn down. In 2009, consumption will remain sluggish, as households continue to raise their saving rate after a long period during which personal wealth was boosted by buoyant capital gains on assets rather than by savings from income. Net exports will continue to be a bright spot, bringing the current account deficit down further to about 4.2 percent of GDP, notwithstanding sustained high oil prices.

Risks around this lower baseline are still somewhat weighted to the downside, particularly for 2009. Negative financial and housing feedbacks could push activity down below the baseline. Nevertheless, concerns have been partially alleviated by vigorous policy responses, particularly the provision of liquidity to financial markets.

Given this outlook, the Federal Reserve may well need to continue easing interest rates for some time, depending on the emerging evidence on the extent of the downturn. The federal funds rate has already been lowered by 300 basis points since summer 2007, and markets expect a further 50-basis-point cut over the next 12 months. With core inflation still somewhat elevated and prospects for continued high and volatile energy and food prices, there are lingering concerns about inflation, but these risks should be blunted by the projected widening output gaps and the soft labor market.

Fiscal policy should also be used to provide valuable support for a faltering economy after several years of consolidation. Automatic stabilizers in the United States are less strong than in western Europe, reflecting the smaller size of government. Government revenues are likely to be quite sensitive to a downturn, and the recent surge in capital gains taxes could be reversed, although the benefits would accrue mainly to higher-income groups with lower marginal propensity to consume. The recently enacted stimulus package provides tax relief to low- and middle-income households, as well as increased incentives for business investment, and should provide an effective boost to demand in the second half of 2008, based on the effects of the stimulus package implemented in 2001 (Box 2.1).

Public support for housing and financial markets could help these markets stabilize, although care should be taken to avoid undue moral hazard. At the same time, however, care should also be taken to avoid weakening the fiscal trajectory on a permanent basis, given continuing long-term pressures on fiscal spending from population aging and rising healthcare costs, which have yet to be seriously addressed. In this respect, the authorities' commitment to achieving a budget surplus by fiscal year 2012

is welcome but will be achieved only with very tight budgetary control.

The authorities are moving to address particular problems in the housing and financial sectors. The Federal Reserve has acted prudently to increase the effectiveness of its instruments for providing liquidity by broadening the range of collateral accepted and the range of institutions with access to its windows and by acting forcefully to maintain systemic stability, while gearing its monetary policy decisions toward its macroeconomic mandates. The government has also helped coordinate an industry agreement to facilitate a freeze on interest-rate resets on subprime loans with excessive loan-to-value ratios, which should help to relieve social strains although without a major effect on market dynamics. Although recent steps to temporarily raise limits on the role of government-sponsored enterprises should provide some support to the mortgage market, they risk eroding already-weak capital cushions. Further initiatives could be considered to facilitate mortgage refinancing in the face of house price declines, including through the judicious use of public funds, in order to reduce the risk that unnecessary foreclosures would put further downward pressure on house prices. In addition, steps will be needed to address systemic weaknesses that have been exposed. Recent proposals to overhaul the fractured financial regulatory system using an objectives-based approach are suitably ambitious, although details will need to be worked out carefully. Also needed are measures to tighten consumer protection against fraudulent lending activity and ensure more prudent lending and securitization practices, as recently proposed by an interagency taskforce.

After several years of strong growth, the Canadian economy also slowed toward the end of 2007. It is expected to grow 1.3 percent in 2008, before regaining momentum in 2009. The slowdown mainly reflects the combined effect of weaker external demand and tighter credit conditions, both of which are sources of additional downside risk. The Bank of Canada has appropriately responded to the more

Box 2.1 When Does Fiscal Stimulus Work?

The idea that discretionary fiscal policy can be an effective countercyclical policy tool is the subject of a long-standing debate among economists. Traditional supporters of an activist approach have argued that economies lack an inherent mechanism to achieve full resource utilization. However, failed policy experiments during the 1970s and theoretical advances led to widespread rejection of this premise. Critics argued that, if markets operated freely, competition would ensure full employment, and a fiscal stimulus would, in any case, be ineffective owing to agents' offsetting responses to anticipated future fiscal reversals (Ricardian equivalence).

A more nuanced view has developed since then in the literature: fiscal policy can be effective, but the necessary conditions may or may not be available at a given time or place. After a period of rising deficits during the 1980s, empirical studies highlighted the stifling effects of high debt levels, deficit bias, and macroeconomic vulnerabilities on the impact of fiscal stimulus.[1] At the same time, theoretical advances identified a variety of circumstances under which fiscal policy can be effective. Models with credit-constrained consumers or finite planning horizons generated positive output effects and were also supported by microstudies. Other modeling approaches relied on nominal wage and price stickiness and imperfect competition among producers, both of which can raise real wages and output in response to a fiscal demand shock.[2] Not only were these assumptions considered realistic extensions of the classical approach, they also generated credible macroeconomic patterns if incorporated into calibrated dynamic general equilibrium models.[3] As these models have grown in number, theory has generated a profusion of possible transmission mechanisms.

It is therefore an empirical question: what impact can discretionary fiscal policy have in stimulating demand? Recent episodes generate a mixed impression about the effectiveness of fiscal policy (table). The 2001 U.S. income tax rebates are generally considered to have been successful in strengthening domestic demand with an estimated multiplier of around 0.5. The tax rebates were, however, part of a larger fiscal package and were given in anticipation of permanent cuts to follow. The 1995 stimulus package in Japan—preceded by a series of smaller programs—is estimated to have raised growth by 1 percent in the short term. However, Japan continued to grow slowly as it struggled to deal with a heavy load of bad bank loans after the collapse of the asset price bubble, and stimulus packages continued to be provided throughout the decade. A third example is Finland's response to the 1991 output shock, which combined a structural fiscal loosening with full operation of automatic stabilizers. The fiscal loosening is thought to have been largely ineffective and possibly even a negative input owing to the concerns it raised about sustainability, given the permanent nature of the shock. Lacking counterfactuals, these experiences offer only anecdotal insights, but they do raise questions about the size and durability of fiscal policy effects, particularly when the underlying reasons for growth slowdowns are permanent in nature.

More generally, cross-country studies based on empirical models find quite small fiscal multipliers. Recent studies using vector autoregression methods conclude that in many large economies, fiscal multipliers have declined over time and may even have become negative (Perotti, 2005; first figure).[4]

Note: The main authors of this box are Stephan Danninger, Michael Kumhof, and Doug Laxton, with input from Steven Symansky.

[1]See, for example, Giavazzi and Pagano (1990).

[2]For other factors, see Blinder (2004).

[3]Even in a frictionless economy, fiscal policy can raise growth via a supply response (Baxter and King, 1993). For other explanations see Ravn, Schmitt-Grohé, and Uribe (2006); Linneman and Schabert (2003); and Galí, López-Salido, and Javier Vallés (2007). Recent applications of calibrated dynamic stochastic general equilibrium models are discussed in Botman, Karam, Laxton, and Rose (2007).

[4]An alternative approach, using historical fiscal expansion episodes to assess output effects (dummy variable approach), finds positive consumption and real wage effects (Perotti, 2007).

Recent Examples of Fiscal Stimulus

Stimulus	Trigger	Measure and Size (percent of GDP)	GDP Growth[1]			Comment
			Previous three years (average)	T	Next three years (average)	
United States 2001–02	Bursting of dot-com bubble and fallout from global terrorism	Income tax rebate: ½ percent	4.1	0.8	2.6	Shapiro and Slemrod (2003) and Johnson, Parker, and Souleles (2004) estimate that between four-tenths and two-thirds of the tax rebate was consumed in the first six months
Japan 1995	Protracted period of slow growth after bursting of asset price bubble and prolonged banking sector stress	Public investment program combined with income tax cut: 1½ percent	0.8	1.9	0.8	Kuttner and Posen (2002) find a short-term growth effect of 1 percent of GDP (in 1996) but argue that the stimulus was ultimately too small to prevent a backsliding of growth. Announcement effects tended to be large, but actual implementation was much smaller (Mühleisen, 2000; Posen, 1998). Bayoumi (2001) uses a vector autoregression methodology and finds a positive but small government expenditure multiplier of 0.6 for the 1990s
Finland 1991	Loss of export market following disintegration of Soviet Union and bursting of real estate and asset bubbles	Full operation of automatic stabilizers (4.2 percent) and structural deterioration (1¾ percent)	4.7	0.1	−3.6	Corsetti and Roubini (1996) find that fiscal policy had little stabilizing effect on output due to the permanent nature of the economic shock

[1]Forward- and backward-looking GDP growth ($T-1$, $T+1$) refer to a three-year average.

Possible explanations are increased leakage through the trade channel as economies have become more open, a decline in the number of credit-constrained consumers as more consumers have gained access to lending, and a stronger focus of monetary policy on curtailing inflation, which offsets some of the fiscal effects. However, there is large cross-country variation in the estimated effects, and this likely reflects difficulties in identifying fiscal shocks and interactions with other policy responses.[5]

[5]In Italy, estimates of spending multipliers are generally larger than 1, while tax multipliers are small and statistically insignificant (Sgherri, 2006; and Giordano and others, 2007). Estimates of spending and tax multipliers in Japan range between 0.5 and 1 (Hemming, Kell, and Mahfouz,

Estimates from macro models—empirical or calibrated—show somewhat stronger multiplier effects, in the range of 0.3 to 1.2 on impact, with expenditure measures generally having a larger effect than tax measures (Hemming, Kell, and Mahfouz, 2002; and Botman, 2006). The size of the effect depends critically, however, on the assumptions about underlying parameters (such as elasticity of substitution, pervasiveness

2002; and Kuttner and Posen, 2002). Impulse responses to fiscal shocks in Spain are small initially but turn negative in the medium term (Catalán and Lama, 2006; and De Castro Fernández and Hernández de Cos, 2006). For Germany, Heppke-Falk, Tenhofen, and Wolff (2006) find that only expenditure measures have positive short-term output effects, with a multiplier of 0.6 on impact, which disappears after three years.

Box 2.1 *(continued)*

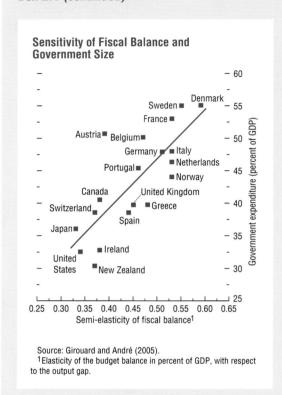

Sensitivity of Fiscal Balance and Government Size

Source: Girouard and André (2005).
[1]Elasticity of the budget balance in percent of GDP, with respect to the output gap.

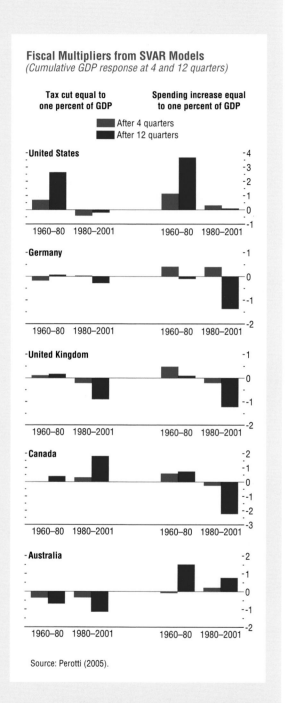

Fiscal Multipliers from SVAR Models
(Cumulative GDP response at 4 and 12 quarters)

Source: Perotti (2005).

of liquidity constraints, and labor supply elasticity) and other factors.

Even if fiscal policy measures have a positive multiplier effect, to be useful they must be implemented at the right time and supported by favorable macroeconomic conditions. Some fiscal measures have implementation lags similar to that of monetary policy, and the cyclical position is often only known with significant lags. For this reason, the first line of fiscal policy response is the use of automatic stabilizers (the variation of revenue and expenditure over the economic cycle). The size of such stabilizers varies across countries, however, and is small in many countries, such as the United States and Japan, that have relatively small governments (second figure). Even when discretionary measures can be adopted in a timely manner, their effectiveness is likely to depend on a range of dimensions such as macroeconomic vulnerabilities (such as external imbalance) and fiscal conditions (such

as sustainability or debt levels). Unfavorable conditions can magnify the offsetting responses to a fiscal stimulus.

Model Simulations

To illustrate these points, the economic effects of discretionary fiscal and monetary policy responses to a sizable demand shock in the United States were modeled using a five-country annual version of the Global Integrated Monetary and Fiscal Model (GIMF).[6]

The baseline scenario, shown as the solid black lines in the third figure, assumes an exogenous shock to domestic U.S. consumption and investment, with maximum impact after one year. Monetary policy is assumed to follow a Taylor rule that responds to lower inflation by lowering nominal and, therefore, real interest rates. As for fiscal policy, the elasticity of the government deficit with respect to the output gap under automatic stabilizers is assumed to be –0.25, which is significantly lower than in other advanced economies, and is assumed to operate through an increase in debt-financed transfers to households. With this set of policies, the baseline scenario generates a contraction of GDP (relative to its trend path) of 1.3 percent in the first year, followed by a slow four-year recovery.[7]

The three alternative scenarios shown in the figure illustrate the effects of a discretion-

[6]GIMF is a multicountry dynamic stochastic general equilibrium model and includes strong non-Ricardian features whereby fiscal policies have significant real effects. It also includes significant nominal and real rigidities, making it a useful tool to study both the short-term and the long-term implications of supply and demand shocks. The country blocks are United States, euro area, Japan, emerging Asia, and remaining countries. Trade linkages among these countries were calibrated using the 2006 matrix of world trade flows. For a description of the structure of the model, see Kumhof and Laxton (2007).

[7]The simulation assumes an equal distribution across households, but the effects would be larger if the transfers were targeted specifically at credit-constrained households. Because the assumed underlying shock is to demand, inflation falls by about 0.8 percentage point in the first two years and then slowly returns to its long-run value. The monetary policy response is to aggressively lower nominal interest rates by 130 basis points to stimulate an early recovery in demand.

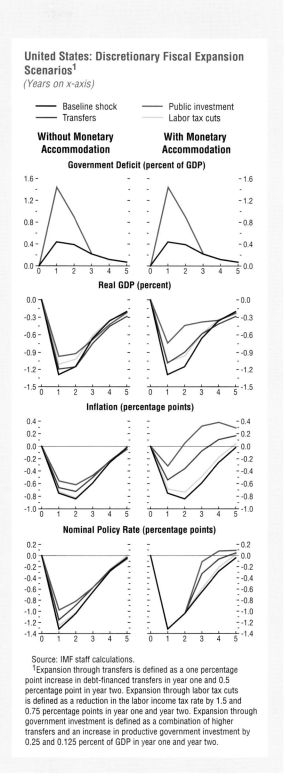

United States: Discretionary Fiscal Expansion Scenarios[1]
(Years on x-axis)

Source: IMF staff calculations.
[1]Expansion through transfers is defined as a one percentage point increase in debt-financed transfers in year one and 0.5 percentage point in year two. Expansion through labor tax cuts is defined as a reduction in the labor income tax rate by 1.5 and 0.75 percentage points in year one and year two. Expansion through government investment is defined as a combination of higher transfers and an increase in productive government investment by 0.25 and 0.125 percent of GDP in year one and year two.

Box 2.1 *(concluded)*

ary fiscal stimulus that raises the government deficit-to-GDP ratio by 1 additional percentage point in the year of the shock and 0.5 additional percentage point in the following year. The main results are as follows.

- Expenditure and tax measures help alleviate the slowdown, but the output effects are small at about 0.1–0.3 percent of GDP on impact (left column of third figure). Expansions involving government investment have the largest effect because they stimulate demand and supply at the same time, although it would be difficult to ensure timely implementation. Expansions that are well targeted to credit-constrained households—such as rebates for low-income workers—are also likely to be more effective (fourth figure).
- If fiscal policy is accommodated by monetary policy, the immediate output effects are twice as large, in the range of 0.2–0.6 percentage point (right column of third figure), with the largest impact again coming from the investment stimulus.[8]
- Larger output effects come at the cost of higher inflation, especially under monetary accommodation. A reduction in labor taxes is the most benign approach because of its positive effects on labor supply and productive capacity, which can help offset the inflation impact.

These results are sensitive to alternative assumptions about the duration of the discretionary stimulus. The size of the short-run effects depends crucially on whether a fiscal expansion is expected to be permanent and what fiscal measures are to be taken in the future to stabilize the deficit-to-GDP ratio. The short-term stimulus to output is generally larger when a fiscal expansion is expected to be temporary rather than permanent, mainly

[8]The results would differ in the event of a supply-side shock. Discretionary demand management may still help to cushion the blow, but inflation would turn out to be higher, with repercussions for longer-term output growth.

United States: Additional Discretionary Fiscal Expansion Scenarios[1]
(GDP and real interest rate in percent; current account in percent of GDP)

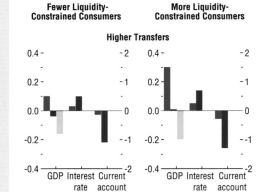

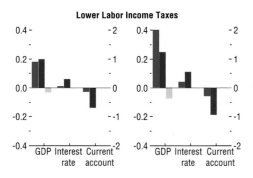

Source: IMF staff calculations.
[1]Interest rate is defined in real terms as nominal interest rate minus consumer price inflation. Short-term effects on output show the direct first-year impact net of the effects of the negative demand shock. A temporary expansion is defined as a deterioration of the deficit by 1 percentage point of GDP in the first year and by half a percentage point in the second year, a permanent expansion by a permanent deterioration of the deficit by 1 percentage point of GDP. The share of liquidity-constrained households was alternated between 25 and 50 percent.
[2]Long-run deviations from baseline—calculated by using the steady-state model—is reported only for GDP.

because a temporary stimulus leads to a lower buildup of public debt and a smaller increase in real interest rates.[9] The crowding-out effect from a persistent deficit can be ameliorated if the stimulus measures reduce distortions—for example, by lowering taxes on labor income, which raises lifetime income (fourth figure, lower left panel). Nonetheless, over the long run, the rising public debt associated with permanent measures and the necessary offsetting measures will lead to a lower growth trajectory. This underscores the advantage of temporary discretionary fiscal actions.

[9]For empirical evidence on the effects of government debt on real interest rates, see Ford and Laxton (1999).

Conclusions

Both empirical work and model simulations suggest that fiscal stimulus can be effective in providing some temporary support to an economy under stress. To be successful, however, a number of factors need to be taken into account: (1) the stimulus must be well timed, requiring early identification of a developing problem; (2) it must avoid undermining long-term fiscal stability, which would weaken multiplier effects; and (3) it must be temporary and well targeted to maximize the impact on aggregate demand. Even satisfying these criteria, there are limits to the boost that fiscal policy can provide, which underlines the importance of dealing directly with the deeper problems that may be holding back economic performance.

unsettled outlook by changing from a tightening to an easing posture, including interest rate cuts in late 2007 and early 2008. A package of tax cuts has provided a timely fiscal stimulus of about ¾ percent of GDP for 2008, while maintaining a small budget surplus consistent with Canada's budget framework. More broadly, the Canadian economy has responded flexibly to terms-of-trade gains and the growing importance of the resource sector, which has contributed to the real appreciation of the Canadian dollar. The Canadian dollar's value seems in line with fundamentals, but moving ahead with the government's structural policy agenda should help increase competitiveness and productivity growth to underpin longer-term prospects.

Western Europe: Can a Sharp Slowdown Be Averted?

For most of 2007, activity in western Europe continued to expand at a robust pace. The euro area grew by 2.6 percent in 2007 as a whole, close to the rapid pace achieved in 2006 and still well above potential. Similarly, growth in the United Kingdom registered a strong 3.1 percent

increase despite woes in the banking sector. Robust domestic demand was fueled by steady employment growth and buoyant investment, supported by healthy corporate balance sheets and strong global demand.

Signs of strain increased toward the end of 2007, however. In the fourth quarter, GDP growth slowed to 1.5 percent in the euro area and to 2.5 percent in the United Kingdom on an annualized basis. Consumer and business sentiment deteriorated in response to financial sector dislocation and the impact of rising oil prices on real disposable income. Euro appreciation and a weaker export market also diminished growth expectations. These effects were not felt equally across Europe. Smaller European countries, such as Austria, the Netherlands, Sweden, and Switzerland, continued to grow well above potential in the second half of 2007. Recent indicators point to a continued deceleration in activity in early 2008, with high oil prices and rising risk spreads beginning to have an increasing impact on investment and consumption growth.

To what extent will the momentum of western European economies be sapped by the U.S. slowdown? Economic links between western Europe and the United States remain significant. The traditional trade channel is still important, although the weight of the U.S. market has declined with the strengthening of trade with Asia, emerging Europe, and the Middle East. But financial sector linkages appear to be the main source of spillovers in the current environment. Exposure to the U.S. subprime mortgage market—directly or through conduits and structured investment vehicles—has already strained banks' capital in a number of countries and forced them to expand their balance sheets. As a result, credit conditions are tightening and risk spreads are rising, with negative repercussions for domestic demand (see Box 1.1).

In the baseline projection, growth in the euro area is forecast to decelerate to 1.4 percent in 2008 and 1.2 percent in 2009. With the impact of the U.S. slowdown feeding through with a short lag, on a fourth-quarter-to-fourth-quarter basis, growth will come down to 0.9 percent in 2008, before picking up to a still-below-par 1.6 percent in 2009. Export growth will likely hold up through the first half of 2008, based on full order books, especially in Germany, but it is projected to taper off thereafter as a moderation of global demand and euro appreciation slow export growth. In the United Kingdom, growth is forecast to slow to 1.6 percent in 2008, as the lagged effects of the 2007 monetary tightening, a turning in the house price cycle, and the financial turbulence are projected to slow activity, despite monetary policy easing. Only a moderate recovery is foreseen for 2009.

Relative to the new lower baseline, risks to the growth outlook are seen as broadly balanced, with financial and external risks to the downside and domestic demand risks to the upside. The most prominent downside risk is a protracted period of strain in the European financial sector. The continuing revelation of losses to European banks from the U.S. housing market downturn has already undermined confidence and prompted a significant tightening of credit standards, and further blows to bank capital could start to have a greater impact on lending for business investment and the housing sector

(Figure 2.2). Corporations in Europe in general rely more heavily on banks for financing than those in the United States, and a slowdown in mortgage lending could accelerate the so-far-gradual adjustment of housing prices in a number of countries with elevated valuations (such as Belgium, the Netherlands, Ireland, Spain, the United Kingdom, and to a lesser extent France), with potentially severe repercussions for private consumption and investment in buildings and structures in some of these countries (see Box 3.1). Moreover, residential investment activity is significantly above trend in a number of countries, especially Belgium, France, Italy, and Spain, and less so in Ireland and the Netherlands. Other sources of downside risk are further euro appreciation, a deeper U.S. recession, high oil price volatility, and bank exposure to losses in emerging Europe if this region were to run into difficulties. On the upside, domestic demand could turn out to be more resilient than projected, supported by a moderation in the food and energy prices projected in the baseline and by relatively strong labor markets.

A concerted effort to improve financial transparency and reduce uncertainty could help calm markets and lower risk spreads. Large write-downs and losses by U.S. banks in early 2008 surprised markets and raised fears of larger-than-anticipated losses by European financial institutions from U.S. subprime markets. These fears were underscored by recent revelations about French and German banks' previously unidentified exposures. In this environment, a coordinated effort by European Union supervisors and regulators to encourage more disclosure and more consistent accounting treatment could allay market concern and help lower risk premiums and financial market volatility.

Despite prospects for moderating growth, inflation pressures remain a major source of concern. Headline inflation in the euro area rose to 3.5 percent (year over year) in March 2008, considerably exceeding the European Central Bank's (ECB's) inflation threshold of 2 percent. The surge was largely in energy and food prices, which have risen sharply since mid-

2007. Core inflation[2] remained stable through-out 2007 at just under 2 percent, against a background of moderate wage increases and the dampening effect of euro appreciation, but it picked up in early 2008. Headline inflation is expected to come down within the ECB's policy ceiling in 2009, reflecting diminished resource utilization, slower food and energy price infla-tion, and the uncertainty of base effects from past administrative price and indirect tax increases. Nonetheless, concerns about second-round price effects have increased, especially with unemployment at its lowest level since the early 1990s and with wage demands having risen recently, especially in Germany. In the United Kingdom, inflation is projected to rise mod-erately from 2.0 percent in December 2007 to 2.5 percent in 2008 because of high energy and food prices. Although core inflation began to decelerate in the second half of 2007, inflation expectations have increased recently despite a weakening of the growth momentum.

Following a period of tightening, the ECB has held rates constant since June 2007. However, given that headline inflation is projected to moderate back below 2 percent during 2009, in the context of an increasingly negative outlook for activity, the ECB can afford some easing of the policy stance. Similarly, while high inflation remains a concern in the United Kingdom, the deterioration in the outlook for activity should alleviate inflation pressures and provide room for further monetary policy easing.

Taking advantage of the economic upswing, most governments in western Europe signifi-cantly lowered their fiscal deficits in 2007. In the euro area, the general government deficit fell by almost 1 percentage point to 0.6 percent of GDP. Large structural fiscal adjustments of more than 1 percent of GDP in Germany and Italy led this effort, while fiscal deficits in France and the United Kingdom remained high at 2.4 percent and 3.0 percent of GDP, respectively. This over-all improvement was an important step toward

[2]Based on Eurostat's harmonized index of consumer prices, excluding energy, tobacco, alcohol, and food.

Figure 2.2. Western Europe: Tightening Lending Standards

Lending standards tightened in the euro area at the end of 2007, for reasons including deteriorating expectations about the economic outlook, sector-specific factors, and weak housing market prospects. Constraints on lending pose risks because corporations in Europe tend to rely more on bank financing, and residential property prices are at elevated levels.

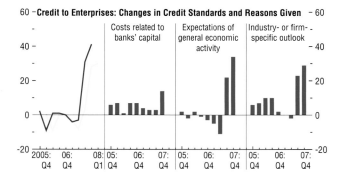

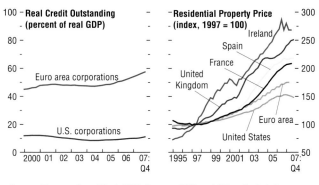

Sources: European Central Bank (ECB); Eurostat; OECD; and IMF staff calculations.
[1]Credit standard is defined as the difference between the sum of the percentages for "tightened considerably" and "tightened somewhat" and the sum of the percentages for "eased somewhat" and "eased considerably." Residential property indices deflated by the consumer price indices are from the OECD for countries, and from the ECB for the euro area.

sustainability and strengthened the credibility of the new Stability and Growth Pact after repeated breaches of the 3 percent deficit ceiling in several countries.

Past fiscal consolidation has created some room for countercyclical fiscal support. Indeed, in 2008 the fiscal deficit in the euro area is expected to widen again by ½ percent of GDP, mainly as a result of the growth slowdown but also because of an increase in the structural deficits in Germany and Italy and a decline in the structural surplus in Spain. Given Europe's larger public sectors and broader safety nets, automatic stabilizers are larger than in other regions and should be the main policy instrument. Countries that are already close to the medium-term objectives laid out in their stability programs could allow these automatic stabilizers to operate in full. However, countries that are close to the 3 percent deficit limit—such as France, Italy, and Greece—should offset at least part of their automatic stabilizers, except in the case of a recession, in which event the Stability and Growth Pact would allow a temporary and small breach of the deficit limit. The hard-won adjustment gains achieved during recent years should not be jeopardized during the coming slowdown, as demographic changes are rapidly affecting the cost of European old-age and health care systems.

Advanced Asia: How Resilient Is Growth in Japan to a Global Slowdown?

Preliminary GDP data for the fourth quarter of 2007 indicate that the Japanese economy remained resilient to the global slowdown through the end of the year. GDP grew at an annualized rate of 3.5 percent, led by robust net exports and business investment. Exports continued to be supported by strong demand from Asia and Europe, and business investment rebounded after contracting during the first half of the year. Following the tightening of building standards in June, the slump in residential investment continued and household spending remained weak. The growth momentum

entering 2008, however, appears to have slowed with deteriorating business and consumer confidence, and export growth shows signs of moderating.

The main direct channel for spillovers to economic activity from a global slowdown would be through slowing export growth, a risk underscored by the strong role of net exports in the recovery of output in recent years (Figure 2.3). In this context, the continued strength of domestic demand—and investment in particular—in emerging Asian economies remains a key support for Japanese exports, as evidenced by the resilience of capital goods shipments in the fourth quarter of 2007. Moreover, emerging Asian economies now account for nearly one-half of Japanese exports, while the share of the United States and the euro area has declined to slightly over a third of the total. Overall, as long as emerging economy growth continues to remain relatively insulated from the slowdown in the United States and western Europe, Japanese export performance should remain well supported.

The prospects for domestic demand are another source of downside risk to the near-term outlook. Higher food and fuel prices and sluggish wages continue to weigh on consumption, and business investment could weaken if the global market turmoil were to intensify and credit conditions were to tighten further. Equity prices have already fallen sharply on concerns over the economic outlook, and further declines represent a potential risk for bank and corporate balance sheets, although the Japanese financial system has limited direct exposure to U.S. subprime securities. On the upside, housing starts appear to have bottomed out in the third quarter of 2007, and residential investment is expected to provide some support to growth in the first half of 2008.

Reflecting the above considerations, growth for Japan is projected at 1.4 percent in 2008 and 1.5 percent in 2009, down from 2.1 percent growth in 2007. Underlying this baseline, export growth is expected to weaken, and consumption is expected to moderate further. Residential investment is expected to start making a positive contribution to growth toward the middle of 2008. Against the considerable uncertainty surrounding global growth, the risks to the lower baseline forecast still appear tilted to the downside. The key risk is a sharper-than-anticipated slowdown in the global economy, which would also adversely affect the demand for Japanese exports from emerging economies and would lower business and consumer confidence.

Rising food and fuel prices contributed to positive headline inflation in Japan in the last three months of 2007, but consumer price inflation, excluding food and energy, remained marginally negative. Looking ahead, high commodity prices are expected to feed through to slightly positive inflation during 2008, but a further weakening of the growth outlook could arrest this trend toward rising prices. Against this background, the Bank of Japan has appropriately maintained an accommodative monetary stance, with policy rates unchanged at about 0.5 percent since February 2007. In light of the prevailing headwinds to growth, monetary policy should maintain its accommodative stance and could be eased further in the face of a serious downturn.

Fiscal adjustment has proceeded ahead of the authorities' plans in recent years, owing to stronger-than-anticipated tax collection and tight spending control. The pace of fiscal consolidation is expected to slow somewhat as the fiscal year 2008 budget envisages only a modest further adjustment. At the same time, the official medium-term fiscal projections now fall slightly short of achieving the earlier goal of a primary balance (at the level of general government excluding social security) by fiscal year 2011. Moreover, despite the substantial progress on fiscal consolidation in recent years, Japan's net public debt remains one of the highest among the major advanced economies. In light of this, there is limited room for fiscal policy to provide a cushion in the event of a stronger-than-anticipated downturn in growth. Indeed, over the medium term, a stronger fiscal adjustment would be desirable to put debt on

Figure 2.3. Japan: Will Domestic Demand Be Able to Support Growth?

Although construction activity is expected to recover, the recent driver of growth—net exports—is vulnerable to weakening global growth prospects. Business sentiment and leading indicators reflect rising concerns over the fallout from weaker global growth.

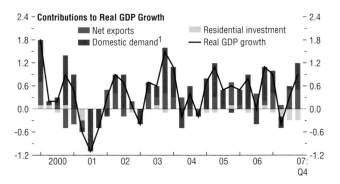

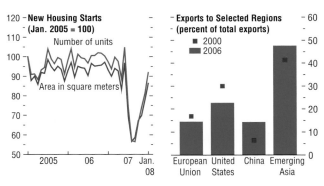

Sources: Haver Analytics; and IMF staff calculations.
[1] Excluding residential investment.
[2] Diffusion indices from Economy Watcher Survey.
[3] Leading indicators from Economic and Social Research Institute.

a firmly declining path. Although there is still some room for further expenditure cuts, consideration needs to be given to revenue measures in the context of a broad reform of the tax system, elements of which could include raising the consumption tax, reforming the corporate tax system, widening the income tax base, and strengthening tax administration.

The growth momentum in Australia and New Zealand remains robust, and the turbulence in global financial markets has thus far had only a limited impact. Although direct exposure to the U.S. subprime market appears to be small, banks have passed on some of the elevated costs of funding in the interbank market in the form of higher lending rates. Despite the implied tightening of financial conditions, the main short-term policy challenge is to keep inflation pressures in check in the face of strong domestic demand, high capacity utilization, and tight labor market conditions. In Australia, the cash rate was appropriately raised in early February. In New Zealand, the official cash rate may need to be maintained at the level in place since July until inflation pressures ease. Prudent fiscal policies and flexible exchange rates continue to provide both Australia and New Zealand with important buffers against any substantial weakening in the external environment.

Emerging Asia: Strong Internal Momentum, but Rising Risks from Spillovers

Growth in emerging Asia remained strong in the second half of 2007, although with some emerging signs of softness. Growth was led by China, where output expanded by 11.4 percent (year over year) in the second half of 2007, driven by strong investment growth and net exports, although the pace of growth moderated somewhat toward the end of the year. Growth in India slowed modestly to 8½ percent (year over year) in the second half of last year as consumption cooled in response to tighter monetary policy, although investment continued at a brisk pace. Robust domestic demand, led by consump-

tion, supported activity in Indonesia, Malaysia, Hong Kong SAR, the Philippines, and Singapore, even while export growth began to show some signs of moderation. Export growth remained strong in Korea and Thailand, but high fuel prices and political uncertainty weighed on domestic demand in Thailand. In Korea, domestic demand was supported by an acceleration in construction and investment activity.

The strength of domestic demand in the region, combined with rising food and energy prices, has contributed to a buildup of inflation pressures in a number of countries. In China, inflation rose to 8.7 percent in February. Inflation largely reflects rising food prices, boosted by a swine epidemic, but there is rising concern that persistent food price increases could spill over into wages and spark a broader pickup in inflation. Inflation pressures have also begun to emerge in Indonesia, Thailand, and the Philippines. In India, monetary tightening earlier in the year led to an easing of inflation by the end of 2007; however, inflation started to pick up in 2008 owing to rising commodity prices.

Growth prospects remain dependent on how resilient the region's financial systems and economies are to the ongoing financial market dislocation and the associated slowdown in the advanced economies. Overall net private capital flows into the region reached record levels in 2007, led by sharp increases in portfolio inflows into China, Hong Kong SAR, and India and by continued very strong foreign direct investment (FDI) flows. Capital inflows are projected to slow this year as a consequence of the tightening of global financial conditions. Thus far, however, the direct impact on regional financial systems has been limited, although in early 2008, regional equity markets gave up an average of 40 percent of their 2007 gains.

A second channel of spillovers is through slowing demand for the region's exports. Exports to the United States and western Europe will likely be most affected, although the impact should be less severe than during previous downturns, because the relative share of exports to these advanced economies has been steadily declining

IMF World Economic Outlook
April 2008

ERRATA
In the lower panels of Figure 2.4, labels for
Hong Kong SAR and India should be reversed

Figure 2.4. Emerging Asia: Trade Patterns and Growth

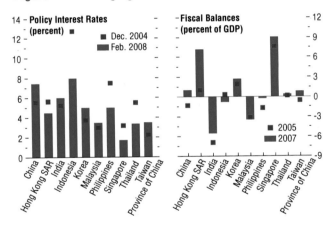

while intra-Asia exports have been rising (Figure 2.4). The overall effect on regional growth of slowing exports is further mitigated by the strength of domestic demand in most countries of the region, which continue to experience strong consumption and investment growth. Exports to China from elsewhere in Asia continue to grow rapidly as Chinese fixed asset investment and consumption both continue to grow vigorously. In India, however, weaker export demand and higher financing costs are expected to dampen growth in private investment.

Against this background, growth in emerging Asia is expected to decelerate but remain robust at about 7.5 percent in 2008 and 7.8 percent in 2009, compared with 9.1 percent in 2007 (Table 2.3). Growth in China is projected to moderate to 9.3 percent in 2008, with rising consumption and continuing strong investment helping to balance slowing export growth. India's economy is expected to expand by 7.9 percent in 2008. Growth in the newly industrialized economies of Asia is expected to slow by about 1½ percentage points to 4 percent in 2008 and then pick up in 2009. Among the ASEAN-5 economies, growth is projected to soften by ½ percentage point in 2008, with activity strengthening in Thailand as domestic demand recovers from recent sluggishness.

Risks to the outlook remain broadly balanced. Given the region's high degree of openness, a sharper-than-anticipated slowdown in the advanced economies could be expected to have a pronounced adverse impact on the region's growth prospects, cooling investment as well as export growth. On the upside, domestic demand could be more resilient than projected in the face of tightening measures and a weaker external environment. In particular, the projected easing of growth in China may be more moderate if consumption continues to gather speed and policy measures aimed at slowing investment growth fail to have the intended effect.

In light of the greater uncertainties associated with the outlook, policymakers face a difficult task in balancing the trade-offs between growth and inflation. In a number of countries, the chal-

Figure 2.4. Emerging Asia: Trade Patterns and Growth Developments

The increase in intra-Asian trade and the strength of domestic demand suggest diminishing vulnerability to a global slowdown. The room for countercyclical fiscal and monetary policies varies across countries. Net exports continue to be an important source of growth for the region.

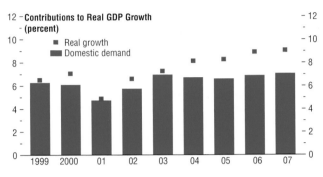

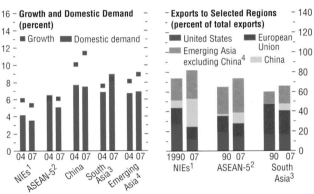

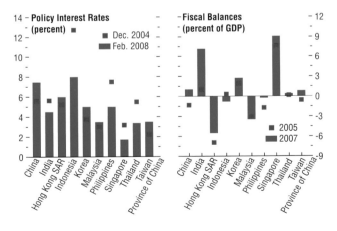

Sources: IMF, *Direction of Trade Statistics;* and IMF staff calculations.
[1]Includes Korea, Hong Kong SAR, Singapore, and Taiwan Province of China.
[2]Includes Indonesia, Malaysia, the Philippines, Thailand, and Vietnam.
[3]Includes Bangladesh, India, Maldives, Nepal, Pakistan, and Sri Lanka.
[4]Includes the NIEs, ASEAN-5, south Asia, Bhutan, Cambodia, China, Fiji, Kiribati, Lao PDR, Mongolia, Myanmar, Papua New Guinea, Samoa, Solomon Islands, Tonga, and Vanuatu.

Table 2.3. Selected Asian Economies: Real GDP, Consumer Prices, and Current Account Balance
(Annual percent change unless noted otherwise)

	Real GDP				Consumer Prices[1]				Current Account Balance[2]			
	2006	2007	2008	2009	2006	2007	2008	2009	2006	2007	2008	2009
Emerging Asia[3]	8.9	9.1	7.5	7.8	3.7	4.8	5.5	3.9	5.7	6.5	5.3	5.2
China	11.1	11.4	9.3	9.5	1.5	4.8	5.9	3.6	9.4	11.1	9.8	10.0
South Asia[4]	9.1	8.6	7.5	7.7	6.5	6.9	5.9	4.7	−1.4	−2.1	−3.4	−3.6
India	9.7	9.2	7.9	8.0	6.2	6.4	5.2	4.0	−1.1	−1.8	−3.1	−3.4
Pakistan	6.9	6.4	6.0	6.7	7.9	7.8	8.5	7.5	−3.9	−4.9	−6.9	−6.1
Bangladesh	6.4	5.6	5.5	6.5	6.5	8.4	9.3	8.1	1.2	0.5	−0.5	−0.7
ASEAN-5	5.7	6.3	5.8	6.0	8.1	4.5	6.1	4.7	4.8	4.8	2.9	1.9
Indonesia	5.5	6.3	6.1	6.3	13.1	6.4	7.1	5.9	3.0	2.5	1.8	1.2
Thailand	5.1	4.8	5.3	5.6	4.6	2.2	3.5	2.5	1.1	6.1	3.4	1.3
Philippines	5.4	7.3	5.8	5.8	6.2	2.8	4.4	3.8	4.5	4.4	2.1	1.0
Malaysia	5.9	6.3	5.0	5.2	3.6	2.1	2.4	2.5	16.2	14.0	11.7	11.1
Vietnam	8.2	8.5	7.3	7.3	7.5	8.3	16.0	10.0	−0.4	−9.6	−13.6	−11.9
Newly industrialized Asian economies	5.6	5.6	4.0	4.4	1.6	2.2	3.0	2.7	5.2	6.0	4.5	4.3
Korea	5.1	5.0	4.2	4.4	2.2	2.5	3.4	2.9	0.6	0.6	−1.0	−0.9
Taiwan Province of China	4.9	5.7	3.4	4.1	0.6	1.8	1.5	1.5	6.7	8.3	7.8	8.1
Hong Kong SAR	7.0	6.3	4.3	4.8	2.0	2.0	3.6	4.5	12.1	12.3	9.9	8.3
Singapore	8.2	7.7	4.0	4.5	1.0	2.1	4.7	2.5	21.8	24.3	20.6	18.9

[1]Movements in consumer prices are shown as annual averages. December/December changes can be found in Table A7 in the Statistical Appendix.
[2]Percent of GDP.
[3]Consists of developing Asia, the newly industrialized Asian economies, and Mongolia.
[4]Includes Maldives, Nepal, and Sri Lanka.

lenge remains to avoid overheating, which may require tighter monetary policy, supported by greater exchange rate flexibility in some countries, including China. Policymakers will need to respond flexibly, however, to evolving developments, with some scope for monetary policy easing in the event of a sharper-than-anticipated slowdown in countries where inflation expectations continue to remain well anchored. In a more adverse global growth environment, countries with strong fiscal positions, such as the newly industrialized economies and China, also have some room for fiscal policy to cushion the impact on activity. However, in other countries, such as India, Pakistan, and the Philippines, continued efforts at fiscal consolidation remain an important priority, despite recent progress, limiting room for countercyclical fiscal policy.

Latin America and the Caribbean: Facing a Cold North Wind

Economic activity in Latin America and the Caribbean grew by a robust 5.6 percent in 2007, slightly stronger than in 2006 (Table 2.4). This capped the region's best four-year performance since the 1970s. The U.S. slowdown took some toll on growth in neighboring Mexico, while activity in the Caribbean slowed as a construction boom wound down. By contrast, growth remained high in Central America and in commodity-exporting countries in South America such as Argentina, Colombia, Peru, and the República Bolivariana de Venezuela. Moreover, growth accelerated markedly in Brazil, amid sustained declines in real interest rates and strong employment. Domestic demand has been the main driver of growth in the region. Current account surpluses have declined, and inflation has accelerated, driven by high capacity utilization in some countries and by rising food and energy prices. This has encouraged a tightening of monetary policy stances in Chile, Colombia, and Peru, and to a lesser extent in Mexico, and an end to easing in Brazil. Capital inflows have generally been maintained, despite some softening in regional equity prices and a widening in risk spreads on bond issues,

Table 2.4. Selected Western Hemisphere Economies: Real GDP, Consumer Prices, and Current Account Balance
(Annual percent change unless noted otherwise)

	Real GDP				Consumer Prices[1]				Current Account Balance[2]			
	2006	2007	2008	2009	2006	2007	2008	2009	2006	2007	2008	2009
Western Hemisphere	**5.5**	**5.6**	**4.4**	**3.6**	**5.3**	**5.4**	**6.6**	**6.1**	**1.5**	**0.5**	**−0.3**	**−0.9**
South America and Mexico[3]	**5.3**	**5.6**	**4.3**	**3.6**	**5.2**	**5.3**	**6.5**	**6.1**	**1.8**	**0.8**	**—**	**−0.6**
Argentina	8.5	8.7	7.0	4.5	10.9	8.8	9.2	9.1	2.5	1.1	0.4	−0.5
Brazil	3.8	5.4	4.8	3.7	4.2	3.6	4.8	4.3	1.3	0.3	−0.7	−0.9
Chile	4.0	5.0	4.5	4.5	3.4	4.4	6.6	3.6	3.6	3.7	−0.5	−1.3
Colombia	6.8	7.0	4.6	4.5	4.3	5.5	5.5	4.6	−2.1	−3.8	−4.9	−4.3
Ecuador	3.9	1.9	2.9	4.1	3.3	2.2	3.3	3.3	3.6	3.3	5.2	3.9
Mexico	4.8	3.3	2.0	2.3	3.6	4.0	3.8	3.2	−0.3	−0.8	−1.0	−1.6
Peru	7.6	9.0	7.0	6.0	2.0	1.8	4.2	2.5	2.8	1.6	−0.2	−0.3
Uruguay	7.0	7.0	6.0	4.0	6.4	8.1	7.4	5.7	−2.4	−0.8	−1.7	−0.8
Venezuela, Rep. Boliv. de	10.3	8.4	5.8	3.5	13.7	18.7	25.7	31.0	14.7	9.8	7.2	5.0
Central America[4]	**6.3**	**6.5**	**4.7**	**4.6**	**6.5**	**6.7**	**8.3**	**6.1**	**−4.9**	**−6.8**	**−7.6**	**−7.6**
The Caribbean[4]	**7.8**	**5.7**	**4.4**	**3.8**	**7.8**	**6.7**	**7.9**	**5.7**	**−0.8**	**−2.5**	**−2.6**	**−2.3**

[1]Movements in consumer prices are shown as annual averages. December/December changes can be found in Table A7 in the Statistical Appendix.
[2]Percent of GDP.
[3]Includes Bolivia and Paraguay.
[4]The country composition of these regional groups is set out in Table F in the Statistical Appendix.

helping to keep exchange rates buoyant and contributing to a continued buildup in international reserves.

Growth in the region is projected to moderate to 4.4 percent in 2008 and to slow further to 3.6 percent in 2009. In some countries, growth will suffer appreciably as capacity constraints are expected to bite. Elsewhere, growth is projected to ease more modestly, responding to the tightening of monetary conditions and to less-favorable external financial conditions, but high commodity prices should help sustain domestic demand across South America. Against this background, inflation rates are expected to rise in a number of countries in 2008 before easing in 2009. In Argentina, although measured inflation has fallen, most private sector analysts believe that actual inflation is considerably higher than reflected in official data. Current account positions are expected to weaken further, and private capital inflows are likely to moderate from the very high rates observed in 2007.

The overall prognosis is that resilient economies will be dampened but not overwhelmed by the slowdown in the United States and other advanced economies and by the dislocations in international financial markets. This would be a very different outcome from past periods of external stress. As shown in Figure 2.5, going back to 1970, Latin America has invariably been hit hard by slowdowns in the United States, its largest trading partner. Many of these episodes were exacerbated by a sharp deterioration of access to external financing in the context of rising risk aversion.

More formal econometric analysis has confirmed the close relationship between the business cycle in Latin America and the external environment. Recent work has found that about one-half of variations in economic activity in Latin America can be explained by a combination of global /U.S. activity, commodity prices, and external financial conditions.[3] Indeed, the spillover from U.S. growth to Latin American growth is as high as 1:1 and even higher for Mexico, while a rise in the U.S. high-yield bond rate has also been found to have a

[3]See for example, Österholm and Zettelmeyer (2007); Izquierdo, Romero, and Talvi (2007); Bayoumi and Swiston (2007); Roache (2007); and Sosa (2007).

Figure 2.5. Latin America: Long Road to Stronger Performance
(Percent of GDP unless otherwise stated)

Latin America's economy grew steadily in recent years in contrast to the volatility in the region beginning in the 1970s. More disciplined macroeconomic policies—together with improved terms of trade—have helped reduce external vulnerabilities and foster rising investment and improving performance.

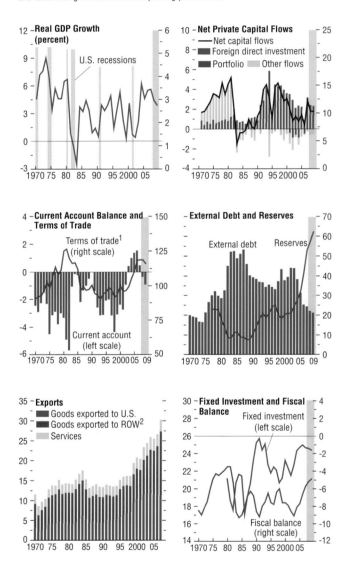

Sources: Haver Analytics; and IMF staff estimates.
[1]Index, 2000 = 100.
[2]ROW = rest of world.

high impact.[4] Recent studies also present evidence that the relevance of external factors has increased over time, as economies have become more open to both trade and capital flows and as domestic shocks have become less intense.[5]

These studies generally do not take account, however, of changes in domestic fundamentals and the global environment that are likely to make Latin America more resilient in the face of external shocks. On the domestic front, generally improved policy performance in the region has helped bring down external debt, build international reserves, and strengthen government and corporate balance sheets (see Figure 2.5). Thus, Latin America has become less vulnerable to increasing risk aversion and financial disruptions. There are also reasons related to the character of the current global business cycle. First, the easing of monetary conditions by the Federal Reserve and the decline in long-term, risk-free interest rates have helped to offset the impact of some widening in risk spreads. Second, sustained strong growth in other emerging economies has kept commodity prices at high levels despite the slowdown in the advanced economies.

Nevertheless, an increasingly open Latin American economy would not be unscathed by a deeper global downturn, and the risks to the outlook are clearly weighted to the downside. The combination of falling commodity prices, weaker growth of external markets, intensifying financial difficulties among U.S. and European banks that are active in Latin America, and a drop in commodity export prices would impose a significant toll on the momentum of growth in Latin America. Even so, the region's external position should be sufficiently robust to avoid the more severe disruptions that occurred in the past. Thus, in the context of a downside scenario such as the one presented in Chapter 1, growth in Latin America would likely be lowered

[4]See Chapter 4 of the April 2007 *World Economic Outlook.*
[5]See also Kose, Meredith, and Towe (2004).

by a further 1–2 percentage points, depending on the extent of financial spillovers.

How should policymakers respond to signs that Latin American economies are weakening in the face of a strong downdraft in global demand? To some degree, sustained good performance has brought room to maneuver, but within limits. The first line of defense against weaker outcomes should be monetary policy, particularly in countries (such as Brazil, Chile, Colombia, and Mexico) where inflation targeting has gained credibility and has succeeded in anchoring inflation expectations more securely than in the past. However, the scope for easing could be hampered by the need to bring inflation back down to within target ranges in a number of countries, especially given the possibility of continued rapid increases in food and energy prices, which weigh heavily in consumption baskets. Flexible exchange rate management should play a supportive role. On the fiscal front, countries that have brought public debt down to more sustainable levels would have some room to let automatic stabilizers work, often for the first time in recent history, mostly by allowing some widening in deficits as revenue performance softens. Chile has a sufficiently robust fiscal framework and low enough public debt to allow this process to work in full. Other countries will need to proceed cautiously, and some could face serious declines in revenues from a turn in commodity prices and in corporate profits, which could require tight control of spending in order to maintain fiscal performance on a sustainable path.

Against this background, there is a continuing need to consolidate and strengthen policy frameworks and lay foundations for higher growth in the medium term in a region that has continued to underperform relative to its peers even in recent years. Even though economic activity remains strong, macroeconomic policymakers should remain cautious. Monetary policymakers should seek to contain inflation, and financial supervisors must ensure that rapid credit growth is not associated with deteriorating credit quality or weakening financial balance sheets. Moreover, more stringent control over government budgets should be combined with reforms to improve the efficiency of government spending, enhance the sustainability of social security systems, and strengthen the foundations of revenue systems. Mexico has made welcome progress toward fiscal reform over the past year, and serious reform efforts are being made elsewhere (for example, in Brazil, Peru, and Uruguay), but to date reform remains very much a "work in progress." Finally, more must be done to establish an environment for sustained growth, including establishing viable frameworks for investment in energy and infrastructure and developing more flexible labor and product markets.

Emerging Europe: Adjusting to a Rougher External Environment

Growth in Emerging Europe moderated by almost a full percentage point to 5.8 percent in 2007 (Table 2.5). The deceleration was most pronounced in Hungary, Turkey, Estonia, and Latvia. In Turkey, slower growth is attributable in part to the strength of the currency and delayed effects of monetary tightening in mid-2006, but also to a drought-related drop in agricultural output. In Hungary, fiscal consolidation to put public finances on a more sustainable path squeezed private consumption and investment. In Estonia and Latvia, a cyclical deceleration was exacerbated by a tightening in financing conditions, after years of exceptionally strong growth. Nonetheless, 2007 marked the sixth consecutive year during which emerging Europe grew substantially faster than western Europe, contributing to a further narrowing of wealth and productivity differentials (Figure 2.6).

In most countries, growth continued to be driven by buoyant domestic demand, which again substantially outpaced production in 2007. As a consequence, the region's overall current account deficit widened to 6.6 percent of GDP, with double-digit external deficits in the Baltic countries, Bulgaria, and Romania. Demand continued to be supported by strong

Table 2.5. Selected Emerging European Economies: Real GDP, Consumer Prices, and Current Account Balance
(Annual percent change unless noted otherwise)

	Real GDP				Consumer Prices[1]				Current Account Balance[2]			
	2006	2007	2008	2009	2006	2007	2008	2009	2006	2007	2008	2009
Emerging Europe	**6.7**	**5.8**	**4.4**	**4.3**	**5.4**	**5.7**	**6.4**	**4.3**	**−6.3**	**−6.6**	**−7.2**	**−6.9**
Turkey	6.9	5.0	4.0	4.3	9.6	8.8	7.5	4.5	−6.1	−5.7	−6.7	−6.3
Excluding Turkey	6.6	6.2	4.7	4.3	3.3	4.1	5.8	4.2	−6.3	−7.1	−7.5	−7.2
Baltics	**9.8**	**8.9**	**4.8**	**3.5**	**4.8**	**7.3**	**10.8**	**6.7**	**−15.5**	**−17.0**	**−12.1**	**−9.9**
Estonia	11.2	7.1	3.0	3.7	4.4	6.6	9.8	4.7	−15.5	−16.0	−11.2	−11.2
Latvia	11.9	10.2	3.6	0.5	6.5	10.1	15.3	9.2	−22.3	−23.3	−15.0	−10.5
Lithuania	7.7	8.8	6.5	5.5	3.8	5.8	8.3	6.1	−10.8	−13.0	−10.5	−8.8
Central Europe	**6.1**	**6.0**	**4.4**	**4.3**	**2.1**	**3.5**	**4.8**	**3.7**	**−4.1**	**−3.9**	**−4.6**	**−4.8**
Czech Republic	6.4	6.5	4.2	4.6	2.5	2.8	6.0	3.5	−3.1	−2.5	−3.0	−2.8
Hungary	3.9	1.3	1.8	2.5	3.9	7.9	5.9	3.5	−6.5	−5.6	−5.5	−5.1
Poland	6.2	6.5	4.9	4.5	1.0	2.5	4.1	3.8	−3.2	−3.7	−5.0	−5.7
Slovak Republic	8.5	10.4	6.6	5.6	4.4	2.8	3.6	3.8	−7.1	−5.3	−5.0	−4.7
Southern and south-eastern Europe	**7.0**	**6.0**	**5.2**	**4.6**	**6.2**	**5.1**	**7.3**	**5.0**	**−10.7**	**−14.0**	**−14.6**	**−13.1**
Bulgaria	6.3	6.2	5.5	4.8	7.4	7.6	9.7	6.0	−15.6	−21.4	−21.9	−18.9
Croatia	4.8	5.8	4.3	4.0	3.2	2.9	5.5	3.5	−7.9	−8.5	−9.0	−8.7
Romania	7.9	6.0	5.4	4.7	6.6	4.8	7.0	5.1	−10.4	−13.9	−14.5	−13.0

[1]Movements in consumer prices are shown as annual averages. December/December changes can be found in Table A7 in the Statistical Appendix.
[2]Percent of GDP.

credit growth fueled by capital inflows and, in many countries, by vigorous wage growth as labor market conditions tightened further. Inflation pressures increased, especially toward year-end, reflecting in part rising food and energy prices but also increasing labor costs. In the Baltic countries, rising inflation significantly reduced the prospects for adoption of the euro in the near term.[6] In several countries, many of them in the Baltics and in southeastern Europe, an accommodative fiscal policy stance added to demand pressures, which were often reinforced by substantial increases in public wages and pensions.

The region's strong performance has been supported by large capital inflows but could be jeopardized by tightening conditions ahead. FDI accounted for about 40 percent of net private capital inflows in 2007, but the remainder was largely in the form of potentially more volatile bank flows, typically from affiliated banks in western Europe.[7] By mid-2007, western European banks held assets of about $1 trillion in the region.[8] These bank inflows, in turn, contributed to fuel rapid domestic credit growth, with loans often denominated in foreign currencies and at variable interest rates. Outstanding claims held by western European banks are

[6]Estonia, Lithuania, Latvia, and the Slovak Republic are currently members of the transitional European exchange rate mechanism (ERM II). Full euro area membership requires that exchange rates be stable over two years and that the four "Maastricht criteria" be met. The fiscal criteria would be met by all countries, but the requirements of the Maastricht reference rate for inflation have turned out to be the main stumbling block: average inflation over the past 12 months must not exceed the average of the three best performers among the EU member countries by more than 1.5 percentage points on a sustainable basis.

[7]Emerging Europe differs markedly from other emerging market regions that have received primarily FDI in recent years (Latin America, Africa) or a mix of FDI and portfolio inflows (emerging Asia; see also Box 2.2). Historically, bank flows have been more volatile than FDI or portfolio flows and have sometimes been subject to sharp reversals, such as during 1997–98 in emerging Asia or during the early 1980s in Latin America. See Box 1.1 of the September 2006 *World Economic Outlook*.

[8]For comparison, the exposure of western European banks to the U.S. subprime mortgage sector is estimated at about $250 billion.

highest for countries whose banking systems are largely foreign-owned (see Figure 2.6). Although local bank lending is funded mainly with local deposits, these countries would be vulnerable in case of problems in parent banks. Since 2002, the ratio of domestic credit to GDP has more than doubled in Latvia, Lithuania, Bulgaria, and Romania and has almost doubled in Estonia. Although patterns differ across countries, foreign credit has often financed activities in the nontradables sector, such as investment in real estate and household consumption. Widespread housing booms have been one consequence. Real house prices have more than tripled since end-2003 in Latvia and have more than doubled in Bulgaria, Estonia, and Lithuania.

The outlook for 2008 is for a further slowing of GDP growth in the region to 4.4 percent. Growth in most economies would ease closer to potential, reflecting a slowing both of domestic demand and of export growth in the face of lower demand from western Europe.

This baseline projection assumes that capital flows to emerging Europe moderate in an orderly manner—with a modest reduction in private capital inflows matched by a slower accumulation of foreign currency reserves. A critical issue for the region's outlook is the degree to which external bank flows could be disrupted by financial turbulence in mature financial markets, especially by losses sustained by western European banks. A sudden capital flow reversal could trigger a credit crunch as well as asset price deflation. The likely consequence would be an undesirably sharp slowdown in domestic absorption, combined with a painful deleveraging of corporate and household balance sheets.

To date, signs of slowing capital inflows have been largely confined to the Baltic countries, notably Latvia and Estonia, where tighter conditions imposed by parent banks have slowed lending—a process that started well before the onset of financial turbulence in August 2007. In addition, spreads on credit default swaps have widened sharply, reflecting these countries' dependence on foreign capital. There are at least three risk factors:

Figure 2.6. Emerging Europe: Macroeconomic Vulnerabilities on the Rise[1]

Strong GDP growth, driven primarily by domestic demand, has supported a substantial narrowing of income differentials with the euro area. At the same time, increasing inflationary pressures, losses in competitiveness, and dependence on external financing flows—especially from western European banks—have given rise to substantial macroeconomic and financial vulnerabilities.

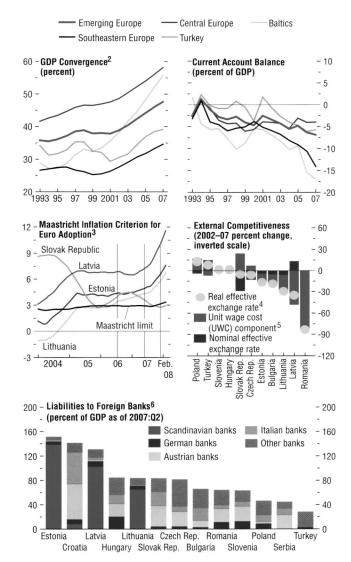

Sources: Bank for International Settlements, *Consolidated Banking Statistics*; European Commission; IMF, *International Financial Statistics*; and IMF staff calculations.
[1]Emerging Europe includes Baltics, central Europe, southeastern Europe, and Turkey. Central Europe includes Czech Republic, Hungary, Poland, Slovak Republic, and Slovenia. Baltics includes Estonia, Latvia, and Lithuania. Southeastern Europe includes Albania; Bosnia and Herzegovina; Bulgaria; Croatia; Macedonia, FYR; Romania; and Serbia.
[2]Purchasing-power-parity-based per capita GDP relative to the euro area.
[3]Twelve-month rolling average of year-over-year inflation. Vertical lines represent assessment dates for Estonia, Lithuania, Latvia, and Slovak Republic.
[4]UWC based. A positive value represents a depreciation.
[5]Differential in the growth of UWC in the manufacturing sector relative to trade partners.
[6]Total financial claims net of interoffice accounts.

- Contagion: Contagion could occur either directly, if banks cut back lending to cover losses from the subprime fallout, or indirectly, if a higher cost of capital and wider risk spreads induce banks to extend fewer loans to emerging Europe and/or to offer less-favorable terms. The potential for direct contagion appears limited, as few banks have (known) exposures both to the U.S. subprime sector and to emerging Europe. Banks affected by the subprime crisis are located primarily in the United Kingdom, Germany, Switzerland, and (to a lesser extent) France, and lending to emerging Europe has been carried out mainly by Scandinavian banks (especially to the Baltic countries) and by banks in Austria and Italy (especially to countries in southeastern Europe). Indirect contagion seems more plausible, however, as lending standards in the euro area have tightened markedly since the outbreak of financial turbulence.
- Concerns about profitability and asset quality: Wage increases in excess of productivity gains have triggered sharp losses of external competitiveness in recent years, especially in the Baltic countries and in southeastern Europe. In most cases, this has occurred in the context of accommodative fiscal policies and fixed exchange rate regimes.[9] This trend threatens to undermine a core motivation for foreign investors' presence in the region. In countries where much of the lending has been in the form of mortgages—such as the Baltic countries and Hungary—slowing housing markets could also trigger a reassessment of credit risk.
- A slowing of petrodollar flows: As discussed in Box 2.2, there is evidence that many funds lent to emerging Europe through banks originated in oil-producing countries and other commodity exporters. These funding sources could dry up if the global economy were to

slow sufficiently to reverse the surge in commodity prices, eroding commodity exporters' surpluses in the process.

The challenge for macroeconomic policymakers is twofold. As long as the current constellation persists—which is still characterized by overheating pressures in most countries—policymakers should steer their economies toward a soft landing. Fiscal policy should take the lead role in the adjustment: in countries with flexible exchange rate regimes, this would lower the burden on monetary policy, and in countries with fixed or tightly managed exchange rates (the Baltic countries, Bulgaria, and Croatia), fiscal tightening is the main tool available to dampen domestic demand and preserve competitiveness. Restraining the growth of public sector wages and pensions also has a role to play (including in Bulgaria, Estonia, and Romania), as do labor market reforms to boost employment (including in the Czech Republic, the Slovak Republic, and Poland). Credit risks should be monitored closely, and prudential and regulatory policies should seek to ensure that banks have sound capital bases to absorb potential losses.

If the external environment deteriorates substantially, some countries would have room for fiscal stimulus, given low levels of public debt, although there would be less room in countries with fiscal sustainability concerns, such as Hungary or Poland. Monetary and exchange rate policies could help in countries with flexible exchange rate regimes, even though balance sheet euroization would limit the scope for depreciation in some countries, including Hungary. Finally, flexible adjustment of wages would be crucial to limit the real impact of a financial contraction.

Commonwealth of Independent States: Containing Inflation Remains the Central Challenge

Real GDP growth was sustained at 8.5 percent in the Commonwealth of Independent States (CIS) during 2007, with high commodity prices, expansionary macroeconomic policies,

---

[9]By contrast, inflation pressures and competitiveness losses have been less pronounced in central Europe, where less-constrained central banks have kept a tighter lid on demand pressures.

Box 2.2. Petrodollars and Bank Lending to Emerging Markets

"Petrodollar recycling" is a phenomenon familiar from the 1970s. When oil prices rose sharply in fall 1973, oil-exporting countries were faced with a windfall in export receipts. A large portion of those receipts was saved and deposited with banks in industrial countries, which, in turn, onlent a large part of the funds to emerging economies, especially in Latin America. When the oil boom subsided in the early 1980s, bank flows to emerging markets reversed sharply, triggering the Latin American debt crisis.

How Important Are Bank Deposits Today for Investing Oil Surpluses?

Bank onlending of petrodollars is rarely considered to be a feature of the current oil price boom.[1] Two factors may contribute to this. First, in contrast to the 1970s, emerging economies as a group have built up sizable current account surpluses in recent years, making a debt buildup comparable to that of the 1970s seem unlikely. Second, bank deposits are widely believed to have lost importance as an instrument for investing oil (and other) surpluses. Recently, much attention has focused instead on vehicles used to invest emerging economy surpluses in global securities markets, including sovereign wealth funds.

Neither point holds up to scrutiny, however. First, not all emerging economies have been running external surpluses. In particular, emerging Europe had an average current account deficit of almost 6 percent of GDP during the past four years—fully comparable to external deficits prevailing in the 1970s. Second, the flow of bank deposits from oil-exporting countries—although less important than in the 1970s—has not become negligible: between 2001 and 2006, deposit outflows from oil exporters to banks in countries reporting to the Bank for International Settlements (BIS) accounted for 27 percent of their total gross

Note: The main author of this box is Johannes Wiegand.

[1]An important exception is Boorman (2006).

Correlation of Quarterly Deposit Outflows with the IMF Average Petroleum Spot Price

Country groups (#)	Correlation Coefficient Average[1]	Total Deposit Outflows, 2001–07 (billions of U.S. dollars)
All countries (210)	0.21 (.02)	10,483
Oil exporters (27)	0.29 (.05)	671
Offshore centers (19)	0.39 (.06)	1,818
Other (164)	0.17 (.02)	7,995
Ten highest correlations		
Libya (oe)	0.90	55
Panama (oc)	0.85	34
Jersey (oc)	0.68	251
Macao SAR (oc)	0.68	14
Samoa (oc)	0.68	3
Nigeria (oe)	0.66	27
Philippines	0.66	8
West Indies, U.K. (oc)	0.61	97
Lao PDR	0.60	1
Russia (oe)	0.60	255
Other major oil exporters		
United Arab Emirates	0.46	35
Kuwait	0.43	29
Iran, I.R. of	0.41	12
Saudi Arabia	0.37	41
Norway	0.25	135
Venezuela, Rep. Boliv. de	0.12	15
Other major offshore centers		
Guernsey	0.50	67
Hong Kong SAR	0.50	58
Cayman Islands	0.31	899
Singapore	0.30	82
Bahamas	0.25	120
Bermuda	−0.04	63

Sources: Bank for International Settlements; and IMF staff calculations.

Note: oe: oil exporter; oc: offshore center.

[1]Standard error in parentheses.

financial outflows. This compares with 44 percent for the period 1973–79 (see Box 2.2 of the April 2006 *World Economic Outlook*).

The degree to which oil exporters use bank deposits to invest surpluses varies across countries, however. As the table shows, between 2001 and 2007, the average correlation coefficient between oil exporters' deposit outflows and the IMF average petroleum spot price (APSP) was 0.29, only slightly higher than the overall

Box 2.2 *(continued)*

cross-country average (0.21). At the same time, deposit outflows from some exporters—notably Libya, Nigeria, and Russia—displayed some of the highest correlations, while for others—including Saudi Arabia and other Middle Eastern oil exporters—the correlations were only modest. Libya, Nigeria, and Russia also accounted for one-half of all deposit outflows from oil-exporting countries, and in each of these countries deposit outflows accounted for one-half or more of total gross capital outflows. This suggests that *some* but *not all* oil-exporting countries deposited oil surpluses regularly with banks in BIS-reporting countries, while other exporters pursued different investment strategies. The table also shows high correlations between outflows from several offshore centers and oil prices. One possible explanation is that some oil surpluses may have first been invested with offshore centers and then deposited with banks in BIS-reporting countries.[2]

Are Petrodollars Onlent to Emerging Markets?

To analyze the extent to which oil surpluses are channeled to emerging economies, quarterly loans to them by banks in BIS-reporting countries were regressed on the various sources of bank funding, including deposit inflows differentiated by country or region of origin and nondeposit inflows (such as debt securities and equity participations), using BIS locational banking statistics. Comovement of loans to emerging economies with specific types of funding is interpreted as an indication of onlending.[3] For the period 2001–07, the results suggest that a large part of bank loans to emerging economies originated from only two sources:

- Oil surpluses: According to the regressions' central estimate, banks in BIS-reporting countries onlent about half of deposits received

---

[2]The correlations for the deposit outflows of Lao PDR and the Philippines with the oil price may be spurious.

[3]See Wiegand (2008) for details.

from oil exporters to emerging economies. Onlending from Russia, Nigeria, and Libya was as much as 80 percent. Overall, oil surpluses accounted for more than half of emerging economies' bank loans.

- Deposits from emerging economies that are not oil exporters: Again, banks in BIS-reporting countries seem to have onlent about half of these funds to other emerging economies. Many countries in this group are non-oil-commodity exporters.

By contrast, deposits from industrial countries and offshore centers displayed little or no statistical relationship with loans to emerging economies. This suggests that funds channeled through offshore centers—including oil surpluses—were largely put to other uses.

Is This Relationship Stable?

Changes in bank loans to emerging economies are determined by two factors: variations in sources of funding and shifts in banks' investment strategies. Shifts in banks' investment strategies would lead to an unstable relationship between sources of funding and bank loans. As the first figure shows, the relationship was indeed unstable between 1996 and 2001. From 1996 until 1998, banks in BIS-reporting countries sharply cut exposure to emerging economies, before reengaging cautiously thereafter. This pattern mirrors the standard narrative of bank lending during and after the Asian and Russian crises. A stable relationship is observed from 2001 until end-2006, a period without major emerging market turbulence. In the first half of 2007, however, loans to emerging economies picked up substantially more than predicted by a model based on unchanged investment strategies. It is quite possible that this signals another structural break, in this case a shift of lending by banks in BIS-reporting countries into loans to emerging economies, perhaps in reaction to financial turbulence in advanced economies. However, there are too few data points after the potential breakpoint to establish this firmly.

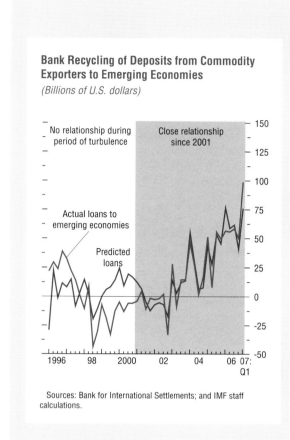

Bank Recycling of Deposits from Commodity Exporters to Emerging Economies

(Billions of U.S. dollars)

Sources: Bank for International Settlements; and IMF staff calculations.

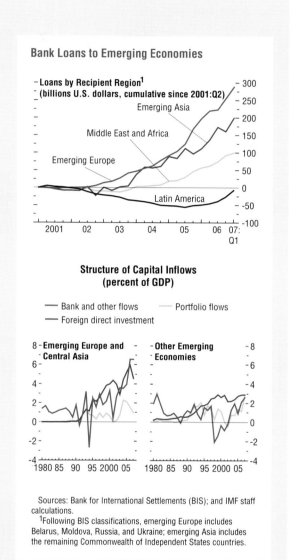

Bank Loans to Emerging Economies

Sources: Bank for International Settlements (BIS); and IMF staff calculations.
[1]Following BIS classifications, emerging Europe includes Belarus, Moldova, Russia, and Ukraine; emerging Asia includes the remaining Commonwealth of Independent States countries.

Who Has Benefited from the Onlending of Petrodollars?

Results from region-specific regressions suggest that almost half the petrodollar surpluses invested in bank deposits were onlent to emerging Europe. This is consistent with the more general pattern of bank lending to emerging economies in recent years, which has evolved quite differently across regions (second figure). Since 2001, about one-half of emerging market loans has gone to emerging Europe, one-third to emerging Asia, and one-sixth to the Middle East and Africa. Latin America did not join the global emerging markets lending boom until very recently. In emerging Europe, bank inflows account also for a much larger share of both GDP and total capital inflows than in other regions, where portfolio inflows are relatively more prevalent.

Some Implications

The current environment of high commodity prices that give rise to large external surpluses, especially in low- and middle-income countries, seems particularly conducive for bank lending to emerging economies. As a consequence, a sharp drop in commodity prices—or higher domestic absorption by commodity-exporting countries—could create substantial risks for emerging economies that depend heavily on bank inflows

Box 2.2 *(concluded)*

to finance external deficits by drying up sources of funding. In contrast to the 1970s and 1980s, the bulk of countries most at risk are not in Latin America but in emerging Europe. This goes at least in part against the conventional view that falling oil prices would *help* non-oil-exporting emerging economies by improving their trade balances and reducing financing needs.

Even if commodity exporters' surpluses persist, however, bank lending could still reverse

if banks reassess the viability of lending to emerging economies, as they did during the Asian and Russian crises. Such a reassessment could in principle go either way, however. There are indeed indications that banks in BIS-reporting countries shifted their lending portfolios *in favor* of emerging economies in early 2007, a move that coincided with increasing credit-quality issues in advanced economies, notably the United States.

strong capital inflows during most of the year, rapid credit growth, and rising asset prices fueling very strong domestic demand growth (Table 2.6). With imports surging, the growth contribution from the external sector was substantially negative, however, and current account balances weakened (smaller surpluses in energy exporters and larger deficits in energy importers). The strong growth of recent years has largely eliminated spare capacity in most economies, and wage growth has picked up. Together with rising food prices—which have particularly affected Kazakhstan, the Kyrgyz Republic, and Tajikistan—this has resulted in a sharp acceleration in inflation across the region in recent months (Figure 2.7). In Russia, inflation rose to almost 12 percent in December 2007, substantially exceeding the central bank's 6.5–8.0 percent year-end target, and was running at nearly 13 percent by February. Inflation is running at about 20 percent in Azerbaijan, Kazakhstan, the Kyrgyz Republic, Tajikistan, and Ukraine.

The turmoil in global financial markets has begun to affect most countries in the region, particularly because bank and portfolio inflows have recently become the dominant source of external financing. In Russia and Ukraine, where banks have borrowed heavily in international markets to finance rapid growth in domestic lending, spreads on external debt have widened. In Kazakhstan, the impact of the financial turmoil has been more severe,

with external financing drying up, credit growth slowing sharply, and reserves initially declining as the central bank intervened in the foreign exchange market to support the exchange rate.

High oil and commodity prices should continue to provide support, but a weaker global economy and slower credit growth would slow the pace of the expansion. Consequently, real GDP growth is expected to ease to 7 percent this year and 6.5 percent in 2009. In Russia, although consumption is expected to moderate, it should remain the main source of demand, spurred by still-strong gains in real incomes, and investment should also rise strongly, led by construction and public capital spending. In Ukraine, growth is projected to slow as wage growth moderates, export demand softens, and the rise in the terms of trade levels off. In Kazakhstan, the construction and real estate sectors are expected to be significantly affected by the sharp slowing in credit growth, and real GDP growth is projected to ease to 5 percent in 2008, from 8.5 percent in 2007. Elsewhere, strong growth is expected to continue in Azerbaijan (as oil output increases further) and Armenia (where the construction and services sectors remain buoyant) and to remain stable in Moldova, Tajikistan, and Uzbekistan.

Risks to the outlook are tilted to the downside. A sharper-than-expected slowdown in the global economy would likely lead to a decline in oil and commodity prices, a key driver of

Table 2.6. Commonwealth of Independent States (CIS): Real GDP, Consumer Prices, and Current Account Balance
(Annual percent change unless noted otherwise)

	Real GDP				Consumer Prices[1]				Current Account Balance[2]			
	2006	2007	2008	2009	2006	2007	2008	2009	2006	2007	2008	2009
Commonwealth of Independent States	**8.2**	**8.5**	**7.0**	**6.5**	**9.5**	**9.7**	**13.1**	**9.5**	**7.5**	**4.5**	**4.8**	**2.4**
Russia	7.4	8.1	6.8	6.3	9.7	9.0	11.4	8.4	9.5	5.9	5.8	2.9
Ukraine	7.1	7.3	5.6	4.2	9.0	12.8	21.9	15.7	−1.5	−4.2	−7.6	−9.7
Kazakhstan	10.7	8.5	5.0	7.0	8.6	10.8	17.1	8.3	−2.2	−6.6	−1.7	−1.0
Belarus	10.0	8.2	7.1	6.8	7.0	8.4	11.2	8.8	−4.1	−6.6	−7.5	−7.7
Turkmenistan	11.1	11.6	9.5	10.0	8.2	6.4	12.0	12.0	15.3	16.8	23.6	28.1
Low-income CIS countries	**14.7**	**14.5**	**11.9**	**10.8**	**10.1**	**12.7**	**14.7**	**13.3**	**8.0**	**12.9**	**19.3**	**19.6**
Armenia	13.3	13.8	10.0	8.0	2.9	4.4	6.8	4.5	−1.8	−6.5	−6.8	−5.0
Azerbaijan	30.5	23.4	18.6	15.6	8.4	16.6	19.6	20.5	17.7	28.8	39.5	39.2
Georgia	9.4	12.4	9.0	9.0	9.2	9.2	9.6	6.4	−15.9	−19.7	−16.6	−13.2
Kyrgyz Republic	3.1	8.2	7.0	6.5	5.6	10.2	18.8	10.2	−6.6	−6.5	−8.3	−7.4
Moldova	4.0	5.0	7.0	8.0	12.7	12.6	11.4	7.9	−12.0	−9.7	−10.3	−10.6
Tajikistan	7.0	7.8	4.1	7.0	10.0	13.2	18.5	10.5	−3.0	−9.5	−8.3	−7.1
Uzbekistan	7.3	9.5	8.0	7.5	14.2	12.3	11.8	10.9	18.8	23.8	24.6	20.8
Memorandum												
Net energy exporters[3]	8.2	8.6	7.1	6.8	9.7	9.4	12.1	8.9	9.1	6.0	6.7	4.1
Net energy importers[4]	7.9	7.9	6.2	5.3	8.4	11.4	18.1	12.9	−3.1	−5.8	−8.1	−9.3

[1]Movements in consumer prices are shown as annual averages. December/December changes can be found in Table A7 in the Statistical Appendix.
[2]Percent of GDP.
[3]Includes Azerbaijan, Kazakhstan, Russia, Turkmenistan, and Uzbekistan.
[4]Includes Armenia, Belarus, Georgia, Kyrgyz Republic, Moldova, Tajikistan, and Ukraine.

regional growth, and could adversely affect external financing conditions. All countries in the region would be negatively affected, although the impact would be largest on those where portfolio and bank inflows are most significant (Kazakhstan, Russia, and Ukraine). Further, links between financial systems in the region would mean that difficulties in the banking systems in larger economies could affect credit availability and growth in other countries (for example, Kazakhstani banks have an important presence in Tajikistan and the Kyrgyz Republic).

The most immediate challenge for policymakers in the region is to rein in rising inflation pressures. Although the anticipated slowdown in growth and some easing of food price increases should help reduce inflation over the course of 2008, it is likely to remain uncomfortably high unless macroeconomic and incomes policies are also tightened. The failure to act swiftly to contain inflation pressures could result in wage and price expectations ratcheting upward,

putting at risk the hard-won gains from earlier disinflation policies.

Fiscal policy has added to demand pressures in a number of countries (including Azerbaijan, Georgia, Russia, and Ukraine), and a tighter budgetary stance will be necessary to cool domestic demand. Income policies should be geared toward achieving wage outcomes consistent with single-digit inflation, given underlying trends in productivity. This will require containing the growth of public sector wages—large increases have taken place in many countries in recent years—and limiting increases in minimum wages. Tighter monetary policy combined with greater exchange rate appreciation will also be necessary in many countries, including Georgia and Russia. In Ukraine, monetary conditions were tightened beginning in the second half of 2007 in response to rising inflation. In Kazakhstan, monetary policy was tightened in December as inflation increased and the exchange rate came under downward pressure, and it can now remain on hold until the impli-

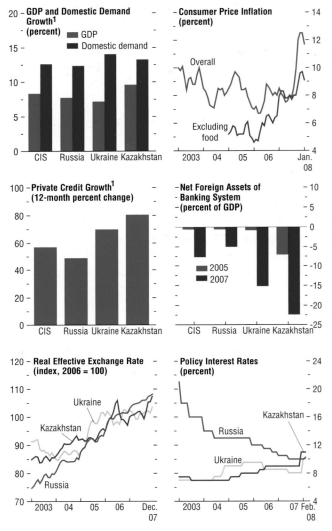

Figure 2.7. Commonwealth of Independent States (CIS): Inflation Pressures Remain the Central Concern

Spurred by rising earnings from commodity exports and rapid credit expansion, domestic demand in the CIS region is growing very strongly. This strong growth, together with rising food prices, has led to a sharp pickup in inflation in recent months.

Sources: IMF, *International Financial Statistics;* and IMF staff calculations.
[1]2006–07 average.

cations of the sharp slowing in credit growth become clearer.

With credit-to-GDP ratios in the region still relatively low, financial deepening is very welcome, but the pace of credit growth has raised concerns about whether a number of countries are experiencing unsustainable credit booms. Rapid credit expansion may be undermining credit quality, particularly if the capacity of banks to assess the creditworthiness of borrowers is failing to keep pace with the expansion of their lending activities, and the potential for sharp reversals of asset prices raises questions about the value of the collateral backing the loans in the event of a downturn. A further concern is that, in many cases, the credit expansion is being financed by bank borrowing in foreign currency, opening exposure to exchange rate movements. To minimize the risks from rapid credit growth, it is important that the authorities upgrade their monitoring and supervisory practices, that banks themselves improve their credit-assessment and risk-management systems, and that borrowers are better educated about the exchange rate and interest rate risks they face.

Over the longer term, the region continues to face the challenge of diversifying its production base away from the current heavy reliance on commodities. Investment in the region remains low—only 22 percent of GDP in 2007—and is concentrated in extractive industries and construction. Efforts to strengthen institutions, improve the business climate, continue trade reforms, and develop more diversified domestic financial systems will be essential to encourage greater private sector investment.

Sub-Saharan Africa: Strong Growth Prospects, but Risks Remain

Building on the best period of sustained economic growth since independence, the pace of economic activity in sub-Saharan Africa (SSA) accelerated to 6.8 percent in 2007, led by very strong growth in oil-exporting countries and supported by robust expansions in the region's other economies. The region's strongest growth was recorded by Angola, where oil and diamond production have both risen sharply. In Nigeria, robust non-oil sector growth offset the drag from a decline in oil production in the Niger Delta. The pace of activity elsewhere in SSA has been supported by domestic demand (investment in particular), the payoff from improvements in macroeconomic stability, and the reforms undertaken in most countries. In South Africa, the region's largest economy, the pace of activity has eased modestly as tighter monetary policy, aimed at containing rising inflation pressures from food and fuel prices, has applied a brake to household spending, but investment continues to grow at a brisk pace in preparation for the 2010 FIFA World Cup. Elsewhere, inflation pressures remain generally well contained, reflecting a variety of factors, including stabilization gains in some countries, improved food supplies, appropriately restrictive monetary policies—with, in some cases, exchange rate appreciation in response to capital inflows—and lower bank financing of fiscal deficits.

The favorable environment has made some countries in SSA increasingly attractive as destinations for private capital inflows. Net private capital inflows reached record levels in 2007, led by strong FDI inflows. However, the bulk of FDI is still focused on a few countries and targeted mainly at extractive industries, particularly the petroleum sector, based on evidence from cross-border mergers-and-acquisition-related inflows—an important fraction of gross FDI inflows.

As discussed in Chapter 5, the current cycle differs in many important ways for commodity exporters, including in Africa. Although commodity export values have risen as a share of regional GDP, the increase in the volume of commodity exports has been much more limited. On the other hand, rising investment—which has benefited from improved policies and a strengthened institutional environment—has provided the basis for a growing manufacturing sector in several countries. Volumes of manufacturing exports now represent a much larger share of regional GDP than commod-

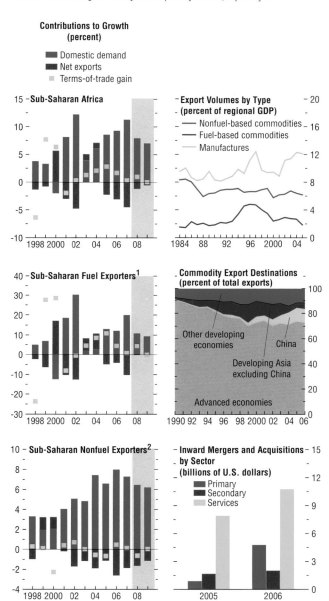

Figure 2.8. Sub-Saharan Africa: Vulnerability of Commodity Exports to Global Demand

Despite strong domestic demand, the region's dependence on commodities underscores continued vulnerability to terms-of-trade shocks. Foreign direct investment is still targeted mainly toward primary sectors, especially oil.

Sources: UNCTAD *World Investment Report*; and IMF staff estimates.
[1]Angola, Republic of Congo, Equatorial Guinea, Gabon, and Nigeria.
[2]Benin, Botswana, Burkina Faso, Burundi, Cameroon, Cape Verde, Central African Republic, Chad, Comoros, Dem. Rep. of Congo, Côte d'Ivoire, Djibouti, Ethiopia, Gambia, Ghana, Guinea, Guinea-Bissau, Kenya, Lesotho, Madagascar, Malawi, Mali, Mauritania, Mauritius, Mozambique, Namibia, Niger, Rwanda, Senegal, Seychelles, Sierra Leone, South Africa, Swaziland, Tanzania, Togo, Uganda, and Zambia.

Table 2.7. Selected African Economies: Real GDP, Consumer Prices, and Current Account Balance
(Annual percent change unless noted otherwise)

	Real GDP				Consumer Prices[1]				Current Account Balance[2]			
	2006	2007	2008	2009	2006	2007	2008	2009	2006	2007	2008	2009
Africa	**5.9**	**6.2**	**6.3**	**6.4**	**6.4**	**6.3**	**7.5**	**5.9**	**3.1**	**0.1**	**1.7**	**0.9**
Maghreb	**4.4**	**4.2**	**5.5**	**5.3**	**3.1**	**3.1**	**3.7**	**3.3**	**14.3**	**12.4**	**13.9**	**10.7**
Algeria	2.0	4.6	4.9	4.9	2.5	3.7	4.3	4.1	25.2	23.2	26.0	20.6
Morocco	8.0	2.2	6.5	5.7	3.3	2.0	2.0	2.0	2.8	−0.1	−1.1	−0.9
Tunisia	5.5	6.3	5.5	5.9	4.5	3.1	4.7	3.5	−2.0	−2.5	−2.7	−2.7
Sub-Sahara	**6.4**	**6.8**	**6.6**	**6.7**	**7.3**	**7.2**	**8.5**	**6.6**	**−0.1**	**−3.3**	**−1.8**	**−1.7**
Horn of Africa[3]	**11.3**	**10.8**	**7.9**	**10.5**	**9.1**	**11.4**	**12.6**	**8.6**	**−13.3**	**−9.8**	**−8.3**	**−5.9**
Ethiopia	11.6	11.4	8.4	7.1	12.3	17.0	20.1	12.9	−9.1	−4.5	−4.3	−6.1
Sudan	11.3	10.5	7.6	12.7	7.2	8.0	8.0	6.0	−15.1	−11.8	−9.8	−5.6
Great Lakes[3]	**6.0**	**6.8**	**5.7**	**6.4**	**10.4**	**9.2**	**9.2**	**6.6**	**−4.4**	**−4.8**	**−8.0**	**−10.0**
Congo, Dem. Rep. of	5.6	6.3	8.8	11.6	13.2	16.7	10.1	11.4	−2.4	−4.0	−10.7	−24.6
Kenya	6.1	7.0	2.5	3.4	14.5	9.8	12.3	7.0	−2.5	−3.5	−5.5	−3.8
Tanzania	6.7	7.3	7.8	8.0	7.3	7.0	7.1	5.2	−7.8	−9.2	−9.7	−10.1
Uganda	5.1	6.5	7.1	7.0	6.6	6.8	5.9	5.0	−4.0	−2.0	−7.7	−9.3
Southern Africa[3]	**10.8**	**12.8**	**11.1**	**9.4**	**11.2**	**10.1**	**9.8**	**7.8**	**15.2**	**6.7**	**5.8**	**6.4**
Angola	18.6	21.1	16.0	13.2	13.3	12.2	11.4	8.9	23.3	11.0	12.0	11.8
Zimbabwe[4]	−5.4	−6.1	−6.6	−6.8	1,016.7	10,452.6	. . .	. . .	−6.0	−1.0	—	. . .
West and Central Africa[3]	**4.6**	**5.1**	**7.0**	**6.9**	**7.0**	**4.6**	**6.7**	**6.1**	**4.2**	**−1.6**	**2.4**	**2.1**
Ghana	6.4	6.4	6.9	7.5	10.9	9.6	8.9	7.9	−10.9	−12.8	−9.8	−7.9
Nigeria	6.2	6.4	9.1	8.3	8.3	5.5	8.6	8.5	9.5	0.7	6.5	5.7
CFA franc zone[3]	**2.2**	**3.6**	**4.8**	**5.2**	**3.6**	**1.6**	**3.9**	**2.9**	**−0.3**	**−2.3**	**−0.6**	**−1.0**
Cameroon	3.2	3.3	4.5	4.6	5.1	0.9	3.0	2.3	0.7	0.4	—	−0.4
Côte d'Ivoire	−0.3	1.6	2.9	5.1	5.0	2.1	4.7	3.2	3.1	1.4	0.6	−0.5
South Africa	**5.4**	**5.1**	**3.8**	**3.9**	**4.7**	**7.1**	**8.7**	**5.9**	**−6.5**	**−7.3**	**−7.7**	**−7.9**
Memorandum												
Oil importers	5.7	5.2	5.1	5.2	6.3	6.7	7.6	5.5	−3.5	−4.8	−5.9	−6.1
Oil exporters[5]	6.3	8.0	8.4	8.3	6.4	5.6	7.2	6.5	13.1	7.4	11.1	9.3

[1]Movements in consumer prices are shown as annual averages. December/December changes can be found in Table A7 in the Statistical Appendix.

[2]Percent of GDP.

[3]The country composition of these regional groups is set out in Table F in the Statistical Appendix.

[4]The inflation figure for 2007 represents an estimate. No inflation projection for 2008 and beyond is shown. No forecast for the current account in percent of GDP is shown for 2009.

[5]Includes Chad and Mauritania.

ity exports (Figure 2.8). Among commodity exporters, manufacturing activity is often in commodity-related sectors, but the rising role of manufacturing exports nevertheless presents an opportunity for a move up the value chain and greater diversification of the economy away from primary exports. As a result of the broadening base of regional economies, terms-of-trade gains now play a smaller role than in the past in explaining the contributions to overall growth of both domestic demand and net exports. Export destinations have also become more diversified, with a greater share of exports now going

to other emerging and developing economies, although advanced economies still account for three-quarters of all exports.

Against this background, growth in SSA during 2008–09 is projected to slow only modestly from the pace recorded in 2007 (Table 2.7). Growth will continue to be led by oil exporters, reflecting the coming onstream of new production facilities in oil-exporting countries. In view of the strength of nonfuel commodity exports and strong investment growth, growth in non-fuel-exporting countries is expected to continue at about the same pace as in 2007. However, in South Africa, rising electricity shortages are expected to weigh on activity during 2008–09.

The balance of risks to the outlook is tilted to the downside. As discussed, regional economies are becoming more diversified and benefiting from improved policies and structural reforms that are under way in many countries. This should strengthen the resilience of the region to a slowdown in the advanced economies. Nonetheless, the region remains sensitive to developments in advanced economy trading partners, especially western Europe. A sharper-than-expected slowdown in the advanced economies that reduces the demand for the region's principal exports is still the key source of risk for the region's commodity exporters, along with the related risk of weaker commodity prices. Tighter global financial market conditions could also slow the pace of capital inflows and investment into the region. In a number of countries, political and security risks remain important.

The main policy challenges for the region are to maintain progress toward increasing integration with the global economy and to reduce poverty in the context of a less-friendly global environment. Globalization is positively associated with a reduction in inequality in developing countries (see Chapter 4 of the October 2007 *World Economic Outlook*), but more needs to be done to allow all segments of the population to benefit from the region's strong growth performance. At the same time, it is important to reduce the region's vulnerabilities to commodity-market-led downturns, which disproportionately affect the poor. Macroeconomic policy frameworks need to be further strengthened and supported by reforms to build on recent progress in improving the business environment and institutions. Further progress in trade integration needs to be complemented with financial sector reform to broaden the private sector's access to financial and banking services and to tools for managing risk, in order to allow economies to take fuller advantage of the increasing opportunities offered by

globalization. Resource-rich countries need to ensure that fiscal policy is carefully calibrated to keep buildups in spending from export earnings in line with the economy's absorptive capacity and consistent with fiscal sustainability. Fiscal policy should be supported by appropriate monetary policies and targeted at improving the economic prospects of the poor and of future generations. Similar strictures apply more broadly to the management of scaled-up aid inflows. In countries where exports remain less diversified, fiscal policy also needs to guard against competitiveness pressures in non-resource-exporting sectors caused by Dutch disease effects.

Middle East: Inflation Is a Growing Concern

Global financial market turmoil has had little direct effect on the Middle East, although the depreciation of the U.S. dollar is complicating policymaking in some countries. Regional growth remains strong, reaching 5.8 percent in 2007 (Table 2.8). In oil-exporting countries, increases in oil production have been limited, but high oil prices are supporting increased government spending, including on infrastructure and social projects, and strong expansion of credit to the private sector. Despite the increase in domestic spending and imports, the large current account surpluses in these countries have narrowed only slightly—to about 22¾ percent of GDP—as higher oil prices have further boosted export revenues. Elsewhere, growth has been even stronger, spurred by trade and financial spillovers from oil-exporting countries as well as domestic reforms. Egypt has been leading the way, with the economy expanding by more than 7 percent in 2007.

Inflation pressures in the region have risen considerably in recent months, owing to strong domestic demand, rising food prices, and higher rents in the Gulf Cooperation Council (GCC) countries, where a large influx of expatriate workers and the growing prosperity of local residents have caused a housing short-

Table 2.8. Selected Middle Eastern Economies: Real GDP, Consumer Prices, and Current Account Balance
(Annual percent change unless noted otherwise)

	Real GDP				Consumer Prices[1]				Current Account Balance[2]			
	2006	2007	2008	2009	2006	2007	2008	2009	2006	2007	2008	2009
Middle East	**5.8**	**5.8**	**6.1**	**6.1**	**7.0**	**10.4**	**11.5**	**10.0**	**20.9**	**19.8**	**23.0**	**19.4**
Oil exporters[3]	**5.8**	**5.6**	**6.0**	**5.9**	**7.6**	**10.5**	**12.2**	**10.4**	**24.0**	**22.8**	**26.3**	**22.4**
Iran, I.R. of	5.8	5.8	5.8	4.7	11.9	17.5	20.7	17.4	9.3	10.4	11.2	8.4
Saudi Arabia	4.3	4.1	4.8	5.6	2.3	4.1	6.2	5.6	27.4	26.8	31.3	24.0
United Arab Emirates	9.4	7.4	6.3	6.4	9.3	11.0	9.0	5.3	22.0	21.6	27.5	26.0
Kuwait	6.3	4.6	6.0	6.2	3.1	5.0	6.5	5.5	51.7	47.4	45.2	42.3
Mashreq	**5.9**	**6.3**	**6.2**	**6.5**	**5.4**	**9.5**	**8.4**	**8.2**	**−2.4**	**−2.8**	**−3.0**	**−3.4**
Egypt	6.8	7.1	7.0	7.1	4.2	11.0	8.8	8.8	0.8	1.5	0.8	−0.5
Syrian Arab Republic	4.4	3.9	4.0	4.8	10.6	7.0	7.0	7.0	−6.1	−5.8	−6.6	−5.5
Jordan	6.3	5.7	5.5	5.8	6.3	5.4	10.9	6.5	−11.3	−17.3	−15.5	−13.4
Lebanon	—	4.0	3.0	4.5	5.6	4.1	5.5	5.3	−6.0	−10.7	−9.8	−10.2
Memorandum												
Israel	5.2	5.3	3.0	3.4	2.1	0.5	2.6	2.0	6.0	3.1	1.8	1.7

[1]Movements in consumer prices are shown as annual averages. December/December changes can be found in Table A7 in the Statistical Appendix.
[2]Percent of GDP.
[3]Includes Bahrain, Islamic Republic of Iran, Kuwait, Libya, Oman, Qatar, Saudi Arabia, Syrian Arab Republic, United Arab Emirates, and Republic of Yemen.

age (Figure 2.9). Consumer price index (CPI) inflation is running at close to 20 percent (year over year) in the Islamic Republic of Iran, is near 14 percent in Qatar, and is above 9 percent in the United Arab Emirates (a 19-year high). Even in Saudi Arabia, where inflation has traditionally been in the 1–2 percent range, prices increased by 6.5 percent in 2007.

The short-term outlook for the region generally remains positive. Growth is projected to rise to over 6 percent in both 2008 and 2009, the current account surplus is expected to remain very large, and inflation pressures should moderate as rents ease with the completion of a large number of new housing units (Qatar and the United Arab Emirates) and limited price controls take effect (caps on rents in the United Arab Emirates and Oman, and subsidies on some food items in Saudi Arabia). Risks to the outlook at this stage appear broadly balanced. Continued high oil prices and/or the large cut in U.S. interest rates could stimulate a stronger-than-expected expansion of domestic demand, although this would likely come at the cost of higher inflation and would create risks of a possible asset price bubble. A broad-based global slowdown that resulted in a substantial drop in

oil prices and regional geopolitical uncertainties are the main near-term downside risks to the outlook.

The key macroeconomic policy challenge is to contain rising inflation pressures. Although the baseline forecast envisages some reduction in inflation over the next year, inflation will still remain uncomfortably high, and risks are on the upside, given strong money and credit growth. The exchange rates of most GCC countries are pegged to the U.S. dollar (Kuwait is the exception, pegging to an undisclosed basket of currencies since May 2007). This constrains the flexibility of monetary policy, given that capital accounts are essentially open.[10] In this context, the recent monetary policy easing in the United States has not been helpful for the GCC countries, leading to increasingly negative real interest rates at a time when the regional economic cycle is moving ahead strongly. Moreover, the weakness of the U.S. dollar has implied real effective depreciation for many Middle Eastern country currencies, while fiscal

[10]The Syrian Arab Republic has also moved away from a peg to the U.S. dollar and now pegs its currency to the SDR.

and incomes policies are turning more expansionary in response to the sharp increase in oil revenues. All these factors add to domestic demand pressures.

It is important that macroeconomic policies be adjusted to put inflation on a firm downward path before wage and price expectations are adversely affected. In the Islamic Republic of Iran, monetary and fiscal policies must be tightened after an extended and significant period of stimulus. In the GCC, especially in Kuwait and Saudi Arabia, monetary policy is constrained by the exchange rate pegs, and it will be important that the current buildup in fiscal spending be calibrated to account for the short-term cyclical position of the economy and that composition of such spending be aimed at maximizing the impact on supply bottlenecks. In addition, the authorities should stay focused on guarding against asset price inflation and a possible buildup in related vulnerabilities on bank balance sheets through appropriate prudential measures.

Looking beyond the immediate short-term macroeconomic challenges, policymakers will need to focus on encouraging the development of vibrant private-sector-led economies in the region, like those already in place in many GCC countries. Central to these efforts will be reforms that help generate jobs for the rapidly growing working-age population. Among the priorities in this regard are reforms to improve the business climate and make investment in the non-oil sector more attractive. Action is needed to reduce barriers to trade, simplify tax systems, reduce pervasive government controls and regulations, and enhance the transparency of legal and administrative systems. Financial sector reforms are also a priority in order to develop financial systems that can support high and sustained growth.

References

Baxter, Marianne, and Robert G. King, 1993, "Fiscal Policy in General Equilibrium," *American Economic Review*, Vol. 83 (June), pp. 315–34.

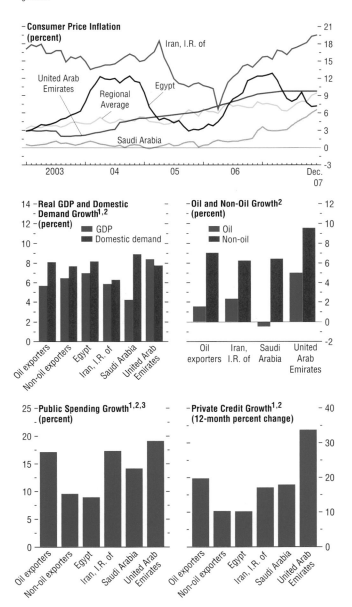

Figure 2.9. Middle East: Strong Growth, Rising Inflation

Inflation in the Middle East is rising as increased public spending and strong credit growth spur domestic demand. Structural reforms will be needed to contain price growth.

Sources: IMF, *International Financial Statistics;* and IMF staff calculations.
[1]2006–07 average.
[2]Oil exporters include Bahrain, Islamic Republic of Iran, Kuwait, Libya, Oman, Qatar, Saudi Arabia, Syrian Arab Republic, United Arab Emirates, and Republic of Yemen. Non-oil exporters include Egypt, Jordan, and Lebanon.
[3]Public spending is defined as consumption and investment.

Bayoumi, Tamim, 2001, "The Morning After: Explaining the Slowdown in Japanese Growth," in *Post-Bubble Blues—How Japan Responded to Asset Price Collapse*, ed. by Tamim Bayoumi and Charles Collyns (Washington: International Monetary Fund).

Bayoumi, Tamim, and Andrew Swiston, 2007, "Foreign Entanglements: Estimating the Source and Size of Spillovers Across Industrial Countries," IMF Working Paper 07/182 (Washington: International Monetary Fund).

Bernanke, Ben, 2007, "Housing, Housing Finance and Monetary Policy," opening speech at the Federal Reserve Bank of Kansas City 31st Economic Policy Symposium, "Housing, Housing Finance and Monetary Policy," Jackson Hole, Wyoming, August 31–September 1.

Blinder, Alan, 2004, "The Case Against Discretionary Fiscal Policy," CEPS Working Paper No. 100 (Princeton, New Jersey: Princeton University Center for Economic Policy Studies). Available via the Internet: www.princeton.edu/~ceps/workingpapers/100blinder.pdf.

Boorman, Jack, 2006, "Global Imbalances and Capital Flows to Emerging Market Countries," paper presented at the Emerging Markets Forum 2006 Global Meeting, "International Capital Flows, Domestic Capital Markets Growth and Development in Emerging Market Countries," Jakarta, September 20–22.

Botman, Dennis, 2006, "Efficiency Gains from Reducing the GST Versus Personal Income Taxation in Canada," in *Canada: Selected Issues*, IMF Country Report 06/229 (Washington: International Monetary Fund).

Botman, Dennis, Philippe Karam, Douglas Laxton, and David Rose, 2007, "DSGE Modeling at the Fund: Applications and Further Developments," IMF Working Paper 07/200 (Washington: International Monetary Fund).

Catalán, Mario, and Ruy Lama, 2006, "Fiscal Policy and the External Balance in Spain," in *Spain: Selected Issues*, IMF Country Report No. 06/213 (Washington: International Monetary Fund).

Corsetti, Giancarlo, and Nouriel Roubini, 1996, "Budget Deficits, Public Sector Solvency and Political Biases in Fiscal Policy: A Case Study of Finland," *Finnish Economic Papers*, Vol. 9 (Spring), pp. 18–36.

Davis, Morris A., Andreas Lehnert, and Robert F. Martin, 2007, "The Rent-Price Ratio for the Aggregate Stock of Owner-Occupied Housing" (unpublished, December). Available via the Internet: morris.marginalq.com/DLM_fullpaper.pdf.

de Castro Fernández, Francisco, and Pablo Hernández de Cos, 2006, "The Economic Effects of Exogenous Fiscal Shocks in Spain: A SVAR Approach," ECB Working Paper No. 647 (Frankfurt am Main: European Central Bank).

Ford, Robert, and Douglas Laxton, 1999, "World Public Debt and Real Interest Rates," *Oxford Review of Economic Policy*, Vol. 15 (Summer), pp. 77–94.

Galí, Jordi, J. David López-Salido, and Javier Vallés, 2007, "Understanding the Effects of Government Spending on Consumption," *Journal of the European Economic Association*, Vol. 5 (March), pp. 227–70.

Giavazzi, Francesco, and Marco Pagano, 1990, "Can Severe Fiscal Contractions Be Expansionary? Tales of Two Small European Countries," *NBER Macroeconomics Annual 1990* (Cambridge, Massachusetts: MIT Press), pp. 75–111.

Giordano, Raffaela, Sandro Momigliano, Stefano Neri, and Roberto Perotti, 2007, "The Effects of Fiscal Policy in Italy: Evidence from a VAR Model," *European Journal of Political Economy*, Vol. 23 (September), pp. 707–33.

Girouard, Nathalie, and Christophe André, 2005, "Measuring Cyclically-Adjusted Budget Balances for OECD Countries," OECD Economics Department Working Paper No. 434 (Paris: Organization for Economic Cooperation and Development).

Hemming, Richard, Michael Kell, and Selma Mahfouz, 2002, "The Effectiveness of Fiscal Policy in Stimulating Economic Activity—A Review of the Literature," IMF Working Paper 02/208 (Washington: International Monetary Fund).

Heppke-Falk, Kirsten H., Jörn Tenhofen, and Guntram B. Wolff, 2006, "The Macroeconomic Effects of Exogenous Fiscal Policy Shocks in Germany: A Disaggregated SVAR Analysis," Deutsche Bundesbank Discussion Paper, Series 1: Economic Studies No. 41/2006 (Frankfurt am Main: Deutsche Bundesbank).

Izquierdo, Alejandro, Randall Romero, Ernesto Talvi, 2008, "Booms and Busts in Latin America: The Role of External Factors," IADB Research Department Working Paper No. 631 (Washington: Inter-American Development Bank).

Johnson, David S., Jonathan A. Parker, and Nicholas S. Souleles, 2004, "The Response of Consumer Spending to the Randomized Income Tax Rebates of 2001," The Wharton School Working Paper (February).

Kose, M. Ayhan, Guy Meredith, and Christopher Towe, 2004, "How Has NAFTA Affected the Mexican Economy? Review and Evidence," IMF Working Paper 04/59 (Washington: International Monetary Fund).

Kumhof, Michael, and Douglas Laxton, 2007, "A Party Without a Hangover? On the Effects of U.S. Fiscal Deficits," IMF Working Paper 07/202 (Washington: International Monetary Fund).

Kuttner, Kenneth N., and Adam S. Posen, 2002, "Fiscal Policy Effectiveness in Japan," *Journal of the Japanese and International Economies*, Vol. 16 (December), pp. 536–58.

Leamer, Edward, 2007, "Housing and the Business Cycle," paper presented at the Federal Reserve Bank of Kansas City 31st Economic Policy Symposium, "Housing, Housing Finance and Monetary Policy," Jackson Hole, Wyoming, August 31–September 1.

Linnemann, Ludger, and Andreas Schabert, 2003, "Fiscal Policy in the New Neoclassical Synthesis," *Journal of Money, Credit and Banking*, Vol. 35 (December), pp. 911–29.

Mühleisen, M., 2000, "Too Much of a Good Thing? The Effectiveness of Fiscal Stimulus," in *Post-Bubble Blues—How Japan Responded to Asset Price Collapse*, ed. by Tamim Bayoumi and Charles Collyns (Washington: International Monetary Fund).

Österholm, Pär, and Jeromin Zettelmeyer, 2007, "The Effect of External Conditions on Growth in Latin America," IMF Working Paper 07/176 (Washington: International Monetary Fund).

Perotti, Roberto, 2005, "Estimating the Effects of Fiscal Policy in OECD Countries," CEPR Discussion Paper No. 4842 (London: Centre for Economic Policy Research).

———, 2007, "In Search of the Transmission Mechanism of Fiscal Policy," NBER Working Paper No. 13143 (Cambridge, Massachusetts: National Bureau of Economic Research).

Posen, Adam, 1998, *Restoring Japan's Economic Growth* (Washington: Institute for International Economics).

Ravn, Morten, Stephanie Schmitt-Grohé, and Martín Uribe, 2006, "Deep Habits," *Review of Economic Studies*, Vol. 73 (January), pp. 195–218.

Roache, Shaun, 2007, "Central America's Regional Trends and U.S. Cycles," paper presented at the Economic and Financial Linkages in the Western Hemisphere Seminar organized by the International Monetary Fund Western Hemisphere Department, Washington, November 26. Available via the Internet: www.imf.org/external/np/seminars/eng/2007/whd/pdf/session2-1a.pdf.

Sgherri, Silvia, 2006, "How Expansionary Are Tax Cuts in Italy?" in *Italy: Selected Issues*, IMF Country Report No. 06/59 (Washington: International Monetary Fund).

Shapiro, Matthew D., and Joel Slemrod, 2003, "Consumer Response to Tax Rebates," *American Economic Review*, Vol. 93 (March), pp. 381–96.

Swiston, Andrew, and Tamim Bayoumi, 2008, "Spillovers Across NAFTA," IMF Working Paper 08/3 (Washington: International Monetary Fund).

Sosa, Sebastian, 2007, "External Shocks and Business Cycle Fluctuations in Mexico: How Important Are U.S. Factors?" IMF Country Report 07/378 (Washington: International Monetary Fund).

Wiegand, Johannes, 2008, "Petrodollars and Bank Lending to Emerging Market Economies during the Current Oil Price Boom," IMF Working Paper (Washington: International Monetary Fund, forthcoming).

THE CHANGING HOUSING CYCLE AND THE IMPLICATIONS FOR MONETARY POLICY

This chapter examines how innovations in housing finance systems in advanced economies over the past two decades have altered the role of the housing sector in the business cycle and in the monetary policy transmission mechanism. It concludes that these changes have broadened the spillovers from the housing sector to the rest of the economy and have amplified their impact by strengthening the role of housing as collateral. This analysis suggests that in economies with more developed mortgage markets, monetary policymakers may need to respond more aggressively to developments in the housing sector, within a risk-management approach that treats house price dynamics as one of the key factors to be considered in assessing the balance of risks to output and inflation.

The recent booms in house prices and residential investment in many advanced economies, and the sharp correction that has followed in a few of them, have reignited the debate over the link between housing and the business cycle and over how monetary policymakers should respond to developments in the housing sector.[1]

Despite general agreement that developments in the housing sector have important implications for the level of economic activity, there is no consensus on why this is the case. In particular, there is disagreement on the dynamics of residential investment, its consequences for the business cycle, and the impact of house price fluctuations on consumer spending.

Note: The main authors of this chapter are Roberto Cardarelli (team leader), Deniz Igan, and Alessandro Rebucci, with support from Gavin Asdorian and Stephanie Denis and under the supervision of Tim Lane. Tommaso Monacelli and Luca Sala provided consultancy support.

[1]See papers presented at "Housing, Housing Finance, and Monetary Policy," Federal Reserve Bank of Kansas City 31st Economic Policy Symposium, Jackson Hole, Wyoming (August 31–September 1, 2007). www.kc.frb.org/publicat/sympos/2007/sym07prg.htm.

Dramatic changes in the systems of housing finance over the past two decades have only increased the uncertainty about the link between housing and economic activity. What is clear is that more widely available and lower-cost housing financing has contributed to the rapid growth of mortgage debt in a number of countries—including among households with impaired or insufficient credit histories, typically referred to as subprime borrowers. What is less clear is whether these changes have weakened the link between housing and the business cycle.

Some authors advanced the hypothesis that these changes have weakened the link between housing and the business cycle—for example, easier access to credit allows households to better smooth temporary downturns in income (Dynan, Elmendorf, and Sichel, 2006). Indeed, the economies that better weathered the cyclical downturn in the early 2000s—such as the United States and the United Kingdom—were those with stronger housing sector performance. With house prices and residential investment softening in a number of countries, however, there is concern that innovations in housing finance may amplify the impact of spillovers from the housing sector to the wider economy.

Against this background, this chapter investigates whether changes in housing finance systems over the past two decades have altered the links between the housing sector and economic activity, and it explores the implications for the conduct of monetary policy. In particular, this chapter addresses the following questions: Has there been a change in the housing sector's contribution to the business cycle in advanced economies over the past two decades? Are cross-country differences in the role of the housing sector in the business cycle related to the institutional characteristics of national mortgage markets? Is there a need for monetary policymakers to change how they respond to developments in the housing sector?

There is a substantial literature on the housing cycle; the main contribution of this chapter is twofold. First, it takes a broad cross-country perspective, rather than focusing on a single or a few countries. Second, it uses a methodology that formally identifies the housing sector as both a source of volatility and a channel through which other shocks are transmitted to the broader economy.

The main conclusion of this analysis is that changes in housing finance systems have affected the role played by the housing sector in the business cycle in two different ways. First, the increased use of homes as collateral has amplified the impact of housing sector activity on the rest of the economy by strengthening the positive effect of rising house prices on consumption via increased household borrowing—the "financial accelerator" effect. Second, monetary policy is now transmitted more through the price of homes than through residential investment. In particular, the evidence suggests that more flexible and competitive mortgage markets have amplified the impact of monetary policy on house prices and thus, ultimately, on consumer spending and output. Furthermore, easy monetary policy seems to have contributed to the recent run-up in house prices and residential investment in the United States, although its effect was probably magnified by the loosening of lending standards and by excessive risk-taking by lenders.

This chapter also offers two intuitions on how monetary policy should take into account the changing nature of the housing cycle and the new characteristics of mortgage markets. First, because its impact is greater in economies with more developed mortgage markets, monetary policy may need to be more aggressively responsive to unexpected developments in the housing sector and mortgage markets in these economies. Second, economic stabilization could be enhanced in economies with more developed mortgage markets by a monetary policy approach that responds to house price inflation

in addition to consumer price inflation and the output gap.

These suggestions, however, do not constitute a recommendation that house price objectives should have a dominant role in the conduct of monetary policy. Given the uncertainty surrounding both the shocks hitting the economy and the effects of interest rates on asset price bubbles, house prices should rather be considered one of the many factors that affect the balance of risks to the economic outlook, albeit an essential one for central banks taking a risk-management approach to monetary policy. Paying increased attention to house price developments does not require any change to the formal mandates of major central banks, but rather could be achieved by interpreting existing mandates in a flexible manner, for instance by extending the time horizon for inflation and output targets.

Developments in Housing Finance

Over the past 30 years, there have been profound changes in the housing finance systems in many advanced economies. Until the 1980s, mortgage markets in general were highly regulated. Mortgage lending was dominated by specialized lenders, who faced limited competition in segmented markets—typically, depository institutions such as savings and loan associations in the United States and building societies in the United Kingdom. Regulations set interest rate ceilings and quantitative limits on mortgage credit and repayment periods. These regulations resulted in chronic or temporary credit rationing in the mortgage market and made it difficult for households to access mortgage credit (Girouard and Blöndal, 2001).

Deregulation of mortgage markets, which began in the early 1980s in many advanced economies, introduced competitive pressures from nontraditional lenders. The result was more responsive pricing and an extended range of services, which broadened households' access to mortgage credit. The process of deregulation, however, took different forms in various countries (Diamond and Lea, 1992).

In the United States, the deregulation of housing finance markets coincided with the phasing out of interest rate controls under Regulation Q in the early 1980s (Green and Wachter, 2007). At the same time, the development of a secondary mortgage market greatly facilitated the funding of mortgage lending via capital markets. Together, these prompted a broad range of banks and other financial institutions to enter the mortgage market. In the United Kingdom, deregulation occurred mainly through the abolition of credit controls ("the corset" was abolished in 1980), which heightened competitive pressures in the mortgage market. In Canada, Australia, and the Nordic countries, deregulation of housing financial markets was also relatively rapid and almost completed by the mid-1980s. In all these countries, the lifting of lending and deposit rate ceilings and of credit controls in the early 1980s opened the way to more competition in new segments of the credit market. In the United States, Canada, and Australia, the share of the total household sector's outstanding loans issued by nonbanking financial institutions had doubled by 2005 compared with the 1980s (Figure 3.1, upper panel). This shift was accompanied by the introduction of new mortgage instruments and easier lending policies, and all these changes contributed to the rapid growth of mortgage credit in these countries (Figure 3.1, middle panel).

By contrast, in some continental European countries and in Japan, the reform process was slower and/or less comprehensive. To be sure, restrictions on interest rates were gradually removed and barriers to entry into mortgage markets were eased in Germany, France, and Italy. However, public sector financial institutions continued to dominate the residential mortgage market in these countries, and this constrained the forces of competition: on average in these countries, nonbank financial institutions accounted for about 1 percent of total outstanding loans to the household sector in 2005 (up only slightly from the mid-1990s), compared with about 30 percent in

Figure 3.1. Mortgage Debt and Financial Innovation

Countries that experienced faster and deeper innovations in mortgage markets (the United States, the United Kingdom, Canada, Australia, and the Nordic countries) tend to have higher shares of household loans from nonbank financial institutions and a higher stock of mortgage debt as a ratio to GDP.

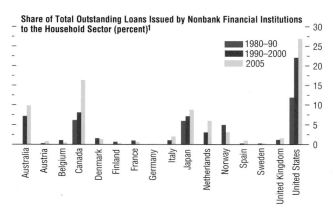

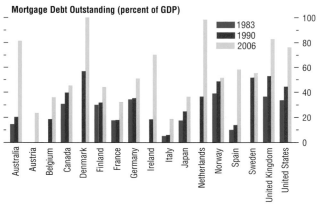

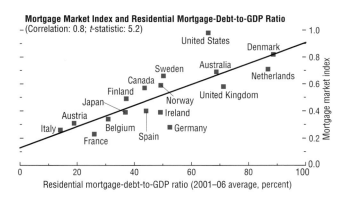

Sources: National accounts; European Mortgage Federation, Hypostat Statistical Tables; Federal Reserve; OECD Analytical Database; Statistics Canada; and IMF staff calculations.
[1]Calculations based on national accounts data. See Chapter 4 of the September 2006 *World Economic Outlook* for an explanation of the methodology used.

the United States. In Japan, interest rate and credit controls began to be removed in the early 1980s, but the process was not completed until the mid-1990s. Mortgage credit did not rise as quickly in the countries that were slower to deregulate their mortgage markets as it did in the previous set of countries (see Figure 3.1, middle panel).

Following the deregulation of mortgage markets, advanced economies all moved toward more competitive housing finance models—in which households have easier access to housing-related credit, thanks to the increased diversity of funding sources, lender types, and loan products. Despite these common patterns, there remain significant cross-country differences in mortgage contracts, which reflect the uneven rates and extent of mortgage market liberalization as well as differences in legal procedures and regulatory structures.[2]

Households' access to housing-related financing depends on certain key institutional features of the mortgage markets:

- The typical loan-to-value (LTV) ratio (the ratio of a mortgage loan to the property's value) and the standard length of mortgage loans: High LTV ratios allow borrowers to take out more debt, whereas longer repayment terms keep debt-service-to-income ratios affordable.
- The ability to make home equity withdrawals and to prepay mortgages without fees: The capacity to borrow against accumulated home equity allows households to tap their housing wealth directly and to borrow more when house prices increase. Early repayment fees constrain households' ability to refinance their mortgage debt in the event interest rates decline.
- Development of secondary markets for mortgage loans: The more developed the second-

ary markets for mortgage loans, the easier it should be for lenders to tap funding via capital markets and, all else being equal, to provide credit to households.

In order to summarize cross-country differences along all these dimensions, a synthetic index of mortgage market development is constructed as a simple average of these five indicators. The index lies between 0 and 1, with higher values indicating easier household access to mortgage credit. The results, shown in Table 3.1, indicate that significant differences remain in the institutional features of mortgage markets across the advanced economies considered in this chapter—differences that may help explain the large inequality in the stock of household mortgage debt (see Figure 3.1, lower panel).[3]

Among these countries, the United States, Denmark, Australia, Sweden, and the Netherlands appear to have the most flexible and "complete" mortgage markets. In these countries, typical LTV ratios are about 80 percent, the standard term of a mortgage is 30 years, mortgage products specifically designed for equity withdrawal are widely marketed, and standard loans include an option to prepay without compensating the lender for capital or market value losses. Moreover, in these countries, financial markets are relatively more important as a source of funding for mortgage lending. For instance, about 60 percent of mortgages were securitized in the United States at end-2004, compared with about 15 percent in the EU-15 (see BIS, 2006). The fact that countries in continental Europe rank at the lower end suggests that mortgage markets in these countries provide more limited access to financing.

---

[2]A crucial factor are the legal protections for collateral. In countries where lenders face high administrative costs and long periods of time in order to realize the value of their collateral in the event of default, they are less likely to make larger loans relative to the value of the property and to lend to higher-risk borrowers.

[3]For "mortgage equity withdrawal" and "refinancing (fee-free prepayment)," values of 0, 0.5, and 1 are assigned to each country depending on whether mortgage equity withdrawal and free prepayment are nonexistent, limited, or widespread, respectively. For the other four variables in Table 3.1, each county is assigned a value between 0 and 1, equal to the ratio to the maximum value across all countries.

Table 3.1. Institutional Differences in National Mortgage Markets and the Mortgage Market Index

	Mortgage Equity Withdrawal[1]	Refinancing (fee-free prepayment)[1]	Typical Loan-to-Value Ratio (percent)[1]	Average Typical Term (years)[1]	Covered Bond Issues (percent of residential loans outstanding)[2]	Mortgage-Backed Security Issues (percent of residential loans outstanding)[2]	Mortgage Market Index[3]
Australia	Yes	Limited	80	25	—	7.9	0.69
Austria	No	No	60	25	2.2	—	0.31
Belgium	No	No	83	20	—	1.9	0.34
Canada	Yes	No	75	25	—	3.6	0.57
Denmark	Yes	Yes	80	30	58.5	0.1	0.82
Finland	Yes	No	75	17	2.6	—	0.49
France	No	No	75	15	1.6	1.0	0.23
Germany	No	No	70	25	3.6	0.2	0.28
Greece	No	No	75	17	—	6.2	0.35
Ireland	Limited	No	70	20	4.0	6.6	0.39
Italy	No	No	50	15	—	4.7	0.26
Japan	No	No	80	25	—	4.7	0.39
Netherlands	Yes	Yes	90	30	0.7	4.6	0.71
Norway	Yes	No	70	17	—	—	0.59
Spain	Limited	No	70	20	11.1	5.7	0.40
Sweden	Yes	Yes	80	25	10.1	0.9	0.66
United Kingdom	Yes	Limited	75	25	0.9	6.4	0.58
United States	Yes	Yes	80	30	—	20.1	0.98

[1]Sources: European Central Bank (2003); Catte and others (2004); Calza, Monacelli, and Stracca (2007).

[2]Average 2003–06. Sources: European Mortgage Federation, Hypostat 2006; Bond Market Association and Federal Reserve for the United States; Dominion Bond Rating Services and Statistics Canada for Canada; Australia Securitization Forum and Reserve Bank of Australia for Australia; FinanceAsia.com and Bank of Japan for Japan.

[3]See text footnote 3 for an explanation of how this index is obtained.

The Housing Sector and the Business Cycle

Some key aspects of the role of the housing sector in the economic cycle of advanced economies have been well established.[4]

- Movements in real house prices have been closely correlated with the economic cycle. As shown in Figure 3.2, however, real house price movements tend to lag cyclical peaks and troughs—generally by one or two quarters, but with some longer lags in some cases (six quarters in Canada, Sweden, Germany, and Italy).[5]

[4]The stylized facts presented in this section are for 18 countries: Australia, Austria, Belgium, Canada, Denmark, Finland, France, Germany, Greece, Ireland, Italy, Japan, Netherlands, Norway, Spain, Sweden, United Kingdom, and United States. See Appendix 1 for a description of the data. See, among others, Case (2000); Girouard and Blöndal (2001); Catte and others (2004); European Commission (2005); European Central Bank (2003); and April 2003 and September 2004 *World Economic Outlook*.

[5]The April 2003 *World Economic Outlook* analyzed the macroeconomic impact of boom-bust housing cycles and showed that housing busts have typically been followed by prolonged periods of very low growth.

- For several economies, there is a clear connection between aggregate economic activity and residential investment. First, residential investment has led the business cycle in several countries, with some exceptions in the euro area (Germany, Italy, and Finland) and the Nordic countries (Sweden and Norway) (see Figure 3.2). Moreover, in some countries—the United States, Ireland, the United Kingdom, Denmark, and the Netherlands—residential investment has added significantly to weakness in the economy on the path to recession (Table 3.2).[6] On average across cycles and countries, residential investment accounted for 10 percent of the weakness in GDP growth a year before the recession, with a peak of 25 percent for the United States (see Leamer, 2007).

[6]To analyze the contributions of residential investment and other GDP components to output fluctuations, the same methodology used by Leamer (2007) is adopted here. See Appendix 1 for further details on Table 3.2.

Figure 3.2. Correlation of Real House Prices and Real Residential Investment with the Output Gap[1]
(X-axis in quarters)

In most countries, real house prices tend to lag the business cycle. Residential investment generally tends to lead the business cycle, with some exceptions in the euro area and Nordic countries.

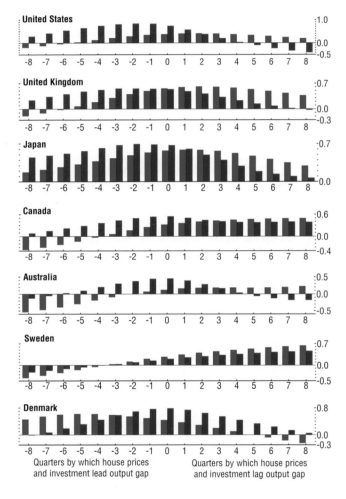

■ Correlations between real house prices and output gap[2]
■ Correlations between real residential investment and output gap[3]

Quarters by which house prices and investment lead output gap

Quarters by which house prices and investment lag output gap

Source: IMF staff calculations.
[1]Real house prices and real residential investment are expressed as deviations from a log-linear trend.
[2]Correlations between output gap at *t* = 0 and real house prices at *t* = –8...+8. For example, a positive correlation at *t* = 2 means house prices lag output gap by two quarters.
[3]Correlations between output gap at *t* = 0 and real residential investment at *t* = –8...+8. For example, a positive correlation at *t* = –2 means residential investment leads output gap by two quarters.

Some studies note, however, that the link between the housing sector and the business cycle appears to have weakened over the past decade. Indeed, with the exception of the euro area countries, housing was a major source of strength over the economic downturn at the beginning of the 2000s. In the United States, for example, the cyclical downturn experienced in 2001 was unusual in that housing investment contributed only mildly to the weakness of GDP before the recession, compared with previous episodes (see Table 3.2). Moreover, in the current housing downturn, a few countries have so far been able to withstand a sharp reversal of the previous housing boom without going into recession. In particular, in the United States, Ireland, Sweden, Finland, Norway, and Canada, the contribution of residential investment to the weakness of GDP growth over the past year has been much larger than during the typical year before a recession over the past three decades (see Table 3.2).[7]

Does this mean that the role of the housing sector in the business cycle has changed? In addressing this question, two factors need to be taken into account. First, recent housing cycles have been unusual in several respects, including in their duration and amplitude. Across the countries considered here, the recent run-up in house prices has lasted on average about twice as long and has been three times stronger than previously (Table 3.3). Second, despite the higher-than-usual synchronization of the housing cycles across countries (see September 2004 *World Economic Outlook*), developments in the housing sector have differed considerably across the set of countries here. House price growth has been particularly strong in Australia, Ireland, the Netherlands, Spain, and the United Kingdom, followed by the United States and some of the Nordic countries. At the other end of the spectrum are Germany and Japan,

[7]All recessions in the United States over the past 35 years, except the recession of the late 1970s, were preceded by a slowdown in residential investment of intensity at least equal to the one experienced since mid-2006.

where prices have remained rather flat or have even declined over the past decade. The current housing sector slowdown also differs widely across countries, as do the prospects for further adjustment (Box 3.1).

These cross-country differences remind us that the dynamics of the housing sector and its link with economic activity can vary substantially depending on the many local factors that affect the supply and demand of housing. For example, in countries with more flexible labor markets and more labor-intensive construction sectors, changes in demand can lead to stronger responses in both housing supply and construction employment, and ultimately can have a larger effect on economic activity. The United States scores high in indices of both labor market flexibility and the labor intensity of the construction sector, which may explain why a weakening of U.S. residential investment is such an important leading indicator of cyclical downturns (Figure 3.3).[8] By contrast, in countries with higher constraints on supply, the housing cycle may involve changes in house price levels more than in construction levels, with possible implications for household wealth and consumer spending.

The characteristics and structure of mortgage markets also play a key role in forging links between housing markets and the business cycle. Indeed, some authors argue that financial deepening over the past two decades may have led to a decoupling of the housing sector from both investment and consumer spending (see Dynan, Elmendorf, and Sichel, 2006; and Campbell and Hercowitz, 2005). Others note that the increased integration of housing finance with capital markets has reduced the interest rate elasticity of residential investment. Together with more stable and predictable monetary policy, this may have reduced the macroeconomic importance

[8]Other local structural factors that are likely to have a role in amplifying or dampening the effects of macroeconomic shocks on the housing sector include land availability, local planning systems, and local taxes on housing (see European Central Bank, 2003).

Figure 3.2 (concluded)[1]

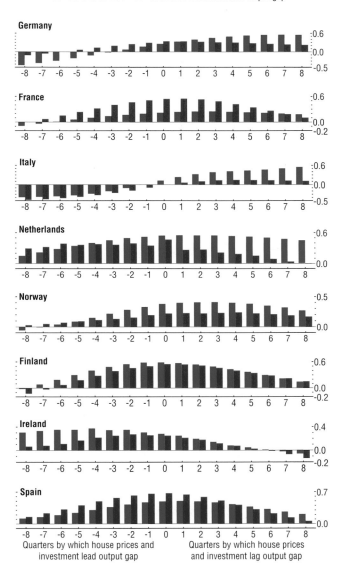

■ Correlations between real house prices and output gap[2]
■ Correlations between real residential investment and output gap[3]

Germany
France
Italy
Netherlands
Norway
Finland
Ireland
Spain

Quarters by which house prices and investment lead output gap

Quarters by which house prices and investment lag output gap

Source: IMF staff calculations.
[1]Real house prices and real residential investment are expressed as deviations from a log-linear trend.
[2]Correlations between output gap at $t = 0$ and real house prices at $t = -8...+8$. For example, a positive correlation at $t = 2$ means house prices lag output gap by two quarters.
[3]Correlations between output gap at $t = 0$ and real residential investment at $t = -8...+8$. For example, a positive correlation at $t = -2$ means residential investment leads output gap by two quarters.

Table 3.2. Abnormal Contributions to GDP Growth Weakness One Year before Recessions
(Percent)[1]

	Average for All Recessions since 1970								Private Residential Investment	
	GDP abnormal cumulative decline (in percentage points)	Consumption		Investment				Net exports	Last recession (after 1995)[2]	Most recent four quarters
		Public	Private	Public	Private residential	Private non-residential	Inventories			
		(relative contributions—sum equals 100)								
United States	−2.6	1	41	3	25	10	8	12	18	56
United Kingdom	−2.2	8	16	3	13	2	13	45	—	0
Japan	−1.7	9	16	35	7	3	3	27	0	0
Germany	−3.3	1	9	4	6	8	22	51	10	0
France	−1.5	11	13	4	10	14	6	42	4	5
Italy	−1.8	13	20	7	8	7	18	28	0	0
Netherlands	−2.6	2	18	3	16	11	18	32	7	0
Canada	−2.7	9	20	2	8	3	5	53	0	9
Norway	−6.4	1	14	1	5	21	35	24	15	28
Australia	−1.7	15	0	6	6	0	15	58	—	0
Sweden	−2.5	14	13	10	9	7	9	39	—	49
Spain	−2.0	5	22	18	11	2	15	28	—	0
Ireland	−5.7	0	33	3	20	15	3	26	—	22
Denmark	−3.1	8	20	4	16	13	2	37	—	0
Finland	−4.8	0	28	1	0	9	0	63	—	2

[1]See Appendix 3.1 for an explanation of the methodology used to calculate the abnormal cumulative contributions to GDP growth weakness before recessions.

[2]Recession timing is as follows: United States: 2001:Q1–2001:Q4; France: 2002:Q3–2003:Q2; Germany: 2002:Q3–2003:Q2; Italy: 2002:Q4–2003:Q2; Netherlands: 2002:Q3–2003:Q2; Norway: 2002:Q2–2003:Q1; Japan: 2001:Q1–2002:Q1. These dates were obtained by updating the April 2002 *World Economic Outlook.*

of the transmission of monetary policy shocks through the housing sector (Bernanke, 2007).[9]

Housing Finance and Spillovers from Housing

The importance of home values as a share of household total wealth suggests that fluctuations in house prices may affect consumer spending through wealth effects. Such effects are complicated, however, because housing has a dual role both as a real asset and as a necessary outlay (a good that produces housing services). As a result, an increase in house prices redistributes wealth within the household sector, rather than boosting net aggregate wealth.[10] Looked at this

[9]Several authors link the decline in the volatility of output and inflation since the early 1980s to improvements in monetary policy (see October 2007 *World Economic Outlook*).

[10]Increases in house prices primarily redistribute wealth from those who intend to consume more housing services in the future toward those who intend to consume fewer.

way, the cyclical impact of house prices on consumer spending reflects the important role of housing as collateral: increases in house prices may raise the value of the collateral available to households, loosen borrowing constraints, and support spending. This effect might be especially strong if income expectations rise at the same time as house prices, giving households an opportunity to borrow against that higher expected income.[11]

Two pieces of cross-country evidence support the hypothesis that the influence of house prices

Because the household sector as a whole is not necessarily made better off by a higher level of house prices, the effect on consumption of higher house prices should be around zero in the long term—but in the short term, a significant net effect would be expected if marginal propensities to consume are substantially different among various groups of households (see Mishkin, 2007; and Muellbauer, 2007).

[11]Both theory and evidence indicate a strong link among income expectations, house price developments, and spending in a range of countries (Benito and others, 2006).

Table 3.3. Features of House Price Cycles[1]

	Duration (quarters)	Amplitude (in percent)
Upturns	26	39.2
Downturns	17	20.4
Recent upturn	59	116.6

[1]Table shows averages across countries. It uses quarterly data for real house prices in the 19 Organization for Economic Cooperation and Development economies considered in the chapter for the period 1970–2007. A peak (trough) is identified as the local high point (low point) in real house prices. If two local peaks are within eight quarters of one another in a particular country, the more extreme of the two is selected.

on household spending stems mainly from housing's role as collateral:

- The correlation between consumption and house prices at business cycle frequencies is stronger in economies with higher values of the mortgage index (Figure 3.4, upper panel).
- The coefficients relating consumer spending to housing wealth in an econometric (error-correction) model for consumption are greater for countries with higher values of the mortgage index (Figure 3.4, lower panel).

Changes in housing finance systems over the past two decades may have increased the potential scope for collateral effects from rising house prices. In principle, however, the resulting impact on consumption and output volatility is ambiguous, because two countervailing effects may be at work. First, households' ability to smooth consumption in the face of adverse shocks to their income may be enhanced through more ready access to financing collateralized by home equity (Dynan, Elmendorf, and Sichel, 2006). Second, macroeconomic fluctuations may be amplified by endogenous variations in collateral constraints tied to real estate values—the financial accelerator analyzed by Kiyotaki and Moore (1997); Bernanke and Gertler (1995); Bernanke and Gilchrist (1999); and Iacoviello (2005).

Although the potential for housing finance to smooth consumption is relevant, it may not fully apply to all households (Dynan and Kohn, 2007). Many households that experience income shortfalls will be unable to borrow to smooth

Figure 3.3. Labor Market Characteristics and the Contribution of Residential Investment to the Business Cycle

The contribution of residential investment to GDP weakness before recessions is larger in economies with lower rigidity in the labor market and a higher share of labor in the construction sector.

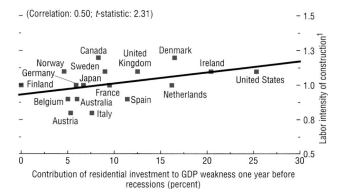

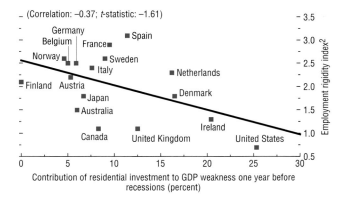

Sources: UNIDO, Industrial Statistics Database; and IMF staff calculations.
[1]Labor intensity of construction is the average over 1979–2005 of the labor share of income in the construction sector relative to the average across countries.
[2]Employment Protection Legislation Index from OECD (2004).

Figure 3.4. Mortgage Market Index, Consumption and House Price Correlation, and the Long-Run Marginal Propensity to Consume out of Housing Wealth

The link between private consumption and housing wealth is stronger in economies with more developed mortgage markets.

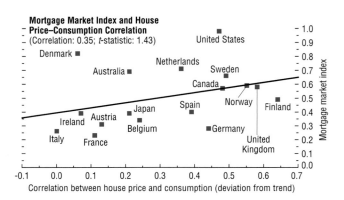

Source: IMF staff calculations.

consumption, even in economies with more flexible mortgage markets. And, if income falls short of expectations at the same time that house prices weaken, some households may need to scale down their spending plans sharply. Furthermore, as illustrated by recent developments among subprime mortgage borrowers in the United States, easier access to housing-related credit may have weakened an important form of discipline on borrowing behavior for some households. The excessive accumulation of debt may mean that for some households an adverse shock to income may bring financial distress and thereby amplify rather than smooth the response of consumption to income (Debelle, 2004). Finally, for consumers who are credit-constrained even when home equity finance is available, innovations that facilitate borrowing against rising home values are likely to increase their consumption response to various economic shocks—consistent with the financial accelerator.[12]

Has there been a change over time in the role of the housing sector in accounting for output fluctuations, and has this varied across countries? To examine these questions more systematically, a vector autoregression (VAR) model for real house prices, residential investment, and other key macroeconomic and monetary policy variables is estimated separately for 18 countries, using quarterly data for the period from 1970 (or the first year for which data are available) to

[12]In the general equilibrium model using housing as collateral that is introduced later in this chapter, such credit-constrained behavior is captured by positing "impatient" households, which have a preference for current consumption rather than consumption smoothing (see also Iacoviello, 2005; and Monacelli, 2008). For example, as house prices increase or interest rates decrease, impatient consumers will desire to raise the amount of their mortgage loans against the greater value of their collateral or to refinance their mortgages and use the additional funds for a variety of purposes—such as consumption, purchase of financial assets, or home improvements. Indeed, housing equity withdrawal seems to have boosted both consumption and residential investment (home improvements) in countries where this product has been prevalent over the past decade (Klyuev and Mills, 2006).

Box 3.1. Assessing Vulnerabilities to Housing Market Corrections

Following a long and pronounced housing boom, several advanced economies have recently experienced symptoms of a cooling housing market (see Figure 1.6, lower panels). In real terms, house price growth has decelerated in many countries, and in a few of them—including the United States, Ireland, and Denmark—real house prices have fallen over the past year. As a share of GDP, real residential investment also has declined in several countries over the recent past, particularly in Australia, the United States, and especially Ireland, where it has fallen by about 3½ percentage points of GDP since its peak over the past five years.

Which countries are most likely to experience a further slowdown in housing prices and residential investment? In this box, the vulnerability to a housing market correction is assessed based on two different indicators: first, the extent to which the increase in house prices in recent years cannot be explained by fundamentals, and second, the size of the increase in the residential investment-to-GDP ratio experienced during the past 10 years.

Assessing Overvaluation in House Prices

For each country, house price growth is modeled as a function of an affordability ratio (the lagged ratio of house prices to disposable incomes), growth in disposable income per capita, short-term interest rates, long-term interest rates, credit growth, and changes in equity prices and working-age population.[1] The unexplained increase in house prices (defined as the "house price gap") might reflect variables omitted from the model—for instance, macroeconomic volatility, household formation, and inward immigration—but could also be interpreted as a measure of overvaluation and, therefore, used to identify which countries may

Note: The main author of this box is Roberto Cardarelli. Gavin Asdorian provided research assistance.

[1]This updates a similar exercise presented in the October 2007 *World Economic Outlook*.

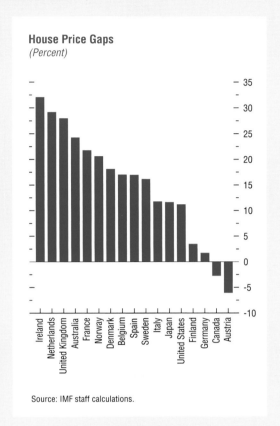

House Price Gaps
(Percent)

Source: IMF staff calculations.

be particularly prone to a correction in house prices.

The first figure shows the percent increase in house prices during the period 1997 to 2007 that is not accounted for by the fundamental drivers of house prices. The countries that experienced the largest unexplained increases in house prices were Ireland, the Netherlands, and the United Kingdom—by the end of the decade, house prices in these countries were about 30 percent higher than justified by fundamentals. A group of other countries, including France, Australia, and Spain, have house price gaps of about 20 percent. Based on this measure, the United States is among the middle-ranked countries in terms of vulnerability to a housing correction, partly reflecting the fact that U.S. house prices have already declined (as measured by the U.S.

Box 3.1 *(continued)*

Office of Federal Housing Enterprise Oversight, OFHEO, in the third quarter of 2007 real house prices were 2¼ percent lower than their peak at end-2006).

Clearly, although a significant house price gap might be expected to be corrected over time, a decline in nominal house prices is only one way for this adjustment to occur. Moderate inflation and support from the fundamental variables driving real house prices may also help close the gap over time. At the same time, negative changes in some of these fundamentals could increase the gap and require an even larger adjustment of house prices. In particular, downward revisions to income expectations and tighter credit conditions may put additional downward pressure on house prices.

Residential Investment

The ratio of residential investment to total output is a measure of the direct exposure of the economy to a weakening housing market. Residential investment, however, does not normally account for a very large share of the economy. Some notable exceptions are Ireland and Spain, where at the end of 2007 residential investment accounted for 12 and 9 percent of GDP, respectively, against an average for advanced economies of about 6½ percent (second figure). The relatively low GDP share of housing construction helps explain why the average contribution of residential investment to economic growth for the advanced economies over the past three decades has been rather low, at about 5 percent.

Still, very large corrections in housing construction may have a nonnegligible impact on economic growth. In the United States, for example, the 1½ percentage points of GDP decline in real residential investment since late 2005 lowered GDP growth by ¾ percent in both 2006 and 2007. Furthermore, as discussed in this chapter, residential investment appears to lead the business cycle in many advanced economies, and a softening of housing construction may be an important factor leading to a cyclical downturn.

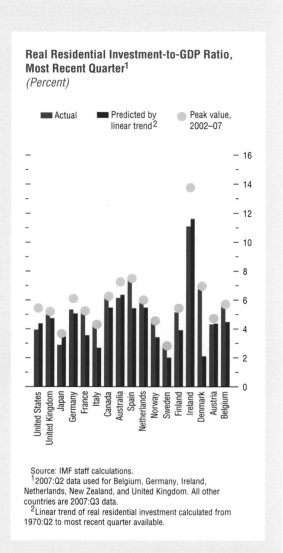

Real Residential Investment-to-GDP Ratio, Most Recent Quarter[1]
(Percent)

Source: IMF staff calculations.
[1] 2007:Q2 data used for Belgium, Germany, Ireland, Netherlands, New Zealand, and United Kingdom. All other countries are 2007:Q3 data.
[2] Linear trend of real residential investment calculated from 1970:Q2 to most recent quarter available.

For these reasons, it may be of interest to assess the exposure of advanced economies to a softening in residential investment. Two pieces of evidence can be used to gauge a country's vulnerability to a decline in housing construction.

First, the residential investment-to-GDP ratio appeared to be significantly above the historical trend in several economies at the end of 2007, especially Spain and Denmark, but also France, Italy, Finland, and Belgium (by about ¾ percentage point of GDP for the euro area) (see second

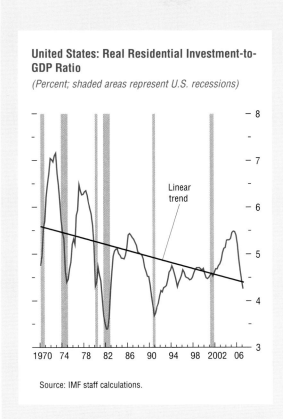

United States: Real Residential Investment-to-GDP Ratio

(Percent; shaded areas represent U.S. recessions)

Source: IMF staff calculations.

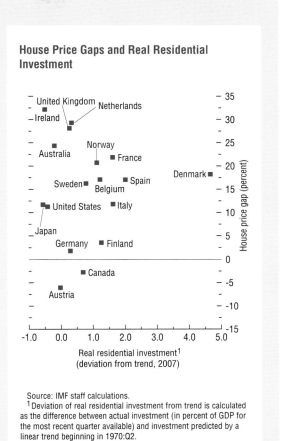

House Price Gaps and Real Residential Investment

Source: IMF staff calculations.
[1] Deviation of real residential investment from trend is calculated as the difference between actual investment (in percent of GDP for the most recent quarter available) and investment predicted by a linear trend beginning in 1970:Q2.

figure). In other economies, the residential investment-to-GDP ratio at mid- or end-2007 seems close to, or even below, the historical trend. In particular, the decline in residential investment since early 2006 seems to have taken the ratio back to trend in Ireland, the United States, and Australia. However, this does not mean that residential investment will not experience a further decline in these countries. As demand for housing cools and inventories build, a below-trend residential investment ratio may be necessary to bring the stock of housing back down to desired levels. Indeed, on average over the past three decades, cyclical downturns in the United States have seen residential investment falling by about 1 percentage point of GDP below trend (with a maximum of 2 percentage points in the recession of the early 1980s) (third figure). Hence, based on historical evidence and the still-high inventories of unsold homes, residential investment in the United States could

decline by another ½ to 1 percentage point of GDP in the coming quarters.

Second, there seems to be a positive association between the increase in residential investment over the past decade and the extent of house price overvaluation (fourth figure). This suggests that countries that experienced the greatest exuberance in house prices also saw the largest acceleration in residential investment, as the supply of housing responded to the price signal. Residential investment in these countries thus may be more exposed to a further correction of house prices, consistent with fundamentals. Based on this approach, Denmark, Spain, and France appear to be the most vulnerable economies, whereas the United Kingdom and the Netherlands seem to be less at risk, because

Box 3.1 *(concluded)*

they have not experienced as pronounced an increase in residential investment over the past decade despite the strong increases in house prices.

Conclusions

Many advanced economies have experienced a remarkably large and long-lasting run-up in their national housing markets in recent years. Nonetheless, housing market developments have varied across countries, reflecting the largely local nature of many factors affecting the demand and supply of housing. The importance of these country-specific factors means that the U.S. housing market correction need not necessarily presage corrections elsewhere. Neverthe-

less, allowing for country-specific influences suggests that similar pressures also exist in other national housing markets.

Countries that look particularly vulnerable to a further correction in house prices are Ireland, the United Kingdom, the Netherlands, and France. In these economies, it is difficult to account for the magnitude of the run-up in house prices on the basis of those countries' fundamentals. Furthermore, a weakening housing market can also present a direct drag on growth from reductions in residential investment. Countries that witnessed the largest run-up in house prices also appear more vulnerable to this effect—in particular, Denmark, Spain, and France.

2006.[13] For countries with sufficiently long data series, the sample period is split into two parts, from 1970 to the mid-1980s and from the mid-1980s to 2006, to examine changes over time.

Within the model, a monetary policy shock is identified through a conventional recursive identification scheme: short-term interest rates are allowed to influence all other variables with a one-quarter lag, but they have an immediate effect on the term spread. A housing demand shock is identified by combining the recursive identification strategy with sign restrictions: that is, housing demand shocks have no contemporaneous effect on output and prices, and they move residential investment and house prices in the same direction.[14]

- On average across the countries considered, housing demand shocks account for a large proportion (one-fourth to about one-half) of

the observed fluctuations in residential investment and house prices (Table 3.4).[15] This suggests that the housing sector tends to have its own distinct dynamics (see also Zhu, 2005). Moreover, these internal dynamics strengthened in the second subperiod, suggesting that the housing sector may have become a more important source of economic volatility over the past two decades than previously.

- The extent to which housing demand shocks explain fluctuations in the aggregate economy varies significantly across countries and over time (Figure 3.5). In the United States and Japan, housing demand shocks account for a share of between 20 and 25 percent of the variance in output (after eight quarters) in the second period, up substantially from the first period. By contrast, housing demand shocks in many European countries account for 5 percent or less of the variation in output. Interestingly, in countries where exogenous housing demand shocks play a more important role in shaping the housing market, these

[13]The model includes six variables: output, inflation (GDP deflator), real house prices, residential investment, the short-term (nominal) interest rate, and the long-term interest rate spread over the short-term rate. See Appendix 3.1 for a description of the data used.

[14]This model is broadly similar to that recently estimated for the United States by Jarociński and Smets (2007). See Appendix 3.1 for further details on the methodology and results of the VAR.

[15]The combined effect of the other variables in the VAR—that is, GDP, inflation, interest rates, and the terms spread—accounts for the rest.

Table 3.4. Forecast Variance Decomposition: Housing Demand Shocks—Average across Countries[1]

Time Horizon (quarters)	1	4	12	18
	(output, in percent)			
First period	4	8	8	9
Second period	1	4	8	12
	(residential investment, in percent)			
First period	40	31	26	25
Second period	49	49	39	33
	(house prices, in percent)			
First period	44	29	21	21
Second period	62	55	38	30

[1]Percent of the variance of the error made in forecasting a variable (e.g., output) at a given time horizon (e.g., 12 quarters) as a result of a housing demand shock.

shocks also have a stronger influence on the overall economy (Figure 3.6).

These patterns suggest that the role of the housing market in providing collateral for loans reinforces the links from the housing market to the wider economy. Figure 3.7 provides further support for this interpretation: it shows that countries with a more flexible system of housing finance tend to experience stronger spillovers from the housing sector.

Housing Finance and Housing as a Transmission Channel for Monetary Policy

Figure 3.8 summarizes the main channels through which monetary policy is transmitted through the housing sector. Changes in interest rates affect domestic demand both directly, by affecting residential construction and household spending plans through the change in cost and availability of credit, and indirectly, by moving house prices. Changes in house prices in turn may affect aggregate demand by altering the incentives for housing investment (Tobin's q effect[16]) and by changing households' ability

[16]According to Tobin's q approach, the profitability of property investment depends on the ratio between house prices and construction costs. When property prices rise above the cost of construction, it is profitable for property developers to construct new buildings.

Figure 3.5. Share of Output Variation Explained by Housing Demand Shocks[1]
(Percent, at eight quarters)

There is great heterogeneity across countries in the share of output fluctuations accounted for by housing demand shocks.

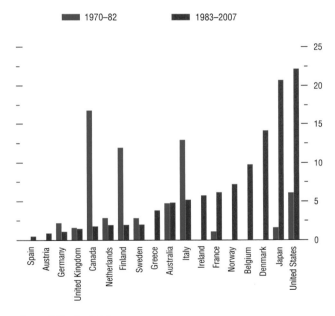

Source: IMF staff calculations.
[1]The absence of values in the first subperiod for some countries reflects a lack of sufficiently long time series on housing variables. See Appendix 3.1 for details on the data used in the vector autoregression.

Figure 3.6. Correlation between the Shares of Output and Housing Sector Variation Explained by Housing Demand Shocks
(Percent, at eight quarters, 1983–2007)

In countries where housing demand shocks explain a larger share of fluctuations in housing variables, they also explain a larger share of output fluctuations.

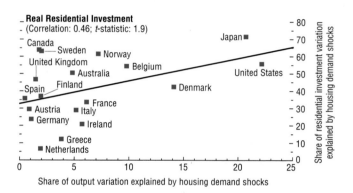

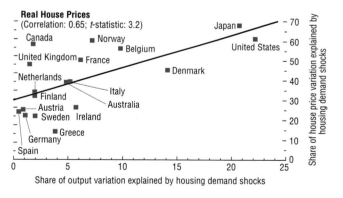

Source: IMF staff calculations.

to use the collateral value of their homes to finance consumption.

Before the deregulation of mortgage markets, changes in monetary policy generally had a strong effect on residential investment by changing the available quantity of housing credit. Housing finance was dominated at that time by specialized lenders who funded long-term mortgages mainly through shorter-term savings deposits that were subject to an interest rate ceiling. Therefore, increases in policy interest rates would trigger an outflow of such savings deposits and squeeze mortgage finance institutions' net incomes—both of which would result in reduced credit availability.

As mortgage markets were integrated into the wider financial system, funding for housing came from a much broader set of investors, and the importance of credit availability as a channel of monetary policy transmission was greatly diminished. Indeed, several authors attribute the decline in the amplitude of housing investment cycles since the mid-1980s in the United States to the reduced importance of the credit volume effects of monetary policy (see Estrella, 2002; Schnure, 2005; and Bernanke, 2007).

At least three other considerations, however, suggest that financial deregulation may have strengthened the role of housing in monetary policy transmission. First, with increased competition in housing finance, mortgage retailers may adjust interest rates more rapidly in response to policy rates. Second, because households and firms have access to a wider array of credit products, residential investment and consumer durable expenditure may respond more strongly to changes in interest rates.[17] Third, greater access to mortgage credit may make house prices more responsive to interest rates, thereby

---

[17]Estimating a consumption equation for the United Kingdom, Muellbauer (2007) shows that the relaxation of credit constraints over the past two decades increased the role of intertemporal substitution and thus the interest rate channel for monetary policy. For example, households have become better able to substitute consumption now for consumption in the future in the wake of a reduction in interest rates.

strengthening the collateral effect of monetary policy (Iacoviello and Minetti, 2002).

In order to assess the net effect of these dynamics on the role of housing in monetary policy transmission in the United States, the VAR model is used to compare the response of residential investment, house prices, and output to monetary policy shocks in the United States in the periods before and after mortgage market deregulation.[18]

The results confirm that there are noticeable differences between the two periods. Monetary policy shocks had a smaller impact on both residential investment and output in the second period, but their effect lasted much longer (Figure 3.9). House prices reacted more slowly during the second period, but their decrease was more persistent and eventually stronger—reaching their maximum decline after about four years, compared with two years during the first period.[19]

These results, however, do not take into account differences in the size and duration of monetary policy shocks in the two sub-samples. Before the mid-1980s, monetary policy was characterized by large swings in interest rates—in the first subsample, the monetary policy shock corresponds to an initial 130-basis-point increase in the federal funds rate, which returns to the initial level after about two years. By contrast, since the mid-1980s monetary policy has become more predictable and systematic in its response—in the second subsample, the increase in the federal funds rate in the period of the shock is much smaller (about 35 basis points) and more persistent (it fades away only after three years).

To take account of these differences in monetary policy shocks, the maximum responses of output and housing variables are normalized by the increase in short-term interest rates during the period of the shock—yielding the elasticity

[18]These are impulse response functions to a monetary policy shock, identified as a one-standard-deviation change in interest rates.

[19]See also McCarthy and Peach (2002).

Figure 3.7. Correlation between the Share of Output Variation Explained by Housing Demand Shocks and the Mortgage Market Index
(Percent, at eight quarters, 1983–2007)

In countries with more developed mortgage markets, housing demand shocks tend to explain a larger share of output fluctuations.

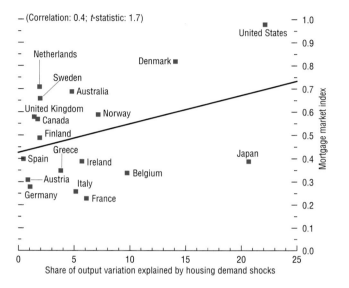

Source: IMF staff calculations.

Figure 3.8. Housing and the Monetary Transmission Mechanism

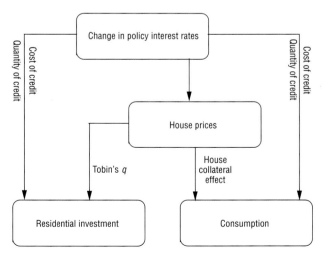

Figure 3.9. Effect of Monetary Policy Shocks on Output and Housing Sector Variables in the United States[1]
(Percent)

In the second period, residential investment and output react less strongly to monetary policy tightening, but their decline is more persistent. Real house prices react more slowly, but their maximum decline is stronger than in the earlier period.

— Output (right scale)
— Real residential investment (left scale)
— Real house prices (left scale)

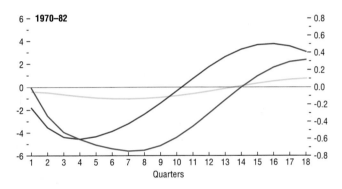

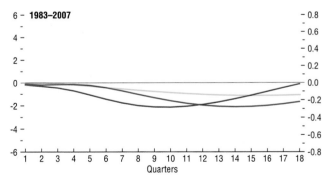

Source: IMF staff calculations.
[1]Monetary policy shocks are defined as a one-standard-deviation increase in short-term interest rates.

of these variables to a 100-basis-point tightening of interest rates. Such normalization suggests that the elasticity of residential investment to monetary policy shocks in the United States has declined only modestly during the second period, whereas the elasticity of house prices and output has increased (Figure 3.10).[20]

For the other economies, there is no clear pattern of change over time in the elasticity of residential investment to monetary policy shocks, although the sensitivity is estimated to have risen somewhat in the United Kingdom, the Netherlands, and France. By contrast, the response of house prices and output to estimated monetary policy shocks is generally stronger during the second period across the countries considered. Of particular relevance for this analysis is that countries with more developed mortgage markets also tend to have higher elasticities of house prices and residential investment to monetary policy shocks during the second period (Figure 3.11).[21] Moreover, the response of output to monetary policy shocks is also greater in economies that have more flexible mortgage markets.

Overall, these results suggest that the housing finance system has an important influence over the role of housing in the monetary transmis-

[20]In particular, a 100-basis-point increase in the policy rate in the United States leads to an estimated reduction in residential investment of about 4 percent in the second period, against a 4½ percent decline in the first period—estimates broadly in line with those in Jarociński and Smets (2007) and Erceg and Levin (2002). On house prices, a 100-basis-point increase in the policy rate in the United States leads to a fall in real house prices of about 3 percent from baseline in the second period, compared with a decline of 1 percent in the first period—broadly similar to Jarociński and Smets (2007) and Iacoviello and Neri (2007).

[21]While positive, the correlation between monetary policy shocks and the peak response of house prices is not statistically significant because of some outliers, such as Spain, France, and Italy, where house prices respond strongly to unexpected changes in monetary policy despite the relatively low level of the mortgage market index for these countries. This may reflect the relevance of direct cash-flow effects in the overall monetary transmission mechanism for the euro area (see Giuliodori, 2004, for similar results regarding France and Italy).

sion mechanism, but that the interrelationship is complex.[22] In particular, the results show that easier access to housing collateral may link house prices more closely to monetary policy shocks, and that the effects of monetary shocks on output are larger in those economies where housing finance markets are relatively more developed and competitive. At the same time, no systematic relationship is found between mortgage market development and the effects of monetary policy shocks on residential investment.

The same VAR framework also can be used to model what would have happened to the recent housing booms if systematically tighter monetary policy had been maintained during the preceding five years. This can be done using two counterfactual scenarios, one that traces the path of house prices and residential investment with interest rates constant throughout that period, and another with rates 100 basis points above the rates actually observed.[23]

Comparing these counterfactuals with the actual path of housing variables suggests that the unusually low level of interest rates in the United States between 2001 and 2003 contributed somewhat to the elevated rate of expansion in the housing market, in terms of both housing investment and the run-up in house prices up to mid-2005 (Figure 3.12), as has been argued by Taylor (2007).[24] The impact of easy monetary conditions on the housing cycle presumably was magnified by the loosening of lending standards and excessive risk-taking by lenders, as suggested by the boom-bust credit cycle in the

---

[22]Calza, Monacelli, and Stracca (2007); Aoki, Proudman, and Vlieghe (2002); and Iacoviello and Minetti (2002).

[23]It is worth mentioning that imposing an alternative path for interest rates is susceptible to the Lucas critique, namely, that spending decisions would be altered by a different policy regime. This effect should be limited by the fact that the counterfactuals are considered for a relatively short period of time. See also Sims (1998).

[24]Iacoviello and Neri (2007) also suggest that monetary conditions explain a nonnegligible portion of the increase in U.S. house prices (more than one-quarter) and residential investment (about one-half) between 2000 and 2005.

Figure 3.10. Elasticity of Real Residential Investment, Real House Prices, and Output to a 100-Basis-Point Increase in Short-Term Interest Rates[1]
(Percent)

Normalizing the maximum decline of output and housing variables by the size of the monetary policy shock suggests that the interest rate elasticity of residential investment and output has declined only modestly in the United States, and that the elasticity of house prices has increased in the majority of countries.

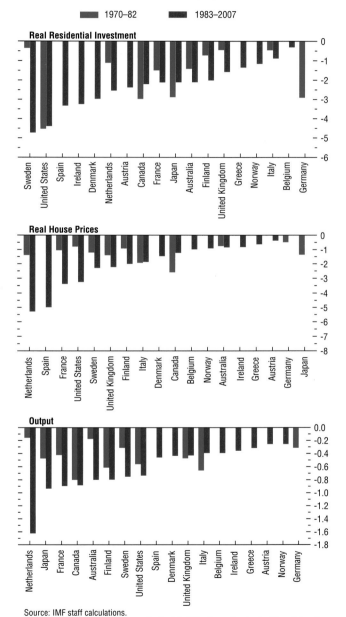

Source: IMF staff calculations.
[1]Peak impulse responses to a one-standard-deviation innovation in short-term interest rates divided by the initial change in interest rates. For Austria, Belgium, Denmark, Greece, Ireland, Norway, and Spain, no data are available for the first period. For Germany, the missing elasticities in the second period reflect the "wrong" sign of the response, possibly reflecting the impact of German unification (see also Calza, Monacelli, and Stracca, 2007).

Figure 3.11. Interest Rate Elasticity of Real Residential Investment, Real House Prices, and Output and the Mortgage Market Index[1]

In the second subperiod (1983–2007) the interest rate elasticity of both housing variables and output tends to be higher in countries with more developed mortgage markets.

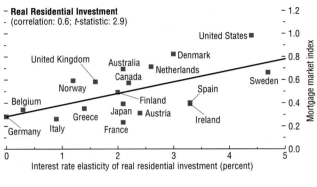

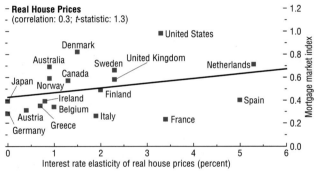

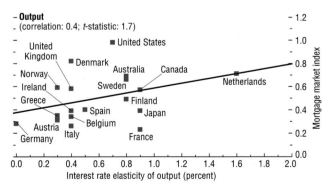

Source: IMF staff calculations.
[1]The interest rate elasticity of real residential investment, for example, is the maximum response (in absolute value) of real residential investment to a one-standard-deviation increase in the interest rate divided by the size of the interest rate increase at the time of the shock.

U.S. subprime mortgage market (Dell'Ariccia, Igan, and Laeven, 2008). A similar analysis has also been carried out for two smaller European economies, Ireland and the Netherlands, whose mortgage markets differ significantly in their degree of flexibility, according to the index used in this chapter (0.34 for Ireland and 0.69 for the Netherlands). For Ireland, which has a less-flexible market, the analysis does not indicate that a tighter monetary policy would have resulted in significantly different housing market outcomes. In the Netherlands, however, the analysis suggests that tighter monetary policy during this period might have contained the housing dynamics, especially with regard to house prices.

Should Changes in the Housing Cycle Affect the Conduct of Monetary Policy?

The recent house price boom in many advanced economies, and the prospect of a global downturn driven by the sharp softening of the housing sector in the United States, have reignited the debate over whether monetary policymakers should respond to asset prices, and in particular to house prices. There is general agreement that when asset prices fall sharply—for example, after the bursting of an asset price bubble—monetary policymakers should react promptly and aggressively to contain inflation and stabilize output. However, there is much less consensus on how best to respond to rising asset prices.

In particular, central bank orthodoxy suggests that monetary policymakers should refrain from targeting any specific level of asset prices and should respond to changes in asset prices only insofar as they affect inflation and output outcomes and expectations (Mishkin, 2007). The difficulties of identifying bubbles in asset prices and the uncertainty over the impact of monetary policy on asset prices are the main arguments against responding to asset price changes over and above the response warranted by their implications for inflation and output.

However, some argue that there are benefits to be derived from "leaning against the wind," that is, increasing interest rates to stem the growth of house price bubbles and help restrain the buildup of financial imbalances (Borio and White, 2004; and Bordo and Jeanne, 2002). Such a preemptive response could diminish the risks that a bigger crash would occur later on, with serious consequences for the real economy and inflation. Moreover, restricting monetary policy to "cleaning up the mess" after a decline in asset prices could encourage excessive asset price swings and could reinforce market perceptions that there are only limited risks to investors' asset price bets (Ahearne and others, 2005).

Based on this view, central banks should be ready to respond to abnormally rapid increases in asset prices by tightening monetary policy even if these increases do not seem likely to affect inflation and output over the short term. This view need not, however, imply any change in the mandate of central banks, particularly those that operate with an inflation target-ing regime: asset price misalignments matter because of the risks they pose for financial stabil-ity and the threat of a severe output contraction should a bubble burst, which would also lower inflation pressure. But given the considerable time it takes for imbalances to build up and unfold, paying attention to asset prices may entail a lengthening of the time horizon for inflation targets beyond the one to two years typical of many inflation targeting regimes (Borio, 2006).[25]

Recently, an increasing number of cen-tral bankers—including some at the Bank of England, Norges Bank, Bank of Canada, and Reserve Bank of New Zealand—have argued that central banks should on rare occasions "lean against" exceptionally large surges in asset prices. A concrete example is provided by the decision of the Swedish central bank in early 2006 to increase its policy rate despite reducing

[25]Although the focus of this chapter is on monetary policy, prudential and regulatory financial policies are also essential tools for constraining the procyclical mechanisms in financial markets that tend to amplify the business cycle (see Borio and White, 2004).

Figure 3.12. Monetary Policy Counterfactuals
(Year-over-year growth rates; percent)

The increase in house prices and residential investment in the United States over the past six years would have been much more contained had short-term interest rates remained unchanged. The difference would have been relatively small in Ireland and, especially for residential investment, in the Netherlands.

—— Actual
—— With no change in short-term interest rates
—— With short-term interest rates 100 basis points higher

United States

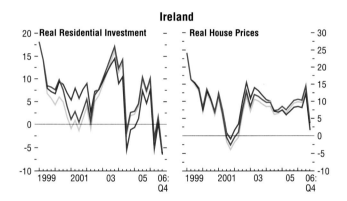

Ireland

Netherlands

Source: IMF staff calculations.

its inflation forecast—a decision justified with an explicit reference to rising household debt and house prices. Furthermore, recent statements from officials in a number of central banks—including at the Bank of England, European Central Bank, and Reserve Bank of Australia—acknowledge that central banks may need to look at the effects of asset prices on inflation and output beyond the usual one- to two-year horizon (see Mishkin, 2007).

The main findings from this analysis are that innovations in housing finance systems have increased the scale of spillovers from the housing sector to the general economy and that housing seems to be particularly important in the monetary transmission mechanism in countries with more developed mortgage markets. These findings raise the question of whether the response of monetary policymakers to changes in the housing sector should differ depending on the level of development of their mortgage markets.

In order to address this issue, a macroeconomic model with a stylized representation of the housing sector, as in Calza, Monacelli, and Stracca (2007), is used to illustrate how the role of housing as collateral in the lending process may affect consumption and output volatility.

This model captures the idea that a fraction of consumers may be credit-constrained by assuming a mix of "patient" and "impatient" consumers: the latter do not smooth consumption based on permanent income, but have preferences tilted toward current consumption.[26] Their access to credit is constrained by the value of their collateral, which is endogenously tied to the evolution of house prices. A more developed mortgage market is represented by a higher LTV ratio—a parameter that determines the extent

to which housing can be used as collateral for borrowing to consume nondurable goods. Monetary policy follows a simple, Taylor-type interest rate rule, responding to changes in the inflation and output gaps.

Despite its stylized nature, this structural model is consistent with the empirical findings from the VAR that output and consumption are more responsive to housing demand shocks in economies with more developed mortgage markets. In economies with a higher LTV ratio (90 percent), as residential investment and house prices increase following a positive housing demand shock, impatient consumers are allowed to borrow more against the rising value of their collateral, and thus to consume more nondurable goods, compared with those in economies with a lower LTV ratio (60 percent) (Figure 3.13, upper panel).[27] Similarly, a higher LTV ratio amplifies the decline in output and consumption following a negative financial shock, identified as an exogenous tightening of lending standards that restricts the ability of households to borrow against collateral for any given level of house prices (Figure 3.13, lower panel).

Having built a model that rationalizes the empirical evidence about the link between housing and economic volatility, the next step is to derive some normative implications for monetary policy. Although the model is highly stylized—abstracting from many factors affecting monetary policy decisions—the exercise is nevertheless instructive because it provides some insight into how monetary policy should vary according to the characteristics of mortgage markets in an economy where borrowing limits are tied to collateral values and where some households do not behave in the farsighted way that is more traditionally supposed.[28]

---

[26]Impatient consumers always borrow the maximum amount possible given their income, although that borrowing may be insufficient to allow them to consume their desired amount of housing services or other goods. Because some households borrow as much as possible, the model allows for the possibility that some households may be shortsighted in their financial planning, which is consistent with the recent lesson from the U.S. subprime market.

[27]It should be noted that the monetary policy responses considered in this section are to changes in fundamental determinants of housing demand, rather than to speculative, bubble-type developments in the housing market.

[28]In particular, the model does not allow for uncertainty concerning the types of shocks hitting the economy and for the possibility of a time-variant, nonnormal

A first result from the model is that, for any given monetary policy objective, monetary policymakers in economies with more developed mortgage markets must respond more aggressively to housing demand and financial shocks, compared with those in economies with less-developed housing finance systems. This is because such shocks have a greater impact on inflation in economies with a higher LTV ratio, reflecting the larger response of consumption and output in these economies. As an example, assuming for simplicity that the sole objective of monetary policy is to stabilize inflation, a positive housing demand shock would require a larger increase in the policy rate of interest in an economy with a higher LTV ratio than in an economy with a lower LTV ratio (Figure 3.14, upper panel). By contrast, offsetting the deflationary impact of a negative financial shock would require a larger decrease in the policy rate in an economy with a higher LTV ratio (Figure 3.14, lower panel).

A second result is that monetary policymakers may need to pay particular attention to house prices in economies with more developed mortgage markets, where house prices play a special role in providing collateral for loans. Indeed, Table 3.5 shows that the monetary policy rule that minimizes the central bank's loss function (with inflation and output gap volatility as arguments) includes *both* the output gap and house price inflation for each type of shock considered in economies with LTV ratios equal to 90 percent. By contrast, when the LTV ratio is lower, at 60 percent, adding house price inflation to the Taylor-type interest rate rule does not improve economic stabilization when the economy is hit by a housing demand shock or a productivity shock. The main reason underlying this result is that, in this model, responding to house price inflation is an effective way of

distribution of these shocks, and thus it is not equipped to address risk-management considerations that are key in monetary policy decision making (see Mishkin, 2008). Moreover, the conclusions presented here might change if the objective of monetary policy were welfare maximization rather than economic stabilization.

Figure 3.13. Macroeconomic Model with Housing as Collateral: Responses of Output and Consumption to Shocks for Different Loan-to-Value (LTV) Ratios
(Percent deviation from model steady state)

Following a positive housing demand shock and a negative financial shock, output and consumption react more strongly in economies with higher LTV ratios than in economies with lower LTV ratios.

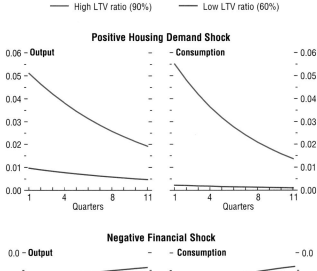

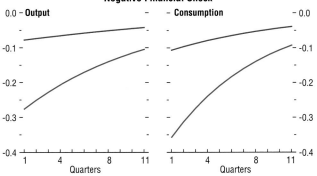

Source: IMF staff calculations.

dampening the output volatility caused by the financial accelerator effect resulting from the endogenous variation in the value of housing as collateral. Because it is precisely in economies with a high LTV ratio that this volatility is strong, the gains from responding to house price movements are large.[29] In contrast, in economies with less-developed mortgage markets, paying special attention to house prices does not provide additional benefits compared with a monetary policy rule that responds to both inflation and the output gap.

Conclusions

The sharp weakening of the housing sector in several advanced economies over the past couple of years, and especially the financial turbulence triggered by increasing defaults in the subprime mortgage market in the United States, have raised concerns that, as a result of innovations in mortgage markets, the housing sector could be a source of macroeconomic instability.

The evidence presented in this chapter indeed suggests that countries where innovation in housing finance systems has advanced the most are more exposed to shocks originating in the housing sector. The reason could be that the greater "liquidity" of housing equity in these economies has amplified the financial accelerator effect from endogenous variations in the collateral constraint tied to the value of homes. The stylized model of the role of housing as collateral provides an explanation of these empirical findings that suggests economies with more developed financial markets and households that are shortsighted in their financial planning are more exposed to housing shocks.

This chapter also suggests that house prices and overall output have become more responsive to monetary policy shocks in the wake of mortgage deregulation and that this responsiveness tends to be greater in economies with

Figure 3.14. Macroeconomic Model with Housing as Collateral: Response of Nominal Interest Rates to a Positive Housing Demand Shock and a Negative Financial Shock for Various Loan-to-Value (LTV) Ratios
(Percent deviation from model steady state)

After a positive housing demand shock and in order to fully stabilize inflation, interest rates have to increase more strongly in economies with higher LTV ratios. In these economies, interest rates have to decrease more following a negative financial shock.

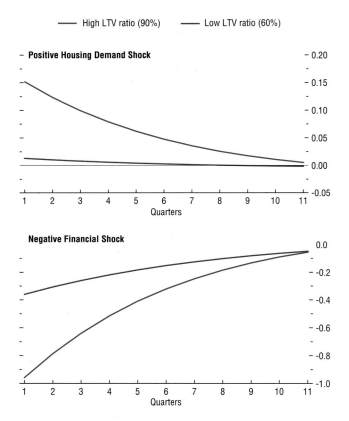

Source: IMF staff calculations.

[29]See Gilchrist and Saito (2006) for similar results in a model with equity prices.

Table 3.5. Optimal Coefficients in the Taylor Rule[1]

	Financial Shocks		Housing Demand Shocks		Productivity Shocks	
	High LTV	Low LTV	High LTV	Low LTV	High LTV	Low LTV
House price growth	0.4	0.75	1.2	0	0.95	0
Output gap	0.35	0.15	0.1	0.1	0	0

[1]The Taylor rule is defined as $i_t = \phi_\pi \pi_t + \phi_x x_t + \phi_q \Delta_q$, where π_t and x_t are deviations of inflation and output gap from their steady-state values, and Δ_q denotes real house price growth. The optimal coefficients on house price growth and output gap are those that minimize a quadratic loss function, with the variance of π_t and x_t as arguments. The inflation coefficient is held constant and equal to 2. High LTV = loan-to-value ratio equal to 90 percent. Low LTV = loan-to-value ratio equal to 60 percent.

more developed mortgage markets. At the same time, the evidence about the responsiveness of residential investment to monetary policy is mixed. For the United States, the results suggest that monetary policy shocks have had a somewhat smaller impact on residential investment since the mid-1980s, presumably because of the reduced importance of the quantity-rationing effect from these shocks and the more predictable and systematic monetary policy pursued during this period. In some other countries, the elasticity of residential investment to monetary policy shocks seems actually to have increased over time. Overall, the results are consistent with the hypothesis that there has been a change in the transmission of monetary policy through housing in economies with more flexible and developed mortgage markets, namely, that monetary policy is now transmitted more through the price of homes than through residential investment.

This chapter also examines the implications for monetary policy of changes in mortgage markets. First, it suggests that monetary policymakers may need to respond more aggressively to housing demand shocks in economies with more developed mortgage markets—that is, with higher LTV ratios and thus, presumably, higher stocks of mortgage debt. They may also need to respond more aggressively to financial shocks that affect the amount of credit available for any given level of house prices. Hence, the model would "predict" a more aggressive reduction of interest rates in the United States compared with the euro area in the face of recent turmoil in the credit markets—and this is in line with what has occurred so far.

Second, this chapter suggests that, in economies with more developed mortgage markets, economic stabilization could be improved by a monetary policy approach that responds to house price developments in addition to consumer price inflation and output developments. In a risk-management framework, such an approach would need to accommodate the uncertainty about what factors drive house price dynamics—in particular, whether house prices reflect changes in fundamentals or speculative forces—and their impact on the economy. House prices would seem relevant for calculating the risks to the outlook for overall economic activity and prices, particularly during periods of rapid change in house prices and when house prices seem to be moving out of line with historical norms.

Such attention to house price developments need not require a change in the formal mandates of major central banks, but could be achieved by interpreting existing mandates more flexibly, for instance, by extending the horizon for inflation and output targets. Moreover, it is important that such an approach be applied symmetrically: while an aggressive easing may be justified in response to a rapid slowdown of the housing sector, some "leaning against the wind" may also prove useful to limit the risk of a buildup of housing market and financial imbalances. In this context, monetary policy certainly should not bear the full weight of responding to possible asset price bubbles; regulatory policy also has a critical role to play in guarding against the inappropriate loosening of lending standards that may fuel extreme house price movements.

Appendix 3.1. Data and Methodology

Data

Variable	Source
Real house prices	Organization for Economic Cooperation and Development (OECD), Bank for International Settlements (BIS)
Real residential investment	OECD Analytical Database
Real private consumption	OECD Analytical Database
Real disposable income	OECD Analytical Database
Consumer price index	OECD Analytical Database
Short-term interest rates	OECD Analytical Database, International Financial Statistics (IFS) database, OECD *Economic Outlook,* Haver Analytics
Long-term interest rates	OECD Analytical Database, IFS Database, OECD *Economic Outlook,* Haver Analytics
Output gap	OECD Analytical Database
Housing wealth	OECD
Share price index	IFS database, Haver Analytics

Note: Nominal house prices are deflated using the Consumer Price Index (BIS data only).

House Prices

Country	Source	Start Date
Australia	OECD	1970:Q1
Austria	BIS	1986:Q3
Belgium	BIS	1988:Q1
Canada	OECD	1970:Q1
Denmark	OECD	1970:Q1
Finland	OECD	1970:Q1
France	OECD	1970:Q1
Germany	OECD	1970:Q1
Greece	BIS	1993:Q1
Ireland	OECD	1970:Q1
Italy	OECD	1970:Q1
Japan	OECD	1970:Q1
Netherlands	OECD	1970:Q1
Norway	OECD	1970:Q1
Spain	OECD	1971:Q1
Sweden	OECD	1970:Q1
United Kingdom	OECD	1970:Q1
United States	OECD	1970:Q1

Contributions to GDP Growth

The contribution of residential investment and other GDP components to output fluctuations around the business cycle, shown in Table 3.2, are calculated as follows:

- The quarterly contribution to total GDP growth of eight different components was cal-
culated for 18 advanced economies. The eight components are (1) government consumption, (2) private consumption, (3) government gross fixed capital formation, (4) private residential investment, (5) private nonresidential investment, (6) inventories, (7) exports, and (8) imports. When possible, contributions from national statistical sources were used. When not available, the contributions were estimated using OECD data on quarterly national accounts and the methodology described in OECD's *Understanding National Accounts,* 2007.

- The "abnormal" contribution of the components to GDP growth was calculated as the difference between the actual and "normal" contributions to GDP—the latter was obtained by smoothing the actual contributions over the whole period using a kernel regression (as in Leamer, 2007).

- The peaks and troughs of the business cycles were determined using the same methodology as in the "Recessions and Recoveries" chapter of the April 2002 *World Economic Outlook.* This methodology uses a simplified Bry-Boschan (1971) dating algorithm, which determines peaks and troughs in log level of real GDP by first searching for maximums and minimums in five-quarter data windows, and then picking pairs of adjacent, locally absolute maximums and minimums that meet the criteria for the minimal duration (five quarters) and phases (two quarters) of cycles.

- The abnormal contributions were then cumulated over the four quarters before business cycle peaks. The average across all business cycles since 1970 of the cumulative GDP growth decline in this period is shown in the first column of Table 3.2 (for example, cumulative GDP growth was on average 2.6 percentage points lower than trend in the year before a recession in the United States).

- The rest of the table shows the contributions to this abnormal cumulative decline of GDP growth from its eight components. For example, in the United States, below-trend growth in private residential investment accounted

Table 3.6. Estimates of the Error-Correction Model of Consumption

	Canada	France	Germany	Italy	Japan	United Kingdom	United States
Long run							
Income	0.547	0.69	0.632	0.271	0.067	−0.194	0.664
	(0.116)	(0.041)	(0.047)	(0.060)	(0.036)	(0.135)	(0.025)
Equity wealth	0.017	0.017	0.086	0.051	−0.038	0.040	0.034
	(0.007)	(0.007)	(0.021)	(0.024)	(0.023)	(0.022)	(0.005)
Housing wealth	0.008	0.008	0.062	−0.010	0.024	0.068	0.137
	(0.003)	(0.003)	(0.018)	(0.003)	(0.003)	(0.009)	(0.005)
Short run							
Change in income	0.494	0.502	0.958	0.194	0.377	0.494	0.643
	(0.072)	(0.141)	(0.120)	(0.101)	(0.061)	(0.199)	(0.060)
Change in equity wealth	0.033	0.006	0.042	0.062	−0.015	0.025	0.007
	(0.036)	(0.008)	(0.016)	(0.028)	(0.011)	(0.017)	(0.006)
Change in housing wealth	0.084	0.017	0.103	0.004	0.014	0.058	0.121
	(0.031)	(0.008)	(0.029)	(0.007)	(0.005)	(0.016)	(0.034)
Inflation	−0.021	−0.001	−0.019	0.005	−2.320	−0.016	−0.010
	(0.004	(0.0005)	(0.018)	(0.005)	(1.060)	(0.010)	(0.033)
Adjustment to long run	−0.350	−0.203	−0.990)	−0.526	−0.506	−0.317	−0.419
	(0.070)	(0.263)	(0.287)	(0.167)	(0.153)	(0.323)	(0.120)
Observations	46	27	15	30	36	19	47

Note: Standard errors are in parentheses. Annual data; sample period varies by country. Coefficients in the short-run equation are short-run marginal propensities to consume. Coefficient and standard-error-on-inflation terms are multiplied by 100.

for 2 percent of the 2.6-percentage-points-below-trend GDP growth in the year before recessions. A value of zero for a particular GDP component means that component was actually adding strength to GDP growth in that period, rather than contributing to its below-trend decline.

Long-Run Propensity to Consume out of Housing Wealth

The long-run propensity to consume out of housing wealth shown in Figure 3.4 is derived from the table below, presenting estimates of an error-correction specification of consumption (Table 3.6), with income, equity wealth, and housing wealth as explanatory variables (see April 2002 *World Economic Outlook,* for a similar methodology).

Vector Autoregression

The vector autoregression (VAR) model estimated in this chapter consists of three blocks.

The first block contains output (real GDP) and the price level (GDP deflator). The second block contains real house prices and residential investment. The third block consists of the short-term (nominal) interest rate and the long-term interest rate spread over the short-term rate.

As usual in the literature, monetary policy shocks are identified using a block recursive identification strategy—that is, shocks to the short-term interest rates are allowed to influence the variables in the first and second blocks, only with a one-quarter lag, but have an immediate effect on the term spread.

Housing demand shocks are identified by combining the block recursive identification strategy with sign restrictions. Reflecting the block recursive identification strategy, housing demand shocks have no contemporaneous effects on output or prices. Moreover, housing demand shocks are those that move house prices and residential investment in the same direction over the four quarters following the shock. There may be several identification schemes consistent with these criteria, so the median across these schemes is reported in this chapter.

As in the vast majority of the monetary literature based on VARs (Christiano, Eichenbaum, and Evans, 1999), although standard unit root tests indicate that some variables used in the models might be integrated of order one, we estimate the systems in levels, without explicitly modeling cointegrating relationships. Sims, Stock, and Watson (1990) show that if cointegration exists among the variables, the system's dynamics can be consistently estimated in a VAR in levels. A time trend was also included, but the results are very similar with and without a time trend.

This model is estimated separately for each of 16 OECD economies using quarterly data for the period 1970 (or the first year for which data are available) to 2006. For economies with all time series starting from 1970:Q1, the sample is broken down into two subperiods, one from 1970:Q1 to 1982:Q4 and the other from 1983:Q1 to 2007:Q1. Results with a 1985:Q4 cutoff are very similar and available on request.

Countries with data from 1970:Q1 are Australia, Canada, Finland, France, Germany, Italy, Japan, the Netherlands, Sweden, the United Kingdom, and the United States. Countries with different starting dates are Austria (1986:Q3), Belgium (1988:Q1), Denmark (1990:Q1), Greece (1994:Q1), Ireland (1997:Q1), Norway (1978:Q1), and Spain (1995:Q1).

References

Ahearne, Alan G., John Ammer, Brian M. Doyle, Linda S. Kole, and Robert F. Martin, 2005, "House Prices and Monetary Policy: A Cross-Country Study," FRB International Finance Discussion Paper No. 841 (Washington: Board of Governors of the Federal Reserve System).

Aoki, Kosuke, James Proudman, and Gertjan Vlieghe, 2002, "House Prices, Consumption, and Monetary Policy: A Financial Accelerator Approach," Bank of England Working Paper No. 169 (London: Bank of England).

Bank for International Settlements (BIS), 2006, "Housing Finance in the Global Financial Market,"

CGFS Publication No. 26 (Basel: Committee on the Global Financial System).

Benito, Andrew, Jamie N.R. Thompson, Matt Waldron, and Rob Wood, 2006, "House Prices and Consumer Spending," *Bank of England Quarterly Bulletin* (Summer).

Bernanke, Ben S., 2007, "Housing, Housing Finance, and Monetary Policy," opening speech at the Federal Reserve Bank of Kansas City 31st Economic Policy Symposium, "Housing, Housing Finance and Monetary Policy," Jackson Hole, Wyoming, August 31–September 1.

———, and Mark Gertler, 1995, "Inside the Black Box: The Credit Channel of Monetary Policy Transmission," *Journal of Economic Perspectives*, Vol. 9 (Autumn), pp. 27–48.

Bernanke, Ben S., and Simon Gilchrist, 1999, "The Financial Accelerator in a Quantitative Business Cycle Framework," in *Handbook of Macroeconomics*, Vol. 1C, ed. by J.B. Taylor and M. Woodford (Amsterdam: North-Holland), Ch. 21.

Bordo, Michael D., and Olivier Jeanne, 2002, "Boom-Busts in Asset Prices, Economic Instability, and Monetary Policy," NBER Working Paper No. 8966 (Cambridge, Massachusetts: National Bureau of Economic Research).

Borio, Claudio, 2006, "Monetary and Financial Stability: Here to Stay?" *Journal of Banking and Finance*, Vol. 30 (December), pp. 3407–14.

———, and William White, 2004, "Whither Monetary and Financial Stability? The Implications of Evolving Policy Regimes," BIS Working Paper No. 147 (Basel: Bank for International Settlements).

Bry, Gerhard, and Charlotte Boschan, 1971, *Cyclical Analysis of Time Series: Selected Procedures and Computer Programs* (New York: National Bureau of Economic Research).

Calza, Alessandro, Tommaso Monacelli, and Livio Stracca, 2007, "Mortgage Markets, Collateral Constraints, and Monetary Policy: Do Institutional Factors Matter?" CEPR Discussion Paper No. 6231 (London: Centre for Economic Policy Research).

Campbell, Jeffrey R., and Zvi Hercowitz, 2005, "The Role of Collateralized Household Debt in Macroeconomic Stabilization," NBER Working Paper No. 11330 (Cambridge, Massachusetts: National Bureau of Economic Research).

Case, Karl E., 2000, "Real Estate and the Macroeconomy," *Brookings Papers on Economic Activity: 2*, pp. 119–62.

Catte, Pietro, Nathalie Girouard, Robert Price, and Christophe André, 2004, "Housing Markets, Wealth and the Business Cycle," OECD Economics Department Working Paper No. 394 (Paris: Organization for Economic Cooperation and Development).

Christiano, Lawrence, Martin Eichenbaum, and Charles Evans, 1999, "Monetary Policy Shocks: What Have We Learned and to What End?" in *Handbook of Macroeconomics*, Vol. 1A, ed. by John B. Taylor and Michael Woodford (Amsterdam: North-Holland).

Debelle, Guy, 2004, "Macroeconomic Implications of Rising Household Debt," BIS Working Paper No. 153 (Basel: Bank for International Settlements).

Dell'Ariccia, Giovanni, Deniz Igan, and Luc Laeven, 2008, "Credit Booms and Lending Standards: Evidence from the Subprime Mortgage Market," CEPR Discussion Paper No. 6683 (London: Centre for Economic Policy Research).

Diamond, Douglas B., Jr., and Michael J. Lea, 1992, "The Decline of Special Circuits in Developed Country Housing Finance," *Housing Policy Debate*, Vol. 3, No. 3, pp. 747–77.

Dynan, Karen E., Douglas W. Elmendorf, and Daniel E. Sichel, 2006, "Can Financial Innovation Help to Explain the Reduced Volatility of Economic Activity?" *Journal of Monetary Economics*, Vol. 53 (January), pp. 123–50.

Dynan, Karen E., and Donald L. Kohn, 2007, "The Rise in U.S. Household Indebtedness: Causes and Consequences," Finance and Economics Discussion Series Working Paper No. 37 (Washington: Board of Governors of the Federal Reserve System).

Erceg, Christopher, and Andrew Levin, 2002, "Optimal Monetary Policy with Durable and Non-Durable Goods," FRB International Finance Discussion Paper No. 748 (Washington: Board of Governors of the Federal Reserve System).

Estrella, Arturo, 2002, "Securitization and the Efficacy of Monetary Policy," Federal Reserve Bank of New York *Economic Policy Review* (May), pp. 243–55.

European Central Bank, 2003, "Structural Factors in the EU Housing Markets" (Frankfurt am Maim, Germany). Available via the Internet: www.ecb. int/pub/pdf/other/euhousingmarketsen.pdf.

European Commission, 2005, "Housing and the Business Cycle," *Quarterly Report on the Euro Area*, Vol. 4 (July), pp. 30–39.

European Mortgage Federation, 2006. *Hypostat* (Brussels). Available via the Internet: www.hypo.org.

Gilchrist, Simon, and Masashi Saito, 2006, "Expectations, Asset Prices, and Monetary Policy: The Role of Learning," NBER Working Paper No. 12442 (Cambridge, Massachusetts: National Bureau of Economic Research).

Girouard, Nathalie, and Sveinbjörn Blöndal, 2001, "House Prices and Economic Activity," OECD Economics Department Working Paper No. 279 (Paris: Organization for Economic Cooperation and Development).

Giuliodori, Massimo, 2004, "Monetary Policy Shocks and the Role of House Prices Across European Countries," DNB Working Paper No. 015 (Amsterdam: Netherlands Central Bank).

Green, Richard K., and Susan M. Wachter, 2007, "The Housing Finance Revolution," paper presented at the Federal Reserve Bank of Kansas City 31st Economic Policy Symposium, "Housing, Housing Finance and Monetary Policy," Jackson Hole, Wyoming, August 31–September 1.

Harding, Don, and Adrian Pagan, 2006, "Synchronization of Cycles," *Journal of Econometrics*, Vol. 132, No. 1, pp. 59–79.

Iacoviello, Matteo, 2005, "House Prices, Borrowing Constraints and Monetary Policy in the Business Cycle," *American Economic Review*, Vol. 95 (June), pp. 739–64.

———, and Raoul Minetti, 2002, "Financial Liberalisation and the Sensitivity of House Prices to Monetary Policy: Theory and Evidence," Working Paper in Economics No. 538 (Boston: Boston College Department of Economics).

Iacoviello, Matteo, and Stefano Neri, 2007, "Housing Market Spillovers: Evidence from an Estimated DSGE Model," Working Paper in Economics No. 659 (Boston: Boston College Department of Economics).

Jarociński, Marek, and Frank R. Smets, 2007, "House Prices and the Stance of Policy," paper presented at the Federal Reserve Bank of St. Louis 32nd Annual Economic Policy Symposium, "Monetary Policy Under Uncertainty," St. Louis, October 18–19. Available via the Internet: research.stlouisfed. org/conferences/policyconf/papers2007/Smets_ Jarocinski.pdf.

Kiyotaki, Nobuhiro, and John Moore, 1997, "Credit Cycles," *Journal of Political Economy*, Vol. 105 (April), pp. 211–48.

Klyuev, Vladimir, and Paul Mills, 2006, "Is Housing Wealth an 'ATM'? The Relationship Between Household Wealth, Home Equity Withdrawal, and

Saving Rates," IMF Working Paper 06/162 (Washington: International Monetary Fund).

Leamer, Edward, 2007, "Housing Is the Business Cycle," paper presented at the Federal Reserve Bank of Kansas City 31st Economic Policy Symposium, "Housing, Housing Finance and Monetary Policy," Jackson Hole, Wyoming, August 31–September 1.

McCarthy, Jonathan, and Richard Peach, 2002, "Monetary Policy Transmission to Residential Investment," Federal Reserve Bank of New York *Economic Policy Review*, Vol. 8 (May), pp. 139–58.

Mishkin, Frederic S., 2007, "Housing and the Monetary Transmission Mechanism," paper presented at the Federal Reserve Bank of Kansas City 31st Economic Policy Symposium, "Housing, Housing Finance and Monetary Policy," Jackson Hole, Wyoming, August 31–September 1.

———, 2008, "Monetary Policy Flexibility, Risk Management, and Financial Disruptions," speech delivered at the Federal Reserve Bank of New York, New York, January 11. Available via the Internet: www.federalreserve.gov/newsevents/speech/mishkin20080111a.htm.

Monacelli, Tommaso, 2008, "New Keynesian Models, Durable Goods, and Collateral Constraints" (unpublished). Available via the Internet: www.igier.uni-bocconi.it/whos.php?vedi=903&tbn=albero&id_doc=177.

Muellbauer, John, 2007, "Housing, Credit and Consumer Expenditure," paper presented at the Federal Reserve Bank of Kansas City 31st Economic Policy Symposium, "Housing, Housing Finance

and Monetary Policy," Jackson Hole, Wyoming, August 31–September 1.

Organization for Economic Cooperation and Development (OECD), 2004, "A Detailed Description of Employment Protection Regulation in Force in 2003," *OECD Employment Outlook* (Paris).

Schnure, Calvin, 2005, "Boom-Bust Cycles in Housing: The Changing Role of Financial Structure," IMF Working Paper 05/200 (Washington: International Monetary Fund).

Sims, Christopher, 1998, "The Role of Interest Rate Policy in the Generation and Propagation of Business Cycles: What Has Changed Since the '30s?" in *Beyond Shocks: What Causes Business Cycles?* ed. by Jeffrey C. Fuhrer and Scott Schuh (Boston: Federal Reserve Bank of Boston).

———, James H. Stock, and Mark W. Watson, 1990, "Inference in Linear Time Series Models with Unit Roots," *Econometrica*, Vol. 58 (January), pp. 113–44.

Taylor, John B., 2007, "Housing and Monetary Policy," paper presented at the Federal Reserve Bank of Kansas City 31st Economic Policy Symposium, "Housing, Housing Finance and Monetary Policy," Jackson Hole, Wyoming, August 31–September 1.

van Els, Peter, Alberto Locarno, Benoît Mojon, and Julian Morgan, 2003, "New Macroeconomic Evidence on Monetary Policy Transmission in the Euro Area," *Journal of the European Economic Association*, Vol. 1 (April/May), pp. 720–30.

Zhu, Haibin, 2005, "The Importance of Property Markets for Monetary Policy and Financial Stability," BIS Paper No. 21 (Basel: Bank for International Settlements).

CLIMATE CHANGE AND THE GLOBAL ECONOMY

This chapter uses a global dynamic model to examine the macroeconomic and financial consequences of policies to address climate change. Although these consequences can be rapid and wide-ranging, this chapter finds that the overall costs of mitigation could be minimized if policies are well designed and accepted by a broad group of countries.

Climate change is a potentially catastrophic global externality and one of the world's greatest collective action problems. The distribution of causes and effects is highly uneven across countries and across generations. Enormous uncertainty surrounds existing estimates of future damages that may result from climate change, but these potential damages are to a considerable extent irreversible and may be catastrophic if global warming is unchecked. The costs of abating climate change also have a sunk component— that is, cannot be fully recovered—and are contingent on a multitude of factors, including the rate at which the global economy grows over the long term and the pace at which low-emission technologies emerge and diffuse across the global economy. The discount rate chosen to

Note: This chapter was prepared by Natalia Tamirisa (team leader), Florence Jaumotte, Ben Jones, Paul Mills, Rodney Ramcharan, Alasdair Scott, and Jon Strand, under the guidance of Charles Collyns. Nikola Spatafora, Eduardo Borensztein, Douglas Laxton, Marcos Chamon, and Paolo Mauro also made significant contributions to the chapter. Warwick McKibbin, Ian Parry, and Kang Yong Tan served as consultants for the project. Angela Espiritu, Elaine Hensle, and Emory Oakes provided research assistance. Joseph Aldy (Resources for the Future), Fatih Birol (International Energy Agency), Kirk Hamilton (World Bank), Helen Mountford and Jan Corfee-Morlot (both Organization for Economic Cooperation and Development, OECD), Georgios Kostakos and Luis Jimenez-McInnis (both Executive Office of the Secretary-General, in the Secretariat of the United Nations), Robert Pindyck (Massachusetts Institute of Technology), and Nicholas Stern (London School of Economics) and his team commented on an earlier draft.

aggregate damages from climate change and the costs of abating them across generations also has important implications for how various policy options are weighed by policymakers.

The macroeconomic consequences of policies to abate climate change can be immediate and wide-ranging, particularly when these policies are not designed carefully. The promotion of biofuels provides a good example. Expansion of biofuel production in the United States and western Europe in recent years has pushed up food prices and boosted inflation, creating serious problems for poor food-importing countries around the world and limiting the ability of central banks to ease monetary policy in response to recent financial turbulence. The main cause of these negative effects is the fact that advanced economies have placed trade restrictions on imports of biofuels, constraining the production of biofuels in lower-cost countries such as Brazil.[1]

This chapter focuses on examining the macroeconomic and financial implications, for the global economy and for individual countries, of policies to address climate change.[2] First, the chapter reviews available estimates of damages from climate change, illustrating the potentially significant benefits of abatement and highlighting the key variations among these estimates.[3] Next, the chapter briefly discusses the need for countries to adapt their ecological, social, and economic systems to climate change. The costs of such adaptation will have significant

[1]Production of biofuels also needs to be environmentally sustainable. For more details on biofuels, see the October 2007 *World Economic Outlook*.

[2]This study builds on the review of climate change issues in the October 2007 *World Economic Outlook*. For an analysis of the fiscal implications of climate change, see IMF (2008).

[3]Abatement is defined here as the reduction in greenhouse gas (GHG) emissions. This term is used interchangeably with the term "mitigation." Adaptation means adjustment to climate change.

bearing on the estimates of potential losses from climate change, and macroeconomic policies and financial markets can play a role in reducing these costs.

The main contribution of this chapter is its analysis of the macroeconomic and financial implications of alternative mitigation policies across countries, using a global dynamic macroeconomic model. An effective mitigation policy must be based on setting a price path for the greenhouse gas (GHG) emissions that drive climate change. The overall costs of such carbon-pricing policies—a global carbon tax, a global cap-and-trade system, or a hybrid policy—could be moderate, provided the policies are well designed.

- Carbon pricing should be credible and long term. If it is, then even small and gradual increases in carbon prices will be sufficient to induce businesses and people to shift away from emission-intensive products and technologies.
- Carbon pricing should be global. It is not feasible to contain climate change unless all major GHG emitters start pricing their emissions.
- Carbon pricing should seek to equalize the price of GHG emissions across countries to maximize the efficiency of abatement. Emissions would then be reduced more where it is cheaper to do so.
- Carbon pricing should be flexible, allowing firms to adjust the amount of abatement in response to changes in economic conditions, to avoid excessive volatility in carbon prices. High carbon price volatility could augment macroeconomic volatility and generate spillovers across the world. Policy frameworks should also provide scope to adjust policy parameters in response to new scientific information and experiences with policy implementation.
- Carbon pricing should be equitable. No undue burdens should be put on countries least able to bear them.

All in all, the analysis highlights the importance of carefully designing mitigation policies to take into account their macroeconomic and financial effects, and thereby to ensure the sus-

tainability of any future international agreement on climate change.[4]

How Will Climate Change Affect Economies?

The global climate is projected to continue to warm in coming decades, as new GHG emissions augment the already large stock of past emissions. Increases in energy-related emissions of carbon dioxide, the largest and fastest-growing source of GHG emissions, are driven by growth in GDP per capita and increases in population, and these increases are only partially offset by improvements in the intensity of energy use (Figure 4.1).[5] Catching-up economies, especially large and fast-growing countries such as China and India, contribute most to the growth in emissions (Box 4.1). Advanced economies account for most past energy-related emissions and thus for most of the current stock of these emissions. However, when changes in land use and deforestation are considered, a different conclusion emerges: advanced economies account for less than half of the current stock of total emissions (den Elzen and others, 2005; Baumert, Herzog, and Pershing, 2005).

Outlook for Climate Change

Without changes in policy, GHG emissions are projected to accelerate. However, these projections are wide-ranging, given uncertainty about the rates at which productivity will grow, energy intensity will improve, and emerging and developing economies will converge toward the living standards of advanced economies. For

[4]Commitments under the central international agreement on emission levels—the Kyoto Protocol—are set to expire in 2012. At a recent conference in Bali, Indonesia, signatories to the United Nations Framework Convention on Climate Change (UNFCCC)—most of which are IMF members—agreed on the agenda for two years of negotiations on a new agreement, with a 2009 deadline.

[5]Intensity of energy use is defined as energy use per unit of output and calculated as the ratio of total energy use to GDP.

example, even studies based on the widely used Special Report on Emissions Scenarios (SRES) developed by the United Nations Intergovernmental Panel on Climate Change (IPCC) show significant variations in projected emission growth. Emission projections in studies based on this source range from 22 percent to 88 percent between 2000 and 2030, and from −40 percent to 237 percent between 2000 and 2100. The estimates based on more recent, "post-SRES" scenarios exhibit a similar range, although the median is lower in 2030 and higher in 2100 (Figure 4.2).

Business-as-usual (BAU) projections imply a sizable risk that global climate would change dramatically by the end of the century. The IPCC projects that, in the absence of emission control policies, global temperatures will increase by 2.8°C on average over the next century, with best-guess increases ranging from 1.8°C to 4°C across SRES scenarios (IPCC, 2007). The probability of higher temperature increases is not negligible. Stern (2008) points out that if BAU concentrations of GHGs stabilize at or above 750 parts per million (ppm) in carbon-dioxide-equivalent (CO₂e) terms by the end of the century, as implied by the latest IPCC scenarios, there would be at least a 50 percent chance that global temperatures would increase by more than 5°C, with potentially disastrous consequences for the planet (also see Weitzman, 2008, on the analysis of catastrophic risks from climate change).[6]

Global warming would have a multifaceted and potentially devastating impact on climate patterns (IPCC, 2007). Precipitation would increase at high latitudes and decrease in most subtropical land regions. Other likely manifestations of warming include increasing acidification of the ocean; melting of snow and sea ice; and

[6]Stern (2008) notes that the latest scenarios may be too optimistic about the likelihood of stabilizing GHG concentrations at these levels, because they do not take into account important feedbacks in the carbon cycle, such as release of methane from permafrost, collapse of the Amazon, and reduction in the absorptive capacity of the oceans.

Figure 4.1. Carbon Dioxide Energy-Related Emissions[1]

Emissions increases are driven by GDP growth per capita and population increases, with improvements in the energy intensity of output providing only a partial offset. Emerging and developing economies contribute most to emissions growth, and advanced economies account for most of past emissions.

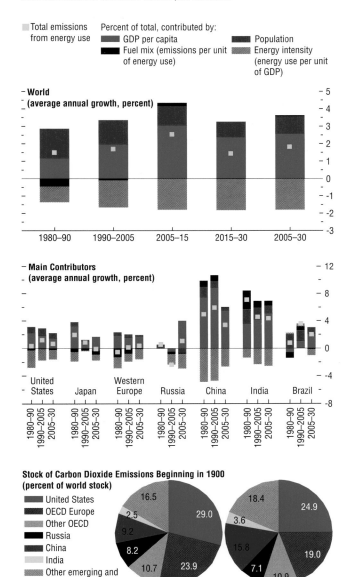

Sources: Energy Information Administration, *International Energy Annual* (2005) and *International Energy Outlook* (2006); International Energy Agency, *World Energy Outlook* (2007); and World Resources Institute's Earth Trends database.
[1]The figure plots emissions of carbon dioxide from energy use.

Figure 4.2. Emission Forecasts[1]

(Gigatons of carbon dioxide equivalent per year)

Emission forecasts cover a wide range of potential scenarios and outcomes, ranging from rapid output growth with developments of new energy technologies (the A1 scenario), less regional development convergence (A2), rapid shifts toward information- and services-based economies (B1), and fewer technological improvements (B2). All these scenarios are considered equally plausible, with no probabilities assigned to them. Even within each type of scenario, there is a wide range of emission projections (not shown), typically diverging by hundreds of percentage points by 2100.

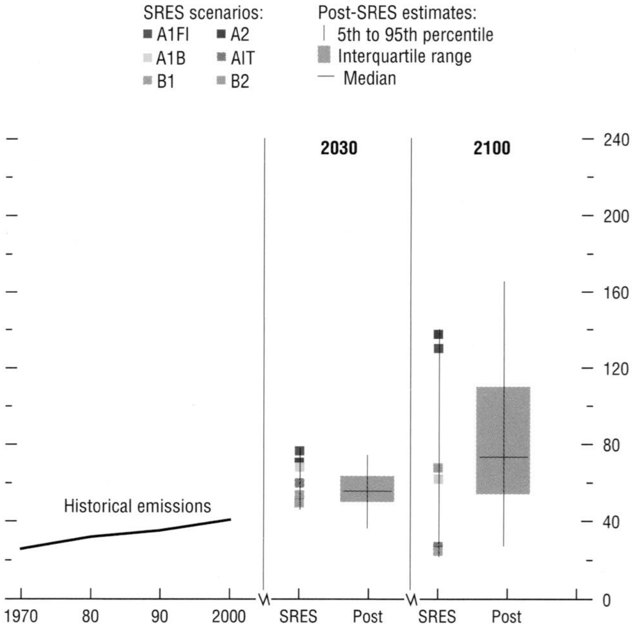

SRES scenarios:
■ A1FI   ■ A2
■ A1B   ■ AIT
■ B1   ■ B2

Post-SRES estimates:
| 5th to 95th percentile
■ Interquartile range
— Median

Sources: EDGAR-HYDE 1.4 database; IPCC (2007); Netherlands Environmental Assessment Agency; Olivier and Berdowski (2001); Van Aardenne and others (2001); and IMF staff calculations.
[1]Global greenhouse gas emissions for 1970–2000 and projected baseline emissions for 2030 and 2100 are from the IPCC's *Special Report on Emissions Scenarios* (SRES) and post-SRES literature. The figure shows emissions from the six illustrative SRES scenarios.

an increase in the intensity of extreme events such as heat waves, droughts, floods, and tropical cyclones. At higher temperatures, the probability of catastrophic climate changes would rise (for example, melting of the west Antarctic ice sheet or permafrost; a change in monsoon patterns in south Asia; or a reversal of the Atlantic Thermohaline Circulation, which would cool the climate of Europe).

Economic Costs of Climate Change

Economic estimates of the impact of climate change are typically based on "damage functions" that relate GDP losses to increases in temperature. The estimates of GDP costs embodied in the damage functions cover a variety of climate impacts that are usually grouped as market impacts and nonmarket impacts. Market impacts include effects on climate-sensitive sectors such as agriculture, forestry, fisheries, and tourism; damage to coastal areas from sea-level rise; changes in energy expenditures (for heating or cooling); and changes in water resources. Nonmarket impacts cover effects on health (such as the spread of infectious diseases and increased water shortages and pollution), leisure activities (sports, recreation, and outdoor activities), ecosystems (loss of biodiversity), and human settlements (specifically because cities and cultural heritage cannot migrate).

Existing studies tend to underestimate economic damages from climate change, particularly the risk of worse-than-expected outcomes. The three main benchmark studies (Mendelsohn and others, 2000; Nordhaus and Boyer, 2000; and Tol, 2002) and the review of the literature in the *Stern Review* (2007) point to mean GDP losses between 0 percent and 3 percent of world GDP for a 3°C warming (from 1990–2000 levels) (Figure 4.3).[7] However, these estimates of damages are often incomplete—they rarely cover nonmarket damages, the risk of local

---

[7]See IPCC (2007) for a detailed review of the literature on damages.

extreme weather, socially contingent events, or the risk of large temperature increases and global catastrophes.[8] Moreover, available estimates tend to be based on a smaller increase in global temperatures than projected in the IPCC's latest scenarios. Studies typically calculate damages for a doubling of CO_2e concentration from pre-industrial levels. Yet the latest IPCC's BAU scenarios are expected to result in a tripling or quadrupling of concentrations by the end of the century, implying higher temperatures than those assumed in most studies. More recent, risk-based approaches to the analysis of damages from climate change point to significantly higher estimates than those suggested in the earlier literature (Stern, 2008).

Estimates of total global damages also mask large variations across countries and regions. Damages tend to be greater for countries with higher initial temperatures, greater climate change, and lower levels of development (Figure 4.4). A moderate rise in temperature increases agricultural productivity in countries with low initial temperatures, but decreases it in hotter countries. Similarly, warming reduces deaths from cold in countries with initially colder climates, but increases mortality and morbidity in countries with warmer climates. Although warming reduces expenditures on winter heating in countries with an initially cooler climate, such countries may incur additional expenditures on summer cooling. Countries with initially warmer climates also incur additional costs for cooling.

Beyond initial temperature, the level of development has a strong effect on the extent of damages from climate change. First, a

[8]Studies are also incomparable in methodology. Mendelsohn covers only market impacts; Tol covers market and nonmarket impacts; Nordhaus and Boyer and the *Stern Review* cover market and nonmarket impacts as well as catastrophic risks. The studies differ in their assumptions about the extent of adaptation to climate change (large in Mendelsohn; smaller in Tol), and about the underlying economy (future or current). Mendelsohn's estimates are based mostly on U.S. data and extrapolated for other countries.

Figure 4.3. Mean GDP Losses at Various Levels of Warming[1]

Estimates of GDP losses from climate change vary depending on the methodology and coverage of impacts and risks. GDP losses increase with temperature.

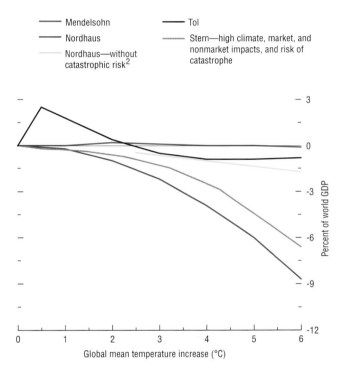

Source: Stern (2007).
[1]The studies presented in the *Stern Review* are from Mendelsohn, Schlesinger, and Williams (2000), Nordhaus and Boyer (2000), and Tol (2002).
[2]Nordhaus and Boyer (2000) data adjusted for catastrophic risk are available only for 2.5°C and 6°C. Observations were interpolated using a linear trend.

Figure 4.4. Damages from 2.5°C Warming by Region[1]

Losses from climate change fall disproportionately on emerging and developing economies.

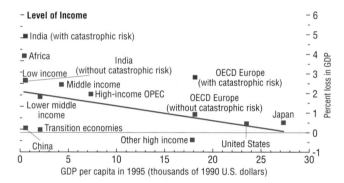

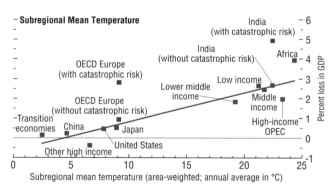

Source: Nordhaus and Boyer (2000).
[1]OECD is the Organization for Economic Cooperation and Development. OPEC is the Organization of Petroleum Exporting Countries. See Nordhaus and Boyer (2000) for information on country group composition. The regression line includes only observations without catastrophic risk.

lower level of development typically implies a larger dependence on climate-sensitive sectors, particularly agriculture. Second, populations in these countries are typically more vulnerable to climate change because of lower income per capita, limited availability of public services (such as health care), less-developed financial markets, and poor governance. Third, the same factors also restrain the adaptive capacity of the economy. Some estimates of damages from climate change explicitly specify costs as a function of income level (Nordhaus and Boyer, 2000). Often, higher initial temperatures and lower levels of development go hand in hand, compounding the damaging impact of climate change on developing economies.

All three of the main benchmark studies suggest a similar distribution of the climate change impact across regions, shown in Figure 4.5 by adjusting regional impacts for the study-specific global impact. The regions likely to experience the most negative effects include Africa, south and southeast Asia (especially India), Latin America, and Organization for Economic Cooperation and Development (OECD) Europe (if catastrophic risk is included). In contrast, China, North America, OECD Asia, and transition economies (especially Russia) should suffer smaller impacts and may even benefit, depending on the actual extent of warming. In India, the large negative impact is due to catastrophic risk (such as a change in the monsoon pattern), agricultural damages, and deteriorating health. In Africa, the main effect estimated by Nordhaus and Boyer is deteriorating health from the spread of tropical disease; however, recent estimates of the likely effects on agricultural potential (discussed herein) also project substantial agricultural damages (Cline, 2007). OECD Europe is largely affected by the risk of catastrophic impact and damages to coastal areas.

Physical estimates of the impact of climate change confirm that Africa and Asia are particularly vulnerable. In these regions, almost 1 billion people would experience shortages of water by 2080, more than 9 million could fall victim to coastal floods, and many could face increased hunger (Figure 4.6). Pacific island countries are perhaps the most immediately vulnerable among the poor countries, as even a small further rise in sea level would dramatically affect their environment.

Two main areas of uncertainty plague estimates of damages from climate change at all levels, as is reflected in the large variation in the present value of damages. The first is the limitation of current scientific knowledge about the physical and ecological processes underlying climate change. For example, there is only incomplete information about how rapidly GHG concentrations will grow in the future, how sensitive climate and biological systems will be to increased concentrations of GHGs, and where the "tipping points" are, beyond which catastrophic climate events can occur.[9]

The second source of uncertainty relates to how best to quantify the economic impact of climate change. The magnitude of losses from climate change depends, for example, on how well people and firms adapt and at what cost, as well as on the extent to which technological innovation can reduce the impact. For example, health effects from the spread of tropical disease may be lower if the spread of malaria can be reduced. Similarly, losses in agricultural yields may be limited if heat- and drought-resistant crops can be developed. Conventional approaches to evaluating damage from climate change also tend to neglect dynamic macroeconomic linkages. Climate change is largely a supply-side shock, but it may have significant effects on trade, capital flows, and

[9]This has implications for measures of economic damage. For example, the effect of climate change on productivity in agriculture and forestry depends to a large extent on the magnitude of carbon fertilization effects (a process by which higher concentrations of carbon dioxide in the atmosphere could result in increased crop yields), which is not known with certainty. Recent downward revisions to carbon fertilization effects have led to higher estimates of diminished world agricultural potential (Cline, 2007).

Figure 4.5. Impact of Warming by Region and Sector

Africa, south and southeast Asia (especially India), Latin America, and European OECD countries are likely to be most affected by climate change.

- Mendelsohn–at 2.0°C warming[1]
- Tol–at 1.0°C warming[2]
- Nordhaus–at 2.5°C warming[3]
- Hope–at 2.5°C warming[4]

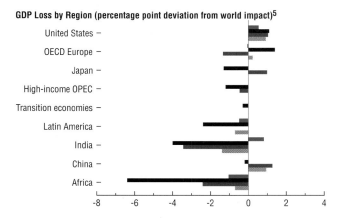

GDP Loss by Region (percentage point deviation from world impact)[5]

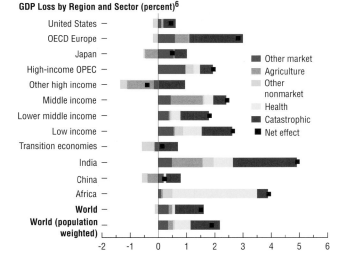

GDP Loss by Region and Sector (percent)[6]

- Other market
- Agriculture
- Other nonmarket
- Health
- Catastrophic
- Net effect

Sources: Hope (2006a); Mendelsohn, Schlesinger, and Williams (2000); Nordhaus and Boyer (2000); and Tol (2002).

[1]Shows the median impact of the Ricardian and Reduced-Form models for a 2°C warming. South and southeast Asia includes Middle East and China. No data are available for Asian Organization for Economic Cooperation and Development (OECD) countries and high-income OPEC (Organization of Petroleum Exporting Countries) countries.

[2]Impact of a 1°C warming. High-income OPEC refers to the Middle East. China includes other centrally planned Asian economies. No data are available for transition economies.

[3]Impact of a 2.5°C warming. North America refers only to the United States. OECD Asia refers only to Japan. South and southeast Asia refers only to India. No data are available for Latin America.

[4]Shows the median impact of models with and without adaptation at 2.5°C warming. North America refers only to the United States. South and southeast Asia refers only to India. No data are available for OECD Asia and high-income OPEC countries.

[5]World impact is estimated as follows: Mendelsohn at 0.13, Tol at 2.30, Nordhaus at -1.50, and Hope at -1.15 percent of GDP.

[6]Estimates from Nordhaus and Boyer (2000).

Figure 4.6. Physical Impact by 2080[1]

Physical estimates of climate change impact confirm that Asia and Africa are particularly vulnerable to climate change.

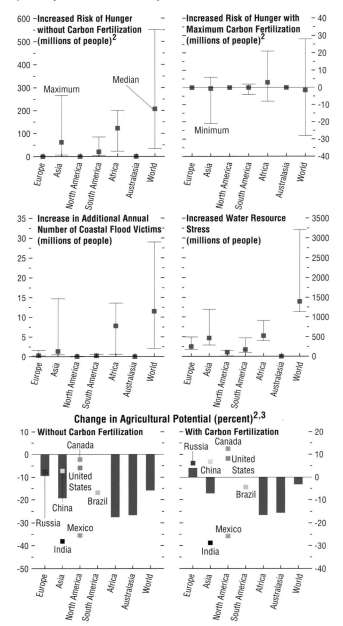

Sources: Cline (2007); and Yohe and others (2007).

[1]Data for panels 1–4 are from Yohe and others (2007); sample includes estimates from A1FI, A2, B1, and B2 *Special Report on Emissions Scenarios* (IPCC, 2007). Data for panels 5–6 are from Cline (2007). All impacts are measured relative to the situation in 2080 with no climate change. Regional compositions may not be comparable across panels.

[2]Carbon fertilization refers to the increase in crop productivity as a result of the effect of carbon dioxide on crops.

[3]Estimates without carbon fertilization are weighted averages of the estimates from a Ricardian model and crop models. Estimates with carbon fertilization include the effect of a uniform boost of 15 percent in yield. See Cline (2007) for more information.

migration, as well as on investment and savings (Box 4.2).[10]

Quantifying the aggregate losses across generations involves use of a single welfare measure and bears on the present value estimates of global losses. The rate at which the welfare of future generations should be discounted to the present (which relates to the marginal product of capital) is the subject of considerable debate. The *Stern Review*'s estimate that climate change would produce a large welfare cost—equivalent to a permanent reduction in consumption of about 14 percent of world output over the next two centuries—is much higher than the average annual estimated output loss.[11] This reflects a low elasticity of marginal utility to consumption and an assumed pure rate of time preference of approximately zero, both of which give a large weight to consumption losses from distant generations.[12] Many consider these assumptions unpersuasive because they imply a much higher-than-observed savings rate and a lower-than-observed rate of return on capital (Nordhaus, 2007a; and Dasgupta, 2007). Stern (2008) points out that discount rates are conditional on the path of future growth in consumption, implying that a lower discount rate should apply in a world with climate change than in a world without it, all other things equal. He also underscores that basing discount rates on market rates is fundamentally inappropriate in cases involving welfare trade-offs across far-apart generations and across countries with different levels of income. Technological change (DeLong, 2006) and uncer-

[10]For instance, as climate lowers output now and in the future, investment may fall because there are fewer resources to invest and because the rate of return on capital is lower. Using simulations, Fankhauser and Tol (2005) show that the capital accumulation effect is important, especially if technological change is endogenous, and may be larger than the direct impact of climate change.

[11]Under the *Stern Review*'s "high-climate scenario" with catastrophic, market, and nonmarket impacts, the mean losses are less than 1 percent of world output in 2050, 2.9 percent in 2100, and 13.8 percent in 2200.

[12]Raising the pure rate of time preference from 0.1 to a still modest 1.5 reduces the range of expected damage costs from 5–20 percent to 1.4–6 percent of global consumption (see the October 2007 *World Economic Outlook*).

tainty over future discount rates may also justify using lower discount rates (Pindyck, 2007).

What is the relative importance of the different sources of variation in damage estimates? The *Stern Review*'s estimate of the percent loss in GDP per capita by 2200 under its baseline climate scenario (which assumes relatively high emissions and includes market impacts, non-market impacts, and catastrophic risk) ranges from about 3 percent to 35 percent (90 percent confidence interval), with a central estimate of 15 percent (Figure 4.7). Hope (2006b) finds that the two most important sources of variation in estimates of welfare losses are the climate sensitivity parameter and the pure rate of time preference.[13] Uncertainty surrounding the nonmarket impacts and the elasticity of marginal utility with respect to income also ranks high, whereas uncertainty about market impacts ranks lower. Weitzman (2007a) concludes that the choice of the discount rate overshadows any uncertainty about the costs and benefits of climate change a century from now. He also argues that the most important source of variation is uncertainty over probability and scale of catastrophes. Webster and others (2003) find that nearly half of the variation is attributable to uncertainty about emission forecasting.

Non-negligible tail risks of large damages from climate change would justify an early and significant policy action. Uncertainty generally increases the benefits of policy delay, but because both the damages from climate change and its costs are irreversible, policy implications of uncertainty are more ambiguous (Pindyck,

---

[13]Hope uses the PAGE 2002 model, but focuses on the social cost of carbon (SCC)—the present value of future climate change damages caused by one extra ton of carbon emissions—as an indicator of damages. Like GDP-based measures, SCC estimates fluctuate widely. In a recent survey, Tol (2005) found a mean SCC of $43 per ton of carbon, with a standard deviation of $83. Using standard assumptions about discounting and aggregation, he concluded that the SCC is unlikely to exceed $50 per ton of carbon. Other surveys, however, point to higher values (a central value of $105 in Clarkson and Deyes, 2002, and a lower benchmark of $50 in Downing and others, 2005). Also see IPCC (2007).

Figure 4.7. Variation in Estimates of Damages from Climate Change

There is considerable uncertainty about estimates of the economic impact of climate change.

Baseline Climate, Market Impacts, Risk of Catastrophe, and Nonmarket Impacts (percent loss in GDP per capita)

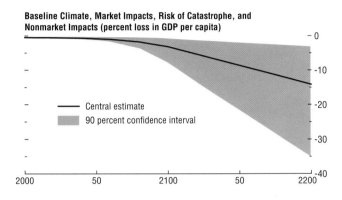

Major Factors Causing Variation in the Social Cost of Carbon (positive values show an increase in cost; negative values show a decrease in cost)

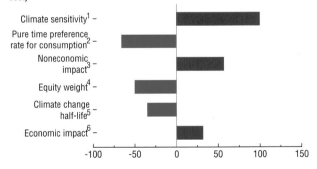

Sources: Hope (2006b); and Stern (2007).
[1]Equilibrium temperature rise for a doubling of carbon dioxide concentration.
[2]Pure time preference for consumption now rather than in one year's time.
[3]Valuation of noneconomic impact for a 2.5°C temperature rise.
[4]Negative of the elasticity of marginal utility with respect to income.
[5]Half-life in years of global response to an increase in radiative forcing.
[6]Valuation of economic impact for a 2.5°C temperature rise.

Box 4.1. Rising Car Ownership in Emerging Economies: Implications for Climate Change

Economic history suggests that as people get richer, they increase their use of private transportation. Accordingly, rapid economic growth in a number of large emerging economies has recently been accompanied by an impressive acceleration in the demand for cars, and these countries may be expected to move quickly toward mass car ownership in the decades ahead. Greater car usage will improve the well-being and broaden the economic opportunities of millions who are being lifted out of poverty, but it will also have major implications for climate change. Cars currently account for 6½ percent of global GHG emissions and a sizable share of oil consumption—for example, gasoline accounts for as much as 45 percent of oil consumption in the United States, one of the most gasoline-reliant economies.

Car ownership is amenable to econometric analysis, and the exercise yields reasonably accurate projections, thereby providing a quantitative illustration of the scale of future challenges related to keeping GHG emissions in check. Indeed, over the past few decades, car ownership has displayed a relatively robust relationship with GDP per capita. More specifically, both the historical experience of economies that are now advanced and cross-country regression analysis suggest that car ownership remains low up to per capita incomes of about $5,000 (a threshold identified through an iterative search for the best regression fit) and then takes off rapidly as incomes grow beyond that threshold.

Several emerging economies—including China and India, the most populous countries in the world—are currently at the stage of development usually associated with such a takeoff (figure). Indeed, while a wide range of consumer durables are commonplace in most urban Chinese households, car ownership remains relatively low beyond a handful of major urban centers. This is indicative of the potential for rising car ownership in the

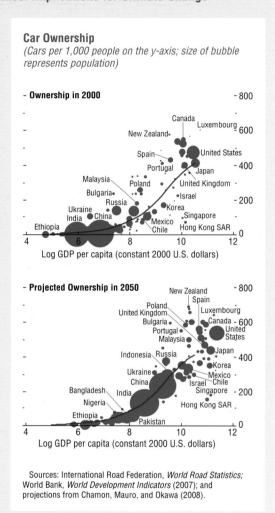

Car Ownership
(Cars per 1,000 people on the y-axis; size of bubble represents population)

Sources: International Road Federation, World Road Statistics; World Bank, World Development Indicators (2007); and projections from Chamon, Mauro, and Okawa (2008).

next few decades, as per capita income grows beyond $5,000 in key emerging and developing economies. Projections derived from regressions based on a panel of countries suggest that the number of cars worldwide will increase by 2.3 billion between 2005 and 2050, and that the number of cars in emerging and developing economies will increase by 1.9 billion.[1] Compa-

Note: The main authors of this box are Marcos Chamon and Paolo Mauro, based on Chamon, Mauro, and Okawa (2008).

[1]The projections are based on a regression model relating car ownership in a panel of countries to the share of the population earning more than $5,000 per capita a year and a trend that captures technological

rable projections are supported by microeconometric estimates based on two surveys of tens of thousands of households in China and India. The results confirm that as more and more households reach income levels that allow them to afford a car, ownership should rise by ½ billion cars in China and ⅓ billion cars in India between now and 2050. The projected increase in car ownership in these emerging market giants (and other countries at a similar stage of development) will not only have substantial fiscal consequences for these countries—which are likely to require infrastructure investment to support such increased demand for transportation—but will also have major implications for emissions and climate change.

A simple back-of-the-envelope calculation regarding GHG emissions may help gauge the implications of an increase in the worldwide car fleet from 0.5 billion in 2000 to 2.9 billion in 2050. According to the *Stern Review* (2007), cars (and vans) accounted for emissions equivalent to 2.6 gigatons of carbon dioxide ($GtCO_2$) in 2000. Relating the projected increase in the number of cars to additional emissions requires strong simplifying assumptions about future improvements in fuel efficiency. Over the past two and a half decades, the average number of miles per gallon has been broadly stable in most advanced economies, as technological improvements have been accompanied by increases in average car weight. Assuming that the growth rate of car emissions is the same as the growth rate of cars, worldwide emissions by cars would amount to 6.8 $GtCO_2$ in 2050. To put this in perspective, the *Stern Review*'s business-as-usual

---

improvements; long-term projections for economic growth are based on published sources. For more details on the methodology and sources, see Chamon, Mauro, and Okawa (2008).

scenario foresees that total emissions (flow) from all sources will rise from 42 $GtCO_2$ in 2000 to 84 $GtCO_2$ in 2050. Emissions from cars as a share of total CO_2 emissions from all sources would thus rise from 6.3 percent in 2000 to 8.1 percent in 2050. To sum up, cars could contribute significantly—and more than proportionately—to an increase in emissions from all sources that would have profound implications for climate change.

Policymakers in emerging and developing economies have an opportunity to "lean against the wind" of greater car ownership that inevitably results from economic development by promoting investment in appropriate subway, rail, and/or public transportation infrastructure. Local pollution concerns also have become an important driver for policy change. The wide variation in gasoline taxes across countries—ranging from $0.4 a gallon in the United States (and even less in some developing economies) to more than $3 a gallon in the United Kingdom—suggests that there may be significant room to increase fuel taxation in various parts of the world. Some countries also have begun to make substantial use of fuel efficiency standards. Notably, China introduced such standards in 2005 and will make them more stringent in 2008. At present, China's fleet average fuel economy standards are more strict than those in Australia, Canada, and the United States, though somewhat less strict than those in Europe and Japan. Additional policy measures include higher taxes on less-fuel-efficient cars.

While such policies seem necessary, they are likely to be insufficient. Ultimately, much will depend on progress with respect to new technologies—such as plug-in hybrids or other breakthroughs that we are unable to foresee—and incentives for innovation may also be considered in this area.

2007). The significant probability of climate catastrophes strengthens the case for earlier abatement—that is, reduction of GHG emissions—with abatement initiatives increasing in

intensity as learning progresses (Stern, 2008; and Weitzman, 2008). Even with aggressive abatement, however, it will be necessary to pursue adaptation—adjustments in ecological, social,

Box 4.2. South Asia: Illustrative Impact of an Abrupt Climate Shock

This box presents some scenarios that illustrate the economic effects on an open economy of an abrupt change in climate. This example examines the impact of changes in the monsoon pattern on a representative south Asian country that is heavily reliant on agriculture, but the arguments are relevant to other countries exposed to major climate shocks.

These scenarios were developed using a six-country[1] annual version of the Global Integrated Monetary and Fiscal Model (GIMF).[2] GIMF is a multicountry dynamic stochastic general equilibrium model that has been designed for multilateral surveillance. It includes strong non-Ricardian features whereby fiscal policies have significant real effects. It also includes significant nominal and real rigidities, making it a useful tool to study both the short- and long-term implications of supply and demand shocks.

Abrupt Climate Shock

The baseline climate change scenario, shown as the red lines in the leftmost column of the figure, assumes that a sudden and permanent deterioration in climate leads to failed harvests and therefore higher mortality rates and emigration to neighboring countries. In the first year 1 percent of the population either perishes or emigrates, followed by 0.2 percent a year over the subsequent five years, leading to a population decline of 2 percent over the long term.

In addition to the population effects, drastic changes in climate could also make obsolete many existing agricultural, distributional, and associated industrial patterns, forcing the relocation or decommissioning of existing capital stocks and the relocation or retraining of labor. This represents a large shock to the stock of a country's technology, which would likely result in a significant decline in total factor productivity.[3] For this south Asian economy, productivity growth would be significantly reduced over the medium term in both the tradable and the nontradable sectors of the economy. This would be accompanied by negative effects on foreign demand for the country's products, due to reduced competitiveness in the new industries in which the country is forced to specialize.

Relative to baseline, these shocks cause an immediate 2 percent and ultimately more than 8 percent contraction in GDP, accompanied by a 2 percent real depreciation as domestic goods prices fall. Policy is accommodative, through both a lowering of interest rates and a deterioration in the fiscal deficit.[4] Both measures reduce national savings and drive the current account into deficit.

Financial Market Response

The blue lines in the leftmost column of the figure show a scenario that adds to the direct climate-related shocks a risk premium shock of 1 percentage point a year, as financial markets respond to the country's deteriorating performance and prospects. Higher interest rates reduce capital accumulation and therefore GDP, which ultimately ends up 3 percent lower than in the baseline scenario. Because a higher risk premium raises domestic savings, it leads to depreciation of the real exchange

Note: The main authors of this box are Michael Kumhof and Douglas Laxton, with support from Susanna Mursula.

[1] The country blocks are emerging Asia, euro area, India, Japan, United States, and the remaining countries. Trade linkages among these countries were calibrated using the 2006 matrix of world trade flows.

[2] For a description of the structure of the model see Kumhof and Laxton (2007).

[3] For estimates of the long-run effects on productivity see Nordhaus (2007b).

[4] Fiscal policy is assumed to target a structural interest-inclusive deficit consistent with the preexisting stock of government debt, with the government's estimate of the permanently sustainable tax base reduced only slowly in response to lower realized tax revenue. As a result, tax rates are raised only gradually when the economy contracts, resulting in several years of deficits and increases in debt. Relative to a balanced budget rule, such a policy is expansionary.

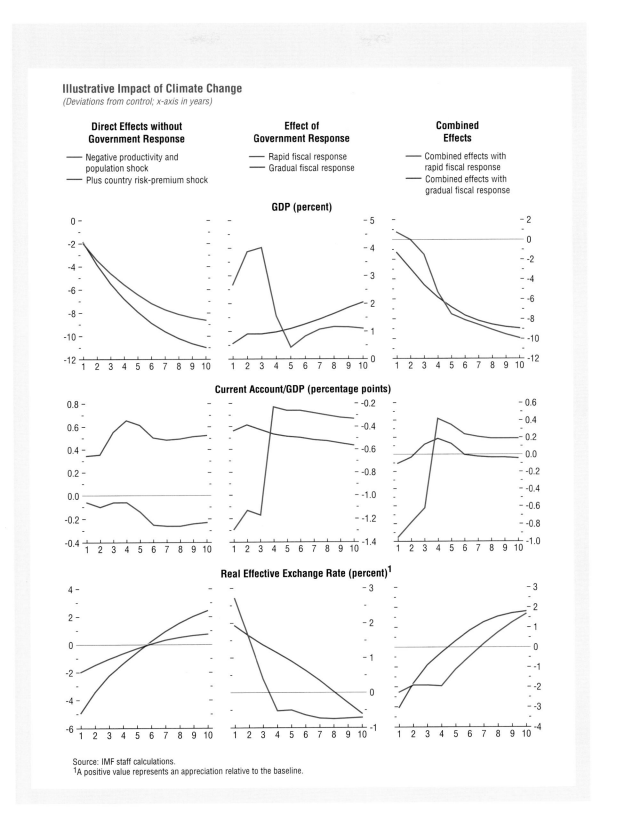

Illustrative Impact of Climate Change
(Deviations from control; x-axis in years)

Source: IMF staff calculations.
[1]A positive value represents an appreciation relative to the baseline.

Box 4.2 *(concluded)*

rate in the short run and causes the current-account-to-GDP ratio to be around 0.7 percentage point higher than in the baseline scenario. After a few years, the improving external asset position causes the real exchange rate to appreciate.

Government Response

Because sufficiently large climate shocks can cause a country's stock of technology to deteriorate significantly, the question arises of how best to rebuild that technology. Clearly, the private sector will have a significant role to play, but private investment may be hampered by the disincentives to capital accumulation stemming from higher real interest rates. Furthermore, the affected economy would require a large-scale investment in public goods such as relief facilities to protect the population, rebuild transportation and communications infrastructure, and retrain the workforce. The middle column of the figure illustrates two such scenarios.[5]

The red lines show the incremental effects of an increase in public investment by 3.3 percent of GDP over a period of three years. This is financed by the issuance of additional government debt, which is allowed to increase by 10 percent of GDP in the long run, accompanied by a 0.5 percent permanent increase in the government-deficit-to-GDP ratio from year four onward. The model assumes that private agents do not save sufficiently to offset such changes in public sector savings. This implies that the issuance of additional government debt crowds out private sector investment in other assets, in this case principally by reducing net foreign assets by 9 percent of GDP in the long run.

Higher public investment increases the stock of public capital by 15 percent at the end of year three. The scenario predicts that GDP increases throughout, initially by about 4 percent as a result of increased government demand, and after a few years by about 1 percent because of the productivity-enhancing effects of a larger public capital stock.[6] The large increase in demand and corresponding decline in national savings causes an initial current account deficit of more than 1 percent of GDP and a 3 percent real appreciation. The current account remains negative as a result of permanently lower government savings, eventually causing the real exchange rate to depreciate enough to generate an export volume sufficient to service the increased external debt.

A policy of rapid government investment may be necessary if the climate shock causes an especially dramatic collapse in activity at the outset. If it does not, as in our baseline scenario, then a more gradual approach may be in order. This is illustrated by the blue lines in the middle column of the figure, which show an increase of public investment by 1 percent of GDP over a period of 10 years. The effects on GDP are similar but are realized much more gradually. The differences are due to the different implications of the two public investment scenarios on the cumulative public capital stock and on the effect of the rate of depreciation.

The red and blue lines in the rightmost column of the figure combine the climate change scenario, including the risk premium response, with either of the two public investment scenarios. Public investment accomplishes two objectives: (1) mitigating the impact of the climate shock, which is most effective when the investment is concentrated in the period immediately following the shock, and (2) mitigating the long-run effects of the shock, which is most effective when the investment is spread over a longer time period.

---

[5]It may be possible to phase in some public investment ahead of a climate shock. But in order to be effective, this would require advance knowledge of exactly when and where such a shock will hit. Given the tremendous uncertainties associated with climate change, there would seem to be only limited scope for such preemptive action.

[6]The elasticity of output with respect to public capital has been calibrated to be consistent with the empirical literature. See Ligthart and Suárez (2005).

or economic systems in response to climatic impacts.[14] If serious efforts to cut emissions were undertaken immediately, some climate warming would still occur, making adaptation unavoidable. However, adaptation is an inadequate response on its own, because there are natural limitations to humans' ability to adapt at higher degrees of warming.

How Can Countries Best Adapt to Climate Change?

Societies have historically adapted to changing environmental conditions, and individuals and firms can be expected to continue altering their behavior in response to changing climate conditions (for example, by planting more drought-resistant crops). However, government involvement is also likely to be needed to spur adaptation, in order to overcome market failures (individual firms and households unable to incorporate the full social benefits of adaptation into their decision making), to meet the need for public goods and services to support adaptation (for example, coastal protection or investment in public health infrastructure), and to augment the private sector's capacity to adapt, for example, in poor countries.

Quantitative analyses of adaptation costs are scant, but studies focusing on public sector costs suggest that adaptation may put a strain on government budgets, especially in developing economies that have weak adaptation capacities and are likely to be more severely affected by climate change. Based on simple extrapolations of current expenditure patterns, the United Nations Framework Convention on Climate Change (2007) estimates additional annual adaptation investment in agriculture, health, water,

and coastal protection of about $40 billion a year in 2030, perhaps half of which might be expected to fall on the public sector. The study also projects additional infrastructure needs of $8 billion–$130 billion, some of which would fall directly on governments.[15] Further refinements of adaptation cost estimates are needed in order to try to narrow the wide range of uncertainty surrounding these estimates and to broaden their coverage where possible—factoring in, for example, the need to adapt to increased climate variability.

Economic and institutional development is perhaps the best means of improving climate-related adaptive capacity. Development promotes diversification away from heavily exposed sectors; improves access to health, education, and water; and reduces poverty. To be effective in fostering adaptation, development strategies need to take climate change vulnerabilities into account, while seeking to avoid maladaptation (IPCC, 2007). Higher-quality institutions also strengthen countries' ability to adapt to climate change (Kahn, 2005).

Fiscal self-insurance against climate change is also needed. Government budgets must include room for adaptation expenditures, and social safety nets must be strengthened, especially in countries that will be severely affected. External financing may be needed to complement domestic resources in cases where the demands of adaptation overwhelm poor countries' capacity.[16] The recent launch of a UN fund to provide

---

[14]More ambitiously, "geoengineering," that is, technological efforts to stabilize the climate system by direct intervention in the energy balance of the Earth, could be used to reduce global warming. But these technologies are at a very early stage of development and, although promising, open a vast range of potential risks to the environment. See Barrett (2006) for a discussion of geoengineering.

[15]The World Bank (2006) puts the cost of "climate-proofing" development investments at $3 billion–$54 billion a year, and the United Nations Development Program (2007) estimates this cost at $44 billion a year in 2015. An additional $2 billion would be needed for disaster response and $40 billion a year to strengthen social safety nets. By comparison, the Japanese government puts the total cost of building coastal defenses to one meter of sea level rise at $93 billion (Government of Japan, 2002). The United Kingdom also reports high cost estimates for flood prevention—about $1 billion annually and a further $8 billion to strengthen the Thames Barrier (UKCIP, 2007).

[16]For example, Easterling and others (2007) conclude that a 3°C regional warming would likely exceed the ability of emerging economies to adapt to the impact on crop yields.

Box 4.3. Macroeconomic Policies for Smoother Adjustment to Abrupt Climate Shocks

Economic theory suggests that macroeconomic policies such as exchange rate flexibility can help reduce the macroeconomic cost of the extreme weather events that are likely to accompany climate change. Such shocks typically destroy capital and disrupt production, and adjusting to them requires reallocating people and capital across and within sectors. Currency depreciation helps reduce the cost of the shock and enables the economy to move more quickly to the new equilibrium by raising the domestic price of exports, while a higher price level facilitates adjustment in real wages (Friedman, 1953; and Mundell, 1961). Adjustment to a negative shock in a fixed-rate regime tends to take longer, with economic activity declining until (sticky) wages and prices fall to their new equilibrium levels (Obstfeld and Rogoff, 2002). The empirical evidence in Ramcharan (2007a) is consistent with these ideas.

However, there are some important caveats to this literature. In part because of concerns about their commitment to price stability, some central banks in developing economies may not have the ability to effectively pursue countercyclical monetary policy. Thus, an important component of the adjustment process in flexible rate regimes may be limited in practice. Also, prices may not be particularly rigid in many developing economies, making adjustment through the nominal exchange rate superfluous. Moreover, fixed-rate regimes can reduce exchange rate variability and lower transaction costs, thereby stimulating trade, investment, and growth. And depending on the balance-sheet exposure of firms, nominal

Note: The main author of this box is Rodney Ramcharan.

exchange rate movements can exacerbate the impact of real shocks.

The reallocation of production factors after a shock also depends on credit market imperfections and labor market rigidities (Caballero and Hammour, 2005; and Matsuyama, 2007). Intuitively, the aggregate economic cost of a shock such as a flood that destroys agricultural production may be lessened if the dislocated farm labor can be readily absorbed in the manufacturing sector. But rigid labor contracts may prevent such a reallocation, idling labor and worsening the shock. Likewise, financial market imperfections that deny firms liquidity to help finance shocks can lead to inefficient closures and economic contractions (Bernanke and Gertler, 1989; Kiyotaki and Moore, 1997; and Wasmer and Weil, 2004). There is also econometric evidence that highlights the importance of flexible financial sector policies in shaping the impact of extreme weather shocks.

However, identifying the role of economic policy in shaping the aggregate economic response to climate change and other adverse shocks can be very difficult. Policymakers often choose policies and regulations based in part on the expected impact of economic events, potentially blurring the lines between cause and effect. For example, because policymakers may choose exchange rate flexibility when they expect costly changes to the terms of trade, more flexible regimes may coincide with sharp output losses, masking the potential impact of floating exchange rate regimes in smoothing these shocks. Bias can also arise because policy choices can determine the frequency and intensity of economic shocks. In this case, exchange rate or financial sector policies may determine

Disasters across High- and Low-Income Countries

Country Income Category	Number of Disasters	Population (million)	Killed in Disasters	Total Damage, as a Percent of GDP	GDP per Capita
High income	1,476	828	75,425	0.007	23,021
Low income	1,533	869	907,810	0.55	1,345

Sources: Centre for Research on the Epidemiology of Disasters; and Stromberg (2007). Disasters include earthquakes, droughts, floods, windstorms, and volcanic eruptions. Total damage is computed for windstorms and floods only.

Regional Differences in Disaster Incidence and Impact

	Number of Disasters	Killed per 100,000	Affected per 100,000
Africa	861	2.61	1,453
Asia	2,352	0.74	4,303
Americas	1,626	0.59	564
Europe	863	0.60	206
Oceania	324	0.46	2,363

Sources: Centre for Research on the Epidemiology of Disasters; and Stromberg (2007).

specialization patterns and thus the intensity and frequency of terms-of-trade shocks.

Natural disasters can, however, provide credible insight into the impact of economic policy in shaping the aggregate economic response to climate change and other shocks. In particular, disasters are easily observed and yet highly unpredictable. They are also, at least in the short run, not determined by economic choices. Thus, in economics jargon, they can be treated as conditionally exogenous with respect to policy choices. That said, these events do cluster geographically (first and second tables), and the general susceptibility of some countries to natural shocks may influence both economic policy and the response to such shocks. But susceptibility is an observable phenomenon that can be included in the estimation framework, reducing the possibility of bias. And even after accounting for geographic clustering, these shocks remain mostly low-probability and unpredictable events for many countries, and therefore are unlikely to be a powerful force in determining economic policy. The Caribbean, for example, is notoriously hurricane prone, yet an Atlantic hurricane on average has struck one of these islands just seven times in the past 100 years.

The methodology in Ramcharan (2007a) can be used to estimate the role of financial sector policies in shaping the output impact of natural disasters. In the case of floods, for example, let S_{it-1} denote a variable that takes on the value of zero if there are no floods in country i in year $t-1$ (the previous year) and the ratio of affected land area to the country's total land

Financial Sector Reforms and the Impact of Floods on Output Growth
(Dependent variable: real per capita GDP growth)

(a)	(b) Baseline	(c) "Constant Policies"	(d) Fixed Effects
Flood ($t-1$)	37.945 [40.916]	70.707 [62.509]	32.146 [51.284]
Index*Flood ($t-1$)	−7.343 [24.954]	−75.724 [100.034]	−0.244 [27.582]
Flood ($t-2$)	13.043 [35.767]	2.490 [36.658]	4.323 [33.569]
Index*Flood ($t-2$)	27.832 [33.379]	40.557 [32.498]	30.428 [28.258]
Flood ($t-3$)	89.142** [36.503]	104.159 [102.895]	86.924** [40.527]
Index*Flood ($t-3$)	−10.844 [26.197]	−150.389 [169.852]	−13.505 [25.770]
Flood ($t-4$)	−37.606 [25.417]	−73.439** [27.862]	−39.671* [23.146]
Index*Flood ($t-4$)	86.859** [37.567]	127.332*** [35.185]	92.125** [36.152]
Flood ($t-5$)	−77.633** [35.548]	−226.517*** [47.327]	−83.121** [35.773]
Index*Flood ($t-5$)	94.267*** [14.572]	70.670*** [10.574]	97.687*** [14.122]
Observations	989	842	989
R-squared	0.28	0.30	0.37

Source: Ramcharan (2007b).
Note: Standard errors, in brackets, are clustered at the country level. *, **, and *** denote significance at the 10 percent, 5 percent, and 1 percent level, respectively.

area if a flood does occur. Let R_{it} denote the Abiad, Detragiache, and Thierry Tressel (2007) de jure financial liberalization index observed in country i on year t. The vector $\mathbf{X}_{it}$ denotes the set of control variables observed for country i in year t.

The estimating equation is

$$y_{it} = \sum_{j=1}^{5} [\alpha_j S_{it-j} + \lambda_j R_{it} + \gamma_j S_{it-j} * R_{it} + \mathbf{X}_{it-j} S_{it-j} \theta_j] + \mathbf{X}_{it}\beta + \nu_t + u_{it},$$

where the parameters γ_j test whether the impact of a shock on the outcome variable, y_{it}, depends on the market orientation of the financial system. Because the financial system as well as the shock can affect the equilibrium level of y_{it}, the specifi-

Box 4.3 *(concluded)*

cation also linearly includes R_{it}, as well as S_{it}. In addition, other variables that are correlated with the decision to reform the financial system might also shape the output response to the shock, and to reduce this potential source of bias, we also estimate these interaction terms, yielding the coefficient θ_j. We consider the effects of the shock over a five-year horizon, beginning in the year immediately after the event is reported. The variable v_t denotes year effects; u_{it} is a residual term that is allowed to be correlated across years for the same country in all regressions.

The third table excerpts some of the main results reported in Ramcharan (2007b). The sample consists of an unbalanced panel of 43 countries, beginning in 1973. The results confirm that financial liberalization can alleviate the impact of a flood on growth. Column b suggests that for two economies experiencing a similar flood, output growth is about 0.65 percentage point

higher in the economy scoring one standard deviation higher on the liberalization index.[1] However, these results can be biased if policy-makers systematically respond to these shocks by changing financial sector policies. Thus, column c excludes those floods that coincided with changes to the liberalization index over a six-year period, beginning in the year prior to the shock. The results are little changed. Finally, column d includes country-specific dummies to absorb time-invariant unobserved heterogeneity among countries. Again, the cumulative effect of financial sector reforms in shaping the output response to the shock is little changed.

[1]The fraction of land area affected by the typical flood in the sample is 0.014, and the standard deviation of the liberalization index is 0.246. Thus, using the significant coefficients from the third table, the estimated impact is (94.267+86.859)*0.014*0.246.

dedicated financing to such countries is a welcome step in this regard.

A flexible exchange rate regime and policies that make capital and labor more flexible may help reduce the macroeconomic cost of the types of abrupt shocks (such as extreme weather events) that are likely to accompany climate change (Box 4.3). Such shocks typically destroy capital and disrupt production, and adjusting to them requires reallocating people and capital across and within sectors. Many of these policies can be implemented fairly quickly and at a small cost to the budget, making them part of an effective adaptation strategy that can dampen the macroeconomic impact of climate shocks.

How Financial Markets Can Foster Adaptation

Financial markets can reduce the macroeconomic costs of adaptation by generating price signals to incentivize the relocation of people to lower-risk areas (for example, through lower insurance premiums) and reallocation of capital to newly productive sectors and regions (factor-

ing in climate-adjusted costs and risks).[17] The financial markets' capacity to reallocate costs and risks to those most willing and able to bear them also will help reduce the social costs of adaptation. However, this capacity is dependent on the quality of macroeconomic and financial policies.

Two types of financial instruments are particularly relevant in the context of responding to climate change.

- Weather derivatives offer a way for producers vulnerable to short-term fluctuations in temperature or rainfall to hedge their exposure.[18] Exchange-traded contracts are typically linked to the number of days hotter or colder than the seasonal average within a future period,

[17]The recent strong performance of water distribution companies suggests that such factors are already being reflected in equity prices (Geman and Kanyinda, 2007).

[18]A weather swap is the transfer of payments between parties under a contract determined by the outcome of a weather-related index. The party who is "long" on the swap pays if the realized index is above the strike price and gets paid if it is below the strike price.

and trading in these contracts has grown strongly (Figure 4.8). Trading has focused on temperatures in selected U.S. and European cities, with liquidity now concentrated in near-term contracts because hedge funds and banks hold a larger share of such positions. Weather derivatives are now complemented by weather swaps and insurance contracts that can be used to hedge adverse weather and agricultural outcomes. Governments in some lower-income countries (for example, India and Mongolia) now offer crop and livestock insurance as a way to protect their most vulnerable farmers. Ethiopia pioneered drought insurance in 2006.

- Catastrophe (Cat) bonds help disperse catastrophic weather risk (Box 4.4). Following Hurricane Katrina, Cat bond issuance rose sharply (see Figure 4.8), benefiting vulnerable sectors, for example, agriculture and coastal property, by offering insurers more flexible instruments to transfer risk, thereby extending insurability and stabilizing premiums.

Nonetheless, there is a possibility that rising climate-related risks may overwhelm the financial sector's capacity (ABI, 2005). What can governments do to help preserve insurability and risk-management capacity? First, governments should refrain from subsidizing or capping flood or hurricane insurance premiums, in order to avoid promoting risky behavior and increasing fiscal risks. Development in areas vulnerable to flooding or wind damage may need to be discouraged in some cases where a high likelihood of damage makes insurance unavailable. In other cases, government investment in flood defenses or water conservation may enable insurers to continue providing flood or drought coverage. Finally, governments can foster the development of weather derivatives, insurance, and Cat bonds by providing reliable and independent data on weather patterns.

Although they are not a panacea—at this point, hedges against weather and catastrophic risks are available only out to five years—recent innovation and deepening in these markets

Figure 4.8. Weather Derivatives and Catastrophe Bonds[1]
(Billions of U.S. dollars)

There has been a strong rise in trading of weather derivatives and issuance of bonds transferring catastrophic risk.

Weather Derivatives: Notional Value Traded[2]

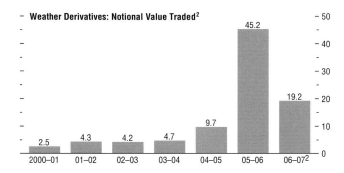

Catastrophe Bonds Issued and Outstanding

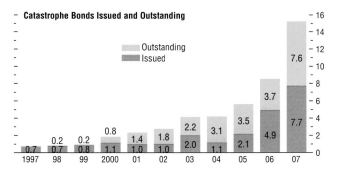

Sources: PricewaterhouseCoopers; and Swiss Re Capital Markets.
[1]Notional value traded is the total value of the derivatives contract transacted, against which weather-related payments are calculated.
[2]Reduction in notional value traded in 2006–07 is largely the result of a move to monthly, rather than seasonal, contracts on the Chicago Mercantile Exchange.

Box 4.4. Catastrophe Insurance and Bonds: New Instruments to Hedge Extreme Weather Risks

Climate change is likely to increase the incidence of extreme weather events. The *Stern Review* (2007) anticipates an increase in the frequency of severe floods, droughts, and storms. Likewise, the Intergovernmental Panel on Climate Change (IPCC) expects an increase in the intensity and duration of droughts and in the severity of hurricanes. Such events often have devastating effects, particularly in low-income and small countries. Financial markets can help these countries to insure against extreme weather risks. Although relatively unexploited to date, a variety of insurance instruments now allow for hedging almost any natural disaster risk.

Over the past decade, the market for global catastrophe reinsurance has grown strongly in volume and in the variety of financial structures, although its geographic coverage has expanded to a more limited degree. The global catastrophe reinsurance market is the wholesale segment of the insurance market. Typically, primary insurers (those that write policies to households and companies) seek coverage for their exposure to natural disasters (first figure). In addition, securitizations—such as catastrophe (Cat) bonds—can be used to transfer ("lay off") risk to the capital markets. Cat bonds are typically issued by reinsurance companies, but are sometimes issued by primary insurers or parties who seek self-insurance, such as governments. Although still relatively small, the Cat bond market has been growing rapidly in the past few years, reaching a total capitalization of more than $15 billion by end-2007. Market sources estimate the overall catastrophe reinsurance volume at about $150 billion.

Most Cat bonds and catastrophe reinsurance contracts are focused on a handful of major risks, but the covered events have widened some over the past two years. The major perils—U.S. wind, U.S. earthquake, European windstorm, Japanese earthquake, and Japanese typhoon—account for about 90 percent

Note: The main author of this box is Eduardo Borensztein.

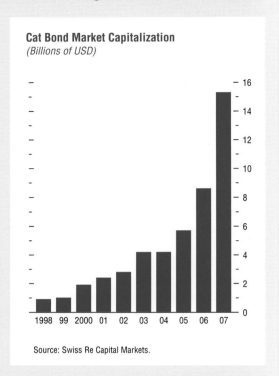

Cat Bond Market Capitalization
(Billions of USD)

Source: Swiss Re Capital Markets.

of the total market volume. Recently, insurers in a wider set of countries have started to seek disaster coverage, including in Australia and New Zealand (wind), and in Taiwan Province of China (earthquake).

A handful of Cat bonds have been issued by governments seeking to hedge the fiscal risks that arise from disasters. For example, in 2006, FONDEN, the Mexican government agency charged with providing relief following natural disasters, placed instruments to cover earthquake risks at three vulnerable locations, with total coverage of $450 million. The operation comprised a direct contract with a reinsurance company and the issuance of two Cat bonds. In 2007, the World Bank launched the Caribbean Catastrophe Risk Insurance Facility (CCRIF)—a regional disaster insurance facility to provide coverage against hurricane risk for 16 Caribbean countries. The countries purchased a total of $120 million in disaster insurance from CCRIF, which then laid off the risk through reinsurers and capital markets. Scale is a significant advantage of pooling multicountry risk. The minimum economically feasible size for a Cat bond is estimated to be about $100 million.

Market instruments typically do not provide full insurance coverage for macro risks. The standard contract or Cat bond, including those used by FONDEN and CCRIF, applies a "parametric" trigger—the insurance payment is triggered by the occurrence of a natural event of a certain magnitude, rather than by a calculation of the losses suffered. The trigger can be a particular wind speed or a certain intensity and/or depth of an earthquake measured at a specified location. The parametric trigger simplifies enormously the monitoring and execution of the insurance contract and permits immediate payment upon the occurrence of the covered disaster.[1] The event can be monitored by a third party, such as the U.S. National Hurricane Center.

Parametric insurance, however, can leave a fair amount of residual risk uncovered ("basis risk" in insurance language). A natural phenomenon may cause considerable damage without crossing the parametric boundary. Indeed, Hurricane Dean, which caused significant damage in Belize and Jamaica in August 2007, did not trigger any payments under the CCRIF because winds did not reach the required speeds at the specified locations. As with any other insurance structure, there is a trade-off between cost and coverage in parametric insurance. Basis risk can be reduced but only at a higher cost, and the insured must choose their preferred trade-off between risk and cost.

Pricing in the Cat market has been punctuated by the impact of large disasters—particularly U.S. hurricanes Andrew in 1993 and Katrina in 2005 (second figure). There has also been an upward trend in insurance premi-

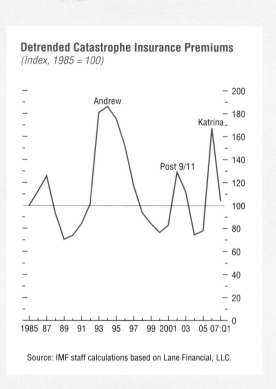

Detrended Catastrophe Insurance Premiums
(Index, 1985 = 100)

Source: IMF staff calculations based on Lane Financial, LLC.

ums, in part related to upward reassessments of disaster risk. The reason for the premium spikes is that, after a large disaster, reinsurance companies need to rebuild capital in order to preserve their solvency and credit ratings. This may be a long process if capital markets are not fluid, and in the meantime insurance premiums remain elevated. Yet the figure also suggests that the post-Katrina rise, although broadly commensurate with the post-Andrew increase, was fairly short lived. The reversal of the premium increase took place despite both a tightening of standards by credit rating agencies and an upward reassessment of disaster risk by weather modeling firms and market participants. Part of the reason for the quick reversal was the rapid entry of new investors such as hedge funds, banks, and private equity investors, who supplied additional capital through various market structures. In addition to Cat bonds, new market instruments include bank loans and equity, especially in the form of "sidecars"—legally

---

[1]A more common feature of standard reinsurance contracts is an "indemnity" trigger—namely, the damage suffered by the insured. There are also intermediate options such as modeled losses and indices based on a parametric occurrence.

Box 4.4 *(concluded)*

separate, special-purpose reinsurance companies that raise short-term capital through private equity and debt.

An Unexploited Opportunity?

Low-income and small countries are especially vulnerable to natural disasters because of more limited geographical diversification, higher percentages of the population living in exposed areas, and higher dependence on natural rainfall and benign weather conditions for agricultural production. According to the World Health Organization's Emergency Events Database, two hurricanes that hit Belize in 2000 and 2001 each caused damage equivalent to more than 30 percent of GDP and impaired public debt sustainability (Borensztein, Cavallo, and Valenzuela, 2008).[2] Even less-extreme events can involve enormous indirect costs. Drought has been linked to higher incidence of armed conflict in low-income countries, essentially through its effect on economic growth and poverty (Miguel, Satyanath, and Sergenti, 2004).

Faced with such catastrophic risk, low-income countries tend to rely on foreign aid or some form of self-insurance (Borensztein, Cavallo, and Valenzuela, 2008). Aid flows, however, are unreliable, may arrive late, and seem somewhat dependent on the extent to which the media covers the disaster. Self-insurance strategies include borrowing when a disaster occurs or accumulating resources in a dedicated fund. But there is a critical difference between insurance and self-insurance. If a country purchases insurance (say by issuing a Cat bond), it will receive ensured payment in a disaster that offsets the loss suffered, albeit imperfectly. By resorting to borrowing, by contrast, the country can spread over time the cost of the disaster but still bears the full economic loss. Moreover, self-insurance strategies may have other problems. For example, self-insurance funds may be appropriated for other uses when they become sizable. There is, in fact, an optimal combination of

insurance and borrowing (or self-insurance), which depends on many factors, including the size of the potential loss, the cost of insurance, interest rates, ease of access to external financing, and the extent to which credit rating agencies incorporate market insurance coverage in their evaluation.

Despite their advantages, few countries have issued Cat bonds or sought disaster insurance. One reason may be cost. Cat premiums can be high owing to various factors, including the required technical studies by modeling agencies, legal costs, and remuneration of the capital requirements for insurance and reinsurance companies under imperfect market conditions (see Froot, 2001). (To some extent, however, the cost of insurance for emerging and developing economies is tempered by the diversification value of these perils within the global financial market.) Another reason may be policymakers' fears of engaging in unusual and complex operations, which they may not fully understand. Politicians also tend to focus on the near term and hence are not motivated to spend money on insurance that may mainly benefit their successors in office.

Catastrophe insurance instruments also can be useful for international financial institutions that seek to provide broad support for such insurance programs, as in the case of CCRIF. The World Bank has other projects under way to provide insurance to farmers in various countries, including India and Mongolia, and it is hedging these risks in global markets. Disaster insurance is a means for aid agencies to deal with the budget limitations that can arise in years when they must respond to several large disasters. In this regard, the United Nations' World Food Program (WFP), in collaboration with the World Bank, ran a pilot program for drought insurance in Ethiopia in 2006, which offered coverage to farmers who could be affected by insufficient rainfall. The WFP laid off the risk in the global reinsurance market. In the event, no payments were triggered because rains were adequate in all the covered areas.

---

[2]Cost estimates should be viewed with appropriate caution and are subject to significant revisions.

holds the promise that they have considerable potential to promote adaptation to climate change. The growth of hedge funds and the strong appetite for risks that are uncorrelated with other financial markets should ensure continuing demand for financial instruments that pay investors a premium for taking weather risk even in the face of climate change (van Lennep and others, 2004; and Bonaccolta, 2007).

All in all, countries' adaptive capacity is likely to increase in the future, as incomes rise, technologies emerge, financial markets develop, and understanding of climate change improves. Nonetheless, at high degrees of warming, the limitations of adaptation are likely to be reached relatively quickly. Together with the rising probability of catastrophic risk, this points to a need for mitigation.

How Can Countries Effectively and Efficiently Mitigate Climate Change?

A successful policy framework for mitigating climate change must satisfy several criteria.

- To be effective, mitigation policy must raise the prices of GHGs to reflect the marginal social damage from emissions. Higher GHG prices would help generate incentives for reducing production and consumption of emission-intensive goods and for development and adoption of new, low-emission technologies.

- Mitigation policy must be applied across all GHGs, firms, countries, sectors, and time periods in order to ensure that policy achieves the desired objectives at the lowest possible cost.

- It is important to address distributional considerations across firms, income groups, and generations, both for reasons of fairness and distributional justice as well as to ensure that policies remain politically viable.

- Mitigation policies must be flexible and robust to changing economic conditions and to new scientific information about climate change, because highly volatile outcomes could increase the economic costs of policies and reduce political support.

- Mitigation policies must be enforceable and have "dynamic consistency," meaning that governments have incentives to keep them in place, in order to induce the needed behavioral response.

Many policy instruments have been considered for reducing emissions. The most prominent have been emission taxes, tradable emission permits, performance standards, incentives for the adoption of energy-saving technologies, and subsidies for the reduction of emissions or introduction of clean technologies (Box 4.5).[19] Market-based policies, such as emission taxes (often called carbon taxes[20]) and permit-trading programs, have an important advantage over performance standards in that they create a common price for emissions. Common pricing encourages emissions to be concentrated in firms that can produce more efficiently.

The choice between carbon taxes and cap-and-trade systems is less clear cut. Carbon taxes have an important advantage over cap-and-trade systems in that they result in a stable price for emissions (cap-and-trade policies seek to stabilize the quantity of emissions, but allow prices to fluctuate). Stable prices for emissions are critical for firms making long-term decisions about investment and innovation in low-emission technologies. Carbon taxes also provide for greater flexibility in the face of changing economic conditions, allowing firms to reduce emissions more during periods of slow demand growth and less during periods of high demand growth, when the cost of doing so would be higher. In contrast, cap-and-trade systems could give rise to volatile emission pricing when demand conditions change. Carbon taxes also generate revenues that can be used to enhance efficiency

---

[19]Performance standards include, for example, limits on emissions per kilowatt hour of electricity and fuel-economy requirements on vehicles.

[20]Taxing the carbon content of emissions is equivalent to taxing carbon dioxide. Carbon dioxide accounts for the largest share of emissions. Emissions of other GHGs (methane, nitrous oxide, and fluorinated gases) are often expressed in terms of their carbon dioxide equivalents.

Box 4.5. Recent Emission-Reduction Policy Initiatives

Under Annex I of the Kyoto Protocol, signatory countries[1] agree to reduce their greenhouse gas (GHG) emissions by 8 percent relative to 1990 levels by 2008–12. This is the principal international policy framework providing incentives to mitigate the impact of global warming. The main implementation mechanism for the Kyoto Protocol in Europe is the European Union Emissions Trading Scheme (EU-ETS). Two additional compliance vehicles, the Clean Development Mechanism (CDM) and Joint Implementation, enable Annex I countries to gain credits for emission reductions arising from investments made in countries not subject to binding targets.

The EU-ETS is an international cap-and-trade system, projected to reduce emissions by 2.4 percent compared to a business-as-usual scenario by 2010,[2] although it needs further reform in order to realize its full potential for large-scale, efficient mitigation. During Phases I (2005–07) and II (2008–12), carbon dioxide (CO_2) emission rights were allocated to about 11,000 energy-intensive installations across the European Union (mostly electric power utilities and major industrial emitters), representing about 40 percent of total EU carbon emissions. The volume of trading in the market was about 1.6 billion tons of CO_2 in 2007 and was valued at about €28 billion (up 55 percent over 2006 values).[3] Intended to minimize abatement costs for a given emission target, the system is subject to a number of design flaws, which have reduced its effectiveness. First, excess quotas and market uncertainty have caused permit prices to be too low and volatile. In fact, prices fell to zero in the second half of 2007 (although prices are generally higher under Phase II). Second, the high share of free allocations (at least 95 per-

cent in Phase I and 90 percent in Phase II) led to windfall profits and forgone public revenues and reduced abatement incentives by creating expectations of future free allocations based on current emissions.[4] These problems were exacerbated by rules under which exiting firms lose their free allocations while new firms typically receive free allocations.[5] Third, the carbon price is poorly coordinated with policies, taxes, and regulations implemented in markets outside the scope of the scheme, such as heating and transportation. Efforts to limit the extent of some of these (and other) problems are under way, for example, by expanding the system to include new industries (including, for example, aviation within the European Union) and new gases; preannouncing future constraints (starting with an 11 percent reduction in Phase III against the previous commitment framework); moving to full auctioning of permits (starting with at least 60 percent in 2013); and harmonizing the rules for cap-setting and entry and exit.

The CDM enables Annex I countries to gain credits for investment in less-carbon-intensive technologies in developing and emerging market economies (currently not subject to mitigation targets), facilitating access to lower-cost abatement opportunities and helping to promote development by adding to the capital stock in these economies. The CDM market has grown rapidly in recent years, with primary markets estimated at 950 million tons of CO_2 and valued at approximately €12 billion in 2007 (up almost 200 percent over 2006 values). Several issues, however, warrant attention. First, the capacity to monitor and verify the "additionality" of emission reductions, formally a condition for CDM project approval, is often unclear. Although emissions may be reduced through a

---

Note: The main authors of this box are Ben Jones and Jon Strand, with input from Paul Mills.

[1]A group of industrialized nations including eastern Europe, the OECD, Russia, and the United States (although the latter did not ratify the treaty).

[2]See Capoor and Ambrosi (2007).

[3]See Point Carbon Research (2008).

[4]See Böhringer and Lange (2005) and Rosendahl (2006) for discussion. Rosendahl points out that when future quotas are updated to reflect current emissions, the quota price could be several times the level of marginal emission abatement cost, indicating that very little abatement is taking place.

[5]See, for example, Åhman and Holmgren (2006); and Åhman, Burtraw, Kruger, and Zetterberg (2007).

particular CDM project, it is difficult to quantify overall emission reductions in economies that are not subject to overarching emission constraints or policies (such counterfactuals are in some sense impossible to ascertain, even given elaborate case-by-case administrative procedures). Second, given the high degree of policy risk after 2012, virtually no abatement has been achieved for projects subject to long investment-return periods, such as in energy supply markets—most investment has targeted emission reductions from industrial processes. Third, forgone deforestation has so far been left out of the CDM, and its inclusion will require overcoming complex administrative and governance problems, especially in relation to establishing a baseline, monitoring and enforcing compliance, and managing "leakage" risks. Finally, few CDM projects have yet been carried out in the poorest countries (with Brazil, China, and India so far dominating), which raises distributional concerns.

In addition, many countries, including non-signatories to the Kyoto Protocol (such as the United States) and major developing economies that are not subject to binding targets under the agreement, have implemented domestic policies that reduce emissions. (The table summarizes these policies for a selected group of countries.) These policies are typically motivated less by climate change concerns than by other considerations, for example, productivity improvements, energy security, and the abatement of local pollution. However, other domestic policies, such as energy subsidies, may have opposing effects, leading to strong overall growth in emissions, particularly from expansion of fossil-fuel-based energy supply in developing economies. Although domestic efforts are welcome—indeed essential—thus far they have provided weak and often poorly coordinated incentives and have also lacked transparency. These factors have impeded effective and efficient international coordination of mitigation efforts. Two primary types of such domestic emission-reduction policies are performance standards and technology subsidies.

Performance standards, though often less attractive than market mechanisms, have resulted in substantial emission reductions in markets for vehicles, buildings, and appliances, for which emissions are diffuse, transaction costs from compliance with market incentives are high, and the credibility of carbon markets is still being established. In road transport, Japan's Top Runner program (see table) has yielded significant energy savings, estimated at 15 percent during 1995–2005 in the case of diesel passenger vehicles (Energy Conservation Centre Japan, 2005). In the United States, Corporate Average Fuel Economy (CAFE) standards, while less demanding than European or Japanese standards, have improved vehicle efficiency since their introduction in 1975. However, laxer restrictions on sport-utility vehicles and small trucks have constrained their overall effectiveness when consumer preferences shifted toward heavier vehicle classes. Regulatory codes applied to buildings, for example in California, are estimated to have saved approximately 10,000 gigawatt hours (GWh) of electricity annually, about 4 percent of total electricity use in 2003 (California Energy Commission, 2005). More stringent commitments to improve the energy efficiency of U.S. federal buildings were announced in December 2007. U.S. standards on appliances are projected to reduce annual residential emissions by about 37 metric tons of CO_2 ($MtCO_2$) by 2020, roughly 9 percent of household emissions (Meyers and others, 2002).

Technology subsidies (including tax incentives) have been widely used to support renewable electricity and biofuel production, but they are not a cost-effective substitute for proper carbon pricing. Even so, they may be an appropriate response to failures in technology markets. Support typically aims to reduce the cost of research and development and capital investment, or to guarantee higher end-user prices. In Germany, for example, a renewable electricity "feed-in" tariff system is expected to impose additional costs of €30 billion–€36 billion on consumers between 2000 and 2012 at a cost of approximately €0.10 a kilowatt hour

Box 4.5 *(concluded)*

Domestic Policy Measures Affecting Emissions

China	Domestic targets to reduce the energy intensity of GDP by 20 percent during 2005–10 and expand renewable energy generation to 30 percent of total capacity by 2020 • Reduced indirect taxation on renewable electricity generation and favorable customs duty rates on imported components • Central and local government research and development support, for example, $28 million expenditure on development of renewables under 10th Five-Year Plan • Various investment subsidies, for example, in renewable village power systems as part of large-scale rural electrification programs • Energy-efficiency standards on vehicles, energy-using products, and some new urban buildings; residential appliances, for example, estimated to conserve about 9 percent of China's residential electricity in 2010[1] • Restructuring of (and closure of the most energy-inefficient) state-owned enterprises
European Union	Kyoto Protocol commitment to reduce emissions by 8 percent against 1990 levels by 2008–12; EU voluntary target of 20 percent below 1990 levels by 2020 • The EU Emissions Trading Scheme (EU-ETS), covering power generation and heavy industry, is projected to reduce emissions by an additional 2.4 percent compared with business as usual in 2010[2] • Extensive taxation of gasoline and diesel, particularly high in the United Kingdom • Support for climate research and technologies amounting to $3 billion, and a further $1.8 billion on nuclear research, under Framework Program 6, 2002–06[3] • Renewables obligations and "feed in" tariffs for diffusion of clean technologies • Regulation of buildings, appliances, and vehicles (for example, the Energy Performance of Buildings Directive) and proposed mandatory regulation of passenger vehicles[4]
India	Domestic targets, including a 20 percent increase in energy efficiency by 2016–17; expanded electricity supply to all villages by 2009; and 5 percent increase in tree and forest cover[5] • Planned subsidies for renewable energy sources, particularly in remote rural areas, totaling $174 million during 2007–12[6] • $38 million investment in research, design, and development in new and renewable energy • Increased forest cover through regulation, incentives, and information on improved forest management[7] • Building codes for large new commercial buildings and government buildings, designed to reduce energy consumption by 20–40 percent[8]
Japan	Kyoto Protocol commitment to reduce emissions by 6 percent from 1990 levels by 2008–12; national objective to reduce energy intensity by 30 percent from 2003 to 2030 • Taxes on gasoline (¥46,800/kiloliter), kerosene (aviation fuel) (¥26,000/kiloliter), coal (¥700/ton), and electricity (¥375/kilowatt-hour sold)[9] • Top Runner Program of performance standards on more than 20 classes of products (including vehicles and appliances), expected to realize savings of 16–25 percent of total national savings by 2010[10] • Supplier obligation to produce 8.7 terawatt hours (tWh) of renewable electricity in 2007, rising to 16 billion tWh by 2014[11] • Voluntary agreements with industry stakeholders covering 39 industries to subsidize one-third of greenhouse gas (GHG) reduction expenditure if targets are met
United States	Voluntary objective to reduce GHG intensity level to 18 percent below 2002 levels by 2012 • Tax incentives totaling $3.6 billion over 2006–11 for use on cleaner, renewable energy and more energy-efficient technology • Support for research and development, domestic and international climate-related programs (for example, "Methane to Markets" and Asia Pacific Partnership) of $37 billion during 2001–07 • Efficiency standards for buildings, vehicles, and appliances. ENERGY STAR performance labeling program covering 1,400 products, and extended through partnerships with six international markets

(International Energy Agency, 2007b). In the United States, repeal of excise taxes for biofuels implies a subsidy of approximately $12 billion during 2007–11 (Metcalf, 2007). Analysis of the returns for various renewable energy subsidies in G7 countries indicates that costs are generally much higher than most current estimates of marginal damage costs related to CO_2 emissions (see, for example, Strand, 2007). This suggests that direct public support for increased renewable energy production is currently an expensive way to mitigate carbon emissions compared with an efficient carbon-pricing regime, although returns may be higher if future cost reductions from induced learning-by-doing are considered.

Domestic Policy Measures Affecting Emissions *(concluded)*

Brazil	National objective to increase the share of renewable energy sources to 10 percent by 2030 and expand availability of electricity to an additional 12 million citizens
	• Roughly 50 percent reduction in deforestation between 2004 and 2006 through improved satellite monitoring, land use controls, and sustainable logging incentives
	• Mandatory 22 percent blend of ethanol in gasoline and 2 percent mix of biosourced diesel (rising to 5 percent in 2013)
	• Subsidized lines of credit for biodiesel production; support for research into biodiesel and expansion of ethanol and sugar program to other products
	• 20-year feed-in tariffs for renewable electricity generators;[12] supplier obligation to invest 1 percent of net operational income in efficiency measures and research and development
	• Adoption of U.S. efficiency standards for light vehicles and EU standards for motorcycles and heavy vehicles
	• Investment in decentralized, renewable electricity as part of "Light for All" electrification program

[1]China Markets Group, Lawrence Berkeley Laboratories: http://china.lbl.gov/china_buildings-asl-standards.html.
[2]See Capoor and Ambrosi (2007).
[3]EU action against climate change: research and development to stimulate climate-friendly technologies.
[4]The Energy Performance of Buildings Directive is designed to realize an estimated cost-effective savings potential of about 22 percent of present consumption in buildings across the European Union by 2010. The European Commission is proposing to reduce the average emissions of CO_2 from new passenger cars in the European Union from about 160 grams a kilometer to 130 grams a kilometer in 2012.
[5]India, Planning Commission (2007).
[6]India, Ministry of New and Renewable Energy (2006).
[7]India, Ministry of Environment and Forests (2006), p. 25.
[8]India, Ministry of Environment and Forests and Ministry of Power Bureau of Energy Efficiency (2007), p. 7.
[9]Japan (2006).
[10]Nordqvist (2006), p. 6.
[11]"Outline of the Renewable Portfolio Standard (RPS) System." www.rps.go.jp/RPS/new-contents/english/outline.html.
[12]Brazil (2007), pp. 22, 27.

(by lowering other taxes) or equity (by compensating groups disadvantaged by the policy). However, under carbon taxes, the quantity of emission reductions is uncertain. Taxes also may be politically difficult to implement.

There are ways to reduce the disadvantages of cap-and-trade systems. Price volatility, for example, can be reduced by introducing safety valves that allow governments to sell some temporary permits if permit prices exceed some prespecified "trigger" levels, by allowing the depositing and borrowing of permits, or by creating a central-bank-type institution for overseeing permit markets. Such hybrid policies—combining elements of a carbon tax and a permit-trading system—could be superior to the respective single policy instruments (Pizer, 2002). Raising the trigger price of the safety valve over time would allow for the simultaneous targeting of emission prices, over the short run, and their quantity, over the long

run.[21] See Box 4.6 for a further discussion of these and other issues that arise in the context of mitigation policies.[22]

Macroeconomic Effects of International Mitigation Policies

The importance of cross-border linkages is assessed by examining the macroeconomic effects of alternative mitigation policies using a dynamic intertemporal global general equilibrium model (the 2007 version of G-Cubed, developed by McKibbin and Wilcoxen, 1998). G-Cubed is well suited for evaluating the short-, medium-, and long-term effects of mitigation

[21]See Aldy and Stavins (2007) for a discussion of alternative mitigation policy proposals, including hybrid schemes proposed by Kopp, Morgenstern, and Pizer (1997) and McKibbin and Wilcoxen (1997, 2002b, 2002c).
[22]See also the October 2007 *World Economic Outlook*.

Box 4.6. Complexities in Designing Domestic Mitigation Policies

This box highlights some broader issues in the design of domestic emission-mitigation policies, beyond the basic choice between an emission tax and a cap-and-trade system (see Kopp and Pizer, 2007, for an in-depth discussion of design issues).

Building Flexibility into Emission-Control Policies

A major concern with rigid annual emission caps is the risk of volatility in emission prices that might be caused, for example, by changes in demand conditions or disruptions in energy markets. Severe volatility in allowance prices may deter investments in emission-saving technologies that have large upfront costs and could undermine political support for a cap-and-trade system. However, there are ways to partly address this problem.

One option is to include a safety-valve mechanism, under which permit prices are prevented from exceeding a certain ceiling price, with the regulator authorized to sell whatever additional allowances must be introduced into the market to prevent prices rising beyond this level (Pizer, 2002). Another option is to allow firms to borrow permits from the government during periods of high permit prices and to deposit such permits when there is downward price pressure, to help smooth out sharp price fluctuations. The European Union Emissions Trading Scheme (EU-ETS) now allows for permit banking (though not borrowing). A further option is government oversight of carbon markets through a new body, much like a central bank, which would intervene to sell or buy permits in response to unexpectedly high or low permit prices. Again, this type of oversight could help to stabilize the permit market while also providing greater confidence in the achievement of longer-run emission goals.

Yet some flexibility in permit prices actually may be beneficial, as this enables future knowledge about the likely impact of global warming to be reflected in real-time permit prices and abatement decisions. For example,

Note: The main author of this box is Ian Parry.

when deciding whether there is a need for intervention, a "climate central bank" could take into account the factors driving changes in emission prices and allow permanent shocks to be reflected in prices. Even without the climate central bank, under a cap-and-trade regime that allowed depositing and borrowing of permits, if new evidence emerges that warming is occurring faster than projected, speculators would anticipate a tightening of the future emission cap, which would instantly shift up the trajectory of current and expected future permit prices (before any adjustment to the cap). In contrast, it may take some time to enact a legislative change in emission tax rates to reflect new scientific information, leaving emission control suboptimal during the period of policy stickiness.

Using Revenues to Keep Policy Costs Down

How the government uses the revenues from carbon taxes or cap-and-trade systems, to the extent that allowances are auctioned, can have a substantial effect on the overall costs of the policy. For example, if revenues are used to lower personal income taxes, this reduces the disincentive effects of these broader taxes on work effort and savings, offsetting the negative effect of higher energy prices on economic activity. Policies that do not exploit the revenue-recycling benefit are more costly, namely, cap-and-trade systems with free allowance allocation or emission taxes and cap-and-trade policies with auctioned allowances, where revenues are not used productively. For example, Parry, Williams, and Goulder (1999) estimate that the overall costs of moderately scaled emission permit systems with free allocation are more than double those for the equivalent, revenue-neutral carbon tax for the United States.

Compensating Low-Income Households and Energy-Intensive Firms

Fairness is a major issue for emission-mitigation policies because low-income households spend a relatively high share of their budgets on energy-intensive goods such as electricity, home heating fuels, and gasoline, and are therefore more vulnerable to increases in the price of these goods. Cap-and-trade systems with free permit allocation provide no mechanism for addressing these concerns. But if allowances are auctioned, or emission taxes are implemented, fairness concerns may be addressed by recycling some of the revenue in ways that particularly benefit low-income households, such as reductions in payroll taxes or increases in income tax thresholds (Metcalf, 2007; and Dinan and Rogers, 2002). Some elderly or other nonworking households may require compensation through other means, such as targeted energy-assistance programs.

On the other hand, free allowance allocations can provide compensation for (politically influential) industries adversely affected by climate policy, which helps to reduce opposition from vested interests. However, according to Bovenberg and Goulder (2001), only a small fraction of allowances must be given away for free to provide such compensation, and so most allowances could still be auctioned. Ideally, any compensation would be progressively phased out over time. This would avoid practical difficulties in updating free allowance allocations as firms grow at different rates over time and would increase the potential fiscal dividend. In fact, after power companies reaped large windfall profits from the allowance giveaway in the initial phase of the EU-ETS, the plan is now to transition to 100 percent allowance auctions by 2020. Transitory compensation for affected industries also could be provided under an emission tax, for example, by applying the tax only to emissions in excess of some threshold level or by providing temporary corporate tax relief for energy-intensive firms downstream of the formal emission tax regime.

Advantages of an Upstream Program

Ideally, a carbon tax or emission trading system would be applied upstream in the fossil fuel supply chain (on petroleum refiners, coal producers, etc.), because this would encompass all possible sources of emissions when fuels are later combusted. Fuel producers would pay a tax, or be required to hold permits, in proportion to a fuel's carbon content, and therefore emission taxes or permit prices would be passed forward into fossil fuel prices and ultimately into the price of electricity and other energy-intensive products. This would provide incentives for emission-reducing behavior throughout the economy. Downstream trading programs, like the EU-ETS, currently cover electricity and large industrial emitters, which account for only about one-half of total CO_2 emissions (Kopp and Pizer, 2007). Therefore, they preclude many low-cost abatement opportunities, for example in the transportation sector. Upstream programs are also easier to administer. In the European Union or the United States, they would involve regulation of only about 2,000–3,000 entities, compared with 12,000 entities or more in a downstream program.

Incorporating All Sources of GHGs and Options for Sequestration

Insofar as possible, it is important to include non-CO_2 greenhouse gases (GHGs) into any emission-mitigation program. In the United States these gases currently account for about 20 percent of total GHGs when gases are expressed on an equivalent basis for warming potential over their atmospheric lifespan, whereas at the global level these gases account for about one-third of total GHGs (US CCSP, 2007). Some of these gases (such as vented methane from underground coal mines and fluorinated gases used as refrigerants and in air conditioners) are fairly straightforward to monitor and incorporate through permit-trading ratios or emission taxes, reflecting their relative global warming potential. Methane and nitrous oxides from landfills, manure management, and soil management might be incorporated into an emission-offset program. In that case, the onus would be on the individual entity to demonstrate valid emission reductions for crediting. However the remaining emission sources, which account for about a third of non-CO_2 GHGs in the United States, are especially

Box 4.6 *(concluded)*

difficult to monitor (for example, methane from ruminants).

Although still in the developmental stage, a potentially important means of reducing emissions from coal plants could be emission capture and storage underground (for example, in depleted oil reservoirs). Incentives for adopting this sequestration technology could be provided through emission offsets or tax credit provisions, although, according to Deutsch and Moniz (2007), the price of carbon would need to be higher than about $25 a ton to make the technology commercially viable. At least for the short term, facilities should be charged for any emission seepage from the underground sink. Because the incorporation and operation of carbon-capture technologies would be fairly easy to verify, emission sources in advanced economies might fund such investments in emerging economies to offset some of their own mitigation obligations.

Biological sequestration could also be a potentially cost-effective way to reduce emissions (Stavins and Richards, 2005). Ideally, farms that increased forestland coverage would be credited, and those that shifted from forests to agriculture would be penalized. For the United States, it would be feasible to incorporate forestry into a national emission-mitigation program, given that transitions between forest and agricultural land in the absence of any carbon policy are relatively small (Sedjo and Toman, 2001). Land use changes might be monitored through remote sensing from satellites or aircraft, with the carbon implications then assessed based on tree species, age in the growth cycle, and so on. Incorporating incentives for reduced deforestation in tropical regions into an international emission-offset program is more challenging, because there would need to be agreement on country baselines indicating forest coverage in the absence of policy. Moreover, major timber-producing regions would need to be covered by the program to lower the risk that reduced harvesting in one area was offset by additional harvesting elsewhere.

Difficulties in Preventing Emission Leakage

Some studies suggest that emission leakage, caused by footloose firms relocating to countries without carbon policies, may be significant, perhaps offsetting about 10 percent or more of the potential effects of abatement policies in developed countries (Gupta and others, 2007). However leakage is difficult to project in practice, as it depends on many factors (including, for example, how strictly abatement policies are enforced, whether potentially footloose firms receive any compensation for forgoing such opportunities, exchange rate risks, and political stability in countries without climate policies).

Preventing this international emission leakage is very tricky. Foreign suppliers from countries without climate policies might be required to pay fines, or purchase domestic permits, to cover the embodied carbon in products they sell domestically. Administratively, however, this would be very complex and contentious and may run afoul of international free-trade obligations. In the EU-ETS, firms are presently deterred from relocating outside the region through confiscation of their (free) allowance allocations. Conversely, so as not to deter new incoming investment, entering firms are granted free emission allowances. But these provisions also have perverse effects (Ellerman and Buchner, 2007). Allowance confiscation retards the exit of inefficient facilities, whereas new firm entry is excessive, given that firms do not pay for their new emission sources.

Complementing Mitigation Policies with Technology Incentives

There is general agreement that, in principle, carbon-abatement policies should be complemented with additional incentives to promote basic and applied clean technology research and development (R&D) at governmental and private institutions. Additional policies are justified on grounds of economic efficiency because of a second source of market failure (in addition to the carbon emission externality), which arises from the inability of innovators to fully appropriate the benefits to other firms of their new knowledge. However, available literature provides limited guidance on how R&D policies might be designed and implemented to complement emission-control policies. For example, it is unclear which is more efficient: subsidies for private R&D, strengthened patent rules, or technology prizes (Wright, 1983). It is also very difficult to project in advance how effective a given package of emission controls and technology incentives will be in bringing forth (as yet undeveloped) emission-saving technologies.

Finally, some analysts argue that, even after the successful development of new technologies or cleaner fuels, further incentives are needed to encourage their diffusion, such as vehicle fuel-economy regulations, energy-efficiency standards for household appliances, or clean fuel subsidies. Such policies would be warranted if there were additional market failures, such as an undervaluation by consumers of energy-efficiency improvements. However, there is little solid empirical evidence either way on the existence and magnitude of such market failures.

policies across countries. Detailed modeling of regions helps account for differences in countries' initial income levels and potential growth rates. Disaggregated production structures summarize the input-output relationships and sectoral cost structures. Forward-looking expectations underscore the importance of policy credibility for inducing changes in behavior.[23] Careful modeling of relative prices helps track the potential implications of rising energy costs for expenditure switching, factor substitution, terms of trade, and balance of payments adjustment. The latter reflects not only trade flows, but also international capital flows—a feature that has so far received little attention in most models used for climate policy analysis.

G-Cubed simulations are intended to illustrate the economic mechanisms at work following the introduction of mitigation policies and should not be taken as long-term macroeconomic forecasts or recommendations on specific emission targets or policies. G-Cubed focuses on modeling energy-related CO_2 emissions, which constitute the largest and the fastest-growing type of GHG emissions. The baseline used in this study broadly matches the stylized facts of the Interna-

tional Energy Agency's latest *World Energy Outlook* (IEA, 2007a). In particular, it assumes stronger growth in the demand for energy from emerging economies than most other studies do. For more details on G-Cubed and how it compares to other models used to analyze mitigation policies, see Appendix 4.1.

The eventual benefits of mitigation policies targeted to reducing emissions are not modeled in G-Cubed, but this is not a major drawback. That is because the focus is on the costs of mitigation policies during the three decades following their introduction, a period during which the benefits of mitigation policies are expected to be small.

Simulation results in G-Cubed are largely driven by assumptions about countries' technologies, particularly their ability to substitute away from emission-intensive inputs. The shift to low-emission technologies is modeled through two channels—exogenous improvements in energy efficiency and endogenous substitution from carbon-intensive inputs such as fossil fuels into other raw materials, intermediate goods, capital, and labor, in response to changes in carbon prices. These technological changes can be interpreted as a shift to alternative sources of energy, such as biofuels, nuclear power, and renewables, and the introduction of carbon capture and storage technologies. Technology is assumed to be freely transferable across countries—if firms

---

[23]To be precise, expectations in G-Cubed are partially forward looking, because some households and firms are assumed to be myopic and to have recursive expectations. For more details, see Appendix 4.1.

Figure 4.9. Global Emission Targets and Paths, 1990–2100

(Gigatons of carbon dioxide)

The baseline path shows the projected level of global energy-based emissions under the assumption of a no-mitigation policy. The target emission path shows the level of global emissions from fossil fuels achieved in the policy simulation results, reaching a level that is 60 percent below the level of global emissions in 2002. The target level in 2100 is 96 percent below the projected level of the baseline in 2100.

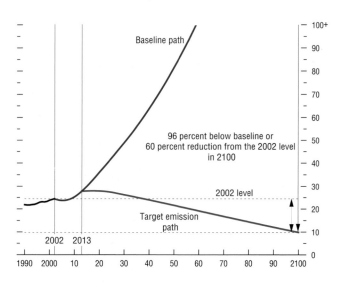

Source: IMF staff estimates.

decide to move away from using fossil fuels and rely more on clean technologies, then they can obtain funding and know-how for such investment without any constraints, although they will face some adjustment costs. Country-specific results in G-Cubed depend to a large extent on assumptions about elasticities of substitution in production, consumption, and trade, which jointly determine the incremental costs at which individual economies can reduce their emissions (see Appendix 4.1).

The modeling exercise starts with an examination of the macroeconomic effects of a global mitigation policy that requires countries to agree on a common carbon price. Such a policy could be implemented through either a uniform global carbon tax or a hybrid policy under which countries commit to a common safety valve (with the price of additional permits tied to the rate of the carbon tax).[24] The effects of these policies are then compared to those of a global policy that requires countries to agree on an initial allocation of emission rights and international trade of these rights—a cap-and-trade system. Next, the study assesses the importance of international allocation rules for the magnitude and direction of international transfers and hence the compatibility of various incentives under a cap-and-trade system. In addition to these main policy experiments, the model is used to explore implications of policy coordination, country participation, technological improvements, and the robustness of mitigation policies to macroeconomic shocks. (Some caveats to the analysis are discussed hereafter.)

Global Carbon Tax and a Hybrid Policy

In this policy experiment, all economies introduce a common carbon price in 2013 and credibly commit to keeping it in place over

---

[24]The hybrid model considered in this chapter is the one proposed by McKibbin and Wilcoxen (1997, 2002c) with an initial allocation of long-term permits and then an annual issuance of permits to target a carbon price equivalent to the tax rate.

the long run, adjusting the rate as necessary to achieve the profile of global emissions depicted in Figure 4.9. Global emissions are assumed to follow a mildly hump-shaped path, peaking around 2018 and then gradually declining to 40 percent of the 2002 levels by 2100 (that is, a 60 percent reduction from the 2002 levels or a 96 percent reduction from the business-as-usual baseline that assumes no policy change).[25] The carbon price rises gradually over time, reaching $86 a ton by 2040 (an average annual rate of about $3 per ton of carbon).[26] This corresponds to a $0.21 increase in the price of a gallon of gasoline by 2040 and a $58 increase in the price of a short ton of bituminous coal. The price is imposed upstream in the fuel production chain, with revenues from carbon pricing used to fund government consumption and investment, and with the budget deficit and debt held constant (Appendix 4.1). Other energy pricing policies are assumed to remain intact.

The macroeconomic effects of the carbon tax and the hybrid system with a safety valve are equivalent in this experiment and are depicted in Figure 4.10. (Note, however, that carbon taxes and hybrid policies generally are not equiva-

---

[25]The profile broadly matches the characteristics of the profiles shown as "Category III" in the Fourth Assessment Report of Working Group III of the IPCC (2007): peaking during 2010–30, and stabilizing CO_2–equivalent concentrations in the range of 535–590 parts per million (ppm) by volume by 2100. The scenario corresponds to a temperature increase of approximately 2.8°C –3.2°C by 2100.

[26]By 2100, carbon prices are projected to rise to $168 a ton of carbon. These estimates are lower, for comparable experiments, than those obtained by Nordhaus (2007a) and US CCSP (2007), where carbon prices range from $300 to $6,000 in 2100. The difference stems mainly from the assumption of free capital flows in G-Cubed and a more flexible technological structure, both of which facilitate an efficient adaptation by firms and individuals to higher carbon prices. Further, G-Cubed models only CO_2 emissions from fossil fuels, which implies that smaller increases in carbon prices are needed to achieve a given reduction in emissions than in multigas models where emission reductions are specified in CO_2-equivalent terms. Comparisons with US CCSP (2007) are also complicated by the fact that the studies covered by that exercise targeted radiative forcings, not concentrations of CO_2-equivalent emissions.

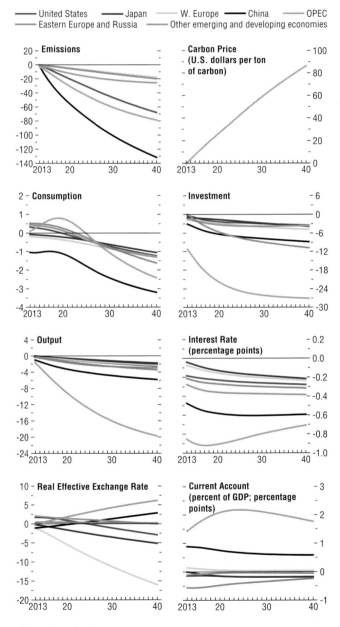

Figure 4.10. Uniform Carbon Tax, 2013–40[1]
(Deviation from the baseline; percent unless otherwise stated)

Each region is assumed to introduce a carbon tax in 2013. The tax rate is common across regions and is calibrated to achieve a 60 percent reduction relative to the 2002 level in world (energy-based) carbon dioxide emissions by 2100. This corresponds to a 96 percent reduction in global emissions relative to the baseline at 2100. The emission profile is mildly hump shaped, allowing for some increases in the medium term, peaking in 2018.

Source: IMF staff estimates.
[1]Output refers to gross national product. Interest rate refers to 10-year real interest rate. For real effective exchange rate, a positive value is an appreciation relative to the baseline.

Figure 4.11. Total Costs of Mitigation, 2013–40
(Deviation of the net present value from the baseline, percent)

This figure shows the costs of mitigation for the three policies shown in Figures 4.10, 4.12, and 4.14. The first panel shows the net present value of the difference between the path for real consumption in the policy experiment and the path for real consumption in the baseline, divided by the net present value of the path for real consumption in the baseline. The bottom panel shows the net present value of output (real gross national product) losses, defined in the same way as for consumption. The discount rate is constant over time and across regions at 2.2 percent, which is the difference between long-term world interest rates and trend GNP growth rates.

■ Uniform carbon tax and hybrid policy
■ Cap-and-trade system, allocation by initial emission shares
■ Cap-and-trade system, allocation by population shares

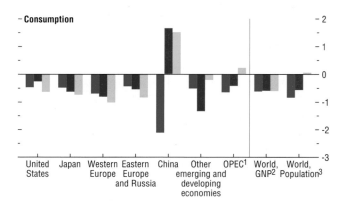

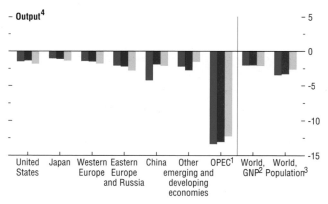

Source: IMF staff estimates.
[1] Organization of Petroleum Exporting Countries.
[2] Weighted by GNP shares in 2013.
[3] Weighted by population shares in 2013.
[4] Average prices of GNP and consumption can differ widely, owing to exchange rate movements. This implies that the rankings of GNP and consumption losses across countries are not necessarily the same.

lent.)[27] Firms change their technology, substituting away from carbon-intensive inputs and into capital (including noncarbon alternative technologies), materials, and labor. Households alter their consumption patterns, also substituting away from carbon-intensive goods. With higher carbon prices raising costs for firms, productivity and output fall. Aggregate investment falls because the average marginal product of capital is lower in each region, while consumption declines, following real incomes. Policy would be more effective to the extent that firms and households are forward looking and react immediately to the anticipated future prices. Although the levels of real activity fall permanently relative to the baseline, the shock has only a temporary effect on GNP growth rates: over time they return to baseline levels.[28]

Changes in national levels of GNP and consumption reflect countries' emission-reduction commitments and the costs of an incremental reduction in emissions. Each economy's marginal abatement costs (MACs) in G-Cubed depend on how intensely it uses carbon-based energy to produce goods for domestic consumption and for export, which in turn are driven by such factors as energy efficiency, factor endowments, and the production and export structure. China, Organization of Petroleum Exporting Countries (OPEC) members, and the United States have low MACs. MACs for eastern Europe and Russia and other emerging and developing economies are in the middle range, and MACs for Japan and western Europe are high. China is

[27] The hybrid policy is not equivalent to the carbon tax under conditions of uncertainty about abatement costs. In a scenario of slower-than-expected growth, the carbon price would fall under the hybrid policy and would remain constant under the tax. Hybrid policies may differ from carbon taxes in other respects as well, for example, in how emission reduction targets are achieved or how new information on damages from climate change is reflected in carbon prices. For a more detailed discussion of hybrid policies, see McKibbin and Wilcoxen (1997, 2002a) and Aldy and Stavins (2007).

[28] The study uses GNP as a measure of output. It is a better comparator of each region's fortunes under different mitigation policies, because, unlike GDP, it takes into account transfer payments.

Table 4.1. Losses in Real GNP, 2040

(Percent deviation from baseline)[1]

	Uniform Carbon Tax and Hybrid Policy	Cap-and-Trade Allocation by Initial Emission Shares	Cap-and-Trade Allocation by Population Shares
United States (130.1)	−2.1	−1.9	−2.6
Japan (80.0)	−1.5	−1.7	−2.1
Western Europe (109.9)	−2.0	−2.0	−2.5
Eastern Europe and Russia (131.8)	−2.8	−3.0	−3.9
China (404.5)	−4.8	−1.6	−2.1
Other emerging and developing economies (353.6)	−2.4	−3.3	−1.7
Organization of Petroleum Exporting Countries (196.0)	−16.2	−15.8	−14.6
World—GNP weighted (169.9)	−2.6	−2.6	−2.8
World—Population weighted (312.8)	−4.0	−3.9	−3.1

Source: IMF staff estimates.

[1]Numbers in parentheses denote the percent change in real GNP between 2007 and 2040 in the baseline.

least efficient in the use of energy, and it has by far the lowest MAC: it is producing nine times more emissions per unit of output than Japan, seven times more than western Europe, five times more than the United States, and three times more than eastern Europe and Russia and other emerging and developing economies (Appendix 4.1). The carbon intensity of the Chinese economy will be reduced as firms and households use energy more efficiently. The same is true for OPEC members and the United States, albeit to a lesser extent. In addition, because the burning of coal generates much higher emissions than the burning of other fossil fuels, rising carbon prices have a particularly strong effect in economies that use coal intensively—China and the United States— encouraging them to substitute alternative, lower-emission technologies. Given a uniform carbon price, economies reduce emissions up to the point at which their MACs are equalized. Economies with lower MACs undertake more emission reductions. China, in particular, reduces emissions by the most, followed by the United States and OPEC members.

Total abatement costs also vary across economies. The costs are highest for China, with the net present value of consumption declining by about 2 percent from the baseline levels by 2040 (Figure 4.11). For other economies, and for the world as a whole, the decline in the net present value of consumption is about 0.6 percent

for the same period. When measured in terms of the bundle of goods produced, the costs are higher, with the net present value of world GNP declining by about 2 percent from the baseline by 2040 (see Figure 4.11). Yet this would still leave the world GNP 2.3 times higher in 2040 than in 2007 (Table 4.1).

Current accounts tend to improve over time in economies with lower MACs (for example, China and OPEC members) because reductions in investment outweigh reductions in savings. An exception to this pattern is the United States, where the current account worsens, because the marginal product of capital declines by less than in other countries, enabling the United States to absorb increased savings from China and OPEC members.[29] These capital inflows help support U.S. investment and consumption.

Changes in real exchange rates are driven by changes in production costs in the short run, whereas the adjustment path over time depends on real interest rate differentials. In western Europe, where energy efficiency is already relatively high, increases in carbon prices result in increases in average unit costs, hurting export competitiveness. The euro and other western European currencies depreciate as a result (the

[29]Owing to the larger size of its capital stock and smaller adjustment costs per unit of capital, the United States experiences fewer "bottleneck" problems with capital inflows.

euro by about 16 percent during 2013–40). By contrast, in China, the marginal costs of reducing emissions are low, and increases in carbon prices can be largely offset by improvements in energy efficiency. The resulting terms-of-trade improvement is reflected in an exchange rate appreciation.

MACs and emission reductions per dollar increase in carbon prices are similar to those obtained by Nordhaus (2007a) but lower than those in many other models (for example, US CCSP, 2007). This is true for three reasons. First, in contrast to models that assume technologies in which energy can be used only in fixed proportions with other inputs of production, G-Cubed allows for substitution between factors of production. Second, forward-looking expectations in G-Cubed make carbon price increases more effective in lowering emissions. The third factor driving down cost estimates is that G-Cubed explicitly models international capital flows, in contrast to most other models in the literature (Appendix 4.1). Free flow of capital implies that capital moves to economies with higher MACs, facilitating both the replacement of old capital stock and the transition to low-emission technology, and allowing the savings of economies with lower MACs to go where expected returns are higher.

The total costs of mitigation in G-Cubed are higher than in many other studies, but they are within the range of estimates reported in IPCC (2007).[30] The main reasons this analysis yields higher estimates is that it assumes relatively strong emission growth in the baseline (benchmarked in IEA, 2007a), and that G-Cubed uses conservative assumptions about the availability of so-called backstop technologies with zero emissions. In many other studies, GDP losses are substantially reduced or even eliminated by 2050 because innovation and the diffusion of backstop technologies and other low-emission

technologies are assumed to proceed rapidly, at a faster pace than in G-Cubed (for example, US CCSP, 2007; Criqui and others, 2003; den Elzen and others, 2005; and Nakicenovic and Riahi, 2003).[31]

A Global Cap-and-Trade System

This experiment assumes that a permanent cap-and-trade policy is put in place in 2013. Emission rights for the world as a whole are assumed to follow the emission profile shown in Figure 4.9—by 2010 the world is allowed to emit only 40 percent of the 2002 emission levels. Individual economies receive emission rights for each year from 2013 onward. These rights are proportional to the economy's share of global emissions in 2012, following the profile depicted in Figure 4.9. Emission permits can be traded internationally, which establishes a common price.[32] Economies with higher MACs buy permits from economies with lower MACs, compensating them for undertaking more abatement than implied by their share of emissions. Hence, the actual emission paths of individual economies differ from their initial allocations of permits, whereas the world emission path is consistent with the targeted profile.

The macroeconomic effects of the global cap-and-trade system are similar to those of the global carbon tax and the hybrid policy with a safety valve, with differences reflecting the various mechanisms through which a common carbon price is established (Figure 4.12). Under the global tax, countries are assumed to agree on a common carbon price, whereas under the

---

[30]In this study, mitigation policies reduce world GDP by 3.8 percent by 2050 compared with the business-as-usual baseline. The range of estimates reported in IPCC (2007) is 0 to 4 percent.

[31]The carbon tax system considered in this study does not require international transfers: governments are assumed to agree on a common tax rate. In practice, however, the establishment of such a system may require side payments, which would alter macroeconomic outcomes. Border tax adjustments also may be used as a way to induce other countries to participate, albeit at the risk of a protectionist response.

[32]Emission permits are allocated to governments, which then sell them to the private sector. Firms are free to trade permits internationally. Governments spend revenues from permit auctioning on consumption and investment, keeping deficits unchanged.

global cap-and-trade system, a common carbon price is established through international trade in emission permits. For most economies, transfers are small and hence the macroeconomic effects are similar; for China (a recipient), other emerging and developing economies (payers), and OPEC members (recipients), transfers reach about 10 percent, –2 percent, and 1 percent of GDP, respectively, by 2040 (Figure 4.13). China receives the largest transfers because it is comparatively inefficient in the use of energy and can reduce emissions at much lower costs than other economies. Advanced economies, as well as other emerging and developing economies, buy emission rights from China because emission reductions are very costly for them. The above findings concerning the direction and magnitude of transfers are highly sensitive to marginal abatement costs assumed in G-Cubed for individual economies (see Appendix 4.1) as well as to the rule used for allocating permits across countries (see below).

Differences in the macroeconomic effects of a global cap-and-trade system, a global carbon tax, and the hybrid with a safety valve are thus most vivid for China. China's consumption rises under a cap-and-trade system, but declines under a carbon tax and under the hybrid (see Figure 4.12). Under cap and trade, the current account remains broadly stable for the first 10 years (and gradually improves after that); there would be an immediate improvement under both a carbon tax and the hybrid (see Figure 4.10). International transfers also result in a larger real appreciation of the renminbi under cap and trade (10 percent by 2040 compared with 3 percent under a carbon tax and the hybrid).

Total (GNP-weighted) world abatement costs are similar under a cap-and-trade system, a carbon tax, and the hybrid policy, but the population-weighted costs are higher under cap and trade, because the increase in costs for other emerging and developing economies outweighs the decrease in costs for China. The costs for economies paying transfers (Europe, Japan, Russia, and other emerging and developing

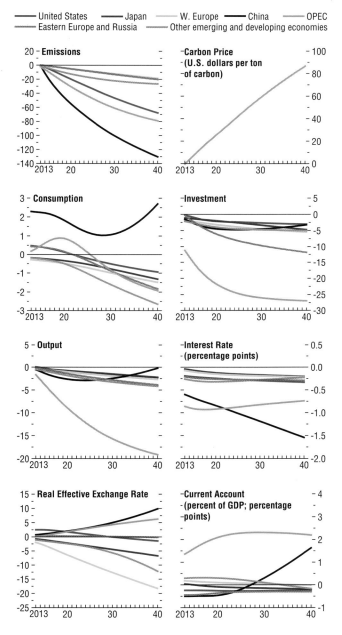

Figure 4.12. Cap-and-Trade System, 2013–40[1]
(Deviation from the baseline; percent unless otherwise stated)

Each region is assumed to introduce a cap-and-trade system in 2013. Each region has to achieve a 60 percent reduction relative to the 2002 level in world (energy-based) carbon dioxide emissions by 2100, but is able to buy and sell emission permits to do so. This corresponds to a 96 percent reduction in global emissions relative to the baseline at 2100. Each region's emission target is mildly hump shaped, allowing for some increases in the medium term, peaking in 2018.

Source: IMF staff estimates.
[1]Output refers to gross national product. Interest rate refers to 10-year real interest rate. For real effective exchange rate, a positive value is an appreciation relative to the baseline.

Figure 4.13. International Transfers under the Cap-and-Trade System
(Percent of GDP)

This figure shows the net value of international transfer payments for emission rights. A positive value denotes a receipt of transfers—that is, the region is selling its emission rights. The top panel summarizes results for a cap-and-trade system under which emission rights are allocated proportionally to emissions in 2012 (see Figure 4.12 for details on this policy experiment). The bottom panel summarizes results for a cap-and-trade system under which emission rights are distributed based on the share of population in each year from 2013 onward (see Figure 4.14).

Annual Emission Rights Allocated to Each Region According to:

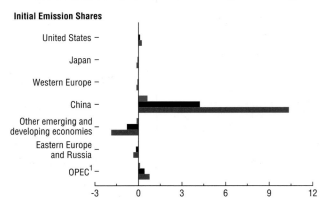

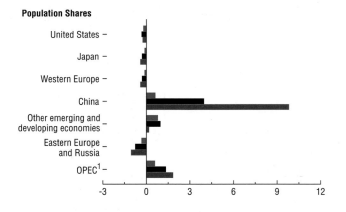

Source: IMF staff estimates.
[1]Organization of Petroleum Exporting Countries.

economies) rise under a cap-and-trade system compared with those under a carbon tax and the hybrid policy, while the costs decline for the economies receiving transfers (China, OPEC members, and the United States).

Although most studies predict that advanced economies—especially western Europe and Japan—would have to pay for emission permits, there is no consensus about international transfers for emerging market economies. Such countries have high growth potential, which implies high future demand for emission rights, but they also emit high levels of carbon per unit of output, which implies a lot of room for efficiency gains and hence the ability to sell emission rights. The latter effect dominates in den Elzen and others (2005) and Criqui and others (2003), which predict that China will sell permits. But Persson, Azar, and Lindgren (2006) project that China will develop so rapidly that it must buy permits. In Grassl and others (2003), China buys permits from other emerging market economies, because Africa, Latin America, and south Asia are assumed to have large innate potential for reduction in emissions through the increased use of solar power and biomass. By contrast, here, China is able to reduce emissions through improvements in the energy efficiency of households and firms, leaving it with a large surplus of emission rights that can be sold.

Alternative Allocations of Emission Permits

The pattern of international transfers and the macroeconomic effects of cap and trade are highly sensitive to how emission rights are allocated. Suppose each economy receives emission rights not according to its initial share of emissions, but according to its share of world population in each year from 2013 onward. For the same global emission target, OPEC members and other emerging and developing economies would receive more permits than under the rule based on the initial share of emissions. This would substantially change the pattern of international trade in permits and the macroeconomic effects, with other emerging and developing economies now selling permits and receiving transfers in the amount of about 1 percent of GDP during 2020–30 (see Figure 4.13). Transfers to OPEC members would also rise to about 2 percent of GDP in 2040, whereas those to China would remain broadly unchanged.

Transfers to other emerging and developing economies would improve their consumption outcomes, but would lead to real exchange rate appreciation and a phenomenon akin to Dutch disease (Figure 4.14). Agriculture and services sectors in other emerging and developing economies would experience a larger contraction than under the emission-based cap-and-trade system. Appreciation would persist during several decades following the introduction of the population-based cap and trade.

Nonetheless, when measured in GNP-weighted terms, world abatement costs would be similar under a population-based cap and trade, under an emission-based cap-and-trade system, and under a uniform global carbon tax, reflecting similar outcomes in terms of increased energy efficiency. In population-weighted terms, world costs decline owing to consumption benefits now accruing to other emerging and developing economies and OPEC members (see Figure 4.11).

Other Findings

Nonharmonized mitigation policies—for example, under which each economy independently chooses its own path for carbon prices in order to achieve a 60 percent reduction from 2002 emission levels by 2100—would be more costly than harmonized policies because they do not provide for an efficient allocation of abatement across the world (Nordhaus, 2007a). Under G-Cubed simulations, total costs at least double for other emerging and developing economies, eastern and western Europe, Russia, and Japan, compared with the costs of the uniform global carbon tax. Although China, OPEC, and the United States would have lower costs than under a uniform carbon tax, the total global costs of uncoordinated policies are still 50 percent higher than those of harmonized policies. Countries with higher MACs would

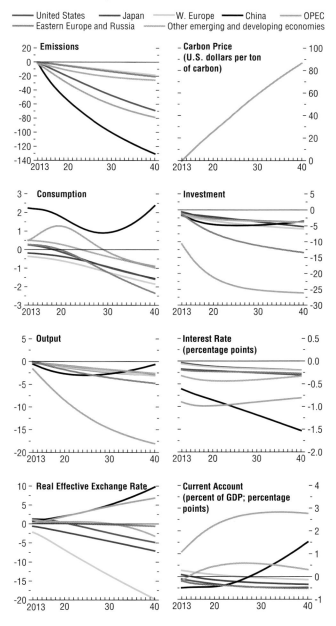

Figure 4.14. Cap-and-Trade System for All Regions Based on Share of World Population, 2013–40[1]
(Deviation from the baseline; percent unless otherwise stated)

Beginning in 2013, there is a cap-and-trade system for all regions to gradually achieve 60 percent reductions in total world (energy-based) carbon dioxide emissions relative to the 2002 level by 2100, allowing for some increases in the medium term, peaking in 2018. This corresponds to a 96 percent reduction in global emissions relative to the baseline at 2100. Emission rights are allocated by share of global population in each year from 2013 onward.

Source: IMF staff estimates.
[1]Output refers to gross national product. Interest rate refers to 10-year real interest rate. For real effective exchange rate, a positive value is an appreciation relative to the baseline.

be particularly adversely affected by the lack of policy coordination, because these countries would no longer be able to relocate abatement to other destinations. This policy experiment suggests that an international policy architecture based on country-specific carbon prices would be less efficient than an architecture establishing a common world carbon price.

An international agreement that does not include emerging and developing economies will be ineffective in stemming climate change. If only Annex I economies[33] (Australia, Canada, eastern and western Europe, Japan, New Zealand, Russia, and the United States) were to assume the full burden of reducing world emissions by 40 percent from 2002 levels by 2100, their emissions would need to be 12½ times lower than in the baseline. This is because they would need to offset the large contribution of non-Annex I countries (China and other emerging and developing economies) to the growth of world emissions. This would represent an unrealistically high cost to Annex I economies. Alternatively, if only Annex I economies decided to reduce their total emissions by 60 percent by 2100, global emissions would be 7½ times higher than in 2002, resulting in greater warming.

The carbon tax and the hybrid policy with a safety valve provide more flexibility for firms and households to respond to fluctuations in abatement costs stemming, for example, from changes in the rate of economic growth. During periods of cyclically high demand and expanding production, cap and trade may become too restrictive, requiring firms to abate to the same extent despite higher abatement costs. When one region experiences unexpectedly higher growth, this would drive up the price of carbon permits for all countries, with the result that those countries that were previously net beneficiaries of transfer payments might find themselves having to pay (McKibbin and

Wilcoxen, 2004). If carbon prices are volatile, variations in growth may put a stress on a global cap-and-trade agreement. This is not the case under the carbon tax or the hybrid policy.[34]

This policy experiment also illustrates that mitigation policies may have important implications for the way macroeconomic shocks are transmitted across countries. For example, under a price-setting policy, unanticipated growth spills over positively to other countries, although this implies that the world misses its emission targets. By contrast, under the global cap-and-trade system, the world global emission target can be achieved, but higher economic growth in one large economy may have negative repercussions across other countries by driving up permit prices.

Energy-efficiency improvements are unlikely to eliminate the need for carbon prices, but they would reduce their level (Nordhaus, 2007a). Even assuming that energy efficiency exogenously improves at a pace that is twice as high as in the baseline, carbon prices would still need to rise to achieve the same reduction in emissions (the carbon price would need to reach $76 by 2040, instead of $86, as in the original policy experiments with the global price-based policies). This points to the potential benefits of complementing carbon pricing with well-designed incentives for innovation and the broad diffusion of clean technologies (see Box 4.6).

Less-stringent emission targets—aiming to stabilize GHG concentrations at about 650 ppm in CO_2e terms, rather than 550 ppm, by 2100—would be less costly to achieve, but the difference in costs would not be dramatic. Analysis of an alternative mitigation scenario, under which emissions were only 40 percent below 2002 levels by 2100 and were allowed to continue to grow for longer before declining,[35] shows that

---

[33]Annex I of the Kyoto Protocol lists the assigned emission targets over the commitment period 2008–12. This does not necessarily mean that the emission targets have been agreed to or met.

[34]The hybrid has a number of advantages under uncertainty, such as directly addressing the problem of time consistency that arises under the cap-and-trade system and carbon-tax approaches.

[35]Matching the "Category IV" scenarios in IPCC (2007) and corresponding to 590–710 ppm in CO_2e terms.

the patterns of macroeconomic responses under carbon taxes, hybrid policies, and cap-and-trade systems remain largely unchanged. However, under the less-stringent scenario, carbon prices would rise more slowly, to $165 by 2100, implying slightly lower consumption and GNP losses (of about 0.5 percent and 1.7 percent in net present value, respectively).

Caveats

Several caveats need to be underlined. The most important is that it is difficult to say anything precise about the state of the world economy and individual country economies in 2040, let alone 2100, especially if there are large and fundamental changes in the price of energy. Many innovations in technology could occur that would change the outlook dramatically over several decades, and these innovations could diffuse at different rates across countries. Results are most sensitive to assumptions about economic growth, autonomous energy-efficiency improvements, and marginal abatement costs—small changes in these assumptions can have a big impact on results in G-Cubed. The direction and magnitude of macroeconomic effects for individual countries, including financial transfers, are particularly sensitive to assumptions about elasticities of substitution in production, consumption, and trade. Using only current technologies, many firms may be unable to react to market demand to the extent estimated in this analysis; yet by basing many of the estimates of the price responsiveness of households and firms on historical experience through econometric estimation, the model attempts to reflect plausible outcomes in technological change. Although G-Cubed does not model when backstop technologies would emerge, it assumes that changes in carbon prices can induce large substitutions away from fossil fuels. Many other models have more rigid technological structures or assume that capital and technology do not flow freely across countries, even over the long run. At the same time, by focusing only on energy-related CO_2 emissions, G-Cubed does not take into account cheap abatement opportuni-

ties that may exist in other areas, for example, by reducing deforestation.

Conclusions

Climate change is a powerful global trend that, along with trade and financial integration, is likely to have profound effects on economies and markets in coming decades. As temperatures and sea levels rise and precipitation patterns change, the global pattern of comparative advantage will shift in tandem. This will prompt structural changes within economies, at the domestic as well as at the global level. There will be shifts in international trade, in capital and migration flows, and in the prices of commodities, other goods and services, and assets.

The macroeconomic effects of climate change will unfold unevenly across time and space. Poor countries will be hit earlier and harder, owing to their geography, heavier reliance on agriculture, and more limited capacity to adapt. Their health and water systems may come under stress from more frequent natural disasters, coasts may be flooded, and populations may migrate. Rich countries may be affected by spillovers from climate change in poor countries, and they would also face severe direct damage if the tail risks of climate catastrophes were to materialize.

The ability of domestic macroeconomic policies to help public and private sectors cope with climate-related risks will be increasingly tested over time. Sound macroeconomic policies and innovative financial and development strategies will be needed to help countries successfully adapt to climate change. Countries with higher incomes, stronger fiscal positions, more developed financial markets, and greater structural policy flexibility will be better positioned to adapt to the adverse consequences of climate change. Countries that are increasingly subject to risks from weather volatility and extreme weather events will need to devise strategies for managing such risks, including the appropriate use of self-insurance through budgetary management, the building of reserves, and the use of weather derivatives, catastrophe bonds, and other forms of disaster insurance. Global cooperation in transferring knowledge about the financial management of weather-related risks would help poor countries better adapt to climate change.

Dealing with climate change also poses enormous multilateral policy challenges. These range from fostering synergies in adaptation and protecting the natural environment to preserving energy security and managing the risks of protectionism. Yet the main task is to address the causes and impacts of climate change by significantly reducing emissions of GHGs over the next several decades, and to do this at the lowest possible cost. This requires joint action by advanced, emerging market, and developing economies.

This chapter concludes that climate change can be addressed without imposing heavy damages either on the global economy or on individual countries. For climate policies to be successful, their potentially adverse economic consequences—slower growth, higher inflation, loss of competitiveness—must be addressed, either through carefully designed climate policies or through supportive macroeconomic and financial policies. Measures to limit the adverse economic effects would strengthen the incentives for a broad range of countries to fully participate in mitigation efforts and would help unleash the potential economic and financial benefits of the transition to a more climate-friendly global economy.

- Carbon-pricing policies need to be long term and credible. They must establish a time horizon for steadily rising carbon prices that people and businesses consider believable. Increases in world carbon prices need not be large—say a $0.01 initial increase in the price of a gallon of gasoline that rises by $0.02 every three years. Such gradual increases, if started early, would allow the cost of adjustment to be spread over a longer period of time. The total cost to the global economy of such policies could be moderate for policies introduced in 2013 that aim to stabilize CO_2e concentrations at 550 ppm by 2100—entailing only a 0.6 percent reduction in the net pres-

ent value of world consumption by 2040. Even with this loss, world GNP would still be 2.3 times higher in 2040 than in 2007.

- Carbon-pricing policies should induce all groups of economies—advanced, emerging, and developing—to start pricing their emissions. Any policy framework that does not include emerging and developing economies (particularly, large and fast-growing economies such as Brazil, China, India, and Russia) in some way (for example, with a lag or with initially less-stringent targets) would be extremely costly and would be politically untenable. That is because during the next 50 years, 70 percent of emissions are projected to come from these and other emerging and developing economies. Some countries may need to strengthen their institutional capacity, however, to implement carbon pricing.

- Carbon-pricing policies should strive to establish a common world price for emissions. This would ensure that emission reduction occurs where it is least costly to do so. Emerging and developing economies, in particular, will likely be able to reduce emissions much more cheaply than advanced economies. For example, if China and India have access to technologies similar to those available in Europe and Japan, they could cut emissions dramatically by improving their intensity of energy use and by reducing their reliance on coal. The difference in costs can be significant—for the world as a whole, costs would be 50 percent lower if carbon prices were the same across countries. Countries would either need to agree to harmonize the rate of a carbon tax, coordinate trigger prices for the safety valve under a hybrid policy, or allow international trading of emission permits under a cap-and-trade system.

- Carbon-pricing policies should be sufficiently flexible to accommodate cyclical economic fluctuations. During periods of high demand, for example, it would be more costly for firms to reduce their emissions, and the opposite would be true when demand is low. Abatement costs would be lower if firms could vary their emissions over the business cycle. That would allow a given average level of emission reductions to be achieved over the medium term. In contrast to carbon taxes and hybrid policies, a cap-and-trade system could prove restrictive in periods of higher growth owing to increased demand and prices for emission permits, unless it incorporates elements that help control price volatility.

- The costs of mitigation should be distributed equitably across countries. Some mitigation policies—for example, a uniform tax, a cap-and-trade system under which permits are allocated based on countries' current shares of emissions, or a hybrid policy combining elements of the two—would impose high costs on some emerging and developing economies. Substantial cross-border transfers may be needed to encourage them to participate and to help them deal with the negative impact. The direction and magnitude of transfers under cap and trade generally depend on the incremental costs of reducing emissions in individual countries (which in turn are a function of countries' domestic technological capabilities and access to foreign technology) as well as on the specific design features of mitigation policies (for example, rules for allocating emission permits, the timing of countries' entry into the climate agreement, supplementary conditions, and the like). If policies were designed so that transfers flow from advanced economies to emerging and developing economies, this would reduce the costs of carbon-pricing policies for the latter two groups, encouraging them to participate. Using border tax adjustments as a way to induce countries to join could elicit a protectionist response that would detract from mitigation efforts.

In addition, countries may need to complement carbon pricing with appropriate macroeconomic and financial policies. For example, under a global cap-and-trade system, transfers from economies that buy permits to economies that sell them could be potentially large—for example, several percentage points of GDP.

Such transfers may cause real exchange rates in the recipient countries to appreciate considerably, making some sectors of their economies less competitive—Dutch disease. Such macroeconomic effects can be reduced if countries save a portion of these inflows, continue to improve their business environments, and, depending on their exchange rate regimes, allow appreciation to take place at least partly through the nominal exchange rate rather than through inflation.

This chapter also points to the supporting role of international capital movements and technology transfer in dealing with climate change. Capital and technology flows can reduce the costs of mitigation by helping allocate abatement to the least costly destinations, while making abatement easier through the use of modern technology. Initiatives by major advanced economies to subsidize the transfer of clean technologies to emerging and developing economies can complement a global commitment to contain carbon emissions through a broadly accepted global carbon-pricing framework. While unlikely to eliminate the need for carbon pricing, well-designed incentives for innovation and the diffusion of clean technologies can help reduce the costs of addressing climate change.

Climate change is a complex global problem that does not lend itself to easy policy solutions. This chapter does not pretend to provide a solution. Its focus has been narrow—on the cross-country macroeconomic dimensions of climate change. Yet its conclusion has broad relevance for ongoing policy debates: climate change can be addressed with minimum damage to the economy, if policy solutions follow some basic principles.

Appendix 4.1. The G-Cubed Model, Baseline Assumptions, and Other Models in the Climate Change Literature

The main author of this appendix is Alasdair Scott.

This appendix outlines the key features of the model used to produce the analysis in Chapter 4, the baseline scenario and its underlying assumptions, the factors affecting the differences in marginal abatement costs (MACs) across countries, and comparisons with some other models that have been prominently used in the literature on climate change mitigation.

The G-Cubed Model

G-Cubed (see McKibbin and Wilcoxen, 1998) is a dynamic general equilibrium model of the global economy. The world is divided into multiple regions linked by international trade and capital flows, with each region divided into multiple production sectors. Decisions about saving, investment, and asset pricing are modeled by assuming that forward-looking households and firms aim to maximize, respectively, consumption utility and profits, but are subject to cash flow constraints, while backward-looking households and firms follow simple rules of thumb.[36] Outputs of different sectors are linked to emissions of carbon dioxide using data for the emission intensity and the energy efficiency of each sector.

Some of the key features of G-Cubed relevant for this study include the following:

- disaggregation of the real sector into an input-output structure to allow for production and trade of multiple goods and services within and across economies, facilitating the examination of how changes in energy prices are transmitted within and across economies;
- "stock-flow" accounting for capital stock and financial assets and enforcement of cash flow and budget constraints;
- integration of real and financial markets, including the modeling of international capital flows along with trade balances; and

- modeling of fiscal and monetary policies.

The 2007 version of G-Cubed used in this study splits the world into the following nine economies:[37]

- United States;
- Japan;
- Western Europe (Austria, Belgium, Denmark, Finland, France, Germany, Greece, Iceland, Ireland, Italy, Luxembourg, Netherlands, Norway, Portugal, Spain, Sweden, Switzerland, and United Kingdom);
- Australia;
- Canada and New Zealand;
- Eastern Europe and Russia (Albania, Bulgaria, Czech Republic, Hungary, Poland, Romania, and Russia);
- China;
- other emerging and developing economies (Argentina, Brazil, Cambodia, Chile, Egypt, Hong Kong SAR, India, People's Democratic Republic of Korea, Republic of Korea, Lao PDR, Malaysia, Mexico, Morocco, Myanmar, Nepal, Pakistan, Philippines, Singapore, South Africa, Sri Lanka, Thailand, Turkey, and Vietnam);
- OPEC economies (Algeria, Indonesia, Islamic Republic of Iran, Iraq, Kuwait, Libya, Niger, Oman, Qatar, Saudi Arabia, and United Arab Emirates).

The six economies covering Australia, Canada and New Zealand, western Europe, eastern Europe and Russia, Japan, and the United States are broadly equivalent to the definition of Annex I under the Kyoto Protocol (United Nations, 1998).

The production structure of each region is the same, with the following 12 production sectors:

- energy sectors: electric utilities, gas utilities, petroleum refining, coal mining, crude oil and gas extraction; and

---

[36]Thirty percent of households are forward looking and 70 percent follow rules of thumb. Expectations play a key role in the effectiveness of carbon prices at reducing emissions, because forward-looking households will factor all future carbon price increases into their current decisions. Hence, for the same carbon price profile, a larger share of forward-looking households would imply earlier reductions in emissions.

[37]Country coverage is constrained by data limitations. Hence, the definition of the "world" may differ from that in other studies, and this may need to be taken into consideration when comparing policy scenarios.

- nonenergy sectors: mining; agriculture, fishing, and hunting; forestry and wood products; durable goods manufacturing; nondurable goods manufacturing; transportation; and services.

The structure of each region is identical but varies in the values of parameters describing shares, weights, and elasticities. Each region consists of several economic agents: households, a consolidated government, the financial sector, and the production sectors listed above. Each firm makes decisions about capital investment and the use of labor, intermediate materials, and energy so as to maximize the value of the firm, given available technology and the prices the firm faces for inputs and outputs. Labor supply is assumed to meet labor demand from firms in the short run—in the long run, it is constrained by population levels—and workers are fully mobile across sectors (they receive the same real wage). By contrast, it takes time to shift and install capital. Each household receives labor and dividend income from firms and (net) transfer income from the government. Given its period-by-period budget constraints and the prices of goods relative to income and other goods, each household makes decisions about total consumption expenditure and the way that expenditure is allocated across a basket of energy and nonenergy goods.

The government administers monetary and fiscal policy. It faces a binding period-by-period fiscal constraint, balancing revenues with expenditures. Each region has the same fiscal rule: given targets for tax rates, transfers, deficits, and expenditures on wages, extra revenues—such as from carbon taxes or sales of emission permits—are used to fund government consumption and investment. To the extent that a rise in carbon prices reduces private demand, this rule will have a small offsetting effect on aggregate demand. The main conclusions in this study are broadly robust to using alternative fiscal rules.[38] There are nominal rigidi-

ties for prices and wages. Governments in the model can use nominal interest rates to achieve targets for inflation, money growth, nominal GDP growth, or exchange rates, or for a mixture of these.

An important aspect of the model is the way in which sectors and economies are linked by trade in goods and services, current transfers, and capital flows. All goods are potentially tradable, but the degree to which they are traded depends on how much they are used as inputs of production in other countries and on their relative prices, which depend in turn on their elasticities of substitution in production and consumption. Relative prices, such as terms of trade and real exchange rates, adjust to clear the worldwide market for goods and services. In addition, capital is assumed to flow freely across borders in search of the highest rate of return. Current flows include transfers from permit trades under a cap-and-trade system, in addition to investment returns on foreign assets.

Baseline Assumptions

The baseline—which is sometimes referred to in other studies as the reference path or business-as-usual (BAU) scenario—is a set of paths, for variables such as GDP and emissions, that is generated by the model and does not include any shocks other than those implicit in assumptions about population and productivity growth and does not include any policy interventions other than those implicit in fiscal and monetary rules. The main assumptions that drive the baseline are those that affect underlying trend growth (here, population and productivity growth), policy assumptions (such as tax rates and spending levels), emission-related assumptions (such as any improvements in energy efficiency), and the structure of the economies

---

[38]For example, the most efficient use of carbon revenues would be to reduce distortionary taxes on capital.

Equity considerations might argue for a reduction in income tax rates for those with lower incomes, as carbon taxes are regressive. Alternatively, carbon revenues could be used to fund research in clean technologies or to pay down debt.

Table 4.2. Baseline Growth Assumptions
(Percent change)

	United States	Japan	Western Europe	Eastern Europe and Russia	China	Other Developing and Emerging Economies	Organization of Petroleum Exporting Countries
Population	0.71	−0.54	0.03	−0.57	0.08	1.29	1.18
	0.18	−0.56	−0.07	−0.53	−0.23	0.20	0.27
Nonenergy sector productivity	1.55	0.52	0.62	1.55	6.78	2.61	0.72
	1.56	1.49	1.50	1.57	1.58	1.71	1.26
Energy sector productivity	0.10	0.06	0.14	0.29	0.94	0.31	0.03
	0.10	0.09	0.11	0.16	0.20	0.21	0.03

Source: IMF staff calculations.
Note: The first row for each category shows the annual average percent change during 2003–30; the second row shows the percent growth rate in 2100.

(as represented by parameters for elasticities and shares).[39]

Table 4.2 summarizes the growth assumptions used in the baseline. Although all regions gradually converge to common trend growth, note that there are substantial differences in the short run (and across sectors within each economy).[40]

[39]Parameter assumptions affect the baseline, including values for the intertemporal elasticity of consumption substitution and the household discount rate. A rise in the discount rate would increase the market rate of interest that households use to evaluate permanent income, but such a change would leave the ordinal comparisons of policies unchanged. This is in contrast to studies that attempt to calculate welfare losses and gains in a full cost-benefit analysis of mitigation policies. See, for example, the *Stern Review* (Stern, 2007) and discussion, such as Nordhaus (2007a).

[40]Some have argued that climate models using GDP measures based on market exchange rates (MER) rather than purchasing power parities (PPP) understate the size of emerging and developing economies and therefore, by assuming convergence, overestimate GDP and emission growth (see, for example, Castles and Henderson, 2003). This point is hotly debated. IPCC (2007) argues that the resulting bias is small compared with other sources of uncertainty. A practical limitation to adopting PPP measures for climate change studies is that PPP-consistent production accounts would be required for the modeling of energy sectors and energy inputs into other sectors, and such accounts are not available. Furthermore, even if they were, comparisons across time would be problematic because PPP-consistent accounts would impose constant weights or relative prices for different goods. For this reason, Nordhaus (2007c) argues that "superlative" PPP accounts are required that would combine PPP exchange rates with actual market prices over time for each country. In this study, relative growth rates are calibrated using PPP-based national income comparisons, but projections for economies' expenditure, income, production, and balance-of-payments variables are made on an MER basis.

For example, data from population projections produced by the United Nations (2006) indicate that other emerging and developing economies will experience substantial population growth over the next quarter century, whereas the populations of Japan, eastern Europe, and Russia will shrink. Similarly, although productivity growth in nonenergy sectors in the developed world is assumed to be modest, there are substantial productivity gains in emerging and developing economies. All other things equal, emission levels reflect activity levels, implying a rising share of emissions produced by developing economies.

Productivity in nonenergy sectors is assumed to exceed the ability to improve the efficiency of producing energy from all sources in each region at all times—this implies that carbon-based energy becomes relatively more expensive over time. Raising energy sector productivity—particularly among OPEC members—would result in higher economic growth and higher emissions in the baseline.

G-Cubed does not explicitly model renewable and low-carbon-emission technologies. But it assumes that there is a constant, albeit modest, improvement in the efficiency with which energy is used by households and firms (sometimes referred to as autonomous energy efficiency improvement) of 0.5 percent each year. This can be thought of as representing advances in clean technologies, which further encourage lower emission intensity—emissions per unit of output—over time. In addition, substitution from

Table 4.3. Carbon-Based Emission Coefficients
(Metric tons of carbon emissions per unit of real GDP in U.S. dollars)

	United States	Japan	Western Europe	Eastern Europe and Russia	China	Other Developing and Emerging Economies	Organization of Petroleum Exporting Countries
Coal	20.88	7.67	7.68	5.48	76.09	15.08	13.62
Crude oil	7.89	2.56	1.75	1.50	7.14	4.90	9.77

Sources: Global Trade Analysis Project database; and IMF staff calculations.

carbon-based energy toward capital as a factor of production can be seen as a type of technological progress toward clean technologies. This plays an important role in reactions to policies and contrasts with some models that model energy sectors and technologies in more detail but implicitly assume that energy and capital must be used in fixed proportions.

In the short run, monetary policy assumptions have an effect on the baseline as regions converge to their trend growth paths. Western Europe, Japan, the United States, Canada, Australia, and New Zealand are assumed to have fully flexible exchange rates, and other regions are assumed to have managed exchange rate regimes. Monetary policy is summarized by an augmented Taylor-type monetary reaction function; in managed exchange rate regimes, a relatively large weight is put on changes in the nominal exchange rate, as well as on output gaps and inflation. Tax rates, transfers, and deficits (the last as a share of GDP) are assumed to stay constant.

In addition to assumptions about economic growth and policy, assumptions made about the structures of the economies—in particular, how intensively and flexibly they use energy, as summarized by share parameters and elasticities—play an important role in determining the baseline paths. One important subset describes the emissions produced from the use of coal or crude oil in each economy to produce a unit of output, which is illustrated by the coefficients in Table 4.3. These parameters are backed out from the model-consistent data to match observed activity levels with measured carbon emissions. China is the most coal intensive, followed by the United States, other emerging and developing economies, and OPEC economies. OPEC economies are the most oil intensive, per unit of output, followed by the United States, China, and other emerging and developing economies.

Elasticities of substitution—the ease with which firms and households can alter the composition of the factors of production they use and the goods they consume—also affect the baseline. Firms have the ability, to some degree, to change the proportions of energy they use to produce a given unit of output by substituting toward capital, labor, and materials. They also can alter the mix of fossil fuels used to produce energy. Production elasticities have otherwise been estimated, where possible, and have been calibrated to match typical values (averaging around 0.5) from other studies. Trade elasticities are about 0.9, except for energy goods, which are more substitutable (2.0).[41] Higher elasticities imply that economies respond more to relative price movements; they also imply that baseline activity grows faster because they allow economies to reduce their reliance on energy earlier than otherwise.

Together, these assumptions generate the baseline scenario summarized in Table 4.4. Most economic growth over the baseline is coming from non-Annex I regions. Although most

[41]The values of these elasticities are standard. But the so-called constant elasticity production functions and consumption bundles used here are vulnerable to the criticism that, in reality, firms and households cannot always substitute away from carbon-based energy (even at a very high price). For example, reducing fossil fuel use by just one more unit might actually imply that completely new technologies—such as renewables, hydro power, or nuclear energy—would have to be installed. This implies that there are nonlinearities that are not addressed in this analysis.

Table 4.4. Summary of the Baseline Scenario

GDP Growth Rates (Annual percent change)		2010	2020	2030	2040
United States		2.60	2.64	2.51	2.40
Japan		2.05	1.70	1.70	1.67
Eastern Europe		1.81	2.78	2.37	2.24
Western Europe		1.89	2.39	2.26	2.19
Annex I economies		2.18	2.46	2.32	2.23
China		10.19	5.04	3.50	2.70
Other developing and emerging economies		4.54	5.39	4.33	3.82
OPEC economies		2.31	3.97	3.39	3.14
Non-Annex I economies		5.19	5.20	4.10	3.58
World		2.83	3.21	2.88	2.71

Emission levels (GtCO$_2$)	2002	2010	2020	2030	2040
United States	5.8	6.2	7.5	9.1	11.0
Japan	1.2	1.4	1.6	1.8	2.1
Eastern Europe	3.1	3.0	3.5	4.1	5.4
Western Europe	3.5	3.7	4.1	4.7	5.4
Annex I economies	14.5	15.1	17.8	21.2	25.0
China	3.3	3.8	8.2	12.3	16.6
Other developing and emerging economies	5.0	5.0	8.2	12.8	18.8
OPEC economies	1.7	1.5	1.9	2.7	3.6
Non-Annex I economies	10.0	10.2	18.2	27.8	39.9
World	24.4	25.3	36.1	48.9	64.0

Emission shares (percent)	2002	2010	2020	2030	2040
United States	23.5	24.3	20.7	18.6	17.2
Japan	4.9	5.5	4.4	3.8	3.3
Eastern Europe	12.7	11.8	9.8	8.4	7.5
Western Europe	14.2	14.5	11.4	9.7	8.4
Annex I economies	59.3	59.7	49.4	43.3	39.1
China	13.5	14.9	22.7	25.2	26.0
Other developing and emerging economies	20.4	19.6	22.6	26.1	29.3
OPEC economies	6.8	5.8	5.3	5.5	5.6
Non-Annex I economies	40.7	40.3	50.6	56.7	60.9

Source: IMF staff calculations.
Note: OPEC = Organization of Petroleum Exporting Countries; GtCO$_2$ = gigatons of carbon dioxide.

emissions are currently produced by Annex I regions, this growth—together with the assumptions about emission intensity—implies that most emissions are produced by non-Annex I regions within the next 30 years.

The levels of emissions from fossil fuels are higher than the median of the levels in the studies published after the Intergovernmental Panel on Climate Change (IPCC) Special Report on Emissions Scenarios in 2001, but are within the 75th percentile (Figure 4.15).[42] The baseline used in this study has slightly higher growth rates than is typical in most other studies, but the main reason for higher emission levels in later periods in this study is higher emission

[42]See IPCC (2007).

intensity, because no explicit assumptions are made about the adoption of zero-emission technologies.[43]

The Determinants of Marginal Abatement Costs

A key determinant of the distribution of the burden of adjustment to policies in the simulations are the MACs, which allow for a compari-

[43]For example, the baseline emission path up to 2050 is very similar to that of the IGSM model from the Massachusetts Institute of Technology Joint Program used in US CCSP (2007). This model has a broadly similar structure to G-Cubed, and similar assumptions are made about population and productivity growth. But baseline emission growth in this study continues strongly after 2050, whereas emission growth from IGSM in US CCSP (2007) falls off considerably even in the absence of any policy intervention.

Table 4.5. Emission Intensities in the Baseline
(Emissions of CO_2 from fossil fuels as a proportion of real GDP)

	2002	2010	2020	2030	2040
United States	0.55	0.51	0.47	0.45	0.43
Japan	0.30	0.28	0.28	0.27	0.26
Eastern Europe	0.85	0.77	0.69	0.63	0.58
Western Europe	0.37	0.35	0.31	0.29	0.26
Annex I economies	0.51	0.47	0.43	0.40	0.38
China	3.11	2.48	2.69	2.72	2.72
Other developing and emerging economies	0.87	0.75	0.71	0.70	0.69
OPEC economies	1.82	1.50	1.36	1.34	1.31
Non-Annex I economies	1.29	1.12	1.14	1.12	1.08
World	0.67	0.61	0.63	0.63	0.63

Source: IMF staff calculations.
Note: OPEC = Organization of Petroleum Exporting Countries.

son of the ease for each economy of changing the intensity with which it uses carbon fuels. MACs are significantly affected by the values for elasticities of substitution. In the baseline, for a given sector, these values are common across regions.[44] MACs are significantly affected by the values for the shares of fossil fuels used by firms and households. Economies that are highly intensive users of energy have more potential for substitution toward other factors (which can be thought of, implicitly, as implementation of clean technologies). Economies that use more coal relative to oil will respond more to an increase in carbon prices, as coal has a higher proportion of carbon. These share parameters are determined by the data. They have a large impact on emission intensity, measured as emissions divided by GDP (Table 4.5).

Even though emission intensities decline over the baseline, reflecting gradual improvements in efficiency, non-Annex I regions are consistently much more intensive in their use of energy than Annex I regions. All else being equal, this implies that the most efficient return on investments in mitigation will come from the non-Annex I regions.

The net effects of substitution elasticities and shares on marginal abatement costs can be seen in Table 4.6, which calculates percentage emis-

[44]This reflects the paucity of data for many of these regions and is one of the major sources of parameter uncertainty in mitigation cost studies.

Figure 4.15. Global Emissions from Energy Only, 2030
(Gigatons of carbon dioxide)

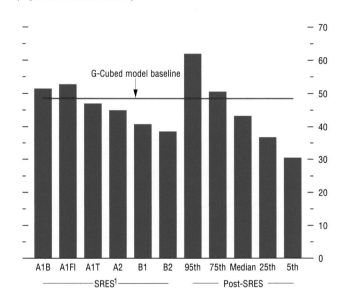

Sources: IPCC (2007); and IMF staff estimates.
[1]IPCC's *Special Report on Emissions Scenarios* (SRES).

Table 4.6. Emission Reductions and Consumption Losses Following a Standardized Carbon Price Shock
(Percent deviations from baseline path)

	United States	Japan	Western Europe	Eastern Europe and Russia	China	Other Developing and Emerging Economies	Organization of Petroleum Exporting Countries
Emission reduction	8.00	2.10	2.30	2.40	15.00	3.00	9.00
Rank	7.00	1.00	2.00	3.00	9.00	4.00	8.00
Consumption loss	0.22	0.12	0.19	0.33	0.50	0.25	2.00
Rank	3.00	1.00	2.00	5.00	8.00	4.00	9.00

Source: IMF staff calculations.

Note: Reduction in emissions and consumption losses measured at 2040, following a permanent unanticipated increase of $10 a ton of carbon beginning in 2013 for each region, leaving all other regions' carbon prices unchanged.

sion reductions and consumption losses from the baseline following a standardized carbon price increase of $10 per ton of carbon.

The table shows that Japan achieves the lowest emission reduction of all economies when it raises carbon prices by the same amount. It has the highest MAC, which implies that it will reduce emissions less than all other regions when faced with a common carbon price, or will find it advantageous to buy emission rights under a cap-and-trade system. On the other hand, China can achieve approximately seven times the emission reduction as Japan for the same cost.[45]

For the world economy, G-Cubed has the same or lower abatement costs compared with other models. The main reason is that it explicitly models capital flows, which makes it easier for economies to install new capital and shift away from carbon-based energy in production.[46]

Comparisons with Other Models

The range of issues implied by climate change economics is reflected in the wide range of models, each of which emphasizes different aspects of the problem. In general, all these models aim to bring climate change analysis into a macroeconomic framework. But they differ substantially in the complexity with which they model the macroeconomy, climate, and technologies.

To illustrate the range of differences, Table 4.7 summarizes features of some prominent models in the climate change literature:[47]

- PAGE, maintained by Chris Hope and Cambridge University and used for the *Stern Review* simulations (Plambeck, Hope, and Anderson, 1997);
- DICE, maintained by William Nordhaus at Yale and used in Nordhaus (2007b);
- EPPA/IGSM, maintained by a team at the Massachusetts Institute of Technology (Paltsev and others, 2005);
- MERGE, maintained by a team at Stanford University (Manne, Mendelsohn, and Richels, 1995); and
- MiniCAM, maintained by a team at Pacific Northwest National Laboratories (Brenkert and others, 2003).

All of these models can claim some comparative advantage, usually because of more elaborate modeling of a particular sector or mechanism. Some of the main differences include the following:

- whether behavior is optimizing and/or forward looking (which can affect the effectiveness of carbon price increases);

[45]In the experiment where a uniform carbon tax is imposed on all countries, this ratio increases to nearly 9:1, which illustrates the importance of reductions in export demand.

[46]The model is solved using linearization methods commonly applied to dynamic macroeconomic models. Linearization implies that responses of endogenous variables are proportional to the shock—a doubling of an increase in carbon taxes produces twice the reduction in emissions, for example. In practice, it may be that there are important nonlinearities in making the transition from old to new energy technologies.

[47]The latter three were used in US CCSP (2007).

Table 4.7. Comparison of Climate Policy Models

	G-Cubed	PAGE	DICE	EPPA/IGSM	MERGE	MiniCAM
Disaggregation	9 regions 5 energy sectors	8 regions Energy sectors not modeled	1 region (world) 2 energy sectors	16 regions 8 energy sectors	9 regions 9 energy sectors	14 regions 9 energy sectors
Expectations	Forward looking	Recursive	Forward looking	Recursive	Forward looking	Recursive
Dynamics and frequency	Annual frequency with intertemporal friction	1- to 50-year steps	10-year steps	5-year steps; vintage capital	10-year steps; putty-clay technologies	15-year steps; vintage capital
Factors used in production	Capital, labor, energy, materials	Not modeled	Capital, labor	Capital, labor, energy, materials	Capital, labor, energy	Energy, land
Equilibrium linkages	Full stock-flow constraints	Limited stock-flow constraints	Full stock-flow constraints	Full stock-flow constraints	Full stock-flow constraints	Limited stock-flow constraints
International linkages	Trade in differentiated goods and services, plus capital flows	Not modeled	Not modeled	Trade in all goods, differentiated by region	Trade in all goods, differentiated by region	Trade in energy and agricultural goods
Emissions and climate	Single gas (CO_2); no feedback from climate	Multiple gases; no feedback from climate	Single gas (CO_2e)[1]; feedback from carbon cycle	Multiple gases; feedback from atmospheric and oceanic climate	Multiple gases; feedback from oceanic climate	Multiple gases; feedback from land and climate models
Technology and energy-efficiency improvements	Both exogenous	Both exogenous	Feedback from climate onto productivity, exogenous AEEI[2]	Exogenous	Exogenous	Exogenous

Note: In models with "vintage" capital, the effective capital stock depends not just on the total cumulative investment over time (net of depreciation), but on the time at which investments were made. Production will therefore depend on the age profile of the capital stock. A closely related concept is "putty clay" technologies, in which investment—putty—is fungible, but once set as capital—clay—it is not.

[1] Carbon dioxide equivalent.

[2] Autonomous energy efficiency improvement.

• whether relative prices are articulated or not (which is important for modeling expenditure switching, factor substitution, external balances, and trade);

• whether there are endogenous monetary and fiscal policy reactions (in particular, the way carbon price revenues are recycled is potentially very important); whether there is stock-flow consistency (which is important to ensure that policies are not able to deliver "free lunches"); and

• whether there is an endogenous feedback mechanism via a carbon cycle model (important for modeling the medium- and long-term implications of policies).

For example, the PAGE model has a relatively simple structure and is designed more as a "meta-model" to quickly incorporate assumptions from other studies about climate change and to be simulated quickly and easily, facilitating the analysis of uncertainty. But it lacks some features that are important for this study, such

as forward-looking expectations, modeling of fiscal policy, and trade and capital linkages. The DICE model is designed to show how agents might respond to endogenous productivity effects from feedback of climate change and some mitigation policies; it simplifies analysis by looking at the world in aggregate using a Ramsey growth model, hence missing regional and sectoral detail. EPPA/IGSM is a large, integrated assessment model that mates a dynamic computable general equilibrium model of many regions and sectors with an elaborate climate change model, but with some loss of tractability. Even then it omits some features, such as forward-looking expectations and international capital flows.[48] MiniCAM is also an integrated assessment model, with detailed modeling of

[48] None of the models described here explicitly model international capital flows. However, free flow of capital is implicit in the DICE model, as it models the world economy as a single sector.

energy, agricultural systems, and land use, but it is not intended for general equilibrium analysis; in particular, only energy and agricultural goods are traded. By contrast, G-Cubed models emissions but not the consequences for GHG concentrations and climate change, and is not suitable for a full cost-benefit analysis of mitigation policies. But G-Cubed includes extensive detail on relative prices and policy linkages for regions and sectors, which is the focus of this study.

A key difference in models used to assess emission policies is the assumptions made about technology. Some models—for example, PAGE—do not make any explicit technology assumptions. Of those that do, there are two main types. In the first, firms have discrete choices of specific technology assumptions (such as nuclear, coal-based, and so on), each requiring inputs to be used in fixed proportions (an example is the MERGE model). In the second, smooth production functions are used and are sometimes nested (see, for example, EPPA/IGSM and G-Cubed). Fixed-proportion models imply that firms must pass cost-benefit thresholds before switching to a new technology, whereas models with smooth production functions allow continual adjustment. In this study, substitution possibilities are very important for determining the costs of emission reductions. Whether the nonlinearities implied by fixed-proportion technologies will be important *in the aggregate* for the reaction to emission policies is an important issue to be resolved.[49]

It is therefore important to realize that models place different emphases on these assumptions of economic behavior, as well as different—though perfectly reasonable—assumptions about population and productivity growth, emission intensity, and clean technologies, as well as about nonclimate policies. Therefore, the models can produce very different scenarios for emissions and for the costs of reducing them. Hence we should put more emphasis on the

[49]For more comment and comparisons, see Weyant (2004) and references therein.

qualitative mechanisms at work than any quantitative predictions.

References

Abiad, Abdul, Enrica Detragiache, and Thierry Tressel, 2007, "A New Database of Financial Reforms" (unpublished; Washington: International Monetary Fund).

Åhman, Markus, and Kristina Holmgren, 2006, "New Entrant Allocation in the Nordic Energy Sectors: Incentives and Options in the EU ETS," *Climate Policy*, Vol. 6, No. 4, pp. 423–40.

Åhman, Markus, Dallas Burtraw, Joseph Kruger, and Lars Zetterberg, 2007, "A Ten-Year Rule to Guide the Allocation of EU Emission Allowances," *Energy Policy*, Vol. 35 (March), pp. 1718–30.

Aldy, Joseph E., and Robert N. Stavins, eds., 2007, *Architectures for Agreement: Addressing Global Climate Change in the Post-Kyoto World* (Cambridge, United Kingdom: Cambridge University Press).

Association of British Insurers (ABI), 2005, *Financial Risks of Climate Change*, Summary Report (London, June). Available via the Internet: www.abi.org.uk/Display/File/Child/552/Financial_Risks_of_Climate_Change.pdf.

Barrett, Scott, 2006, "Climate Treaties and 'Breakthrough' Technologies," *American Economic Review*, Vol. 96 (May), pp. 22–25.

Baumert, Kevin A., Timothy Herzog, and Jonathan Pershing, 2005, *Navigating the Numbers: Greenhouse Gas Data and International Climate Policy* (Washington: World Resources Institute).

Bernanke, Ben, and Mark Gertler, 1989, "Agency Costs, Net Worth and Business Fluctuations," *American Economic Review*, Vol. 79 (March), pp. 14–31.

Böhringer, Christoph, and Andreas Lange, 2005, "On the Design of Optimal Grandfathering Schemes for Emission Allowances," *European Economic Review*, Vol. 49 (November), pp. 2041–55.

Bonaccolta, John, 2007, "Come Rain and Shine," *Investment & Pensions in Europe* (November), pp. 63–64.

Borensztein, Eduardo, Eduardo A. Cavallo, and Patricio Valenzuela, 2008, "Debt Sustainability under Catastrophic Risk: The Case for Government Budget Insurance," IMF Working Paper 08/44 (Washington: International Monetary Fund).

Borensztein, Eduardo, Daniel Cohen, Julia Cage, and Cécile Valadier, 2008, "Aid Volatility and

Macroeconomic Risks in Low-Income Countries (unpublished; Washington: International Monetary Fund).

Bovenberg, A. Lans, and Lawrence H. Goulder, 2001, "Neutralizing the Adverse Industry Impacts of CO_2 Abatement Policies: What Does It Cost?" in *Behavioral and Distributional Effects of Environmental Policy*, ed. by C. Carraro and G. Metcalf (Chicago: University of Chicago Press), pp. 45–85.

Brazil, Ministries of External Relations, Science and Technology, Environment, Mines and Energy, and Development, Industry and Foreign Trade, 2007, "Brazil's Contribution to Prevent Climate Change," White Paper (Brasilia). Available via the Internet: www.mct.gov.br/upd_blob/0018/18294.pdf.

Brenkert, Antoinette L., Steven J. Smith, Son H. Kim, and Hugh M. Pitcher, 2003, "Model Documentation for the MiniCAM," Report No. 14337 (Richmond, Washington: Pacific Northwest National Library).

Caballero, Ricardo, and Mohamad L. Hammour, 2005, "The Cost of Recessions Revisited: A Reverse-Liquidationist View," *Review of Economic Studies*, Vol. 72 (April), pp. 313–41.

California Energy Commission (CEC), 2005, "Implementing California's Loading Order for Electricity Resources," Staff Report No. CEC-400-2005-043 (Sacramento). Available via the Internet: www.energy.ca.gov/2005publications/CEC-400-2005-043/CEC-400-2005-043.PDF.

Capoor, Karan, and Philippe Ambrosi, 2007, "State and Trends of the Carbon Market" (Washington: World Bank). Available via the Internet: carbonfinance.org/docs/Carbon_Trends_2007-_FINAL_-_May_2.pdf.

Castles, Ian, and David Henderson, 2003, "Economics, Emissions Scenarios and the Work of the IPCC," *Energy and Environment*, Vol. 14 (July 1), pp. 415–35.

Chamon, Marcos, Paolo Mauro, and Yoki Okawa, forthcoming, "Cars—Mass Car Ownership in the Emerging Market Giants," *Economic Policy*.

Clarkson, Richard, and Kathryn Deyes, 2002, "Estimating the Social Cost of Carbon Emissions," Government Economic Service Working Paper No. 140 (London: HM Treasury, Department of Environment Food and Rural Affairs, January). Available via the Internet: www.hm-treasury.gov.uk/media/5/F/SCC.pdf.

Cline, William, 2007, *Global Warming and Agriculture: Impact Estimates by Country* (Washington: Center for Global Development).

Criqui, Patrick, Alban Kitous, Marcel Berk, Michel den Elzen, Bas Eickhout, Paul Lucas, Detlef van Vuuren, Nikolaos Kouvaritakis, Denise Vanregemorter, 2003, "Greenhouse Gas Reduction Pathways in the UNFCCC Process up to 2025" (Brussels: European Commission). Available via the Internet: ec.europa.eu/environment/climat/pdf/pm_techreport2025.pdf.

Dasgupta, Partha, 2007, "Commentary: The Stern Review's Economics of Climate Change," *National Institute Economic Review*, Vol. 199 (January), pp. 4–7.

DeLong, Brad, 2006, "Partha Dasgupta Makes a Mistake in His Critique of the *Stern Review*" (November 20). Available via the Internet: http://delong.typepad.com/sdj/2006/11/partha_dasgaptu.html.

den Elzen, Michel, Jan S. Fuglestvedt, Niklas Höhne, Cathy Trudinger, Jason Lowe, Ben Matthews, Bård Romstad, Christiano Pires de Campos, and Natalia Andronova, 2005, "Analysing countries' contribution to climate change: Scientific and policy-related choices," Environmental Science and Policy, Vol. 8, No. 6, pp. 614–36.

Deutsch, John, and Ernest J. Moniz, 2007, *The Future of Coal: Options for a Carbon-Constrained World* (Cambridge, Massachusetts: MIT Press).

Dinan, Terry M., and Diane L. Rogers, 2002, "Distributional Effects of Carbon Allowance Trading: How Government Decisions Determine Winners and Losers," *National Tax Journal*, Vol. 55 (June), pp. 199–222.

Downing, Thomas, and others, 2005, "Social Cost of Carbon: A Closer Look at Uncertainty, Final Project Report" (Oxford: Stockholm Environment Institute for the UK Department for Environment, Food and Rural Affairs). Available via the Internet: www.defra.gov.uk/environment/climatechange/research/carboncost/pdf/sei-scc-report.pdf.

Easterling, William, Pramod Aggarwal, Punsalmaa Batima, Keith Brander, Lin Erda, Mark Howden, Andrei Kirilenko, John Morton, Jean-François Soussana, Josef Schmidhuber, and Francesco Tubiello, 2007, "Food, Fibre and Forest Products," in *Climate Change 2007: Impacts, Adaptation and Vulnerability, Contribution of Working Group II to the Fourth Assessment Report of the Intergovernmental Panel on Climate Change*, ed. by M.L. Parry, O.F. Canziani, J.P. Palutikof, P.J. van der Linden, and C.E. Hanson (Cambridge, United Kingdom: Cambridge University Press), pp. 273–313.

Ellerman, A. Denny, and Barbara Buchner, 2007, "The European Union Emissions Trading Scheme:

Origins, Allocation, and Early Results," *Review of Environmental Economics and Policy*, Vol. 1 (Winter), pp. 66–87.

Energy Conservation Centre Japan (ECCJ), 2005, "Top Runner Programme: Developing the World's Best Energy Efficient Appliance" (Tokyo). Available via the Internet: www.eccj.or.jp/top_runner/index. html.

Energy Information Administration, 2005, *International Energy Annual* (Washington). Available via the Internet: www.eia.doe.gov/iea.

———, 2006, *International Energy Outlook 2006* (Washington). Available via the Internet: www.eia.doe. gov/oiaf/archive/ieo06/index.html.

Fankhauser, Samuel, and Richard S.J. Tol, 2005, "On Climate Change and Economic Growth," *Resource and Energy Economics*, Vol. 27, pp. 1–17.

Friedman, Milton, 1953, "The Case for Flexible Exchange Rates," in *Essays in Positive Economics* (Chicago: University of Chicago).

Froot, Kenneth, 2001, "The Market for Catastrophe Risk: A Clinical Examination," *Journal of Financial Economics*, Vol. 60 (May), pp. 529–71.

Geman, Hélyette, and Alois Kanyinda, 2007, "Water as the Next Commodity," *Journal of Alternative Investments*, Vol. 10, No. 2, pp. 23–30.

Government of Japan, 2002, "Japan's Third National Communication Under the United Nations Framework Convention on Climate Change" (Tokyo). Available via the Internet: unfccc.int/resource/docs/natc/japnc3.pdf.

———, 2007, "Outline of the Renewable Portfolio Standard (RPS) System" (Tokyo).

Grassl, Hartmut, Renate Schubert, Juliane Kokott, Margareta Kulessa, Joachim Luther, Franz Nuscheler, Rainer Sauerborn, Hans-Joachim Schellnhuber, and Ernst-Detlef Schulze, 2003, "Climate Protection Strategies for the 21st Century: Kyoto and Beyond," WBGU Special Report (Berlin: German Advisory Council on Global Change). Available via the Internet: www.wbgu.de/wbgu_sn2003_engl.pdf.

Gupta, Sujata, Dennis A. Tirpak, Nicholas Burger, Joyeeta Gupta, Niklas Höhne, Antonina Ivanova Boncheva, Gorashi Mohammed Kanoan, Charles Kolstad, Joseph A. Kruger, Axel Michaelowa, Shinya Murase, Jonathan Pershing, Tatsuyoshi Saijo, and Agus Sari, 2007, "Policies, Instruments and Co-operative Arrangements," in *Climate Change 2007: Mitigation. Contribution of Working Group III to the Fourth Assessment Report of the Intergovernmental Panel on Climate Change*, ed. by Bert Metz, Ogunlade

Davidson, Peter Bosch, Rutu Dave, and Leo Meyer (Cambridge, United Kingdom: Cambridge University Press). Available via the Internet: www.mnp. nl/ipcc/pages_media/FAR4docs/final_pdfs_ar4/Chapter13.pdf.

Hope, Chris, 2006a, "The Marginal Impact of CO_2 from PAGE2002: An Integrated Assessment Model Incorporating the IPCC's Five Reasons for Concern," *Integrated Assessment*, Vol. 6, No. 1, pp. 19–56.

———, 2006b, "The Social Cost of Carbon: What Does It Actually Depend on?" *Climate Policy*, Vol. 6, No. 5, pp. 565–72.

India, Ministry of Environment and Forests, 2006, *National Environment Policy 2006* (Mumbai). Available via the Internet: www.envfor.nic.in/nep/nep2006.html.

———, and Ministry of Power Bureau of Energy Efficiency, 2007, "India: Addressing Energy Security and Climate Change" (Mumbai). Available via the Internet: envfor.nic.in/divisions/ccd/Addressing_CC_09-10-07.pdf.

India, Ministry of New and Renewable Energy, 2006, "11th Plan Proposals" (Mumbai).

India, Planning Commission, 2007, *Eleventh Five-Year Plan, 2007–2012* (New Delhi). Available via the Internet: planningcommission.nic.in/plans/planrel/11thf.htm.

Intergovernmental Panel on Climate Change (IPCC), 2007, *Climate Change 2007: Mitigation. Contribution of Working Group III to the Fourth Assessment Report of the Intergovernmental Panel on Climate Change*, ed. by B. Metz, O.R. Davidson, P.R. Bosch, R. Dave, and L.A. Meyer (Cambridge, United Kingdom: Cambridge University Press). Available via the Internet: www. ipcc.ch/ipccreports/ar4-wg3.htm.

International Energy Agency (IEA), 2007a, *World Energy Outlook 2007: China and India Insights* (Paris, November).

———, 2007b, *Energy Policies of IEA Countries: Germany 2007 Review* (Paris).

International Monetary Fund (IMF), 2008, "The Fiscal Implications of Climate Change" (Washington, forthcoming).

International Road Federation, various issues, *World Road Statistics* (Geneva).

Japan, Ministry of Finance, 2006, "Comprehensive Handbook of Japanese Taxes 2006" (Tokyo). Available via the Internet: www.mof.go.jp/english/tax/taxes2006e.htm.

Kahn, Matthew E., 2005, "The Death Toll from Natural Disasters: The Role of Income, Geography, and

Institutions," *Review of Economics and Statistics*, Vol. 87 (May), pp. 271–84.

Kiyotaki, Nobuhiro, and John Moore, 1997, "Credit Cycles," *Journal of Political Economy*, Vol. 105 (April), pp. 211–48.

Kopp, Raymond, Richard Morgenstern, and William Pizer, 1997. "Something for Everyone: A Climate Policy that Both Environmentalists and Industry Can Live With" (Washington: Resources for the Future). Available via the Internet: www.weather-vane.rff.org/SomethingForEveryone.pdf.

Kopp, Raymond J., and William A. Pizer, eds., 2007, *Assessing U.S. Climate Policy Options* (Washington: Resources for the Future). Available via the Internet: www.rff.org/rff/Publications/CPF_AssessingUSClimatePolicyOptions.cfm.

Kumhof, Michael, and Douglas Laxton, 2007, "A Party Without a Hangover? On the Effects of U.S. Government Deficits," IMF Working Paper 07/202 (Washington: International Monetary Fund).

Ligthart, Jenny, and Rosa Martín Suárez, 2005, "The Productivity of Public Capital: A Meta Analysis," (unpublished; Tilburg, Netherlands: Tilburg University). Available via the Internet: center.uvt.nl/staff/ligthart/meta.pdf.

Manne, Alan S., Robert Mendelsohn, and Richard G. Richels, 1995, "MERGE—A Model for Evaluating Regional and Global Effects of GHG Reduction Policies," *Energy Policy*, Vol. 23 (January), pp. 17–34.

Matsuyama, Kiminori, 2007, "Aggregate Implications of Credit Market Imperfections," NBER Working Paper No. 13209 (Cambridge, Massachusetts: National Bureau of Economic Research).

McKibbin, Warwick J., and Peter J. Wilcoxen, 1997, "A Better Way to Slow Global Climate Change," Policy Brief No. 17 (Washington: The Brookings Institution).

———, 1998, "The Theoretical and Empirical Structure of the G-Cubed Model" *Economic Modelling*, Vol. 16 (January 1), pp. 123–48.

———, 2002a, "An Alternative to Kyoto?" *New Economy*, Vol. 9 (September), pp. 133–38.

———, 2002b, *Climate Change Policy After Kyoto: A Blueprint for a Realistic Approach* (Washington: Brookings Institution Press).

———, 2002c, "The Role of Economics in Climate Change Policy," *Journal of Economic Perspectives*, Vol. 16 (Spring), pp. 107–29.

———, 2004, "Estimates of the Costs of Kyoto-Marrakesh Versus the McKibbin-Wilcoxen Blueprint," *Energy Policy*, Vol. 32 (March), pp. 467–79.

Mendelsohn, Robert, Michael Schlesinger, and Larry Williams, 2000, "Comparing Impacts Across Climate Models," *Integrated Assessment*, Vol. 1 (March), pp. 37–48.

Metcalf, Gilbert E., 2007, "A Proposal for a U.S. Carbon Tax Swap: An Equitable Tax Reform to Address Global Climate Change," Hamilton Project Discussion Paper No. 2007-12 (Washington: The Brookings Institution). Available via the Internet: www.brookings.edu/~/media/Files/rc/papers/2007/10carbontax_metcalf/10_carbontax_metcalf.pdf.

Meyers, Stephen, James McMahon, Michael McNeil, and Xiaomin Liu, 2002, "Realized and Prospective Impacts of U.S. Energy Efficiency Standards for Residential Appliances," Report No. LBNL-49504 (Berkeley, California: Lawrence Berkeley National Laboratory).

Miguel, Edward, Shanker Satyanath, and Ernest Sergenti, 2004, "Economic Shocks and Civil Conflict: An Instrumental Variables Approach," *Journal of Political Economy*, Vol. 112 (August), pp. 725–53.

Mundell, Robert A., 1961, "A Theory of Optimum Currency Areas," *American Economic Review*, Vol. 51 (September), pp. 657–65.

Nakicenovic, Nebosja, and Keywan Riahi, 2003, "Model Runs with MESSAGE in the Context of the Further Development of the Kyoto Protocol," Expertise for the WBGU Special Report "Climate Protection Strategies for the 21st Century: Kyoto and Beyond" (Berlin). Available via the Internet: www.wbgu.de/wbgu_sn2003_ex03.pdf.

Nordhaus, William D., 2007a, "A Review of the *Stern Review of the Economics of Climate Change*," *Journal of Economic Literature*, Vol. 45 (September), pp. 686–702.

———, 2007b, "The Challenge of Global Warming: Economic Models and Environmental Policy" (unpublished). Available via the Internet: nordhaus.econ.yale.edu/dice_mss_091107_public.pdf.

———, 2007c, "Alternative Measures of Output in Global Economic-Environmental Models: Purchasing Power Parity or Market Exchange Rates?" *Energy Economics*, Vol. 29 (May), pp. 349–72.

———, and Joseph Boyer, 2000, *Warming the World: Economic Models of Global Warming* (Cambridge, Massachusetts: MIT Press).

Nordqvist, Joakim, 2006, "Evaluation of Japan's Top Runner Programme Within the Framework of the AID-EE Project," Active Implementation of the European Directive on Energy Efficiency. Available via the Internet: www.aid-ee.org/documents/018TopRunner-Japan.pdf.

Obstfeld, Maurice, and K. Rogoff, 2002, *Foundations of International Macroeconomics*, Fifth Edition (Cambridge, Massachusetts: MIT Press).

Olivier, Jos, and Jan Berdowski, 2001, "Global Emission Sources and Sinks," in *The Climate System*, ed. by Jan Berdowski, Robert Guicherit, and BertJan Heij (Lisse, Netherlands: Swets & Zeitlinger B.V.), pp. 33–78.

Paltsev, Sergey, John M. Reilly, Henry D. Jacoby, Richard S. Eckaus, James McFarland, Marcus Sarofim, Malcolm Asadoorian, and Mustafa Babiker, 2005, "The MIT Emissions Prediction and Policy Analysis (EPPA) Model: Version 4," Report No. 125 (Cambridge, Massachusetts: Massachusetts Institute of Technology, Joint Program on the Science and Policy of Global Change).

Parry, Ian W.H., Roberton C. Williams, III, and Lawrence H. Goulder, 1999, "When Can Carbon Abatement Policies Increase Welfare? The Fundamental Role of Distorted Factor Markets," *Journal of Environmental Economics and Management*, Vol. 37 (January), pp. 52–84.

Persson, Tobias, Christian Azar, and Kristian Lindgren, 2006, "Allocation of CO_2 Emission Permits— Economic Incentives for Emissions Reductions in Developing Countries," *Energy Policy*, Vol. 34 (September), pp. 1889–99.

Pindyck, Robert S., 2007, "Uncertainty in Environmental Economics," *Review of Environmental Economics and Policy*, Vol. 1, No. 1, pp. 45–65.

Pizer, William A., 2002, "Combining Price and Quantity Controls to Mitigate Global Climate Change," *Journal of Public Economics*, Vol. 85 (September), pp. 409–34.

Plambeck, Erica L., Chris Hope, and John Anderson, 1997, "The [PAGE95] Model: Integrating the Science and Economics of Global Warming," *Energy Economics*, Vol. 19 (March), pp. 77–101.

Point Carbon Research, 2008, "A Review of 2007," *Carbon Market Monitor* (January).

Ramcharan, Rodney, 2007a, "Does the Exchange Rate Regime Matter for Real Shocks? Evidence from Windstorms and Earthquakes," *Journal of International Economics*, Vol. 73 (September), pp. 31–47.

———, 2007b, "Floods, Windstorms, and the Financial System" (unpublished; Washington: International Monetary Fund).

Rosendahl, Knut Einar, 2007, "Incentives and Quota Prices in an Emission Trading Scheme with

Updating," Research Department Working Paper No. 495 (Oslo: Statistics Norway). Available via the Internet: www.ssb.no/publikasjoner/DP/pdf/dp495.pdf.

Sedjo, Roger A., and Michael Toman, 2001, "Can Carbon Sinks Be Operational? RFF Workshop Proceedings," Discussion Paper No. 01–26 (Washington: Resources for the Future). Available via the Internet: www.rff.org/rff/Documents/RFF-DP-01-26.pdf.

Stavins, Robert N., and Kenneth R. Richards, 2005, "The Cost of U.S. Forest-Based Carbon Sequestration" (Arlington, Virginia: Pew Center on Global Climate Change). Available via the Internet: http://www.pewclimate.org/docUploads/Sequest_Final.pdf.

Stern, Nicholas, 2008, "The Economics of Climate Change," Richard T. Ely Lecture, American Economic Association Meetings, New Orleans, Louisiana (January 4).

Stern, Nicholas, and others, 2007, *The Economics of Climate Change: The Stern Review* (London: HM Treasury).

Strand, Jon, 2007, "Energy Efficiency and Renewable Energy Supply for the G-7 Countries, with Emphasis on Germany," IMF Working Paper 07/299 (Washington: International Monetary Fund).

Stromberg, David, 2007, "Natural Disasters, Economic Development, and Humanitarian Aid," *Journal of Economic Perspectives*, Vol. 21 (Summer), pp. 199–222.

Tol, Richard S.J., 2002, "Estimates of the Damage Costs of Climate Change. Part 1: Benchmark Estimates," *Environmental and Resource Economics*, Vol. 21 (January), pp. 47–73.

———, 2005, "The Marginal Damage Costs of Carbon Dioxide Emissions: An Assessment of the Uncertainties," *Energy Policy*, Vol. 33 (November), pp. 2064–74.

United Kingdom Climate Impacts Programme (UKCIP), 2007, *UKCIP Climate Digest: April 2007* (Oxford). Available via the Internet: www.ukcip.org.uk/news_releases/38.pdf.

United Nations, 1998, "Kyoto Protocol to the United Nations Framework Convention on Climate Change" (New York). Available via the Internet: unfccc.int/resource/docs/convkp/kpeng.pdf.

———, 2006, "World Population Prospects: The 2006 Revision Population Database" (New York). Available via the Internet: esa.un.org/unpp.

United Nations Development Program (UNDP), 2007, *Human Development Report 2007/2008, Fighting*

Climate Change: Human Solidarity in a Divided World (New York).

United Nations Framework Convention on Climate Change (UNFCCC), 2007, *Investment and Financial Flows to Address Climate Change* (Bonn).

U.S. Climate Change Science Program (US CCSP), 2007, *Scenarios of Greenhouse Gas Emissions and Atmospheric Concentrations and Review of Integrated Scenario Development and Application*, Synthesis and Assessment Product 2.1 (Washington: Department of Energy). Available via the Internet: www.climatescience.gov/Library/sap/sap2-1/default.php.

van Aardenne, J.A., F.J. Dentener, J.G.J. Olivier, C.G.M. Klein Goldewijk, and J. Lelieveld, 2001, "A 1 Degree x 1 Degree Resolution Dataset of Historical Anthropogenic Trace Gas Emissions for the Period 1890–1990," *Global Biogeochemical Cycles*, Vol. 15, No. 4, pp. 909–28.

van Lennep, David, Teddy Oetomo, Maxwell Stevenson, and André de Vries, 2004, "Weather Derivatives: An Attractive Additional Asset Class," *Journal of Alternative Investments*, Vol. 7 (Fall), pp. 65–74.

Wasmer, Etienne, and Philippe Weil, 2004, "The Macroeconomics of Labor and Credit Market Imperfections," *American Economic Review*, Vol. 94 (September), pp. 944–63.

Webster, Mort, Chris Forest, John Reilly, Mustafa Babiker, David Kicklighter, Monika Mayer, Ronald Prinn, Marcus Sarofim, Andrei Sokolov, Peter Stone, and Chien Wang, 2003, "Uncertainty Analysis of Climate Change and Policy Response," *Climatic Change*, Vol. 61, No. 3, pp. 295–320.

Weitzman, Martin, 2007a, "The Role of Uncertainty in the Economics of Catastrophic Climate Change," Working Paper 07-11 (Washington: AEI-Brookings Joint Center).

———, 2007b, "A Review of the *Stern Review of the Economics of Climate Change*," *Journal of Economic Literature*, Vol. 45 (September), pp. 703–24.

———, 2008, "On Modeling and Interpreting the Economics of Catastrophic Climate Change" (unpublished). Available via the Internet: www.economics.harvard.edu/faculty/weitzman/files/modeling.pdf.

Weyant, John P., 2004, "Introduction and Overview," *Energy Economics*, Vol. 26, "EMF 19 Alternative Technology Strategies for Climate Change Policy" (July), pp. 501–15.

World Bank, 2006, *Clean Energy and Development: Towards an Investment Framework* (Washington).

Wright, Brian D., 1983, "The Economics of Invention Incentives: Patents, Prizes and Research Contracts," *American Economic Review*, Vol. 73 (September), pp. 691–707.

Yohe, Gary, Rodel Lasco, Qazi Ahmad, Nigel Arnell, Stewart Cohen, Chris Hope, Anthony Janetos, and Rosa Perez, 2007, "Perspectives on Climate Change and Sustainability," in *Climate Change 2007: Impacts, Adaptation, and Vulnerability. Contributions of Working Group II to the Fourth Assessment Report of the Intergovernmental Panel on Climate Change*, ed. by Martin Parry, Osvaldo Canziani, Jean Palutikof, Paul van der Linden, and Clair E. Hanson (Cambridge, United Kingdom: Cambridge University Press), pp. 811–41. Available via the Internet: www.ipcc.ch/pdf/assessment-report/ar4/wg2/ar4-wg2-chapter20.pdf.

GLOBALIZATION, COMMODITY PRICES, AND DEVELOPING COUNTRIES

This chapter examines the role of soaring commodity prices in contributing to emerging and developing economies' growing trade and financial integration into the global economy. It finds that improvements in institutions and policy frameworks help explain why the current commodity price boom is proving more favorable to developing economies than previous booms, bringing rapid growth in exports (especially manufacturing exports), investment (both domestic and foreign), and output. Continued progress in trade and financial integration will require sustained efforts to further strengthen institutions and economic policies in developing countries.

O ver the past couple of decades, and in particular over the past few years, many developing and emerging economies have become steadily more integrated into the world economy. International trade, in both manufactures and commodities, has become substantially more important to most of these economies (Figures 5.1 and 5.2). At the same time, they have become more open to international capital flows, in particular through foreign direct investment (FDI) (Figure 5.3). This chapter discusses some characteristics and causes of this growing integration, with a view to assessing its sustainability. More specifically, the chapter focuses on the following issues.

First, have the extent and the pace of trade and financial integration differed among developing economies and regions? Have these countries diversified their production between commodities and manufactures? Have they diversified their export destinations between

Note: The main authors of this chapter are Nikola Spatafora and Irina Tytell, with support from Patrick Hettinger and Ercument Tulun. The project was supervised by Jonathan Ostry. Arvind Subramanian and Shang-Jin Wei provided consultancy support. We also thank Tim Callen, Paul Cashin, Paul Collier, Gian Maria Milesi-Ferretti, and Alessandro Prati for their comments.

Figure 5.1. Trade in Goods and Services

Over the past two decades, international trade has become substantially more important to most developing economies.

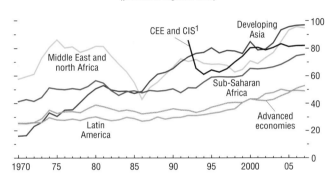

**Trade in Goods and Services
(percent of regional GDP)**

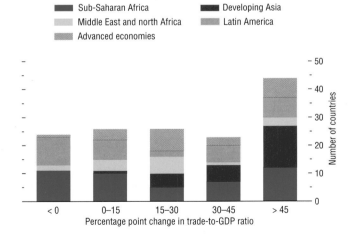

Trade Growth, 1970–2007

Sources: World Bank, World Development Indicators database; and IMF staff calculations.
[1]Central and eastern Europe, and Commonwealth of Independent States.

191

Figure 5.2. Merchandise Exports of Emerging and Developing Economies

Manufacturing exports have been growing especially fast, particularly in volume terms.

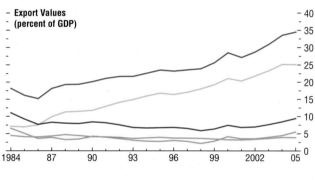

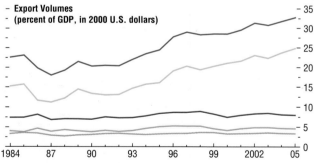

Sources: World Bank, World Development Indicators database; and IMF staff calculations.

advanced and other developing economies? Has the emergence of China and India as major players in the global marketplace helped pull other developing economies into the international markets, or has it displaced them?

Second, the surge of globalization across developing economies has coincided with booming prices for oil and other primary commodities. To what extent have increased trade and capital flows to these countries been driven by rising prices for the commodities they export? Have other, potentially more permanent factors, such as improved domestic institutions and policy frameworks, played a role in fostering these countries' economic integration? Has rising trade openness in nearby economies contributed to their export growth?

The existing literature on the determinants of international trade and capital flows emphasizes the role of institutional and political factors within countries (including direct restrictions on current and capital account transactions), as well as historical, cultural, and geographical links across countries (including bilateral or multilateral agreements).[1] This literature has paid far less attention to the terms of trade or to commodity prices. This stands in sharp contrast to, say, the literature on economic growth, in which the role of commodity prices has been hotly debated, with some studies linking commodity booms and increased growth and others suggesting the existence of a "resource curse" that undercuts sustainable growth.[2]

This chapter takes a closer look at the role of commodity market developments in driving globalization in developing economies. Price fluctuations have direct effects on the values of commodity exports and imports and can also encourage changes in the volume of such trade. Furthermore, there can be indirect effects on

[1]See, for example, Baier and Bergstrand (2007) and Dell'Ariccia and others (2007).
[2]See Deaton (1999) for Africa's experience, and Blattman, Hwang, and Williamson (2007) for a historical account. On the resource curse more particularly, see Collier and Goderis (2007), as well as a literature survey by van der Ploeg (2006).

investment (both domestic and foreign) in commodity-related and other export sectors. In addition, commodity price movements can affect real exchange rates and competitiveness, especially in non-resource-exporting sectors (Dutch disease), and thereby can affect the extent of trade integration.[3] In a similar vein, commodity price booms may promote public spending and external borrowing by commodity exporters, potentially setting the stage for subsequent crises, which could negatively affect trade and financial globalization. Moreover, any change in trade and capital flows associated with commodity market developments could motivate policymakers to extend or curtail their economies' external openness. Through all these channels, changes in commodity prices may have lasting effects on the degree to which commodity-dependent economies integrate further into the global economy.

The rest of the chapter is organized as follows. The first section presents key stylized facts concerning developing economies' trade and financial integration. Then, an event-study methodology is used to assess how specific variables of interest behaved during previous commodity price booms and busts and whether the current boom differs significantly from previous episodes. Finally, formal econometric techniques are used to analyze the historical evidence on the determinants of developing economies' integration into the global economy, with an emphasis on the respective roles of evolving institutions and policies versus developments in commodity markets. While the focus throughout is on those factors driving integration, it is also important to recognize the impact of globalization, and in particular trade integration and FDI, on growth and welfare in developing economies (Box 5.1).

Overall, this chapter finds that, in important ways, the current commodity price boom is

[3]Dutch disease occurs when increased revenues from natural resources raise the real exchange rate and thereby make other exports, particularly manufactures, less competitive. See Corden and Neary (1982) and Corden (1984) for classic discussions of Dutch disease. See also Ostry (1988) and Edwards and Ostry (1990).

Figure 5.3. Gross Foreign Capital and Gross Foreign Liabilities
(Percent of regional GDP)

Developing economies have become more open to international capital flows, in particular through foreign direct investment (FDI).

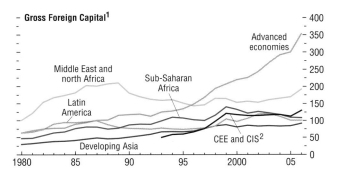

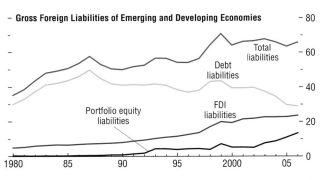

Sources: Lane and Milesi-Ferretti (2006); and IMF staff calculations.
[1]Total assets and liabilities of FDI, portfolio equity, and debt.
[2]Central and eastern Europe, and Commonwealth of Independent States.

Box 5.1. How Does the Globalization of Trade and Finance Affect Growth? Theory and Evidence

The implications of trade and financial globalization for economic growth have long been of interest to economists and policymakers alike. This box summarizes the results of recent research on this topic. There are multiple theoretical channels through which trade and financial integration can generate growth benefits, but the empirical evidence for such direct growth effects is hardly decisive, particularly in the case of financial integration. However, recent empirical research suggests that both trade and financial integration can play catalytic roles for a variety of indirect growth benefits. Moreover, recent studies also indicate that countries that employ appropriate structural and macroeconomic policies appear better equipped to enjoy these benefits.

Trade Integration

Trade theory has traditionally emphasized the link between trade liberalization and economic efficiency. A trade barrier alters consumption and production decisions, leading to a misallocation of resources. Therefore, liberalization will generally raise real incomes, except perhaps in cases in which externalities or preexisting distortions are present or a terms-of-trade deterioration outweighs efficiency gains. The results from simulation models suggest that, with few exceptions, trade liberalization raises the level of a country's real income.[1]

In addition, recent models of international trade and growth demonstrate how trade liberalization can lead to dynamic gains. Greater openness to international trade can affect an economy's growth rate by making a wider range of goods available to an economy. Trade liberalization not only increases the volume of existing goods that are traded, it also allows a country to import and export new varieties of goods (see Broda and Weinstein, 2004). Other channels through which trade liberalization can raise a country's growth rate include (1) stimulating capital and labor inflows (including foreign direct investment, FDI); (2) raising the productivity of domestic firms through the transfer of new technologies; and (3) creating dynamic externalities through learning.

Empirical studies have generally uncovered a positive relationship between trade liberalization and growth, albeit with some exceptions.[2] However, many methodological problems complicate any effort to quantify the relationship between trade and growth, including how best to measure the extent of a country's openness to trade. This and other issues have prompted some authors, most visibly Rodriguez and Rodrik (2002), to question the robustness of the empirical "evidence" linking trade liberalization and growth.

In general, the impact of trade liberalization on an economy's growth rate will depend on the broader policy environment. For instance, trade liberalization generates benefits for an economy by reducing the price of imports. If prices in an economy are not free to change and resources (for example, labor and capital) are not mobile across sectors, then an economy will not reap the full benefits of the liberalization. Therefore, trade liberalization should be accompanied by policies that enhance both price flexibility and factor mobility.

In a study of 13 countries that undertook trade liberalization, Wacziarg and Welch (2003) identified several characteristics that accompanied successful trade reform. First, the majority of countries that experienced higher growth rates following trade liberalization continued to deepen their reforms following the initial period of liberalization. This was especially

Note: The main authors of this box are M. Ayhan Kose and Stephen Tokarick.

[1] For instance, Anderson Martin, and van der Mensbrugghe (2005) calculate that complete trade liberalization by all countries would raise real world income by about ½ percent of global GDP in 2015, with about 30 percent of this gain accruing to developing economies as a group.

[2] See Hallaert (2006), Table 3. For detailed reviews, see also Winters (2004), Baldwin (2003), Berg and Krueger (2003), and Rodriguez and Rodrik (2002). Other relevant studies include Dollar and Kraay (2003) and Frankel and Romer (1999).

true for Taiwan Province of China, Republic of Korea, Chile, and Uganda. Second, some of the countries where trade liberalization was unsuccessful implemented policies that counteracted the trade reform. For instance, in Israel, coalitions of labor, government, and industry set guidelines for prices, wages, and the exchange rate in ways that offset the benefits of trade reform. Third, macroeconomic stability, and particularly an appropriate exchange rate policy, greatly enhances the efficacy of trade liberalization.[3] Johnson, Ostry, and Subramanian (2007) have emphasized the importance of avoiding overvaluation in order to sustain growth.

Financial Globalization

There are a number of channels through which financial globalization—the phenomenon of rising cross-border financial flows—can generate growth benefits. For instance, theory predicts that international financial flows can complement domestic savings in capital-poor developing economies, and, by reducing the cost of capital, foster increased investment. Certain types of financial flows can also generate technology spillovers and serve as a conduit for transferring managerial and other forms of organizational expertise to developing economies.

However, the empirical literature about the existence of such benefits has been inconclusive (see Kose and others, 2006). On the surface, there appears to be a positive association between embracing financial globalization and attaining rapid economic growth (see figure). For example, the group of developing economies that have participated most actively in financial globalization has clearly achieved better growth outcomes on average than other developing economies. However, the majority of studies using cross-country growth regres-

[3]See, for instance, Harrison and Tang (2005), Wacziarg and Welch (2003) on Mexico's trade liberalizations between the 1970s and the early 1990s, Krueger (1998), and Edwards (1993) on Chile's trade liberalizations between 1950 and 1970.

Financial Openness and GDP Growth

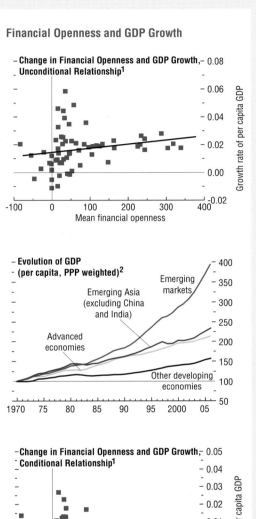

Source: IMF staff calculations.
[1]Change in financial openness is defined as the change over the same period in the ratio of gross stocks of foreign assets and liabilities to GDP. The conditional relationship uses residuals from a cross-section regression of growth on initial income, population growth, human capital, and the investment rate.
[2]PPP = purchasing power parity.

Box 5.1 *(concluded)*

sions to analyze the relationship between growth and financial openness have been unable to show that capital account liberalization produces measurable growth benefits after accounting for other determinants of growth (see figure).

Several factors explain the inconclusive nature of these empirical studies. One major reason is the difficulty of measuring financial openness.[4] Recent studies that are based on improved measures of financial integration are beginning to find evidence of positive growth effects of financial integration (see Quinn and Toyoda, 2006). An alternative line of inquiry is based on the notion that not all types of capital flows are created equal (see Dell'Ariccia and others, 2007). This notion is particularly relevant because the composition of financial flows has shifted markedly over time, from riskier debt flows to more stable flows of FDI and portfolio equity. Studies examining the growth effects of equity market liberalization generally suggest that it has a significant, positive impact on output growth (see Henry, 2007). An expanding body of evidence based on industry- and firm-level data supports the growth benefits of equity liberalization and FDI inflows.

Recent studies also argue that successful financial globalization does not simply enhance access to financing for domestic investment, but that its benefits are catalytic and indirect (see Kose and others, 2006; and Dell'Ariccia and others, 2007). Far more important than the direct

growth effects of access to more capital is how capital flows generate potential collateral benefits. For example, a growing number of studies are finding that financial openness can promote development of the domestic financial sector, impose discipline on macroeconomic policies, generate efficiency gains among domestic firms by exposing them to competition from foreign entrants, and unleash forces that result in better government and corporate governance. These collateral benefits could enhance efficiency and, by extension, total factor productivity growth.

There is also a growing number of studies on a range of supporting conditions associated with structural and policy-related factors (thresholds) that appear to play an important role in the relationship between growth and financial openness (see Kose and others, 2007). For instance, structural policies that promote financial sector development, improve institutional quality, and increase trade openness are important not only in their own right, but also because they help developing economies realize the potential benefits of globalization. Similarly, sound macroeconomic policies appear to be an important prerequisite for ensuring that financial integration is beneficial.[5]

[4]Kose and others (2006) argue that widely used de jure measures of capital controls (restrictions on capital account transactions) fail to capture how effectively countries enforce those controls and do not always reflect the actual (de facto) degree of an economy's financial integration.

[5]Ishii and others (2001) and Dell'Ariccia and others (2007) document a number of country cases showing that the implementation of prudent macroeconomic policies has been an important factor in improving the growth benefits of financial integration while minimizing the potential risks. For instance, Austria was successful in maintaining policies consistent with its exchange rate regime during the process of financial integration and thereby protected itself from a crisis. However, Mexico, Sweden, and Turkey, while opening up their capital accounts, employed expansionary policies incompatible with their exchange rate regimes and experienced financial crises.

proving more beneficial to developing economies than previous booms. Exports (including manufacturing exports), FDI, and domestic investment have all risen relatively rapidly, government borrowing has slowed, and output

growth has accelerated. A key factor behind this robust performance, and a crucial reason why a large majority of developing economies are enjoying rapid trade and financial integration into the global economy, is the general improvement in their institutional and policy environments, including greater fiscal restraint as well as trade liberalization (both domestically and in their trading partners). As a corollary, continued progress toward integration will require sustained efforts to further improve institutions and policy frameworks in order to help minimize the risks associated with abrupt future changes in commodity prices.

Commodity Prices and Patterns of Integration

The global level of commodity prices (relative to manufactures unit values) had been on the decline for a couple of decades, but has been rising since the turn of the 21st century (Figure 5.4).[4] The current boom in the prices of energy and industrial inputs, including agricultural raw materials and metals, is particularly notable. The prices of food and beverages have also increased, although somewhat less dramatically until recently. Overall, the current boom seems largely associated with increased demand for commodities on the part of China and other fast-growing economies in Asia, which is outpacing the increases in supply, including from Russia and other countries of the former Soviet bloc (see Appendix 1.2). Box 5.2 compares the current boom to previous episodes of rising commodity prices and shows that this boom has been notable for both its broad coverage and its duration. Nonetheless, risks remain that the current boom, like its predecessors, eventually will be reversed as supply responses gain momentum, particularly in the food and metals sectors, where long-term supply elasticities should be substantial, albeit less so in energy (see Chapter 4 of the September 2006 *World Economic Outlook*).

Movements in commodity prices affect countries differently depending on the composition

---

[4]The behavior of commodity prices has remained a subject of controversy in the literature, ever since Prebisch (1950) and Singer (1950) found a downward trend in the data. See, among others, Cashin and McDermott (2002).

Figure 5.4. Commodity Prices

Commodity prices, especially for energy and industrial inputs, have been rising sharply since the turn of the century. The Middle East and north Africa, and to a somewhat lesser extent sub-Saharan Africa and Latin America, have been the main beneficiaries of the current boom.

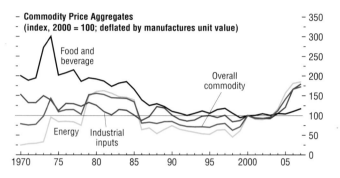

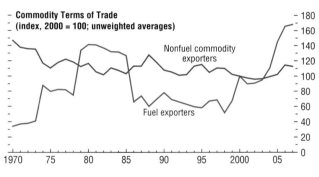

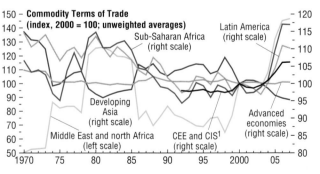

Sources: UNCTAD, Handbook of Statistics database; and IMF staff calculations.
[1]Central and eastern Europe, and Commonwealth of Independent States.

Box 5.2. The Current Commodity Price Boom in Perspective

Commodity markets have been booming, and the prices of many commodities have reached new record highs in recent months. Buoyant global growth has been only one of the reasons behind high commodity prices, but the expectation that global activity will slow noticeably in 2008–09 has nevertheless prompted concerns about the prospects for commodity markets. Against this backdrop, this box compares key features of the current boom with those of earlier booms.

At the general (global) market level, a commodity price boom is defined as a period of at least 12 months during which the spot price of a commodity or a group of similar commodities increases in real terms.[1] Accordingly, the booms

and slumps in commodity prices are identified here on the basis of peaks and troughs in inflation-adjusted commodity prices.[2] In contrast with the analysis in the rest of Chapter 5, in this box booms are considered to be commodity- rather than country-specific.[3]

On the basis of this definition, the table compares the current boom with earlier booms using the monthly price indices of four major

typically used in business-cycle analysis, these authors argue that for commodities, a longer minimum is needed because harvest seasons for major crops tend to be 12 months apart. A unit value index for the exports of manufactures by industrial economies is used to make the inflation adjustment.

[2]The analysis is based on a business-cycle-dating procedure developed by the National Bureau of Economic Research (NBER). See Chapter 3 in both the April 2002 and April 2003 *World Economic Outlook*.

[3]The rest of Chapter 5 identifies booms and busts using the annual commodity terms of trade of each country, rather than monthly global prices of individual commodities or commodity groups.

Note: The main author of this box is Thomas Helbling.
[1]This approach follows the example of Pagan and Sossounov (2003) for the case of equity price booms. The restriction of using a minimum phase duration of 12 months follows Cashin, McDermott, and Scott (2002). While a minimum restriction of 6 months is

Properties of Commodity Price Booms, 1960–2007[1]

	Current phase	Latest turning point[2]		Price Changes (percent)		Duration (months)		Synchronization with industrial production[5]
				From latest turning point	Average of past booms[3]	From latest turning point	Average of past booms[4]	
Crude oil (IMF APSP)[6]	Boom	December 2001	T	210.1	54.0	73	18	0.189***
Metals	Boom	March 2003	T	104.8	43.0	58	22	0.236***
Aluminum	Boom	April 2003	T	29	41.0	57	22	0.025
Copper	Boom	October 2001	T	212.5	61.0	75	21	0.259***
Nickel	Boom	October 2005	T	74.9	84.0	19	29	0.301***
Food	Boom	November 2004		30.4	21.0	38	18	0.103
Maize (corn)	Boom	November 2004	T	62.2	39.0	38	19	−0.139
Wheat	Boom	April 2005	T	124.1	38.0	32	20	−0.103
Soybeans	Boom	January 2005	T	83.9	42.0	36	18	0.11
Palm oil	Boom	January 2005	T	116.8	61.0	36	20	−0.015
Soybean oil	Boom	January 2005	T	100.9	50.0	36	18	0.066
Beef	Slump	September 2004	P	−25.1	35.0	. . .	20	0.091
Beverages	Slump	February 2006	P	0.0	47.0	. . .	19	0.109
Agricultural raw materials	Boom	December 2004	T	2.2	28.0	37	20	0.128
Rubber	Boom	January 2005	T	77.2	56.0	36	21	0.07

Sources: IMF commodity price database; and current IMF staff calculations.
[1]See text for details.
[2]T stands for trough, P for peak.
[3]Average price increase during past booms (excluding the current boom).
[4]Average duration of past booms (excluding the current boom).
[5]Coefficient of a regression of the cyclical state in the commodity price on the cyclical state in global industrial production (see Harding and Pagan, 2006, for details); *** denotes significance at the 1 percent level.
[6]IMF average petroleum spot price.

commodity groups and prices of a number of individual commodities, based on data for the period 1960–2007. As a caveat, the prices for some commodities began to fall in 2007, and therefore a slump—that is, a period of falling prices lasting at least 12 months—cannot yet be identified. The main results are as follows.

- The current commodity price boom has been broadly based and includes oil, metals, major food crops, and some beverages. Within these groups, price increases during the current boom have typically been well above average, and the period of sustained price increases has been longer than usual. In contrast, prices for some meats and many agricultural raw materials have remained relatively weak (with the notable exception of natural rubber, a substitute for petroleum-based synthetic rubber). This weakness is surprising, given that prices of these commodities have tended to boom in tandem with those of metals.

- The current boom also has been unusual in that oil prices and the price indices of three major commodity groups—metals, foods, and agricultural raw materials—have been jointly booming since early 2005 (beverages were booming in 2005 and early 2006). Although broad-based booms have occurred previously, they have typically been much shorter than the current one (see figure). Indeed, out of 74 months of broad-based boom periods since 1960, almost one-half have been recorded since 2005. Crude oil and metals prices have been booming for even longer—since 2003—which is also unusual.

- Previous broad-based booms have emerged toward the end of relatively long periods of expansion in global industrial activity—especially in 1973 and 2000—and have ended with a subsequent downturn in activity. In contrast, the current boom started earlier in the cycle. In all cases, however, broad-based booms have emerged during times of very strong global growth.

- More generally, although slumps in commodity prices have been more frequent than global industrial downturns, the prices of many com-

Number of Major Commodity Groups in Boom Phase and Global Industrial Production[1]

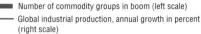

Number of commodity groups in boom (left scale)

Global industrial production, annual growth in percent (right scale)

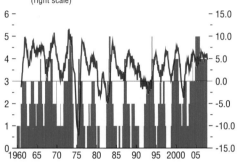

Sources: IMF, Commodity Price System; IMF, International Financial Statistics; and IMF staff calculations.
[1]Major commodity groups are defined as oil, metals, food, beverages, and agricultural raw materials.

modities tend to be in sync with global industrial activity, in particular crude oil, metals, and some agricultural raw materials.

In sum, the comparison of the current commodity price boom with earlier ones suggests that the current boom has been more broad-based and longer lasting and that prices have risen by more than usual. This suggests that the current boom reflects a confluence of mutually reinforcing demand and supply factors, as well as the effects both of increasingly important links among commodity markets (such as between the prices for oil and food and the production of biofuels) and of supportive financial conditions, including U.S. dollar depreciation and low real interest rates (see Appendix 1.2 for details). Some of these factors obviously played a role in earlier booms as well. In the 1973 boom, for example, commodity prices were pushed up by the combination of very strong global growth and U.S. dollar depreciation. However, the current boom is characterized by the extended period during which these factors have interacted. As a result, the prospects for global commodity markets depend importantly on how long these underlying, mutually reinforcing forces continue to prevail.

Figure 5.5. Values of Exports of Commodities and Manufactures[1]
(Percent of regional GDP)

The recent increase in the values of commodity exports relative to GDP largely reflects increases in the price of fuel. However, nonfuel commodity exporters in sub-Saharan Africa and Latin America have also benefited.

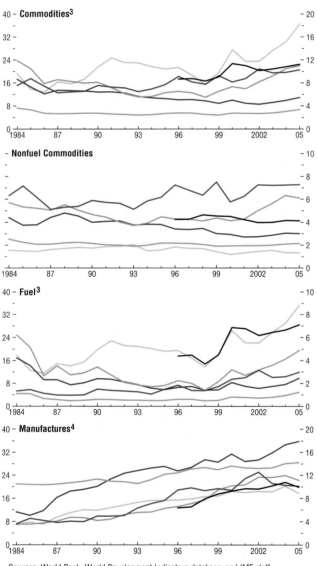

Sources: World Bank, World Development Indicators database; and IMF staff calculations.

[1]The data on exports of commodities and manufactures in this figure are not necessarily consistent with the data on total trade in goods and services in Figure 5.1, nor with the data on merchandise trade in Figure 5.2, because some countries do not provide a complete breakdown of trade data.

[2]Central and eastern Europe, and Commonwealth of Independent States.

[3]Left scale for Middle East and north Africa. Right scale for all others.

[4]Left scale for Asia, and CEE and CIS. Right scale for all others.

of their exports and imports. Because many developing economies export nonfuel primary commodities but import energy, booms in commodity prices do not translate directly into terms-of-trade booms for all commodity exporters. It is useful to consider the country-specific commodity terms of trade: the ratio of commodity export prices to commodity import prices, with each price weighted by the (time-averaged) share of the relevant commodity in the country's (average) total trade.[5] It is also useful at this stage to draw a distinction between countries exporting primarily fuel and those exporting other primary commodities.[6] Commodity terms of trade have moved in different ways in fuel exporters and nonfuel commodity exporters over the past decades (see Figure 5.4, middle panel). The current boom in energy prices gave a sizable boost to the commodity terms of trade of fuel exporters. Those of nonfuel commodity exporters have also risen, but more modestly.

At a regional level, the Middle East and north Africa and, to a somewhat lesser extent, sub-Saharan Africa and Latin America have been the main beneficiaries of the current commodity price boom (see Figure 5.4, lower panel).[7] Differences in trade composition are behind these regional patterns. Fuel exports play the most critical role in the Middle East and north Africa, where they now account for more than one-

[5]Deaton and Miller (1996) and Cashin, Céspedes, and Sahay (2004) construct country-specific commodity export prices in a similar way. The terms-of-trade measure used here takes into account both commodity export and import prices, and also adjusts for the importance of commodities in the overall trade of each country. A similar terms-of-trade measure is used in Lee and others (2008). See Appendix 5.1 for more details.

[6]Fuel exporters are defined as countries for which fuel constitutes more than 50 percent of total exports. Nonfuel primary commodity exporters are similarly defined as countries for which other primary commodities constitute more than 50 percent of total exports. Finally, commodity exporters are defined to include both fuel and nonfuel primary commodity exporters.

[7]It is important to note that terms-of-trade effects vary within regions. Because the current boom benefits fuel exporters more than nonfuel commodity exporters, not all countries in sub-Saharan Africa and Latin America have gained from it. See, for example, IMF (2007a).

third of regional GDP. Latin America depends on both fuel and nonfuel commodities to broadly similar degrees, whereas nonfuel commodities are especially important in sub-Saharan Africa (although fuels also account for a significant share of the regional economy). Globally, the recent increase in the value of commodity exports relative to GDP reflects trade in fuel more so than nonfuel commodities, although the value shares of nonfuel commodities also rose in sub-Saharan Africa and Latin America (Figure 5.5). The current commodity price boom has had a comparatively limited impact on the volume of commodity exports relative to GDP (Figure 5.6). The volume share of fuel has increased in central and eastern Europe and the Commonwealth of Independent States (CIS),[8] and in Latin America, but it has declined somewhat in the Middle East and north Africa.

Importantly, the recent growth in trade across emerging and developing economies has not been limited to commodities. Manufacturing exports relative to GDP have grown steadily in both value and volume terms (see Figures 5.5 and 5.6). Asia saw an especially dramatic rise in the share of manufacturing exports over the past couple of decades, but a significant upsurge occurred also in central and eastern Europe and the CIS, and other regions have experienced steady growth too. Even commodity exporters have significantly stepped up their manufacturing trade (Figure 5.7). Some of this may reflect commodity-related manufacturing, such as relatively low-value-added metal or mineral products.[9] Nonetheless, for commodity-dependent nations, a move from exports of unprocessed

[8]This finding reflects fuel-exporting countries in the CIS. The CIS includes large fuel and nonfuel commodity exporters, while countries of central and eastern Europe tend to be net importers of primary commodities.

[9]For instance, in sub-Saharan Africa nonmetallic mineral manufactures (mainly diamonds) account for a substantial share of manufacturing exports, although exports of transport equipment and clothing are currently growing fast (see IMF, 2007a). Clothing exports are also rising rapidly in Latin America and in the Middle East and north Africa, although natural-resource-related manufactures are an important export category in the latter.

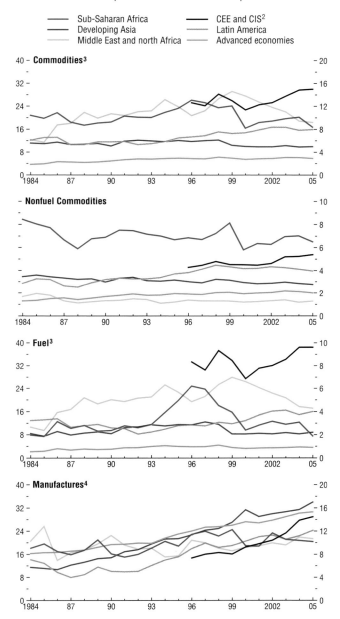

Figure 5.6. Volumes of Exports of Commodities and Manufactures[1]
(Percent of regional GDP in 2000 U.S. dollars)

Volumes of commodity exports relative to GDP have remained broadly stable, while those of manufacturing exports have risen steadily, especially in Asia, as well as in central and eastern Europe and the Commonwealth of Independent States.

— Sub-Saharan Africa
— Developing Asia
— Middle East and north Africa
— CEE and CIS[2]
— Latin America
— Advanced economies

Commodities[3]

Nonfuel Commodities

Fuel[3]

Manufactures[4]

Sources: World Bank, World Development Indicators database; and IMF staff calculations.
[1]Export volume indices are divided by real GDP indices; the values in 2000 are set equal to export shares of regional GDP in current U.S. dollars.
[2]Central and eastern Europe, and Commonwealth of Independent States.
[3]Left scale for Middle East and north Africa. Right scale for all others.
[4]Left scale for Asia, and CEE and CIS. Right scale for all others.

Figure 5.7. Patterns of Regional Trade[1]

The export destinations of developing economies have become more diversified over time. Although advanced economies remain the most important market, trade with other developing economies, especially China and other countries in Asia, has grown rapidly. Manufacturing trade has risen substantially more than commodity trade, with manufacturing exports to advanced economies tripling in real terms since the early 1990s. Commodity exporters have also stepped up their trade, not just in commodities but also in manufactures.

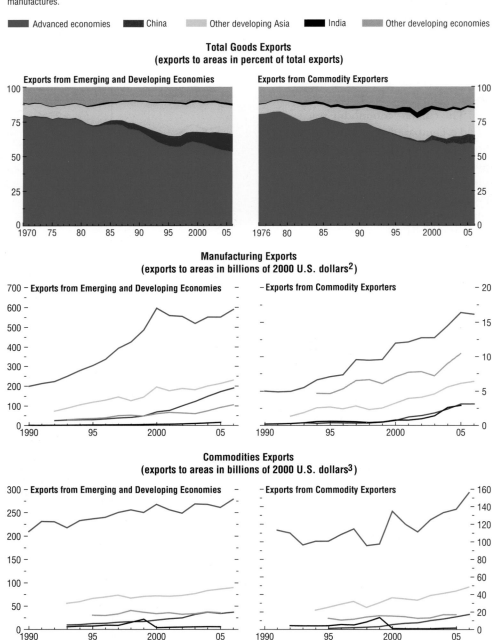

Sources: IMF, Commodity Price System; IMF, Direction of Trade Statistics; UNCOMTRADE; and IMF staff calculations.
[1] Sources of exports are defined as emerging and developing economies excluding China and India. Values are shown only if data are available for at least 80 percent of all countries.
[2] Nominal dollar values deflated by manufactures unit value.
[3] Nominal dollar values deflated by overall commodity price index.

raw materials to those of somewhat higher-value-added products is a natural and important first step toward broader-based industrialization, even though it does not eliminate these economies' vulnerability to commodity price shocks.

The export destinations of developing economies have become more diversified over time. Advanced economies remain the most important markets for developing economies, which continue to penetrate these markets with both commodities and manufactures. However, there has been rapid growth in trade with other developing economies, especially in Asia (see Figure 5.7; see also Akin and Kose, 2007).[10] Commodity exports to China and other Asian economies have risen substantially. Perhaps less well known, growth in China and elsewhere in Asia has also significantly expanded the developing economies' markets for manufactures. Indeed, while manufacturing exports to advanced economies have tripled in real terms since the early 1990s, those to China have grown even more dramatically, albeit from a very low initial level.[11]

Developing economies have attracted substantially more FDI in recent years in all economic sectors (Figure 5.8). While the largest increase has occurred in services, manufacturing and commodity sectors have also enjoyed a sizable inflow of FDI. The stock of FDI in developing economies' manufacturing has been consistently greater and has recently grown by a somewhat larger amount than the stock of FDI in commodities. Developing economies have also become a significantly more important source of FDI for advanced and other developing economies, especially in services. Although the role of these economies as providers of global investment is still relatively small, it is clearly on the rise.

[10]Intraregional trade in Asia has been an important component of the broad-based rise in trade among developing countries (see IMF, 2007b).

[11]The implications of China's and India's emergence for the integration of other developing economies into the global economy are the subject of a growing and, as yet, not fully conclusive literature. See, among others, Lederman, Olarreaga, and Soloaga (2007) and Cravino, Lederman, and Olarreaga (2007) for Latin America and Goldstein and others (2006) for Africa.

Figure 5.8. Foreign Direct Investment in Emerging and Developing Economies[1]
(Share of GDP in percent)

Emerging and developing economies have attracted greater amounts of foreign direct investment in all sectors. They have also become a much more important source of foreign direct investment.

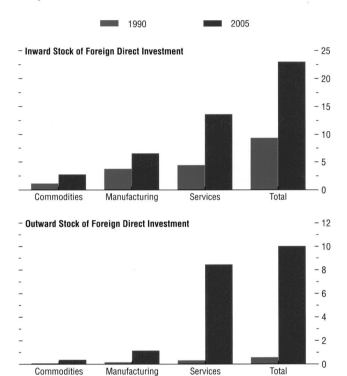

Sources: UNCTAD (2007); and IMF staff calculations.
[1]Sectoral aggregations are based on different classifications than those used elsewhere in the chapter; thus the sectors are not fully comparable with those elsewhere. Commodities include the primary sector; food, beverages, and tobacco; and coke, petroleum products, and nuclear fuel.

Figure 5.9. Policy and Institutional Environment
(Mean; all variables on right scale unless indicated otherwise)

Developing economies have pursued external liberalization by reducing trade tariffs and restrictions on current and capital account transactions. Macroeconomic policies have also improved, with fewer large government and current account deficits, stronger overall institutions, and deeper financial systems.

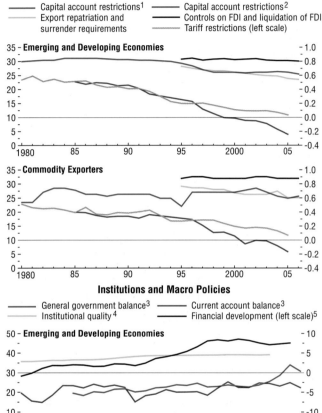

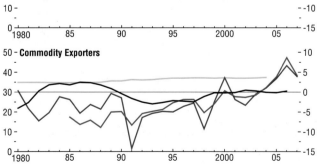

Sources: Beck, Demirgüç-Kunt, and Levine (2007); Chinn and Ito (2006); Grilli and Milesi-Ferretti (1995); Marshall, Jaggers, and Gurr (2004); World Bank, World Development Indicators database; and IMF staff calculations.
[1]Grilli and Milesi-Ferretti measure.
[2]Chinn and Ito measure; 1993–95 data interpolated owing to irregularities in the underlying data.
[3]Percent of GDP.
[4]Institutional quality is measured by the Marshall, Jaggers, and Gurr "executive constraints" variable (see Appendix 5.1 for details).
[5]Financial development is measured using the ratio of private sector credit by banks and other financial institutions to GDP (see Appendix 5.1 for details).

The rising integration of developing economies into the world economy has been accompanied by significant improvements in domestic policies and institutions (Figure 5.9). Emerging and developing economies—both those that export commodities and those that export other goods and services—have pursued external liberalization by reducing trade tariffs and restrictions on current and capital account transactions (although about 80 percent of all countries still maintain restrictions on FDI). Macroeconomic policies also have improved, with fewer large government and current account deficits, as has the overall quality of institutions and the depth of financial systems (see Appendix 5.1 for details). Compared with other countries, commodity exporters have achieved larger government and current account surpluses, but they have lagged in terms of broad institutional quality and financial development.[12]

In sum, commodity prices continue to play an important role in developing economies, with the current boom benefiting predominantly fuel exporters. However, the importance of manufacturing exports to developing economies has increased, with an especially dramatic rise in Asia and, on a somewhat smaller scale, in central and eastern Europe and the CIS. Both commodity and noncommodity exporters have stepped up their manufacturing exports both to advanced economies, which remain their most important export destinations, and to China and other Asian countries. Commodity exports to China and elsewhere in Asia have also risen sharply, although less so than manufacturing exports. Developing economies have attracted more FDI, including in their manufacturing sectors, and have become more important as a source for FDI. External liberalization has continued unabated across the developing world, and macroeconomic policies and institutions

[12]Clearly, improvements in government and current-account balances among commodity exporters may in part reflect the direct impact of commodity exports, as opposed to more structural changes. See below for a more direct comparison of the current commodity boom with previous booms.

have improved steadily, including in commodity exporters.

Globalization and Commodity Price Cycles

This section turns to the historical record on the consequences of commodity price cycles and, in particular, compares the current boom with previous booms. A modified measure of the commodity terms of trade is used to identify commodity price cycles, taking into account cross-country differences not just in the composition of commodity export and import baskets, but also in the importance of commodities to the over-all economy.[13] Booms and busts are defined as periods of relatively large increases and decreases, respectively, in the commodity terms of trade.[14] This exercise yielded over 300 booms and busts since 1970, with sub-Saharan Africa accounting for the largest number of booms, and the Middle East and north Africa accounting for the biggest booms (Figure 5.10). By historical standards, the current boom is long and large: for the average country, it has lasted over four years, with the commodity terms of trade rising by 9.1 percent, compared with two years and 3.3 percent, respectively, during past booms.[15]

[13]The weights on individual commodity prices in the commodity terms of trade are scaled by the (time-averaged) share of (average) total trade in a country's GDP. Appendix 5.1 provides more details.

[14]A boom (bust) is defined as any period starting with a commodity terms-of-trade trough (peak) and ending with a peak (trough), and such that the cumulative change in the commodity terms of trade during the period falls into the top quartile of all such episodes across the sample. Appendix 5.1 provides more details. See also Cashin, McDermott, and Scott (2002).

[15]Because the weights on individual commodity prices in the commodity terms of trade are scaled to reflect the importance of commodities to the overall economy, the increases in the modified index appear small. Without the adjustment for the share of total trade in GDP, the rise in the commodity terms of trade is 25.3 percent during the current boom and 9.2 percent during past booms for the average country. These numbers would be higher still if the commodity terms of trade were not adjusted for the importance of commodities in the overall trade of each country.

Figure 5.10. Commodity Price Booms

Most large commodity price booms occurred in the mid-1970s and in recent years. Sub-Saharan Africa was home to the largest number of booms, but the biggest booms were in the Middle East and north Africa.

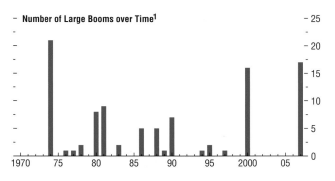

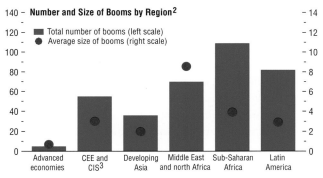

Sources: IMF, Commodity Price System database; UNCOMTRADE database; World Bank, World Development Indicators database; and IMF staff calculations.
[1]Large booms are defined as episodes with a cumulative increase in the commodity terms of trade in the top quartile of all booms. The dates shown correspond to the last year of each boom. See Appendix 5.1 for details.
[2]Size refers to the cumulative increase in the commodity terms of trade during a boom. See Appendix 5.1 for details.
[3]Central and eastern Europe, and Commonwealth of Independent States.

An event study was then conducted to examine how trade and capital flows, exchange rates, investment, government spending and borrowing, and other important variables responded to booms in commodity terms of trade and whether the current boom appears to be significantly different. Specifically, the event study compares (1) average annual percentage changes in the indicators of interest during past booms with changes during past busts and (2) changes during the current boom with changes during past booms. To account for the likely heterogeneity of responses across different events and different countries, the analysis focuses separately on large commodity price events and on fuel and nonfuel commodity exporters.[16] To keep the focus on developing economies, advanced economies are excluded from the study.

As expected, the total value of exports grew much faster during terms-of-trade booms than during busts (Figure 5.11). The difference in growth rates was especially marked (exceeding 40 percentage points a year) during large booms and among fuel exporters. As for the current boom, export value growth has been faster than during past booms for the full sample (by about 18 percentage points a year), although it has been somewhat slower than during past large booms. During the present boom, total export volumes, except for fuel exports, have responded much more strongly than in the past, when the impact on export volumes was substantially smaller in magnitude than the impact on export values.

The improvement in export performance during the current boom reflects differences in the growth of commodities versus manufactures exports. In the past, real commodity exports grew faster during booms than busts, but manufacturing exports changed little in the full sample. During past booms, manufacturing exports tended to rise faster for fuel exporters and more slowly for nonfuel commodity exporters. During the current boom, commodity exports have generally grown more slowly than during previous booms, but manufacturing exports have grown faster, producing higher real export growth overall.[17]

A look at relative changes in real effective exchange rates and tariff rates provides further insights into these trade patterns.[18] During past booms, nonfuel commodity exporters experienced relatively strong real exchange rate appreciations, with adverse effects for their manufacturing exports and import-competing sectors owing to Dutch disease (see Figure 5.11). Probably related to this, their tariff rates fell relatively less. Conversely, during busts, these countries had relatively weaker real exchange rates, which allowed them to undertake relatively larger tariff reductions. The picture is very different for fuel exporters. These countries experienced less nominal and real appreciation during commodity price booms than during busts. This largely reflected the widespread tendency of these countries to peg their exchange rates to the dollar,[19] which tends to depreciate when commodity prices rise.[20]

---

[16]Appendix 5.1 provides more details on the calculations behind this event study, as well as precise definitions of the relevant subsets of events and countries. Because the current boom is concentrated in fuel exporters, the comparison with past booms in nonfuel commodity exporters is based on few observations and should be treated with some caution.

[17]The shift in real export growth from commodities to manufactures has not been sufficiently strong in the case of fuel exporters (where the composition of exports is more heavily skewed toward commodities) to yield faster increases in total export volumes.

[18]The links between commodity prices and real exchange rates in commodity-dependent countries are explored in the "commodity currencies" literature (see Chen and Rogoff, 2003; and Cashin, Céspedes, and Sahay, 2004). This literature finds that commodity export prices tend to have a strong influence on real exchange rates for many commodity producers, although in countries with pegged nominal exchange rates the relationship is subject to structural shifts and may be weakened.

[19]In fuel exporters, half of all booms occurred in countries with dollar pegs. In contrast, none of the nonfuel commodity exporters that experienced booms had dollar pegs.

[20]The correlation between the nominal effective exchange rate of the United States and the overall index of commodity prices in real terms is negative and over 40 percent in absolute value.

Figure 5.11. Event Study of the Commodity Terms of Trade, 1970–2007[1,2]

(Median differences in average annual percent change in selected variables; advanced economies excluded)

During past booms (compared with busts) stronger export growth tended to reflect prices much more than volumes. Commodity exports rose, whereas manufacturing exports showed mixed patterns consistent with Dutch disease and protectionist pressures. In the current boom, export volumes have responded more and manufacturing exports have grown significantly faster, reflecting in part less real appreciation in fuel exporters and greater tariff reduction in nonfuel commodity exporters.

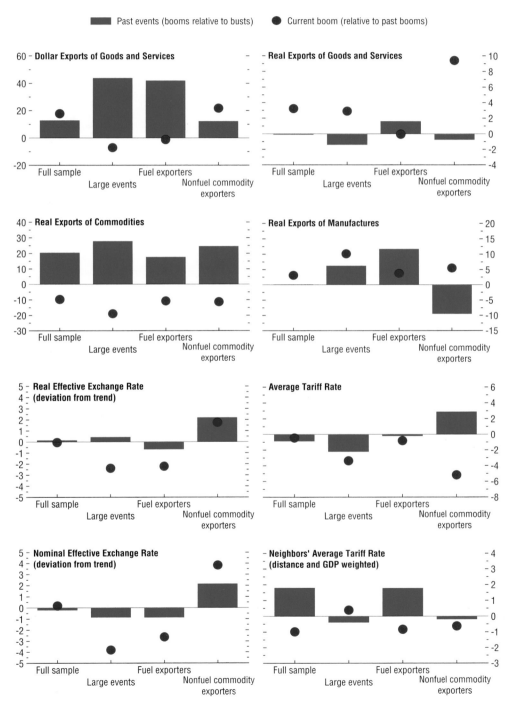

Figure 5.11 *(concluded)*

During past booms (compared with busts) foreign investment accelerated, reflecting primarily portfolio inflows, while domestic investment responded weakly. Governments tended to pursue procyclical fiscal policies and not to engage in consumption smoothing. In the current boom, FDI and domestic investment have grown substantially more. Government borrowing has slowed, and government consumption has moderated slightly relative to private consumption. Finally, real economic growth has accelerated.

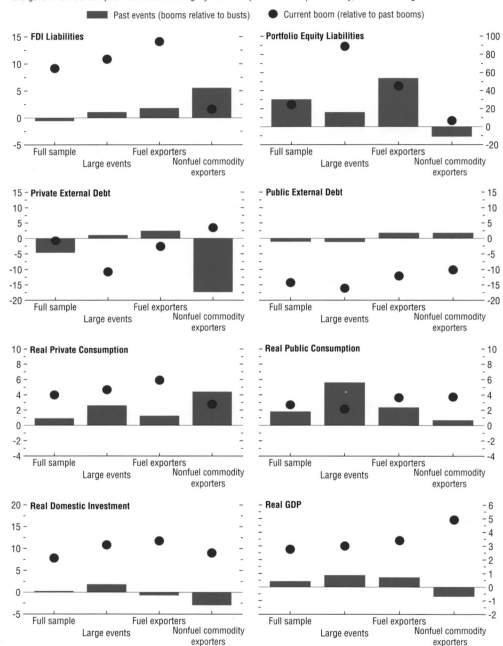

Sources: IMF, Commodity Price System; UNCOMTRADE; World Bank, World Development Indicators database; and IMF staff calculations.
[1] Some of the series are not available after 2005 or 2006; effective exchange rates are available starting in the late 1970s; tariff rates are available starting in 1980.
[2] Because the current boom is concentrated in fuel exporters, its comparison to past booms in nonfuel commodity exporters is based on few observations and should be treated with caution.

By way of comparison, during the current boom, real exchange rates have appreciated less for fuel exporters, but more for nonfuel exporters, in part reflecting the differential effects on these two groups of the recent dollar plunge.[21] This may provide one reason why manufacturing exports have increased substantially faster for fuel exporters. In nonfuel commodity exporters, the recent rise in manufacturing exports may reflect a greater commitment to trade liberalization. For example, in Chile, since the beginning of the current boom in 2002 and compared with the average of past booms, trade tariffs have decreased more than 6 percentage points a year faster, and manufacturing exports have grown more than 6 percentage points a year faster. In addition, tariff reductions in neighboring countries may have played a positive role, creating broader opportunities for intraregional trade.[22]

Turning to foreign capital inflows, portfolio equity liabilities responded markedly more than FDI during past commodity price booms, relative to busts.[23] However, during the current boom, inward FDI has increased much faster than during past booms. The rise in FDI is especially apparent among fuel exporters, for which it has grown by over 14 percentage points a year faster than in previous booms (for a median country).

Foreign borrowing exhibited mixed patterns. In nonfuel commodity exporters, private debt grew less during booms than during busts. In fuel exporters, both governmental and private entities tended to borrow more during booms. In the full sample, the dynamics of public debt were similar in booms and in busts, whereas private debt

tended to grow somewhat more during busts. These patterns suggest that fuel exporters have been more successful in attracting foreign capital during booms than nonfuel commodity exporters, which suffered more from protectionism and Dutch disease, as noted. Also, governments did not generally use borrowing to smooth consumption during busts, though private borrowing was used to some extent for this purpose. During the current boom, external debt has risen more slowly than during past booms, with government borrowing showing considerably slower growth than private borrowing. Such fiscal restraint during the current boom is likely to have reduced these economies' vulnerability to Dutch disease and contributed to stronger manufacturing and overall export growth.

Both private and public consumption increased more during past booms than during past busts, suggesting that fiscal policies were procyclical in many countries. However, during the present boom, public consumption has tended to grow somewhat more slowly than private consumption, when compared with past booms, although this tendency has been less pronounced among nonfuel commodity exporters than among fuel exporters. For example, in Chile both types of consumption have grown faster than in previous booms (with public consumption lagging only slightly behind private consumption), whereas in Saudi Arabia government consumption has grown by 3 percentage points a year more slowly, but private consumption has grown by more than 7 percentage points a year faster than in previous booms.

Both domestic investment and output growth increased during past large booms relative to busts, but the response was weak in the full sample. Slower investment and growth in nonfuel commodity exporters likely reflected their weaker export performance and contributed to their difficulty in attracting foreign capital (except FDI), as discussed. During the current boom, investment has risen at a dramatically faster rate (especially in fuel exporters), and GDP has grown significantly more than during past booms.

[21]While many fuel exporters have continued to peg their currencies to the dollar, nonfuel commodity exporters (such as Chile) suffered from currency depreciation in their trading partners, including the United States.

[22]It is important to note that buoyant global demand of the recent years has contributed to stronger growth in manufacturing exports during the current commodity price boom.

[23]While FDI flowed into a wide range of developing economies, portfolio investment was narrower in scope. Accordingly, the country coverage is more limited for portfolio equity.

In sum, during past commodity price booms (compared with busts) stronger export growth tended to reflect export prices much more than export volumes. Still, real commodity exports rose, whereas manufacturing exports showed mixed patterns consistent with Dutch disease and protectionist pressures. Foreign investment accelerated, reflecting primarily portfolio inflows, while domestic investment responded weakly. Governments tended to pursue procyclical fiscal policies and to forgo consumption smoothing. Along several dimensions, the current boom appears quite different. Export volumes have responded more strongly and manufacturing exports have grown at a significantly faster rate, reflecting in part less real exchange rate appreciation in fuel exporters and more tariff reduction in nonfuel commodity exporters. Increasing trade openness in neighboring countries, as well as improved fiscal management and better policies and institutions more generally, likely contributed to stronger performance. FDI and domestic investment have grown at substantially higher rates than during past booms. Foreign borrowing, especially by governments, has slowed, and government spending has moderated slightly. Finally, real economic growth has accelerated.

Explaining the Patterns

This section takes a longer-term view to analyze the determinants of the success by developing economies in integrating into the global economy. It focuses on the contribution of domestic institutions and policies, as compared with the terms of trade or geographic location. A key question is whether, over the long run, the dynamics of the terms of trade and commodity endowments account for a significant share of cross-country and cross-regional differences in globalization.

To a lesser extent, this analysis also assesses the importance of spillover effects from other countries' openness to trade and capital flows, as well as from their institutions and policies.

In other words, is a given country more likely to liberalize internally and/or externally when other nearby countries do? In this sense, does globalization help developing countries create a basis for sustainable growth?

In turn, the above analyses are used to examine whether developing economies' increasing integration into the global economy is likely to be sustained in the future, even in the face of adverse movements in the terms of trade. Put differently, because globalization has proven to be an important driver of growth in developing economies, it is important to know what factors can hold it back.

Specifically, the analysis considers a broad sample of about 80 countries, including both advanced and developing economies, over the period 1970–2005. It examines the determinants of several aspects of integration, including in particular total trade, exports, imports, and FDI. It analyzes trade both of merchandise as a whole and of commodities alone, in both value and volume terms. The econometric framework consists of both cross-sectional and (five-year-average) panel regressions.

Building on the existing literature, the analysis encompasses a broad range of variables that could explain integration, including institutions, policies, commodity prices, and geographic factors. Specifically, the variables include the following (see Appendix 5.1 for details).

- Quality of domestic institutions: As is well understood, this can have major effects on a country's productivity and output across all sectors (see, for instance, Chapter 3 of the April 2003 *World Economic Outlook*). The effects may be disproportionately large in tradable sectors; for instance, production for export may require large, visible, up-front investments, which may be particularly susceptible to expropriation. Likewise, financial investments by foreign residents may be particularly vulnerable to perceptions of a poor investment climate (see also Dell'Ariccia and others, 2007).

- Structural features: A better-developed financial infrastructure (measured using the ratio of private sector credit to GDP) may boost output across all sectors. Tradable sectors may derive particular benefits to the extent that they are either relatively capital intensive or else involve relatively large-scale plants and firms that find it harder to rely on informal credit markets. In addition, some specifications also consider the role of exchange-regime flexibility (based on Reinhart and Rogoff, 2004).

- Quality of domestic macroeconomic policies: This is assessed (as in Chapter 5 of the October 2007 *World Economic Outlook)* through an index measuring the success of the monetary framework in maintaining low inflation, as well as through a measure of the stability of fiscal policy (the volatility of cyclically adjusted government expenditures).

- Direct policy barriers to integration: The role of three separate policy variables is considered. These are (1) "trade openness," an index of (both tariff and nontariff) barriers to international trade; (2) "exchange restrictions," a measure of overall current- and capital-account exchange restrictions; and (3) exchange rate "overvaluation" (measured by the deviation of a country's real exchange rate from its trend value, calculated using the Hodrick-Prescott filter). This third variable aims to capture any Dutch disease effects on an economy's tradables sector.

- Commodity prices: The country-specific indices of commodity export and import prices are included separately, to test for differential effects. To control for cross-country differences in the importance of commodity trade, commodity prices are weighted by the average share of the relevant commodity in the country's GDP.

- Location and external spillover effects: Depending on the specification, these are captured through a mixture of the following variables: (1) "neighbors' trade openness," a distance- and size-weighted average of neighboring countries' policy barriers to trade; (2) an index of geographical remoteness; (3) a trade-weighted measure of external

Table 5.1. Cross-Sectional Regressions: Overall Trade

	Trade to GDP	Net Exports to GDP	Exports to GDP	Imports to GDP
Broad institutions	**6.9****	−0.56	**3.2***	**3.7****
Financial development[1]	**1.2*****	−0.4	**0.67*****	**0.54*****
Trade openness	10.1	2.92	6.5	3.6
Exchange restrictions	**−47****	−2.09	**−25****	**−23****
Overvaluation	4.3	−0.79	1.8	2.5
Neighbors' trade openness	**1.7***	**0.38****	**1.0****	0.66
R-squared	0.61	0.47	0.57	0.64

Note: Statistically significant coefficients are in boldface; *, **, and *** denote significance at, respectively, the 10, 5, and 1 percent level (based on robust standard errors). Other controls include monetary policy quality and fiscal policy volatility (always insignificant); exchange-rate-regime flexibility; initial GDP; landlocked status; land size; population; distance. Number of countries = 81.

[1]In order to allow for nonlinearities, regressions employ both the level and the square of financial development; the joint coefficient presented represents the marginal value, evaluated at the sample mean.

demand; and (4) a measure of world interest rates.

Overall, both the cross-sectional analysis (Tables 5.1 and 5.2) and the panel regressions (Tables 5.3 and 5.4) suggest the following broad findings (subject to the usual caveats about the direction of causality).

- Greater institutional quality is significantly associated with greater overall trade, in both value and volume terms. Institutional quality is also associated with greater FDI.

- Financial deepening is also significantly associated with increased trade and FDI. There is also evidence that the impact diminishes beyond a threshold level of financial development, which is greater however than the values observed in emerging and developing economies.

- The quality of domestic monetary and fiscal policy does not have a statistically significant impact on integration. Put differently, any impact on trade and FDI is no larger than the overall impact on GDP.

- As for direct policy barriers to integration, the impact of the different measures is often hard to disentangle, but there is some evidence that exchange restrictions in particular are significantly correlated with lower overall trade and FDI.

Table 5.2. Cross-Sectional Regressions: Commodity Trade, Foreign Direct Investment (FDI)

	Trade to GDP	Net Exports to GDP	Exports to GDP	Imports to GDP	FDI to GDP
Broad institutions	**3*****	−0.32	**1.8****	**1.5*****	0.16
Financial development[1]	**4****	−0.79	−0.1	**0.81****	**1.9***
Trade openness	7.3	−0.29	3.7	3.3	0.8
Exchange restrictions	−3.5	−0.33	−2.1	−2.2	**−2.5****
Overvaluation	−1.3	1.8	1.5	0.16	0.51
Neighbors' trade openness	244	49	156	93	41
R-squared	0.48	0.32	0.30	0.65	0.4

Note: Statistically significant coefficients are in boldface; *, **, and *** denote significance at, respectively, the 10, 5, and 1 percent level (based on robust standard errors). Other controls include monetary policy quality and fiscal policy volatility (always insignificant); exchange-rate-regime flexibility; initial GDP; landlocked status; land size; population; distance. Number of countries = 81.

[1]In order to allow for nonlinearities, regressions employ both the level and the square of financial development; the joint coefficient presented represents the marginal value, evaluated at the sample mean.

- Trade barriers in neighboring countries are associated with lower exports and trade, confirming the importance of external spillover effects. This effect is more statistically significant in the panel.
- Commodity prices do not exert a statistically significant impact either on overall trade volumes or on commodity trade volumes. Put differently, and in line with the earlier event analysis, the impact, if any, of commodity prices on trade volumes (as opposed to values) is not a dominant feature of the data. The limited impact on commodity trade volumes likely reflects both the inelastic demand for many commodities, especially in the short run, and the presence of significant constraints to expanding supply.

These results can be applied to explain the large increase in trade and FDI over time, both for the world as a whole and for advanced and developing economies separately.[24] In light of these results, as well as the previously illustrated improvements over time in domestic institutions and policies, it may not be surprising that most of the explained variation in trade and financial integration reflects the impact of institutions, financial development,

[24]Formally, for any given integration variable of interest, the economic significance of the results may be gauged by splitting the sample into two subperiods. Given the coefficient estimates based on the overall sample, it can then be calculated which regressors explain most of the variation in the dependent variable between the subperiods.

Table 5.3. Panel Regressions: Overall Trade

	Trade Volume to GDP	Net Export Volume to GDP	Export Volume to GDP	Import Volume to GDP
Broad institutions	**0.019****	−0.038	**0.028*****	**0.022***
Financial development[1]	**0.07***	0.01	**0.13****	**0.13***
Trade openness	**−0.03***	−1.7*	**−0.09***	0.002
Exchange restrictions	**−0.15*****	**−2.5*****	**−0.14*****	**−0.13****
Overvaluation	−0.0033	−0.27	**−0.025****	0.0032
Neighbors' trade openness	**0.20*****	**0.7*****	**0.33*****	**0.20***
Commodity export prices	5.4	−1.4	0.02	1.8
Commodity import prices	−2.0	1.8	6.1	12.0
R-squared	0.46	0.07	0.52	0.35

Note: Statistically significant coefficients are in boldface; *, **, and *** denote significance at, respectively, the 10, 5, and 1 percent level (based on robust standard errors). Other controls include monetary policy quality and fiscal policy volatility (always insignificant); exchange-rate-regime flexibility; initial GDP; country effects; time trend; trade-weighted world real GDP growth; London interbank offered rate. Number of countries = 79; number of observations = 342.

[1]In order to allow for nonlinearities, regressions employ both the level and the square of financial development; the joint coefficient presented represents the marginal value, evaluated at the sample mean.

Table 5.4. Panel Regressions: Commodity Trade, Foreign Direct Investment (FDI)

	Trade Volume to GDP	Net Export Volume to GDP	Export Volume to GDP	Import Volume to GDP	FDI to GDP
Broad institutions	0.0011	1.0	0.07	0.02	**0.6***
Financial development[1]	**0.8***	1.2	0.2	0.3	**0.2***
Trade openness	0.012	−1.5	**−0.18***	0.3	0.19
Exchange restrictions	**−0.18****	−9.9	**−0.18***	**−0.15****	**−1.5*****
Overvaluation	0.01	0.62	0.014	0.001	−0.03
Neighbors' trade openness	**0.23****	−4.3	0.55	0.17	**3.1*****
Commodity export prices	0.03	0.7	0.0	**2.1***	4.0
Commodity import prices	−0.0002	5.1	0.12	**−1.1***	0.3
R-squared	0.19	0.02	0.18	0.22	0.33

Note: Statistically significant coefficients are in boldface; *, **, and *** denote significance at, respectively, the 10, 5, and 1 percent level (based on robust standard errors). Other controls include monetary policy quality and fiscal policy volatility (always insignificant); exchange-rate-regime flexibility; initial GDP; country effects; time trend; trade-weighted world real GDP growth; London interbank offered rate. Number of countries = 79; number of observations = 363.

[1]In order to allow for nonlinearities, regressions employ both the level and the square of financial development; the joint coefficient presented represents the marginal value, evaluated at the sample mean.

policy distortions, and exogenous factors such as geography, rather than the direct impact of commodity prices. For instance, export volumes (relative to real GDP) grew in the sample by an average 30 percent between the 1980s and 2000s. Institutions and financial development accounted for almost one-quarter of this overall increase (Figure 5.12). Reduced policy distortions, including fewer exchange restrictions, lower tariffs, and diminished overvaluation, accounted for another quarter. In contrast, commodity export and import prices accounted for very little of the increase in export volumes, in either advanced or developing economies.

A broader issue concerns the relationship between the various explanatory variables. In particular, there may be important political-economy links between institutions and policy distortions, on the one hand, and commodity prices on the other. A full discussion lies beyond the scope of this chapter. Nevertheless, simple correlation analysis brings up one interesting finding: increases in commodity export prices have historically been associated with increased trade barriers (Table 5.5). One interpretation of this response, largely driven by nonfuel commodity exporters (as shown in the event analysis), is that it reflected policymakers' past concerns about the potential Dutch disease effects of positive terms-of-trade shocks on noncommodity tradable sectors.

Conclusions

The analysis in this chapter suggests that, along several dimensions, the current commodity price boom is proving more favorable to developing economies than previous booms. Exports are rising faster, reflecting substantially higher growth in manufacturing exports. Strikingly, even commodity exporters have increased their manufacturing exports, including to Asia. This observed acceleration has coincided with less real exchange rate appreciation in fuel exporters and more tariff reduction in nonfuel commodity exporters, which in previous booms tended to increase their trade barriers. FDI and domestic investment are increasing at a substantially faster rate than during past booms, and government borrowing has slowed at the same time that government spending has moderated somewhat. Against this background, real economic growth has accelerated across the developing world, and large majorities of countries in all regions are enjoying rapid trade and financial integration into the global economy.

That said, the analysis also suggests that commodity prices are a relatively minor contributor to the long-run trend toward globaliza-

Table 5.5. Panel Regressions: Institutions and Policies

	Broad Institutions	Trade Openness	Exchange Restrictions	Over-valuation
Commodity export prices	19	**−19****	1.2	9.3
Commodity import prices	1.6	**2.3*****	−0.84	−4.8
R-squared	0.05	. . .	0.11	0.05

Note: Results for "trade openness" are based on a probit regression. Statistically significant coefficients are in boldface; *, **, and *** denote significance at, respectively, the 10, 5, and 1 percent level (based on robust standard errors). Other controls include initial GDP; country effects; time trend; trade-weighted world real GDP growth; London interbank offered rate. Number of countries = 89; number of observations = 801.

Figure 5.12. Explaining the Increase in Integration from the 1980s to the 2000s

(Dependent variable and total difference in percentage points on the x-axis; share of total difference on the y-axis; based on panel regressions)

Most of the explained variation over time reflects the impact of institutions, financial development, policy distortions, and exogenous factors such as geography, rather than the direct impact of commodity prices. Institutions and financial development accounted for almost one-quarter of the overall increase.

Selected contributions:

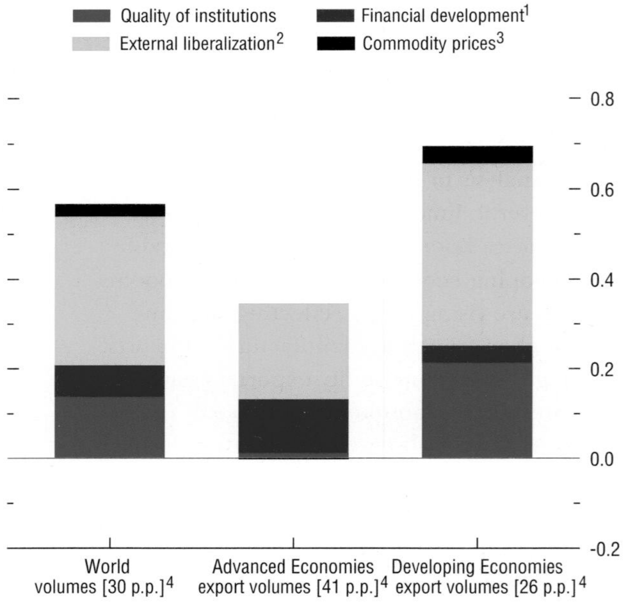

■ Quality of institutions   ■ Financial development[1]
▨ External liberalization[2]   ■ Commodity prices[3]

World volumes [30 p.p.][4]
Advanced Economies export volumes [41 p.p.][4]
Developing Economies export volumes [26 p.p.][4]

Sources: Beck, Demirgüç-Kunt, and Levine (2007); Heston, Summers, and Aten (2006); Marshall, Jaggers, and Gurr (2004); Reinhart and Rogoff (2004); Wacziarg and Welch (2003); World Bank, World Development Indicators database; and IMF staff calculations (see Appendix 5.1 for details).
[1]Combines contributions of financial development and its square.
[2]Combines contributions of trade openness, exchange restrictions, and overvaluation.
[3]Combines contributions of commodity export prices and import prices.
[4]Throughout, export volumes are deflated by a real GDP index; p.p. = percentage points.

tion. Linked to this, one key reason developing economies have performed relatively well during the current commodity price boom has been the general improvement in their institutional and policy environments, including greater financial development, trade liberalization, and fiscal restraint. Many developing economies also have benefited from liberalization and rapid growth in their neighbors, including through the effects on demand for their exports (of both commodities and manufactures). All this has two main implications.

• Even if commodity prices were to lose their buoyancy, such a development would be unlikely on its own to reverse many developing economies' growing integration into the global economy. This is significant, because the favorable changes in commodity exporters' terms of trade observed over the past few years should not necessarily be regarded as a permanent feature of the economic landscape.

• Continued progress toward trade and financial integration will require sustained ongoing efforts by policymakers to further improve institutions and policy frameworks. For instance, it will be important to extend progress toward trade liberalization and ensure that observed improvements in fiscal positions do not turn out to be purely cyclical.

More generally, it should be emphasized that the increased participation of low-income countries in the world economy has created new challenges for policymakers. Many economies remain heavily dependent on commodity exports and could prove significantly vulnerable to commodity price shocks. This provides an important motivation to increase diversification over time, and many developing economies are moving in this direction. Continued reforms that serve this end also will help cushion these economies against abrupt changes in the external environment, including in commodity prices.

Appendix 5.1. Data and Methodology

The main authors of this appendix are Patrick Hettinger, Nikola Spatafora, Ercument Tulun, and Irina Tytell.

Country Coverage and Country Groupings

Chapter 5 covers 171 advanced and developing economies (subject to data availability). Country coverage is held constant across time in each figure, although it may differ from figure to figure depending on data availability. The countries are grouped as follows (the number of countries is in parentheses).

Advanced Economies (23)

Australia, Austria, Belgium, Canada, Denmark, Finland, France, Germany, Greece, Iceland, Ireland, Italy, Japan, Luxembourg, Netherlands, New Zealand, Norway, Portugal, Spain, Sweden, Switzerland, United Kingdom, and United States.

Emerging and Developing Economies (148)

Sub-Saharan Africa (45)

Angola, Benin, Botswana, Burkina Faso, Burundi, Cameroon, Cape Verde, Central African Republic, Chad, Comoros, Democratic Republic of Congo, Republic of Congo, Côte d'Ivoire, Djibouti, Equatorial Guinea, Ethiopia, Gabon, The Gambia, Ghana, Guinea, Guinea-Bissau, Kenya, Lesotho, Madagascar, Malawi, Mali, Mauritania, Mauritius, Republic of Mozambique, Namibia, Niger, Nigeria, Rwanda, São Tomé and Príncipe, Senegal, Seychelles, Sierra Leone, South Africa, Sudan, Swaziland, Tanzania, Togo, Uganda, Zambia, and Zimbabwe.

Central and Eastern Europe and Commonwealth of Independent States (27)

Albania, Armenia, Azerbaijan, Belarus, Bulgaria, Croatia, Cyprus, Czech Republic, Estonia, Georgia, Hungary, Kazakhstan, Kyrgyz Republic, Latvia, Lithuania, former Yugoslav Republic of Macedonia, Moldova, Poland, Romania, Russia, Slovak Republic, Slovenia, Tajikistan, Turkey, Turkmenistan, Ukraine, and Uzbekistan.

Developing Asia (27)

Bangladesh, Bhutan, Cambodia, China, Fiji, Hong Kong SAR, India, Indonesia, Kiribati, Republic of Korea, Lao People's Democratic Republic, Malaysia, Maldives, Myanmar, Nepal, Pakistan, Papua New Guinea, Philippines, Samoa, Singapore, Solomon Islands, Sri Lanka, Taiwan Province of China, Thailand, Tonga, Vanuatu, and Vietnam.

Latin America (32)

Antigua and Barbuda, Argentina, The Bahamas, Barbados, Belize, Bolivia, Brazil, Chile, Colombia, Costa Rica, Dominica, Dominican Republic, Ecuador, El Salvador, Grenada, Guatemala, Guyana, Haiti, Honduras, Jamaica, Mexico, Nicaragua, Panama, Paraguay, Peru, St. Kitts and Nevis, St. Lucia, St. Vincent and the Grenadines, Suriname, Trinidad and Tobago, Uruguay, and República Bolivariana de Venezuela.

Middle East and North Africa (17)

Algeria, Bahrain, Egypt, Islamic Republic of Iran, Israel, Jordan, Kuwait, Lebanon, Libya, Morocco, Oman, Qatar, Saudi Arabia, Syrian Arab Republic, Tunisia, United Arab Emirates, and Republic of Yemen.

Fuel Exporters (24)[25]

Algeria, Angola, Azerbaijan, Bahrain, Republic of Congo, Ecuador, Equatorial Guinea, Gabon, Islamic Republic of Iran, Kazakhstan, Kuwait, Libya, Nigeria, Oman, Qatar, Russia,

---

[25]Countries are classified as fuel exporters if fuels constitute more than 50 percent of their exports.

Saudi Arabia, Sudan, Syrian Arab Republic, Trinidad and Tobago, Turkmenistan, United Arab Emirates, República Bolivariana de Venezuela, and Republic of Yemen.

Nonfuel Primary Commodity Exporters (21)[26]

Botswana, Burkina Faso, Burundi, Chad, Chile, Democratic Republic of Congo, Guinea, Guinea-Bissau, Guyana, Malawi, Mauritania, Mongolia, Republic of Mozambique, Papua New Guinea, Sierra Leone, Solomon Islands, Suriname, Tajikistan, Uzbekistan, Zambia, and Zimbabwe.

Data Sources and Definitions of Variables

Trade Flows

The overall trade data (and the GDP data used to obtain ratios) are from *World Development Indicators* (World Bank, 2007)[27] and the IMF's World Economic Outlook database. Data from these sources are combined and spliced to produce the best possible coverage across countries and over time. The data on manufacturing and commodity trade (including fuel and nonfuel) are from the World Bank's World Development Indicators database; missing values in these data are interpolated. Volumes of exports and imports of manufactures and commodities are created, respectively, by deflating the nominal values by the manufacturing unit value index and by the corresponding commodity price index (see below).

Foreign Capital

The data on the stocks of foreign direct investment (FDI), portfolio equity, and debt are from Lane and Milesi-Ferretti (2006).[28] These data are extended back in time for several coun-

tries. The GDP data are from the World Bank's World Development Indicators database and the IMF's World Economic Outlook database, as above. Public and private external debt used in the event study are from the World Bank's World Development Indicators database.

Manufacturing Unit Value

The United Nations' Manufacturing Unit Value index (MUV) measures the unit values of exports of manufacturing goods (Standard Industrial Trade Classification, SITC, 5–8) by 24 developed market economies. The data are from UNCTAD's Handbook of Statistics database[29] and the IMF's World Economic Outlook database.

Commodity Prices

Commodity price indices (overall, food and beverage, energy, and industrial inputs) are from the IMF's Commodity Price System database.[30] These price aggregates are available starting in 1980 and are extended back in time using available data on individual commodity prices and their weights in the aggregates. Country-specific export and import prices used in the regressions are 32 individual real commodity prices geometrically weighted by the respective shares of exports and imports of these commodities in GDP, averaged over 1980–2006 (see the description of the commodity terms of trade below).

Commodity Terms of Trade

The country-specific commodity terms of trade are defined as a ratio of commodity export prices to commodity import prices, as follows:

$$TOT_{jt} = \prod_i (P_{it}/MUV_t)^{X_{ij}} / \prod_i (P_{it}/MUV_t)^{M_{ij}},$$

where P_{it} are individual commodity prices, MUV_t is the manufacturing unit value index, X_{ij} is the share of exports of commodity i in country j's

---

[26]Countries are classified as nonfuel commodity exporters if nonfuel primary commodities constitute more than 50 percent of their exports.

[27]For more details on the *World Development Indicators* data, see http://go.worldbank.org/3JU2HA60D0.

[28]See www.imf.org/external/pubs/ft/wp/2006/wp0669.pdf for more information.

[29]See www.unctad.org/Templates/Page.asp?intItemID=1890&lang=1 for more information.

[30]See www.imf.org/external/np/res/commod/index.asp for more information.

(average) total trade, and M_{ij} is the share of imports of commodity i in country j's (average) total trade.[31]

This terms-of-trade index uses prices of 32 individual commodities from the IMF's Commodity Price System database: shrimp, beef, lamb, wheat, rice, corn (maize), bananas, sugar, coffee, cocoa, tea, soybean meal, fish meal, hides, soybeans, natural rubber, hardlog, cotton, wool, iron ore, copper, nickel, aluminum, lead, zinc, tin, soy oil, sunflower oil, palm oil, coconut oil, gold, and crude oil.

Exports and imports of the individual commodities are obtained from the United Nations' COMTRADE database. These exports and imports are divided by total (average) trade, and the resultant shares are averaged over 1980–2006. For use in the event study and the regressions, the weights are further scaled by the share of (average) total trade in each country's GDP (averaged over 1980–2006) from the World Bank's World Development Indicators databases and the IMF's World Economic Outlook database.

Bilateral Trade

Bilateral goods trade data are from the IMF's Direction of Trade Statistics database. The data by sector are from the UNCOMTRADE database and use SITC Revision 3. The manufacturing sector combines SITC 5–8, excluding group 68 (nonferrous metals). The commodities sector combines SITC 0–4, including 68. Missing values are interpolated. Volumes are obtained by deflating the nominal values by, respectively, the manufacturing unit value index and by the overall commodity price index, as above.

Trade Restrictions

Export repatriation, surrender requirements, controls on FDI, and liquidation of FDI are from the IMF's *Annual Report on Exchange Arrangements and Exchange Restrictions* (various years). Average tariff rate is the average of the effective rate (the ratio of tariff revenues to import values) and the average unweighted tariff rates from a database prepared by IMF staff. In some cases, this series is based on either the effective rate or the average unweighted rate, depending on data availability; missing values are interpolated. The regressions use the Wacziarg and Welch (2003) index of trade openness, based on average tariff rates, average nontariff barriers, the average parallel market premium for foreign exchange, the presence of export marketing boards, and the presence of a socialist economic system (the index is equal to zero prior to liberalization and to unity from the beginning of liberalization).[32]

Capital Account Restrictions

One measure is from Chinn and Ito (2006)[33] and is based on principal components extracted from several capital and current account restriction measures from the IMF's *Annual Report on Exchange Arrangements and Exchange Restrictions*. Another measure is an updated version of Grilli and Milesi-Ferretti (1995) and includes restrictions on capital account transactions from the IMF's *Annual Report on Exchange Arrangements and Exchange Restrictions*.

Effective Exchange Rates and Overvaluation

The real and nominal effective exchange rates are from the IMF's Information Notice System. The data are spliced with data from the World Bank's World Development Indicators database to produce the best possible coverage across countries and over time. In the event study, effective exchange rates are measured as percent deviations from trend, based on the Hodrick-Prescott filter. In the regressions, the overvaluation measure uses the log difference of the real effective exchange rate from trend, calculated using the Hodrick-Prescott filter.

---

[31]See also Lee and others (2008), which uses a similar measure.

[32]For more details on the openness variable, see http://papers.nber.org/papers/w10152.pdf.

[33]For more information about this measure, see www.ssc.wisc.edu/~mchinn/Readme_kaopen163.pdf.

Exchange Rate Flexibility

This is measured using the Reinhart-Rogoff coarse index of de facto exchange rate flexibility, collapsed to a three-value indicator (where 1 denotes a fixed or pegged exchange rate regime, 2 denotes an intermediate regime, and 3 denotes free float). The Reinhart-Rogoff classification takes into account the existence in some economies of dual rates or parallel markets, and uses the volatility of market-determined exchange rates to classify an exchange rate regime statistically.[34]

Macroeconomic Policies and Institutions

Institutional quality is measured using the "executive constraint" variable from Marshall, Jaggers, and Gurr's Polity IV data set (2004).[35] The variable follows a seven-category scale, with higher values denoting better checks and balances in place on the executive branch of the government. A score of 1 indicates that the executive branch has unlimited authority in decision making, and a score of 7 represents the highest possible degree of accountability to another group of at least equal power, such as a legislature. The general government balance and the current account balance are from the World Bank's World Development Indicators database and the IMF's World Economic Outlook database.

Key Macroeconomic Indicators

Real GDP, domestic investment, and public and private consumption are from the World Bank's World Development Indicators database and the IMF's World Economic Outlook database. Data from these sources are combined and spliced to produce the best possible coverage across countries and over time.

Financial Development

This is measured using the ratio of private sector credit by banks and other financial

institutions to GDP. The data are from Beck, Demirgüç-Kunt, and Levine's Financial Development and Structure database (2007).[36] In order to allow for nonlinearities, regressions employ both the level and the square of this variable.

Neighbors' Trade Openness and Average Tariff Rate

The regressions use neighbors' trade openness measured by the weighted average of the Wacziarg and Welch (2003) index of trade openness (see above) in other countries. The event study uses neighbors' average tariff rate measured by the weighted average of the average tariff rates (see above) in other countries. In both cases, the weights are related to other countries' GDP in 2000 U.S. dollars and to the inverse of their distance from the country in question. Distances are great circle distances, computed using the geographic coordinates provided in the Central Intelligence Agency (CIA) *World Factbook*.[37]

Economic Remoteness

This is measured by (log) distances from a given country to other countries, weighted by other countries' GDP in 2000 U.S. dollars relative to total GDP of all other countries in 2000 U.S. dollars. The distances are great circle distances computed using geographic coordinates provided in the CIA *World Factbook*.

Landlocked Status and Land Size

Landlocked status equals unity if a country has no coastline and zero otherwise. Land size is the area in square kilometers. These data are from the CIA *World Factbook*.

Event Study Methodology

The event study of commodity price booms and busts uses the commodity terms of trade

---

[34]For more details on the Reinhart-Rogoff index, see www.wam.umd.edu/~creinhar/Links.html.
[35]For more details on the Polity IV data set, see www.cidcm.umd.edu/polity.

[36]For more details on the Financial Development and Structure database, see http://go.worldbank.org/X23UD9QUX0.
[37]For more information, see https://www.cia.gov/library/publications/the-world-factbook/index.html.

described above. This measure is used to identify country-specific booms and busts during the period from 1970 to 2007. The dating procedure largely follows Cashin, McDermott, and Scott (2002) and is based on finding turning points (peaks and troughs) in the series.[38] These turning points are determined using annual country-specific data, which means that the cycles cannot be too short and that their timing may differ from country to country. Once the turning points are found, their duration and amplitude (the cumulative change in the commodity terms of trade) from trough to peak and from peak to trough are computed. Then booms and busts are identified as periods of increases or decreases, respectively, in the commodity terms of trade with amplitudes that fall into the top quartile of all such episodes across the sample. This procedure yields 327 booms and 321 busts.

The current episode is treated in a similar manner although, because it is still ongoing, 2007 is taken as the peak year for all the countries involved. Several peaks that occurred in 2006 are also considered part of the current boom. Its beginning is dated as the most recent country-specific trough that comes after the most recent peak. Then the associated country-specific amplitudes are computed, and the booms are selected as episodes with the cumulative increases in the commodity terms of trade above the top quartile threshold, as described above. The result is 30 booms, of which 19 are happening in fuel exporters and 6 in nonfuel commodity exporters.

These country-specific booms and busts are the basis of the event study, the results of which are shown in Figure 5.11. For each variable of interest, the average annual percent change (average annual change in the case of effective exchange rates measured as percentage deviations from trend) is computed during each boom and each bust, subject to data availability. Then the medians of all such changes are obtained separately for past booms, past busts,

and the current boom. Finally, the differences between the medians of past booms and busts and of the current and past booms are found and reported.

The event study focuses on three separate subsamples, in addition to the full sample of booms and busts: large booms, fuel exporters, and nonfuel commodity exporters. Large booms (busts) are defined as booms (busts) with amplitudes that fall into the top quartile of all booms (busts). By this definition, 17 of the current booms qualify as large. The definitions of fuel exporters and nonfuel commodity exporters are given above.

Econometric Analysis

The econometric analysis (see Tables 5.1–5.5) considers the following dependent variables.

- Trade to GDP, Net Exports to GDP, Exports to GDP, and Imports to GDP, in value terms (Table 5.1)
- Commodity Trade to GDP, Commodity Net Exports to GDP, Commodity Exports to GDP, and Commodity Imports to GDP, in value terms (Table 5.2)
- Trade to GDP, Net Exports to GDP, Exports to GDP, and Imports to GDP, in volume terms (Table 5.3)
- Commodity Trade to GDP, Commodity Net Exports to GDP, Commodity Exports to GDP, and Commodity Imports to GDP, in volume terms (Table 5.4)
- Broad Institutions, measured using the "executive constraint" variable described above (Table 5.5)
- Trade Openness, measured using the Welch and Wacziarg (2003) index of trade openness (Table 5.5)
- Exchange Restrictions, measured using the mean of the restrictions on current and on capital account transactions, from the IMF's *Annual Report on Exchange Arrangements and Exchange Restrictions* (Table 5.5)
- Exchange Rate Overvaluation (Table 5.5)

Explanatory variables employed in the analysis are as discussed above.

---

[38]See also Pagan and Sossounov (2003), who use a similar approach to date equity price booms and busts.

All cross-sectional regressions are estimated using average values over the period 1970–2005. Panel regressions are estimated using all available five-year-average observations, starting in 1970, and use country-fixed effects.

Figure 5.12 is constructed as follows. First, each regression is estimated using the whole sample. Then, the sample is split into the 1980s and the 2000s, and mean values of the dependent and explanatory variables are calculated for each subsample. For each explanatory variable, the difference in its mean value across subsamples is multiplied by the relevant coefficient (estimated using the whole sample). This yields the contribution of the relevant explanatory variable to the (mean) difference of the dependent variable between decades.

References

Akin, Çigdem, and M. Ayhan Kose, 2007, "Changing Nature of North-South Linkages: Stylized Facts and Explanations," IMF Working Paper 07/280 (Washington: International Monetary Fund).

Anderson, Kym, Will Martin, and Dominique van der Mensbrugghe, 2006, "Market and Welfare Implications of Doha Reform Scenarios," in *Agricultural Trade Reform and the Doha Development Agenda*, ed. by Kym Anderson and Will Martin (New York: Palgrave Macmillan).

Baier, Scott L., and Jeffrey H. Bergstrand, 2007, "Do Free Trade Agreements Actually Increase Members' International Trade?" *Journal of International Economics*, Vol. 71 (March), pp. 72–95.

Baldwin, Robert E., 2003, "Openness and Growth: What's the Empirical Relationship?" NBER Working Paper No. 9578 (Cambridge, Massachusetts: National Bureau of Economic Research).

Beck, Thorsten, Asli Demirgüç-Kunt, and Ross Levine, 2000 (revised: October 17, 2007), "A New Database on Financial Development and Structure," *World Bank Economic Review*, Vol. 14 (September), pp. 597–605. Available via the Internet: www.econ.worldbank.org/staff/tbeck.

Berg, Andrew, and Anne Krueger, 2003, "Trade, Growth, and Poverty: A Selective Survey," IMF Working Paper 03/30 (Washington: International Monetary Fund).

Blattman, Christopher, Jason Hwang, and Jeffrey G. Williamson, 2007, "Winners and Losers in the Commodity Lottery: The Impact of Terms of Trade Growth and Volatility in the Periphery 1870–1939," *Journal of Development Economics*, Vol. 82 (January), pp. 156–79.

Broda, Christian, and David Weinstein, 2004, "Globalization and the Gains from Variety," NBER Working Paper No. 10314 (Cambridge, Massachusetts: National Bureau of Economic Research).

Cashin, Paul, and C. John McDermott, 2002, "The Long-Run Behavior of Commodity Prices: Small Trends and Big Variability," *IMF Staff Papers*, Vol. 49 (July), pp. 175–99.

———, and Alasdair Scott, 2002, "Booms and Slumps in World Commodity Prices," *Journal of Development Economics*, Vol. 69 (October 1), pp. 277–96.

Cashin, Paul, Luis F. Céspedes, and Ratna Sahay, 2004, "Commodity Currencies and the Real Exchange Rate," *Journal of Development Economics*, Vol. 75 (October), pp. 239–68.

Chen, Yu-chin, and Kenneth Rogoff, 2003, "Commodity Currencies," *Journal of International Economics*, Vol. 60 (May), pp. 133–60.

Chinn, Menzie, and Hiro Ito, 2006, "What Matters for Financial Development? Capital Controls, Institutions, and Interactions," *Journal of Development Economics*, Vol. 81 (October), pp. 163–92. Available via the Internet: www.web.pdx.edu/~ito.

Collier, Paul, and Benedikt Goderis, 2007, "Commodity Prices, Growth, and the Natural Resource Curse: Reconciling a Conundrum," CSAE Working Paper No. 2007-15 (Oxford: University of Oxford, Center for the Study of African Economies). Available via the Internet: www.csae.ox.ac.uk/workingpapers/pdfs/2007-15text.pdf.

Corden, W. Max, 1984, "Booming Sector and Dutch Disease Economics: Survey and Consolidation," *Oxford Economic Papers*, Vol. 36 (November), pp. 359–80.

———, and J. Peter Neary, 1982, "Booming Sector and De-Industrialisation in a Small Open Economy," *Economic Journal*, Vol. 92 (December), pp. 825–48.

Cravino, Javier, Daniel Lederman, and Marcelo Olarreaga, 2007, "Substitution Between Foreign Capital in China, India, the Rest of the World, and Latin America: Much Ado about Nothing?" Policy Research Working Paper No. 4361 (Washington: World Bank).

Deaton, Angus, 1999, "Commodity Prices and Growth in Africa," *Journal of Economic Perspectives*, Vol. 13 (Summer), pp. 23–40.

———, and Ronald Miller, 1996, "International Commodity Prices, Macroeconomic Performance, and Politics in Sub-Saharan Africa," *Journal of African Economies*, Vol. 5 (October), pp. 99–191.

Dell'Ariccia, Giovanni, Julian di Giovanni, André Faria, M. Ayhan Kose, Paolo Mauro, Jonathan Ostry, Martin Schindler, and Marco Terrones, 2007, "Reaping the Benefits of Financial Globalization" (Washington: International Monetary Fund). Available via the Internet: www.imf.org/external/np/res/docs/2007/0607.htm.

Dollar, David, and Aart Kraay, 2003, "Institutions, Trade, and Growth," *Journal of Monetary Economics*, Vol. 50 (January), pp. 133–62.

———, 2004, "Trade, Growth, and Poverty," *Economic Journal*, Vol. 114 (February), pp. F22–F49.

Edwards, Sebastian, 1993, "Openness, Trade Liberalization, and Growth in Developing Countries," *Journal of Economic Literature*, Vol. 31 (September), pp. 1358–93.

———, and Jonathan Ostry, 1990, "Anticipated Protectionist Policies, Real Exchange Rates, and the Current Account: The Case of Rigid Wages," *Journal of International Money and Finance*, Vol. 9 (June), pp. 206–19.

Frankel, Jeffrey A., and David Romer, 1999, "Does Trade Cause Growth?" *American Economic Review*, Vol. 89 (June), pp. 379–99.

Goldstein, Andrea, Nicolas Pinaud, Helmut Reisen, and Xiaobao Chen, 2006, "The Rise of China and India: What's in It for Africa?" OECD Development Center Study (Paris: Organization for Economic Cooperation and Development).

Grilli, Vittorio, and Gian Maria Milesi-Ferretti, 1995, "Economic Effects and Structural Determinants of Capital Controls," *Staff Papers*, International Monetary Fund, Vol. 42 (September), pp. 517–51.

Hallaert, Jean-Jacques, 2006, "A History of Empirical Literature on the Relationship Between Trade and Growth," *Mondes en Développement*, Vol. 34 (March), pp. 63–77.

Harding, Don, and Adrian Pagan, 2006, "Synchronization of Cycles," *Journal of Econometrics*, Vol. 132, No. 1, pp. 59–79.

Harrison, Ann, and Helena Tang, 2005, "Trade Liberalization: Why So Much Controversy?" in *Economic Growth in the 1990s: Learning from a Decade of Reform*, ed. by N. Roberto Zagha (Washington: World Bank), pp. 131–56.

Henry, Peter B., 2007, "Capital Account Liberalization: Theory, Evidence, and Speculation," *Journal of Economic Literature*, Vol. 45 (December), pp. 887–935.

Heston, Alan, Robert Summers, and Bettina Aten, 2006, "Penn World Table Version 6.2," Center for International Comparisons of Production, Income and Prices at the University of Pennsylvania (Philadelphia: University of Pennsylvania, September). Available via the Internet: pwt.econ.upenn.edu/php_site/pwt_index.php.

International Monetary Fund (IMF), 2007a, *Regional Economic Outlook: Sub-Saharan Africa*, April (Washington).

———, 2007b, *Regional Economic Outlook: Asia and Pacific*, October (Washington).

Ishii, Shogo, Karl Habermeier, and others, 2002, "Capital Account Liberalization and Financial Sector Stability," IMF Occasional Paper No. 211 (Washington: International Monetary Fund).

Johnson, Simon, Jonathan D. Ostry, and Arvind Subramanian, 2007, "The Prospects for Sustained Growth in Africa: Benchmarking the Constraints," NBER Working Paper No. 13120 (Cambridge, Massachusetts: National Bureau of Economic Research).

Kose, M. Ayhan, Eswar S. Prasad, Kenneth Rogoff, and Shang-Jin Wei, 2006, "Financial Globalization: A Reappraisal," IMF Working Paper 06/189 (Washington: International Monetary Fund).

———, 2008, "Financial Globalization and Economic Policies," forthcoming IMF Working Paper (Washington: International Monetary Fund).

Krueger, Anne, 1998, "Why Trade Liberalisation Is Good for Growth," *Economic Journal*, Vol. 108 (September), pp. 1513–22.

Lane, Philip R., and Gian Maria Milesi-Ferretti, 2006, "The External Wealth of Nations Mark II: Revised and Extended Estimates of Foreign Assets and Liabilities, 1970–2004," IMF Working Paper 06/69 (Washington: International Monetary Fund).

Lederman, Daniel, Marcelo Olarreaga, and Isidro Soloaga, 2007, "The Growth of China and India in World Trade: Opportunity or Threat for Latin America and the Caribbean?" Policy Research Working Paper No. 4320 (Washington: World Bank).

Lee, Jaewoo, Gian Maria Milesi-Ferretti, Jonathan Ostry, Alessandro Prati, and Luca Antonio Ricci, 2008, *Exchange Rate Assessments: CGER Methodologies,*

IMF Occasional Paper No. 261 (Washington: International Monetary Fund).

Marshall, Monty, Keith Jaggers, and Ted Gurr, 2004, "Polity IV Project: Political Regime Characteristics and Transitions, 1800–2004" (College Park, Maryland: University of Maryland, Center for International Development and Conflict Management). Available via the Internet: www.cidcm.umd.edu/polity.

Ostry, Jonathan, 1988, "Balance of Trade, Terms of Trade, and Real Exchange Rate: An Intertemporal Optimizing Framework," *Staff Papers*, International Monetary Fund, Vol. 35, pp. 541–73.

———, and Andrew Rose, 1992, "An Empirical Evaluation of the Macroeconomic Effects of Tariffs," *Journal of International Money and Finance*, Vol. 11 (February), pp. 63–79.

Pagan, Adrian R., and Kirill A. Sossounov, 2003, "A Simple Framework for Analysing Bull and Bear Markets," *Journal of Applied Econometrics*, Vol. 18 (January/February), pp. 23–46.

Prebisch, Raul, 1950, "The Economic Development of Latin America and Its Principal Problems" (New York: United Nations).

Quinn, Dennis, and A. Maria Toyoda, 2006, "Does Capital Account Liberalization Lead to Growth?" (unpublished; Washington: Georgetown University). Available via the Internet: faculty.msb.edu/quinnd/papers/capital_liberalization_growth_Dec2006.pdf.

Reinhart, Carmen, and Kenneth Rogoff, 2004, "The Modern History of Exchange Rate Arrangements: A Reinterpretation," *Quarterly Journal of Economics*, Vol. 119 (February), pp. 1–48.

Rodriguez, Francisco, and Dani Rodrik, 2002, "Trade Policy and Economic Growth: A Skeptic's Guide to the Cross-National Evidence," in *NBER Macroeconomics Annual 2000*, ed. by Ben S. Bernanke and Kenneth Rogoff (Cambridge, Massachusetts: MIT Press).

Singer, Hans W., 1950, "The Distribution of Gains between Investing and Borrowing Countries," *American Economic Review, Papers and Proceedings*, Vol. 40 (May), pp. 473–85.

United Nations Conference on Trade and Development (UNCTAD), 2007, *World Investment Report 2007: Transnational Corporations, Extractive Industries and Development* (New York).

van der Ploeg, Frederick, 2006, "Challenges and Opportunities for Resource Rich Economies," CEPR Discussion Paper No. 5688 (London: Centre for Economic Policy Research).

Wacziarg, Romain, and Karen Horn Welch, 2003, "Trade Liberalization and Growth: New Evidence," NBER Working Paper No. 10152 (Cambridge, Massachusetts: National Bureau of Economic Research).

Winters, L. Alan, 2004, "Trade Liberalisation and Economic Performance: An Overview," *Economic Journal*, Vol. 114 (February), pp. F4–F21.

IMF EXECUTIVE BOARD DISCUSSION OF THE OUTLOOK, MARCH 2008

The following remarks by the Acting Chair were made at the conclusion of the Executive Board's discussion of the World Economic Outlook *on March 21, 2008.*

Global Prospects and Policies

Executive Directors discussed global economic developments and prospects against the background of exceptional uncertainties about the likely duration and cost of the financial crisis, which has now spread far beyond the U.S. subprime mortgage market. In recent months, growth has slowed in the advanced economies in the face of tightening financial conditions, while remaining strong thus far in the rapidly globalizing emerging economies. Directors agreed that global growth prospects for 2008 have deteriorated markedly since the January 2008 *World Economic Outlook Update,* although a number of Directors felt that the staff's new baseline forecast has been marked down too sharply, particularly given the flexibility and resilience of the U.S. economy and the still-robust official data from several western European economies. Clear communication as these forecasts evolve remains essential, particularly at this juncture.

Directors emphasized that the greatest risk to the outlook comes from the still-unfolding events in financial markets, and particularly the concern that the deep losses related to the U.S. subprime mortgage sector and other structured credits can seriously impair financial capital and transform a credit squeeze into a full-blown credit crunch. In the view of most Directors, the interaction between negative financial shocks and slowing domestic demand remains a serious downside risk in the United States, and to a lesser degree in western Europe and elsewhere. At the same time, many Directors still saw positive momentum driven by the potential strength of domestic demand in fast-growing emerging economies, while recognizing their exposure to negative external risks through both the trade and the financial channels. Directors also cautioned that the risks related to inflationary pressures and the oil market have risen, notwithstanding the economic slowdown, as commodity prices have soared in the context of continued tight supply-demand conditions as well as increased investor interest in commodities as an asset class and other financial factors. A number of Directors also saw a continued risk of a disorderly unwinding of global imbalances despite the recent depreciation of the U.S. dollar against other flexible currencies and the narrowing of the U.S. current account deficit.

Against this backdrop, Directors underscored that policymakers around the world face a fast-moving set of challenges. In the advanced economies, the key priorities are to deal effectively with the financial crisis and counter downside risks to growth, while taking due account of the recent elevated inflation readings and the need to preserve longer-term fiscal sustainability. In many emerging and developing economies, the challenge is to control inflationary pressures while ensuring that strong domestic demand does not lead to a buildup in vulnerabilities. At the same time, Directors noted that a number of these countries are already facing fallout from the advanced economy slowdown, and an intensified or prolonged global slowdown will require judicious responses from policymakers in the affected economies. Directors considered that it will be important to ensure consistency of policy approaches across countries in these difficult global conditions.

Advanced Economies

Directors agreed that the U.S. economy has been slowed by the impact of tightening credit, a deterioration in labor market conditions, and a continuing deep correction in the housing market. Some Directors observed that lending could be constrained by losses experienced by core U.S. financial institutions. Directors considered that economic activity is likely to remain weak through 2009, and will recover gradually thereafter. Consumption will be held back by wealth effects and weakening employment, while residential investment will continue to drop. Most Directors noted that the recently approved fiscal stimulus package will help contain the downturn during the course of the year. Most Directors welcomed the aggressive actions by the Federal Reserve to ease interest rates and inject liquidity into the financial system. They considered that further easing of interest rates may be necessary, depending on the incoming evidence on the extent of the downturn and the deterioration in credit conditions. At the same time, a number of Directors underscored that monetary policy decisions will need to pay careful attention to inflation risks, given the somewhat elevated core inflation and prospects for continued high and volatile energy and food prices—although it was recognized that such trends could well be alleviated by the projected widening of output gaps and the softening labor market. While noting the staff's assessment that the dollar is still on the strong side, a few Directors considered that recent market moves are likely to have significantly reduced the degree of overvaluation.

Directors recognized that activity in western Europe had also slowed starting in late 2007, reflecting high oil prices, tighter financial conditions, and weaker export growth. They observed that lending activity may be constrained due to the losses experienced by some major European banks from their exposure to structured credits. Directors also noted that growth will likely continue to decelerate in the period ahead. Noting the relatively heavy reliance of corporations in Europe on banks for financing, Directors considered that a key downside risk to the regional outlook is the possible effects on the financial sector in Europe of the spreading credit crisis, although some Directors observed that employment has continued to rise, and money and credit growth rates have remained strong despite a tightening of lending standards. Against this background, and with recent structural reforms bearing fruit, several Directors saw the region as generally well equipped to cope with the fallout from further financial market turbulence. With continuing inflation risks, and the considerable uncertainty in financial markets, the European Central Bank (ECB) continues to attach priority to ensuring that inflation expectations remain firmly anchored. Noting that the ECB is appropriately keeping interest rates on hold for now, most Directors considered that the ECB should stand ready to ease policy if inflation concerns moderate and downside risks to growth intensify. Directors generally agreed that, in the euro area, automatic stabilizers should be allowed to play in full, while bearing in mind the need for steady advancement toward these countries' medium-term fiscal objectives. Countries where medium-term objectives are well in hand could also have scope for some additional discretionary stimulus. However, in other euro area countries, most Directors noted, the scope to allow even automatic stabilizers to operate in full may be limited by high levels of public debt and adjustment plans that are insufficient for medium-term sustainability.

Directors welcomed the strength of activity in Japan through the end of 2007. While noting the limited direct impact of the credit market turbulence on the Japanese financial system, Directors were of the view that weakening business sentiment, sluggish personal income growth, high oil prices, and lower global growth will weigh on activity in 2008 and 2009. Most Directors saw merit in keeping interest rates on hold for now, but saw some scope, albeit limited, to reduce interest rates from already low levels if there is a substantial deterioration in growth prospects. Directors noted that net public debt levels remain high despite consolidation efforts, with little scope for additional discretionary fiscal action. Although automatic stabilizers could be allowed to operate in the event of a sharp downturn, their impact on domestic demand will likely be limited.

Directors welcomed the liquidity injections by major central banks and recognized that monetary policy actions have provided an important first line of defense in the current troubled financial environment. They noted the particular challenges to monetary policy implementation at the present juncture. One such challenge is the delicate balance between alleviating downside risks to growth and guarding against a buildup in inflation. With rising threats to price stability, several Directors stressed that central banks should not risk their hard-earned inflation-fighting credibility. Another aspect of monetary policy implementation is that the ongoing financial dislocations may have weakened the normal monetary policy transmission mechanism in some countries, thus raising questions about the impact of monetary easing on the economy. Directors acknowledged, however, that liquidity injections do not solve the underlying financial market problems—involving repricing of risky assets, lack of confidence and counterparty trust, and solvency issues—but could buy time to address these issues. Directors looked forward to returning to financial sector issues in the context of the discussion of the April 2008 *Global Financial Stability Report.*

Directors welcomed the analysis of the connections between housing cycles and monetary policy in Chapter 3. They noted that the impact of house price movements on overall economic activity is likely to be affected by a range of factors that vary over time and across countries. Directors agreed with the analysis that one important factor may be the degree of development of the mortgage market. Many Directors emphasized that house prices matter for central banks to the extent that they affect inflation and the output gap. In addition, it was noted that central banks with an inflation target can incorporate concerns about asset price bubbles by extending the monetary policy horizon. A

number of Directors stressed that monetary policy should continue to be focused on the prospects for inflation and activity. Several Directors also cautioned that monetary policy alone should not bear the full weight of responding to possible asset price bubbles, emphasizing the role of regulatory policy.

Emerging and Developing Economies

Directors noted that emerging and developing economies have been relatively resilient in the face of the spreading crisis in global financial markets, owing in large part to the stabilization gains from improved macroeconomic policy frameworks and the strong growth momentum from productivity gains associated with continuing integration into the global economy and the broadening of export bases. As a result, the advanced economy business cycle may play a less-dominant role, even as these economies have become increasingly more open to trade. Nevertheless, Directors recognized that a protracted weakening of growth in the advanced economies will likely have an appreciable negative impact on these countries. Moreover, a broadening of the problems in financial markets could lead to global deleveraging that could increasingly constrain financial flows to emerging economies that are seen as vulnerable.

Directors agreed that, while many emerging and developing economies continue to face the challenge of containing inflation and avoiding a buildup in vulnerabilities, policymakers in these countries should be ready to respond to a more negative external environment. Although in a number of countries there seems to be more room than in the past to use countercyclical monetary and fiscal policies, Directors emphasized that the appropriate mix will need to be judged country by country. In particular, they noted that countries with large current account deficits or other vulnerabilities may need to respond by tightening policies promptly, so as to maintain confidence and avoid external crises familiar from earlier decades.

In emerging Asian economies, growth is expected to decelerate but will remain strong, led by China and India. Most Directors viewed the risks to the outlook as being broadly balanced—with some upside potential from domestic demand, but downside risks from the external environment. Some Directors expressed concern that a number of countries could face sustained inflation and overheating problems, particularly if consumption continues to gather pace and policy measures to slow investment prove ineffective. Countries in this region with heavily managed exchange rate regimes would benefit from shifting to more flexible exchange rate regimes that provide greater scope for monetary tightening.

In Latin America, stronger policy frameworks, improved debt management, and the development of domestic capital markets have reduced vulnerabilities, and the region has shown resilience to the increasing risk aversion and disruptions in international financial markets. However, Directors considered that the risks to the outlook for the region are weighted to the downside, particularly in the event of a reversal of the recent commodity price boom associated with a deeper global downturn. Directors agreed that in countries where inflation targeting has gained credibility, monetary policy is the first line of defense against weaker outcomes, whereas for other countries the scope for easing will be constrained by the need to contain inflationary pressures. Many Directors also agreed that flexible exchange rate management should play a supportive role, and that countries with public debt at sustainable levels should let automatic stabilizers work.

For most countries in emerging Europe, containment of inflation remains the main policy challenge. Countries that have built up large current account deficits relying on short-term and debt-related financing could be vulnerable to a reversal of capital inflows. For these countries, Directors underscored the importance of prudent macroeconomic policies, aimed at steering these economies toward a "soft landing," as well as of prudential and regulatory policies to contain balance sheet vulnerabilities.

In the Commonwealth of Independent States, domestic demand has continued to expand rapidly, fueled by high commodity prices, expansionary macroeconomic policies, rapid credit growth, and rising asset prices. In this context, Directors agreed that the most immediate challenge for policymakers in the region is to rein in rising inflation pressures. Directors agreed that risks to the regional outlook are tilted to the downside, as a sharper-than-expected slowdown in the global economy will likely lead to a decline in oil and commodity prices, and could adversely affect external financing conditions.

In sub-Saharan Africa, Directors were encouraged by the sustained expansion, led by very strong growth in oil-exporting countries and supported by robust expansion elsewhere. In some countries, rising inflationary pressures from food and fuel prices are of concern. Directors welcomed the analysis in Chapter 5 showing that developing economies in Africa and elsewhere are becoming more diversified and are benefiting from improved policies and structural reforms that are under way in many countries. Although these reforms should strengthen the resilience of the region to a slowdown in the advanced economies, Directors saw the balance of risks to the outlook as tilted to the downside, owing to the risks of a significant drop in commodity prices when the present boom ends and of a possible slowdown in capital inflows and investment. The main policy priorities for the region are to maintain progress toward increasing integration with the global economy and to improve the business environment, infrastructure, and institutions.

In the Middle East, high oil prices have supported buoyant growth, strong external balances, and a buildup in government spending in oil-exporting countries, while strong growth in the region's other economies has been spurred by trade and financial linkages with oil-exporting countries as well as by domestic reforms. However, inflation pressures have risen considerably due to strong domestic demand, rising food prices, and higher rents. Directors recommended focusing public spending from oil revenues on addressing supply bottlenecks, and some Directors emphasized that rising inflationary pressures may require exercising fiscal restraint in the short term to counterbalance strong private demand growth. At the same time, Directors emphasized the need to continue pursuing long-term development objectives, through reforms that encourage investment in the non-oil sector and develop financial systems that can support high and sustained growth.

Multilateral and Other Issues

Directors emphasized that reducing the risks associated with global current account imbalances remains an important task. Progress is being made toward trimming the U.S. current account deficit and implementing detailed policy plans consistent with the strategy endorsed by the International Monetary and Financial Committee that were laid out by the participants in the IMF-sponsored Multilateral Consultation. However, recent currency market movements underline the potential for disorderly adjustments. Several Directors stressed that the present environment heightens the importance of continued actions in line with the policy plans and of IMF monitoring of their implementation. Although policies aimed at rebalancing domestic demand across countries remain relevant, they should be approached flexibly to take account of individual country circumstances and the changing global context. Directors agreed that temporary fiscal relaxation in the United States will provide useful insurance against a deeper slowdown but should not jeopardize medium-term consoli-

dation goals. A number of Directors stressed that further tightening of monetary policy in China, alongside greater upward flexibility of the exchange rate, would help relieve the burden being borne by other major currencies in response to the depreciating dollar and would also serve China's aim to control inflation. Directors emphasized the importance of tackling supply bottlenecks in oil-exporting countries and of further pursuing growth-enhancing structural reforms of product and labor markets in the euro area and Japan.

More generally, Directors welcomed the ongoing consultations among countries, especially by the monetary authorities of the advanced economies with each other and with international bodies such as the IMF and the Financial Stability Forum, in dealing with the present financial turmoil. Joint efforts could prove more effective in bolstering confidence and demand than individual efforts. Directors agreed that the IMF is uniquely placed for adding a multilateral perspective to policy responses to the current crisis, including through the *World Economic Outlook* and the *Global Financial Stability Report;* for providing a forum for ongoing discussion and exchange of views, especially with regard to possible contingency actions; and for promoting consistency of national policies and assessing their spillovers in an increasingly integrated global economy.

Directors welcomed the staff's analysis in Chapter 4 drawing out the short- and medium-term macroeconomic consequences of measures to mitigate the buildup of greenhouse gases. They considered that the analysis adds value to the debate on climate change and underlines the role of multilateral efforts in addressing this issue in an effective, efficient, and equitable manner.

The Statistical Appendix presents historical data, as well as projections. It comprises five sections: Assumptions, What's New, Data and Conventions, Classification of Countries, and Statistical Tables.

The assumptions underlying the estimates and projections for 2008–09 and the medium-term scenario for 2010–13 are summarized in the first section. The second section presents a brief description of changes to the database and statistical tables. The third section provides a general description of the data and of the conventions used for calculating country group composites. The classification of countries in the various groups presented in the *World Economic Outlook* is summarized in the fourth section.

The last, and main, section comprises the statistical tables. Data in these tables have been compiled on the basis of information available through end-March 2008. The figures for 2008 and beyond are shown with the same degree of precision as the historical figures solely for convenience; because they are projections, the same degree of accuracy is not to be inferred.

Assumptions

Real effective *exchange rates* for the advanced economies are assumed to remain constant at their average levels during the period January 30 to February 27, 2008. For 2008 and 2009, these assumptions imply average U.S. dollar/SDR conversion rates of 1.504 and 1.510, U.S. dollar/euro conversion rates of 1.47 and 1.48, and yen/U.S. dollar conversion rates of 106.7 and 105.9, respectively.

It is assumed that the *price of oil* will average $95.50 a barrel in 2008 and $94.50 a barrel in 2009.

Established *policies* of national authorities are assumed to be maintained. The more specific policy assumptions underlying the projections for selected advanced economies are described in Box A1.

With regard to *interest rates*, it is assumed that the London interbank offered rate (LIBOR) on six-month U.S. dollar deposits will average 3.1 percent in 2008 and 3.4 percent in 2009, that three-month euro deposits will average 4.0 percent in 2008 and 3.6 percent in 2009, and that six-month Japanese yen deposits will average 1.0 percent in 2008 and 0.8 percent in 2009.

With respect to *introduction of the euro*, on December 31, 1998, the Council of the European Union decided that, effective January 1, 1999, the irrevocably fixed conversion rates between the euro and currencies of the member states adopting the euro are as follows.

1 euro	= 13.7603	Austrian schillings
	= 40.3399	Belgian francs
	= 0.585274	Cyprus pound[1]
	= 1.95583	Deutsche mark
	= 5.94573	Finnish markkaa
	= 6.55957	French francs
	= 340.750	Greek drachma[2]
	= 0.787564	Irish pound
	= 1,936.27	Italian lire
	= 40.3399	Luxembourg francs
	= 0.42930	Maltese lira[3]
	= 2.20371	Netherlands guilders
	= 200.482	Portuguese escudos
	= 239.640	Slovenian tolars[4]
	= 166.386	Spanish pesetas

See Box 5.4 of the October 1998 *World Economic Outlook* for details on how the conversion rates were established.

[1]The conversion rate for Cyprus was established prior to inclusion in the euro area on January 1, 2008.

[2]The conversion rate for Greece was established prior to inclusion in the euro area on January 1, 2001.

[3]The conversion rate for Malta was established prior to inclusion in the euro area on January 1, 2008.

[4]The conversion rate for Slovenia was established prior to inclusion in the euro area on January 1, 2007.

Box A1. Economic Policy Assumptions Underlying the Projections for Selected Economies

The short-term *fiscal policy assumptions* used in the *World Economic Outlook* are based on officially announced budgets, adjusted for differences between the national authorities and the IMF staff regarding macroeconomic assumptions and projected fiscal outturns. The medium-term fiscal projections incorporate policy measures that are judged likely to be implemented. In cases where the IMF staff has insufficient information to assess the authorities' budget intentions and prospects for policy implementation, an unchanged structural primary balance is assumed, unless otherwise indicated. Specific assumptions used in some of the advanced economies follow (see also Tables B5–B7 in the Statistical Appendix for data on fiscal and structural balances).[1]

United States. The fiscal projections are based on the administration's fiscal year 2009 budget. Adjustments are made to account for differences in macroeconomic projections as well as IMF staff assumptions about (1) additional defense spending based on analysis by the Congressional Budget Office, (2) slower compression in the growth rate of discretionary spending, (3) continued alternative minimum tax relief beyond fiscal year 2009, and (4) an economic stimulus package similar to recent proposals by the president and members of

Congress. Projections also assume that proposed Medicare savings are achieved only partially and that personal retirement accounts are not introduced.

Japan. The medium-term fiscal projections assume that expenditure and revenue of the general government (excluding social security) are adjusted in line with the current government target to achieve primary fiscal balance (excluding social security) by fiscal year 2011.

Germany. Projections reflect the measures announced in the Stability Program Update 2007. Projections for 2008 include a loss in revenue owing to corporate tax reform and a cut in social security contribution rates (unemployment insurance). Over the medium term, the path of health expenditures accelerates as a result of aging and cost increases because significant health care reform measures have not been taken.

France. The 2007 fiscal estimates incorporate the end-year corrective budget law. For 2008, the fiscal projections are based on the budget law and assume higher social security spending growth, largely owing to higher-than-targeted increases in health care outlays. Medium-term projections reflect the authorities' official tax revenue forecast but assume different spending (less deceleration) and nontax revenue profiles, consistent with an unchanged policy assumption.

Italy. For 2007, the deficit number reflects the IMF staff's estimated outcome. For 2008, the deficit projection is based on the IMF staff's assessment of this year's budget, adjusted for recent macroeconomic and fiscal developments, specifically lower growth and prior spending commitments that would have to be executed in 2008. For 2009–12, a constant structural primary balance (net of one-off measures) is assumed.

United Kingdom. The projection for 2007–08 assumes that the pattern seen through December will continue in the last quarter of the fiscal year. The medium-term revenue projections are based on economic assumptions, with some modest buoyancy built in, although not as much as assumed by the authorities. The expenditure

[1]The output gap is actual minus potential output, as a percent of potential output. Structural balances are expressed as a percent of potential output. The structural budget balance is the budgetary position that would be observed if the level of actual output coincided with potential output. Changes in the structural budget balance consequently include effects of temporary fiscal measures, the impact of fluctuations in interest rates and debt-service costs, and other noncyclical fluctuations in the budget balance. The computations of structural budget balances are based on IMF staff estimates of potential GDP and revenue and expenditure elasticities (see the October 1993 *World Economic Outlook*, Annex I). Net debt is defined as gross debt minus financial assets of the general government, which include assets held by the social security insurance system. Estimates of the output gap and of the structural balance are subject to significant margins of uncertainty.

projections assume that after some slippage in 2007–08, the planned consolidation, set out in the Pre-Budget Report, will continue in terms of the percent of GDP through 2012–13.

Canada. Projections use the baseline forecast in the 2007 Economic Statement. The IMF staff makes some adjustments to this forecast for differences in macroeconomic projections. The IMF staff forecast also incorporates the most recent data releases from Statistics Canada, including provincial and territorial budgetary outturns through the second quarter of 2007.

Australia. The fiscal projections through fiscal year 2010/11 are based on the Mid-Year Economic and Fiscal Outlook published in October 2007. For the remainder of the projection period, the IMF staff assumes unchanged policies.

Austria. Projections for 2007 and beyond are IMF staff projections based on current policies.

Brazil. The fiscal projections for 2008 are based on the 2008 budget guidelines law and recent pronouncements by the authorities regarding their policy intentions. For the outer years, the IMF staff assumes unchanged policies, with a further increase in public investment in line with the authorities' intentions.

Belgium. After the June 2007 federal elections, disagreements on reforms of fiscal federalism arrangements have led to more than six months of political division. At the date of submission, the Budget Report for 2008 was not yet available. Projections for 2008 and 2009 are IMF staff estimates adjusted for macroeconomic assumptions and assuming unchanged policies.

China. Projections for 2007 are based on IMF staff estimates and data for the first 11 months, with some adjustment for the IMF staff's definition of overall budget balance. For 2008–13, IMF staff projections assume that spending, especially in social sectors, will increase, with the deficit roughly constant at its projected 2008 level (about 1 percent of GDP).

Denmark. Estimates for 2007 and projections for 2008 are aligned with the latest official budget estimates and the underlying projections, adjusted where appropriate for the IMF staff's

macroeconomic assumptions. For 2009–13, the projections incorporate key features of the prior medium-term fiscal plan as embodied in the authorities' November 2007 Convergence Program submitted to the European Union (EU). The projections imply convergence of the budget toward a close-to-balanced position from an initial surplus position. This is consistent with the authorities' projection of a closure of the output gap over the medium term, as well as being in line with their objectives for long-term fiscal sustainability and debt reduction.

Greece. Projections are based on the 2008 budget, the latest Stability Program, and other forecasts provided by the authorities. According to preliminary estimates by the European Commission, the revision of gross national income could lead to a permanent increase of Greece's contribution to the EU budget of less than ¼ percent of GDP, as well as a one-off payment of arrears of such a contribution of about ¾ percent of GDP, which could accrue to the 2007 balance. These possible contributions are not reflected in the IMF staff projections.

Hong Kong SAR. Fiscal projections for 2007–10 are consistent with the authorities' medium-term strategy as outlined in the fiscal year 2007/08 budget, with projections for 2011–12 based on the assumptions underlying the IMF staff's medium-term macroeconomic scenario.

India. Estimates for 2007 are based on data on budgetary execution. Projections for 2008 and beyond are based on available information on the authorities' fiscal plans (the 2008–09 budget was expected on February 29, 2008), with some adjustments for the IMF staff's assumptions.

Korea. Projections reflect advance GDP estimates for 2007, as well as the 2008 budget, and the five-year medium-term budget for 2009–13, with some adjustment for the IMF staff's assumptions and macroeconomic projections.

Mexico. Fiscal projections for 2008 build on the authorities' budget. Projections for 2009 and beyond are based on IMF staff calculations in line with the Federal Government Fiscal Responsibility Law, requiring a zero overall balance on the traditional (budget) definition.

Box A1 *(concluded)*

Netherlands. The fiscal projections build on the 2007 budget, the latest Stability Program, and other forecasts provided by the authorities.

New Zealand. The fiscal projections through fiscal year 2010/11 are based on the Half-Year Economic and Fiscal Update released in December 2007. For the remainder of the projection period, the IMF staff assumes unchanged policies. The New Zealand fiscal account switched to new Generally Accepted Accounting Principles beginning in fiscal year 2006/07, with no comparable back data.

Portugal. Fiscal projections through 2010 are based on the IMF staff's assessment of the 2007 budget and the authorities' projections presented in the 2007 Stability Program. In subsequent years, the fiscal projections assume maintaining the primary balance excluding age-related expenditures.

Singapore. For fiscal year 2007/08, expenditure projections are based on budget numbers, whereas revenue projections reflect the IMF staff's estimates of the impact of new policy measures, including an increase in the goods and services tax. Medium-term revenue projections assume that capital gains on fiscal reserves will be included in investment income.

Spain. Fiscal projections through 2010 are based on the 2008 budget; policies outlined in the authorities' updated Stability Program 2007–10, adjusted for the IMF staff's macroeconomic assumptions, information from recent statistical releases, and official announcements. In

subsequent years, the fiscal projections assume unchanged policies.

Sweden. The fiscal projections are based on information provided in the 2008 Budget Bill (October 2007), with adjustments reflecting incoming fiscal data and the IMF staff's views on the macroeconomic environment.

Switzerland. Projections for 2007–12 are based on IMF staff calculations, which incorporate measures to restore balance in the federal accounts and strengthen social security finances.

Monetary policy assumptions are based on the established policy framework in each country. In most cases, this implies a nonaccommodative stance over the business cycle: official interest rates will therefore increase when economic indicators suggest that inflation will rise above its acceptable rate or range, and they will decrease when indicators suggest that prospective inflation will not exceed the acceptable rate or range, that prospective output growth is below its potential rate, and that the margin of slack in the economy is significant. On this basis, the London interbank offered rate (LIBOR) on six-month U.S. dollar deposits is assumed to average 3.1 percent in 2008 and 3.4 percent in 2009 (see Table 1.1). The rate on three-month euro deposits is assumed to average 4.0 percent in 2008 and 3.6 percent in 2009. The interest rate on six-month Japanese yen deposits is assumed to average 1.0 percent in 2008 and 0.8 percent in 2009.

What's New

On January 1, 2008, Cyprus and Malta became members of the euro area, bringing the total number of euro countries to 15; the country composition of the fuel-exporting group has been revised to reflect the periodic update of the classification criteria; and the purchasing-power-parity (PPP) weights have been updated to reflect the most up-to-date PPP conversion factor provided by the International Comparison Program.

Data and Conventions

Data and projections for 183 countries form the statistical basis for the *World Economic Outlook* (the World Economic Outlook database). The data are maintained jointly by the IMF's Research Department and area departments, with the latter regularly updating country projections based on consistent global assumptions.

Although national statistical agencies are the ultimate providers of historical data and definitions, international organizations are also involved in statistical issues, with the objective of harmonizing methodologies for the national compilation of statistics, including the analytical frameworks, concepts, definitions, classifications, and valuation procedures used in the production of economic statistics. The World Economic Outlook database reflects information from both national source agencies and international organizations.

The comprehensive revision of the standardized *System of National Accounts 1993 (SNA)*, the IMF's *Balance of Payments Manual, Fifth Edition (BPM5)*, the *Monetary and Financial Statistics Manual (MFSM)*, and the *Government Finance Statistics Manual 2001 (GFSM 2001)* represented significant improvements in the standards of economic statistics and analysis.[5] The IMF was actively involved in all these projects, particularly the *Balance of Payments, Monetary and Financial Statistics*, and *Government Finance Statistics* manuals, which reflects the IMF's special interest in countries' external positions, financial sector stability, and public sector fiscal positions. The process of adapting country data to the new definitions began in earnest when the manuals were released. However, full concordance with the manuals is ultimately dependent on the provision by national statistical compilers of revised country data, and hence the *World Economic Outlook* estimates are still only partially adapted to these manuals.

In line with recent improvements in standards for reporting economic statistics, several countries have phased out their traditional *fixed-base-year* method of calculating real macroeconomic variables levels and growth by switching to a *chain-weighted* method of computing aggregate growth. Recent dramatic changes

in the structure of these economies have caused these countries to revise the way in which they measure real GDP levels and growth. Switching to the chain-weighted method of computing aggregate growth, which uses current price information, allows countries to measure GDP growth more accurately by eliminating upward biases in new data.[6] Currently, real macroeconomic data for Albania, Australia, Austria, Azerbaijan, Belgium, Canada, Cyprus, the Czech Republic, Denmark, the euro area, Finland, France, Georgia, Germany, Greece, Hong Kong SAR, Iceland, Ireland, Italy, Japan, Kazakhstan, Lithuania, Luxembourg, Malta, the Netherlands, New Zealand, Norway, Poland, Portugal, Russia, Slovenia, Spain, Sweden, Switzerland, the United Kingdom, and the United States are based on chain-weighted methodology. However, data before 1996 (Albania), 1994 (Azerbaijan), 1995 (Belgium), 1995 (Cyprus), 1995 (Czech Republic), 1995 (euro area), 1996 (Georgia), 1991 (Germany), 2000 (Greece), 1990 (Iceland), 1995 (Ireland), 1994 (Japan), 1994 (Kazakhstan), 1995 (Luxembourg), 2000 (Malta), 1995 (Poland), 1995 (Russia), 1995 (Slovenia), and 1995 (Spain) are based on unrevised national accounts and subject to revision in the future.

The members of the European Union have adopted a harmonized system for the compilation of national accounts, referred to as ESA 1995. All national accounts data from 1995 onward are presented on the basis of the new system. Revision by national authorities of data prior to 1995 to conform to the new system has progressed but, in some cases, has not been completed. In such cases, historical *World Economic Outlook* data have been carefully adjusted to avoid breaks in the series. Users of EU national accounts data prior to 1995 should nevertheless exercise caution until such time as the revision of historical data by national statistical

---

[5]Commission of the European Communities, International Monetary Fund, Organization for Economic Cooperation and Development, United Nations, and World Bank, *System of National Accounts 1993* (Brussels/Luxembourg, New York, Paris, and Washington, 1993); International Monetary Fund, *Balance of Payments Manual, Fifth Edition* (Washington, 1993); International Monetary Fund, *Monetary and Financial Statistics Manual* (Washington, 2000); and International Monetary Fund, *Government Finance Statistics Manual* (Washington, 2001).

[6]Charles Steindel, 1995, "Chain-Weighting: The New Approach to Measuring GDP," *Current Issues in Economics and Finance* (Federal Reserve Bank of New York), Vol. 1 (December).

agencies has been fully completed. See Box 1.2 of the May 2000 *World Economic Outlook*.

Composite data for country groups in the *World Economic Outlook* are either sums or weighted averages of data for individual countries. Unless otherwise indicated, multiyear averages of growth rates are expressed as compound annual rates of change.[7] Arithmetically weighted averages are used for all data except inflation and money growth for the emerging and developing economies group, for which geometric averages are used. The following conventions apply.

- Country group composites for exchange rates, interest rates, and the growth rates of monetary aggregates are weighted by GDP converted to U.S. dollars at market exchange rates (averaged over the preceding three years) as a share of group GDP.

- Composites for other data relating to the domestic economy, whether growth rates or ratios, are weighted by GDP valued at PPPs as a share of total world or group GDP.[8]

- Composites for data relating to the domestic economy for the euro area (15 member countries throughout the entire period unless otherwise noted) are aggregates of national source data using GDP weights. Annual data are not adjusted for calendar day effects. For data prior to 1999, data aggregations apply 1995 European currency unit exchange rates.

- Composite unemployment rates and employment growth are weighted by labor force as a share of group labor force.

[7]Averages for real GDP and its components, employment, per capita GDP, inflation, factor productivity, trade, and commodity prices are calculated based on the compound annual rate of change, except for the unemployment rate, which is based on the simple arithmetic average.

[8]See Box A2 of the April 2004 *World Economic Outlook* for a summary of the revised PPP-based weights and Annex IV of the May 1993 *World Economic Outlook*. See also Anne-Marie Gulde and Marianne Schulze-Ghattas, "Purchasing Power Parity Based Weights for the *World Economic Outlook*," in *Staff Studies for the World Economic Outlook* (International Monetary Fund, December 1993), pp. 106–23.

- Composites relating to the external economy are sums of individual country data after conversion to U.S. dollars at the average market exchange rates in the years indicated for balance of payments data and at end-of-year market exchange rates for debt denominated in currencies other than U.S. dollars. Composites of changes in foreign trade volumes and prices, however, are arithmetic averages of percent changes for individual countries weighted by the U.S. dollar value of exports or imports as a share of total world or group exports or imports (in the preceding year).

For central and eastern European countries, external transactions in nonconvertible currencies (through 1990) are converted to U.S. dollars at the implicit U.S. dollar/ruble conversion rates obtained from each country's national currency exchange rate for the U.S. dollar and for the ruble.

All data refer to calendar years, except for the following countries, which refer to fiscal years: Australia (July/June), Egypt (July/June), Haiti (October/September), Islamic Republic of Iran (April/March), Mauritius (July/June), Myanmar (April/March), Nepal (July/June), New Zealand (July/June), Pakistan (July/June), Samoa (July/June), and Tonga (July/June).

Classification of Countries

Summary of the Country Classification

The country classification in the *World Economic Outlook* divides the world into two major groups: advanced economies, and emerging and developing economies.[9] Rather than being based on strict criteria, economic or otherwise, this classification has evolved over time with the objective of facilitating analysis by providing a

[9]As used here, the term "country" does not in all cases refer to a territorial entity that is a state as understood by international law and practice. It also covers some territorial entities that are not states, but for which statistical data are maintained on a separate and independent basis.

Table A. Classification by *World Economic Outlook* Groups and Their Shares in Aggregate GDP, Exports of Goods and Services, and Population, 2007[1]

(Percent of total for group or world)

	Number of Countries	GDP		Exports of Goods and Services		Population	
		Advanced economies	World	Advanced economies	World	Advanced economies	World
Advanced economies	**31**	**100.0**	**56.4**	**100.0**	**66.4**	**100.0**	**15.3**
United States		37.9	21.4	14.4	9.6	30.7	4.7
Euro area	15	28.6	16.1	44.4	29.5	32.3	4.9
Germany		7.7	4.3	13.8	9.2	8.4	1.3
France		5.6	3.2	6.0	4.0	6.3	1.0
Italy		4.9	2.8	5.6	3.7	6.0	0.9
Spain		3.7	2.1	3.4	2.2	4.6	0.7
Japan		11.7	6.6	7.2	4.7	13.0	2.0
United Kingdom		5.9	3.3	6.4	4.2	6.2	0.9
Canada		3.5	2.0	4.4	2.9	3.3	0.5
Other advanced economies	12	12.5	7.0	23.3	15.4	14.5	2.2
Memorandum							
Major advanced economies	7	77.2	43.5	57.8	38.4	73.8	11.3
Newly industrialized Asian economies	4	6.6	3.7	13.5	8.9	8.4	1.3
		Emerging and developing economies	World	Emerging and developing economies	World	Emerging and developing economies	World
Emerging and developing economies	**141**	**100.0**	**43.6**	**100.0**	**33.6**	**100.0**	**84.7**
Regional groups							
Africa	47	6.9	3.0	7.4	2.5	15.1	12.8
Sub-Sahara	44	5.3	2.3	5.5	1.9	13.7	11.6
Excluding Nigeria and South Africa	42	2.8	1.2	2.8	1.0	10.2	8.6
Central and eastern Europe	13	9.3	4.1	13.8	4.6	3.3	2.8
Commonwealth of Independent States[2]	13	10.2	4.5	10.2	3.4	5.1	4.3
Russia		7.3	3.2	6.8	2.3	2.6	2.2
Developing Asia	23	46.0	20.1	39.3	13.2	62.0	52.6
China		24.8	10.8	23.3	7.8	24.2	20.5
India		10.5	4.6	4.0	1.3	20.6	17.5
Excluding China and India	21	10.6	4.6	12.1	4.1	17.2	14.6
Middle East	13	8.7	3.8	14.0	4.7	4.4	3.7
Western Hemisphere	32	19.0	8.3	15.2	5.1	10.1	8.6
Brazil		6.4	2.8	3.2	1.1	3.5	2.9
Mexico		4.8	2.1	5.1	1.7	1.9	1.6
Analytical groups							
By source of export earnings							
Fuel	24	19.4	8.4	26.5	8.9	11.1	9.4
Nonfuel	117	80.6	35.2	73.5	24.7	88.9	75.3
of which, primary products	20	1.7	0.7	2.2	0.7	4.0	3.4
By external financing source							
Net debtor countries	116	55.0	24.0	47.5	16.0	64.5	54.6
of which, official financing	30	3.4	1.5	2.4	0.8	10.6	9.0
Net debtor countries by debt-servicing experience							
Countries with arrears and/or rescheduling during 2002–06	49	9.6	4.2	6.9	2.3	17.2	14.5
Other net debtor countries	67	45.4	19.8	40.5	13.6	47.3	40.1
Other groups							
Heavily indebted poor countries	31	1.8	0.8	1.3	0.4	8.5	7.2
Middle East and North Africa	19	10.6	4.6	16.1	5.4	6.5	5.5

[1]The GDP shares are based on the purchasing-power-parity (PPP) valuation of country GDPs. The number of countries comprising each group reflects those for which data are included in the group aggregates.

[2]Mongolia, which is not a member of the Commonwealth of Independent States, is included in this group for reasons of geography and similarities in economic structure.

Table B. Advanced Economies by Subgroup

Major Currency Areas	Other Subgroups					
	Euro area		Newly industrialized Asian economies	Major advanced economies	Other advanced economies	
United States	Austria	Italy	Hong Kong SAR[1]	Canada	Australia	New Zealand
Euro area	Belgium	Luxembourg	Korea	France	Denmark	Norway
Japan	Cyprus	Malta	Singapore	Germany	Hong Kong SAR[1]	Singapore
	Finland	Netherlands	Taiwan Province of China	Italy	Iceland	Sweden
	France	Portugal		Japan	Israel	Switzerland
	Germany	Slovenia		United Kingdom	Korea	Taiwan Province of China
	Greece	Spain		United States		
	Ireland					

[1]On July 1, 1997, Hong Kong was returned to the People's Republic of China and became a Special Administrative Region of China.

reasonably meaningful organization of data. Table A provides an overview of these standard groups in the *World Economic Outlook*, showing the number of countries in each group and the average 2007 shares of groups in aggregate PPP-valued GDP, total exports of goods and services, and population.

A few countries are currently not included in these groups, either because they are not IMF members and their economies are not monitored by the IMF or because databases have not yet been fully developed. Because of data limitations, group composites do not reflect the following countries: the Islamic Republic of Afghanistan, Bosnia and Herzegovina, Brunei Darussalam, Eritrea, Iraq, Liberia, the Republic of Montenegro, Serbia, Somalia, Timor-Leste, and Zimbabwe. Cuba and the Democratic People's Republic of Korea are examples of countries that are not IMF members, whereas San Marino, among the advanced economies, and Aruba, Marshall Islands, Federated States of Micronesia, and Palau, among the developing economies, are examples of countries for which databases have not been completed.

General Features and Composition of Groups in the World Economic Outlook Classification

Advanced Economies

The 31 advanced economies are listed in Table B. The seven largest in terms of GDP—the United States, Japan, Germany, France, Italy, the United Kingdom, and Canada—constitute the subgroup of *major advanced economies,* often referred to as the Group of Seven (G7). The 15 members of the *euro area* and the four *newly industrialized Asian economies* are also distinguished as subgroups. Composite data shown in the tables for the euro area cover the current members for all years, even though the membership has increased over time.

In 1991 and subsequent years, data for *Germany* refer to west Germany *and* the eastern Länder (that is, the former German Democratic Republic). Before 1991, economic data were not available on a unified basis or in a consistent manner. Hence, in tables featuring data expressed as annual percent change, these apply to west Germany in years up to and including 1991, but to unified Germany from 1992 onward. In general, data on national accounts and domestic economic and financial activity through 1990 cover west Germany only, whereas data for the central government and balance of payments apply to west Germany

Table C. European Union

Austria	Finland	Latvia	Romania
Belgium	France	Lithuania	Slovak Republic
Bulgaria	Germany	Luxembourg	Slovenia
Cyprus	Greece	Malta	Spain
Czech Republic	Hungary	Netherlands	Sweden
Denmark	Ireland	Poland	United Kingdom
Estonia	Italy	Portugal	

Table D. Middle East and North African Countries

Algeria	Jordan	Morocco	Syrian Arab Republic
Bahrain	Kuwait	Oman	Tunisia
Djibouti	Lebanon	Qatar	United Arab Emirates
Egypt	Libya	Saudi Arabia	Yemen, Rep. of
Iran, I.R. of	Mauritania	Sudan	

Table E. Emerging and Developing Economies by Region and Main Source of Export Earnings

	Fuel	Nonfuel Primary Products
Africa	Algeria Angola Congo, Rep. of Equatorial Guinea Gabon Nigeria Sudan	Botswana Burkina Faso Burundi Chad Congo, Dem. Rep. of Guinea Guinea-Bissau Malawi Mauritania Mozambique Sierra Leone Zambia
Commonwealth of Independent States	Azerbaijan Kazakhstan Russia Turkmenistan	Mongolia Tajikistan Uzbekistan
Developing Asia		Papua New Guinea Solomon Islands
Middle East	Bahrain Iran, I.R. of Kuwait Libya Oman Qatar Saudi Arabia Syrian Arab Republic United Arab Emirates Yemen, Rep. of	
Western Hemisphere	Ecuador Trinidad and Tobago Venezuela, Rep. Boliv. de	Chile Guyana Suriname

Note: Mongolia, which is not a member of the Commonwealth of Independent States, is included in this group for reasons of geography and similarities in economic structure.

through June 1990 and to unified Germany thereafter.

Table C lists the member countries of the European Union, not all of which are classified as advanced economies in the *World Economic Outlook.*

Emerging and Developing Economies

The group of emerging and developing economies (141 countries) includes all countries that are not classified as advanced economies.

The *regional breakdowns* of emerging and developing economies—*Africa, central and eastern Europe, Commonwealth of Independent States, developing Asia, Middle East, and Western Hemisphere*—largely conform to the regional breakdowns in the IMF's *International Financial Statistics.* In both classifications, Egypt and the Socialist People's Libyan Arab Jamahiriya are included in the *Middle East* region rather than in Africa. In addition, the *World Economic Outlook* sometimes refers to the regional group of Middle East and North African countries, also referred to as the MENA countries, whose composition straddles the Africa and Middle East regions. This group is defined as the Arab League countries plus the Islamic Republic of Iran (see Table D).

Emerging and developing economies are also classified according to *analytical criteria*. The analytical criteria reflect countries' composition of export earnings and other income from abroad; exchange rate arrangements; a distinction between net creditor and net debtor countries; and, for the net debtor countries, financial criteria based on external financing sources and experience with external debt servicing. The detailed composition of emerging and developing economies in the regional and analytical groups is shown in Tables E and F.

The analytical criterion, by *source of export earnings*, distinguishes between categories: *fuel* (Standard International Trade Classification—SITC 3) and *nonfuel* and then focuses on *nonfuel primary products* (SITCs 0, 1, 2, 4, and 68).

The financial criteria focus on *net creditor countries, net debtor countries,* and *heavily indebted poor countries (HIPCs).* Net debtor countries are further differentiated on the basis of two additional financial criteria: by *official external*

Table F. Emerging and Developing Economies by Region, Net External Position, and Status as Heavily Indebted Poor Countries

	Net External Position		Heavily Indebted Poor Countries		Net External Position		Heavily Indebted Poor Countries
	Net creditor	Net debtor[1]			Net creditor	Net debtor[1]	
Africa				**Central and eastern Europe**			
Maghreb				Albania		*	
Algeria	*			Bulgaria		*	
Morocco		*		Croatia		*	
Tunisia		*		Czech Republic		*	
Sub-Sahara				Estonia		*	
South Africa		*		Hungary		*	
Horn of Africa				Latvia		*	
Djibouti		*		Lithuania		*	
Ethiopia		•	*	Macedonia, FYR		*	
Sudan		*		Poland		*	
Great Lakes				Romania		*	
Burundi		•	*	Slovak Republic		*	
Congo, Dem. Rep. of		*	*	Turkey		*	
Kenya		*					
Rwanda		•	*	**Commonwealth of Independent States[2]**			
Tanzania		•	*	Armenia		•	
Uganda		*	*	Azerbaijan		*	
Southern Africa				Belarus		*	
Angola	*			Georgia		*	
Botswana	*			Kazakhstan		*	
Comoros		•		Kyrgyz Republic		*	
Lesotho		*		Moldova		*	
Madagascar		•	*	Mongolia		•	
Malawi		•	*	Russia	*		
Mauritius		*		Tajikistan		*	
Mozambique		*	*	Turkmenistan	*		
Namibia	*			Ukraine	*		
Seychelles		*		Uzbekistan	*		
Swaziland		*					
Zambia		•	*	**Developing Asia**			
West and Central Africa				Bhutan		•	
Cape Verde		*		Cambodia		•	
Gambia, The		*	*	China	*		
Ghana		•	*	Fiji		*	
Guinea		*	*	Indonesia		*	
Mauritania		*	*	Kiribati	*		
Nigeria	*			Lao PDR		*	
São Tomé and Príncipe		*	*	Malaysia	*		
Sierra Leone		•	*	Myanmar		*	
CFA franc zone				Papua New Guinea	*		
Benin		*	*	Philippines		*	
Burkina Faso		•	*	Samoa		*	
Cameroon		*	*	Solomon Islands		•	
Central African Republic		•	*	Thailand		*	
Chad		*	*	Tonga		•	
Congo, Rep. of		•	*	Vanuatu		*	
Côte d'Ivoire		*		Vietnam		•	
Equatorial Guinea		*		**South Asia**			
Gabon	*			Bangladesh		•	
Guinea-Bissau		*	*	India		*	
Mali		*	*	Maldives		*	
Niger		•	*	Nepal		•	
Senegal		*	*	Pakistan		*	
Togo		*		Sri Lanka		*	

Table F *(concluded)*

	Net External Position		Heavily Indebted Poor Countries		Net External Position		Heavily Indebted Poor Countries
	Net creditor	Net debtor¹			Net creditor	Net debtor¹	
Middle East				Peru		*	
Bahrain	*			Uruguay		•	
Iran, I.R. of	*			Venezuela, Rep. Boliv. de	*		
Kuwait	*			**Central America**			
Libya	*			Costa Rica		*	
Oman	*			El Salvador		•	
Qatar	*			Guatemala		*	
Saudi Arabia	*			Honduras		*	*
United Arab Emirates	*			Nicaragua		*	*
Yemen, Rep. of	*			Panama		*	
Mashreq				**Caribbean**			
Egypt		*		Antigua and Barbuda		*	
Jordan		*		Bahamas, The		*	
Lebanon		*		Barbados		*	
Syrian Arab Republic		*		Belize		*	
				Dominica		*	
Western Hemisphere				Dominican Republic		*	
Mexico		*		Grenada		•	
South America				Guyana		*	*
Argentina		*		Haiti		•	*
Brazil		*		Jamaica		*	
Bolivia		•	*	St. Kitts and Nevis		*	
Chile		*		St. Lucia		*	
Colombia		*		St. Vincent and the Grenadines		•	
Ecuador		*		Suriname		*	
Paraguay		*		Trinidad and Tobago	*		

¹Dot instead of star indicates that the net debtor's main external finance source is official financing.

²Mongolia, which is not a member of the Commonwealth of Independent States, is included in this group for reasons of geography and similarities in economic structure.

financing and by *experience with debt servicing.*[10] The HIPC group comprises the countries considered by the IMF and the World Bank for their debt initiative, known as the HIPC Initiative, with the aim of reducing the external debt burdens of all the eligible HIPCs to a "sustainable" level in a reasonably short period of time.[11]

[10]During 2002–06, 49 countries incurred external payments arrears or entered into official or commercial bank debt-rescheduling agreements. This group of countries is referred to as *countries with arrears and/or rescheduling during 2002–06.*

[11]See David Andrews, Anthony R. Boote, Syed S. Rizavi, and Sukwinder Singh, *Debt Relief for Low-Income Countries: The Enhanced HIPC Initiative*, IMF Pamphlet Series, No. 51 (Washington: International Monetary Fund, November 1999).

List of Tables

Table A1. Summary of World Output[1]
(Annual percent change)

	Average 1990–99	2000	2001	2002	2003	2004	2005	2006	2007	2008	2009	2013
World	**2.9**	**4.7**	**2.2**	**2.8**	**3.6**	**4.9**	**4.4**	**5.0**	**4.9**	**3.7**	**3.8**	**4.9**
Advanced economies	**2.7**	**3.9**	**1.2**	**1.6**	**1.9**	**3.2**	**2.6**	**3.0**	**2.7**	**1.3**	**1.3**	**2.9**
United States	3.1	3.7	0.8	1.6	2.5	3.6	3.1	2.9	2.2	0.5	0.6	3.2
Euro area	. . .	3.8	1.9	0.9	0.8	2.1	1.6	2.8	2.6	1.4	1.2	2.4
Japan	1.5	2.9	0.2	0.3	1.4	2.7	1.9	2.4	2.1	1.4	1.5	1.7
Other advanced economies[2]	3.3	5.2	1.7	3.2	2.5	4.1	3.2	3.8	3.9	2.5	2.7	3.4
Emerging and developing economies	**3.2**	**5.9**	**3.8**	**4.7**	**6.2**	**7.5**	**7.1**	**7.8**	**7.9**	**6.7**	**6.6**	**7.0**
Regional groups												
Africa	2.3	3.5	4.9	6.1	5.3	6.5	5.7	5.9	6.2	6.3	6.4	5.3
Central and eastern Europe	1.2	4.9	0.4	4.2	4.8	6.9	6.1	6.6	5.8	4.4	4.3	5.0
Commonwealth of Independent States[3]	. . .	9.1	6.1	5.2	7.8	8.2	6.5	8.2	8.5	7.0	6.5	5.7
Developing Asia	7.2	6.9	5.8	6.9	8.1	8.6	9.0	9.6	9.7	8.2	8.4	8.9
Middle East	4.3	5.4	3.0	3.9	6.9	5.9	5.7	5.8	5.8	6.1	6.1	6.0
Western Hemisphere	2.9	4.1	0.7	0.4	2.1	6.2	4.6	5.5	5.6	4.4	3.6	4.0
Memorandum												
European Union	2.0	3.9	2.1	1.4	1.5	2.7	2.1	3.3	3.1	1.8	1.7	2.8
Analytical groups												
By source of export earnings												
Fuel	−0.2	7.0	4.5	4.8	6.8	7.7	6.8	7.2	7.3	6.7	6.4	5.3
Nonfuel	4.2	5.6	3.7	4.7	6.0	7.5	7.1	7.9	8.0	6.7	6.7	7.4
of which, primary products	3.1	3.3	4.0	3.5	4.8	7.2	5.9	4.9	5.7	5.4	5.6	5.3
By external financing source												
Net debtor countries	3.1	4.7	2.2	3.2	4.5	6.4	5.9	6.7	6.5	5.6	5.5	5.8
of which, official financing	4.3	4.8	4.2	3.9	5.3	6.5	7.0	7.1	6.8	6.4	6.5	6.5
Net debtor countries by debt-servicing experience												
Countries with arrears and/or rescheduling during 2002–06	3.2	3.2	2.4	1.4	5.5	6.6	6.5	6.5	6.5	6.1	6.0	5.7
Memorandum												
Median growth rate												
Advanced economies	3.0	3.9	1.9	1.8	1.9	3.7	3.1	3.4	3.5	2.0	1.9	2.8
Emerging and developing economies	3.3	4.5	3.7	4.0	4.8	5.4	5.5	6.1	6.0	5.4	5.2	5.0
Output per capita												
Advanced economies	2.0	3.3	0.6	0.9	1.2	2.5	1.9	2.4	2.1	0.8	0.8	2.4
Emerging and developing economies	1.6	4.5	2.4	3.4	4.9	6.2	5.8	6.5	6.6	5.4	5.4	5.8
World growth based on market exchange rates	**2.4**	**4.1**	**1.5**	**1.9**	**2.6**	**4.0**	**3.4**	**3.9**	**3.7**	**2.6**	**2.6**	**4.0**
Value of world output in billions of U.S. dollars												
At market exchange rates	27,333	31,823	31,583	32,854	36,931	41,546	44,881	48,436	54,312	60,109	63,354	81,978
At purchasing power parities	31,715	41,583	43,494	45,457	48,052	51,775	55,703	60,295	64,903	68,624	72,449	94,384

[1]Real GDP.

[2]In this table, "other advanced economies" means advanced economies excluding the United States, euro area countries, and Japan.

[3]Mongolia, which is not a member of the Commonwealth of Independent States, is included in this group for reasons of geography and similarities in economic structure.

Table A2. Advanced Economies: Real GDP and Total Domestic Demand
(Annual percent change)

	Average 1990–99	2000	2001	2002	2003	2004	2005	2006	2007	2008	2009	2013	Fourth Quarter[1] 2007	2008	2009
Real GDP															
Advanced economies	**2.7**	**3.9**	**1.2**	**1.6**	**1.9**	**3.2**	**2.6**	**3.0**	**2.7**	**1.3**	**1.3**	**2.9**	**2.6**	**0.5**	**2.1**
United States	3.1	3.7	0.8	1.6	2.5	3.6	3.1	2.9	2.2	0.5	0.6	3.2	2.5	−0.7	1.6
Euro area	. . .	3.8	1.9	0.9	0.8	2.1	1.6	2.8	2.6	1.4	1.2	2.4	2.2	0.9	1.6
Germany	2.3	3.1	1.2	—	−0.3	1.1	0.8	2.9	2.5	1.4	1.0	2.0	1.8	0.8	1.6
France	1.9	3.9	1.9	1.0	1.1	2.5	1.7	2.0	1.9	1.4	1.2	2.6	2.1	0.9	1.9
Italy	1.4	3.6	1.8	0.5	—	1.5	0.6	1.8	1.5	0.3	0.3	1.4	−0.1	0.2	—
Spain	2.8	5.1	3.6	2.7	3.1	3.3	3.6	3.9	3.8	1.8	1.7	3.8	3.5	0.9	2.4
Netherlands	3.1	3.9	1.9	0.1	0.3	2.2	1.5	3.0	3.5	2.1	1.6	2.3	4.3	0.2	3.1
Belgium	2.3	3.9	0.7	1.4	1.0	2.8	2.0	2.9	2.7	1.4	1.2	2.0	2.4	0.8	1.7
Austria	2.7	3.4	0.8	0.9	1.2	2.3	2.0	3.3	3.4	1.9	1.7	2.2	3.0	1.1	2.2
Finland	1.5	5.0	2.6	1.6	1.8	3.7	2.8	4.9	4.4	2.4	2.1	2.4	3.8	1.7	2.9
Greece	1.9	4.5	4.5	3.9	5.0	4.6	3.8	4.2	4.0	3.5	3.3	3.5	3.7	3.5	3.2
Portugal	3.4	3.9	2.0	0.8	−0.8	1.5	0.9	1.3	1.9	1.3	1.4	2.3	2.0	1.1	1.6
Ireland	6.9	9.1	5.9	6.4	4.3	4.3	5.9	5.7	5.3	1.8	3.0	4.1	3.9	3.6	4.6
Luxembourg	4.7	8.4	2.5	4.1	2.1	4.9	5.0	6.1	5.4	3.1	3.2	3.5	4.3	2.9	3.7
Slovenia	. . .	4.1	3.1	3.7	2.8	4.4	4.1	5.7	6.1	4.1	3.5	4.3	4.6	3.4	5.4
Cyprus	3.7	5.0	4.0	2.1	1.9	4.2	3.9	4.0	4.4	3.4	3.5	4.0	4.3	3.2	3.7
Malta	5.0	−1.0	−1.6	2.6	−0.3	0.2	3.4	3.4	3.8	2.2	2.0	3.1	3.7	1.6	2.3
Japan	1.5	2.9	0.2	0.3	1.4	2.7	1.9	2.4	2.1	1.4	1.5	1.7	1.7	1.3	1.5
United Kingdom	2.1	3.8	2.4	2.1	2.8	3.3	1.8	2.9	3.1	1.6	1.6	2.7	2.9	0.9	2.3
Canada	2.4	5.2	1.8	2.9	1.9	3.1	3.1	2.8	2.7	1.3	1.9	2.6	2.9	0.9	2.8
Korea	6.1	8.5	3.8	7.0	3.1	4.7	4.2	5.1	5.0	4.2	4.4	4.6	5.9	2.6	5.9
Australia	3.3	3.4	2.1	4.1	3.0	3.8	2.8	2.8	3.9	3.2	3.1	3.5	3.9	3.4	2.8
Taiwan Province of China	6.5	5.8	−2.2	4.6	3.5	6.2	4.2	4.9	5.7	3.4	4.1	5.0	6.4	1.0	8.4
Sweden	1.7	4.4	1.1	2.4	1.9	4.1	3.3	4.1	2.6	2.0	1.7	2.4	2.6	1.3	2.2
Switzerland	1.1	3.6	1.2	0.4	−0.2	2.5	2.4	3.2	3.1	1.3	0.9	1.8	3.6	−0.4	2.2
Hong Kong SAR	3.5	8.0	0.5	1.8	3.0	8.5	7.1	7.0	6.3	4.3	4.8	5.0	6.8	2.6	8.1
Denmark	2.4	3.5	0.7	0.5	0.4	2.3	2.5	3.9	1.8	1.2	0.5	1.6	2.0	0.6	0.5
Norway	3.6	3.3	2.0	1.5	1.0	3.9	2.7	2.5	3.5	3.1	2.3	1.8	4.6	2.2	2.2
Israel	5.2	8.9	−0.4	−0.6	2.3	5.2	5.3	5.2	5.3	3.0	3.4	3.7	6.8	2.5	4.0
Singapore	7.5	10.1	−2.4	4.2	3.5	9.0	7.3	8.2	7.7	4.0	4.5	5.5	5.4	4.9	4.9
New Zealand	2.5	3.9	2.7	5.2	3.4	4.5	2.8	1.5	3.0	2.0	2.1	2.8	3.1	2.5	2.3
Iceland	2.3	4.3	3.9	0.1	2.4	7.7	7.5	4.4	3.8	0.4	0.1	3.2	12.7	0.5	−1.8
Memorandum															
Major advanced economies	2.5	3.6	1.0	1.2	1.8	3.0	2.3	2.7	2.2	0.9	0.9	2.6	2.1	0.1	1.6
Newly industrialized Asian economies	6.1	7.7	1.2	5.5	3.2	5.9	4.8	5.6	5.6	4.0	4.4	4.8	6.1	2.4	6.8
Real total domestic demand															
Advanced economies	**2.7**	**4.0**	**1.1**	**1.7**	**2.1**	**3.3**	**2.6**	**2.8**	**2.2**	**0.9**	**1.2**	**2.8**	. . .	. . .	. . .
United States	3.3	4.4	0.9	2.2	2.8	4.1	3.1	2.8	1.5	−0.6	0.1	3.1	1.6	−1.7	1.5
Euro area	. . .	3.4	1.2	0.4	1.5	1.9	1.8	2.6	2.0	1.4	1.2	2.4	1.9	1.1	1.4
Germany	2.3	2.2	−0.5	−2.0	0.6	−0.2	0.3	1.9	0.9	0.8	0.8	2.3	0.9	1.4	0.7
France	1.6	4.3	1.8	1.1	1.7	3.2	2.3	2.4	1.5	1.9	1.5	2.6	2.0	2.7	3.9
Italy	1.4	2.7	1.6	1.3	0.8	1.4	0.9	1.8	1.3	0.3	0.4	1.4	2.2	−1.1	1.2
Spain	2.7	5.3	3.8	3.2	3.8	4.8	5.1	4.9	4.3	1.7	1.6	3.7	3.7	0.6	2.5
Japan	1.4	2.4	1.0	−0.4	0.8	1.9	1.7	1.6	1.0	0.9	1.6	1.8	0.2	1.5	1.5
United Kingdom	2.1	3.9	2.9	3.1	2.8	3.8	1.6	2.8	3.7	1.3	1.0	2.7	3.4	0.1	2.1
Canada	1.8	4.8	1.2	3.2	4.6	4.3	5.1	4.4	4.3	4.0	2.3	2.5	6.5	1.8	2.8
Other advanced economies	4.1	5.5	0.3	3.9	1.4	4.8	3.3	3.7	4.5	3.4	3.4	3.9	. . .	. . .	. . .
Memorandum															
Major advanced economies	2.5	3.7	1.1	1.3	2.1	3.1	2.4	2.5	1.7	0.4	0.7	2.6	1.7	−0.3	1.7
Newly industrialized Asian economies	5.9	7.8	−0.1	4.5	0.1	5.0	2.6	4.0	4.5	4.0	4.3	4.8	5.4	2.9	6.5

[1]From fourth quarter of preceding year.

Table A3. Advanced Economies: Components of Real GDP
(Annual percent change)

	Ten-Year Averages		2000	2001	2002	2003	2004	2005	2006	2007	2008	2009
	1990–99	2000–09										
Private consumer expenditure												
Advanced economies	**2.8**	**2.3**	**3.8**	**2.3**	**2.2**	**1.9**	**2.8**	**2.5**	**2.6**	**2.6**	**1.2**	**1.4**
United States	3.3	2.7	4.7	2.5	2.7	2.8	3.6	3.2	3.1	2.9	0.4	0.9
Euro area	. . .	1.6	3.1	2.0	0.9	1.2	1.6	1.5	1.7	1.4	1.4	1.2
Germany	2.4	0.5	2.4	1.9	−0.8	0.1	0.2	−0.1	1.0	−0.4	0.7	0.3
France	1.6	2.2	3.6	2.6	2.4	2.0	2.5	2.2	2.0	2.0	1.7	1.4
Italy	1.6	1.0	2.4	0.7	0.2	1.0	0.7	0.9	1.1	1.4	0.9	0.8
Spain	2.5	3.4	5.0	3.4	2.8	2.9	4.2	4.2	3.8	3.2	2.0	2.2
Japan	1.9	1.3	0.7	1.6	1.1	0.4	1.6	1.3	2.0	1.4	0.7	1.7
United Kingdom	2.3	2.6	4.6	3.0	3.5	2.9	3.4	1.5	2.1	3.1	1.4	1.0
Canada	2.2	3.5	4.0	2.3	3.6	3.0	3.4	3.8	4.2	4.7	3.5	2.3
Other advanced economies	4.1	3.4	5.6	2.6	3.9	1.1	3.5	3.4	3.4	4.3	3.1	3.0
Memorandum												
Major advanced economies	2.6	2.1	3.5	2.2	2.0	2.0	2.7	2.3	2.5	2.3	0.8	1.1
Newly industrialized Asian economies	5.9	3.6	7.4	3.3	5.1	−0.3	2.4	3.4	3.8	4.3	3.3	3.5
Public consumption												
Advanced economies	**1.9**	**2.2**	**2.5**	**2.8**	**3.4**	**2.3**	**1.7**	**1.5**	**1.7**	**2.1**	**1.9**	**1.9**
United States	1.1	2.1	1.7	3.1	4.3	2.5	1.5	0.8	1.4	1.9	1.7	1.7
Euro area	. . .	1.9	2.3	2.0	2.4	1.8	1.4	1.5	2.0	2.2	1.9	1.9
Germany	2.0	0.9	1.4	0.5	1.5	0.4	−1.5	0.5	0.9	2.1	1.3	2.0
France	1.7	1.6	1.9	1.2	1.9	2.0	2.3	0.9	1.4	1.4	1.4	1.6
Italy	0.1	1.8	2.3	3.9	2.4	1.9	2.2	1.9	0.8	1.2	0.7	0.3
Spain	3.3	5.1	5.3	3.9	4.5	4.8	6.3	5.5	4.8	5.1	5.7	4.9
Japan	3.0	1.8	4.3	3.0	2.4	2.3	1.9	1.6	−0.4	0.8	1.1	0.9
United Kingdom	1.2	2.7	3.1	2.4	3.5	3.5	3.2	2.7	1.9	1.9	2.4	2.6
Canada	0.9	3.0	3.1	3.9	2.5	3.1	2.5	2.2	3.3	3.6	3.4	2.5
Other advanced economies	3.6	2.7	2.3	3.2	3.6	2.1	1.9	2.5	3.2	2.9	2.4	2.7
Memorandum												
Major advanced economies	1.5	1.9	2.3	2.7	3.2	2.3	1.5	1.2	1.2	1.8	1.6	1.6
Newly industrialized Asian economies	5.2	3.1	2.9	3.7	4.5	2.4	1.8	3.0	4.0	3.6	2.4	3.2
Gross fixed capital formation												
Advanced economies	**3.4**	**1.8**	**5.0**	**−0.8**	**−1.5**	**2.2**	**4.6**	**4.3**	**4.0**	**1.7**	**−0.7**	**−0.6**
United States	5.1	0.6	6.1	−1.7	−3.5	3.2	6.1	5.8	2.6	−2.0	−5.1	−4.6
Euro area	. . .	2.3	4.9	0.6	−1.5	1.4	2.3	2.9	5.0	4.4	1.8	1.0
Germany	2.7	0.8	3.0	−3.6	−6.1	−0.3	−0.2	1.0	6.1	5.0	2.6	0.9
France	1.4	2.9	7.2	2.4	−1.7	2.2	3.6	4.0	3.7	3.9	2.4	1.7
Italy	1.0	2.0	6.4	2.7	3.7	−1.2	2.3	0.7	2.5	1.2	0.9	0.8
Spain	3.3	4.2	6.6	4.8	3.4	5.9	5.1	6.9	6.8	5.9	−1.1	−1.8
Japan	—	0.3	1.2	−0.9	−4.9	−0.5	1.4	3.1	1.3	−0.3	1.1	2.0
United Kingdom	2.3	3.0	2.7	2.6	3.6	1.1	5.9	1.5	7.9	5.0	−0.6	0.2
Canada	1.9	4.9	4.7	4.0	1.6	6.2	7.7	8.5	7.2	4.1	2.9	2.3
Other advanced economies	4.9	4.1	6.8	−4.4	3.8	2.8	7.2	4.6	5.3	6.4	4.2	4.5
Memorandum												
Major advanced economies	3.2	1.2	4.8	−0.6	−2.6	1.9	4.4	4.3	3.4	0.4	−1.8	−1.6
Newly industrialized Asian economies	7.1	3.9	10.5	−5.9	2.2	2.3	7.8	2.0	4.0	5.3	5.2	6.5

Table A3 *(concluded)*

	Ten-Year Averages		2000	2001	2002	2003	2004	2005	2006	2007	2008	2009
	1990–99	2000–09										
Final domestic demand												
Advanced economies	**2.5**	**2.1**	**3.6**	**1.8**	**1.5**	**2.1**	**2.9**	**2.7**	**2.7**	**2.2**	**0.8**	**1.0**
United States	3.3	2.2	4.5	1.8	1.8	2.8	3.8	3.3	2.7	1.8	−0.4	0.1
Euro area	...	1.8	3.3	1.7	0.6	1.3	1.6	1.6	2.6	2.3	1.8	1.7
Germany	2.4	0.7	2.3	0.4	−1.5	0.1	−0.2	0.3	2.0	1.2	1.2	0.8
France	1.6	2.4	3.9	2.2	1.4	2.1	2.7	2.2	2.2	2.1	2.7	2.4
Italy	1.2	1.4	3.1	1.7	1.3	0.7	1.3	1.1	1.3	1.4	0.9	0.7
Spain	2.8	3.9	5.4	3.9	3.2	4.0	4.8	5.2	4.8	4.3	1.7	1.6
Japan	1.5	1.1	1.4	1.2	−0.2	0.5	1.6	1.9	1.4	0.9	0.9	1.6
United Kingdom	2.1	2.7	4.0	2.8	3.5	2.7	3.7	1.8	3.0	3.2	1.3	1.2
Canada	1.8	3.7	4.0	2.9	3.0	3.7	4.1	4.5	4.7	4.3	3.3	2.3
Other advanced economies	4.2	3.4	5.4	0.9	3.7	1.7	4.0	3.4	3.8	4.6	3.3	3.4
Memorandum												
Major advanced economies	2.5	2.0	3.6	1.7	1.3	2.0	2.8	2.5	2.4	1.8	0.6	0.8
Newly industrialized Asian economies	6.1	3.6	7.6	0.8	4.1	0.8	3.5	3.0	3.9	4.6	3.8	4.3
Stock building[1]												
Advanced economies	**—**	**—**	**0.1**	**−0.6**	**—**	**0.1**	**0.3**	**−0.1**	**0.1**	**−0.2**	**−0.1**	**—**
United States	0.1	−0.1	−0.1	−0.9	0.4	—	0.4	−0.2	0.1	−0.3	−0.2	—
Euro area	...	−0.1	—	−0.4	−0.3	0.2	0.3	0.2	—	−0.3	−0.4	−0.5
Germany	−0.1	−0.2	−0.1	−0.9	−0.6	0.5	—	0.1	−0.1	−0.3	−0.4	—
France	—	—	0.5	−0.4	−0.3	−0.3	0.6	—	0.2	−0.6	−0.1	—
Italy	—	—	−0.2	0.1	—	0.1	−0.1	−0.2	1.1	—	−0.6	−0.3
Spain	−0.1	—	−0.1	−0.1	—	−0.1	—	−0.1	0.1	—	—	—
Japan	−0.1	0.1	1.0	−0.2	−0.3	0.2	0.3	−0.1	0.2	0.1	—	—
United Kingdom	—	—	−0.1	0.1	−0.3	0.2	0.1	−0.1	−0.2	0.4	0.1	−0.2
Canada	—	0.1	0.8	−1.7	0.2	0.8	0.1	0.3	−0.2	—	0.6	—
Other advanced economies	—	—	0.1	−0.5	0.1	−0.2	0.7	−0.1	−0.1	—	0.2	—
Memorandum												
Major advanced economies	—	—	0.1	−0.6	0.1	0.1	0.3	−0.1	0.1	−0.2	−0.2	—
Newly industrialized Asian economies	−0.1	—	0.1	−0.8	0.3	−0.6	1.1	−0.4	0.1	−0.1	0.2	—
Foreign balance[1]												
Advanced economies	**—**	**—**	**−0.1**	**0.1**	**−0.2**	**−0.5**	**−0.3**	**−0.2**	**—**	**0.4**	**0.5**	**0.2**
United States	−0.2	−0.1	−0.9	−0.2	−0.7	−0.4	−0.7	−0.2	−0.1	0.6	1.2	0.4
Euro area	...	0.2	0.5	0.7	0.5	−0.6	0.2	−0.2	0.2	0.5	0.2	—
Germany	—	0.9	1.0	1.7	2.0	−0.8	1.3	0.5	1.1	1.7	0.7	0.3
France	0.3	−0.3	−0.5	0.1	−0.1	−0.7	−0.9	−0.7	−0.5	0.4	−0.2	−0.2
Italy	0.1	−0.1	0.8	0.2	−0.8	−0.8	0.2	−0.3	—	0.1	—	−0.2
Spain	−0.2	−0.7	−0.4	−0.2	−0.6	−0.8	−1.7	−1.6	−1.2	−0.7	—	—
Japan	0.1	0.5	0.5	−0.8	0.7	0.7	0.8	0.3	0.8	1.2	0.5	—
United Kingdom	—	−0.2	−0.1	−0.5	−1.1	−0.1	−0.6	—	—	−0.6	0.3	0.6
Canada	0.6	−1.0	0.6	0.7	−0.1	−2.5	−1.0	−1.7	−1.4	−1.6	−2.5	−0.3
Other advanced economies	0.3	0.6	0.7	0.9	0.2	1.2	0.6	0.9	1.0	0.6	—	0.3
Memorandum												
Major advanced economies	—	—	−0.2	—	−0.2	−0.4	−0.2	−0.2	0.1	0.6	0.6	0.2
Newly industrialized Asian economies	0.1	1.5	0.3	1.2	1.1	3.0	1.8	2.6	2.2	1.8	0.4	0.6

[1]Changes expressed as percent of GDP in the preceding period.

Table A4. Emerging and Developing Economies, by Country: Real GDP[1]

(Annual percent change)

	Average 1990–99	2000	2001	2002	2003	2004	2005	2006	2007	2008	2009	2013
Africa	**2.3**	**3.5**	**4.9**	**6.1**	**5.3**	**6.5**	**5.7**	**5.9**	**6.2**	**6.3**	**6.4**	**5.3**
Algeria	1.5	2.2	2.7	4.7	6.9	5.2	5.1	2.0	4.6	4.9	4.9	5.1
Angola	0.6	3.0	3.1	14.5	3.3	11.2	20.6	18.6	21.1	16.0	13.2	0.4
Benin	4.9	4.9	6.2	4.5	3.9	3.1	2.9	3.8	4.2	5.4	5.7	5.7
Botswana	6.0	8.3	4.9	5.7	6.0	6.3	4.7	3.6	5.4	5.0	4.3	5.0
Burkina Faso	5.1	1.8	6.6	4.7	8.0	4.6	7.1	5.5	4.2	4.0	6.3	5.8
Burundi	−1.3	−0.9	2.1	4.4	−1.2	4.8	0.9	5.1	3.6	5.9	5.7	6.1
Cameroon[2]	0.3	4.2	4.5	4.0	4.0	3.7	2.3	3.2	3.3	4.5	4.6	5.3
Cape Verde	6.1	7.3	6.1	5.3	4.7	4.4	5.7	10.8	6.9	7.7	7.4	6.7
Central African Republic	0.4	1.8	0.3	−0.6	−7.6	1.0	2.4	4.0	4.2	4.9	5.0	5.0
Chad	3.2	−0.9	11.7	8.5	14.7	33.6	7.9	0.2	0.6	1.8	2.5	1.9
Comoros	1.5	1.4	3.3	4.1	2.5	−0.2	4.2	1.2	−1.0	1.6	3.0	4.5
Congo, Dem. Rep. of	−5.6	−6.9	−2.1	3.5	5.8	6.6	7.9	5.6	6.3	8.8	11.6	6.3
Congo, Rep. of	0.8	7.6	3.8	4.6	0.8	3.5	7.8	6.2	−1.6	9.2	10.6	1.8
Côte d'Ivoire	3.5	−4.6	—	−1.6	−1.7	1.6	1.8	−0.3	1.6	2.9	5.1	6.0
Djibouti	−1.2	0.5	2.0	2.6	3.2	3.0	3.2	4.8	5.2	6.5	7.6	6.7
Equatorial Guinea	29.2	18.6	62.3	20.6	13.1	32.2	6.9	−5.6	12.4	10.1	4.9	6.6
Eritrea	...	−12.4	8.8	3.0	−2.7	1.5	2.6	−1.0	1.3	1.2	2.0	3.5
Ethiopia	2.6	5.9	7.7	1.2	−3.5	9.8	12.6	11.6	11.4	8.4	7.1	7.7
Gabon	2.4	−1.9	2.1	−0.3	2.4	1.1	3.0	1.2	5.6	4.2	3.8	2.7
Gambia, The	4.2	5.5	5.8	−3.2	6.9	7.0	5.1	6.5	7.0	6.5	6.5	5.5
Ghana	4.5	3.7	4.2	4.5	5.2	5.6	5.9	6.4	6.4	6.9	7.5	7.0
Guinea	4.2	2.9	3.8	4.2	1.2	2.7	3.3	2.2	1.5	4.9	5.2	5.2
Guinea-Bissau	0.6	7.5	0.2	−7.1	−0.6	2.2	3.2	1.8	2.5	3.2	3.1	3.9
Kenya	2.1	0.6	4.7	0.3	2.8	4.6	5.8	6.1	7.0	2.5	3.4	6.2
Lesotho	4.0	2.3	1.8	2.8	2.7	4.2	2.9	7.2	4.9	5.2	5.4	4.4
Liberia	...	29.3	2.9	3.7	−31.3	2.6	5.3	7.8	9.4	9.5	10.2	3.7
Madagascar	1.6	4.5	6.0	−12.4	10.8	5.3	4.4	5.0	6.3	6.8	7.3	7.3
Malawi	3.9	0.8	−4.1	1.9	4.2	5.0	2.3	7.9	7.4	7.1	6.2	5.5
Mali	5.5	−3.2	12.1	4.3	7.2	2.4	6.1	5.3	2.5	4.3	5.1	5.6
Mauritania	2.6	1.9	2.9	1.1	5.6	5.2	5.4	11.4	0.9	6.1	6.8	6.3
Mauritius	5.8	7.2	4.2	1.5	3.8	4.7	3.1	3.6	4.6	7.0	6.0	5.0
Morocco	2.6	1.8	7.6	3.3	6.1	5.2	2.4	8.0	2.2	6.5	5.7	5.9
Mozambique	6.4	1.5	12.3	9.2	6.5	7.9	8.4	8.0	7.0	7.0	7.0	6.5
Namibia	3.8	3.5	2.4	6.7	3.5	6.6	4.8	4.1	4.4	4.7	4.5	4.6
Niger	1.1	−2.6	7.4	5.3	7.7	−0.8	7.4	5.2	3.2	4.4	4.5	3.3
Nigeria	2.6	5.3	8.2	21.2	10.3	10.6	5.4	6.2	6.4	9.1	8.3	6.5
Rwanda	−0.5	6.0	3.9	11.0	0.3	5.3	7.1	5.5	6.0	6.0	5.6	5.7
São Tomé and Príncipe	1.2	0.4	3.1	11.6	5.4	6.6	5.7	6.7	6.0	6.0	6.0	8.0
Senegal	2.7	3.2	4.6	0.7	6.7	5.8	5.3	2.1	5.0	5.4	5.9	5.0
Seychelles	4.8	4.3	−2.3	1.2	−5.9	−2.9	1.2	5.3	5.3	4.6	4.2	3.6
Sierra Leone	−7.8	3.8	18.2	27.4	9.5	7.4	7.3	7.4	6.8	6.5	6.5	5.6
South Africa	1.4	4.2	2.7	3.7	3.1	4.9	5.0	5.4	5.1	3.8	3.9	4.8
Sudan	2.7	8.4	6.2	5.4	7.1	5.1	6.3	11.3	10.5	7.6	12.7	5.2
Swaziland	3.7	2.0	1.0	1.8	3.9	2.5	2.2	2.8	2.4	2.0	2.0	2.1
Tanzania	3.1	4.9	6.0	7.2	6.9	7.8	7.4	6.7	7.3	7.8	8.0	7.0
Togo	1.6	−1.3	−2.3	−0.3	5.2	2.4	1.3	4.1	2.1	3.0	4.0	4.0
Tunisia	5.0	4.7	5.0	1.7	5.6	6.0	4.0	5.5	6.3	5.5	5.9	6.4
Uganda	6.3	5.4	5.0	6.4	4.7	5.4	6.8	5.1	6.5	7.1	7.0	6.0
Zambia	−0.6	3.6	4.9	3.3	5.1	5.4	5.2	6.2	5.3	6.3	6.3	5.9
Zimbabwe[3]	2.0	−7.3	−2.7	−4.4	−10.4	−3.6	−4.0	−5.4	−6.1	−6.6	−6.8	...

Table A4 (continued)

	Average 1990–99	2000	2001	2002	2003	2004	2005	2006	2007	2008	2009	2013
Central and eastern Europe[4]	**1.2**	**4.9**	**0.4**	**4.2**	**4.8**	**6.9**	**6.1**	**6.6**	**5.8**	**4.4**	**4.3**	**5.0**
Albania	−0.5	7.3	7.0	4.2	5.8	5.7	5.5	5.0	6.0	6.0	6.1	6.3
Bosnia and Herzegovina	. . .	5.2	3.6	5.0	3.5	6.3	4.3	6.2	5.8	5.5	5.5	4.5
Bulgaria	−5.4	5.4	4.1	4.5	5.0	6.6	6.2	6.3	6.2	5.5	4.8	6.5
Croatia	. . .	2.9	4.4	5.6	5.3	4.3	4.3	4.8	5.8	4.3	4.0	4.8
Czech Republic	−0.3	3.6	2.5	1.9	3.6	4.5	6.4	6.4	6.5	4.2	4.6	4.0
Estonia	. . .	9.6	7.7	8.0	7.2	8.3	10.2	11.2	7.1	3.0	3.7	5.2
Hungary	0.1	5.2	4.1	4.4	4.2	4.8	4.1	3.9	1.3	1.8	2.5	4.3
Latvia	. . .	6.9	8.0	6.5	7.2	8.7	10.6	11.9	10.2	3.6	0.5	3.0
Lithuania	. . .	4.1	6.6	6.9	10.3	7.3	7.9	7.7	8.8	6.5	5.5	5.8
Macedonia, FYR	. . .	4.5	−4.5	0.9	2.8	4.1	4.1	3.7	5.0	4.5	5.0	6.0
Montenegro, Rep. of	. . .	. . .	. . .	. . .	2.3	4.2	4.1	6.5	7.5	7.2	5.4	4.5
Poland	2.6	4.3	1.2	1.4	3.9	5.3	3.6	6.2	6.5	4.9	4.5	4.9
Romania	−2.5	2.1	5.7	5.1	5.2	8.4	4.1	7.9	6.0	5.4	4.7	6.0
Serbia	. . .	4.5	4.8	4.2	2.5	8.4	6.2	5.7	7.3	4.0	6.0	5.5
Slovak Republic	. . .	1.4	3.4	4.8	4.8	5.2	6.6	8.5	10.4	6.6	5.6	4.8
Turkey	3.9	6.8	−5.7	6.2	5.3	9.4	8.4	6.9	5.0	4.0	4.3	5.0
Commonwealth of Independent States[4,5]	. . .	**9.1**	**6.1**	**5.2**	**7.8**	**8.2**	**6.5**	**8.2**	**8.5**	**7.0**	**6.5**	**5.7**
Russia	. . .	10.0	5.1	4.7	7.3	7.2	6.4	7.4	8.1	6.8	6.3	5.6
Excluding Russia	. . .	6.6	8.9	6.6	9.0	10.8	6.7	10.1	9.6	7.4	7.0	5.8
Armenia	. . .	6.0	9.6	13.2	14.0	10.5	14.0	13.3	13.8	10.0	8.0	4.0
Azerbaijan	. . .	6.2	6.5	8.1	10.5	10.4	24.3	30.5	23.4	18.6	15.6	−2.6
Belarus	. . .	5.8	4.7	5.0	7.0	11.4	4.0	10.0	8.2	7.1	6.8	4.8
Georgia	. . .	1.9	4.7	5.5	11.1	5.9	9.6	9.4	12.4	9.0	9.0	5.0
Kazakhstan	. . .	9.8	13.5	9.8	9.3	9.6	9.7	10.7	8.5	5.0	7.0	8.0
Kyrgyz Republic	. . .	5.4	5.3	−0.0	7.0	7.0	−0.2	3.1	8.2	7.0	6.5	4.5
Moldova	. . .	2.1	6.1	7.8	6.6	7.4	7.5	4.0	5.0	7.0	8.0	6.0
Mongolia	−0.4	3.9	1.9	1.8	5.4	13.3	7.6	8.6	9.9	8.7	8.1	6.0
Tajikistan	. . .	8.3	10.2	9.1	10.2	10.6	6.7	7.0	7.8	4.1	7.0	7.0
Turkmenistan	. . .	18.6	20.4	15.8	17.1	14.7	12.9	11.1	11.6	9.5	10.0	9.1
Ukraine	. . .	5.9	9.2	5.2	9.6	12.1	2.7	7.1	7.3	5.6	4.2	6.5
Uzbekistan	. . .	3.8	4.2	4.0	4.2	7.7	7.0	7.3	9.5	8.0	7.5	6.0

246

Table A4 *(continued)*

	Average 1990–99	2000	2001	2002	2003	2004	2005	2006	2007	2008	2009	2013
Developing Asia	**7.2**	**6.9**	**5.8**	**6.9**	**8.1**	**8.6**	**9.0**	**9.6**	**9.7**	**8.2**	**8.4**	**8.9**
Afghanistan, I.R. of	...	...	...	...	15.1	9.4	16.4	6.1	12.4	8.6	8.4	5.6
Bangladesh	4.8	5.6	4.8	4.8	5.8	6.1	6.3	6.4	5.6	5.5	6.5	7.0
Bhutan	5.6	7.6	7.2	10.0	7.6	6.8	6.9	11.0	22.4	7.8	6.7	6.8
Brunei Darussalam	...	2.9	2.7	3.9	2.9	0.5	0.4	5.1	0.4	−0.5	2.8	3.0
Cambodia	...	8.8	8.1	6.6	8.5	10.3	13.3	10.8	9.6	7.2	7.0	6.6
China	9.9	8.4	8.3	9.1	10.0	10.1	10.4	11.1	11.4	9.3	9.5	10.0
Fiji	5.8	−1.8	2.0	3.2	1.1	5.4	0.7	3.6	−4.4	2.0	2.8	2.9
India	5.6	5.4	3.9	4.6	6.9	7.9	9.1	9.7	9.2	7.9	8.0	8.0
Indonesia	4.1	5.4	3.6	4.5	4.8	5.0	5.7	5.5	6.3	6.1	6.3	6.7
Kiribati	4.3	3.9	3.2	8.1	−1.3	−1.5	1.7	2.4	2.0	3.7	2.5	1.1
Lao PDR	6.4	5.8	5.7	5.9	6.1	6.4	7.1	8.1	7.5	7.9	8.2	6.2
Malaysia	7.1	8.7	0.5	5.4	5.8	6.8	5.0	5.9	6.3	5.0	5.3	6.0
Maldives	6.5	4.8	3.5	6.5	8.5	9.5	−4.5	19.1	6.6	4.5	4.0	3.5
Myanmar	6.0	13.7	11.3	12.0	13.8	13.6	13.6	12.7	5.5	4.0	4.0	4.0
Nepal	4.9	6.1	5.6	0.1	3.9	4.7	3.1	2.8	2.5	4.0	4.5	5.5
Pakistan	4.0	4.3	2.0	3.2	4.8	7.4	7.7	6.9	6.4	6.0	6.7	7.2
Papua New Guinea	4.5	−2.5	−0.1	−0.2	2.2	2.7	3.4	2.6	6.2	5.8	4.7	2.6
Philippines	2.8	6.0	1.8	4.4	4.9	6.4	4.9	5.4	7.3	5.8	5.8	6.2
Samoa	2.0	5.0	8.1	5.5	2.1	2.4	6.0	1.8	6.0	4.5	4.0	3.5
Solomon Islands	4.3	−14.3	−9.0	−1.6	6.4	8.0	5.0	6.1	5.4	4.2	2.8	1.7
Sri Lanka	5.2	6.0	−1.5	4.0	6.0	5.4	6.0	7.4	6.3	6.4	5.6	5.5
Thailand	5.1	4.8	2.2	5.3	7.1	6.3	4.5	5.1	4.8	5.3	5.6	6.0
Timor-Leste	...	15.5	16.5	−6.7	−6.2	0.3	2.3	−3.4	19.8	2.5	0.6	3.8
Tonga	1.5	5.4	2.6	3.0	3.2	1.4	2.3	1.3	−3.5	0.8	1.3	1.2
Vanuatu	3.6	2.7	−2.5	−7.4	3.2	5.5	6.5	7.2	5.0	4.0	3.5	2.5
Vietnam	7.4	6.8	6.9	7.1	7.3	7.8	8.4	8.2	8.5	7.3	7.3	8.0
Middle East	**4.3**	**5.4**	**3.0**	**3.9**	**6.9**	**5.9**	**5.7**	**5.8**	**5.8**	**6.1**	**6.1**	**6.0**
Bahrain	4.8	5.2	15.1	5.2	7.2	5.6	7.9	6.5	6.6	6.2	6.6	6.3
Egypt	4.1	5.4	3.5	3.2	3.2	4.1	4.5	6.8	7.1	7.0	7.1	7.8
Iran, I.R. of	5.1	5.1	3.7	7.5	7.2	5.1	4.7	5.8	5.8	5.8	4.7	4.7
Iraq	...	...	...	...	...	...	...	...	...	...	...	...
Jordan	4.2	4.3	5.3	5.8	4.2	8.6	7.1	6.3	5.7	5.5	5.8	6.0
Kuwait	0.1	4.7	0.2	3.0	17.3	10.7	11.4	6.3	4.6	6.0	6.2	6.0
Lebanon	5.4	1.7	4.5	3.3	4.1	7.5	1.1	—	4.0	3.0	4.5	5.0
Libya	−0.9	3.4	5.9	1.4	5.9	5.0	6.3	5.2	6.8	8.8	9.8	7.4
Oman	4.9	5.5	7.5	2.6	2.0	5.3	6.0	6.8	6.4	7.4	6.0	5.6
Qatar	4.2	10.9	6.3	3.2	6.3	17.7	9.2	10.3	14.2	14.1	13.1	7.9
Saudi Arabia	3.1	4.9	0.5	0.1	7.7	5.3	6.1	4.3	4.1	4.8	5.6	5.8
Syrian Arab Republic	5.6	2.3	3.7	5.9	1.1	2.8	3.3	4.4	3.9	4.0	4.8	4.2
United Arab Emirates	5.4	12.4	1.7	2.6	11.9	9.7	8.2	9.4	7.4	6.3	6.4	7.7
Yemen, Rep. of	...	6.2	3.8	3.9	3.7	4.0	5.6	3.2	3.1	4.1	8.1	4.8

Table A4 (concluded)

	Average 1990–99	2000	2001	2002	2003	2004	2005	2006	2007	2008	2009	2013
Western Hemisphere	**2.9**	**4.1**	**0.7**	**0.4**	**2.1**	**6.2**	**4.6**	**5.5**	**5.6**	**4.4**	**3.6**	**4.0**
Antigua and Barbuda	3.3	3.3	1.5	2.0	4.3	5.2	5.5	12.2	6.1	2.1	4.0	4.5
Argentina	4.2	−0.8	−4.4	−10.9	8.8	9.0	9.2	8.5	8.7	7.0	4.5	3.0
Bahamas, The	1.8	1.9	0.8	2.3	1.4	1.8	2.5	3.4	3.1	4.0	3.8	3.8
Barbados	0.4	2.3	−2.6	0.6	2.0	4.8	4.1	3.9	4.2	2.7	2.5	2.5
Belize	5.8	13.0	5.0	5.1	9.3	4.6	3.1	5.6	2.2	3.0	2.3	2.5
Bolivia	4.0	2.5	1.7	2.5	2.7	4.2	4.0	4.6	4.2	4.7	5.0	5.0
Brazil	1.7	4.3	1.3	2.7	1.1	5.7	3.2	3.8	5.4	4.8	3.7	4.0
Chile	6.4	4.5	3.5	2.2	4.0	6.0	5.7	4.0	5.0	4.5	4.5	5.0
Colombia	2.9	2.9	1.5	1.9	3.9	4.9	4.7	6.8	7.0	4.6	4.5	5.0
Costa Rica	5.4	1.8	1.1	2.9	6.4	4.3	5.9	8.8	6.8	4.1	4.0	5.5
Dominica	2.6	1.3	−4.2	−5.1	0.1	3.0	3.3	4.0	0.9	3.5	3.0	3.0
Dominican Republic	4.5	8.1	3.6	4.4	−1.9	2.0	9.3	10.7	8.5	4.8	3.3	5.0
Ecuador	2.2	2.8	5.3	4.2	3.6	8.0	6.0	3.9	1.9	2.9	4.1	4.4
El Salvador	4.9	2.2	1.7	2.3	2.3	1.9	3.1	4.2	4.7	3.0	3.4	4.5
Grenada	4.3	7.0	−3.0	1.6	7.1	−5.7	11.0	−2.4	3.1	4.3	4.0	4.0
Guatemala	3.7	2.5	2.4	3.9	2.5	3.2	3.3	5.2	5.7	4.8	4.5	4.5
Guyana	4.7	−1.3	2.3	1.1	−0.7	1.6	−1.9	5.1	5.4	4.6	4.5	3.6
Haiti	0.2	0.9	−1.0	−0.3	0.4	−3.5	1.8	2.3	3.2	3.7	4.0	4.0
Honduras	2.7	5.7	2.7	3.8	4.5	6.2	6.1	6.3	6.3	4.8	4.6	4.2
Jamaica	0.9	0.7	1.5	1.1	2.3	1.0	1.4	2.5	1.4	2.4	2.8	3.4
Mexico	3.3	6.6	—	0.8	1.4	4.2	2.8	4.8	3.3	2.0	2.3	3.8
Nicaragua	3.1	4.1	3.0	0.8	2.5	5.3	4.4	3.9	3.7	4.0	4.2	5.0
Panama	6.1	2.7	0.6	2.2	4.2	7.5	7.2	8.7	11.2	7.7	7.2	6.5
Paraguay	2.4	−3.3	2.1	—	3.8	4.1	2.9	4.3	6.4	4.0	4.5	5.0
Peru	3.1	3.0	0.2	5.0	4.0	5.1	6.7	7.6	9.0	7.0	6.0	5.5
St. Kitts and Nevis	4.0	4.3	2.0	1.0	0.5	7.6	4.8	6.4	3.3	3.5	2.7	2.0
St. Lucia	3.1	0.1	−3.7	0.8	3.1	4.5	3.8	5.0	3.2	4.4	4.4	4.9
St. Vincent and the Grenadines	3.5	2.0	−0.1	3.2	2.8	6.8	2.6	6.9	6.6	5.0	4.9	4.3
Suriname	0.5	−0.1	6.8	2.6	6.0	8.2	4.5	4.8	5.5	6.8	5.5	4.7
Trinidad and Tobago	3.9	6.9	4.2	7.9	14.4	8.8	8.0	12.0	5.5	5.9	5.6	4.0
Uruguay	3.2	−1.4	−3.4	−11.0	2.2	11.8	6.6	7.0	7.0	6.0	4.0	3.2
Venezuela	2.4	3.7	3.4	−8.9	−7.8	18.3	10.3	10.3	8.4	5.8	3.5	2.2

[1]For many countries, figures for recent years are IMF staff estimates. Data for some countries are for fiscal years.

[2]The percent changes in 2002 are calculated over a period of 18 months, reflecting a change in the fiscal year cycle (from July–June to January–December).

[3]Extrapolating existing trends would indicate a further decline of at least this magnitude.

[4]Data for some countries refer to real net material product (NMP) or are estimates based on NMP. For many countries, figures for recent years are IMF staff estimates. The figures should be interpreted only as indicative of broad orders of magnitude because reliable, comparable data are not generally available. In particular, the growth of output of new private enterprises of the informal economy is not fully reflected in the recent figures.

[5]Mongolia, which is not a member of the Commonwealth of Independent States, is included in this group for reasons of geography and similarities in economic structure.

Table A5. Summary of Inflation

(Percent)

	Average 1990–99	2000	2001	2002	2003	2004	2005	2006	2007	2008	2009	2013
GDP deflators												
Advanced economies	**2.6**	**1.5**	**1.9**	**1.6**	**1.7**	**2.0**	**2.1**	**2.1**	**2.1**	**1.8**	**1.8**	**1.7**
United States	2.2	2.2	2.4	1.7	2.1	2.9	3.2	3.2	2.7	2.0	1.8	1.8
Euro area	...	1.5	2.4	2.6	2.2	1.9	1.9	1.9	2.2	2.2	1.7	1.9
Japan	0.5	−1.7	−1.2	−1.5	−1.6	−1.1	−1.2	−1.0	−0.8	−0.7	1.0	1.3
Other advanced economies[1]	3.3	2.1	2.0	1.7	2.1	2.2	2.0	1.9	2.3	2.2	2.6	1.7
Consumer prices												
Advanced economies	**3.0**	**2.2**	**2.1**	**1.5**	**1.8**	**2.0**	**2.3**	**2.4**	**2.2**	**2.6**	**2.0**	**2.1**
United States	3.0	3.4	2.8	1.6	2.3	2.7	3.4	3.2	2.9	3.0	2.0	2.2
Euro area[2]	...	2.2	2.4	2.3	2.1	2.1	2.2	2.2	2.1	2.8	1.9	1.9
Japan	1.2	−0.7	−0.7	−0.9	−0.3	—	−0.3	0.3	—	0.6	1.3	1.5
Other advanced economies	3.5	1.8	2.1	1.7	1.8	1.7	2.1	2.1	2.1	2.6	2.4	2.2
Emerging and developing economies	**51.4**	**8.5**	**7.6**	**6.7**	**6.6**	**5.9**	**5.7**	**5.4**	**6.4**	**7.4**	**5.7**	**4.5**
Regional groups												
Africa	24.9	11.7	11.0	9.1	8.6	6.3	7.1	6.4	6.3	7.5	5.9	4.5
Central and eastern Europe	60.1	24.9	21.5	16.4	10.1	6.3	5.1	5.4	5.6	6.4	4.3	3.1
Commonwealth of Independent States[3]	...	24.1	20.3	14.0	12.3	10.4	12.1	9.5	9.7	13.1	9.5	5.9
Developing Asia	8.6	1.9	2.7	2.0	2.5	4.1	3.8	4.1	5.3	5.9	4.1	3.6
Middle East	10.9	4.1	3.8	5.3	6.1	7.0	6.2	7.0	10.4	11.5	10.0	7.1
Western Hemisphere	98.4	8.3	6.5	8.7	10.5	6.6	6.3	5.3	5.4	6.6	6.1	6.2
Memorandum												
European Union	10.0	3.1	3.0	2.5	2.2	2.3	2.3	2.3	2.4	3.1	2.2	2.0
Analytical groups												
By source of export earnings												
Fuel	76.0	14.4	13.4	11.8	11.5	9.7	9.6	8.5	9.7	12.1	10.1	7.7
Nonfuel	45.2	7.1	6.3	5.5	5.4	5.0	4.8	4.6	5.5	6.3	4.6	3.8
of which, primary products	55.0	17.8	15.4	8.4	6.7	4.0	7.2	7.4	6.5	7.9	5.7	4.5
By external financing source												
Net debtor countries	52.2	9.4	8.3	8.0	7.2	5.4	5.9	6.0	5.9	6.4	5.0	4.0
of which, official financing	17.5	3.8	4.1	4.8	6.1	7.2	7.8	7.3	9.1	11.1	8.1	5.3
Net debtor countries by debt-servicing experience												
Countries with arrears and/or rescheduling during 2002–06	28.5	7.3	8.0	10.5	7.3	5.9	8.6	9.6	6.8	7.5	6.4	4.5
Memorandum												
Median inflation rate												
Advanced economies	2.8	2.7	2.5	2.3	2.1	1.9	2.1	2.2	2.1	2.9	2.1	2.0
Emerging and developing economies	10.1	4.0	4.7	3.3	4.2	4.5	5.7	5.6	6.3	7.0	5.4	4.0

[1]In this table, other advanced economies means advanced economies excluding the United States, euro area countries, and Japan.

[2]Based on Eurostat's harmonized index of consumer prices.

[3]Mongolia, which is not a member of the Commonwealth of Independent States, is included in this group for reasons of geography and similarities in economic structure.

Table A6. Advanced Economies: Consumer Prices
(Annual percent change)

	Average 1990–99	2000	2001	2002	2003	2004	2005	2006	2007	2008	2009	2013	End of Period 2007	End of Period 2008	End of Period 2009
Consumer Prices															
Advanced economies	**3.0**	**2.2**	**2.1**	**1.5**	**1.8**	**2.0**	**2.3**	**2.4**	**2.2**	**2.6**	**2.0**	**2.1**	**2.9**	**2.2**	**2.0**
United States	3.0	3.4	2.8	1.6	2.3	2.7	3.4	3.2	2.9	3.0	2.0	2.2	4.1	2.0	2.1
Euro area[1]	...	2.2	2.4	2.3	2.1	2.1	2.2	2.2	2.1	2.8	1.9	1.9	3.1	2.2	1.7
Germany	2.4	1.4	1.9	1.4	1.0	1.8	1.9	1.8	2.3	2.5	1.6	1.8	−0.2	4.8	1.9
France	1.9	1.8	1.8	1.9	2.2	2.3	1.9	1.9	1.6	2.5	1.7	1.7	2.8	2.5	1.7
Italy	4.1	2.6	2.3	2.6	2.8	2.3	2.2	2.2	2.0	2.5	1.9	2.0	2.6	2.5	1.9
Spain	4.3	3.5	2.8	3.6	3.1	3.1	3.4	3.6	2.8	4.0	3.0	2.2	4.3	3.4	2.6
Netherlands	2.3	2.3	5.1	3.8	2.2	1.4	1.5	1.7	1.6	2.4	1.8	2.0	1.6	2.4	1.8
Belgium	2.0	2.7	2.4	1.6	1.5	1.9	2.5	2.3	1.8	3.1	1.9	1.8	3.1	2.5	1.6
Austria	2.1	2.0	2.3	1.7	1.3	2.0	2.1	1.7	2.2	2.8	1.9	1.7	3.5	2.1	1.9
Finland	2.1	3.0	2.7	2.0	1.3	0.1	0.8	1.3	1.6	2.8	1.9	2.0	1.9	2.4	2.3
Greece	10.8	2.9	3.7	3.9	3.4	3.0	3.5	3.3	3.0	3.5	2.7	2.5	3.9	3.0	2.7
Portugal	5.7	2.8	4.4	3.7	3.3	2.5	2.1	3.0	2.4	2.4	2.0	2.1	2.4	2.4	2.0
Ireland	2.4	5.3	4.0	4.7	4.0	2.3	2.2	2.7	3.0	3.2	2.1	2.0	3.5	2.6	2.0
Luxembourg	2.2	3.2	2.7	2.1	2.0	2.2	2.5	2.7	2.3	2.9	2.1	2.0	3.4	2.2	2.0
Slovenia	...	8.8	8.4	7.5	5.6	3.6	2.5	2.5	3.6	4.0	2.4	2.4	5.6	2.5	2.4
Cyprus	3.7	4.9	2.0	2.8	4.0	1.9	2.0	2.2	2.2	4.0	2.9	2.0	3.7	3.3	2.5
Malta	3.1	3.0	2.5	2.6	1.9	2.7	2.5	2.6	0.7	3.4	2.5	2.0	3.1	3.4	2.5
Japan	1.2	−0.7	−0.7	−0.9	−0.3	—	−0.3	0.3	—	0.6	1.3	1.5	0.7	0.6	1.3
United Kingdom[1]	3.3	0.9	1.2	1.3	1.4	1.3	2.0	2.3	2.3	2.5	2.1	2.0	2.0	2.2	2.1
Canada	2.2	2.7	2.5	2.3	2.7	1.8	2.2	2.0	2.1	1.6	2.0	2.0	2.5	1.8	2.0
Korea	5.7	2.3	4.1	2.8	3.5	3.6	2.8	2.2	2.5	3.4	2.9	2.5	3.6	3.0	2.9
Australia	2.5	4.5	4.4	3.0	2.8	2.3	2.7	3.5	2.3	3.5	3.3	2.8	3.0	3.4	3.2
Taiwan Province of China	2.9	1.3	—	−0.2	−0.3	1.6	2.3	0.6	1.8	1.5	1.5	1.5	3.4	0.6	1.5
Sweden	3.6	1.3	2.7	1.9	2.3	1.0	0.8	1.5	1.7	2.8	2.1	2.0	2.5	2.4	2.0
Switzerland	2.3	1.6	1.0	0.6	0.6	0.8	1.2	1.0	0.9	2.0	1.4	1.0	2.7	1.2	1.4
Hong Kong SAR	6.8	−3.7	−1.6	−3.0	−2.6	−0.4	0.9	2.0	2.0	3.6	4.5	5.4	3.8	3.4	4.5
Denmark	2.1	2.9	2.4	2.4	2.1	1.2	1.8	1.9	1.7	2.3	2.0	1.9	2.3	2.0	1.9
Norway	2.4	3.1	3.0	1.3	2.5	0.4	1.6	2.3	0.8	3.1	2.6	2.5	2.8	1.3	2.4
Israel	11.2	1.1	1.1	5.7	0.7	−0.4	1.3	2.1	0.5	2.6	2.0	2.0	3.4	2.0	2.0
Singapore	1.9	1.3	1.0	−0.4	0.5	1.7	0.5	1.0	2.1	4.7	2.5	1.7	3.9	2.8	2.9
New Zealand	2.1	2.6	2.6	2.6	1.7	2.3	3.0	3.4	2.4	3.4	2.7	2.0	3.2	3.1	2.5
Iceland	4.1	5.1	6.6	4.8	2.1	3.2	4.0	6.8	5.0	5.5	2.7	2.5	5.9	3.2	2.5
Memorandum															
Major advanced economies	2.6	2.1	1.9	1.3	1.7	2.0	2.3	2.4	2.2	2.4	1.8	2.0	2.7	2.1	1.9
Newly industrialized Asian economies	4.7	1.2	1.9	1.0	1.4	2.4	2.2	1.6	2.2	3.0	2.7	2.5	3.6	2.3	2.7

[1]Based on Eurostat's harmonized index of consumer prices.

Table A7. Emerging and Developing Economies, by Country: Consumer Prices[1]

(Annual percent change)

	Average 1990–99	2000	2001	2002	2003	2004	2005	2006	2007	2008	2009	2013	End of Period 2007	2008	2009
Africa	**24.9**	**11.7**	**11.0**	**9.1**	**8.6**	**6.3**	**7.1**	**6.4**	**6.3**	**7.5**	**5.9**	**4.5**	**7.1**	**6.7**	**5.5**
Algeria	17.3	0.3	4.2	1.4	2.6	3.6	1.6	2.5	3.7	4.3	4.1	2.9	4.4	4.2	3.9
Angola	463.0	325.0	152.6	108.9	98.3	43.6	23.0	13.3	12.2	11.4	8.9	4.5	11.8	10.0	8.0
Benin	7.2	4.2	4.0	2.4	1.5	0.9	5.4	3.8	2.0	2.4	2.6	2.9	2.1	2.7	2.7
Botswana	10.9	8.5	6.6	8.0	9.2	7.0	8.6	11.6	7.1	8.0	6.8	5.1	8.1	7.5	6.3
Burkina Faso	4.3	−0.3	4.7	2.3	2.0	−0.4	6.4	2.4	−0.2	6.4	2.5	2.0	2.3	3.3	2.2
Burundi	13.5	24.3	9.3	−1.3	10.7	8.0	13.4	2.8	8.4	11.8	8.2	4.0	14.4	7.8	5.7
Cameroon[2]	4.9	0.8	2.8	6.3	0.6	0.3	2.0	5.1	0.9	3.0	2.3	2.0	3.5	2.5	0.4
Cape Verde	7.3	−2.4	3.7	1.9	1.2	−1.9	0.4	5.4	4.4	3.3	2.2	2.3	3.8	2.0	2.3
Central African Republic	3.5	3.2	3.8	2.3	4.4	−2.2	2.9	6.7	0.9	2.7	4.1	2.5	−0.2	5.1	3.1
Chad	4.1	3.8	12.4	5.2	−1.8	−5.4	7.9	7.9	−8.8	3.0	3.0	3.0	0.8	2.9	3.0
Comoros	2.5	5.9	5.6	3.6	3.7	4.5	3.0	3.4	3.0	3.0	3.0	3.0	3.0	3.0	3.0
Congo, Dem. Rep. of	848.4	550.0	357.3	25.3	12.8	4.0	21.4	13.2	16.7	10.1	11.4	10.0	10.0	12.1	11.5
Congo, Rep. of	7.3	0.4	0.8	3.1	1.5	3.8	2.5	4.7	2.6	3.0	3.5	3.0	−1.7	4.0	3.0
Côte d'Ivoire	6.0	−0.4	4.2	5.1	1.3	0.6	4.2	5.0	2.1	4.7	3.2	1.6	1.9	3.8	2.6
Djibouti	4.2	1.6	1.8	0.6	2.0	3.1	3.1	3.5	5.0	6.1	4.5	3.0	5.0	6.1	4.5
Equatorial Guinea	6.1	4.8	8.8	7.6	7.3	4.2	5.7	4.5	4.6	5.5	4.7	4.1	5.9	4.9	4.8
Eritrea	...	19.9	14.6	16.9	22.7	25.1	12.5	15.1	9.3	11.0	10.5	8.5	12.3	11.0	10.0
Ethiopia	7.1	6.2	−5.2	−7.2	15.1	8.6	6.8	12.3	17.0	20.1	12.9	7.8	15.7	18.6	15.0
Gabon	4.9	0.5	2.1	0.2	2.1	0.4	1.2	−1.4	5.0	4.0	3.0	2.5	5.9	3.5	2.5
Gambia, The	5.4	0.9	4.5	8.6	17.0	14.3	5.0	2.1	5.0	5.0	5.0	4.0	5.0	5.0	5.0
Ghana	26.8	25.2	32.9	14.8	26.7	12.6	15.1	10.9	9.6	8.9	7.9	3.0	12.7	8.7	7.1
Guinea	8.5	6.8	5.4	3.0	12.9	17.5	31.4	34.7	22.9	13.2	7.3	5.0	12.8	10.0	7.0
Guinea-Bissau	35.6	8.6	3.3	3.3	−3.5	0.8	3.4	2.0	3.8	3.3	2.5	3.0	4.3	2.4	2.5
Kenya	16.0	10.0	5.8	2.0	9.8	11.6	10.3	14.5	9.8	12.3	7.0	5.0	12.0	7.9	8.4
Lesotho	11.1	6.1	6.9	12.5	7.3	5.0	3.4	6.1	8.0	9.6	6.9	5.0	10.5	9.3	6.2
Liberia	...	5.3	12.1	14.2	10.3	3.6	6.9	7.2	11.2	9.0	8.0	5.0	9.5	8.5	7.5
Madagascar	16.4	10.7	6.9	16.2	−1.1	14.0	18.4	10.8	10.3	9.0	6.6	5.0	8.2	7.8	5.0
Malawi	29.0	29.6	27.2	17.3	9.6	11.4	15.5	13.9	8.1	6.9	6.3	6.0	7.5	6.5	6.2
Mali	3.8	−0.7	5.2	5.0	−1.3	−3.1	6.4	1.9	2.5	2.5	2.5	2.5	2.5	2.5	2.5
Mauritania	5.0	6.8	7.7	5.4	5.3	10.4	12.1	6.2	7.3	7.1	6.0	5.0	7.4	6.0	6.0
Mauritius	8.2	4.2	5.4	6.5	3.9	4.7	4.9	5.6	10.7	9.5	8.2	5.0	10.0	9.0	7.5
Morocco	4.4	1.9	0.6	2.8	1.2	1.5	1.0	3.3	2.0	2.0	2.0	2.0	2.0	2.0	2.0
Mozambique	31.8	12.7	9.1	16.8	13.5	12.6	6.4	13.2	7.9	5.7	5.4	5.0	5.5	5.3	5.0
Namibia	10.2	9.3	9.3	11.3	7.2	4.1	2.3	5.1	6.7	7.5	6.5	5.5	7.1	7.0	6.5
Niger	4.5	2.9	4.0	2.7	−1.8	0.4	7.8	0.1	0.1	4.5	2.0	2.0	4.7	1.0	2.0
Nigeria	28.5	6.9	18.0	13.7	14.0	15.0	17.8	8.3	5.5	8.6	8.5	8.5	6.6	8.5	8.5
Rwanda	16.3	3.9	3.4	2.0	7.4	12.0	9.2	8.8	9.4	7.1	5.0	5.0	7.5	7.3	5.0
São Tomé and Príncipe	39.2	11.0	9.2	10.1	9.8	13.3	17.2	23.1	19.9	14.1	8.2	4.0	19.6	9.5	7.0
Senegal	4.1	0.7	3.0	2.3	—	0.5	1.7	2.1	5.9	4.5	2.2	1.8	6.2	2.9	2.1
Seychelles	2.0	6.3	6.0	0.2	3.3	3.9	0.8	−1.4	5.7	23.3	7.6	3.0	16.8	15.6	7.2
Sierra Leone	42.6	−0.9	2.6	−3.7	7.5	14.2	12.1	9.5	11.7	12.4	9.8	5.0	13.8	11.0	8.5
South Africa	9.8	5.4	5.7	9.2	5.8	1.4	3.4	4.7	7.1	8.7	5.9	4.5	9.0	7.8	5.2
Sudan	75.2	8.0	4.9	8.3	7.7	8.4	8.5	7.2	8.0	8.0	6.0	4.0	8.8	7.0	5.0
Swaziland	9.5	7.2	7.5	11.7	7.4	3.4	4.8	5.3	8.2	9.8	7.0	5.5	9.8	8.4	6.5
Tanzania	21.3	6.2	5.1	4.6	4.4	4.1	4.4	7.3	7.0	7.1	5.2	5.0	6.4	5.5	5.0
Togo	6.0	1.9	3.9	3.1	−0.9	0.4	6.8	2.2	1.0	4.1	3.8	3.2	3.4	2.3	4.2
Tunisia	4.8	2.3	2.0	2.7	2.7	3.6	2.0	4.5	3.1	4.7	3.5	2.7	5.3	3.0	3.5
Uganda	16.3	5.8	4.5	−2.0	5.7	5.0	8.0	6.6	6.8	5.9	5.0	4.7	4.4	6.5	3.7
Zambia	68.3	26.1	21.7	22.2	21.4	18.0	18.3	9.0	10.7	6.6	5.9	2.7	8.9	7.0	5.0
Zimbabwe[3]	28.1	55.6	73.4	133.2	365.0	350.0	237.8	1,016.7	10,452.6	...	...	...	108,844.1	...	...

Table A7 (continued)

	Average 1990–99	2000	2001	2002	2003	2004	2005	2006	2007	2008	2009	2013	End of Period 2007	End of Period 2008	End of Period 2009
Central and eastern Europe[4]	**60.1**	**24.9**	**21.5**	**16.4**	**10.1**	**6.3**	**5.1**	**5.4**	**5.6**	**6.4**	**4.3**	**3.1**	**6.7**	**5.3**	**3.9**
Albania	34.7	—	3.1	5.2	2.3	2.9	2.4	2.4	2.9	4.2	2.9	2.8	3.1	3.8	3.0
Bosnia and Herzegovina	...	5.0	3.2	0.3	0.5	0.3	3.6	7.5	1.3	4.8	2.7	2.5	...	...	...
Bulgaria	110.3	10.3	7.4	5.8	2.3	6.1	6.0	7.4	7.6	9.7	6.0	3.5	11.6	7.2	5.0
Croatia	...	4.6	3.8	1.7	1.8	2.0	3.3	3.2	2.9	5.5	3.5	3.0	5.8	3.8	3.5
Czech Republic	13.9	3.8	4.7	1.8	0.1	2.8	1.8	2.5	2.8	6.0	3.5	2.0	5.4	5.5	3.5
Estonia	...	4.0	5.8	3.6	1.3	3.0	4.1	4.4	6.6	9.8	4.7	2.9	9.6	7.1	3.6
Hungary	22.0	9.8	9.2	5.3	4.6	6.8	3.6	3.9	7.9	5.9	3.5	3.0	7.4	4.7	3.0
Latvia	...	2.6	2.5	1.9	2.9	6.2	6.7	6.5	10.1	15.3	9.2	3.1	14.1	11.8	7.9
Lithuania	...	1.1	1.6	0.3	−1.1	1.2	2.7	3.8	5.8	8.3	6.1	2.7	8.2	7.0	4.5
Macedonia, FYR	...	6.4	5.5	2.2	1.2	−0.4	0.5	3.2	2.2	7.0	2.5	2.5	6.1	3.0	2.5
Montenegro, Rep. of	...	...	...	...	...	3.1	3.4	2.1	3.4	4.8	4.1	3.0	...	...	...
Poland	51.4	10.1	5.5	1.9	0.8	3.5	2.1	1.0	2.5	4.1	3.8	2.5	4.0	3.9	3.7
Romania	110.3	45.7	34.5	22.5	15.3	11.9	9.0	6.6	4.8	7.0	5.1	2.7	6.6	6.3	4.0
Serbia	...	70.0	91.8	19.5	11.7	10.1	17.3	12.7	6.8	11.3	8.9	5.7	10.1	10.5	8.0
Slovak Republic	...	12.0	7.1	3.3	8.5	7.5	2.8	4.4	2.8	3.6	3.8	2.5	3.4	3.3	3.6
Turkey	76.1	55.0	54.2	45.1	25.3	8.6	8.2	9.6	8.8	7.5	4.5	4.0	8.4	6.0	4.0
Commonwealth of Independent States[4,5]	**...**	**24.1**	**20.3**	**14.0**	**12.3**	**10.4**	**12.1**	**9.5**	**9.7**	**13.1**	**9.5**	**5.9**	**13.0**	**11.1**	**8.1**
Russia	...	20.8	21.5	15.8	13.7	10.9	12.7	9.7	9.0	11.4	8.4	5.2	11.9	10.0	7.0
Excluding Russia	...	34.1	17.1	9.2	8.6	9.1	10.6	8.8	11.6	17.3	12.4	7.6	15.8	13.9	10.9
Armenia	...	−0.8	3.1	1.1	4.7	7.0	0.6	2.9	4.4	6.8	4.5	5.0	6.6	5.0	5.0
Azerbaijan	...	1.8	1.5	2.8	2.2	6.7	9.7	8.4	16.6	19.6	20.5	19.0	19.5	22.0	19.0
Belarus	...	168.6	61.1	42.6	28.4	18.1	10.3	7.0	8.4	11.2	8.8	5.2	12.1	10.2	7.3
Georgia	...	4.0	4.7	5.6	4.8	5.7	8.3	9.2	9.2	9.6	6.4	5.0	11.0	8.0	5.0
Kazakhstan	...	13.3	8.4	5.9	6.4	6.9	7.6	8.6	10.8	17.1	8.3	6.0	18.8	10.0	7.0
Kyrgyz Republic	...	18.7	6.9	2.1	3.1	4.1	4.3	5.6	10.2	18.8	10.2	5.0	20.1	15.0	7.0
Moldova	...	31.3	9.8	5.3	11.7	12.5	11.9	12.7	12.6	11.4	7.9	4.5	13.4	9.0	7.0
Mongolia	...	11.6	6.2	0.9	5.1	7.9	12.5	5.1	9.0	10.6	5.8	5.2	15.1	6.0	5.5
Tajikistan	...	32.9	38.6	12.2	16.4	7.2	7.3	10.0	13.2	18.5	10.5	6.0	19.8	15.0	9.0
Turkmenistan	...	8.0	11.6	8.8	5.6	5.9	10.7	8.2	6.4	12.0	12.0	6.0	10.0	12.0	12.0
Ukraine	...	28.2	12.0	0.8	5.2	9.0	13.4	9.0	12.8	21.9	15.7	7.6	16.6	17.1	13.4
Uzbekistan	...	25.0	27.3	27.3	11.6	6.6	10.0	14.2	12.3	11.8	10.9	8.0	11.9	12.1	10.0

Table A7 (continued)

	Average 1990–99	2000	2001	2002	2003	2004	2005	2006	2007	2008	2009	2013	End of Period 2007	2008	2009
Developing Asia	**8.6**	**1.9**	**2.7**	**2.0**	**2.5**	**4.1**	**3.8**	**4.1**	**5.3**	**5.9**	**4.1**	**3.6**	**6.3**	**4.6**	**4.0**
Afghanistan, I.R. of	...	...	...	5.1	24.1	13.2	12.3	5.1	13.0	19.6	9.2	5.0	20.7	15.0	6.0
Bangladesh	6.4	2.5	1.9	3.7	5.4	6.1	7.0	6.5	8.4	9.3	8.1	4.0	9.2	9.4	7.0
Bhutan	9.8	4.0	3.4	2.5	2.1	4.6	5.3	5.0	4.9	4.7	4.3	3.9	4.8	4.5	4.2
Brunei Darussalam	...	1.2	0.6	−2.3	0.3	0.9	1.1	0.2	0.4	0.7	1.0	1.2	...	...	...
Cambodia	...	−0.8	0.2	3.3	1.2	3.8	5.9	4.7	5.9	9.0	5.0	3.5	10.8	7.5	5.0
China	7.5	0.4	0.7	−0.8	1.2	3.9	1.8	1.5	4.8	5.9	3.6	3.4	6.6	3.9	3.6
Fiji	4.2	1.1	4.3	0.8	4.2	2.8	2.4	2.5	4.8	3.0	3.0	3.0	7.0	2.5	3.0
India	9.5	4.0	3.8	4.3	3.8	3.8	4.2	6.2	6.4	5.2	4.0	3.9	5.5	4.6	3.9
Indonesia	13.6	3.8	11.5	11.8	6.8	6.1	10.5	13.1	6.4	7.1	5.9	3.2	6.6	6.7	5.5
Kiribati	3.4	0.4	6.0	3.2	2.5	−1.9	−0.5	−0.2	0.2	1.0	1.5	2.5	3.7	2.8	2.5
Lao PDR	22.6	23.2	9.3	10.6	15.5	10.5	7.2	6.8	4.5	6.9	6.1	5.0	5.6	7.0	5.5
Malaysia	3.7	1.6	1.4	1.8	1.1	1.4	3.0	3.6	2.1	2.4	2.5	2.5	2.2	2.4	2.5
Maldives	8.4	−1.2	0.7	0.9	−2.8	6.3	3.3	3.7	5.0	6.0	6.0	6.0	7.0	6.0	6.0
Myanmar	26.9	−1.7	34.5	58.1	24.9	3.8	10.7	25.7	34.4	25.0	20.0	15.0	30.0	20.0	20.0
Nepal	9.8	3.4	2.4	2.9	4.8	4.0	4.5	8.0	6.4	6.4	4.9	4.0	5.1	6.4	5.3
Pakistan	9.6	3.6	4.4	2.5	3.1	4.6	9.3	7.9	7.8	8.5	7.5	4.0	7.0	8.2	7.0
Papua New Guinea	8.6	15.6	9.3	11.8	14.7	2.1	1.7	2.3	1.7	5.0	5.0	4.0	4.5	5.5	4.5
Philippines	9.6	4.0	6.8	3.0	3.5	6.0	7.7	6.2	2.8	4.4	3.8	3.5	3.9	3.4	3.5
Samoa	4.4	−0.2	1.9	7.4	4.3	7.9	1.9	3.8	6.0	5.5	5.1	3.0	5.1	4.8	4.7
Solomon Islands	10.7	6.9	7.6	9.3	10.0	6.9	7.3	8.1	6.3	7.3	6.6	5.0	7.0	6.7	6.5
Sri Lanka	11.1	1.5	12.1	10.2	2.6	7.9	10.6	9.5	19.7	11.5	9.0	7.0	21.8	11.0	9.0
Thailand	5.0	1.6	1.7	0.6	1.8	2.8	4.5	4.6	2.2	3.5	2.5	2.0	3.2	1.9	3.0
Timor-Leste	...	63.6	3.6	4.8	7.0	3.2	1.8	4.1	7.8	4.0	3.5	3.2	7.8	4.0	3.5
Tonga	4.4	5.3	6.9	10.4	11.1	11.7	9.7	7.0	5.9	5.3	5.6	6.0	5.6	5.4	5.6
Vanuatu	3.2	2.5	3.7	2.0	3.0	1.4	1.2	2.1	3.9	3.2	2.5	2.5	4.0	3.0	2.5
Vietnam	19.2	−1.6	−0.4	4.0	3.2	7.7	8.3	7.5	8.3	16.0	10.0	6.0	12.6	14.0	8.5
Middle East	**10.9**	**4.1**	**3.8**	**5.3**	**6.1**	**7.0**	**6.2**	**7.0**	**10.4**	**11.5**	**10.0**	**7.1**	**10.9**	**11.7**	**10.0**
Bahrain	0.8	−0.7	−1.2	−0.5	1.7	2.3	2.6	2.2	3.4	3.3	3.1	2.9	3.4	3.2	3.1
Egypt	10.7	2.8	2.4	2.4	3.2	8.1	8.8	4.2	11.0	8.8	8.8	6.7	8.6	9.4	7.8
Iran, I.R. of	23.5	12.8	11.3	15.7	15.6	15.3	10.4	11.9	17.5	20.7	17.4	11.8	19.0	20.7	17.4
Iraq	...	...	...	...	...	...	...	...	...	...	...	...	...	...	...
Jordan	5.0	0.7	1.8	1.8	1.6	3.4	3.5	6.3	5.4	10.9	6.5	2.5	5.7	9.0	6.3
Kuwait	3.6	1.6	1.4	0.8	1.0	1.3	4.1	3.1	5.0	6.5	5.5	4.5	5.0	6.5	5.5
Lebanon	24.9	−0.4	−0.4	1.8	1.3	1.7	−0.7	5.6	4.1	5.5	5.3	2.7	2.0	5.0	5.5
Libya	6.2	−2.9	−8.8	−9.9	−2.1	−2.2	2.0	3.4	6.7	8.0	7.5	6.0	8.1	8.0	7.5
Oman	1.6	−1.2	−0.8	−0.3	0.2	0.7	1.9	3.2	5.5	6.0	6.8	5.0	5.8	6.4	6.4
Qatar	2.9	1.7	1.4	0.2	2.3	6.8	8.8	11.8	13.8	12.0	10.0	4.5	13.8	12.0	10.0
Saudi Arabia	1.2	−1.1	−1.1	0.2	0.6	0.4	0.6	2.3	4.1	6.2	5.6	4.5	4.1	6.2	5.6
Syrian Arab Republic	7.2	−3.9	3.4	−0.5	5.8	4.4	7.2	10.6	7.0	7.0	7.0	5.0	23.0	5.0	5.0
United Arab Emirates	3.6	1.4	2.7	2.9	3.2	5.0	6.2	9.3	11.0	9.0	5.3	3.0	...	...	...
Yemen, Rep. of	37.0	10.9	11.9	12.2	10.8	12.5	11.8	18.2	12.5	10.3	11.0	14.5	8.6	12.0	10.0

Table A7 (concluded)

	Average 1990–99	2000	2001	2002	2003	2004	2005	2006	2007	2008	2009	2013	End of Period 2007	2008	2009
Western Hemisphere	**98.4**	**8.3**	**6.5**	**8.7**	**10.5**	**6.6**	**6.3**	**5.3**	**5.4**	**6.6**	**6.1**	**6.2**	**6.3**	**6.3**	**6.1**
Antigua and Barbuda	3.4	−0.6	1.7	2.4	2.0	2.0	2.1	1.8	1.5	3.0	2.0	2.0	1.5	3.0	2.0
Argentina	59.3	−0.9	−1.1	25.9	13.4	4.4	9.6	10.9	8.8	9.2	9.1	9.0	8.5	9.0	9.0
Bahamas, The	2.8	1.6	2.0	2.2	3.0	0.9	2.2	1.8	2.4	2.4	2.3	2.0	2.6	2.4	2.2
Barbados	2.9	2.4	2.6	−1.2	1.6	1.4	6.0	7.3	5.5	3.6	2.1	2.0	5.7	2.3	2.0
Belize	2.0	0.7	1.2	2.2	2.6	3.1	3.7	4.3	3.0	2.8	2.6	2.5	3.0	2.6	2.5
Bolivia	10.4	4.6	1.6	0.9	3.3	4.4	5.4	4.3	8.7	15.1	14.3	14.9	11.7	16.0	14.0
Brazil	325.4	7.1	6.8	8.4	14.8	6.6	6.9	4.2	3.6	4.8	4.3	4.5	4.5	4.5	4.5
Chile	11.5	3.8	3.6	2.5	2.8	1.1	3.1	3.4	4.4	6.6	3.6	3.0	7.8	4.2	3.0
Colombia	22.0	9.2	8.0	6.3	7.1	5.9	5.0	4.3	5.5	5.5	4.6	3.4	5.7	5.0	4.0
Costa Rica	16.7	11.0	11.3	9.2	9.4	12.3	13.8	11.5	9.4	9.5	7.0	3.0	10.8	8.0	6.0
Dominica	2.3	0.9	1.6	0.1	1.6	2.4	1.6	2.6	2.7	2.2	1.5	1.5	3.4	2.4	1.5
Dominican Republic	14.2	7.7	8.9	5.2	27.4	51.5	4.2	7.6	6.1	6.2	4.8	4.0	8.9	7.0	4.0
Ecuador	38.6	96.1	37.7	12.6	7.9	2.7	2.1	3.3	2.2	3.3	3.3	3.3	2.9	3.3	3.3
El Salvador	10.4	2.3	3.8	1.9	2.1	4.5	4.7	4.0	3.9	5.5	4.4	3.0	4.9	4.9	4.0
Grenada	2.9	0.6	1.7	1.1	2.2	2.3	3.5	4.3	3.7	5.0	2.0	2.0	6.7	2.0	2.0
Guatemala	14.5	6.0	7.3	8.1	5.6	7.6	9.1	6.6	6.8	8.0	6.0	4.2	8.7	6.2	5.8
Guyana	21.8	6.1	2.7	5.4	6.0	4.7	6.9	6.6	12.2	6.2	6.5	5.0	13.9	6.8	6.3
Haiti	20.7	11.5	16.5	9.3	26.7	28.3	16.8	14.2	9.0	9.7	7.5	5.0	7.9	9.0	7.0
Honduras	19.5	11.0	9.7	7.7	7.7	8.1	8.8	5.6	6.9	9.5	8.6	5.5	8.9	9.0	7.9
Jamaica	26.7	8.1	7.0	7.1	10.5	13.4	15.1	8.5	9.3	19.0	10.2	7.2	16.8	14.4	9.3
Mexico	20.1	9.5	6.4	5.0	4.5	4.7	4.0	3.6	4.0	3.8	3.2	3.0	3.8	3.5	3.0
Nicaragua	66.5	9.9	4.7	4.0	6.5	8.5	9.6	9.1	11.1	13.8	7.5	3.0	16.9	9.5	7.5
Panama	1.1	1.4	0.3	1.0	0.6	0.5	2.9	2.5	4.2	7.4	4.9	4.0	6.4	6.5	4.8
Paraguay	16.2	9.0	7.3	10.5	14.2	4.3	6.8	9.6	8.1	7.6	3.8	3.0	6.0	5.0	3.0
Peru	112.1	3.8	2.0	0.2	2.3	3.3	1.6	2.0	1.8	4.2	2.5	2.5	3.9	3.5	2.5
St. Kitts and Nevis	3.5	2.1	2.1	2.1	2.3	2.2	3.4	8.5	4.5	1.6	2.3	2.2	2.1	2.5	2.2
St. Lucia	3.2	3.7	5.4	−0.3	1.0	1.5	3.9	3.6	1.9	3.4	3.1	2.5	6.8	2.9	2.6
St. Vincent and the Grenadines	3.1	0.2	0.8	0.8	0.2	3.0	3.7	3.0	6.1	4.1	2.8	2.8	5.8	3.2	3.0
Suriname	70.9	58.6	39.8	15.5	23.0	9.1	9.9	11.3	6.4	8.0	7.0	5.0	8.4	7.0	6.0
Trinidad and Tobago	5.9	3.6	5.5	4.2	3.8	3.7	6.9	8.3	7.9	7.3	6.8	5.0	7.6	7.0	6.5
Uruguay	45.1	4.8	4.4	14.0	19.4	9.2	4.7	6.4	8.1	7.4	5.7	3.3	8.5	7.0	5.0
Venezuela	46.1	16.2	12.5	22.4	31.1	21.7	16.0	13.7	18.7	25.7	31.0	40.0	22.5	29.0	33.0

[1]In accordance with standard practice in the *World Economic Outlook*, movements in consumer prices are indicated as annual averages rather than as December/December changes during the year, as is the practice in some countries. For many countries, figures for recent years are IMF staff estimates. Data for some countries are for fiscal years.

[2]The percent changes in 2002 are calculated over a period of 18 months, reflecting a change in the fiscal year cycle (from July–June to January–December).

[3]2007 represents an estimate. No projections for 2008 and beyond are shown because Zimbabwe is in hyperinflation and inflation can no longer be forecasted in a meaningful way. Unless policies change, inflation can increase without limit.

[4]For many countries, inflation for the earlier years is measured on the basis of a retail price index. Consumer price indices with a broader and more up-to-date coverage are typically used for more recent years.

[5]Mongolia, which is not a member of the Commonwealth of Independent States, is included in this group for reasons of geography and similarities in economic structure.

Table A8. Major Advanced Economies: General Government Fiscal Balances and Debt[1]
(Percent of GDP)

	Average 1992–2001	2002	2003	2004	2005	2006	2007	2008	2009	2013
Major advanced economies										
Actual balance	−2.8	−4.0	−4.8	−4.2	−3.5	−2.6	−2.2	−3.4	−3.2	−2.1
Output gap[2]	0.1	−0.5	−0.9	−0.3	−0.3	0.1	0.1	−1.1	−2.3	—
Structural balance[2]	−2.7	−3.8	−4.3	−4.0	−3.4	−2.6	−2.3	−3.0	−2.4	−2.1
United States										
Actual balance	−1.8	−3.8	−4.8	−4.4	−3.6	−2.6	−2.5	−4.5	−4.2	−2.8
Output gap[2]	0.2	−0.4	−0.6	0.0	0.3	0.5	0.1	−1.8	−3.6	—
Structural balance[2]	−1.9	−3.7	−4.6	−4.3	−3.7	−2.8	−2.6	−3.8	−2.8	−2.8
Net debt	48.0	38.4	41.4	43.1	43.8	43.3	44.0	47.9	51.6	55.5
Gross debt	64.2	56.1	59.4	60.4	60.8	60.1	60.8	63.2	66.5	69.9
Euro area										
Actual balance	−3.5	−2.6	−3.1	−2.9	−2.6	−1.4	−0.6	−1.1	−1.1	−0.4
Output gap[2]	−0.3	0.2	−0.9	−0.8	−1.1	−0.4	0.1	−0.4	−1.1	—
Structural balance[2]	−3.0	−2.6	−2.7	−2.4	−2.1	−1.2	−0.6	−0.9	−0.6	−0.2
Net debt	58.4	58.4	59.8	60.3	60.7	58.8	56.7	55.9	55.4	50.6
Gross debt	70.3	68.2	69.3	69.7	70.3	68.6	66.3	65.4	64.8	59.3
Germany[3]										
Actual balance	−2.2	−3.7	−4.0	−3.8	−3.4	−1.6	—	−0.7	−0.4	—
Output gap[2]	0.2	−0.2	−1.7	−2.0	−2.4	−1.0	—	−0.2	−0.8	—
Structural balance[2,4]	−1.8	−2.9	−3.2	−2.8	−2.4	−1.1	0.0	−0.6	−0.1	0.4
Net debt	46.8	54.3	57.7	60.0	61.7	60.2	57.7	57.0	56.6	55.2
Gross debt	54.3	59.6	62.8	64.7	66.3	66.0	63.2	62.4	61.9	59.9
France										
Actual balance	−3.7	−3.1	−4.1	−3.6	−3.0	−2.5	−2.4	−2.8	−3.0	−1.2
Output gap[2]	−0.8	0.7	−0.2	0.2	−0.2	−0.2	−0.5	−1.2	−2.1	—
Structural balance[2,4]	−3.1	−3.5	−3.8	−3.5	−3.1	−2.3	−2.0	−2.0	−1.8	−1.2
Net debt	44.8	49.1	53.2	55.3	57.0	54.4	54.3	54.9	55.9	52.9
Gross debt	54.1	58.8	62.9	65.0	66.7	64.1	64.0	64.6	65.6	62.6
Italy										
Actual balance	−5.5	−2.9	−3.5	−3.5	−4.2	−3.4	−1.9	−2.5	−2.5	−2.2
Output gap[2]	−0.6	0.7	−0.5	−0.2	−0.8	−0.2	0.2	−0.2	−0.6	—
Structural balance[2,4]	−5.2	−4.1	−3.5	−3.7	−4.0	−3.3	−2.1	−2.4	−2.3	−2.2
Net debt	109.5	102.1	101.5	100.8	102.7	102.7	100.3	100.0	100.4	99.0
Gross debt	114.8	105.6	104.4	103.8	105.8	106.5	104.0	103.6	104.0	102.6
Japan										
Actual balance	−4.6	−8.0	−8.0	−6.2	−5.0	−3.8	−3.4	−3.4	−3.3	−2.4
Excluding social security	−6.2	−7.9	−8.1	−6.6	−5.4	−3.8	−2.9	−2.8	−3.0	−2.5
Output gap[2]	−0.5	−2.3	−2.2	−1.2	−0.9	−0.2	0.2	−0.0	−0.2	—
Structural balance[2]	−4.4	−7.0	−7.1	−5.7	−4.7	−3.7	−3.5	−3.4	−3.2	−2.4
Excluding social security	−6.8	−7.3	−7.6	−6.3	−5.2	−3.7	−2.9	−2.8	−2.9	−2.5
Net debt	36.9	72.6	76.5	82.7	84.6	88.4	90.8	93.8	94.7	94.6
Gross debt	108.4	160.9	167.2	178.1	191.6	194.7	195.5	197.5	196.0	186.1
United Kingdom										
Actual balance	−3.0	−1.9	−3.3	−3.4	−3.4	−2.6	−3.0	−3.1	−3.2	−2.1
Output gap[2]	−0.4	−0.1	−0.1	0.5	−0.2	−0.1	0.4	−0.7	−1.6	—
Structural balance[2]	−2.5	−2.0	−3.0	−3.6	−3.2	−2.6	−3.1	−3.1	−3.2	−1.9
Net debt	35.2	32.5	34.2	35.9	37.8	38.4	38.3	38.9	38.8	38.6
Gross debt	40.8	37.7	39.0	40.5	42.4	43.0	43.0	43.5	43.5	43.3
Canada										
Actual balance	−2.7	−0.1	−0.1	0.8	1.6	1.0	1.0	0.1	0.0	0.5
Output gap[2]	3.5	0.2	−0.7	−0.3	0.2	0.3	0.3	−1.0	−1.8	—
Structural balance[2]	−2.6	−0.2	0.2	0.9	1.5	0.9	0.8	0.5	0.8	0.4
Net debt	60.3	42.6	38.6	34.4	30.1	27.6	25.1	24.2	23.3	17.2
Gross debt	104.7	89.4	85.2	80.2	78.4	73.5	68.4	66.2	63.8	50.4

Note: The methodology and specific assumptions for each country are discussed in Box A1 in this Statistical Appendix.
[1]Debt data refer to end of year. Debt data are not always comparable across countries.
[2]Percent of potential GDP.
[3]Beginning in 1995, the debt and debt-service obligations of the Treuhandanstalt (and of various other agencies) were taken over by general government. This debt is equivalent to 8 percent of GDP, and the associated debt service to ½ to 1 percent of GDP.
[4]Excludes one-off receipts from the sale of mobile telephone licenses (the equivalent of 2.5 percent of GDP in 2000 for Germany, 0.1 percent of GDP in 2001 and 2002 for France, and 1.2 percent of GDP in 2000 for Italy). Also excludes one-off receipts from sizable asset transactions, in particular 0.5 percent of GDP for France in 2005.

Table A9. Summary of World Trade Volumes and Prices

(Annual percent change)

	Ten-Year Averages		2000	2001	2002	2003	2004	2005	2006	2007	2008	2009
	1990–99	2000–09										
Trade in goods and services												
World trade[1]												
Volume	6.5	6.7	12.2	0.3	3.5	5.4	10.7	7.6	9.2	6.8	5.6	5.8
Price deflator												
In U.S. dollars	—	4.5	−0.4	−3.6	1.1	10.4	9.6	5.5	4.9	8.2	8.6	1.1
In SDRs	−0.7	3.4	3.3	−0.1	−0.6	2.0	3.7	5.8	5.4	4.1	10.4	0.8
Volume of trade												
Exports												
Advanced economies	6.5	5.4	11.7	−0.5	2.4	3.3	9.0	6.0	8.2	5.8	4.5	4.2
Emerging and developing economies	7.5	9.4	13.7	2.6	6.9	10.5	14.1	11.1	10.9	8.9	7.1	8.7
Imports												
Advanced economies	6.3	5.1	11.7	−0.5	2.7	4.1	9.3	6.3	7.4	4.2	3.1	3.7
Emerging and developing economies	6.5	11.0	13.7	3.1	6.3	10.1	16.1	12.0	14.4	12.8	11.8	10.7
Terms of trade												
Advanced economies	—	−0.4	−2.6	0.3	0.8	1.0	−0.1	−1.5	−1.1	—	−1.0	0.1
Emerging and developing economies	−0.7	2.3	6.0	−2.5	0.6	1.1	3.0	5.6	4.7	1.4	4.5	−0.5
Trade in goods												
World trade[1]												
Volume	6.7	6.7	12.8	−0.5	3.6	6.3	10.8	7.5	9.1	6.4	5.9	6.0
Price deflator												
In U.S. dollars	−0.2	4.6	0.4	−3.7	0.6	9.9	9.9	6.3	5.7	8.4	8.7	1.0
In SDRs	−0.9	3.6	4.0	−0.3	−1.1	1.6	3.9	6.5	6.1	4.3	10.5	0.7
World trade prices in U.S. dollars[2]												
Manufactures	0.3	4.1	−5.3	−3.4	2.1	14.4	9.5	3.6	3.8	9.7	6.4	1.4
Oil	—	18.0	57.0	−13.8	2.5	15.8	30.7	41.3	20.5	10.7	34.3	−1.0
Nonfuel primary commodities	−2.2	6.5	4.2	−4.8	1.9	5.9	15.2	6.1	23.2	14.0	7.0	−4.9
Food	−2.3	6.4	2.5	−2.0	3.5	6.3	14.0	−0.9	10.5	15.2	18.2	−0.9
Beverages	−0.5	3.2	−18.4	−13.3	24.3	4.8	−0.9	18.1	8.4	13.8	9.0	−5.0
Agricultural raw materials	−0.6	1.8	5.5	−3.4	−0.2	0.6	4.1	0.5	8.8	4.9	−2.3	−0.2
Metals	−4.1	11.1	13.2	−10.3	−3.5	11.8	34.6	22.4	56.2	17.4	−1.3	−12.2
World trade prices in SDRs[2]												
Manufactures	−0.3	3.0	−1.8	0.1	0.4	5.7	3.6	3.9	4.2	5.6	8.1	1.0
Oil	−0.6	16.9	62.8	−10.7	0.8	7.1	23.6	41.6	21.0	6.5	36.5	−1.4
Nonfuel primary commodities	−2.9	5.4	8.1	−1.3	0.2	−2.1	9.0	6.3	23.8	9.7	8.7	−5.2
Food	−2.9	5.4	6.2	1.5	1.8	−1.7	7.8	−0.7	11.0	10.8	20.1	−1.2
Beverages	−1.1	2.2	−15.4	−10.2	22.2	−3.1	−6.3	18.3	8.8	9.5	10.8	−5.4
Agricultural raw materials	−1.2	0.8	9.4	0.1	−1.9	−7.0	−1.6	0.8	9.3	0.9	−0.7	−0.5
Metals	−4.8	10.0	17.4	−7.0	−5.1	3.3	27.3	22.7	56.9	12.9	0.3	−12.4
World trade prices in euros[2]												
Manufactures	0.7	0.7	9.3	−0.3	−3.1	−4.5	−0.4	3.4	2.9	0.5	−0.9	0.9
Oil	0.4	14.3	81.3	−11.1	−2.8	−3.3	18.9	41.0	19.5	1.4	25.1	−1.5
Nonfuel primary commodities	−1.9	3.1	20.4	−1.8	−3.3	−11.6	4.8	5.9	22.3	4.5	−0.3	−5.3
Food	−2.0	3.0	18.3	1.1	−1.8	−11.2	3.7	−1.1	9.6	5.6	10.1	−1.3
Beverages	−0.1	−0.1	−5.7	−10.5	17.9	−12.5	−9.9	17.8	7.5	4.2	1.6	−5.5
Agricultural raw materials	−0.3	−1.5	21.8	−0.4	−5.4	−16.0	−5.3	0.3	8.0	−3.9	−9.0	−0.6
Metals	−3.8	7.6	30.7	−7.4	−8.4	−6.7	22.4	22.2	55.0	7.5	−8.1	−12.5

Table A9 *(concluded)*

	Ten-Year Averages		2000	2001	2002	2003	2004	2005	2006	2007	2008	2009
	1990–99	2000–09										
Trade in goods												
Volume of trade												
Exports												
Advanced economies	6.4	5.4	12.5	−1.5	2.3	3.9	8.7	5.5	8.6	5.3	4.8	4.3
Emerging and developing economies	7.4	9.4	14.0	1.9	6.9	11.4	14.0	10.8	10.8	8.7	7.0	8.8
Fuel exporters	2.6	5.2	7.0	0.5	2.8	11.3	8.8	5.9	3.6	1.7	4.4	5.9
Nonfuel exporters	9.5	10.9	16.2	2.5	8.3	11.5	15.8	12.6	13.7	11.7	8.0	9.9
Imports												
Advanced economies	6.7	5.2	12.3	−1.5	3.0	5.0	9.5	6.2	7.6	3.8	3.5	3.6
Emerging and developing economies	6.8	11.2	14.6	3.1	6.2	11.4	16.9	12.4	12.5	12.3	12.2	11.3
Fuel exporters	−0.6	13.8	11.0	16.0	8.5	10.1	15.9	17.6	13.2	14.2	17.8	14.4
Nonfuel exporters	9.0	10.7	15.2	0.9	5.8	11.7	17.1	11.4	12.3	11.9	10.9	10.6
Price deflators in SDRs												
Exports												
Advanced economies	−1.1	2.7	0.5	−0.1	−0.8	2.5	3.1	3.8	4.1	4.0	9.3	1.1
Emerging and developing economies	0.1	6.5	14.6	−0.9	0.1	1.5	7.5	13.9	10.7	5.1	14.3	−0.1
Fuel exporters	0.6	13.4	44.1	−7.3	0.8	4.8	17.1	32.4	18.1	8.0	28.0	−1.3
Nonfuel exporters	−0.2	3.9	5.7	1.5	−0.1	0.4	4.2	7.2	7.6	3.9	9.1	0.3
Imports												
Advanced economies	−1.4	3.2	3.6	−0.6	−1.9	1.2	3.2	5.8	5.7	4.2	10.4	1.1
Emerging and developing economies	0.7	3.8	6.6	1.2	−0.6	0.2	4.3	7.0	6.7	4.1	8.9	0.1
Fuel exporters	1.0	3.6	2.2	0.3	1.1	0.3	4.5	7.2	7.9	4.6	8.4	—
Nonfuel exporters	0.5	3.8	7.4	1.3	−0.9	0.2	4.2	6.9	6.4	4.0	9.0	0.1
Terms of trade												
Advanced economies	0.3	−0.5	−3.1	0.5	1.1	1.3	−0.1	−1.9	−1.5	−0.1	−1.1	—
Emerging and developing economies	−0.7	2.6	7.5	−2.1	0.7	1.2	3.1	6.4	3.8	0.9	5.0	−0.2
Regional groups												
Africa	−0.4	5.4	13.2	−3.5	0.2	2.8	4.1	14.2	9.3	3.6	11.6	−0.1
Central and eastern Europe	−0.7	0.1	−2.3	3.6	1.0	−0.3	1.2	−0.9	−1.6	1.1	−0.9	0.4
Commonwealth of Independent States[3]	−2.1	7.5	24.2	−2.7	−2.2	11.0	12.3	15.3	8.5	2.2	12.1	−2.3
Developing Asia	−0.2	−0.6	−4.3	0.9	0.5	−0.4	−2.3	−0.6	−0.4	−1.0	0.4	1.2
Middle East	0.3	8.3	39.7	−8.2	1.7	−0.1	10.3	23.6	6.3	1.9	16.5	−1.2
Western Hemisphere	−0.8	3.1	7.3	−4.2	1.6	2.9	6.0	5.5	8.3	2.3	4.3	−2.2
Analytical groups												
By source of export earnings												
Fuel exporters	−0.4	9.5	41.0	−7.5	−0.3	4.5	12.1	23.6	9.5	3.2	18.1	−1.3
Nonfuel exporters	−0.7	0.1	−1.5	0.2	0.7	0.2	—	0.3	1.1	−0.1	0.1	0.2
Memorandum												
World exports in billions of U.S. dollars												
Goods and services	5,752	12,898	7,879	7,607	7,986	9,298	11,280	12,817	14,700	17,019	19,535	20,855
Goods	4,584	10,388	6,348	6,074	6,353	7,425	9,016	10,290	11,887	13,729	15,836	16,923
Average oil price[4]	—	18.0	57.0	−13.8	2.5	15.8	30.7	41.3	20.5	10.7	34.3	−1.0
In U.S. dollars a barrel	18.20	52.29	28.2	24.3	25.0	28.9	37.8	53.4	64.3	71.1	95.5	94.5
Export unit value of manufactures[5]	0.3	4.1	−5.3	−3.4	2.1	14.4	9.5	3.6	3.8	9.7	6.4	1.4

[1]Average of annual percent change for world exports and imports.

[2]As represented, respectively, by the export unit value index for the manufactures of the advanced economies; the average of U.K. Brent, Dubai, and West Texas Intermediate crude oil prices; and the average of world market prices for nonfuel primary commodities weighted by their 2002–04 shares in world commodity exports.

[3]Mongolia, which is not a member of the Commonwealth of Independent States, is included in this group for reasons of geography and similarities in economic structure.

[4]Average of U.K. Brent, Dubai, and West Texas Intermediate crude oil prices.

[5]For the manufactures exported by the advanced economies.

Table A10. Summary of Balances on Current Account

(Billions of U.S. dollars)

	2000	2001	2002	2003	2004	2005	2006	2007	2008	2009	2013
Advanced economies	**−263.3**	**−205.0**	**−208.8**	**−207.0**	**−224.2**	**−438.7**	**−525.2**	**−463.3**	**−464.2**	**−460.1**	**−603.3**
United States	−417.4	−384.7	−459.6	−522.1	−640.2	−754.9	−811.5	−738.6	−614.7	−605.5	−676.0
Euro area[1]	−35.1	8.4	50.1	45.2	108.2	23.6	−6.4	−30.0	−98.0	−121.1	−180.1
Japan	119.6	87.8	112.6	136.2	172.1	165.7	170.4	212.8	193.3	198.5	189.1
Other advanced economies[2]	69.6	83.5	88.1	133.6	135.7	126.9	122.2	92.6	55.2	68.0	63.6
Memorandum											
Newly industrialized Asian economies	38.9	46.8	54.6	79.2	80.6	73.5	82.7	102.3	82.0	84.7	100.2
Emerging and developing economies	**86.9**	**41.1**	**76.6**	**144.3**	**213.6**	**439.5**	**606.7**	**630.9**	**729.4**	**662.2**	**694.0**
Regional groups											
Africa	8.3	1.3	−8.6	−3.9	2.0	15.8	29.6	1.6	21.7	12.7	−8.0
Central and eastern Europe	−31.3	−15.8	−24.0	−37.2	−59.3	−61.3	−90.9	−121.5	−150.3	−151.9	−164.5
Commonwealth of Independent States[3]	48.3	33.1	30.2	36.0	63.8	88.3	97.8	76.1	106.2	62.8	−90.2
Developing Asia	38.5	36.7	64.8	82.6	89.2	161.4	277.5	383.5	367.5	407.1	702.4
Middle East	71.5	39.9	30.3	59.1	97.1	200.3	247.3	274.6	398.3	370.3	317.6
Western Hemisphere	−48.3	−54.0	−16.0	7.7	20.8	35.0	45.4	16.4	−14.1	−38.9	−63.3
Memorandum											
European Union	−81.4	−26.4	22.2	23.6	63.0	−32.4	−113.1	−202.8	−294.5	−310.0	−422.3
Analytical groups											
By source of export earnings											
Fuel	151.7	83.6	61.6	106.4	185.9	349.7	432.4	423.5	619.6	548.0	326.6
Nonfuel	−64.8	−42.5	15.0	37.9	27.7	89.8	174.3	207.3	109.8	114.2	367.4
of which, primary products	−2.4	−3.5	−4.5	−2.9	—	0.6	9.9	9.2	0.3	−3.7	−10.1
By external financing source											
Net debtor countries	−95.4	−72.6	−34.9	−30.9	−70.3	−102.1	−109.3	−187.8	−282.6	−319.2	−404.1
of which, official financing	−5.1	−3.9	−4.2	−5.7	−5.6	−6.1	−6.5	−17.2	−24.8	−24.8	−33.8
Net debtor countries by debt-servicing experience											
Countries with arrears and/or rescheduling during 2002–06	−8.4	−5.1	12.0	15.0	0.1	−9.1	0.1	−16.1	−27.9	−34.0	−58.1
World[1]	**−176.4**	**−163.8**	**−132.2**	**−62.8**	**−10.5**	**0.9**	**81.5**	**167.6**	**265.2**	**202.1**	**90.6**
Memorandum											
In percent of total world current account transactions	−1.1	−1.1	−0.8	−0.3	—	—	0.3	0.5	0.7	0.5	0.2
In percent of world GDP	−0.6	−0.5	−0.4	−0.2	—	—	0.2	0.3	0.4	0.3	0.1

[1]Reflects errors, omissions, and asymmetries in balance of payments statistics on current account, as well as the exclusion of data for international organizations and a limited number of countries. Calculated as the sum of the balance of individual euro area countries. See "Classification of Countries" in the introduction to this Statistical Appendix.

[2]In this table, other advanced economies means advanced economies excluding the United States, euro area countries, and Japan.

[3]Mongolia, which is not a member of the Commonwealth of Independent States, is included in this group for reasons of geography and similarities in economic structure.

Table A11. Advanced Economies: Balance on Current Account

(Percent of GDP)

	2000	2001	2002	2003	2004	2005	2006	2007	2008	2009	2013
Advanced economies	**−1.0**	**−0.8**	**−0.8**	**−0.7**	**−0.7**	**−1.3**	**−1.5**	**−1.2**	**−1.1**	**−1.1**	**−1.1**
United States	−4.3	−3.8	−4.4	−4.8	−5.5	−6.1	−6.2	−5.3	−4.3	−4.2	−3.8
Euro area[1]	−0.6	0.1	0.7	0.5	1.1	0.2	−0.1	−0.2	−0.7	−0.9	−1.0
Germany	−1.7	—	2.0	1.9	4.3	4.6	5.0	5.6	5.2	4.9	3.7
France	1.6	1.9	1.4	0.8	0.5	−0.9	−1.3	−1.3	−2.4	−2.5	−2.0
Italy	−0.5	−0.1	−0.8	−1.3	−0.9	−1.6	−2.6	−2.2	−2.4	−2.3	−2.0
Spain	−4.0	−3.9	−3.3	−3.5	−5.3	−7.4	−8.6	−10.1	−10.5	−10.3	−9.2
Netherlands	1.9	2.4	2.5	5.5	7.5	7.2	8.3	6.6	5.9	5.6	5.1
Belgium	4.0	3.4	4.6	4.1	3.5	2.6	2.7	3.2	2.9	2.8	1.6
Austria	−0.7	−0.8	2.7	1.7	2.1	2.0	2.4	2.7	2.9	2.9	1.8
Finland	8.1	8.6	8.8	5.1	6.5	3.6	4.6	4.6	3.8	3.9	3.5
Greece	−7.8	−7.2	−6.5	−6.4	−5.8	−7.4	−11.0	−13.9	−13.9	−14.1	−12.4
Portugal	−10.2	−9.9	−8.1	−6.1	−7.7	−9.7	−9.4	−9.4	−9.5	−9.5	−8.3
Ireland	−0.4	−0.6	−1.0	—	−0.6	−3.5	−4.2	−4.5	−3.2	−2.9	−2.0
Luxembourg	13.2	8.8	11.7	8.0	11.6	10.9	10.3	9.5	8.2	7.3	5.8
Slovenia	−2.7	0.2	1.0	−0.8	−2.7	−2.0	−2.8	−4.8	−4.8	−4.9	−4.1
Cyprus	−5.3	−3.3	−3.7	−2.2	−5.0	−5.6	−5.9	−7.1	−7.7	−7.1	−4.8
Malta	−13.1	−4.1	2.5	−3.1	−6.0	−8.7	−6.7	−6.2	−6.1	−5.8	−4.1
Japan	2.6	2.1	2.9	3.2	3.7	3.6	3.9	4.9	4.0	3.9	3.3
United Kingdom	−2.6	−2.2	−1.6	−1.3	−1.6	−2.5	−3.9	−4.9	−4.8	−4.4	−4.7
Canada	2.7	2.3	1.7	1.2	2.3	2.0	1.6	0.9	−0.9	−1.2	0.7
Korea	2.4	1.7	1.0	2.0	4.1	1.9	0.6	0.6	−1.0	−0.9	−1.1
Australia	−3.8	−2.0	−3.8	−5.4	−6.0	−5.8	−5.5	−6.2	−6.3	−5.3	−5.7
Taiwan Province of China	2.8	6.3	8.6	9.6	5.6	4.5	6.7	8.3	7.8	8.1	8.2
Sweden	4.0	4.3	5.0	7.2	6.7	6.8	8.5	8.3	6.4	6.7	7.5
Switzerland	12.3	7.8	8.3	12.9	12.9	13.5	15.1	17.2	15.4	13.8	14.5
Hong Kong SAR	4.1	5.9	7.6	10.4	9.5	11.4	12.1	12.3	9.9	8.3	6.4
Denmark	1.4	3.1	2.5	3.4	3.1	4.3	2.7	1.1	0.7	1.3	1.1
Norway	15.0	16.1	12.6	12.3	12.7	16.3	17.3	16.3	20.0	20.4	18.0
Israel	−0.8	−1.1	−0.8	1.2	2.4	3.3	6.0	3.1	1.8	1.7	1.1
Singapore	11.6	12.5	12.6	23.2	16.7	18.6	21.8	24.3	20.6	18.9	15.1
New Zealand	−5.1	−2.8	−3.9	−4.3	−6.4	−8.5	−8.6	−8.1	−7.1	−7.1	−6.2
Iceland	−10.2	−4.3	1.5	−4.8	−9.8	−16.1	−25.4	−15.6	−8.0	−5.3	−2.6
Memorandum											
Major advanced economies	−1.6	−1.4	−1.4	−1.5	−1.4	−2.0	−2.3	−1.8	−1.6	−1.5	−1.5
Euro area[2]	−1.5	−0.3	0.8	0.4	0.8	0.1	−0.2	0.1	−0.5	−0.8	−1.0
Newly industrialized Asian economies	3.5	4.6	5.0	6.8	6.3	5.1	5.2	6.0	4.5	4.3	3.8

[1]Calculated as the sum of the balances of individual euro area countries.
[2]Corrected for reporting discrepancies in intra-area transactions.

Table A12. Emerging and Developing Economies, by Country: Balance on Current Account

(Percent of GDP)

	2000	2001	2002	2003	2004	2005	2006	2007	2008	2009	2013
Africa	**1.9**	**0.3**	**−1.9**	**−0.7**	**0.3**	**1.9**	**3.1**	**0.1**	**1.7**	**0.9**	**−0.4**
Algeria	16.7	12.9	7.7	13.0	13.1	20.6	25.2	23.2	26.0	20.6	12.6
Angola	8.7	−16.0	−1.3	−5.2	3.5	16.8	23.3	11.0	12.0	11.8	8.0
Benin	−7.7	−6.4	−8.4	−8.3	−7.2	−5.9	−6.2	−5.7	−6.1	−6.0	−6.2
Botswana	8.8	9.9	3.3	5.6	2.9	15.3	17.6	16.8	8.6	8.3	7.3
Burkina Faso	−12.3	−11.2	−9.9	−8.9	−10.4	−11.3	−9.6	−9.9	−11.5	−10.7	−9.9
Burundi	−8.6	−4.6	−3.5	−4.6	−8.1	−9.6	−14.4	−12.4	−12.0	−12.2	−13.0
Cameroon	−1.4	−3.6	−5.1	−1.8	−3.8	−3.4	0.7	0.4	—	−0.4	−2.7
Cape Verde	−10.9	−10.6	−11.1	−11.1	−14.3	−3.4	−5.1	−10.1	−11.6	−12.8	−15.5
Central African Republic	−1.3	−1.7	−1.6	−2.2	−1.8	−6.6	−2.7	−4.5	−6.4	−6.7	−5.4
Chad	−15.4	−30.8	−92.9	−46.8	−16.0	2.1	−9.5	−4.3	−2.2	−4.0	−10.0
Comoros	1.7	3.0	−1.7	−3.8	−4.6	−6.5	−5.2	1.9	−3.5	−4.3	−5.4
Congo, Dem. Rep. of	−4.0	−4.0	−1.6	1.0	−2.4	−10.5	−2.4	−4.0	−10.7	−24.6	−8.4
Congo, Rep. of	7.9	−5.6	0.6	−4.1	12.7	11.4	1.6	−19.5	6.0	10.9	−3.8
Côte d'Ivoire	−2.8	−0.6	6.7	2.1	1.6	0.2	3.1	1.4	0.6	−0.5	−3.4
Djibouti	−9.0	−2.9	−1.6	3.4	−1.3	1.3	−14.2	−25.2	−22.6	−17.8	−9.3
Equatorial Guinea	−15.7	−41.1	0.9	−33.2	−22.3	−5.4	4.5	1.8	2.9	1.5	−3.3
Eritrea	−0.6	−4.6	6.8	9.7	−0.7	0.3	−3.3	−4.7	−5.1	−5.5	−0.4
Ethiopia	−4.2	−3.0	−4.7	−1.4	−4.0	−6.3	−9.1	−4.5	−4.3	−6.1	−2.5
Gabon	19.7	11.0	6.8	9.5	11.2	19.8	18.0	12.8	15.3	14.3	11.5
Gambia, The	−3.1	−2.6	−2.8	−5.1	−6.1	−15.1	−11.5	−10.7	−12.1	−10.9	−7.7
Ghana	−8.4	−5.3	0.5	1.7	−2.7	−7.0	−10.9	−12.8	−9.8	−7.9	−9.7
Guinea	−6.4	−2.7	−2.5	−3.4	−5.8	−4.5	−5.9	−9.2	−10.9	−9.8	−14.4
Guinea-Bissau	−5.6	−22.1	−10.7	−2.8	2.4	−5.1	−11.3	−1.7	7.0	2.8	−3.9
Kenya	−2.3	−3.1	2.2	−0.2	0.1	−0.8	−2.5	−3.5	−5.5	−3.8	−2.8
Lesotho	−18.0	−12.4	−19.4	−12.3	−5.5	−7.0	4.4	4.8	5.0	4.5	3.5
Liberia	−15.6	−14.9	1.0	−14.2	−5.6	−13.3	−31.0	−30.7	−42.1	−36.2	−8.1
Madagascar	−5.6	−1.3	−6.0	−4.9	−9.2	−11.1	−8.7	−15.1	−27.4	−16.7	−7.1
Malawi	−5.3	−6.8	−12.9	−7.2	−8.5	−12.3	−6.2	−3.2	−2.9	−4.4	−4.9
Mali	−10.0	−10.4	−3.1	−6.2	−8.4	−8.3	−4.9	−6.6	−7.5	−6.7	−6.4
Mauritania	−9.0	−11.7	3.0	−13.6	−34.6	−47.2	−1.3	−6.7	−8.6	−12.0	5.1
Mauritius	−1.5	3.4	5.7	2.4	0.8	−3.5	−5.3	−7.9	−6.3	−5.8	−2.5
Morocco	−1.3	4.3	3.6	3.2	1.7	1.9	2.8	−0.1	−1.1	−0.9	−0.3
Mozambique	−12.1	−11.7	−13.5	−10.5	−6.3	−11.4	19.7	−9.4	−11.3	−10.3	−9.6
Namibia	9.0	1.9	3.7	6.7	8.2	5.5	15.9	18.4	12.8	10.0	5.1
Niger	−6.7	−5.1	−6.6	−8.3	−7.8	−9.3	−8.6	−7.7	−9.7	−14.0	−9.0
Nigeria	11.7	4.9	−13.1	−6.1	5.0	7.1	9.5	0.7	6.5	5.7	4.9
Rwanda	−5.0	−6.0	−7.4	−7.4	−2.8	−2.9	−6.5	−4.8	−9.5	−12.7	−8.8
São Tomé and Príncipe	−17.5	−21.0	−16.4	−13.2	−17.3	−13.6	−45.7	−35.5	−36.1	−32.9	−34.6
Senegal	−6.6	−4.4	−5.7	−6.1	−6.1	−7.8	−9.8	−8.1	−10.3	−11.1	−10.5
Seychelles	−7.3	−23.4	−16.3	0.4	−7.0	−23.6	−17.2	−38.7	−44.9	−41.4	−30.0
Sierra Leone	−8.8	−6.3	−2.0	−4.8	−5.8	−7.1	−3.6	−3.8	−6.4	−5.9	−5.9
South Africa	−0.1	0.3	0.8	−1.1	−3.2	−4.0	−6.5	−7.3	−7.7	−7.9	−6.5
Sudan	−8.2	−12.5	−10.3	−7.8	−6.5	−10.9	−15.1	−11.8	−9.8	−5.6	−6.2
Swaziland	−4.9	−4.3	4.8	6.8	2.2	−3.1	−3.7	1.2	−1.4	−1.6	−2.4
Tanzania	−4.8	−4.5	−6.2	−4.2	−3.6	−4.1	−7.8	−9.2	−9.7	−10.1	−10.0
Togo	−9.0	−9.3	−5.5	−4.2	−3.0	−5.3	−6.0	−6.4	−7.9	−6.7	−5.2
Tunisia	−4.2	−5.1	−3.6	−2.9	−2.0	−1.1	−2.0	−2.5	−2.7	−2.7	−2.6
Uganda	−7.1	−3.9	−4.9	−5.8	−2.2	−3.2	−4.0	−2.0	−7.7	−9.3	−5.5
Zambia	−18.2	−19.9	−15.3	−14.8	−11.8	−9.1	1.1	−6.7	−5.5	−3.9	−7.1
Zimbabwe[1]	0.4	−0.3	−0.6	−2.9	−8.3	−11.0	−6.0	−1.0	—	. . .	. . .

Table A12 *(continued)*

	2000	2001	2002	2003	2004	2005	2006	2007	2008	2009	2013
Central and eastern Europe	**–4.7**	**–2.5**	**–3.3**	**–4.2**	**–5.4**	**–4.7**	**–6.2**	**–6.6**	**–7.2**	**–6.9**	**–5.5**
Albania	–3.7	–3.7	–7.2	–5.2	–4.0	–6.6	–5.9	–8.3	–8.3	–5.5	–4.2
Bosnia and Herzegovina	–6.9	–12.5	–17.8	–19.4	–16.3	–18.0	–8.4	–13.0	–14.0	–15.3	–13.1
Bulgaria	–5.6	–5.6	–2.4	–5.5	–6.6	–12.0	–15.6	–21.4	–21.9	–18.9	–6.7
Croatia	–2.9	–3.7	–8.4	–6.2	–4.9	–6.2	–7.9	–8.5	–9.0	–8.7	–6.4
Czech Republic	–4.7	–5.3	–5.7	–6.3	–5.3	–1.6	–3.1	–2.5	–3.0	–2.8	–2.8
Estonia	–5.4	–5.2	–10.6	–11.3	–12.3	–10.0	–15.5	–16.0	–11.2	–11.2	–10.0
Hungary	–8.4	–6.0	–7.0	–7.9	–8.4	–6.8	–6.5	–5.6	–5.5	–5.1	–4.2
Latvia	–4.8	–7.6	–6.6	–8.2	–12.8	–12.5	–22.3	–23.3	–15.0	–10.5	–4.8
Lithuania	–5.9	–4.7	–5.2	–6.9	–7.7	–7.1	–10.8	–13.0	–10.5	–8.8	–8.0
Macedonia, FYR	–1.9	–7.2	–9.4	–3.3	–7.7	–1.3	–0.4	–2.7	–6.8	–6.0	–3.4
Montenegro, Rep. of	. . .	. . .	. . .	–7.3	–7.2	–8.6	–30.4	–37.0	–32.7	–29.1	–18.2
Poland	–5.8	–2.8	–2.5	–2.1	–4.2	–1.6	–3.2	–3.7	–5.0	–5.7	–6.2
Romania	–3.7	–5.5	–3.3	–5.8	–8.4	–8.9	–10.4	–13.9	–14.5	–13.0	–8.5
Serbia	–1.7	–2.4	–7.9	–7.0	–11.7	–8.5	–12.5	–16.5	–16.1	–15.8	–14.8
Slovak Republic	–3.3	–8.3	–8.0	–5.9	–7.8	–8.5	–7.1	–5.3	–5.0	–4.7	–3.8
Turkey	–3.7	1.8	–0.7	–2.6	–4.0	–4.7	–6.1	–5.7	–6.7	–6.3	–4.8
Commonwealth of Independent States[2]	**13.7**	**8.0**	**6.5**	**6.3**	**8.2**	**8.8**	**7.5**	**4.5**	**4.8**	**2.4**	**–2.0**
Russia	18.0	11.1	8.4	8.2	10.1	11.0	9.5	5.9	5.8	2.9	–2.1
Excluding Russia	1.5	–0.8	0.9	0.4	2.3	1.6	1.1	–0.1	1.5	0.9	–1.8
Armenia	–14.6	–9.5	–6.2	–6.8	–0.5	–1.0	–1.8	–6.5	–6.8	–5.0	–5.7
Azerbaijan	–3.5	–0.9	–12.3	–27.8	–29.8	1.3	17.7	28.8	39.5	39.2	0.9
Belarus	–3.2	–3.3	–2.2	–2.4	–5.2	1.4	–4.1	–6.6	–7.5	–7.7	–5.5
Georgia	–7.9	–6.4	–6.8	–8.6	–8.9	–11.9	–15.9	–19.7	–16.6	–13.2	–10.6
Kazakhstan	3.0	–5.4	–4.2	–0.9	0.8	–1.8	–2.2	–6.6	–1.7	–1.0	1.2
Kyrgyz Republic	–4.3	–1.5	–4.0	1.7	4.9	3.2	–6.6	–6.5	–8.3	–7.4	–6.3
Moldova	–7.6	–1.7	–4.0	–6.6	–2.3	–10.3	–12.0	–9.7	–10.3	–10.6	–10.5
Mongolia	–5.0	–6.6	–8.5	–6.8	1.5	1.3	7.0	–0.6	–17.1	–17.6	–1.6
Tajikistan	–1.6	–4.9	–3.5	–1.3	–3.9	–2.7	–3.0	–9.5	–8.3	–7.1	–3.9
Turkmenistan	8.2	1.7	6.7	2.7	0.6	5.1	15.3	16.8	23.6	28.1	32.2
Ukraine	4.7	3.7	7.5	5.8	10.6	2.9	–1.5	–4.2	–7.6	–9.7	–9.2
Uzbekistan	1.8	–1.0	1.2	8.7	10.1	13.6	18.8	23.8	24.6	20.8	7.3

Table A12 (continued)

	2000	2001	2002	2003	2004	2005	2006	2007	2008	2009	2013
Developing Asia	**1.7**	**1.5**	**2.4**	**2.7**	**2.6**	**4.0**	**5.9**	**6.7**	**5.5**	**5.4**	**6.2**
Afghanistan, I.R. of	...	...	−3.7	−10.3	−4.9	−2.8	−6.3	−0.8	0.0	−1.0	−4.2
Bangladesh	−1.4	−0.9	0.3	0.3	−0.3	—	1.2	0.5	−0.5	−0.7	−1.8
Bhutan	−9.7	−9.0	−12.0	−13.3	−10.3	−26.1	−3.1	8.8	9.5	2.3	−6.0
Brunei Darussalam	50.0	48.4	41.2	47.7	48.6	52.8	55.9	57.3	56.5	56.1	55.2
Cambodia	−2.8	−1.1	−2.4	−3.6	−2.2	−4.2	−2.0	−0.9	−5.4	−6.2	−6.8
China	1.7	1.3	2.4	2.8	3.6	7.2	9.4	11.1	9.8	10.0	10.9
Fiji	−4.8	−4.7	1.4	−3.8	−11.0	−11.5	−17.4	−14.9	−17.9	−17.9	−18.3
India	−1.0	0.3	1.4	1.5	0.1	−1.3	−1.1	−1.8	−3.1	−3.4	−2.1
Indonesia	4.8	4.3	4.0	3.5	0.6	0.1	3.0	2.5	1.8	1.2	−1.1
Kiribati	−1.2	22.2	10.5	12.6	−3.4	−42.2	−27.6	−31.1	−43.7	−47.0	−53.6
Lao PDR	−10.6	−8.2	−7.2	−8.1	−14.3	−18.8	−12.6	−23.1	−21.7	−15.5	−0.6
Malaysia	9.0	7.9	8.0	12.0	11.9	14.6	16.2	14.0	11.7	11.1	8.5
Maldives	−8.2	−9.4	−5.6	−4.6	−16.5	−35.8	−40.7	−45.0	−35.7	−19.2	−6.0
Myanmar	−0.8	−2.4	0.2	−1.0	2.4	3.7	7.3	4.0	2.9	2.0	−2.2
Nepal	2.7	4.2	3.9	2.2	2.7	2.0	2.2	0.6	0.5	0.2	−1.1
Pakistan	−0.3	0.4	3.9	4.9	1.8	−1.4	−3.9	−4.9	−6.9	−6.1	−4.0
Papua New Guinea	8.5	6.5	−1.0	4.5	2.2	4.2	2.9	4.3	3.3	1.7	−3.7
Philippines	−2.9	−2.4	−0.4	0.4	1.9	2.0	4.5	4.4	2.1	1.0	−0.4
Samoa	1.0	0.1	−1.1	−95.3	−6.8	−1.7	−6.1	−6.1	−7.8	−6.8	3.5
Solomon Islands	−10.6	−10.9	−10.2	−2.5	3.1	−24.2	−26.5	−40.0	−27.5	−13.9	−9.9
Sri Lanka	−6.5	−1.1	−1.4	−0.4	−3.2	−2.8	−5.0	−4.6	−5.7	−4.9	−2.9
Thailand	7.6	4.4	3.7	3.4	1.7	−4.3	1.1	6.1	3.4	1.3	−0.6
Timor-Leste	−15.0	−19.3	−22.9	−21.4	14.8	61.0	192.2	253.3	230.5	178.1	94.3
Tonga	−6.2	−9.5	5.1	−3.1	4.2	−2.6	−8.2	−10.5	−19.0	−17.2	−6.7
Vanuatu	2.0	2.0	−9.7	−10.7	−7.3	−10.0	−8.0	−13.2	−13.7	−10.1	−7.0
Vietnam	3.5	2.1	−1.7	−4.9	−3.5	−1.1	−0.4	−9.6	−13.6	−11.9	−9.6
Middle East	**11.4**	**6.3**	**4.8**	**8.3**	**11.8**	**19.7**	**20.9**	**19.8**	**23.0**	**19.4**	**11.7**
Bahrain	10.6	2.8	−0.7	2.0	4.2	11.0	13.3	19.9	20.4	18.6	9.5
Egypt	−1.2	—	0.7	2.4	4.3	3.2	0.8	1.5	0.8	−0.5	−2.5
Iran, I.R. of	13.0	5.2	3.1	0.6	0.9	8.8	9.3	10.4	11.2	8.4	0.5
Iraq	...	...	...	...	...	...	...	...	...	...	...
Jordan	0.7	0.1	5.7	12.2	0.8	−17.4	−11.3	−17.3	−15.5	−13.4	−9.2
Kuwait	38.9	23.9	11.2	19.7	30.6	42.5	51.7	47.4	45.2	42.3	40.3
Lebanon	−17.2	−19.3	−14.2	−13.2	−15.5	−13.6	−6.0	−10.7	−9.8	−10.2	−6.2
Libya	31.5	13.0	3.3	21.9	24.3	41.8	51.6	42.5	42.6	38.5	32.4
Oman	15.5	9.8	6.7	3.8	2.4	15.2	12.1	10.0	11.7	10.8	7.3
Qatar	23.2	27.3	21.9	25.3	22.4	33.2	30.6	34.6	44.6	40.7	39.2
Saudi Arabia	7.6	5.1	6.3	13.1	20.7	28.5	27.4	26.8	31.3	24.0	6.9
Syrian Arab Republic	5.2	5.7	7.2	0.8	−3.2	−4.1	−6.1	−5.8	−6.6	−5.5	−7.9
United Arab Emirates	17.3	9.5	5.0	8.6	10.0	18.3	22.0	21.6	27.5	26.0	23.5
Yemen, Rep. of	13.8	6.8	4.1	1.5	1.6	3.8	1.1	−4.3	−1.4	0.9	−4.1

Table A12 *(concluded)*

	2000	2001	2002	2003	2004	2005	2006	2007	2008	2009	2013
Western Hemisphere	**−2.4**	**−2.8**	**−0.9**	**0.4**	**1.0**	**1.4**	**1.5**	**0.5**	**−0.3**	**−0.9**	**−1.2**
Antigua and Barbuda	−9.8	−8.0	−11.5	−12.9	−8.3	−12.4	−16.1	−19.4	−18.2	−14.6	−11.6
Argentina	−3.2	−1.4	8.9	6.3	2.1	2.0	2.5	1.1	0.4	−0.5	−0.8
Bahamas, The	−10.4	−11.6	−7.8	−8.6	−5.4	−14.3	−25.3	−21.9	−18.5	−13.8	−7.7
Barbados	−5.7	−4.4	−6.8	−6.3	−12.4	−12.5	−8.1	−6.8	−7.5	−7.5	−7.5
Belize	−20.3	−21.9	−17.7	−18.2	−14.8	−14.4	−2.2	−4.0	−4.0	−4.3	−6.1
Bolivia	−5.3	−3.4	−4.1	1.0	3.8	6.5	11.7	13.3	12.3	8.6	5.5
Brazil	−3.8	−4.2	−1.5	0.8	1.8	1.6	1.3	0.3	−0.7	−0.9	−0.3
Chile	−1.2	−1.6	−0.9	−1.1	2.2	1.1	3.6	3.7	−0.5	−1.3	−3.0
Colombia	0.9	−1.3	−1.7	−1.2	−0.9	−1.5	−2.1	−3.8	−4.9	−4.3	−2.8
Costa Rica	−4.3	−3.7	−4.9	−4.8	−4.5	−5.2	−4.9	−5.8	−6.6	−6.1	−5.8
Dominica	−19.7	−18.5	−13.7	−13.0	−17.3	−29.5	−19.4	−23.3	−26.6	−23.9	−17.8
Dominican Republic	−5.1	−3.4	−3.7	6.0	6.1	−1.4	−3.5	−5.6	−4.6	−3.9	−1.9
Ecuador	5.3	−3.2	−4.8	−1.5	−1.7	0.8	3.6	3.3	5.2	3.9	1.5
El Salvador	−2.8	−1.1	−2.8	−4.7	−4.0	−4.2	−3.8	−4.8	−5.8	−5.3	−3.4
Grenada	−20.5	−24.9	−29.2	−30.0	−11.4	−22.8	−23.0	−23.5	−25.4	−25.8	−25.1
Guatemala	−6.1	−6.7	−6.1	−4.6	−4.9	−4.5	−5.0	−5.0	−5.5	−5.4	−5.3
Guyana	−14.1	−15.0	−11.9	−8.6	−9.3	−14.8	−19.4	−18.2	−16.6	−15.8	−9.0
Haiti	−1.0	−2.0	−0.9	−1.6	−1.6	2.6	−0.4	0.2	−1.3	−2.5	−2.8
Honduras	−7.1	−6.3	−3.6	−6.8	−7.7	−3.0	−4.7	−10.0	−9.5	−9.0	−6.0
Jamaica	−4.9	−10.7	−10.3	−9.4	−5.8	−11.2	−11.5	−14.5	−13.6	−11.9	−8.0
Mexico	−3.2	−2.8	−2.2	−1.3	−1.0	−0.7	−0.3	−0.8	−1.0	−1.6	−2.1
Nicaragua	−20.1	−19.4	−17.7	−15.7	−12.6	−14.1	−13.2	−17.3	−24.8	−24.4	−20.4
Panama	−5.9	−1.5	−0.8	−4.5	−7.5	−4.9	−3.2	−8.0	−7.8	−9.8	−5.0
Paraguay	−2.3	−4.1	1.8	2.3	2.1	0.6	−1.2	1.5	1.0	0.4	—
Peru	−2.8	−2.1	−1.9	−1.5	—	1.4	2.8	1.6	−0.2	−0.3	−0.9
St. Kitts and Nevis	−21.0	−32.0	−39.1	−34.9	−20.2	−22.6	−29.0	−31.0	−30.2	−28.3	−22.2
St. Lucia	−13.4	−15.7	−15.1	−19.7	−10.9	−17.1	−32.2	−20.7	−18.5	−17.9	−16.6
St. Vincent and the Grenadines	−7.1	−10.4	−11.5	−20.8	−24.8	−22.3	−24.0	−26.7	−26.7	−23.3	−19.5
Suriname	−3.8	−15.2	−5.6	−10.8	−2.1	−4.3	0.1	1.0	1.1	−0.6	0.4
Trinidad and Tobago	6.6	5.9	1.6	8.8	13.0	23.7	25.6	20.2	14.9	12.5	6.0
Uruguay	−2.8	−2.9	3.2	−0.5	0.3	—	−2.4	−0.8	−1.7	−0.8	−0.1
Venezuela	10.1	1.6	8.2	14.1	13.8	17.7	14.7	9.8	7.2	5.0	0.5

[1]Given recent trends, it is not possible to forecast nominal GDP with any precision and consequently no projections beyond 2008 are shown.
[2]Mongolia, which is not a member of the Commonwealth of Independent States, is included in this group for reasons of geography and similarities in economic structure.

Table A13. Emerging and Developing Economies: Net Capital Flows[1]
(Billions of U.S. dollars)

	Average 1997–99	2000	2001	2002	2003	2004	2005	2006	2007	2008	2009
Emerging and developing economies											
Private capital flows, net[2]	116.9	74.8	79.5	89.8	168.6	241.9	251.8	231.9	605.0	330.7	441.5
Private direct investment, net	162.4	171.3	186.3	157.2	166.2	188.7	259.8	250.1	309.9	306.9	322.4
Private portfolio flows, net	52.0	15.9	−78.7	−92.2	−13.2	16.4	−19.4	−103.8	48.5	−72.2	31.0
Other private capital flows, net	−97.3	−112.2	−27.1	25.1	17.1	38.5	13.3	87.5	248.8	98.0	90.0
Official flows, net[3]	20.9	−33.9	0.9	−0.6	−50.0	−70.7	−109.9	−160.0	−149.0	−162.3	−149.8
Change in reserves[4]	−72.8	−135.7	−124.0	−194.8	−363.3	−509.3	−595.1	−752.8	−1236.2	−1004.1	−1071.4
Memorandum											
Current account[5]	−27.3	124.8	86.6	130.3	224.9	297.2	517.3	698.0	738.1	814.7	750.0
Africa											
Private capital flows, net[2]	8.6	1.7	6.5	5.7	7.0	16.0	30.5	39.6	47.1	57.5	64.2
Private direct investment, net	7.4	7.7	23.2	14.4	17.8	16.6	23.6	21.5	32.0	38.3	37.1
Private portfolio flows, net	6.9	−2.1	−7.9	−1.6	−0.4	5.8	3.7	18.5	11.5	9.4	10.4
Other private capital flows, net	−5.5	−3.8	−7.9	−6.7	−9.0	−4.8	5.1	1.5	5.8	11.8	18.6
Official flows, net[3]	3.9	1.5	1.4	4.3	1.4	−1.2	−5.3	−18.2	−1.6	4.4	6.1
Change in reserves[4]	−2.5	−13.4	−10.6	−5.7	−11.5	−31.8	−43.3	−54.2	−61.4	−87.6	−87.0
Central and eastern Europe											
Private capital flows, net[2]	32.4	38.6	11.1	53.7	53.3	74.3	118.1	120.4	170.5	162.5	158.2
Private direct investment, net	18.1	23.5	24.0	24.5	17.0	36.0	51.5	64.7	73.2	74.7	75.7
Private portfolio flows, net	4.3	3.8	0.9	2.1	8.0	28.4	21.5	9.9	−6.8	12.1	12.3
Other private capital flows, net	10.0	11.4	−13.8	27.2	28.2	10.0	45.1	45.8	104.2	75.6	70.1
Official flows, net[3]	−1.5	1.6	6.0	−7.5	−4.8	−6.0	−8.1	−4.6	−2.6	−0.9	−2.5
Change in reserves[4]	−10.1	−6.2	−2.7	−18.1	−12.8	−14.7	−45.9	−22.7	−42.9	−25.1	−21.7
Commonwealth of Independent States											
Private capital flows, net[2]	−7.0	−27.4	6.9	15.6	18.4	6.7	32.5	57.9	115.1	59.1	89.1
Private direct investment, net	5.4	2.3	4.9	5.2	5.4	13.0	11.3	23.5	16.7	29.5	35.4
Private portfolio flows, net	1.0	−10.0	−1.2	0.4	−0.5	8.1	−4.7	12.5	7.7	12.4	14.9
Other private capital flows, net	−13.5	−19.7	3.2	10.0	13.5	−14.5	25.8	21.9	90.7	17.2	38.8
Official flows, net[3]	−0.5	−5.8	−5.0	−10.5	−9.3	−7.4	−20.3	−29.7	−4.2	−4.6	−3.7
Change in reserves[4]	1.6	−20.4	−14.4	−15.1	−32.7	−55.0	−77.2	−128.8	−170.9	−154.5	−143.0
Emerging Asia[6]											
Private capital flows, net[2]	−0.9	5.3	23.0	23.6	64.5	146.6	90.8	47.9	193.5	40.7	116.2
Private direct investment, net	62.1	60.8	53.2	53.4	70.3	64.1	103.9	97.4	90.5	93.4	94.3
Private portfolio flows, net	23.4	19.7	−50.1	−60.0	7.5	13.4	−9.3	−110.7	18.4	−129.3	−15.5
Other private capital flows, net	−86.4	−75.2	19.9	30.3	−13.2	69.1	−3.8	61.2	84.6	76.5	37.4
Official flows, net[3]	11.6	−1.9	−13.1	2.8	−18.0	−13.4	−21.0	−22.6	−38.0	−18.7	−25.9
Change in reserves[4]	−57.5	−57.7	−87.0	−154.4	−236.0	−339.2	−288.3	−372.4	−669.3	−470.2	−580.8
Middle East[7]											
Private capital flows, net[2]	9.3	−5.3	−7.4	−22.3	2.3	−17.0	−56.7	−43.4	−21.0	−62.1	−63.0
Private direct investment, net	7.2	6.0	12.3	9.2	17.5	10.1	18.2	15.3	20.4	13.2	19.7
Private portfolio flows, net	−5.0	3.0	−12.6	−17.6	−17.3	−20.7	−36.0	−20.1	−14.0	−16.7	−31.8
Other private capital flows, net	7.1	−14.2	−7.1	−13.8	2.1	−6.3	−38.9	−38.6	−27.4	−58.6	−50.8
Official flows, net[3]	1.3	−23.5	−13.9	−8.1	−24.2	−33.7	−24.4	−66.4	−103.6	−145.5	−124.4
Change in reserves[4]	−3.4	−31.3	−11.1	−2.9	−36.7	−46.2	−107.1	−125.2	−159.2	−192.3	−183.2
Western Hemisphere											
Private capital flows, net[2]	74.4	61.9	39.3	13.6	23.0	15.2	36.7	9.5	99.7	73.0	76.8
Private direct investment, net	62.3	71.0	68.7	50.6	38.1	48.9	51.3	27.8	77.0	57.8	60.2
Private portfolio flows, net	21.3	1.5	−7.9	−15.3	−10.6	−18.6	5.4	−14.0	31.8	39.9	40.8
Other private capital flows, net	−9.1	−10.6	−21.4	−21.7	−4.5	−15.0	−20.0	−4.3	−9.1	−24.6	−24.1
Official flows, net[3]	5.9	−5.8	25.5	18.4	4.9	−8.9	−30.9	−18.6	1.0	2.9	0.6
Change in reserves[4]	−0.9	−6.7	1.7	1.4	−33.6	−22.4	−33.2	−49.5	−132.6	−74.3	−55.7
Memorandum											
Fuel exporting countries											
Private capital flows, net[2]	−4.8	−43.3	−6.7	−15.4	9.9	−16.0	−37.6	3.5	64.7	−37.0	−6.9
Other countries											
Private capital flows, net[2]	121.7	118.1	86.3	105.3	158.7	257.9	289.5	228.5	540.3	367.8	448.4

[1]Net capital flows comprise net direct investment, net portfolio investment, and other long- and short-term net investment flows, including official and private borrowing. In this table, Hong Kong SAR, Israel, Korea, Singapore, and Taiwan Province of China are included.
[2]Because of data limitations, flows listed under private capital flows, net, may include some official flows.
[3]Excludes grants and includes overseas investments of official investment agencies.
[4]A minus sign indicates an increase.
[5]The sum of the current account balance, net private capital flows, net official flows, and the change in reserves equals, with the opposite sign, the sum of the capital account and errors and omissions.
[6]Consists of developing Asia and the newly industrialized Asian economies.
[7]Includes Israel.

Table A14. Emerging and Developing Economies: Private Capital Flows[1]

(Billions of U.S. dollars)

	Average 1997–99	2000	2001	2002	2003	2004	2005	2006	2007	2008	2009
Emerging and developing economies											
Private capital flows, net	116.9	74.8	79.5	89.8	168.6	241.9	251.8	231.9	605.0	330.7	441.5
Inflow	252.4	321.7	164.8	173.6	418.6	630.4	826.8	1,161.2	1,633.8	1,425.5	1,465.8
Outflow	−88.2	−246.4	−90.2	−83.2	−252.7	−388.9	−574.0	−927.4	−1,027.0	−1,093.0	−1,022.3
Africa											
Private capital flows, net	8.6	1.7	6.5	5.7	7.0	16.0	30.5	39.6	47.1	57.5	64.2
Inflow	20.5	10.7	19.5	17.6	22.2	30.1	49.7	71.3	73.0	84.9	92.8
Outflow	−7.1	−8.9	−12.1	−11.6	−13.7	−12.5	−17.4	−29.8	−23.6	−25.4	−26.7
Central and eastern Europe											
Private capital flows, net	32.4	38.6	11.1	53.7	53.3	74.3	118.1	120.4	170.5	162.5	158.2
Inflow	38.1	48.6	20.4	55.0	63.8	103.9	139.1	175.6	211.2	186.6	182.9
Outflow	−1.5	−9.9	−9.3	−1.3	−10.5	−29.6	−21.1	−55.2	−40.7	−24.1	−24.7
Commonwealth of Independent States											
Private capital flows, net	−7.0	−27.4	6.9	15.6	18.4	6.7	32.5	57.9	115.1	59.1	89.1
Inflow	11.3	−2.2	10.8	22.3	46.0	66.2	112.3	163.1	261.4	201.9	231.8
Outflow	−1.4	−25.2	−3.9	−6.7	−27.6	−59.5	−79.9	−105.2	−146.3	−142.8	−142.8
Emerging Asia[2]											
Private capital flows, net	−0.9	5.3	23.0	23.6	64.5	146.6	90.8	47.9	193.5	40.7	116.2
Inflow	60.6	138.7	47.9	63.6	208.0	308.1	367.3	512.0	719.9	682.7	686.0
Outflow	−57.5	−133.1	−30.2	−39.9	−147.7	−163.6	−278.6	−464.3	−527.0	−642.4	−569.9
Middle East[3]											
Private capital flows, net	9.3	−5.3	−7.4	−22.3	2.3	−17.0	−56.7	−43.4	−21.0	−62.1	−63.0
Inflow	17.1	41.1	−3.8	−11.9	31.9	57.1	69.9	131.2	159.4	112.7	111.5
Outflow	−7.1	−46.4	−4.1	−10.3	−29.4	−74.0	−125.3	−174.5	−180.3	−174.6	−174.3
Western Hemisphere											
Private capital flows, net	74.4	61.9	39.3	13.6	23.0	15.2	36.7	9.5	99.7	73.0	76.8
Inflow	104.8	84.8	70.0	27.0	46.8	65.0	88.5	108.0	208.9	156.7	160.8
Outflow	−13.6	−23.0	−30.6	−13.4	−23.7	−49.8	−51.8	−98.5	−109.2	−83.7	−84.0

[1]Private capital flows comprise direct investment, portfolio investment, and other long- and short-term investment flows. In this table, Hong Kong SAR, Israel, Korea, Singapore, and Taiwan Province of China are included.

[2]Consists of developing Asia and the newly industrialized Asian economies.

[3]Includes Israel.

Table A15. Emerging and Developing Economies: Reserves[1]

	2000	2001	2002	2003	2004	2005	2006	2007	2008	2009
					Billions of U.S. dollars					
Emerging and developing economies	**800.9**	**895.8**	**1,072.6**	**1,395.3**	**1,848.3**	**2,339.3**	**3,095.5**	**4,283.4**	**5,271.4**	**6,319.6**
Regional groups										
Africa	54.0	64.3	72.0	90.2	126.2	160.3	221.3	282.7	370.3	457.3
Sub-Sahara	35.0	35.5	36.0	39.9	62.3	83.0	115.9	144.9	187.8	236.4
Excluding Nigeria and South Africa	18.7	18.7	22.5	26.1	31.9	35.9	50.3	62.2	77.0	96.0
Central and eastern Europe	91.2	91.3	121.7	149.1	172.0	202.2	240.2	283.1	308.2	329.9
Commonwealth of Independent States[2]	33.2	43.9	58.1	92.4	148.7	214.4	357.1	527.9	682.5	825.5
Russia	24.8	33.1	44.6	73.8	121.5	176.5	296.2	445.3	583.0	708.1
Excluding Russia	8.4	10.8	13.5	18.5	27.2	37.9	60.8	82.6	99.4	117.3
Developing Asia	320.7	379.5	496.2	669.7	933.9	1,155.5	1,489.1	2,108.4	2,562.0	3,118.9
China	168.9	216.3	292.0	409.2	615.5	822.5	1,069.5	1,531.4	1,911.4	2,411.4
India	38.4	46.4	68.2	99.5	127.2	132.5	171.3	256.8	287.5	301.2
Excluding China and India	113.4	116.9	136.0	161.1	191.2	200.5	248.2	320.2	363.1	406.3
Middle East	146.1	157.9	163.9	198.3	246.7	351.6	477.2	638.1	830.9	1,014.8
Western Hemisphere	155.7	158.8	160.7	195.6	220.8	255.5	310.7	443.3	517.6	573.3
Brazil	31.5	35.8	37.7	49.1	52.8	53.6	85.6	180.1	219.9	250.5
Mexico	35.5	44.8	50.6	59.0	64.1	74.1	76.3	86.6	97.0	105.0
Analytical groups										
By source of export earnings										
Fuel	192.0	216.6	232.8	310.2	436.7	626.1	931.6	1,281.8	1,700.9	2,097.0
Nonfuel	608.9	679.2	839.8	1,085.2	1,411.6	1,713.2	2,163.9	3,001.6	3,570.5	4,222.7
of which, primary products	25.9	24.9	26.3	27.3	28.9	31.6	39.8	43.1	49.1	55.5
By external financing source										
Net debtor countries	419.8	443.4	526.7	644.4	745.2	825.6	1,023.7	1,368.8	1,540.0	1,678.2
of which, official financing	17.3	18.4	18.8	26.1	30.0	33.8	44.0	55.5	59.8	66.0
Net debtor countries by debt-servicing experience										
Countries with arrears and/or rescheduling during 2002–06	76.4	72.3	81.3	98.2	110.4	122.3	150.7	194.8	220.4	250.8
Other groups										
Heavily indebted poor countries	10.3	11.0	13.4	16.2	19.4	20.5	26.7	31.4	36.9	43.3
Middle East and north Africa	165.5	187.1	200.6	249.6	312.4	431.3	585.0	777.8	1,015.9	1,240.2

Table A15 *(concluded)*

	2000	2001	2002	2003	2004	2005	2006	2007	2008	2009
					Ratio of reserves to imports of goods and services[3]					
Emerging and developing economies	**44.7**	**49.5**	**55.3**	**60.4**	**62.7**	**66.5**	**73.8**	**84.5**	**87.2**	**93.7**
Regional groups										
Africa	39.7	46.1	46.7	48.0	54.1	57.5	68.1	71.6	79.3	89.4
Sub-Sahara	34.1	33.8	31.1	27.7	35.1	38.3	45.1	47.1	51.9	60.1
Excluding Nigeria and South Africa	34.3	32.1	36.6	35.3	34.8	31.7	38.2	38.9	40.8	46.8
Central and eastern Europe	34.5	34.7	40.9	39.1	34.6	35.1	34.2	32.1	29.1	28.2
Commonwealth of Independent States[2]	30.5	34.3	40.9	52.5	65.3	76.9	101.6	113.1	114.4	120.4
Russia	40.6	44.6	52.9	71.5	93.0	107.4	141.5	159.6	159.6	167.6
Excluding Russia	17.5	20.0	23.3	25.5	28.0	33.0	42.8	44.0	43.0	44.6
Developing Asia	49.1	58.3	68.1	74.5	79.4	81.8	89.8	107.2	111.2	119.8
China	67.4	79.7	89.0	91.1	101.5	115.5	125.4	149.0	159.0	173.6
India	52.6	65.0	90.0	107.1	97.0	72.8	76.3	91.7	85.1	80.2
Excluding China and India	34.5	37.9	41.8	45.1	43.7	38.6	42.7	48.6	47.5	48.5
Middle East	75.6	78.7	74.2	78.0	77.4	91.3	102.9	119.1	129.9	138.6
Western Hemisphere	35.8	37.1	40.4	47.4	44.6	43.6	44.9	54.0	52.7	54.8
Brazil	43.5	49.2	61.1	77.2	65.9	54.8	71.0	114.7	102.6	110.7
Mexico	18.6	24.2	27.3	31.4	29.8	30.5	27.4	28.2	28.3	29.3
Analytical groups										
By source of export earnings										
Fuel	64.6	66.3	63.8	72.4	81.0	93.8	114.1	128.0	137.6	148.5
Nonfuel	40.8	45.8	53.3	57.6	58.6	60.1	64.1	73.8	74.2	79.2
of which, primary products	64.6	61.9	62.6	58.3	48.7	43.5	48.1	43.0	42.5	43.4
By external financing source										
Net debtor countries	36.6	39.3	45.4	48.0	44.1	40.8	42.7	47.2	44.7	44.6
of which, official financing	24.7	26.4	25.9	30.8	28.7	27.8	30.1	30.4	27.5	27.9
Net debtor countries by debt-servicing experience										
Countries with arrears and/or rescheduling during 2002–06	41.8	41.0	48.2	51.0	45.3	39.9	42.8	46.4	44.8	47.0
Other groups										
Heavily indebted poor countries	27.7	28.2	31.7	33.9	33.2	29.2	32.3	31.7	32.4	34.9
Middle East and north Africa	72.0	78.3	76.4	82.5	82.1	94.4	107.6	122.3	133.7	142.9

[1]In this table, official holdings of gold are valued at SDR 35 an ounce. This convention results in a marked underestimate of reserves for countries that have substantial gold holdings.
[2]Mongolia, which is not a member of the Commonwealth of Independent States, is included in this group for reasons of geography and similarities in economic structure.
[3]Reserves at year-end in percent of imports of goods and services for the year indicated.

Table A16. Summary of Sources and Uses of World Savings
(Percent of GDP)

	Averages 1986–93	Averages 1994–2001	2002	2003	2004	2005	2006	2007	2008	2009	Average 2010–13
World											
Savings	22.7	22.1	20.5	20.8	21.9	22.5	23.3	23.7	23.8	23.8	24.4
Investment	22.4	22.4	20.8	21.1	21.9	22.4	23.0	23.3	23.4	23.5	24.2
Advanced economies											
Savings	22.2	21.6	19.2	19.1	19.8	19.7	20.0	20.0	19.7	19.3	19.5
Investment	22.7	21.8	19.9	19.9	20.5	20.9	21.3	21.1	20.8	20.4	20.6
Net lending	–0.5	–0.2	–0.7	–0.8	–0.7	–1.2	–1.4	–1.1	–1.1	–1.1	–1.1
Current transfers	–0.4	–0.5	–0.6	–0.6	–0.7	–0.7	–0.7	–0.8	–0.7	–0.7	–0.7
Factor income	–0.3	0.1	0.2	0.2	0.5	0.5	0.5	0.4	0.4	0.2	0.2
Resource balance	0.1	0.2	–0.4	–0.4	–0.5	–1.0	–1.2	–0.8	–0.8	–0.6	–0.6
United States											
Savings	16.3	17.0	14.2	13.3	13.8	14.0	14.1	13.6	13.0	12.2	12.8
Investment	18.8	19.6	18.4	18.4	19.4	19.9	20.0	18.8	17.4	16.4	16.8
Net lending	–2.6	–2.6	–4.2	–5.1	–5.5	–6.0	–5.9	–5.1	–4.3	–4.2	–3.9
Current transfers	–0.4	–0.6	–0.6	–0.6	–0.7	–0.7	–0.7	–0.8	–0.7	–0.7	–0.7
Factor income	–0.4	0.1	0.5	0.1	0.5	0.5	0.5	0.7	0.8	0.4	0.4
Resource balance	–1.7	–2.2	–4.0	–4.5	–5.2	–5.7	–5.7	–5.1	–4.4	–3.9	–3.6
Euro area											
Savings	. . .	21.3	20.7	20.7	21.4	20.9	21.4	21.8	21.4	20.9	21.1
Investment	. . .	21.0	20.0	20.1	20.4	20.8	21.6	22.2	22.2	21.9	22.2
Net lending	. . .	0.3	0.7	0.6	1.1	0.2	–0.2	–0.4	–0.9	–1.0	–1.1
Current transfers[1]	–0.5	–0.7	–0.7	–0.8	–0.8	–0.9	–1.0	–1.0	–0.9	–0.9	–0.9
Factor income[1]	–0.2	–0.4	–0.9	–0.8	–0.2	–0.3	–0.2	–0.4	–0.5	–0.6	–0.7
Resource balance[1]	1.0	1.6	2.4	2.1	2.2	1.5	1.1	1.2	0.8	0.7	0.6
Germany											
Savings	23.8	20.5	19.3	19.3	21.3	21.7	22.8	23.8	23.3	22.5	22.3
Investment	21.8	21.4	17.3	17.4	17.1	17.1	17.8	18.3	18.1	17.5	18.2
Net lending	2.0	–0.9	2.0	1.9	4.3	4.6	5.0	5.6	5.2	4.9	4.2
Current transfers	–1.6	–1.4	–1.3	–1.3	–1.3	–1.3	–1.2	–1.4	–1.3	–1.3	–1.3
Factor income	0.8	–0.3	–0.8	–0.7	0.6	0.9	1.0	1.0	1.0	1.0	1.0
Resource balance	2.8	0.8	4.1	3.9	5.0	4.9	5.2	6.0	5.5	5.2	4.4
France											
Savings	20.2	20.3	20.2	19.7	19.8	19.0	19.3	20.4	20.1	20.0	20.7
Investment	20.4	18.5	18.8	18.9	19.3	19.9	20.5	21.7	22.4	22.5	22.9
Net lending	–0.2	1.8	1.4	0.8	0.5	–0.9	–1.3	–1.3	–2.4	–2.5	–2.1
Current transfers	–0.6	–0.8	–1.0	–1.1	–1.1	–1.3	–1.2	–1.2	–1.0	–1.0	–1.0
Factor income	–0.3	0.6	0.6	0.8	1.1	1.1	1.2	1.5	1.3	1.3	1.4
Resource balance	0.8	2.1	1.7	1.1	0.5	–0.7	–1.2	–1.6	–2.7	–2.8	–2.5
Italy											
Savings	20.3	21.1	20.4	19.4	19.8	18.9	18.6	19.3	19.5	19.7	19.3
Investment	21.7	19.8	21.1	20.7	20.8	20.6	21.2	21.6	21.9	22.0	21.4
Net lending	–1.3	1.4	–0.8	–1.3	–0.9	–1.6	–2.6	–2.2	–2.4	–2.3	–2.1
Current transfers	–0.4	–0.5	–0.4	–0.5	–0.6	–0.7	–0.9	–0.6	–0.7	–0.7	–0.7
Factor income	–1.6	–1.1	–1.2	–1.3	–1.1	–1.0	–0.9	–0.9	–0.9	–0.9	–0.9
Resource balance	0.7	3.0	0.8	0.6	0.7	—	–0.7	–0.7	–0.8	–0.7	–0.5
Japan											
Savings	33.4	29.3	25.9	26.1	26.8	27.2	27.8	28.6	28.1	28.2	27.7
Investment	30.7	26.9	23.1	22.8	23.0	23.6	24.0	23.8	24.1	24.3	24.2
Net lending	2.7	2.3	2.9	3.2	3.7	3.6	3.9	4.8	4.0	3.9	3.5
Current transfers	–0.1	–0.2	–0.1	–0.2	–0.2	–0.2	–0.2	–0.3	–0.2	–0.2	–0.2
Factor income	0.7	1.2	1.7	1.7	1.9	2.3	2.7	3.1	2.7	2.9	3.0
Resource balance	2.1	1.3	1.3	1.7	2.0	1.5	1.4	2.0	1.4	1.2	0.7
United Kingdom											
Savings	16.4	16.4	15.8	15.7	15.9	15.0	14.1	13.6	13.6	13.8	13.8
Investment	19.1	17.7	17.4	17.1	17.5	17.5	18.0	18.5	18.5	18.2	18.5
Net lending	–2.7	–1.3	–1.6	–1.3	–1.6	–2.5	–3.9	–4.9	–4.8	–4.4	–4.6
Current transfers	–0.7	–0.8	–0.9	–0.9	–0.9	–1.0	–0.9	–0.9	–0.9	–1.0	–1.0
Factor income	–0.1	0.6	2.2	2.2	2.2	2.0	0.6	–0.5	–0.4	–0.5	–0.6
Resource balance	–1.9	–1.1	–2.9	–2.6	–3.0	–3.6	–3.6	–3.5	–3.5	–2.9	–3.0
Canada											
Savings	17.2	19.8	21.0	21.2	22.9	23.8	24.2	23.7	22.5	22.3	23.3
Investment	20.6	19.6	19.3	20.0	20.7	21.7	22.5	22.8	23.4	23.5	23.4
Net lending	–3.4	0.2	1.7	1.2	2.3	2.0	1.6	0.9	–0.9	–1.2	—
Current transfers	–0.2	0.1	—	—	—	–0.1	—	—	—	—	—
Factor income	–3.4	–3.2	–2.6	–2.5	–1.9	–1.6	–0.8	–1.0	–1.1	–1.2	–1.1
Resource balance	0.2	3.4	4.3	3.7	4.2	3.7	2.5	2.0	0.2	–0.1	1.1

Table A16 (continued)

	Averages		2002	2003	2004	2005	2006	2007	2008	2009	Average 2010–13
	1986–93	1994–2001									
Newly industrialized Asian economies											
Savings	35.7	33.0	29.7	31.5	32.8	31.3	31.4	32.0	30.9	31.0	31.0
Investment	29.8	29.9	24.7	24.7	26.5	25.9	26.0	25.7	26.3	26.7	27.0
Net lending	5.9	3.1	5.0	6.8	6.3	5.3	5.3	6.3	4.5	4.4	4.1
Current transfers	0.1	−0.3	−0.7	−0.8	−0.7	−0.7	−0.7	−0.7	−0.7	−0.7	−0.7
Factor income	1.3	0.6	0.5	0.9	0.6	—	0.4	1.0	0.5	0.3	0.4
Resource balance	4.5	2.8	5.1	6.6	6.5	6.0	5.7	5.9	4.8	4.7	4.4
Emerging and developing economies											
Savings	24.3	24.1	25.9	27.7	29.4	31.3	32.7	33.0	33.5	33.6	34.0
Investment	25.4	24.8	24.7	25.7	27.1	27.2	27.9	28.8	29.3	30.2	31.2
Net lending	−2.5	−0.7	1.2	1.9	2.4	4.1	4.8	4.2	4.1	3.4	2.8
Current transfers	0.5	0.9	1.4	1.6	1.5	1.6	1.6	1.5	1.3	1.3	1.1
Factor income	−1.5	−1.6	−2.0	−2.0	−2.0	−1.9	−1.8	−1.6	−1.6	−1.4	−0.7
Resource balance	−0.8	—	1.8	2.4	2.9	4.4	5.1	4.3	4.4	3.5	2.4
Memorandum											
Acquisition of foreign assets	1.1	3.7	3.6	5.8	7.0	9.1	10.3	12.5	10.1	8.9	7.3
Change in reserves	0.4	1.1	2.3	3.9	4.8	5.0	5.6	7.8	5.5	5.3	3.9
Regional groups											
Africa											
Savings	18.0	18.5	20.3	21.4	22.9	24.3	26.3	24.8	26.1	26.4	26.3
Investment	19.5	20.1	22.0	21.8	22.8	22.5	23.5	24.5	24.3	25.4	26.1
Net lending	−1.5	−1.6	−1.7	−0.4	0.1	1.8	2.8	0.3	1.9	1.0	0.2
Current transfers	2.4	2.6	3.1	3.1	3.2	3.0	3.1	3.0	2.8	2.6	2.5
Factor income	−3.6	−3.9	−4.6	−4.4	−5.0	−5.4	−5.0	−5.5	−6.1	−6.2	−4.8
Resource balance	−0.3	−0.3	−0.1	0.9	1.9	4.1	4.7	2.8	5.2	4.6	2.4
Memorandum											
Acquisition of foreign assets	0.1	2.6	2.7	3.3	4.3	5.6	7.1	6.2	7.6	6.7	5.7
Change in reserves	0.1	1.4	1.2	2.0	4.5	5.2	5.7	5.6	6.8	6.2	5.0
Central and eastern Europe											
Savings	25.4	20.2	17.9	17.0	17.2	17.5	17.8	18.7	18.5	19.3	21.3
Investment	26.3	22.8	21.3	21.2	22.5	22.2	23.9	25.0	25.4	25.9	26.8
Net lending	−0.8	−2.6	−3.3	−4.2	−5.3	−4.6	−6.1	−6.4	−6.9	−6.6	−5.5
Current transfers	1.4	1.7	1.7	1.5	1.5	1.5	1.5	1.4	1.2	1.3	1.3
Factor income	−1.4	−0.9	−1.5	−1.9	−2.7	−2.3	−2.7	−2.8	−2.6	−2.5	−2.3
Resource balance	−0.8	−3.4	−3.5	−3.9	−4.1	−3.8	−4.9	−4.9	−5.6	−5.3	−4.5
Memorandum											
Acquisition of foreign assets	1.2	2.1	3.2	2.1	3.2	4.8	4.6	4.6	2.0	1.8	2.1
Change in reserves	−0.3	1.9	2.5	1.4	1.3	3.5	1.6	2.3	1.2	1.0	1.4
Commonwealth of Independent States[2]											
Savings	...	24.6	26.6	27.5	29.7	29.7	29.5	29.0	29.4	28.0	26.4
Investment	...	21.0	20.2	21.2	21.4	21.0	22.1	24.5	24.7	25.7	27.4
Net lending	...	3.6	6.4	6.3	8.3	8.6	7.4	4.5	4.7	2.3	−1.0
Current transfers	...	0.4	0.6	0.6	0.5	0.6	0.5	0.4	0.3	0.2	0.1
Factor income	...	−2.0	−2.0	−2.8	−2.1	−2.9	−3.5	−2.8	−2.2	−1.7	−1.5
Resource balance	...	5.2	7.9	8.4	9.9	11.0	10.4	6.9	6.6	3.8	0.5
Memorandum											
Acquisition of foreign assets	...	4.8	5.5	11.6	14.3	15.2	16.3	16.5	12.0	9.6	5.6
Change in reserves	...	1.1	3.3	5.7	7.1	7.7	9.9	10.1	7.0	5.5	3.0

Table A16 *(continued)*

	Averages		2002	2003	2004	2005	2006	2007	2008	2009	Average 2010–13
	1986–93	1994–2001									
Developing Asia											
Savings	28.9	32.7	33.6	36.6	38.4	41.3	43.8	44.7	44.7	45.5	46.8
Investment	31.5	32.4	31.2	33.8	35.9	37.2	37.9	37.9	39.1	39.9	40.7
Net lending	−2.6	0.3	2.4	2.8	2.6	4.1	5.9	6.8	5.6	5.5	6.1
Current transfers	0.8	1.3	1.9	2.1	2.0	2.1	2.1	2.0	2.0	1.9	1.7
Factor income	−1.8	−1.4	−1.5	−1.1	−1.0	−0.6	−0.6	−0.2	−0.5	−0.5	0.1
Resource balance	−1.6	0.4	2.1	1.8	1.6	2.6	4.4	5.0	4.2	4.2	4.4
Memorandum											
Acquisition of foreign assets	2.4	5.8	5.1	6.2	7.3	9.6	11.5	15.5	12.6	11.5	10.4
Change in reserves	0.9	1.7	4.2	5.5	7.4	5.9	6.8	10.8	6.7	7.5	5.8
Middle East											
Savings	17.4	25.2	27.7	31.3	34.9	42.0	42.8	44.7	48.6	46.5	42.6
Investment	23.6	22.1	23.0	23.0	23.2	22.3	22.0	24.9	25.6	27.2	27.8
Net lending	−6.2	3.1	4.8	8.3	11.8	19.7	20.9	19.8	23.0	19.4	14.8
Current transfers	−3.5	−2.9	−2.5	−2.2	−1.9	−1.8	−1.7	−1.7	−1.5	−1.5	−1.7
Factor income	2.4	2.6	0.5	0.2	0.3	1.1	2.2	2.4	1.8	2.4	4.4
Resource balance	−5.1	3.4	6.8	10.4	13.4	20.4	20.4	19.1	22.7	18.5	12.1
Memorandum											
Acquisition of foreign assets	−0.5	4.8	2.6	12.8	16.4	24.6	26.6	27.4	26.0	22.3	16.9
Change in reserves	−0.4	1.2	0.6	5.0	5.6	10.4	10.5	11.6	11.1	9.6	6.2
Western Hemisphere											
Savings	18.7	17.0	17.8	18.7	20.8	21.1	21.9	21.2	20.6	20.3	20.1
Investment	19.2	20.1	18.7	18.2	19.9	19.7	20.3	20.8	20.9	21.2	21.2
Net lending	−0.5	−3.0	−0.9	0.5	0.9	1.4	1.6	0.4	−0.3	−0.9	−1.2
Current transfers	0.8	1.0	1.7	2.0	2.1	2.0	2.1	1.9	1.7	1.6	1.6
Factor income	−2.3	−2.7	−3.1	−3.3	−3.4	−3.2	−3.2	−2.9	−2.6	−2.3	−1.9
Resource balance	1.0	−1.3	0.6	1.7	2.2	2.6	2.7	1.4	0.6	−0.2	−0.8
Memorandum											
Acquisition of foreign assets	0.7	1.8	1.4	3.0	2.9	3.0	3.2	6.0	2.9	2.3	1.6
Change in reserves	0.6	0.2	−0.1	1.9	1.1	1.3	1.7	3.8	1.8	1.3	0.7
Analytical groups											
By source of export earnings											
Fuel											
Savings	26.5	26.0	28.3	30.3	33.6	37.8	38.2	37.4	39.1	37.2	33.9
Investment	28.7	22.3	23.1	22.7	23.0	22.2	22.7	25.1	25.2	26.4	27.5
Net lending	−2.2	3.7	5.2	7.7	10.6	15.6	15.5	12.3	13.9	10.8	6.4
Current transfers	−1.5	−1.9	−1.7	−1.4	−1.1	−0.9	−0.9	−0.9	−0.9	−0.9	−1.0
Factor income	—	−0.7	−1.9	−2.5	−2.3	−2.3	−1.9	−1.8	−2.0	−1.4	−0.2
Resource balance	−0.7	6.4	8.9	11.6	14.0	18.8	18.4	15.0	16.7	13.2	7.6
Memorandum											
Acquisition of foreign assets	0.2	5.0	3.1	11.7	14.4	19.1	19.8	19.6	17.6	14.9	10.2
Change in reserves	−0.3	0.9	1.1	5.2	6.9	9.2	10.3	10.3	9.5	7.9	4.8
Nonfuel											
Savings	23.3	23.7	25.3	27.1	28.4	29.6	31.1	31.8	31.7	32.4	34.1
Investment	25.2	25.3	25.0	26.4	28.1	28.5	29.4	29.9	30.7	31.5	32.5
Net lending	−2.1	−1.6	0.3	0.7	0.4	1.1	1.8	1.9	1.0	0.9	1.6
Current transfers	1.2	1.5	2.1	2.3	2.2	2.2	2.3	2.2	2.1	2.0	1.9
Factor income	−1.7	−1.8	−2.0	−1.9	−2.0	−1.8	−1.8	−1.5	−1.5	−1.4	−0.9
Resource balance	−0.8	−1.3	0.3	0.3	0.2	0.6	1.3	1.2	0.4	0.3	0.7
Memorandum											
Acquisition of foreign assets	1.3	3.4	3.7	4.4	5.2	6.4	7.7	10.5	7.6	6.9	6.3
Change in reserves	0.5	1.1	2.5	3.6	4.2	3.9	4.2	7.1	4.2	4.4	3.5

Table A16 *(concluded)*

	Averages		2002	2003	2004	2005	2006	2007	2008	2009	Average 2010–13
	1986–93	1994–2001									
By external financing source											
Net debtor countries											
Savings	20.8	19.3	19.5	20.5	21.2	21.5	22.3	22.6	22.3	22.7	23.9
Investment	22.9	21.9	20.3	21.1	22.6	23.1	23.9	24.7	25.0	25.6	26.6
Net lending	−2.1	−2.6	−0.9	−0.6	−1.4	−1.6	−1.6	−2.1	−2.7	−2.9	−2.7
Current transfers	1.5	1.8	2.6	2.8	2.6	2.7	2.8	2.7	2.6	2.6	2.5
Factor income	−2.4	−2.4	−2.4	−2.4	−2.7	−2.8	−2.9	−2.6	−2.4	−2.3	−2.1
Resource balance	−1.1	−2.5	−1.1	−0.9	−1.3	−1.6	−1.5	−2.1	−2.9	−3.1	−3.2
Memorandum											
Acquisition of foreign assets	0.8	1.7	2.5	3.0	2.9	3.0	4.2	5.8	2.8	2.2	1.9
Change in reserves	0.5	0.8	1.6	2.1	1.6	1.8	2.3	4.1	1.8	1.3	1.2
Official financing											
Savings	14.0	17.1	19.9	21.1	22.2	23.1	23.2	23.0	22.4	22.7	23.3
Investment	16.9	20.4	22.0	23.4	24.2	24.6	25.3	26.4	26.3	26.2	26.7
Net lending	−2.9	−3.3	−2.1	−2.3	−1.9	−1.6	−2.1	−3.4	−3.9	−3.6	−3.4
Current transfers	4.2	5.7	7.0	7.6	7.9	8.6	8.7	8.9	8.7	8.4	8.2
Factor income	−0.8	−1.0	−1.8	−1.7	−1.2	−1.8	−2.4	0.1	0.8	0.4	—
Resource balance	−6.3	−8.0	−7.4	−8.2	−8.6	−8.3	−8.4	−12.4	−13.4	−12.3	−11.7
Memorandum											
Acquisition of foreign assets	0.5	1.5	1.1	5.0	2.5	4.1	4.3	5.8	2.6	2.8	2.5
Change in reserves	0.5	0.5	−0.2	3.0	1.2	2.0	2.8	3.1	1.0	1.3	1.2
Net debtor countries by debt-servicing experience											
Countries with arrears and/or rescheduling during 2002–06											
Savings	17.2	19.4	21.1	23.2	21.6	22.0	23.9	23.2	23.0	23.6	23.9
Investment	23.2	22.3	18.7	20.8	21.4	22.7	23.7	24.2	24.6	25.5	26.2
Net lending	−6.0	−2.9	2.3	2.4	0.2	−0.7	0.2	−1.0	−1.6	−1.9	−2.3
Current transfers	1.6	2.1	4.0	4.0	3.9	4.5	4.3	4.1	3.8	3.6	3.4
Factor income	−5.6	−3.1	−4.0	−3.4	−4.2	−3.7	−3.4	−3.3	−3.2	−3.1	−2.8
Resource balance	−1.9	−2.0	2.3	1.8	0.4	−1.4	−0.7	−1.7	−2.3	−2.4	−2.9
Memorandum											
Acquisition of foreign assets	1.0	2.1	3.7	3.8	2.3	2.4	3.1	4.0	2.5	2.3	1.6
Change in reserves	0.2	0.4	0.8	2.2	1.6	1.7	2.2	3.3	1.7	1.8	1.3

Note: The estimates in this table are based on individual countries' national accounts and balance of payments statistics. Country group composites are calculated as the sum of the U.S dollar values for the relevant individual countries. This differs from the calculations in the April 2005 and earlier *World Economic Outlooks,* where the composites were weighted by GDP valued at purchasing power parities (PPPs) as a share of total world GDP. For many countries, the estimates of national savings are built up from national accounts data on gross domestic investment and from balance-of-payments-based data on net foreign investment. The latter, which is equivalent to the current account balance, comprises three components: current transfers, net factor income, and the resource balance. The mixing of data source, which is dictated by availability, implies that the estimates for national savings that are derived incorporate the statistical discrepancies. Furthermore, errors, omissions, and asymmetries in balance of payments statistics affect the estimates for net lending; at the global level, net lending, which in theory would be zero, equals the world current account discrepancy. Despite these statistical shortcomings, flow of funds estimates, such as those presented in these tables, provide a useful framework for analyzing development in savings and investment, both over time and across regions and countries.

[1]Calculated from the data of individual euro area countries.

[2]Mongolia, which is not a member of the Commonwealth of Independent States, is included in this group for reasons of geography and similarities in economic structure.

Table A17. Summary of World Medium-Term Baseline Scenario

	Eight-Year Averages		Four-Year Average 2006–09	2006	2007	2008	2009	Four-Year Average 2010–13
	1990–97	1998–2005						
	Annual percent change unless otherwise noted							
World real GDP	**2.9**	**3.6**	**4.4**	**5.0**	**4.9**	**3.7**	**3.8**	**4.9**
Advanced economies	2.6	2.6	2.1	3.0	2.7	1.3	1.3	2.9
Emerging and developing economies	3.3	5.1	7.2	7.8	7.9	6.7	6.6	7.0
Memorandum								
Potential output								
Major advanced economies	2.6	2.4	2.2	2.3	2.2	2.2	2.1	2.1
World trade, volume[1]	**6.8**	**6.2**	**6.8**	**9.2**	**6.8**	**5.6**	**5.8**	**7.3**
Imports								
Advanced economies	6.2	5.9	4.6	7.4	4.2	3.1	3.7	5.7
Emerging and developing economies	8.0	7.7	12.4	14.4	12.8	11.8	10.7	10.8
Exports								
Advanced economies	6.9	5.2	5.7	8.2	5.8	4.5	4.2	5.6
Emerging and developing economies	8.2	8.4	8.9	10.9	8.9	7.1	8.7	9.8
Terms of trade								
Advanced economies	−0.1	−0.1	−0.5	−1.1	−0.0	−1.0	0.1	0.1
Emerging and developing economies	−0.6	1.4	2.5	4.7	1.4	4.5	−0.5	—
World prices in U.S. dollars								
Manufactures	1.3	1.6	5.3	3.8	9.7	6.4	1.4	1.7
Oil	0.9	13.6	15.4	20.5	10.7	34.3	−1.0	−0.5
Nonfuel primary commodities	0.0	0.5	9.4	23.2	14.0	7.0	−4.9	−3.4
Consumer prices								
Advanced economies	3.4	1.9	2.3	2.4	2.2	2.6	2.0	2.1
Emerging and developing economies	62.9	8.3	6.2	5.4	6.3	7.4	5.6	4.7
Interest rates (in percent)								
Real six-month LIBOR[2]	3.1	1.6	1.8	2.1	2.6	1.1	1.6	3.1
World real long-term interest rate[3]	4.0	2.4	1.6	1.7	2.0	1.1	1.8	2.8
	Percent of GDP							
Balances on current account								
Advanced economies	0.0	−0.7	−1.2	−1.5	−1.2	−1.1	−1.1	−1.1
Emerging and developing economies	−1.6	1.2	4.1	4.8	4.2	4.0	3.3	2.8
Total external debt								
Emerging and developing economies	34.5	36.2	25.9	27.0	26.6	25.1	24.9	24.1
Debt service								
Emerging and developing economies	4.7	6.2	4.5	5.7	4.4	3.9	3.9	3.9

[1]Data refer to trade in goods and services.
[2]London interbank offered rate on U.S. dollar deposits minus percent change in U.S. GDP deflator.
[3]GDP-weighted average of 10-year (or nearest maturity) government bond rates for the United States, Japan, Germany, France, Italy, the United Kingdom, and Canada.

WORLD ECONOMIC OUTLOOK AND *STAFF STUDIES FOR THE WORLD ECONOMIC OUTLOOK,* SELECTED TOPICS, 2000–2008

I. Methodology—Aggregation, Modeling, and Forecasting

II. Historical Surveys

III. Economic Growth—Sources and Patterns

IV. Inflation and Deflation, and Commodity Markets

V. Fiscal Policy

VI. Monetary Policy, Financial Markets, and Flow of Funds

VII. Labor Markets, Poverty, and Inequality

VIII. Exchange Rate Issues

IX. External Payments, Trade, Capital Movements, and Foreign Debt

X. Regional Issues

XI. Country-Specific Analyses

XII. Special Topics

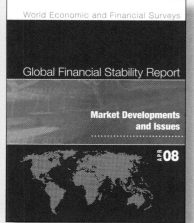